H.E. Schneiderman
N.Y.C.
17 November '85

American Puritan Studies

AMERICAN PURITAN STUDIES

An Annotated Bibliography
of Dissertations,
1882–1981

COMPILED BY

MICHAEL S. MONTGOMERY

Bibliographies and Indexes in American History, Number 1

GREENWOOD PRESS
Westport, Connecticut • London, England

Library of Congress Cataloging in Publication Data

Main entry under title:

American Puritan studies.

   (Bibliographies and indexes in American history, ISSN 0742-6828 ; no. 1)
   Includes indexes.
   1. Puritans—New England—Bibliography. 2. New England—History—Colonial period, ca. 1600–1775— Bibliography. 3. Dissertations, Academic—Bibliography. I. Montgomery, Michael S. (Michael Stewart), 1948- II. Series.
Z1251.E1A54 1984 [F7] 016.974'02   84-6553
ISBN 0-313-24237-2 (lib. bdg.)

Library of Congress Catalog Card Number: 84-6553
ISBN: 0-313-24237-2
ISSN: 0742-6828

First published in 1984

Greenwood Press
A division of Congressional Information Service, Inc.
88 Post Road West, Westport, Connecticut 06881

Printed in the United States of America

10 9 8 7 6 5 4 3 2 1

To John J. Gatta and Donald W. Krummel,
whose respective enthusiasms for
the Puritans and for bibliography
inspired me to undertake this project

CONTENTS

PREFACE

This bibliography comprises 940 American, British, Canadian, and German doctoral dissertations relating to the American Puritans from 1882, the year the first thesis was accepted, through 1981. During the first fifty years such scholars as Charles McLean Andrews (Johns Hopkins, 1889) and Kenneth B. Murdock (Harvard, 1923) received their Ph.D.'s for work on Puritan New England, and at the end of this period, in 1931, a University of Chicago student named Perry Miller submitted his thesis on "The Establishment of Orthodoxy in Massachusetts." During the ensuing half-century appeared nearly 90 percent of the dissertations cited herein, more than half of them in the last fifteen years. Due to imposing growth rates for published books and articles in American Puritan Studies, the total literature of the field has become so intractably immense that no single bibliographic effort could hope to cover adequately the entire mass of relevant material.

Much important bibliographic work has been done with the primary literature of the field, but for nearly a century after Henry Martyn Dexter's The Congregationalism of the Last Three Hundred Years, as Seen in Its Literature (New York: Harper, 1880) no major compilation including secondary materials appeared. Then in the 1970s there was an abrupt surge of interest in the secondary bibliography of American Puritanism; not only was Dexter reprinted (New York: Burt Franklin, 1970), but several new contributions were published. Edward J. Gallagher and Thomas Werge compiled Early Puritan Writers: A Reference Guide (Boston: G. K. Hall, 1976), devoted to works on William Bradford, John Cotton, Thomas Hooker, Edward Johnson, Richard Mather, and Thomas Shepard. William J. Scheick and JoElla Doggett's Seventeenth-Century American Poetry: A Reference Guide (Boston: G. K. Hall, 1977) included references to studies on over forty Puritan poets. Roger Williams and Edward Taylor each served as the subject of a bibliographic monograph: Wallace Coyle's Roger Williams: A Reference Guide (1977; see 1974-4) and Constance J. Gefvert's Edward Taylor: An Annotated Bibliography, 1668-1970 (1971; see 1971-8). Finally, since 1975, the Committee for a New England Bibliography has been producing an important series of Bibliographies of New England History (Boston: G. K. Hall; Hanover, N.H.: University Press of New England).

In the present work I have endeavored to bring into good bibliographic order one major genre of research in American Puritan

Studies--doctoral dissertations and published monographs based on them--
in the hope of facilitating access to many significant but often
neglected studies, and of displaying per exemplum the remarkably broad
array of topics that have interested students of the American Puritans.

Scope

   In selecting citations for this bibliography I have had to ask
myself many times, "Is this dissertation--or part of it--central to the
study of the American Puritans and their world, or is it peripheral?"
And, if peripheral: "Is it nevertheless a plausible source of
information or insight for the American Puritan scholar?   Is it
reasonable to suppose that it might be sought in a bibliography of
American Puritan Studies?" If the answer to any of these questions was
affirmative I have included the thesis. Most of the time I have been in
no doubt, but in view of the substantial minority of doubtful cases I
owe it to the user to explain here in some detail what my basic criteria
for selection have been.

   The nucleus of "Puritanism," from the American point of view, was
the Non-Separating Congregationalism of John Winthrop, his followers,
and their descendants.   To their right on the English religious
spectrum, just within the scope of this bibliography, were the
Presbyterian Puritans. Farther right, and beyond the bibliography's
scope, were the Anglican adherents of episcopacy, and farther yet the
Roman Catholics.   Just to the left of the Winthrop group, and
comprehensively included herein, were the Separatist followers of
William Bradford in Plymouth Colony. Also included as reluctant leftist
offshoots of the Massachusetts Bay settlers were the founders of Rhode
Island--Roger Williams, Anne Hutchinson, and their disciples.
Dissertations treating of Roman Catholics and Anglicans on the one hand
and Quakers, Baptists, Seekers, and other sectaries on the other have
been included only if they focus clearly--at least in part--on the
treatment received by these groups from the Puritans, or on the
theological differences between members of these sects and the Puritans.
In recognition of the international character of Puritanism, I have
included dissertations on several representative English Independents
whose works either directly influenced the Americans or were read on
this side of the Atlantic; similarly, the English Puritan right is
represented by Richard Baxter, and the left by Thomas Cartwright, Robert
Browne, Henry Jacob, and John Robinson. Theses on aspects of Puritan
theology in general were often found to be equally applicable to both
English and American believers. If so, I have included them, as I have
for similar reasons included dissertations concerning Calvinism, and the
publication of Calvin's works, in England; the Geneva Bible; Puritan
education at Cambridge and Oxford; and the debates at the Westminster
Assembly of Divines.

   Since New England was the area of the New World in which Puritans
were most thickly settled I have of course concentrated most of my
attention on events and circumstances in that region. Yet, when I have
encountered theses on American Puritans elsewhere--on Long Island, or in
East Jersey, Maryland, or Virginia--I have included them. New England's
relations with the mother country, with the native Americans within and
beyond the region's frontiers, and with such important trading partners

as New France and the West Indies have also been judged relevant to a full understanding of the American Puritans during the period in question.

That period extends basically from 1620 to 1730, from the sailing of the Mayflower through the decade that witnessed the deaths of Richard Steere (1721); Increase Mather (1723); John Leverett and Gurdon Saltonstall (1724); John Wise (1725); Samuel Danforth II and Sarah Kemble Knight (1727); Cotton Mather (1728); Solomon Stoddard, Edward Taylor, and John Williams (1729); and John Danforth and Samuel Sewall (1730). In addition, however, I have selectively included some works treating events prior to 1620 if they provided valuable information on the English background of American Puritan theology and ecclesiology or on English colonialism as practiced in North America. The year 1730 also is only an approximate terminus ad quem. Many included dissertations deal with matters extending over a very long period of time--for example, from 1619 to 1970; or the time period covered by the dissertation might only marginally overlap with the period emphasized here--say, from 1729 to 1754, or 1730 to 1755. In such cases as these I have included the theses if the subject matter was clearly relevant. Similarly, not all important Puritans died conveniently before the fourth decade of the eighteenth century. In instances of individuals whose careers extended over the entire eighteenth century I have made case by case judgments. For example, theses on Samuel Johnson (1696-1772), Ebenezer Gay (1697-1787), and Charles Chauncy (1705-1787) have been included because their student years and early ministerial careers are substantially treated; Jonathan Edwards (1703-1758), whose ministry began (like Chauncy's) in 1727, has been excluded both because his name is associated most closely with the later religious history of New England and because theses on his life and work may be found cited in M. X. Lesser's Jonathan Edwards: A Reference Guide (Boston: G. K. Hall, 1981). Similarly, I have included the career of James Franklin (1697-1735), the Boston printer of the influential New-England Courant from 1721 to 1726, while I have excluded studies of his more illustrious half-brother Benjamin (1706-1790).

Although 1730 represents the point after which, for the purposes of this bibliography, "Puritanism" is assumed to metamorphose into something else, the influence of Puritanism--and to an even greater extent the belief later Americans had in its influence--continued well past that date. I have attempted to do some justice to this fact by including works on the perceived influence of Puritanism on later American history and culture, and also historiographical studies of the idea of "Puritanism" as various later generations of Americans have interpreted it. By midcentury, indeed, the field of American Puritan Studies had become self-reflective, and its own history became the object of doctoral-level study. However, I have generally eschewed tracing the strictly theological influences of Puritanism on later religious thought: to have relentlessly pursued its every influence on, say, the minds of Jonathan Edwards and Isaac Backus, the transformations and defections of the Great Awakenings, the rise of Unitarianism, and the formation of the United Church of Christ would have required broadening the scope of this bibliography to include far more of the later history of Reformed churches in America than was my intent.

While I have thus limited my scope respecting the later evolution of American Puritan theology, I have interpreted liberally the notion of what is relevant to the study of "American Puritans" during the seventeenth and early eighteenth centuries. These men and women spent a great deal of time on religious matters--in their churches, on their knees at home in familial or private prayer, or otherwise actively about their God's business. But they had the world's business to transact as well, and many had lives that were even by our standards full and rich. Below, roughly following the order and terminology of Library of Congress classification, is briefly outlined the subject scope of this bibliography.

Philosophy. Puritan logic, epistemology, and ethics.

Psychology. The psychology of Puritans and Puritanism; the influence of Puritanism on the history of psychology.

Religion. The history of the Congregational Church and its Platforms; biographies of Puritanism's prominent religious figures; the Puritans' Bible, its exegesis, and the uses of typology; doctrinal theology (e.g., preparation for grace, conversion, the covenant); practical theology (forms of worship, church and state issues, the ministry, sermons, the sacraments, religious education, missions); pastoral theology; sectarians, schismatics, and heretics; demonology and witchcraft.

History. The Elizabethan and Jacobean Puritan movements; early British exploration of North America and the promotion of and reasons for emigration; the native Americans of British North America, especially of New England, and their relations with the Puritan settlers; the general history of Puritan North America and its confederations, colonies, provinces, counties, towns, and villages; ethnic minorities in the Puritan colonies; the Puritan historians; the depiction of Puritans in American historical writing.

Geography. Physical geography (influences of environment and climate); human ecology and the attitudes and responses of the Puritan settlers to the environment.

Recreation. Physical training; sports; games and amusements; Sabbatarianism.

Economics. Economic history and conditions; land and agriculture; industries (e.g., fishing, iron, lumber, shipbuilding); roads and highways; trade (the British Board of Trade, directions and content of trade, advertising); finance (currency, banking, speculation, public revenue and taxation); Puritans in the light of Karl Marx and Max Weber.

Sociology. Social history and the relation of the church to social problems; social groups (the family, marriage, women, children, minorities); the sexual life; town life and town planning; social welfare (charity, poor relief, treatment of the handicapped); criminology (crimes, punishments, juvenile offenders); slavery and the indenture system.

Political science.   The organs and functions of government
(executives and their agents, administrative bodies, legislative bodies)
at colonial or local levels; political rights and guarantees
(citizenship, suffrage, electoral systems, representation); colonialism;
migration, emigration, and immigration.

Law.   English common law in the colonies; colonial codes and
legislation; courts and adjudication; lawyers.

Education.   The history of colonial elementary and secondary
education; teaching and teaching methods; textbooks and primers;
religion in education; apprenticeship and vocational education;
education of special groups (native Americans, blacks, the handicapped);
Harvard and Yale.

Music.   Instruments and instrumental music; psalmody.

Art.   Architecture (dwellings and other buildings); decorative arts
(cloth window hangings, wall coverings, silverwork, stonecarving).

Editions.   Scholarly editions of seventeenth- and early eighteenth-
century American Puritan books and manuscripts.

Language.   Puritans as students of native American languages;
Puritan vocabulary and syntax; early New England pronunciation.

Literature.   Rhetoric; literary aesthetics; sermons and tracts;
poetry; diaries; almanacs; newspapers; wit and humor; juvenile
literature; the depiction of Puritans in the periodical press, poetry,
drama, and prose fiction of later generations of Americans; the literary
influences of Puritanism.

Science.   Puritan attitudes toward and contributions to science.

Medicine.   Public health; epidemics; the practice of medicine;
medicine as a profession.

Military affairs.   The British Army in the colonies; the colonial
militias; military policies; defense; warfare against native Americans
and foreign colonials.

Bibliography.   Books and printing; libraries.

Sources

By far the richest source for these citations was the Comprehensive
Dissertation Index (Ann Arbor, Mich.:   University Microfilms
International, 1973-June 1983), the computerized version of which I
found more convenient, more up-to-date, and somewhat more complete in
retrospective listings than the hard copy or microfiche editions.   While
other sources turned up a few verifiable American dissertations not
listed in CDI, that work is indeed very nearly "comprehensive" for
American theses and was a useful supplementary source for Canadian
citations.   Dissertation Abstracts International (Ann Arbor: UMI, 1938-
June, 1983)--called Microfilm Abstracts from 1938 to 1951 and

Dissertation Abstracts from 1952 to 1969--supplied me with a superlative source for many of the extracts quoted below in the annotations of American and Canadian theses and enabled me to determine quickly the relevancy of many dissertations with uninformative or ambiguous titles.

For foreign theses various national bibliographies were found to be more complete than CDI or DAI. In seeking Canadian dissertations I used the Canadian Bibliographic Centre's Canadian Graduate Theses in the Humanities and Social Sciences, 1921-1946 (Ottawa: E. Cloutier, 1951) and the National Library of Canada's Canadian Theses/Thèses canadiennes (Ottawa: NLC, 1962-1982). The first volume (Social Sciences and Humanities) of Roger R. Bilboul's Retrospective Index to Theses of Great Britain and Ireland, 1716-1950 (Santa Barbara, Calif.: American Bibliographic Center-Clio Press, 1975) and Aslib's Index to Theses Accepted for Higher Degrees in the Universities of Great Britain and Ireland (London: Aslib, 1953-1982) were the best sources for the dissertations of the United Kingdom. Other British works referred to were British Books in Print (London: Whitaker, 1925-1982); the British National Bibliography (London: British Museum, 1950-1981); and the General Catalogue of Printed Books (London: British Museum, 1959-1981). For German works I consulted the Jahresverzeichnis der deutschen Hochschulschriften (Leipzig: VEB Verlag für Buch- und Bibliothekswesen, 1887-1971); its continuations, the Jahresverzeichnis der Hochschulschriften der DDR, der BRD und Westberlins and the Jahresverzeichnis der Hochschulschriften; and Deutsche Bibliographie: Hochschulschriften-Verzeichnis (Frankfurt am Main: Buchhändler-Vereinigung, 1972-1981). It may be mentioned here that study of the Catalogue des thèses et écrits académiques (1884-1959) and the Catalogue des thèses de doctorat soutenues devant les universités françaises (1960-1976) turned up no relevant French dissertations. In all, some sixty-four relevant foreign dissertations were identified (or about 7 percent of the total), of which forty-two were British, twelve German, and ten Canadian.

In addition to these multi-disciplinary works a number of subject bibliographies of doctoral dissertations were used. Warren F. Kuehl's Dissertations in History: An Index to Dissertations Completed in History Departments of United States and Canadian Universities, 1873-1970, 2 vols. (Lexington: Univ. of Kentucky Press, 1965 and 1972) and Phyllis M. Jacobs's History Theses 1901-70: Historical Research for Higher Degrees in the Universities of the United Kingdom (London: Univ. of London, Institute of Historical Research, 1976) were excellent sources for historical works. In the area of literature I examined the following: Ernest E. Leisy and Jay B. Hubbell, "Doctoral Dissertations in American Literature," American Literature, 4 (1933), 419-65; Lewis Leary, "Doctoral Dissertations in American Literature, 1933-1948," American Literature, 202 (1948), 169-229; L. Balla-Cayard, "German Dissertations on American Literature Accepted between 1900 and 1945," American Literature, 24 (1952), 384-88; Richard Mummendey, Language and Literature of the Anglo-Saxon Nations as Presented in German Doctoral Dissertations, 1885-1950: A Bibliography (Charlottesville: Bibliographical Society of the Univ. of Virginia, 1954); James L. Woodress, Dissertations in American Literature, 1891-1966, revised ed. (Durham, N.C.: Duke Univ. Press, 1968); and Lawrence F. McNamee, Dissertations in English and American Literature: Theses Accepted by

American, British and German Universities, 1865-1964 (New York: R. R. Bowker, 1968) and its Supplements covering 1964-1968 and 1969-1973.

Finally, the large bibliographic database developed by OCLC Online Computer Library Center, Inc., of Columbus, Ohio, and the National Union Catalog, Pre-1956 Imprints (London: Mansell, 1968-1980), its Supplement (1980-1982), and its quinquennial and annual continuations through 1982 were used to verify citations and served as the principal sources of information about the publication, in monographic form, of the original dissertations.

The Entries

The arrangement adopted for this bibliography is chronological. Each citation is given an entry number consisting of the dissertation's year followed by a second number representing the entry's order within those entries assigned that date: this order is determined by the author's last name.   For example, O. L. Abbott's dissertation, the first alphabetically for 1953, is assigned the entry number 1953-1, and the thesis of M. W. Zuckerman becomes 1967-36 as the alphabetical last of the 1967 entries.

The choice of date as the essential determinant of the ordering of these citations is in a way a perverse one, since the notion of the "date of a dissertation" is one that has been variously--and inconsistently--interpreted by authors, academic departmental examiners, university graduate school administrators, librarians, and bibliographers.   The phrase can refer to the date of completion, submission, approval, the official awarding of the degree, the Commencement exercises at which the parchment is physically turned over to the grantee--or none of these.   Three or even four different dates for the same dissertation might appear in different bibliographic sources and on the title page.   An archival typescript dated "1940-41" in one egregious instance was recognized with the award of a Ph.D. only after war and victory had intervened, in 1946.   The "date" of a doctoral thesis is, in short, the least definite thing about it.   Nevertheless, I have preferred a chronological arrangement, which can provide the interested user with a sense of the historical development of American Puritan Studies, to its alternatives: an alphabetical author arrangement (meaningless in itself and adding nothing substantive to the bibliography as a whole); a geographical or alphabetical arrangement by the institutions granting the degrees (unfamiliar to American scholars); a broad subject classification system (requiring, redundantly, an additional, detailed subject index); or a narrow subject classification system (in which some interdisciplinary studies would inevitably be lost).   In general I have chosen for each dissertation the latest date given in any source as that most likely to represent the date the degree was officially granted, unless the preponderance of other evidence suggests that the date is inaccurate.   My preferred sources, in descending order, are the NUC, OCLC, DAI, CDI, Canadian Theses, Canadian Graduate Theses, Bilboul's Retrospective Index, the Jahresverzeichnis, the title pages of the dissertations themselves (which commonly reflect only the date of completion or submission), and the Aslib Index (which until quite recent years unhelpfully gave the user the choice of two different dates--e.g., "1960/61").   Whatever may be the ambiguities inherent in the chronological order employed here, I am confident that they are compensated for by thorough indexing (described below) and by the great likelihood that the "real" date is no more than a year or two away from the one under which a citation might be sought.

The basic citations consist of five parts. First is the fullest and latest available form of the author's name, followed by the fullest known form of the title of the thesis. Next are the degree earned (Ph.D., Th.D., D.Phil., Dr. phil., etc.) and the institution granting the degree, to which some clarifying parenthetical element may be added--for example, "Boston Univ. (School of Theology)" or "Univ. of London (Royal Holloway College)." Last appear, if known, the number of volumes and pagination of the original dissertation, in recording which, as with imprint and series information, I have been guided by the forms recommended by the Anglo-American Cataloguing Rules, 2d ed. (Chicago: American Library Assn., 1978). As the source of pagination I have preferred, in order, the thesis itself, the NUC, OCLC, DAI, and CDI.

The basic entries are followed by annotations. The content of these annotations varies considerably owing to the differing amounts and types of information from which the annotations could be constructed. For purposes of description it is convenient to consider the theses as being either published or unpublished.

Broadly speaking I have judged a dissertation to have been "published" if a monographic version of the original dissertation has appeared that is substantially like it or clearly based on it. In some cases, especially when more than five years have intervened between the degree and publication, it has been difficult to determine the precise genetic link between thesis and book. In cases of doubt I have generally assumed a substantial relationship, especially when the interval is less than ten years. Two special cases should be mentioned: if a book is based on a portion (a chapter or two, say) of the thesis that is outside the subject scope of this bibliography, then I have at most mentioned the book briefly (see 1976-11); if, on the other hand, any relevant part of a dissertation is expanded into a published book, I have treated that book as the published dissertation (see 1969-13). Reference to portions of theses published as journal articles has been made only if the original, unpublished dissertation itself is no longer extant and no other access to its contents exists (see 1910-3).

Having determined according to these guidelines that a given dissertation has in fact been "published," I have noted for that version the title, imprint information (publisher and place and date of publication of the original edition, subsequent editions, and reprints), pagination, and publisher's series information. Then, normally using the latest published edition, I have provided an extract (usually from the book's "Preface," "Introduction," or "Conclusion") that sheds light on the scope or focus of the work as a whole, and/or I have quoted the titles of the book's relevant chapters and appendixes. Also sometimes included in annotations of published theses are DAI references (if available) and mention of noteworthy chapters or appendixes accepted as part of the original thesis but not included in the published version(s). I have also regularly noted the inability of the degree-granting institution's library or archives to locate the original dissertation, and the absence of citation of an American thesis in CDI.

Annotation of unpublished theses I have handled in two different ways. In the case of those abstracted in DAI I have quoted sufficient portions of those abstracts relevant to focus, scope, and/or contents to provide the user with a degree of information intermediate between bare, unannotated citation of the dissertations' titles and the full authors' abstracts presented in DAI; these extracts should by no means be construed as replacing the DAI abstracts, for which complete references are given and to which the interested reader should refer for further information. In a few instances I have supplemented these extracts with further content information. When the dissertations were not abstracted in DAI, I have quoted from the dissertation itself and authorial statements of intent and scope descriptions, and/or provided contents notes. As with the published works, I have noted when dissertations are no longer extant or, if from American institutions, not cited in CDI.

The results of my decision to employ to as great an extent as possible the author's own words in these annotations, rather than to paraphrase and thereby reinterpret them in abstracts of my own, have in most cases satisfied me. The method has served to preserve my editorial objectivity and to supply the user with a more direct expression of the author's point of view than would have otherwise been possible. Unfortunately, however, not all authors have included terse thesis statements and succinct summaries of their conclusions; some have provided one but not the other; and some have not articulated their intentions or reviewed their findings at all. I have consequently been able to provide only contents notes for some theses. I have tried in general to keep these annotations at least indicative of the purpose of the dissertations, but owing to constraints of time and space they cannot always be informative--that is, the author's actual findings or conclusions are not always included in the extracts.

With respect to editorial policy, I should state that in both annotations and in the thesis titles I have silently emended obvious typographical errors in my sources and, sparingly, changed original punctuations (especially commas) in the interests of clarity or standardization. I have retained, however, with an editorial "[sic]," authorial mistakes of diction, syntax, or spelling. In editing the extracts I have frequently had recourse to ellipsis to exclude from within a quotation irrelevant, redundant, or prolix material.

Access to Theses

More than a quarter of the dissertations included herein were commercially published and should therefore be available from the publishers (if the works are in print), or from libraries or their interlibrary loan departments. Slightly more than half of the theses were unpublished but included in DAI, which provides either an order number by which a microfilm or photographic copy can be purchased from University Microfilms International or, more rarely, a note about alternative sources of access. A substantial number of university libraries will lend their own institution's dissertations (particularly ones accepted before the 1950s) on interlibrary loan or permit UMI to copy and sell them, and academic libraries that have purchased microform or photographic copies of other universities' theses will usually lend these as well. Finally, some major universities (most notably Harvard and Chicago) that neither participate in the UMI copying service nor lend their own original dissertations will sell photo- or microcopies produced by their own photographic services departments. Many Canadian dissertations are available from the National Library of Canada, and British and German theses are often obtainable through participating libraries from the British Lending Library (Wetherby, West Yorkshire) or the Center for Research Libraries (Chicago). A few unpublished dissertations whose relevancy is clearly indicated by their titles appear no longer to exist in either original or copy; in these cases I have briefly mentioned the bibliographic sources consulted and individuals applied to in my attempts to locate them.

Indexes

Four indexes are provided: of authors, short titles, institutions, and subjects.

In the first index are included the authors of the dissertations themselves, as well as the editors of scholarly editions of seventeenth- or early eighteenth-century works presented as dissertations, and the compilers of bibliography-dissertations. Where I have thought it useful, I have given cross-references to the married names of women scholars.

The titles in the second index are those of unpublished theses, of the published versions of theses, and of the original dissertations upon which published versions were based if the original titles differed significantly from the published ones. Titles have usually been shortened in this index, and subtitles have in general been dropped. The short-title index entries consist of the titles, the author's last name in brackets, and the entry number. Published book titles are underlined.

The 145 universities, colleges, and seminaries included in the third index are those granting the doctoral degrees for the theses of which this bibliography is composed. They are arranged first by country, then alphabetically by name of institution; the number of degrees granted in each country and by each institution is also entered here.

Nearly all of these theses were book-length productions, each one of which could plausibly have been furnished by its author with a detailed index of subjects (although in fact only a few of the unpublished ones were). I have felt justified, therefore, in making my subject index rather detailed. It by no means claims to comprehend all subjects covered in the theses or even to provide an equal degree of indexing for all dissertations. It does, however, attempt to cover the major subjects referred to in the annotations--quoted extracts and contents notes--as well as in the theses' titles. Authors and institutions considered as subjects of study (e.g., Kenneth Murdock or Perry Miller as historians, or the early years of Harvard and Yale) are found in this fourth index.

ACKNOWLEDGMENTS

In compiling this work I have had various sorts of help from many different people whom I wish gratefully to mention in the paragraphs that follow. These persons, however, are in no way responsible for any errors of omission or commission that despite all care have doubtless crept in. The responsibility for these is exclusively my own.

Initial thanks must be offered to those individuals at the University of Missouri-St. Louis whose encouragement and support enabled me to begin and to complete this project: Blanche M. Touhill, Associate Vice-Chancellor for Academic Affairs; K. Peter Etzkorn, Director of Research Administration; Ronald D. Krash, Director of Libraries; and Barbara Lehocky, head of the Thomas Jefferson Library's Reference Services Division. Special gratitude must be extended to the library's Interlibrary Loan staff, especially to Carolyn Huston, Sandra Fortune Brandt, Linda Garvey, and Tyrona Rowland, upon whose diligence and patience I had constantly to rely; and to Steven Falk and Sandra Snell, who advised me in planning my online searches. The speed, accuracy, and patience of Deloris Licklider, who prepared the camera-ready copy, have earned her the right of first refusal of the typing of the second edition.

Patricia M. Colling of University Microfilms International has very generously granted me permission to quote from a substantial number of Dissertation Abstracts.

Mention should also be made of my debt to the librarians and archivists who helped me to locate and obtain the dissertations I sought when I solicited them in person, at Boston University, Harvard, the University of Connecticut, the Hartford Seminary Foundation, Yale, Columbia, Union Theological Seminary, and New York University. I am also grateful to the Reference staff at Washington University in St. Louis for use of their collection. And, for special favors and courtesies extended to me in connection with my interlibrary loan requests, I wish to thank the members of the library staffs at Brown University, the University of Chicago, Eden-Webster College, Johns Hopkins University, McMaster University, the University of Missouri-Columbia, Temple University, the University of Toronto, and the University of Wisconsin-Madison.

For his careful work in the Pusey Archives, Daniel Lepow has earned a paragraph of his own. The hours he spent there saved me the trouble of a third visit to Cambridge.

Finally, I must of course thank again my wife, Lauren Lepow, who helped and encouraged me in innumerable ways, and my young son, Thomas Montgomery, who ate not one index card.

ABBREVIATIONS

BBIP	British Books in Print, 1874-1982
BMGC	British Museum, General Catalogue of Printed Books, 1959-1981
BNB	British National Bibliography, 1950-1981
Bd.	Band (volume)
Bilboul	Roger R. Bilboul, Retrospective Index to Theses of Great Britain and Ireland, 1975
CDI	Comprehensive Dissertation Index, 1973-1983
CRL	Center for Research Libraries (Chicago)
Cf.	Confer (compare)
D.A.	Doctor of Arts
DA	Dissertation Abstracts, 1952-1969
DAI	Dissertation Abstracts International, 1969-1983
D.D.	Doctor of Divinity
D.M.A.	Doctor of Musical Arts
D.Min.	Doctor of Ministry
D.Phil.	Doctor of Philosophy
D.R.E.	Doctor of Religious Education
diss.	dissertation
Dr. phil.	Doctor philosophiae (German degree)
Ed.D.	Doctor of Education

Ed.R.D.   Doctor of Religious Education

GPO   United States Government Printing Office (Washington, D.C.)

Jacobs   Phyllis M. Jacobs, History Theses 1901-70, 1976

MA   Microfilm Abstracts, 1938-1951

n.p.   no page number given; page not numbered

NUC   National Union Catalog, 1968-1982

OCLC   database of OCLC Online Computer Library Center, Inc. (Columbus, Ohio)

Ped.D.   Doctor of Pedagogy

Ph.D.   Doctor of Philosophy

s.l.   sine loco (no place of publication given)

s.n.   sine nomine (no publisher given)

S.T.D.   Doctor of Sacred Theology

sec.   section

ser.   series

Th.D.   Doctor of Theology

UMI   University Microfilms International (Ann Arbor, Mich.)

Univ.   Universität; University

AMERICAN PURITAN STUDIES

DISSERTATIONS, 1882–1981

1882-1   Bowen, Clarence Winthrop. "The Boundaries of Connecticut."
Ph.D., Yale Univ.

Revision published as The Boundary Disputes of Connecticut. --
Boston : J. R. Osgood, 1882. -- vi, 90 p. "Introduction" (published
version): "One would hardly suppose that the boundary line of . . .
Connecticut has been a subject of dispute for nearly two hundred and
fifty years. Islands on the south have been claimed and reclaimed,
only to be lost again. How the boundary on the east was ever fixed
seems a puzzle, in the light of the bitter quarrels extending through
several generations between the people of Connecticut and Rhode
Island. The northern boundary of Connecticut was thought to be
settled three or four times, but almost a hundred years passed before
the question was finally determined. The western line . . . and the
southern boundary were established at last about a year ago by Act of
Congress. The State, too, has been subdivided, each portion claiming
a jurisdiction of its own. The boundary lines have been in perpetual
motion since the founding of the Colony--a strange inconsistency for
'the land of steady habits'" (p. 9). Relevant chapters:
"Introduction"; Part I. "Claims to the Soil of Connecticut": I.
"Historical Statement, and the Controversy with the Dutch," II. "The
Woodward and Saffery Survey of 1642, and the Necessity for a Colonial
Charter," III. "The Duke of Hamilton's Claim," IV. "The Controversy
with New Haven," V. "The Mohegan Claim," and VI. "The Controversy
concerning Long Island"; Part II. "Connecticut's Boundary Disputes
with Rhode Island": I. "The Claims of Connecticut and Massachusetts
to the Territory of Rhode Island," II. "Disturbances and Disputes up
to 1685," III. "The Appeal of Connecticut and Rhode Island to
England," and IV. "The Disputes between Connecticut and Rhode Island
from 1700 to 1840"; Part III. "Connecticut's Boundary Disputes with
Massachusetts": I. "The Controversy concerning Windsor, and the
Survey of the Inter-Colonial Line," II. "The Memorials of
Massachusetts and Connecticut to the Crown, and the Boundary
Settlement of 1713," and III. "The Controversy concerning Woodstock,
Enfield, and Suffield"; and Part IV. "Connecticut's Boundary Disputes
with New York": I. "Disputes between New York and Connecticut from
1664 until 1731." Other chapters deal with later events. The Yale
Univ. Libraries no longer possessed a copy of the original diss. on
December 29, 1981.

1886-1   Levermore, Charles Herbert.   "The Republic of New Haven: A
History of Municipal Evolution."   Ph.D., Johns Hopkins Univ.

Published under same title: Baltimore : N. Murray, 1886. -- 342
p. -- (Johns Hopkins Univ. Studies in Historical and Political
Science; extra vol. I). Reprinted with an introduction by Ellis A.
Johnson: Port Washington, N.Y. : Kennikat Press, 1966. -- 342 p.
"Preface" (1966 ed.):   The work's "purpose has been to depict the
steady evolution of various forms of local government from the
assembly of freemen, to detect the far-reaching influence of the
Church organization at the center of social activity, to describe the
gradual differentiation that took place within the official structure,
to observe the operation of political and social agencies, whether
external or internal, and to discern . . . the permanent
characteristics which made up New Haven's strong individuality"
(n.p.). Relevant chapters: I. "The Genesis of New Haven," II. "The
Evolution of Town Government," III. "The Land Question," IV. "The
Union with Connecticut--The Birth of Newark," V. "The Work of the
Courts in Judicature and Legislation," VI. "New Haven, a Connecticut
Town, 1664-1700," and VII. "New Haven, a Connecticut Town, 1700-1784."
Chapters VIII and IX cover later periods. Relevant appendices: A.
"Mr. [Abraham] Pierson's Elegy," B. "The Town of Naugatuck," and D. "A
Town Court of Elections, New Haven, A.D. 1656."

1887-1   Randall, Daniel Richard.   "The Puritan Colony at Annapolis,
Maryland." Ph.D., Johns Hopkins Univ.

According to Johns Hopkins Univ. interlibrary loan unit, on
October 29, 1981, diss. is "not owned" by the Univ. Part of diss.
published as A Puritan Colony in Maryland. -- Baltimore : N. Murray,
1886. -- (Johns Hopkins Univ. Studies in Historical and Political
Science ; 4th ser., VI, pp. 5-47 [pp. 215-57]). Reprinted: New York:
Johnson Reprint Corp., 1973. -- 47 p. Contents (published portion):
"Puritans in Virginia," "Significance of Puritan Emigration," "Growth
of Puritan Settlement in Virginia," "Puritan Ministers from
Massachusetts," "Beginnings of Persecution in Virginia," "Effect of
the Indian Massacre [1644]," "Continued Persecution," "Early
Settlements upon Kent Island," "Two Classes of Settlers in Maryland,"
"Lord Baltimore's Colonial Policy," "Puritans of Virginia Invited to
Maryland," "Beginnings of Puritan Migration," "Puritan Meeting-House,"
"Puritans in Politics," "Puritan Independence," "Revolution in
Virginia and Maryland," "Indian Policy," "Puritan Conquest of
Maryland," "Puritan Legislation," "[Gov. William] Stone's Campaign
Against the Puritans," "The Battle upon Severn," "Puritan Supremacy
Re-established," "A Proprietary Governor and A Puritan Government,"
"Compromise with Lord Baltimore," "Advent of the Quakers," "[Gov.
Josias] Fendall's Conspiracy," "Beginnings of Annapolis," "Importance
of the Puritan Factor in Maryland History," "Drift toward Democracy,"
"Political Parties," and "A Historical Parallel."

1889-1   Andrews, Charles McLean. "The River Towns of Connecticut: A Study of Wethersfield, Hartford, and Windsor." Ph.D., Johns Hopkins Univ.

Published under same title: Baltimore : Publishing agency of the Johns Hopkins Univ., 1889. -- 129 p. -- (Johns Hopkins Univ. Studies in Historical and Political Science ; 7th ser., VII-IX). Reprinted: New York : Johnson Reprint Corp., 1973 -- 126 p. Covers period from 1627 through early eighteenth century; consists mainly of the histories of the three towns. Contents: I. "Early Settlements," II. "The Land System," and III. "The Town and the People."

1890-1   Gardner, Henry Brayton. "A History of Taxation in Rhode Island." Ph.D., Johns Hopkins Univ.

No abstract available. Diss. may no longer be extant: cited in CDI, vol. 34, p. 570; but not in DAI, NUC, OCLC, or Johns Hopkins Univ. Library catalog. In February, 1982, that institution's Interlibrary Loan Librarian also checked the Johns Hopkins Studies in Historical and Political Science series (cf. #1896-1, below), but the title and author did not appear there.

1890-2   Peters, Thomas McClure. "A Picture of Town Government in Massachusetts Bay Colony at the Middle of the Seventeenth Century, as Illustrated by The Town of Boston." Ph.D., Columbia Univ.

Published under same title: New York : McWilliams Printing Co., 1890. -- 74 p. A history of Boston to 1655. Contents: I. "The General Court and the Judiciary," II. "Elections and Naturalization," III. "The Town," IV. "The Militia and the Church," and V. "Taxation, Education, and the Poor Laws."

1892-1   Douglas, Charles Henry James. "Financial History of Massachusetts, from the Organization of the Massachusetts Bay Colony to the American Revolution." Ph.D., Columbia Univ.

Published under same title: New York : Columbia Univ., 1892. -- 148 p. -- (Columbia Univ., Faculty of Political Science, Studies in History, Economics, and Public Law ; vol. I, no. 4). Reprinted in 1897 as 2nd ed. of "Studies" ser. (vol. I, no. 4, pp. 251-396). Also reprinted: New York : AMS Press, 1969. -- 148 p. Contents (1969 ed.): Book I. "The Colony of Massachusetts Bay"; and Book II. "The Province of Massachusetts Bay": I. "Direct Taxation," II. "Indirect Taxation," III. "The Lotteries," IV. "Currency and Banking," and "Conclusion." "Introduction" refers to "the relatively large proportion of space which I have devoted to the exposition of administrative features, and the correspondingly small space to numerical statements. . . . [Massachusetts'] financial records are all but worthless for purposes of accurate and valuable generalization, on account of their fragmentary and unsystematic character" (p. v).

1892-2   Lauer, Paul Erasmus. "Church and State in New England."
     Ph.D., Johns Hopkins Univ.

     Published under same title: Baltimore : Johns Hopkins Press,
1892. -- 106 p. -- (Johns Hopkins Univ. Studies in Historical and
Political Science ; 10th ser., II-III). Reprinted: New York :
Johnson Reprint Corp., 1973. -- 106 p. "Preface" (1973 ed.): "The
design of this monograph is to give the history of the establishment
[of the Congregational Church], to point out the causes that led to
the dis-establishment and also the stages by which the latter was
brought about" (p. 5). Relevant chapters: I. "Introductory," II.
"The Civil and Ecclesiastical Beginnings of New England," III. "The
Development of Religious Liberty in the Seventeenth Century to 1691,"
and IV. "Development of Religious Liberty in the Eighteenth Century to
1787." Remaining chapters cover later periods.

1893-1   Bishop, Cortlandt Field. "History of Elections in the
     American Colonies." Ph.D., Columbia Univ.

     Published under same title: New York : Columbia Univ., 1893. --
v, 297 p. -- (Columbia Univ., Faculty of Political Science, Studies in
History, Economics, and Public Law ; vol. III, no. 1). Reprinted:
New York : Burt Franklin, 1968. -- v, 297 p. -- (Research and Source
Works Ser. ; no. 183) (American Classics of History and Social
Science ; no. 26). Also reprinted: New York : AMS Press, 1970. -- v,
297 p. Relevant chapters: Part I. "General Elections": I. "History
of General Elections" (includes sections on Massachusetts and
Plymouth, New Hampshire, Rhode Island, and Connecticut and New Haven),
II. "The Suffrage," and III. "The Management of Elections"; Part II.
"Local Elections": I. "History of Local Elections," II. "The
Suffrage," and III. "The Management of Local Elections." Relevant
appendices: A. "Writs, Returns, and Oaths," B. "Unpublished Statutes
Relating to Elections," and D. "Tables of Regnal and Proprietary
Years."

1893-2   Greene, Evarts Boutell. "The American Provincial Governor:
     A Study in the Constitutional History of the American Colonies."
     Ph.D., Harvard Univ. 230, 30 leaves.

     Revision published as The Provincial Governor in the English
Colonies of North America. -- New York : Longmans, Green, 1898. -- x,
292 p. -- (Harvard Historical Studies ; 7). Reprinted: New York :
Longmans, Green, 1907. -- x, 292 p. Also reprinted: New York :
Russell & Russell, 1966. -- x, 292 p. Also reprinted: Gloucester,
Mass. : Peter Smith, 1966. -- x, 292 p. "Preface" (1966 eds.): Diss.
was "revised and considerably rewritten" for publication (p. v).
Contents: I. "The Evolution of the Provincial Government," II. "The
Evolution of the Provincial Executive," III. "The Governor's
Appointment, Tenure of Office, and Emoluments," IV. "The Governor as
the Agent of the Home Government," V. "The Governor's Council," VI.
"The Governor's Executive Powers," VII. "The Governor's Relation to

the Judiciary," VIII. "The Governor's Power over the Assembly," IX.
"The Assembly's Power over the Governor," X. "The Encroachments of the
Assembly upon the Executive," XI. "The Governor's Legal and Political
Accountability," and "Conclusion."

1893-3   Haynes, George Henry.   "Representation and Suffrage in
     Massachusetts, 1620-1691." Ph.D., Johns Hopkins Univ.

     Published under same title: Baltimore : Johns Hopkins Press,
1894. -- 90 p. -- (Johns Hopkins Univ. Studies in Historical and
Political Science ; 12th ser., VIII-IX). Reprinted: New York :
Johnson Reprint Corp., 1973. -- 90 p. Contents (1973 ed.):   I.
"Introduction," II. "Beginnings of Representation in Massachusetts,"
III. "The First Decade of Representative Government--1634-1644," IV.
"Representation and Suffrage--1644-1688," V. "Representation and
Suffrage in Plymouth--1620-1691," and VI. "Changes Introduced by the
Charter of 1691." Appendices: A. "Disenfranchisement in
Massachusetts" and B. "The Confederation of 1643."

1894-1   Rogers, Sara Bulkley. "The Rise of Civil Government and
     Federation in Early New England." Ph.D., Yale Univ. 68, [3]
     leaves.

     "Introduction": "It is the object of this thesis to discover, if
possible, some of the causes which were responsible for the phenomenon
of civil government and federation in New England. Under what subtle
and powerful influences arose a form of government at once so unique
and so extraordinary? Was it entirely fortuitous in its origin,
chance-led by reason of natural and inevitable circumstances, or was
it a thoroughly-well-conceived and well-wrought-out design?" (n.p.).
Part II: "The Mayflower Compact, the Fundamental Orders of
Connecticut, and the Articles of Confederation of 1643 were decisive
steps in the movement, steps which led inevitably to the establishment
of the doctrine of the ultimate sovereignty of the people, and the
division of power between the states and the general government" (p.
67). Diss. is divided into two untitled "Parts," with no chapter
divisions.

1895-1   Greene, Maria Louise. "Church and State in Connecticut, to
     1818; or, The Rise of Religious Sects and Their Development of
     Religious Liberty." Ph.D., Yale Univ. 298, 25 leaves.

     Revision published in The Development of Religious Liberty in
Connecticut. -- Boston : Houghton Mifflin, 1905. -- xiii, 552 p.
Reprinted: New York : Da Capo Press, 1970. -- xiii, 552 p. -- (Civil
Liberties in American History). Also reprinted: Freeport, N.Y. :
Books for Libraries Press, 1970. -- xiii, 552 p. "Preface" (1905
ed.): "The following monograph is the outgrowth of three earlier and
shorter essays. The first, 'Church and State in Connecticut to 1818,'
was presented to Yale University as a doctor's thesis." Relevant
chapters (1970 eds.):   I. "The Evolution of Early Congregationalism,"
II. "The Transplanting of Congregationalism," III. "Church and State

in New England," IV. "The Cambridge Platform and the Half-Way
Covenant," V. "A Period of Transition," VI. "The Saybrook Platform,"
VII. "The Saybrook Platform and the Toleration Act," and VIII. "The
First Victory for Dissent." Chapters IX-XV treat of later events.

1895-2   Perrin, John William. "The History of Compulsory Education
    in New England." Ph.D., Univ. of Chicago. 923 leaves.

    Revision published under same title: Meadville, Pa. : [s.n.],
1896. -- 71 p. Published version: "Compulsory education . . . had
its origins in the desire for universal education which accompanied
the Reformation" (p. 30). Relevant chapters: I. "Introductory: The
Origin of Compulsory Education, and the Progress of Universal
Education and the Principle of Compulsion in the Sixteenth Century"
and II. "The Principle of Compulsion in New England, 1620-1800."
Chapters III-V deal with later periods.

1896-1   Jones, Frederick Robertson. "History of Taxation in
    Connecticut, 1636-1776." Ph.D., Johns Hopkins Univ.

    Published under same title: Baltimore : Johns Hopkins Press,
1896. -- 70 p. -- (Johns Hopkins Univ. Studies in Historical and
Political Science ; 14th ser., VIII). Reprinted: New York : Johnson
Reprint Corp., 1973. -- 70 p. Contents: I. "Introduction," II.
"Basis of Taxation," III. "The Grand List," IV. "Rates," V.
"Collection of Taxes," VI. "Indirect Taxation," and VII. "Local
Taxation."

1896-2   Riley, Franklin Lafayette. "Colonial Origins of New England
    Senates." Ph.D., Johns Hopkins Univ.

    Published under same title: Baltimore : Johns Hopkins Press,
1896. -- 76 p. -- (Johns Hopkins Univ. Studies in Historical and
Political Science ; 14th ser., III). Reprinted: New York : Johnson
Reprint Corp., 1973. -- 76 p. "Introduction" (1973 ed.): The
"research is designed to trace ultimately the successive steps of [the
development of the American Senate] from its inception in colonial
institutions to its final results as embodied in our Senate and
Federal Constitutions. . . . The Colonial Councils, from which the
State Senates evolved, originally exercised a power which was three-
fold,--executive, judicial, and legislative. In the course of time,
however, they lost their executive and judicial authority" (p. 7).
Contents: I. "Massachusetts," II. "Connecticut," III. "New
Hampshire," IV. "Rhode Island," and V. "Conclusions." First four
chapters are subdivided into sections on governmental beginnings and
on the executive, judicial, and legislative functions.

1897-1   Duniway, Clyde Augustus. "The History of Restrictions upon
    Freedom of the Press in Massachusetts." Ph.D., Harvard Univ.
    249 leaves.

"An extended revision" of diss. published as The Development of
Freedom of the Press in Massachusetts. -- Cambridge, Mass. : Harvard
Univ. Press, 1906. -- xv, 202 p. -- (Harvard Historical Studies ; 12).
Reprinted: New York : Burt Franklin, 1968 . -- xv, 202 p. -- (Burt
Franklin Bibliography and Reference Ser. ; 93). In 1968 ed. the
"gradual relaxation of restraints upon the freedom of the press in
Massachusetts is . . . traced through two hundred years of
development" (p. 1). Relevant chapters: I. "Control of the Press in
England to 1603," II. "Restriction of Discussion in England and
Massachusetts, 1603-1640," III. "Supervision of the Press, 1638-1662,"
IV. "Restrictive Censorship, 1662-1685," V. "Lax Enforcement of
Censorship, 1686-1716," VI. "Last Efforts to Maintain Censorship,
1716-1723," and VII. "Limited Freedom of the Press, 1723-1763."
Relevant appendices: A. "Illustrative Documents": I. "James Franklin
and the New England Courant, 1722-1723" and II. "The Case of John
Checkley, 1724." Subsequent chapters and appendices deal with later
periods. Diss. includes several appendices not in published version,
including I. "Early Printers, Printing Presses, and Printing, 1639-
1670."

1897-2   Strong, Frank R. "Cromwell's Colonial and Foreign Policy,
          with Special Reference to the West Indies Expedition of 1654-
          1655." Ph.D., Yale Univ. 399 leaves.

Abstract in DAI, vol. 31 (1), sec. A, p. 329: "This Thesis is to
show . . . [:] Cromwell's relation to the Colonial, Navigation, and
Mercantile System of his time. . . . That Cromwell was entirely
controlled by the economic ideas of the seventeenth century, and made
no attempts whatever to break away from the economic dogmas of his
time. . . . That he had no conception of the true relation of
Colonies to the mother country. . . . The influence of the religious
movement on Cromwell's political actions and how far religious motives
were a determining factor in his colonial and foreign policy. . . .
The transportation policy as carried out by Cromwell in connection
with his colonial policy, especially as to New England."

1898-1   Reinsch, Paul Samuel. "The Attitude of the American Colonies
          to the English Common Law." Ph.D., Univ. of Wisconsin at
          Madison.

Published as English Common Law in the Early American Colonies.
-- Madison : [s.n.], 1899. -- 64 p. -- (Bulletin of the Univ. of
Wisconsin ; no. 31) (Economics, Political Science, and History Ser. ;
vol. 2. no. 4, pp. 393-456). Reprinted: New York : Da Capo Press,
1970. -- 64 p. Also reprinted: New York : Gordon Press, 1977. -- 64
p. "Introduction" (1970 ed.): "The object . . . is to present the
attitude of the colonists during the 17th century, and in some cases
during the 18th, towards the common law of England" (p. 9).
"Conclusion": "The process which we may call the reception of the
English common law by the colonies was not so simple as the legal
theory would lead us to assume. While their general legal conceptions
were conditioned by, and their terminology derived from, the common
law, the early colonists were far from applying it as a technical

system, they often ignored it or denied its subsidiary force, and they consciously departed from many of its most essential principles" (p. 58). The relevant chapter, I. "New England," contains sections on Massachusetts, Connecticut and New Haven, New Hampshire, and Rhode Island.

1899-1   Behan, Warren Palmer. "The Social Ideals and Institutions of the Church-State of Plymouth Colony, 1620-1691." Ph.D., Univ. of Chicago. 10 ["Contents"], 212, 16 ["Bibliography"], ix ["Abstract"] leaves.

"Abstract": "This study has a two-fold purpose: first, from the standpoint of history, to discover and set forth facts hitherto unknown or unnoted regarding that institution around which the life of the Pilgrims in New England centred--the church; secondly, from the standpoint of sociology, to discover and set forth the lines of social service which, directly or indirectly, emerge from this ecclesiastical institution" (p. ii). Contents: "Introduction"; Part I. "Social Ideals": I. "The Elements of Human Welfare and their Relative Values," II. "The Forces Making for Human Welfare," and III. "The Institutions Through Which These Forces Operate"; Part II. "Social Institutions": I. "The Organization of the Church," II. "The State and Church," III. "The Church-State and the Family," IV. "The Church-State and Education," V. "The Church-State and Industry," VI. "The Church-State and the Poor and Suffering," and VII. "The Church-State and the Criminal"; and "General Conclusions."

1899-2   Day, Clive. "Industrial Organisation and Regulations in the American Colonies." Ph.D., Yale Univ. 239 leaves.

Abstract in DAI, vol. 30 (6), sec. A, p. 2223: "I have essayed in the following pages to describe some features of the industrial organisation of the colonies, and some attempts at government control of the organisation. . . . For the government regulations I have relied mainly upon the colonial statutes and New England town records. . . . I have limited my study of the industrial organisation to New England colonies, but I have felt myself justified in citing facts from the other colonies, and I have made use on many points of material dating from a considerably later period than that indicated in the title of the essay."

1899-3   Prince, Walter Franklin. "Three Studies in the History of Crime and Punishment in the Colonial Period." Ph.D., Yale Univ. 97, 106, 72 leaves.

DA, vol. 28 (4), p. 1360: "Abstract not available." Relevant "Study," Part III. "An Examination of Peters' 'Blue Laws,'" published separately: American Historical Assn. -- Annual Report . . . for the Year 1898. -- Washington, D. C. : The Assn., 1899. -- pp. 95-138. Study defends the Rev. Samuel Peters' description of the blue laws in his General History of Connecticut (1781) and discusses the origin and history of the blue laws of Connecticut, New Haven Colony, and

Massachusetts.

1900-1   Proper, Emberson Edward. "Colonial Immigration Laws: A
     Study of the Regulation of Immigration by the English Colonies in
     America." Ph.D., Columbia Univ.

     Published under same title: New York : Columbia Univ. Press,
     1900. -- 91 p. -- (Columbia Univ., Faculty of Political Science,
     Studies in History, Economics, and Public Law ; vol. XII, no. 2).
     Reprinted: New York : AMS Press, 1967. -- 91 p. "Introduction"
     (published ed.): "Our purpose is to study the regulation of colonial
     immigration exclusively from the American standpoint, [but] we shall
     find ourselves compelled to observe it more or less in connection with
     the European conditions" (p. 10). "Conclusion": "The rigorous
     measures of the New England colonies practically excluded immigration
     from other nations than England, and even limited those from the
     mother country to persons of a definite political and religious
     belief" (p. 89). Relevant chapters: Part I. "General Survey": I.
     "Introductory," II. "Encouragement of Immigration," and III.
     "Restriction of Immigration"; Part II. "Detailed Survey": IV.
     "Immigration Laws of the New England Colonies" and VII. "Attitudes of
     England toward Immigration"; Part III. "Reflective Analysis": VIII.
     "Distribution and Characteristics of Nationalities" and IX.
     "Conclusion."

1901-1   Geis, Silas Wright. "The Colonial Agent in England." Ph.D.,
     Yale Univ.   207 leaves.

     "Conclusion": "The end of our journey with the colonial agent is
     near at hand. We have followed him as he labored to preserve the
     domain of his province undespoiled; we have seen him humbly
     petitioning for a written guarantee of personal rights, obtaining and
     defending it. His exertions to establish the constitutional
     prerogatives of America on the foundation of charter grants and the
     'rights of Englishmen' have perhaps evoked our sympathy. He has stood
     forth as the champion of the spiritual and material concerns of the
     colony; and through it all he has kept his constituents constantly
     posted on the hopes and fears they might entertain from their mother
     country. We shall now have a few remarks to make in reference to the
     results that he accomplished, the importance of his office and his
     part in the union of the colonies" (p. 170). Contents: I.
     "Appointment," II. "Financial Relations between Colony and Agent,"
     III. "Functions in Relation to Colonial Domain and Jurisdiction," IV.
     "Functions in Relation to Constitutional Rights of the Colony," V.
     "Functions in Relation to Ecclesiastical Rights of Colony," VI.
     "Economic Functions," VII. "Processes of Agental Action," and VIII.
     "Conclusion." Relevant appendix: I. "Instructions to [Simon]
     Bradstreet and [John] Norton, January 24, 1661."

1902-1   Kellogg, Louise Phelps. "The Colonial Charter: A Study in
     English Colonial Administration." Ph.D., Univ. of Wisconsin at
     Madison.

Revision published as "The American Colonial Charter: A Study of English Administration in Relation Thereto, Chiefly After 1688" in American Historical Assn. -- Annual Report . . . for the Year 1903. -- Washington, D. C. : The Assn., 1904. -- vol. I, pp. 185-341. Reprinted separately: Washington, D. C. : GPO, 1904. -- "185-341" on cover title. Also reprinted: New York : Da Capo Press, 1971. -- 155 p. -- (The Era of the American Revolution). Contents (1971 ed.): "Introduction," I. "The Inception and Control of the English Colonies," II. "Treatment of Individual Colonies," III. "Attempts at Internal Control," IV. "Parliamentary Proceedings Against the Charters," and "Conclusion." Documentary appendices: "Reply of Rhode Island to Request for Surrendering Charter, Nov. 26, 1723," and "Reply of Connecticut to Surrender of Charter, Oct. 28, 1723."

1904-1   Camp, Olinda Anne. "The Pioneering of New York and Massachusetts in Education." Ped.D., New York Univ. xix, 77 [11] leaves.

Relevant chapters: I. "Introduction: Public School Pioneering," II. "Popular Education in Europe during the Sixteenth Century," III. "Education in Massachusetts: Legislation--Schools--Certification of Teachers--Supervision--Support of Schools--Attendance," and V. "New York and Massachusetts as Pioneers in Education." Chapter IV treats of education in New York only. Cf. #1905-3, below.

1904-2   Capen, Edward Warren. "The Historical Development of the Poor Law in Connecticut." Ph.D., Columbia Univ.

Published under same title: New York : Columbia Univ. Press : Macmillan [distributor] ; London : P. S. King & Son, 1905. -- 520 p. -- (Columbia Univ., Faculty of Political Science, Studies in History, Economics, and Public Law ; vol. XXII). Reprinted: New York : AMS Press, 1968. -- 520 p. -- (Columbia Univ. Studies in Social Sciences ; 57). "Preface" (1968 ed.): The work's intention is "to trace [the Poor Law's] development from its beginnings in the early colonial period to its present form" (p. 5). Relevant chapters: "Introduction"; Part I. "Early Colonial Period, 1634-1712": I. "Chief characteristics: establishment of principle of relief by towns; first step toward relief by colony or state," II. "Preventive measures," III. "Methods of relief," IV. "Special legislation," and V. "Summary"; Part II. "Late Colonial Period, 1713-1784": I. "Chief characteristic: workhouse laws," II. "Preventive measures," III. "Methods of relief," IV. "Special legislation," and V. "Summary"; and Part VI. "Conclusion." Parts III-V deal with later periods.

1904-3   Kimball, Everett. "The Public Life of Joseph Dudley, (1672-1715)." Ph.D., Harvard Univ. 135 leaves.

Revision published as The Public Life of Joseph Dudley: A Study of the Colonial Policy of the Stuarts in New England, 1660-1715. -- New York : Longmans, Green, 1911. -- vii, 239 p. -- (Harvard

Historical Studies ; XV). "Preface" (1911 ed.): "I have . . .
attempted to examine the Stuart colonial policy and to set forth the
practical political problems connected with its application in New
England, and to show the parts played by the various agencies
connected with its development. I have viewed Dudley as an English
official charged with the execution of English policy, and . . . I
have investigated . . . particularly the problems and difficulties
that faced all royal officials in New England at that period" (p. v).
Contents: I. "The Early Life of Joseph Dudley and the Loss of the
Massachusetts Charter, 1660-1686," II. "The Temporary Policy of the
Restoration: Joseph Dudley President of the Massachusetts Council,
May to December, 1686," III. "New England Regulated: Joseph Dudley and
the Rule of Andros, 1686-1689," IV. "Scheming for Office: Joseph
Dudley Member of Council for New York, Deputy-Governor of the Isle of
Wight, Member of Parliament, 1689-1702," V. "Joseph Dudley Governor of
Massachusetts: Parliamentary Relations with the General Court," VI.
"Joseph Dudley Captain-General of Massachusetts: Military and Indian
Affairs," VII. "Dudley's Relations with the Colonies of New Hampshire,
Rhode Island, and Connecticut," VIII. "The Currency and Banking
Problems During Dudley's Administration as Governor," IX. "Dudley's
Fight to Retain Office," and X. "The Motives of Dudley's Conduct."
Appendix: A. "Royal Commission to Joseph Dudley, Governor of the
Province of Massachusetts Bay in New England, April 1, 1702."

1905-1   Rowe, Henry Kalloch. "Rise and Development of Religion in
    New England." Ph.D., Boston Univ. (Graduate School). ix, 161
    leaves, handwritten.

    "Introductory": "Human history presents certain periods of rapid
growth in religious thought and life. Among these it is doubtful if
any period . . . has been so productive as the last three centuries,
or any soil more fruitful than that of New England. Here freedom is
in the air, and the earnestness of the Pilgrim Fathers is the heritage
of these hills and valleys. In the cycle of the centuries the
Congregational simplicity of the early faith and practice was restored
in the first settlement at Plymouth, and here has developed a higher
type of thinking and living than the world elsewhere has seen" (p. 1).
Relevant chapters: "Introductory"; Part I. "The Rise of New England
Congregationalism": "The Faith and Practice of the Pilgrims," "The
Puritans of Massachusetts Bay Become Separatists," "Congregationalism
Becomes the Standing Order," "The Straight and Narrow Way of
Puritanism," "The Place of Religion in the Early History of the Other
New England Colonies," "The Importance of Religion in the Colonial
Life of the First Generation," and "The Halfway Covenant"; and Part
II. "The Decline of Spirituality, 1662-1740": "The Decline of
Spiritual Fervor in the Second Generation," "Progress of the
Baptists," "The Age of the Mathers," "The End of the Theocracy," and
"Tendencies towards Liberalism." Parts III and IV deal with later
events to 1834.

1905-2   Spencer, Henry Russell. "Constitutional Conflict in
     Provincial Massachusetts: A Study of Some Phases of the
     Opposition Between the Massachusetts Governor and General Court
     in the Early Eighteenth Century." Ph.D., Columbia Univ.

     Published under same title: Columbus, Ohio : Press of Fred J.
Heer, 1905. -- 135 p. Chapter I (published version): "The present
study is concerned with some phases of the . . . provincial period.
The new system was a mixture of two diverse, frequently opposed, sets
of institutions, those of the normal British province, and those
commonwealth institutions which Massachusetts had developed in her
seventeenth-century independence. In the antagonism soon found and
developed between them there appeared a constant tendency to reaction
toward colonial autonomy, a tendency which was constantly opposed and
hampered in its progress by the progressive elements in the system"
(p. 6). Contents: I. "Antagonistic Colonial Ideas," II. "Compromise
in the Charter," III. "The Prerogative Bodies," IV. "The Popular
House," V. "The Salary Question," VI. "Control of the Treasury," and
VIII. "Control of the Military and Domestic Affairs."

1905-3   Suzzallo, Henry. "The Rise of Local School Supervision in
     Massachusetts (The School Committee, 1635-1827)." Ph.D. Columbia
     Univ.

     Published under same title: New York: [s.n.], 1905. ("Printed
for the author.") -- vii, 155 p. -- (Teachers College, Columbia Univ.,
Contributions to Education ; vol. 1, no. 3). Reprinted: New York :
Teachers College, Columbia Univ., 1906. -- vii, 154 p. -- (Teachers
College, Columbia Univ., Contributions to Education ; vol. 1, no. 3).
Also reprinted: New York : Arno Press, 1969. -- vii, 154 p. --
(American Education: Its Men, Ideas, and Institutions). Also
reprinted: New York : AMS Press, 1972. -- vii, 154 p. "Introduction"
(1969 ed.): "The development of school supervision in the
commonwealth of Massachusetts accompanied the evolution of a state
system of public schools. As more and more public money was devoted
to the fostering of education, it was natural that people should
desire to control and supervise the schools to which such money was
given. The outcome of increasing support of education was a system of
public schools. The outcome of the tendency in the direction towards
controlling the schools supported by public funds was the evolution of
the special functions and agencies of school supervision" (p. 1).
Relevant chapters: I. "Introduction," II. "The Control of the Town
Meeting," III. "The Delegation of Power to the Selectmen," IV. "The
Minister and Others in School Affairs," V. "The Early School
Committees, 1639-1725," VI. "The Development of the Committee for
Promising Teachers, 1700-1789," and VII. "The Development of the
Committees for School Inspection, 1700-1789." Chapters VIII and IX
deal with a later period.

1905-4   Whitney, William T. "New York and Massachusetts as Pioneers
     in Education." Ped.D., New York Univ. [140] leaves.

     Relevant chapters: I. "Introduction: Early Educational Activity

in Massachusetts and New York," II. "Education at the Reformation--
Elementary Education in Germany--Popular Education in Switzerland,
Scotland, Sweden, and Holland--Public Elementary Education in
England," III. "Rise of the Puritan Movement in England--The Principle
for which it Stood--the Exodus to America in 1620-1629," and IV. "Rise
of Education in Massachusetts: Early Legislation--Schools--
Certification of Teachers--Supervision--School Support--Compulsory
Attendance--General Conclusion." The remaining chapters treat of
education in Holland and New York and of later events in
Massachusetts. Cf. #1904-1, above.

1906-1   Mead, Nelson Prentiss.   "Connecticut as a Corporate Colony."
    Ph.D., Columbia Univ.

    Published under same title: Lancaster, Pa. : New Era Printing
Co., 1906. -- 119 p. "Introduction" (published version): "It is the
purpose of this study to trace out, in considerable detail, the
internal development of Connecticut as a type of the corporate colony.
Emphasis will naturally be laid on constitutional questions; economic
and social considerations only being touched upon as they affected or
were affected by the constitutional development of the colony.
Secondly an attempt will be made to consider Connecticut as part of
the British Empire; to show her position was, from the standpoint of
imperial control, an anomalous one; how the English administration
tried to bring the colony into closer and more harmonious relations
with the home government, and finally, how the colony was enabled to
avert these attacks and preserve its institutions intact throughout
the colonial period" (p. 6). Contents: I. "Organs of Legislation and
Administration," II. "Finance and Currency," III. "Land System," and
IV. "Military Affairs."

1906-2   Rosenberry, Lois Kimball Mathews. "Study of the Spread of
    New England Settlement and Institutions, 1620-1865." Ph.D.,
    Harvard Univ. (Radcliffe College). [228] leaves.

    Revision published as The Expansion of New England: The Spread
of New England Settlements and Institutions to the Mississippi River,
1620-1865. -- Boston : Houghton Mifflin, 1909. -- xiv, 303 p.
Reprinted: New York : Russell & Russell, 1962. -- xiv, 303 p.
Relevant chapters (1962 ed.): I. "Introduction," II. "The Beginnings
of an American Frontier," III. "The Influence of Indian Warfare upon
the Frontier, 1660-1713," IV. "Forty Years of Strife with the
Wilderness, 1713-1754," and X. "Two Centuries and a Half of New
England Pioneering, 1620-1865." Diss. includes several appendices not
in published version, including B. "Plymouth Compact; Agreement of
Springfield Settlers." This diss. is not included in CDI.

1908-1   Fry, William Henry. "New Hampshire as a Royal Province."
    Ph.D., Columbia Univ.

    Published under same title: New York : Columbia Univ. :
Longmans, Green [distributor], 1908. -- 526 p. -- (Columbia Univ.,

Faculty of Political Science, Studies in History, Economics, and Public Law ; vol. XXIX, no. 2). Reprinted: New York : AMS Press, 1970. -- 526 p. -- (Columbia Univ. Studies in the Social Sciences ; 79). Principally covers the period 1679-1741. Contents: I. "Introduction," II. "The Executive," III. "The Legislature," IV. "The Land System," V. "Finance," VI. "Justice," and VII. "Military Affairs." Appendices: "Royal Commissions, 1679-1741," "Speakers of the House, 1692-1775," and "Assemblies, 1692-1775."

1908-2   MacLear, Anne Bush. "Early New England Towns: A Comparative Study of Their Development." Ph.D., Columbia Univ.

Published under same title: New York : Columbia Univ. : Longmans, Green [distributor], 1908. -- 183 p. -- (Columbia Univ., Faculty of Political Science, Studies in History, Economics, and Public Law ; vol. XXIX, no. 1). Reprinted: New York : AMS Press, 1967. -- 181 p. "Preface" (1967 ed.): "The purpose of this work is to give in some detail an account of the institutional life of a Massachusetts town in the seventeenth century by means of a comparison of the institutions of five of the earliest of these towns,--Salem, Dorchester, Watertown, Roxbury and Cambridge." Contents: I. "The Town as a Whole," II. "Town Courts," III. "Town Finances," IV. "Town Lands," V. "Town Government," VI. "The Church," and VII. "The Schools."

1908-3   Otis, William Bradley. "American Verse, 1625-1807: A History." Ph.D., New York Univ.

Published under same title: New York : Moffat Yard, 1909. -- xiv, 303 p. Reprinted: New York : Haskell House, 1966. -- xiv, 303 p. "Preface" (1966 ed.): "The present work includes all important American verse between 1625 and 1807 which is worthy of note because of its connection with American history, or because of the light which it throws upon the social and intellectual characteristics of the time" (p. vii). Includes poetry by William Bradford, Anne Bradstreet, Benjamin Colman, Cotton Mather, Urian Oakes, and Michael Wigglesworth. Contents: I. "Historical Verse," II. "Religious Verse," III. "Political and Satirical Verse," IV. "Imaginative Verse," and V. "Translation, Paraphrase, etc."

1908-4   Updegraff, Harlan. "The Origin of the Moving School in Massachusetts." Ph.D., Columbia Univ.

Published under same title: New York : [s.n.], 1907. ("Printed for the author.") -- 186 p. -- (Teachers College, Columbia Univ., Contributions to Education ; no. 17). Reprinted: New York : Teachers College, Columbia Univ., 1908. -- 186 p. -- (Teachers College, Columbia Univ., Contributions to Education ; no. 17). Also reprinted: New York : Arno Press, 1969. -- 186 p. -- (American Education: Its Men, Ideas, and Institutions). Also reprinted: New York : AMS Press, 1972. "Introduction" (1972 ed.): "This study is an attempt to account for the establishment of the moving school.

Speaking generally, it was wanted because the central original fixed, or standing, school failed to satisfy longer the new conditions arising in the development of colonial life. Many of these new conditions were in themselves a product of slow growth, extending back over the entire latter half of the seventeenth century. As a result this treatment deals for the most part with the life of this earlier period" (p. 7). Contents: "Introduction," I. "Control and Support of the Church-Town School: Methods of Support," II. "Control and Support of the Church-Town School: Agencies of Control," III. "Control and Support of the Civil School: Methods of Support," IV. "Control and Support of the Civil School: Agencies of Control," V. "Social Disintegration," VI. "Dispersion of Population," VII. "Intellectual Decline," VIII. "Decentralizing Tendencies of Democracy," IX. "The Dame School," X. "The Abolition of the Tuition-Tax," and "Conclusion." Appendices: A. "Entries in Town Records Concerning Schools to 1648"-- i.e., the towns of Boston, Charlestown, Dedham, Dorchester, Newbury, Salem, and Ipswich; and B. "A portion of the Agreement entered into by the inhabitants of Roxbury in the 'last of August 1645' at the time of the establishment of 'The Free School of 1645 in Roxburie.'"

1909-1   Jackson, George Leroy. "The Development of School Support in
      Colonial Massachusetts." Ph.D., Columbia Univ.

      Published under same title: New York : Teachers College, Columbia Univ., 1909. -- 95 p. -- (Teachers College, Columbia Univ., Contributions to Education ; no. 25). Reprinted: New York : Arno Press, 1969. -- 95 p. -- (American Education: Its Men, Ideas, and Institutions). Also reprinted: New York : AMS Press, 1972. "Introduction" (1969 ed.): "The aim of this study is, first, to trace the various methods through which the early schools of Massachusetts were supported--showing at the same time the basis of experience for dealing with the problem of support through the close relationship existing between--1) education and religion and 2) education and the support and apprenticeship of the poor; and, second, after partial support by general taxation had become customary, to point out the main causes which made general taxation the sole method of school support and hence gave rise to the 'free school'--publicly controlled and publicly supported" (p. 5). Contents: I. "Introduction," II. "School Support by Contribution," III. "Free Education for the Poor," IV. "Records of Town Action with Respect to School Support," V. "School Support by General Taxation," and VI. "The 'Free School.'"

1910-1   Hilkey, Charles Joseph. "Legal Development in Colonial
      Massachusetts, 1630-1686." Ph.D., Columbia Univ.

      Published under same title: New York : Columbia Univ., 1910. -- 148 p. -- (Columbia Univ., Faculty of Political Science, Studies in History, Economics, and Public Law ; vol. XXXVII, no. 2 ; whole no. 98). Reprinted: New York : AMS Press, 1967. -- 148 p. "Preface" (1967 ed.): "According to the accepted legal theory, the American colonists claimed the English common law as their birthright, brought with them its general principles and adopted so much of it as was applicable to their condition. Although this theory is universally adopted by the courts, a close study of the subject reveals among the early colonists a far different attitude toward the common law from that which is usually attributed to them. In none of the colonies, perhaps, was this more marked than in early Massachusetts. Here the binding force of English law was denied, and a legal system largely different came into use. It is the purpose of this work to trace the development of that system during the period of the first charter" (p. 5). Contents: I. "The Law-making Factors: --The Legislative Department --The Judicial System --The Church --Lawyers --Law Books" and II. "The Law: --Civil Procedure --Criminal Procedure --Criminal Law --Torts --Contracts --Property --Family --Succession."

1910-2   Pearson, George Edward. "The Great and General Court of Massachusetts, 1628-1691: A Study of Its Early History with Special Reference to Its Organization." Ph.D., Tufts Univ. vii, 116 leaves.

"Foreword": "The early history of Massachusetts is virtually the history of its General Court. . . . The early history of the Great and General Court of Massachusetts is of more than local importance, and is of special interest to those who wish to make a thorough study of our political institutions, as it affords not only an excellent example of the form of government of that time, but it also shows the transition from the old established principles and institutions of the government in England to the new and changed conditions applicable to the needs of the colonists in the new world" (pp. vi-vii). Contents: I. "Introduction," II. "From the Organization of the Company to the Establishment of Government in America," III. "From the Transfer of the Government until the Separation of the Legislature into Two Houses," IV. "Struggle for Independence," V. "Organization of the General Court 1630-1644," and VI. "Organization of the General Court 1644-1686."

1910-3   Phelps, Vergil Vivian. "The Pastor and Teacher, with Special Reference to the Pastor and Teacher in the New England Churches." Ph.D., Yale Univ.

Diss. may no longer be extant. Cited in CDI, vol. 36, p. 546; but not in DAI, NUC, or OCLC. Yale Univ. diss. catalog (April 24, 1980) notes "No copies," and refers user to excerpt or summary published as "The Pastor and Teacher in New England," Harvard Theological Review, 4 (1911), pp. 388-99. Article examines "a unique institution of early New England by which religion was linked to education, and religious education was given a high place in the life of the churches. . . . The pastor was the administrative head of the church, who was expected to inspire its life and activities; the teacher was undoubtedly the distinctive feature of the New England system. . . . As far as it is possible to make a comparison, the teacher may be described as a kind of theological professor whose sphere of work was exclusively a church" (p. 388).

1911-1   Dickerson, Oliver Morton. "American Colonial Government, 1696-1765: A Study of the British Board of Trade in Its Relation to the American Colonies, Political, Industrial, Administrative." Ph.D., Univ. of Illinois at Urbana-Champaign.

Published under same title: Cleveland, Ohio : Arthur H. Clark Co., 1912. -- 390 p. Reprinted: New York : Russell & Russell, 1962. -- 390 p. "Preface" (1962 ed.): "The period covered by this volume . . . is one of the most important in the growth of the American nation. It was during this period that the original colonies developed their traditions of political liberty, and acquired by steady encroachments on the part of the assemblies practically complete self-government" (p. 10). [This work is] a study of the British Board of Trade and the machinery of imperial control: what it was, the men who directed it, their ideas of the relations of the mother country to the colonies, the relations of the colonial office to other branches of government, and the conditions under which colonial affairs were administered" (pp. 12-13). Contents: I. "Organization and Personnel of the Board of Trade," II. "Relations of the Board of Trade to Other Departments of Administration," III. "Difficulties of Colonial Administration," IV. "The Imperialistic Policy of the Board of Trade," V. "Treatment of Colonial Legislation," and VI. "Boundaries, Trade, Defense, and Indian Affairs."

1911-2   Inglis, Alexander James. "The Rise of the High School in Massachusetts." Ph.D., Columbia Univ.

Published under same title: New York : Teachers College, Columbia Univ., 1911. -- v, 166 p. -- (Teachers College, Columbia Univ., Contributions to Education ; no. 45). Reprinted: New York : AMS Press, 1972. -- v, 166 p. "Introduction" (1972 ed.): "The present discussion has for its aim a consideration of the high schools of Massachusetts up to the beginning of the Civil War" (p. iv). Relevant chapter: I. "The Educational Situation in Massachusetts Previous to 1827." The remaining chapters treat of later developments.

1912-1   Cook, Elizabeth Christine. "Literary Influences in Colonial Newspapers, 1704-1750." Ph.D., Columbia Univ.

Published under same title: New York : Columbia Univ. Press, 1912. -- 279 p. -- (Columbia Univ. Studies in English and Comparative Literature). Reprinted with an introduction by Donald D. Stewart: Port Washington, N. Y. : Kennikat Press, 1966. -- xv, 279 p. "Preface" (1966 ed.): "The following study aims to give a fairly comprehensive survey of the literary contributions in colonial newspapers from 1704 to 1750" (p. vii). Relevant chapters: "Introduction," I. "The New England Courant" (Boston, 1721-1726) and II. "The New England Weekly Journal" (Boston, 1727-1741).

1912-2   Seymour, J. A. "The Development of New England Thought." S.T.D., Temple Univ.   37 leaves.

Very briefly summarizes "New England thought" from the English Reformation--through Elizabethan and Jacobean Puritanism, the founding and history of the Plymouth, Massachusetts Bay, and Connecticut colonies, and the Great Awakening--to Horace Bushnell.

1914-1   Colman, George Tilden. "Certain Movements in England and America Which Influenced the Transition from the Ideals of Personal Righteousness of the Seventeenth Century to the Modern Ideals of Social Service." Ph.D., Univ. of Chicago.

Published under same title: Menasha, Wis. : George Banta Publishing Co. ; Chicago : Univ. of Chicago Libraries [distributor], 1917. -- vii, 107 p. Chapter I: "Well into the eighteenth century, the Puritan ideals of salvation were still exerting a wide sway over the purposes of the English people. The author is seeking in this treatise to trace the fundamental factors which, in a single century, transformed the popular aims for individual salvation into the social ideals which began to touch all ranks during the nineteenth century" (p. 4). Relevant chapters: "Summary," I. "Introduction," II. "The Ethical Ideal of Puritanism," III. "The Rise of Commerce and Industry--The Settlement of the New World," IV. "Deism and Rationalism," VI. "The Early Eighteenth-Century Moralists," and VII. "Social Unrest--The Decline of Puritanism 1700-1750." Chapters V, VIII-XII deal exclusively with later periods.

1914-2   Stifler, Susan Martha Reed. "Church and State in Massachusetts, 1691-1740." Ph.D., Univ. of Illinois at Urbana-Champaign.

Published under same title: Urbana : Univ. of Illinois, 1914. -- 208 p. -- (Univ. of Illinois Studies in the Social Sciences ; vol. III, no. 4). "Introduction": "The opposition to the established church of Massachusetts which had been opened by the intruders in the mid-seventeenth century was renewed soon after 1691 and now had an altered basis for attack in the terms of the new chapter. . . . The elaborate ecclesiastical structure reared in order to meet the situation was artificial, and had no strength of its own to resist continual pressure on it. The nature of this artificial structure and the scheme of attack made against it by outside forces will be treated" (pp. 17-18). Contents: I. "Introduction," II. "The Ecclesiastical System of Provincial Massachusetts," III. "Opposing Elements," IV. "The System in Practice," V. "The Quakers and Their Allies," VI. "The Church of England," and "Conclusion."

1915-1   Carroll, Charles. "A History of Public Education in Rhode Island." Ph.D., Brown Univ.

Revision published as Public Education in Rhode Island with an introduction by Walter E. Ranger. -- Providence : E. L. Freeman, 1918. -- 500 p. -- (Rhode Island Education Circulars). Chapter I of published version, "Rhode Island Colonial Schools, 1640-1776," is relevant; chapters II-X concern later periods.

1915-2   Russell, Elmer Beecher. "The Review of American Colonial
    Legislation by the King in Council." Ph.D., Columbia Univ.

    Published under same title: New York: Columbia Univ., 1915. --
227 p. -- (Columbia Univ., Faculty of Political Science, Studies in
History, Economics, and Public Law ; vol. LXIV, no. 2 ; whole no.
155). Reprinted: New York : Octagon Books, 1976. -- 227 p. Also
reprinted: Buffalo, N. Y. : W. S. Hein, 1981. -- 227 p. --
(Historical Writings in Law and Jurisprudence ; vol. 31). "Preface"
(1976 ed.): The work "is primarily a study of the action taken upon
colonial legislation by the English government" (p. 5). Contents: I.
"Introductory: The Review of Colonial Legislation Prior to 1696," II.
and III. "The Procedure of the English Government in Legislative
Review," IV. and V. "The Policy of the Government in Legislative
Review" in "Trade, Shipping and Finance" and in "Insistence upon
Conformity to the Law of England," VI. and VII. "The Policy of the
British Government in Legislative Review" in "Attitude Toward
Encroachments on the Prerogative" and in "Attitude Toward Laws Deemed
Inexpedient," and VIII. "The Results of Legislative Review."

1916-1   Jackson, Elizabeth. "Reaction Against Puritanism in American
    Periodicals of the Eighteenth Century." Ph.D., Harvard Univ.
    (Radcliffe College). 2 vols. (257 leaves + extra sequence for
    notes numbered 2a-228a: notes for each page appear on a separate
    pale blue page immediately following the page to which the notes
    refer).

    "Introduction": "These pages have suggested a few of the
essential elements of early New England thought as it is
distinguished, though never dissociated, from Puritan theology. In
the course of the eighteenth century all these ideas suffered
modifications that have been variously defined, described, and
explained" (p. 8). Diss. treats of eighteenth-century reaction
against Puritan views of man's relation to God and a future life; the
natural depravity of man; the Calvinistic doctrine of reason; and the
relation between church and state. Contents: I. "Introduction," II.
"Massachusetts, 1700-1750," III. "Massachusetts, 1750-1780," IV.
"Massachusetts, 1780-1800. Newspapers," V. "Massachusetts, 1780-1800.
Magazines," VI. "Connecticut before 1780," VII. "Connecticut, 1780-
1800," VIII. "New Hampshire and Vermont," IX. "Rhode Island," and X.
"Conclusion." This diss. does not appear in CDI.

1916-2   Powell, Chilton Latham. "English Domestic Relations, 1487-
    1653: A Study of Matrimony and Family Life in Theory and
    Practice as Revealed by the Literature, Law, and History of the
    Period." Ph.D., Columbia Univ.

    Published under same title: New York : Columbia Univ. Press,
1917. -- xii, 271 p. -- (Columbia Univ. Studies in English and
Comparative Literature). Reprinted: New York : Russell & Russell,

1974. -- 274 p. "Preface" (1974 ed.): "The subject of my investigation here is that of domestic relations in England, including both the contract of marriage (its making and breaking) and the subsequent life of the family" (n.p.). Relevant chapters: I. "Introduction"; II. "Controversies Regarding Marriage": I. "Historical Situation," II. "The Puritan Platform in regard to Marriage," III. "The Position and Practice of the Independents," and IV. "Continental, Scottish, and American Churches"; III. "The Attempted Reform of Divorce": II. "The Puritan-Anglican Controversy on Divorce"; IV. "The Domestic Conduct Book": II. "Puritan and Romish Attitudes towards Marriage"; V. "Contemporary Attitudes towards Women"; and VI. "Wider Ranges of Domestic Literature." Relevant appendix: D. "Contents of Typical Domestic Books."

1916-3   Seybolt, Robert Francis. "Apprenticeship and Apprenticeship Education in Colonial New England and New York." Ph.D., Columbia Univ.

Published under same title: New York : Teachers College, Columbia Univ., 1917. -- 121 p. -- (Teachers College, Columbia Univ., Contributions to Education ; no. 85). Reprinted: New York : Arno Press, 1969. -- 121 p. -- (American Education: Its Men, Ideas, and Institutions). Also reprinted: New York : AMS Press, 1972. -- 121 p. "Conclusion" (1969 ed.): "In New England . . . the first laws concerning education, and the first compulsory education laws were contained in apprenticeship enactments. . . . The apprenticeship system took care of the entire problem of public elementary education during the colonial period" (p. 107). Relevant chapters: I. "The Apprenticeship System in England," II. "The Practice of Apprenticeship in the New Plymouth and Massachusetts Bay Colonies," III. "The Educational Aspects of the Practice of Apprenticeship in the New Plymouth and Massachusetts Bay Colonies," IV. "Apprenticeship and Apprenticeship Education in the Connecticut, New Haven, and Rhode Island Colonies," and IX. "Conclusion." Chapters V-VIII deal with New York.

1916-4   Young, James Reed. "Relation of the Church and Clergy to Education in the American Colonies." Ph.D., Univ. of Chicago. [187] leaves.

Final "Summary": "The purpose of this study was to trace the educational history of the various sects settling in the American colonies; to formulate, as definitely as possible, the educational policy of each church; and to determine the effect of religious doctrine and tradition upon the evolution of our schools during the colonial period" (p. 1, last numerical sequence). Relevant chapters: I. "Religious and Educational Traditions of the Colonists," II. "Calvinism and Education," V. "Educational Activities of the Clergy," and VI. "Summary and Conclusions." Chapters III and IV treat of various non-Calvinist sects.

1917-1   Keir, Robert Malcolm. "Some Influences of Environment in Massachusetts." Ph.D., Univ. of Pennsylvania.

Published under same title: Lancaster, Pa. : Press of the New Era Printing Co., 1917. -- 18, [7-]25 p. Published version is reprint of article "Some Responses to Environment in Massachusetts," first published in The Bulletin of the Geographical Society of Philadelphia, vol. 15 (July, 1917), pp. 121-38, and vol. 15 (Oct., 1917), pp. 167-85. Conclusion: "The main features of life in Massachusetts have been controlled by two environmental factors, the first of which--the general north-south trend of the hills and valleys--was responsible for the early grouping of population along the seaboard and the Connecticut valley. . . . Manufacturing, agriculture, and even summer visitors have been segregated by the tendency of the hills and valleys to open northward and southward. Along with this feature of the environment and fully as influential, are the changes brought about by the visitation of the glacier. The creation of water power, the alteration of the soil and baring of rocks have done much to direct industry; for manufacturing, agriculture, and quarrying in their present form, and in their positions of relative importance may be traced to these causes. Since the history, politics, the prestige and the present problems of the state have all turned about one or the other of these two environmental factors or the results that have flowed from them, we may safely grant them a place of paramount importance" (p. 25).

1917-2   Perrine, Fred J. "Significance of the English and the American Almanacs of the Seventeenth and Eighteenth Centuries." Ph.D., New York Univ. 329 numbered leaves + 139 unnumbered leaves following leaf 267.

"Summary and Conclusion": "I have tried to make plane [sic] in the foregoing chapters my contention that the almanac . . . has a distinct and peculiar value that no other publication can quite satisfy" (p. 308). Contents: "Introduction," I. "Description of the English and American Almanacs of the 17th and 18th Centuries," II. "Miscellaneous Literature," III. "Literature Pertaining to the Life and Customs of the People," IV. "Literature Pertaining to the Sciences and Medical Knowledge of the Period," V. "Literature Pertaining to the History of the Period," VI. "Poetry," and VII. "Summary and Conclusion."

1917-3   Wright, Thomas Goddard. "Aspects of Culture in New England During the First Century of Colonization, with Special Reference to Literary Culture and the Production of Literature." Ph.D., Yale Univ. 444 leaves.

Published version: Literary Culture in Early New England, 1620-1730, edited by his widow, Mabel Hyde Kingsbury Wright, with a "Memorial Note" by William Lyon Phelps. -- New Haven : Yale Univ. Press, 1920. -- 322 p. Reprinted: New York : Russell & Russell, 1966. -- 322 p. "Introduction" (1966 ed.): "The pages which follow . . . will attempt to determine that which lies back of any literature, the

culture of the people themselves, and to study the relation between
their culture and the literature which they produced. . . . [The]
general state of culture in the colonies will be shown to be higher
than it has usually been rated" (p. 11). Contents: Part I. "The
Early Settlers": I. "Education," II. "Libraries and the Circulation
of Books," III. "Intercourse with England and English Literary Men,"
IV. "Other Phases of Culture," and V. "The Production of Literature";
Part II. "The End of the Seventeenth Century": VI. "Education," VII.
"Books and Libraries," VIII. "Quotations by New England Writers," IX.
"Relations with England and Other Phases of Literary Culture," and X.
"The Production of Literature"; and Part III. "The New Century": XI.
"Education," XII. "Books and Libraries," XIII. "Other Phases of
Literary Culture," and XIV. "The Production of Literature."
Appendices: "Items Illustrating the Movement of Books to and Among
New Englanders," "Invoices," "Book References in Increase Mather's
Writings," "Inventory of the Library of William Brewster," "Books
Bequeathed to Harvard College by John Harvard," "Selected Titles from
the 1723 Catalogue of the Harvard Library," and "Selected Titles from
the 1725 Catalogue of the Harvard Libraries." Diss. includes several
appendices not in published version: catalogs of the libraries of
William Bradford, Thomas Dudley, Samuel Eaton, Increase and Cotton
Mather, Thomas Prince, Miles Standish, William Tyng, and John
Winthrop, Jr.

1918-1   Mead, Arthur Raymond. "The Development of Free Schools in
     the United States as Illustrated by Connecticut and Michigan."
     Ph.D., Columbia Univ.

     Published under same title: New York : Teachers College,
Columbia Univ., 1918. -- xi, 236 p. -- (Teachers College, Columbia
Univ., Contributions to Education ; no. 91). Reprinted: New York :
AMS Press, 1972. -- xi, 236 p. Part I. "Connecticut" begins with
section on "Colonial Beginnings in Connecticut."

1919-1   Barnes, Viola Florence. "The Dominion of New England: A
     Study in British Colonial Policy." Ph.D., Yale Univ.   350
     leaves.

     Revision published under same title: New Haven : Yale Univ.
Press, 1923. -- 303 p. -- (Yale Historical Publications. Miscellany ;
11). Reprinted: New York : F. Ungar, 1960. -- 303 p. -- (American
Classics). "Preface" (1960 ed.): "The aim of this study is to show
(1) the purpose of the British colonial policy of consolidation, (2)
the characteristics of the Andros Administration, and (3) the effect
of this policy on subsequent relations between New England and the
mother country to 1691 when the Massachusetts charter was granted" (p.
ii). Contents: "Introduction: British Colonial Policy to 1665," I.
"The Refusal of Massachusetts to Become a Part of the British Colonial
System," II. "An Experiment in Consolidation," III. "Establishment of
the Dominion of New England," IV. "Legislation and Taxation," V.
"Administration of Justice," VI. "Liberty of Conscience," VII.
"Trade," VIII, "The Land System," IX. "Defense," X. "Revolution," and
XI. "Abandonment of the Policy of Consolidation."

1919-2 Gabriel, Ralph Henry. "The Evolution of Long Island: A Story of Land and Sea." Ph.D., Yale Univ.

Revision published under same title: New Haven : Yale Univ. Press, 1921. -- 194 p. -- (Yale Historical Studies. Miscellany ; IX). Reprinted: Port Washington, N.Y. : I. J. Friedman, 1960. -- 194 p. Friedman ed. reprinted 1968 as: (Empire State Historical Publications; no. 1). "Foreword" (1921 ed.): "The problem of the present study is to trace the development of a people as it has been affected, not only by its social and economic, but also by its natural surroundings" (p. 12). Relevant chapters: I. "An Unfinished Play," II. "The Struggle for Existence," and III. "The Influence of the Hinterland." Chapters IV-XVI deal mainly with later events but touch on the development of the Long Island fishing and whaling industries.

1921-1 Stewart, George, Jr. "A History of Religious Education in Connecticut to the Middle of the the Nineteenth Century." Ph.D., Yale Univ.

Revision published under same title: New Haven : Yale Univ. Press, 1924. -- xiv, 402 p. -- (Yale Studies in the History and Theory of Religious Education ; I). Reprinted: New York : Arno Press, 1969, -- xiv, 402 p. -- (American Education: Its Men, Ideas, and Institutions). "Introduction" (1969 ed.): "The history of the relations of religion and education in Connecticut is of especial interest and value because it exhibits in bold relief factors and processes of development which have characterized American life generally. Connecticut supported an established Church until 1818, and religion dominated the early life of its schools. It was the first state to establish a permanent public school fund; and its system of common schools was for a time considered the best in the country. Immigration . . . of dissenting Protestants . . . added new elements to the population, and has been largely responsible for the secularization of the public schools. Connecticut was the stronghold of the New England Theology, and the scene of its passing" (p. vii). Relevant chapters: "Introduction"; Part I. "The Period 1633-1712": I. "The Union of Church and State," II. "Legislation Bearing upon Religious Education" (includes New Haven Colony), III. "Status of Religious Education, 1636-1721," and IV. "The Materials of Religious Education in the Period 1633-1712"; and Part II. "The Period 1712-1798": V. "Growth of Dissent and Toleration in the Period 1712-1798," VI. "Legislation Bearing upon Religious Education in the Period 1712-1798," VII. "The Status of Religious Education in the Period 1712-1798," and VIII. "Materials of Religious Instruction in the Period 1712-1798," Part III covers 1798-1861. Diss. was awarded the John Addison Porter Prize in 1921.

1922-1 Clune, Mary Catherine. "The Geographic Factors in the Development of the Massachusetts Towns of the Connecticut Valley." Ph.D., Clark Univ. 110, 3 leaves.

"Preface": "The physiographic and geologic facts incorporated in this study have been obtained in part from published maps, in part from direct observation in the Connecticut Valley. Historical data have been gathered from original sources especially from the town records of Springfield and Northampton. . . . The published histories of several towns have been helpful. . . . My work has been in the field and in the library to ascertain by independent research much of the material here presented, to compile and interpret all available information, and then to show the relations which exist between the several sets of facts involved; to indicate the influence of geographic conditions upon the settlement and upon the agricultural and industrial development within the Connecticut River Valley" (n.p.). Relevant chapters: "Introduction," I. "The Geology of the Connecticut Valley," II. "Surface Characteristics," III. "Climate," IV. "Historical Geography," V. "Early Industries in the Valley Towns," and X. "Summary."

1922-2   Grizzell, Emit Duncan. "Origin and Development of the High
       School in New England before 1865." Ph.D., Univ. of Pennsylvania.

       Published with an "Introduction" by Arthur J. Jones under same
title: Philadelphia : [s.n.] ; New York : Macmillan, 1923. -- xv,
428 p. "Foreword" (1923 ed.): "The aim of this study is to present
as fully as possible the facts concerning the origin and development
of the high school in New England during the formative period of its
history. At the same time attention is called wherever possible to
those social and economic forces that affected high school origins,
theory, and practice" (p. xi). Relevant chapter: I. "Early Secondary
Education in New England." The remaining chapters deal with later
events.

1923-1   Akagi, Roy Hidemichi. "The Town Proprietors of the New
       England Colonies: A Study of Their Development, Organization,
       Activities and Controversies, 1620-1770." Ph.D., Univ. of
       Pennsylvania.

       Revision published under same title: Philadelphia : Press of the
Univ. of Pennsylvania, 1924. -- xiii, 348 p. Reprinted: Gloucester,
Mass. : Peter Smith, 1963. -- 348 p. Contents (1963 ed.): I.
"Introduction"; Part I. "The Town Proprietors": II. "The Method by
Which the Town Proprietors Acquired Title to Land in the New England
Colonies," III. "The Organization of the Town Proprietors," IV. "The
Activities of the Town Proprietors," and V. "The Controversies of the
Town Proprietors"; Part II: VI. "The Background of Land Speculation
in New England in the Eighteenth Century," VII. "The Speculative Town
Proprietors of the Eighteenth Century," VIII. "The Revival of the
Ancient Patents," and IX. "Conclusions."

1923-2   Branom, Frederick Kenneth. "The Economic Geography of the
       Boston Region: A Study of Regional Geography." Ph.D., Clark
       Univ.   287 leaves.

"Preface":   "The attempt is made here to explain from the geographic viewpoint the economic development of the Boston Region" (n.p.).   Relevant chapters: Part One.   "The Geographic Setting of the Boston Region":   I. "The Boston Region Defined" and II. "How Geographic Factors Influenced the Early Settlement of the Boston Region"; Part Two. "The Boston Region as a Workshop of New England": VIII. "The Importance of the Water Supply . . . in the Life of the Boston Region," XII. "The Shipbuilding Industry," XIV. "The Fishing Industry," and XV. "Boston as a Market and Business Center"; and Part Three. "The Port of Boston":   XVI. "The Character of the Port of Boston" and XVII. "The Commerce at the Port of Boston during the Colonial Period." The other chapters deal with later events.

1923-3   Burns, John Francis. "Controversies Between Royal Governors and Their Assemblies in the Northern American Colonies." Ph.D., Catholic Univ. of America.

Published under same title: Boston : Wright & Potter, 1923. -- 447 p. Reprinted: New York : Russell & Russell, 1969. -- 447 p. "Preface" (1969 ed.): The work covers the period "between the English Revolution of 1688 and the American Revolution of 1775-1783"; the study was "undertaken in the hope of bringing into more distinct relief the origins of the gradually increasing political divergence between England and British North America, through investigation of the relations between colonial royal governors and representative assemblies" (p. 3).   "Conclusion":   "The causes underlying this perennial dissatisfaction [of the colonies] with the agents of the Crown were founded in the prevalent longstanding and unmistakable tendencies toward complete political freedom" (p. 415).   Relevant chapters: Part I. "Massachusetts":   I. "Early Democratic Opposition, 1644-1730"; Part II. "New Hampshire, New York, New Jersey": IV. "New Hampshire."

1923-4   Dexter, Elisabeth Williams Anthony. "Colonial Women of Affairs: A Study of Women in Business and the Professions in America before 1776." Ph.D., Clark Univ.

Revision published under same title: Boston ; New York : Houghton Mifflin, 1924. -- 203 p. The 2nd ed., revised, published: Boston ; New York : Houghton Mifflin, 1931. -- xxii, 223 p. Reprint of 2nd ed.: Clifton, N.J. : A. M. Kelley, 1972. -- xxii, 223 p. "Preface" (2nd ed.): "Conditions for women, in some respects at least, were more favorable in the colonial days than they became in the early nineteenth century" (p. vii). "Introduction": The work intends to show "how some of our ancestors met the ever-present problem of women's place in the economic and social life of their time" (p. xxii). Contents: I. "My Hostess of the Tavern," II. "The 'She-Merchant,'" III. "The Artificer," IV. "The Ministering Angel," V. "The School Dame," VI. "The Landed Proprietor," VII. "With Tongue, Pen, and Printer's Ink," and "Conclusion."

1923-5   Ferrell, Clyde Miser. "The Massachusetts Colonial Agents in
        England." Ph.D., Univ. of Wisconsin at Madison. iv, 263 leaves.

    "Introduction": "The purpose of this investigation is to
consider the various aspects of the Massachusetts colonial agency
throughout the whole colonial period. It will be shown why the agents
were found to be necessary and how the agency originated. The various
experiments and developments which occurred from time to time as
conditions and circumstances dictated will be pointed out.
Considerable emphasis will be placed upon the work and functions of
the agents in their efforts to serve the colony, the personnel of the
agency, and the importance of the agency as an institution in the
conduct of Anglo-Massachusetts relations" (p. iv). Relevant chapters:
"Introduction," I. "The Beginnings of the Agency," II. "The Agents and
the Restoration," III. "The Loss of the Charter," IV. "The Provincial
Charter of 1691," V. "Anglo-Massachusetts Relations under William III
and Anne," and VI. "An Era of Constitutional Controversy." Chapters
VII and VIII treat of a later period.

1923-6   Murdock, Kenneth Ballard. "The Life and Works of Increase
        Mather." Ph.D., Harvard Univ. 2 vols. (xii, 835, 28 leaves).

    Revision published as Increase Mather, the Foremost American
Puritan. -- Cambridge, Mass. : Harvard Univ. Press, 1925. -- xv, 422
p. Reprinted: New York : Russell & Russell, 1963. -- xv, 442 p.
Contents (1963 ed.): I. "Introduction," II. "The Mathers in England,"
III. "Puritan Emigrants," IV. "The Mathers in New England," V.
"Boyhood," VI. "Harvard College. The Choice of a Life Work," VII.
"Experimental Years--England, Ireland, and Guernsey," VIII.
"Beginnings in Boston," IX. "The Teacher of the Second Church," X.
"Public Life," XI. "Literary Leader and Spokesman of the People," XII.
"'Illustrious Providences,' and the Flight to England," XIII. "The
Court of James the Second," XIV. "The Negotiation with William III,"
XV. "The New Charter," XVI. "The Bostonian in London," XVII.
"'Dolefull Witchcraft,'" XVIII. "Defending the Faith," XIX. "The First
Defeat," XX. "Old Age and the New Century," and XXI. "Increase
Mather." Relevant appendices: A. "Mather's Agency and the Plymouth
Colony," B. "The Return of the Ministers upon Witchcraft," and D.
"Check List of Mather's Writings."

1923-7   Washburne, George Adrian. "Imperial Control of the
        Administration of Justice in the Thirteen American Colonies,
        1684-1776." Ph.D., Columbia Univ.

    Published under same title: New York : Columbia Univ., 1923. --
191 p. -- (Columbia Univ., Faculty of Political Science, Studies in
History, Economics, and Public Law ; vol. CV, no. 2 ; whole no. 238).
Reprinted: New York : AMS Press, 1967. -- 191 p. Relevant chapters:
I. "Imperial Development of a Colonial Legal System," II. "The King in
Council," III. "Appeals to the King in Council, 1684-1745," and V.
"The Working of the Imperial System." Chapter IV deals with period
1745-1776.

1924-1   Lanier, Mary Jean. "The Earlier Development of Boston as a Commercial Center." Ph.D., Univ. of Chicago. v, 122 leaves.

Chapter I: "Within three decades of its founding, Boston gave evidence of the growing significance of those commercial activities which were the dominant factors in its economic life for at least two centuries" (p. 1).   Contents: I. "Boston at the End of Three Decades," II. "Environmental Relations: The Site and Situation of Boston," III. "Commercial Adjustments of the First Decade: Boston as Market Town of the Basin," IV. "Commercial Readjustments during the Second and Third Decades; Boston Develops an Export Trade" (ships, lumber, fish, beaver), and V. "Summary." Appendix: "Typical cargoes shipped to [Gov. John] Winthrop in the first decade."

1925-1   Buffinton, Arthur Howland. "The Policy of the Northern English Colonies Towards the French to the Peace of Utrecht." Ph.D., Harvard Univ. 466 leaves.

Chapter I: "The struggle of the French and English in North America was . . . the result, partly of a class of interests, conceivably capable of adjustment, and partly consciously adopted policies which made such adjustment practically impossible. . . . In the common task of exploiting the resources of soil, ocean, and forest, rivalry developed which either deepened into antagonism, or, as in the case of the fur trade, was reconciled by the adoption of a mutually advantageous policy of intercolonial trade" (p. 1). Contents: I. "Heredity and Environment," II-V. "New England and Acadia, 1620-1654," "1654-1670," and "1670-1686," VI. "Consolidation and Imperial Control, 1683-1689," VII. "The Attempt of the Northern Colonies to Conquer Canada, 1689-90," VIII. "The Failure of Colonial Efforts, 1690-1697," IX. "The Struggle for the West, 1698-1702," and X. "The Close of a Century of Rivalry, 1702-1713." "Annex" to diss.: Buffinton's "New England and the Western Fur Trade, 1629-1675," reprinted from Publications of the Colonial Society of Massachusetts, XVIII (1916), pp. 61-192, by Cambridge, Mass. : John Wilson & Son, 1916.

1925-2   Gatke, Robert Moulton. "Plans of American Colonial Union, 1643 to 1754." Ph.D., American Univ. ii, 312 leaves.

Relevant chapters: I. "The United Colonies of New England, 1643-1684," II. "Attempts to Secure the Military Union of the Colonies, 1689-1713," and III. "Colonial Union and the Development of Empire, 1721-1751." Remaining chapters deal with later events.

1925-3   Wilson, S. K. "American Colonial Colleges." Ph.D., Univ. of Cambridge (U.K.).

Cited in Bilboul, vol. I, p. 66. Not in CDI, NUC, BMGC, or OCLC. CRL (September 8, 1982): "We are sorry but we have not been able to get a copy of this dissertation for you. We have not been able to obtain the author's permission for a copy to be made and no such copy can be made without his permission. We have exhausted all means of contacting the author."

1926-1   Ernst, James Emanuel. "The Political Thought of Roger Williams." Ph.D., Univ. of Washington.

Revision published under same title: Seattle : Univ. of Washington Press, 1929. -- iii, 229 p. -- (Univ. of Washington Publications in Language and Literature : vol. 6, no. 1). Reprinted: Port Washington, N.Y. : Kennikat Press, 1966. -- iii, 229 p. Contents (1966 ed.): I. "Roger Williams," II. "Williams' Concept of the State, Its Origin and Nature," III. "The Sovereignty of the State," IV. "The Relation of State to State," V. "The Purpose of the State," VI. "Activities of the State," and VII. "Limits of State Power."

1926-2   Hubbard, Clifford Chesley. "Constitutional Development in Rhode Island." Ph.D., Brown Univ. 260 leaves.

"Preface": The "thesis attempts to present the constitutional development of Rhode Island through the entire history of the colony and state from 1636 to 1926" (n.p.). Relevant chapter: I. "Constitutional Foundations in the Colony, 1636-1776": "Government under the Parliamentary Charter," "Analysis of the Charters," "Constitutional Changes in Colonial Days," and "Absence of Judicial Control in Colonial Days."

1926-3   Sly, John Fairfield. "Town Government in Massachusetts: A Survey of its Development and Contemporary Aspects." Ph.D., Harvard Univ. 287, xl leaves.

Revision published as Town Government in Massachusetts (1620-1930). -- Cambridge, Mass. : Harvard Univ. Press, 1930. -- vii, 244 p. Reprinted: Hamden, Conn. : Archon Books, 1967. -- vii, 244 p. "Preface": "The steady and continuous unfolding of a local institutional pattern contains within it the historic facts from which spring many of the generalizations which form the fibre of political thought. There is a new understanding that comes with a long perspective; there is a judicious tolerance towards contemporary institutions that flows from a grasp of the past usefulness; and there is an impetus to orderly progress in the description and analyses of those present-day adjustments through which perplexed communities aim to regulate the rapid and often extreme transitions that are a phenomenon of modern life. Broadly, the application of these observations to one of America's most distinguished political experiments--the Massachusetts town meeting--forms the purpose of this brief study" (p. vii). Relevant chapters: I. "Settlement," II. "Institutional Beginnings," III. "A Critique of Town Origins," and IV. "The Town of the Eighteenth Century." Chapters V-IX deal with later periods.

1927-1   Armitage, Frank Guy. "Reconsideration of Puritan Recreation in Massachusetts, 1620-1763." Ph.D., Clark Univ. iii, 221 leaves.

"Foreword": "The object of this dissertation is simple. It is an attempt to dissipate an unkind mist that has obscured the Fathers of New England and of Massachusetts in particular; --a mist that has distorted them and caused them to appear as a dour, sad and lacklustre people. It is an attempt to take a forbidding frown from the face of the Puritan, and to leave in its place a cheerful, benignant smile" (p. 1). Contents: One. "Introduction," Two. "Recreation in Puritan Life," Three. "Games of the Inns," Four. "Public Amusements. Dancing," Five. "Innocuous Diversions," Six. "Games of the Open Air," Seven. "Sabbath Restrictions," and Eight. "Conclusion."

1927-2   Brebner, John Bartlet. "New England's Outpost: Acadia before the Conquest of Canada." Ph.D., Columbia Univ.

Published under same title: New York : Columbia Univ. Press ; London : P. S. King & Son, 1927. -- 291 p. -- (Columbia Univ., Faculty of Political Science, Studies in History, Economics, and Public Law ; no. 293). Reprinted: Hamden, Conn. : Archon Books, 1965. -- 291 p. Also reprinted: New York : Burt Franklin, 1974. -- 291 p. -- (Burt Franklin Research and Source Work Ser.) (American Classics in History and Social Science ; 249). "Introduction" (1965 ed.): The work proposes "to tell primarily of the genesis and character of the Acadian people and of the strategic problem which grew up around their country in the seventeenth century: to explain the implication of New England in the affairs of the province and its peculiar results" (p. 8). Relevant chapters: I. "Noble Proprietors and Merchant Adventurers (1640-1670)," II. "Acadians, Real and Unreal (1670-1710)," III. "A Phantom Rule and 'Neutral' Subjects (1710-1723)," and IV. "Counterfeit Suzerainty (1724-1739)." Remaining chapters concern later periods.

1927-3   Deshmukh, Ramakrishna Ganesh. "The Development of Highways in Massachusetts: with Special Reference to the Financial Aspects." Ph.D., Harvard Univ. v, 251, vi leaves.

Relevant chapters: I. "Introduction: An Historical Summary": (A) "The Early Colonial Period: Seventeenth Century. First Settlements near coast: no pressing need for superior highways: Indian trails: their development by the Colonists: famous old roads in Massachusetts: first American road laws: difficulties in the way of road-making: poor standard of roads in the period" and (B) "The Later Colonial and Post-Revolutionary Period: 1700-1790. Increased Travel: widening the trails: appearance of carts and wagons on public roads: the stagecoach and the freight-wagon: more attention given to 'roads': macadamized road ushered in: poor condition of roads in New England until the Revolution: Postal service: causes of tardiness in road-building" and V. "Conclusion. A retrospect." Chapters II-IV deal with later periods.

1927-4   Hertzler, Silas. "The Rise of the Public High School in
          Connecticut." Ph.D., Yale Univ. 281 leaves.

          Revision published under same title: Baltimore : Warwick & York,
1930. -- xx, 258 p. -- (Univ. Research Monographs ; no. 10). Relevant
chapters (1930 ed.): I. "Introduction" and II. "Origin of the Public
High School in Connecticut." Chapter II covers 1638-1838 and treats
of the roots of public support and control in the Latin grammar
school, and (in the diss. version) is divided into sections on 1.
"Earliest Grammar Schools," 2. "The Connecticut Code of 1650," and 3.
"Country Grammar Schools." The remaining chapters treat of later
events.

1927-5   Highfill, Robert David. "The Vocabulary of Samuel Sewall
          from 1673 to 1699." Ph.D., Univ. of Chicago. xii, 393 leaves.

          "Introduction": "The study of Samuel Sewall's vocabulary was
undertaken with the purpose of comparing it with the evidence
furnished by existing dictionaries, and of compiling such evidence as
Sewall furnishes to supplement them" (p. iii). Contents: I.
"Seventeenth-Century Words Used by Samuel Sewall," II. "Old-Fashioned
or Obsolescent Words Used by Sewall," III. "Words for Which Sewall is
Later Evidence," IV. "Sewall is Earlier Evidence," V. "Sewall Fills a
Gap in the Evidence," and VI. "Evidence Supplementary to That Found
in Dictionaries."

1927-6   Knappen, Marshall Mason. "Richard Greenham and the Practical
          Puritans under Elizabeth." Ph.D., Cornell Univ. ii, 266 leaves.

          Contents: I. "Introduction," II. "Life and Character," III.
"Greenham's Contemporaries at Christ's College," IV. "Greenham's
Practical Influence," V. "Attitude to the Prophane [sic] and Others of
Divergent Views," VI. "Pastoral Advice," and VII. "The Sabbath, the
Third Sacrament."

1927-7   Orbeck, Anders. "Early New England Pronunciation, as
          Reflected in Some Seventeenth-Century Town Records of Eastern
          Massachusetts." Ph.D., Columbia Univ.

          Published under same title: Ann Arbor, Mich. : George Wahr,
1927. -- x, 148 p. "Preface": "The present investigation seeks to
find evidence for seventeenth-century pronounciation in eastern
Massachusetts in the occasional spellings of naive--more or less
illiterate--scribes. . . . The documents in question are the town
records of Plymouth, Watertown, Dedham, and Groton" (pp. v-vi). The
period covered is 1634-1707. Contents: I. "The Interpretation of
Naive Forms," II. "The Pronunciation of Stressed Vowels," III. "The
Pronunciation of Unstressed Vowels," IV. "The Pronunciation of
Consonants," and V. "The Sources of New England Speech."

1928-1   Appleton, Marguerite. "The Relations of the Corporate Colony
    of Rhode Island to the British Government." Ph.D., Brown Univ.
    ii, 292 leaves.

"Introduction": "It is the purpose of this thesis to present a
study of the relations of Rhode Island to the British government.
Rhode Island occupied a peculiar position in the empire, because, with
the exception of Connecticut, it was the only colony that retained its
corporate form unchanged throughout the colonial period. Unlike its
neighbor, agricultural Connecticut, however, it had many points of
contact with the mother country. . . . It is the interplay of . . .
two forces, the colonial and the imperial, that forms the main theme
of the relations of Rhode Island to the home government" (p. i).
Relevant chapters: I. "Introduction," II. "The Attacks on the
Charter," III. "Boundaries," IV. "Defense," V. "Rhode Island and the
Acts of Trade," VI. "The Admiralty Court," VII. "The Colonial Agent,"
and IX. "Conclusion." Relevant appendices: A. "Map showing disputed
boundaries" and B. "Chronology of the Admiralty Court." Chapter VIII
treats of the Revolutionary period.

1928-2   Chadbourne, Ava Harriet. "The Beginnings of Education in
    Maine." Ph.D., Columbia Univ. (Teachers College).

Published under same title: New York : Bureau of Publication,
Teachers College, Columbia Univ., 1928. -- vi, 135 p. -- (Teachers
College, Columbia Univ., Contributions to Education ; no. 336).
Reprinted: New York : AMS Press, 1972. -- vi, 135 p. "Preface" (1972
ed.):   "The purpose of this study is to show the beginnings of
education in Maine from the time of settlement, during the periods
when it was a province and a district until the separation from
Massachusetts in 1820. . . . The first chapter attempts to explain
the reasons why Maine allowed the long period of nearly a century to
elapse between the first settlement and the establishment of schools
within her borders while Massachusetts began the establishment of her
schools fifteen or sixteen years after her first permanent settlement.
. . . Chapters II and III take up the records of schools in the towns
in the order of their incorporation and show what were the principles
and practices developed in regard to education in this frontier
province and district and then . . . what changes were necessitated by
changing conditions" (p. iii). Relevant chapters: I. "Maine's
Indifference to Education, 1602 to 1692"; II. "Maine as a District,
1692 to 1785--The Beginnings of Schools": "Agencies of Educational
Control," "Methods of School Support," and "Beginnings of the District
System"; and VI. "Conclusion." Chapters III-V are concerned with
later periods.

1928-3   Griffin, Orwin Bradford. "The Evolution of the Connecticut
    State School System, with Special Reference to the Emergence of
    the High School." Ph.D., Columbia Univ.

Published under same title: New York : Teachers College,
Columbia Univ., 1928. -- 261 p. -- (Teachers College, Columbia Univ.,
Contributions to Education ; no. 293). Reprinted: New York : AMS

Press, 1972. -- 261 p. Relevant chapter (1972 ed.): I. "Connecticut School Laws, 1650 to 1842, Preparing the Way for the High School." Chapters II-IX cover later periods.

1928-4   Schimmelpfeng, Hans. "The Conception of Church in Earliest American Congregationalism, from 1620-1650." Ph.D., Hartford Seminary Foundation. ii, 160 leaves.

Chapter I: Author uses work of Georg Jellinek, Max Weber, Ernst Troeltsch, and Heinrich Frick as four "approaches" to the period, chosen "because this time is most clearly still in touch with both medieval and modern ages; moreover, the theologians of this period had the fiction of erecting a Theocracy. They made the grand attempt . . . to establish a kingdom of God here on earth, and in doing so they made the still greater attempt of combining their theocratical ideals with the idea of a self-evidencing Bible" (p. 10). Contents: I. "General Introduction," II. "Special Introduction: Biblicism and Christocracy in Church," III-V. "The Formality of the Church: The Covenant": a: "Freedom and equality of believers," b: "The local character of the congregation," and c: "congregation and synod," VI. "The Materiality of Church: Visible Saints," VII. "Church and State," and VIII. "Congregationalism: its historical position and contribution to modern thought."

1929-1   Calder, Isabel MacBeath. "The Jurisdiction of New Haven, a Seventeenth-Century Puritan Colony." Ph.D., Yale Univ.   300 leaves.

Revision published as The New Haven Colony. -- New Haven : Yale Univ. Press ; London : H. Milford, Oxford Univ. Press, 1934. -- vi, 301 p. -- (Yale Historical Publications. Miscellany ; XXVIII). Reprinted: Hamden, Conn. : Archon Books, 1970. -- vi, 301 p. Contents (1970 ed.): I. "St. Stephen's, Colman Street," II. "Massachusetts Bay," III. "Staking Out a Colony," IV. "Settlers of the Outlying Plantations," V. "The Congregational Way," VI. "Moses His Judicials," VII. "For the Service of God in Church and Commonwealth," VIII. "Farmers, Artisans, and Merchants," IX. "New England Confederates," X. "Puritan England," XI. "The End of Christ's Kingdom," and XII. "Epilogue."

1929-2   Fleming, Sandford. "Children in the Life and Thought of the New England Churches, 1620-1847." Ph.D., Yale Univ.

Revision published as Children & Puritanism: The Place of Children in the Life and Thought of the New England Churches, 1620-1847. -- New Haven : Yale Univ. Press ; London : H. Milford, Oxford Univ. Press, 1933. -- xii, 236 p. -- (Yale Studies in Religious Education ; VIII). Reprinted: New York : Arno Press, 1969. -- xii, 236 p. -- (American Education: Its Men, Ideas, and Institutions). "Introduction" (1969 ed.): "The purpose of this book is to present the situation with respect to the religious education of children among the Puritans of New England from the coming of the Pilgrims to the epoch-making work of Horace Bushnell at the middle of the

nineteenth century. From an examination of the records it seeks to
show how children were regarded, what place was afforded them in the
churches, and what sort of experiences were considered desirable for
their entrance into church membership and into the family of God. Its
general questions are: 'What religious appeal was made to the children
of Puritans?' and 'What response did the children make to this
appeal?'" (p. 1). Relevant chapters: "Introduction"; Part One.
"History and Characteristics of the New England Churches": I. "The
Establishment of the New England Churches," II. "Sabbath Observance
and Public Worship," III. "Uniting with the Church," IV. "Excessive
Emotionalism," and V. "The New England Theology"; Part Two. "Children
in the New England Churches--The Religious Appeal": VI. "Implications
of the Historical Situations," VII. "The Church Membership of
Children," VIII. "Children's Books," IX. "Children's Sermons," and X.
"Religious Education"; and Part Three. "Children in the New England
Churches--The Religious Response": XI. "General Statements Concerning
the Religious Experiences of Children," XII. "Meetings of Children and
Young People," XIII. "The Emotional Response of Children," and XIV.
"Religious Precocity." Part IV deals with later developments.

1929-3   Johnson, Edgar Augustus Jerome. "American Economic Thought
           in the Seventeenth Century." Ph.D., Harvard Univ.   412 leaves.

        Revision published under same title: London : P. S. King & Son,
1932. -- 292 p. Reprinted: New York : Russell & Russell, 1961. --
292 p. "Preface" (1961 ed.): The author's aim is "to bring together
the scattered colonial references to economic questions in the hope
that, in assembled form, this economic philosophy will give us a more
accurate understanding of the formative influences in American
civilization . . . [and] to assemble the crude ideas of a century of
pioneers in order to understand the subsequent differences between
American and European economic thought" (p. ix). Contents: I.
"Heritage and Circumstance," II. "The Control of Economic Activity,"
III. "English Theories of Colonization," IV. "American Theories of
Colonization," V. "Ethical Economics: The Vindication of Wealth," VI.
"The Way of Wealth's Increase," VII. "The Morality of the Market-
Place," VIII. "Trade, Fettered and Free," IX. "Monetary Principles and
Monetary Proposals," X. "Lombard Banks and Land Banks," XI. "Wages and
Usury," XII. "The Condemnation of Communism," XIII. "The Support of
Government," and XIV. "The Fruits of Economic Philosophy." Diss. is
not listed in CDI.

1929-4   Judah, Charles Burnet, Jr. "English Colonial Policy and the
           North American Fishing Industry, 1498-1713." Ph.D., Univ. of
           Illinois at Urbana-Champaign.

        Revision published as The North American Fisheries and British
Policy to 1713. -- Urbana : Univ. of Illinois, 1933. -- 183 p. --
(Univ. of Illinois. Illinois Studies in the Social Sciences ; vol.
XVII, no. 3-4 ; vol. XXXI, no. 1). "Preface" (1933 ed.): "The
following study is an attempt to trace and account for the policy of
the British government toward the North American fishing industry from
the time English fishermen first went to Newfoundland to the signing
of the peace of Utrecht. . . . Though Newfoundland is the center of

interest, New England has been included, as there is no reason to believe that English officials made a theoretical distinction toward the two great North American fishing banks" (p. 5). Contents: I. "The Discovery and Early Exploration of the Newfoundland Fisheries," II. "Strife in the Fisheries, and the Rise of English Influence," III. "Home and Colonial Rivalry in the North American Fisheries," IV. "First Effort at Governmental Control in Newfoundland," V. "The Policy of the Commonwealth and Protectorate in Regard to the Fisheries," VI. "The Dutch Wars and the Government's Decision Against Colonization in Newfoundland," VII. "The Reversal of Governmental Policy Toward Newfoundland," and VIII. "The Newfoundland Fisheries in the Peace of Utrecht."

1929-5   Warren, Alice Farwell. "John Cotton: The Father of Boston." Ph.D., Univ. of Wisconsin at Madison. 111, vii leaves.

"Introduction": "It is the purpose of this thesis to study the life of John Cotton in order to gain a clearer perception of him as an individual personality and as a representative of the first generation of the founders of the colony of Massachusetts Bay" (p. 1). Contents: "Introduction"; I. "Choosing a Life's Profession"; II. "St. Botolphs"; III. "The Garden of the Lord": I. "The Voyage," II. "The Setting Down," and III. "Utopia"; IV. "Bryars and Thorns"; V. "The Scholar": "Science," "History," "Government," and "Economics"; VI. "'The Word'": I. "Theology" and II. "Church Government"; and "Conclusion."

1930-1   Bigelow, Bruce Macmillan. "The Commerce of Rhode Island with the West Indies before the American Revolution." Ph.D., Brown Univ. 2 vols. (v, [279]; ii, [163] leaves).

Abstract in DAI, vol. 30 (4), sec. A, p. 1490: "The subject is divided into two parts: History and Development, and Commercial Organization and Practices. Introductory chapters briefly describe the geographical and economic background of colonial Rhode Island and the West Indies. They are followed by . . . chronological chapters which discuss The Beginnings of Rhode Island Commerce, 1636-1713; . . . [and] from Utrecht to the Molasses Act, 1713-1733. . . . The thesis concludes with three topical chapters on The Rhode Island Merchant and his Commercial Organization; Trade Routes and Commodities; and Smuggling."

1930-2   Bishop, Eugene Alfred. "The Development of a State School System: New Hampshire." Ph.D., Columbia Univ.

Published under same title: New York : Teachers College, Columbia Univ., 1930. -- 159 p. -- (Teachers College, Columbia Univ., Contributions to Education ; no. 391). Reprinted: New York : AMS Press, 1972. -- 159 p. Relevant chapter: IV. "Colonial Period: The Old New Hampshire Town Schools." Other chapters are concerned with other matters, later periods.

1930-3   Morris, Richard Brandon. "Studies in the History of American
   Law, with Special Reference to the Seventeenth and Eighteenth
   Centuries." Ph.D., Columbia Univ.

   Published under same title: New York : Columbia Univ. Press ;
London : P.S. King & Son, 1930. -- 285 p. -- (Columbia Univ., Faculty
of Political Science, Studies in History, Economics, and Public Law ;
no. 316). A 2nd ed. published: Philadelphia : J. M. Mitchell Co.,
1959. -- xiii, 285 p. Reprint of 2nd ed.: New York : Octagon Books,
1963. -- xiii, 285 p. Contents (1963 ed.): I. "An Introduction to
the Early History of American Law": A. "The Problem for the Legal
Historian," B. "Seventeenth-century Influences in American Law," and
C. "The Conservative Reaction of the Eighteenth Century"; II.
"Colonial Laws Governing the Distribution and Alienation of Land": A.
"The Security and Alienability of Land," B. "Primogeniture and
Entailed Estates in America," and C. "The Customary Character of
American Land Tenure"; III. "Women's Rights in Early American Law":
A. "The Colonial Concept of Marriage in Relation to the Legal Position
of Women," B. "The Married Woman's Proprietary Capacity," C. "The
Married Woman's Contractual Capacity," D. "The Married Woman's
Capacity in Tort," and E. "The Married Woman's Evidential Capacity";
IV. "Responsibility for Tortious Acts in Early American Law": A. "The
Doctrine of No Liability without Fault," B. "Exceptions to the
Doctrine of No Liability without Fault," and C. "Liability for Death
by Wrongful Act in Colonial Law"; and V. "Bibliographical Essay."

1930-4   Volckmar, Wilhelm Paul Ernst. "Soziologische Studien zur
   neuenglischen Syntax: Ein Versuch, den Einfluss des Puritanismus
   auf die Entwicklung der englischen Sprache festzulegen." Dr.
   phil., Univ. Jena.

   "Verkürzter Druck" published under same title: Halle (Saale) :
Eduard   Klinz, 1930. -- 75 p. Relevant chapters (published version):
1. "Die Problemstellung," 2. "Das Gesamtergebnis," 3. "Kritische
Bemerkungen zur Methode Spezieller Teil," 3. "Die Umschreibung mit to
do," and 5. "Aus dem Gebiete des Relativpronomens."

1931-1   Diettrich, Sigismond de Rüdesheim. "Historical Geography of
   the Thames River Valley, Connecticut." Ph.D., Clark Univ.
   6 ["Abstract"], ix, 273 leaves.

   "Abstract": "The Thames River Valley, since Capt. Adrian Block
discovered it in 1614, witnessed great changes in man's adjustment to
the environment. The analysis of these changing conditions of human
life and the investigation of the influences of geographic environment
upon the history of the Valley is the aim of this work" (p. 1).
Contents: I. "The Thames River Valley and the Problem of Its
Development"; II. "Indian [i.e., Pequot] Life"; III. "Pioneer Days";
IV. "Maritime Activities: Fishing, Ship building, Agriculture,
Coasting Trade, West Indies Trade, British and Triangular Trade,
Readjustments to the Changed Conditions"; V. "War Times"; VI.
"Whaling"; VII. "Industrial Age"; and VIII. "Conclusions and Future."

1931-2   Donovan, George Francis. "The Pre-Revolutionary Irish in Massachusetts, 1620-1775." Ph.D., St. Louis Univ.

Published under same title: Menasha, Wis. : George Banta Publishing Co., 1932. -- 158 p. Chapter I (1932 ed.): "The purpose of this work is to set forth the facts concerning the Irish element in Massachusetts during the seventeenth and eighteenth centuries, correct wrong impressions and finally, establish a firmer basis from which future research or activity in the same or similar fields will begin" (p. 1). Relevant chapters: I. "Plymouth and Boston," II. "Northeastern and Southeastern Massachusetts," III. "Central and Western Massachusetts," and IV. "King Philip's War and the Irish Donation." Remaining chapters treat of later periods.

1931-3   McKinley, Samuel Justus. "The Economic History of Portsmouth, N.H., from Its First Settlement in 1630, Including a Study of Price Movements There, 1723-1770 and 1804-1830." Ph.D., Harvard Univ. x, 463 leaves.

"Preface": "An effort has been made to consider all the factors that affected the commerce of the port and special attention has been paid to the methods of business which were revealed in the mercantile accounts" (p. i). Relevant chapters: I. "Introduction," II. "Settlement [c.1623]," III. "The Lower Piscataqua Settlement, 1635-1680," IV. "Portsmouth, 1680-1725," V. "Portsmouth, 1725-1775," IX. "The New Hampshire Powder Duties, Imposts, and Export Duties and Their Relation to the Commerce of the Maine Side of the River and the Coasting Trade with Boston," X. "Ship Building on the Piscataqua River," XI. "Fishing, Lumber, and Commerce," and XII. "Price Movement in Portsmouth, N.H., 1723-1770 and 1804-1830." Chapters VI-VIII deal with later history.

1931-4   Miller, Perry Gilbert Eddy. "The Establishment of Orthodoxy in Massachusetts." Ph.D., Univ. of Chicago. 405 leaves.

Revision published as Orthodoxy in Massachusetts, 1630-1650: A Genetic Study. Cambridge, Mass. : Harvard Univ. Press, 1933. -- xvi, 353 p. Reprinted with a new preface by the author: Boston : Beacon Press, 1959. -- 319 p. -- (Beacon Paperbacks). Also reprinted: Gloucester, Mass. : Peter Smith, 1965. -- 319 p.   Also reprinted with an introduction by David D. Hall: New York : Harper & Row, 1970. -- xxxiv, 319 p. -- (Harper Torchbooks). Contents (1970 ed.): I. "Supremacy and Uniformity," II. "Discipline Out of the Word," III. "Separatist Congregationalism," IV. "Non-Separatist Congregationalism," V. "A Wide Door of Liberty," VI. "The New England Way," VII. "The Supreme Power Politicke," and VIII. "Tollerating Times."

1932-1   Andrews, George Angell. "History of the Puritan Discipline, 1554-1593." Ph.D., Washington Univ. 391 leaves.

Chapter XII: "What . . . was accomplished by the quarter century of disciplinarian propaganda and organization? The failure of the presbyterian discipline . . . determined that the English church would

not undertake further reformation. . . . It further determined that
the English protestant sects must find their origin outside the
established church, and for an indefinite time, outside the law. The
dissensions which arose in the English church in the course of the
Vestiarian Controversy and the attempt to establish the Book of
Discipline, drove into separation the fore-runners of
congregationalism,--the puritans of New England and the independents
of the Commonwealth" (pp. 331-32). Contents: I. "The Problem of
Discipline in the Reformed Church of England," II. "The Congregational
Form of Discipline Developed at Frankfort, 1554-1559," III. "The Early
Disciplinarian Movement and Conformity, 1559-1566," IV. "The
Congregational Phase of the Disciplinarian Movement and Its Opposition
to the Episcopate, 1567-1570," V. "The Formulation of the New
Disciplinarian Platform and Its Suppression, 1570-1573," VI. "The
Undertree Conspiracy, 1574," VII. "The Presbyterian Propaganda and
Separation of the Brownists, 1574-1582," VIII. "The Drafts of
Discipline, 1575-1589," IX. "The Bill and the Book," X. "The
Presbyterian Discipline in Relation to the Classis Movement, 1582-
1589," XI. "Puritan Synods and Subscription to the Discipline," and
XII. "Failure and Disintegration, 1588-1593."

1932-2   Bining, Arthur Cecil. "British Regulation of the Colonial
         Iron Industry." Ph.D., Univ. of Pennsylvania.

        Published under same title: Philadelphia : Univ. of Pennsylvania
Press ; London : Oxford Univ. Press, 1933. -- 163 p. Reprinted:
Clifton, N.J., : A. M. Kelley, 1973. -- 163 p. -- (Library of Early
American Business and Industry). Includes discussion of colonial New
England iron industry from 1641, especially in Chapter I. "A Survey of
the Colonial Iron Industry." Chapters II. "The Opening Battle" and
III. "The Conflict Between Groups" are also relevant.

1932-3   Clarke, Mary Patterson. "Parliamentary Privilege in the
         American Colonies." Ph.D., Yale Univ.

        Revision published under same title: New Haven : Yale Univ.
Press ; London : H. Milford, Oxford Univ. Press, 1943. -- xi, 303 p.
-- (Yale Historical Publications. Miscellany ; XLIV). Reprinted: New
York : Da Capo Press, 1971. -- xi, 303 p. -- (Da Capo Press Reprints
in American Constitutional and Legal History). "Preface" (1971 ed.):
"The study covers a wide range of territory, including the colonies
. . . [and] also England itself, since the parliament had to be
studied as the background of younger representative bodies. . . .
[The] treatment of the [colonial] assemblies, which is the main
interest of the book, covers the period from 1619 . . . till 1783.
. . . In the present work the interest is in the lower, or elected,
house, and the terms 'assembly' and 'house,' or 'lower house,' are
used interchangeably" (pp. x-xi). Contents: "Introduction: The
British Background of Parliamentary Privilege," I. "The Assembly as a
Court," II. "The Speaker's Petition," III. "The Enforcement of the
Speaker's Petition," IV. "The Determination of Disputed Elections," V.
"The Control of the House over its Members," VI. "Incidental Features
of Parliamentary Privilege," VII. "Conflicts in Jurisdiction," and
VIII. "The Significance of Privilege."

1932-4   Waentig, Karl. "Die Self-Komposita der Puritanersprache."
    Dr. phil., Univ. Leipzig (Germany).

    Published under same title: Leipzig : Druckerei der
Werkgemeinschaft, 1932. -- viii, 123 p. Concentrates on the use of
English and American Puritans (especially Thomas Hooker) of the word
"self" and its compounds and on the significance of such usage.
Relevant chapters: 1. "Der Stand der self-Komposita um 1600," 2. "Die
Lehre vom Selbst," and 3. "Die self-Komposita der Puritaner."

1933-1   Gibson, Martha Jane. "Early Connecticut Pronunciation:
    Guilford, 1639-1800; Branford, 1644-1800." Ph.D., Yale Univ.
    231 leaves.

    "Summary of Results": "The classification and interpretation of
the thousands of items . . . gathered has revealed many facts of
interest from two points of view: (a) as casting new light upon or as
corroborating the work of older investigators in the field of the
history of the English language: (b) as revealing the background of
present-day American speech" (first leaf of diss., tipped in).
Contents: I. "Introduction": A. "Historical Background," B. "The
Method," C. "Materials," and D. "Plan of Arrangement"; II. "Stressed
Vowels"; III. "Unstressed Vowels"; IV. "Consonants"; and V.
"Conclusion."

1933-2   MacFarlane, Ronald Oliver. "Indian Relations in New England,
    1620-1760: A Study of a Regulated Frontier." Ph.D., Harvard
    Univ. xv, 694 leaves.

    "Summary": "In providing adequate defense, in acquiring land, in
prosecuting trade, in spreading Christianity, and in administering
justice: in all these relations with the natives, the New England
frontier, in comparison to that of other sections of America, can only
be regarded as one that was well regulated. In this regulation lies
the explanation of New England's success in handling her Indian
problem" (p. 662). Contents: I. "Introduction," II. "Defense: The
Art of War," III. "Defense: Methods of Maintaining Peace," IV.
"Defense: Political Aspects," V. "The Acquisition of Indian Lands: By
Purchase," VI. "The Acquisition of Indian Lands: By Conquest and
Squatting," VII. "Land: Indian Reservations," VIII. "Indian Trade,"
IX. "Trade: Regulation and Prohibition," X. "Trade: Public Trade
Houses," XI. and XII. "Missions and Education," XIII. and XIV. "The
Administration of Justice," XV. "Slavery," and XVI. "Conclusion."
Appendices: A. "Indian Tribes of New England and Nova Scotia," B.
"Scalp Bounties Offered by New Hampshire and Massachusetts," and C.
"Prices Paid for Indian Slaves."

1933-3   Moody, Robert Earle. "The Maine Frontier, 1607 to 1763."
    Ph.D., Yale Univ. iv, 462 leaves.

    Abstract in DA, vol. 28 (8), sec. A, p. 3117: "The Province of

Maine has a more varied history than any other English colony in the
New World. . . .   Maine was an important factor in the colonial
history of Massachusetts. The successful attempts by the Bay Colony
to possess Maine were a major cause of the revocation of the first
Massachusetts charter. In Maine primarily were fought the Indian Wars
in New England. The traders planned and led the assaults upon the
citadels of New France. The defense of Maine and the control of its
forest resources were among the most important causes of conflict
between England and Massachusetts before 1763."

1933-4   Shipton, Clifford Kenyon. "Part I, New England in Social
     Transition, 1680-1740: An Historical Introduction to Volume Four
     of Sibley's Harvard Graduates. Part II, Biographical Sketches of
     Harvard Graduates of the Classes of 1690-1700 (Alumni
     Harvardienses)." Ph.D., Harvard Univ. Part I: 156 leaves; Part
     II: 4 vols. (394 leaves).

     Part I: "This introduction offers a synthesis of the secondary
material available on such aspects as have been worked out, and offers
new conclusions based upon primary materials for the many questions
which are still open. . . .   The years covered by the lives of these
men are still the most neglected in American history, at least on the
social side; yet . . . , in New England, the social complex that is
modern America . . . was then taking shape. The period has been
neglected because our historians have found it unpleasant to study the
decaying carcass of the great Puritan movement, and because the
glories of the Revolution have blinded them to its confused and
relatively uninteresting precedents. . . . [This] was a period of
transition from an exceptionally religious and non-materialistic
century to an unusually skeptical and practical one" (pp. 1-2). Part
II published with an "Introduction" by Samuel Eliot Morison as vol.
IV, 1690-1700, of Sibley's Harvard Graduates: Biographical Sketches
of Those Who Attended Harvard College . . . with Bibliographical and
Other Notes. -- Cambridge, Mass. : Harvard Univ. Press, 1933. -- x,
574 p. Published version consists of 155 biographical sketches and
includes lists of subjects' printed works; arrangement is by class
date. (Vols. I-III written by John Langdon Sibley and   published:
Cambridge, Mass. : C. W. Sever, 1873-85. Vols. V-XVII written by
Shipton and published, in continuous series: Boston : Massachusetts
Historical Society, 1937-75). Cf. also Shipton's New England Life in
the 18th Century: Representative Biographies from Sibley's Harvard
Graduates. -- Cambridge, Mass. : Harvard Univ. Press, 1963. -- vi, 626
p.; which includes "Foreword" by Samuel Eliot Morison and ten
biographies from diss.: Benjamin Wadsworth (Class of 1690), Henry
Flynt (1693), William Vesey (1693), Jedediah Andrews (1695), Richard
Saltonstall (1695), Samuel Vassall (1695), Peter Thacher (1696), John
Read (1697), Jonathan Belcher (1699), and Jeremiah Dummer (1699).

1933-5   Tilley, Winthrop. "The Literature of Natural and Physical
     Science in the American Colonies from the Beginnings to 1765."
     Ph.D., Brown Univ. v, 236 leaves.

     "Introduction": "The work which follows undertakes a survey of
the printed literature of natural and physical science in the American

colonies from the beginnings to 1765.   It has so happened that of the group of men in the colonies interested in research of one sort or another, the names of only two or three--Benjamin Franklin, Cadwallader Colder, John Winthrop--are generally associated with scientific work; it will be shown, however, that these men were only a few of the many and that the work of the other men was quite as sound and quite as interesting" (p. 1). Contents: I. "Introduction," II. "The Literature of Natural History and of Agriculture," III. "The Literature of Medicine," IV. "The Literature of Astronomy and of Unusual Phenomena," V. "The Literature of Physics, Chemistry, and Manufacturing," VI. "Science and the Colonial College," VII. "American Relations with the Royal Society of London; Learned Societies in the Colonies," and VIII. "Conclusion."

1933-6   Wrinn, Louise Gertrude.   "The Development of the Public
           School System in New Haven, 1639-1930: A Problem in Historical
           Research." Ph.D., Yale Univ. v, 448, 69 leaves.

"Digest": "This dissertation traces the history of public school education in New Haven from 1639, when Ezekiel Cheever taught a few scholars in his own house, till 1931." Relevant chapters: "Introduction"; Part I: "Education in a Theocracy 1638-1665": I. "The Latin Grammar School," II. "The Experiment of the Colony School," and III. "The Origin of the Hopkins Grammar School"; Part II. "Education under the Town, and the Ecclesiastical Societies 1665-1798": IV. "New Haven as Part of the Colony of Connecticut," V. "'Ye Ancient Hopkins Records,'" and VI. "The Ecclesiastical Societies." Parts III and IV deal with later periods. Appendices include a "Chronology" and some twenty-one tables.

1934-1   Balsam, Louis.   "A Study of the Changes in Punishment for
           Crime in Massachusetts from 1630-1934." Ph.D., Harvard Univ.
           iii, 435 leaves.

"Introduction": "This thesis is a historical account of punishments inflicted upon those convicted of crimes in Massachusetts from 1630 when the first governor brought over the charter from England, to the present time. . . . The construction of such an account required a detailed examination of hundreds of penal statutes and of statutes allied to penal matters. . . . The next step was to discover, if possible, what relationship existed between statutory punishments and those pronounced by the courts. . . . The attempt . . . to find out what punishments judges actually did inflict meant a search through and an analysis of court records" (pp. 1-2). "Conclusion": "In the whole of the three hundred years reviewed, there have been very few really fundamental changes in punishment. The very concept of punishment still remains the basis for dealing with criminals. What changes there have been, thus, have been changes within punishment, itself; changes of ways and means; changes of emphasis and proportion, almost entirely" (p. 419).   Relevant chapters: "Introduction," I. "Statutory Punishments for Crime," II. "Judicial Punishment for Crime," III. "Jails and Houses of Correction," IX. "Pardon, Parole and the Indeterminate Sentence," and "Conclusion." Chapters IV-VIII deal with later events only.

1934-2   Brown, George Edward.   "Catechists and Catechisms of Early
     New England." D.R.E., Boston Univ. (School of Theology). [900]
     leaves.

     "Statement of Thesis": "The Puritans who settled in New England
during the early part of the Seventeenth Century were staunch
advocates of Catechising. The considered Catechetical Instruction a
most effective method by which to inculcate the fundamental teachings
of Puritanism, and also an invaluable weapon of defence against any
teaching contrary to their faith. . . .   In this study we consider
only those Catechists and Catechisms which were the product of the
first century of colonial life in New England. . . .   We have divided
our study into three parts: Book I, Catechetical Instruction Among
the Puritans; Book II, Cotton Mather; Book III, The Catechetical
Instruction of the Indians" (n.p.).   Some thirty New England
"catechists" are treated.

1934-3   Chakerian, Charles Garabed.   "The Development of State Care
     of Dependents and Defectives in New England." Ph.D., Yale Univ.
     ix, 536 leaves.

     Relevant chapters: Part I.   "The Development of State Poor
Relief":   I. "Historical Sketch of Poor Relief," II. "State Outdoor
Poor Relief in New England," and III. "State Indoor Poor Relief in New
England"; Part II. "The Development of State Care of Dependents and
Neglected Children in New England":   VI. "The Background of State Care
of Dependents and Neglected Children in New England"; Part III. "The
Development of State Care and Training of the Physically Handicapped
in New England":   IX. "State Care and Training of the Deaf," X. "State
Maintenance and Education of the Blind," and XI. "State Training and
Care of the Crippled"; Part IV. "The Development of State Care of the
Mentally Handicapped in New England":   XII. "State Care of the
Insane"; Part V. "The Development of State Care of the Dependent Sick
in New England":   XIV. "State Care of the Dependent Sick"; and
"General Conclusion." Other chapters deal with later periods.

1934-4   Hornberger, Theodore R.   "American Puritanism and the Rise of
     the Scientific Mind: A Study of Science and American Literature
     in the Seventeenth and Early Eighteenth Centuries." Ph.D., Univ.
     of Michigan. 2 vols. (vi, 659 leaves).

     "Conclusion":   An "effort has been made to trace the effect of
the advance of science upon the thought of the New England clergy
during the colonial time. We have dealt not only with science, . . .
but with . . . pseudo-science, and most of all with the great variety
of philosophical and theological ideas which were in the seventeenth
and eighteenth centuries more or less related to the spread of the
scientific mind" (p. 597). Contents: One: "The Problem," Two: "Trial
by Scripture: The First Generation," Three: "Comets, Fires, and Indian
Wars: The Second Generation," Four: "Bearers of the New Science from
Oxford to New England," Five: "Cotton Mather and His Contemporaries,"
Six: "Eighteenth-Century Gentlemen of the Clergy," Seven: "The Triumph

of Final Ends," and Eight: "Conclusion."

1934-5   Newcombe, Alfred W.   "The Organization and Procedure of the
        S.P.G. with Special Reference to New England." Ph.D., Univ. of
        Michigan. 245 leaves.

        "Summary and Conclusion":   "The S.P.G. [i.e., Society for the
    Propagation of the Gospel] was the last of a series of organizations
    formed in the Seventeenth Century by the clergy and supporters of the
    Church of England to correct the spiritual decline that accompanied
    the Restoration. Its origin in 1701 was largely due to Dr. Thomas
    Bray's appreciation of the religious needs of the American Colonies.
    . . . Though subject to modification in the presence of new
    circumstances its purpose was essentially to aid the Anglican
    colonists in the formation and support of churches and to minister to
    the needs of Negroes and Indians" (p. 225). Contents: I. "The Origin
    and Formation of the S.P.G.," II. "The Organization and Procedure of
    the Home Office," III. "The Appointment and Instruction of the
    Missionaries," IV. "The Supervision and Control of the Missionaries,"
    V. "The Remuneration of the Missionaries," VI. "Other Activities of
    the Society," VII. "The Finances of the Home Office," VIII. "The Aims
    of the Society," and "Summary and Conclusion."

1934-6   Sheridan, Marion Campbell.   "The Teaching of Reading in the
        Public Schools of New Haven, 1638-1930." Ph.D., Yale Univ. 543
        leaves.

        Relevant chapters: I. "Introduction," II. "The Eradication of
    Current Ideas," III. "As Things Were," and IX. "Conclusion." Chapters
    IV-VIII treat of later events.

1934-7   Shores, Louis.   "Origins of the American College Library,
        1638-1800." Ph.D., George Peabody College for Teachers.

        Published under same title: Nashville, Tenn. : George Peabody
    College for Teachers, 1934. -- xi, 290 p. -- (Contributions to
    Education ; no. 134). Reprinted: New York : Barnes & Noble, 1935. --
    xi, 290 p. Also reprinted: Hamden, Conn. : Shoe String Press, 1966.
    -- xi, 290 p. Also reprinted: Boston : Gregg Press, 1972. -- xi, 290
    p. -- (Library Reference Ser. Library History and Biography).
    Relevant chapters (1966 ed.): I. "History of Colonial College
    Libraries" (including sections on "Colonial Higher Education" and on
    nine "Colonial College Libraries," of which Harvard and Yale are two),
    II. "Book Collecting and Selecting," III. "Library Benefactors," IV.
    "Libraries in Colonial Education," and a "Recapitulation."
    Appendices: I. "Chronological Checklist of Colonial College Library
    Donations," II. "Notable Private Libraries Donated to Colonial
    Colleges," and III. "Colonial College Librarians."

1934-8   Stearns, Raymond Phineas.   "Hugh Peter: A Biography."
        Ph.D., Harvard Univ. 2 vols. (v, 809, xlix, xxi, ii, ii leaves).

Revision published as <u>The Strenuous Puritan: Hugh Peter, 1598-1660</u>. -- Urbana : Univ. of Illinois Press, 1954. -- x, 463 p. "Preface" (1954 ed.): "To comprehend Hugh Peter we must explore some parts of Puritan theology and enter into an amazing labyrinth of political intrigue on both sides of the Atlantic. . . . There are paradoxes ahead. . . . He was said to despise learning; yet he was a founder of Harvard College. He helped to exile Anne Hutchinson from the Massachusetts Bay Colony; yet he advocated religious toleration in the English Commonwealth. He was said to be giddy, without fixed principles; yet he was steadfast throughout his life to Congregationalist tenets. He preached otherworldliness; yet he was the father of the New England fisheries and the triangular trade" (pp. vii-viii). Relevant chapters: Part 1: "Old World Beginnings": One: "Cornish Boyhood, 1598-1613," Two: "The Making of a Puritan," and Three: "Congregationalist in Exile"; and Part 2: "New World Interlude": Four: "Agent to New England," Five: "Salem Ministry," Six: "Builder of the Bay Colony," and Seven: "Agent for the Massachusetts Bay Colony, 1641-45." Part 3 deals with Peter's later career in England. An Appendix gives "The Paternal Ancestry of Hugh Peter."

1934-9   Wainger, Bertrand Max. "Liberal Currents in Provincial Massachusetts, 1692-1766." Ph.D., Cornell Univ. 277 leaves.

"Conclusion": "This essay is a study, through the lives and works of Benjamin Colman, John Wise, and Jonathan Mayhew, of the currents of liberal thought in Massachusetts from 1692 to 1766. The period is dull and prosaic. To understand it one must dig through innumerable and interminable sermons and treatises of theological dispute, all doubtless of vital significance in their own day but to us bleak and dreary. Yet the labor is not without its fruits. One learns to recognize the wider import of disputes over 'dumb reading,' the aggrandizement of ministerial authority, and human inability in regeneration. One comes to understand that changes in theological thought were the expression of the slow triumph of rationalism and equalitarianism, the two forces which molded the revolutionary era. . . . Perhaps the most progressive change that took place during the period was the discrediting of Calvinistic theology" (p. 264). Relevant chapters: I. "Brattle Street Liberalism," II. "The Triumph of Democratic Polity" (deals largely with John Wise), III. "Colman's Career," IV. "The Long Sleep and the Great Awakening," and VI. "Conclusion." Chapter V deals with a later period.

1935-1   Burns, James Joseph. "The Colonial Agents of New England." Ph.D., Catholic Univ. of America.

Published under same title: Washington, D.C. : Catholic Univ. of America, 1935. -- v, 156 p. Reprinted: Philadelphia : Porcupine Press, 1975. -- v, 156 p. -- (Perspectives in American History ; no. 26). Relevant chapters: I. "The Colonial Agency," II. "The Early Agents of New England," and III. "The Eighteenth Century." The final two chapters concern later periods. Appendix: "List of Agents."

1935-2   Butler, Vera Minnie. "Education as Revealed by New England
     Newspapers prior to 1850." Ed.D., Temple Univ.

     Published under same title: Philadelphia : Majestic Press, 1935.
-- ix, 503 p. Reprinted: New York : Arno Press, 1969. -- ix, 503 p.
-- (American Education: Its Men, Ideas, and Institutions). "Preface"
(1969 ed.): "At the present time, when much of public opinion is
molded by our newspapers, ample space is given to education. . . . Did
the early school use the early newspaper in this same way? Was early
advertising alert to the needs of education? Were the editors of early
news sheets interested in the educational institutions in their midst?
What was this attitude, and did it in any way reveal to the people the
changes as they came in the schools? . . . To discover the answers to
these questions; to examine the columns of these early New England
newspapers, in order to find revealed therein the story of an evolving
school system; to see the field of education expand from a local
nucleus to a wider interest; in short, to rediscover education through
the medium of the household news sheet: such is the problem and the
purpose of this thesis" (pp. v-vi). Contents: Part I. "Higher
Education," Part II. "Academies and Special Education," and Part III.
"The Rise of the Common Schools," and "Conclusion." Includes the
Boston News-Letter (1704-1776) and The New England Courant (1721-1726).

1935-3   Creech, Margaret D. "Three Centuries of Poor Law
     Administration in Rhode Island." Ph.D., Univ. of Chicago.

     Revision published as Three Centuries of Poor Law Administration:
A Study of Legislation in Rhode Island with an introductory note by
Edith Abbott. -- Chicago : Univ. of Chicago Press, 1936. -- xxii, 331
p. -- (Social Science Monographs ; no. 24). Reprinted: College Park,
Md. : McGrath Publishing Co., 1969. -- xxii, 331 p. "Preface" (1969
ed.): "In order to understand the development of [laws providing for
the care of the destitute] it is necessary to trace their adoption and
their adaptation from the Elizabethan law brought from England. . . .
Rhode Island offers an opportunity for a study of three hundred years
of legislation and of the means by which this legislation was
administered" (p. xiii). Relevant chapters: Part I. "The Colonial
Period": I. "The Colony and the State of Rhode Island," II. "The
Colonial Poor Law: Provisions and Administration," III. "Colonial
Settlement and Removal," IV. "The Dependent Child, the Sick, and the
Insane," and V. "Methods of Financing Early Relief of the Poor." Part
II deals with the modern period. Relevant appendices: I. "List of
Laws of Rhode Island Relating to the Poor," II. "List of Judicial
Decisions under the Poor Law," III. "Select Documents Relating to the
History of Poor Relief in the Colonial Period and the Late Eighteenth
Century," and IV. "Thirteen Case Histories, 1644-1724."

1935-4   James, May Winsor Hall. "Schooling and Education in Old
     Lyme, Connecticut, 1635-1935." Ph.D., Yale Univ.

     Revision published as The Educational History of Old Lyme,
Connecticut, 1635-1935. -- New Haven : Published for the New Haven
Historical Society by Yale Univ. Press ; H. Milford, Oxford Univ.
Press, 1939. -- viii, 259 p. "Introduction" (1939 ed.): "The primary

object of the study has been to reveal in retrospect the evolving conditions which have affected and directed education and schooling in a given political unit within the state.... [This] study was made as a type study of education and schooling in the state of Connecticut" (p. 1). Relevant chapters: "Introduction," I. "Early Settlements at the Mouth of the Connecticut River, 1635-1667," II. "Lyme during the Seventeenth Century. A Period of Town Control. The Beginnings of Public Schooling, 1667-1712," III. "A Century of Expansion, Warfare and Internal Growth. Ecclesiastical Control of Church and School, 1713-1794," and "Summary." Chapters IV-VI cover later developments.

1935-5   Miller, Donald George. "A Critical Appraisal of Richard Baxter's Views of the Church and Their Applicability to Contemporary Church Problems." Ph.D., New York Univ. (School of Education). 303 leaves.

"Introduction": "It is the purpose of this thesis to single [Baxter] out for special study, centering particular attention on his views of the Church, and their validity and applicability to contemporary Church problems. Who was Baxter and what was his relation to his times? What, to him, is the true Church, and what are its characteristics? What is the faith of the Church and how shall it be propagated? Who are the true ministers of the Church? What form of organization and what type of polity should the Church adopt? What ordinances are valid, and of what type shall Church worship be?" (p. 2). Contents: I. "Introduction," II. "The Life and Times of Baxter," III. "The Nature of the Church," IV. "The Teaching Office of the Church," V. "The Government of the Church" (treats the ministry, Church polity, Church discipline), VI. "The Ordinances and Worship of the Church," VII. "A Critical Evaluation of Baxter's Views and Their Applicability to Contemporary Church Problems."

1935-6   Platz, Mabel Beulah. "The Relation of Speech to the Colonial Policies of Massachusetts, 1620-1692." Ph.D., Univ. of Southern California. 293 leaves.

"Introduction": "The aims of the study are: I. To show the relation of public speech to the settlement of the Massachusetts colony. ... This can best be accomplished by studying the motives which prompted the colonists in coming to America and by designating the leaders who prompted the migration and the means they used to convince their colleagues. ... II. In the absence of the press and newspaper the needs for social intercourse were met by establishing institutions fostering public discussion. The second purpose of this study is therefore to designate the institutions which were set up by the leaders within the colony conducive to influencing their fellow colonists through public speech. ... III. To study the crucial events in the history of the colony which were influenced by these institutions set up for public speech. ... These events will be studied under two general headings: a. Affairs of the Church [and] b. Secular affairs. ... The dominant theme of the study will be to show how public speech was a factor in the establishment of American democratic foundations" (pp. 10-11). Contents: I. "The

Introduction," II. "The Historical Background of American Colonial Oratory," III. "Institutions in the Massachusetts Colony Conducive to Public Speech [i.e., town meetings, the Assembly, the court, pulpit and occasional sermons]," IV. "Controversies over Toleration and Liberation," V. "The Voice of the Church," VI. "Secular Controversies in the Massachusetts Colony," and VII. "Conclusions."

1935-7   Poppers, Hirsch Leib.   "Die Entstehung des Kongregationalismus aus der puritanischen Bewegung und seine Bedeutung als Independentismus für die englische Staatsgeschichte des 17. Jahrhunderts." Dr. phil., Humboldt-Univ. zu Berlin (Germany).

Revision published as Der religiöse Ursprung des modernen englischen Freiheits- und Staatsideals: Die Geschichtsgestaltung des Independentismus. -- Berlin : Buchdruckerei Hanns Michel, 1936. -- x, 127 p. "Vorwort" (1936 ed.): "Vorliegende Arbeit will ein Beitrag sein zum Problem des Wirkens der Religion und des religiösen Denken auf die staatspolitische Gestaltung Englands. . . . Nach einem knappen Ueberblick über die grossen Ideen, welche im Hintergrunde des puritanisch-kongregationalistischen Handelns standen, gebe ich im zweiten Teil meiner Arbeit neben einer Lebensgeschichte Robert Brownes eine Darstellung seiner fast unbekannten Hauptschrift 'A Booke which sheweth.' . . . Im dritten Teil meiner Arbeit behandle ich die allgemeinen puritanischen Tendenzen und Forderungen, die sich aus ihnen ergebenden Zusammenstösse mit der Stattsgewalt, deren Massnahmen und schliesslich die Radikalisierung des Puritanismus und den Sieg des Independentismus. . . . In der vorliegenden Arbeit versuche ich . . . die zarten Fäden sowie die theoretischen und historischen Zwangsläufigkeiten festzuhalten, welche zwischen dem frühen Stadium des Brownismus und den das Staatsgeschehen gestaltenden Independenten Cromwellischer Art bestanden" (pp. V-VII). Contents: "Einleitung"; "Lehre und Praxis des religiösen Independentismus als politisch wirkende Kraftzentren"; "Robert Browne"; "Die puritanischen Reformbestregungen, die kirchenpolitischen Massnahmen des englischen Staates und die Entwicklung der Independenten zur politische revolutionären Partei"; and "Historischer Ausblick."

1935-8   Réti, Elisabeth. "Hawthorne's [sic] Vehältnis zur Neu-Englandtradition." Dr. phil., Georg-August-Univ. zu Göttingen (Germany).

Published under same title: Rüstrigen : Chr. Wiechmann, 1935. -- iv, 117 p. "Einleitung": "Puritaner sind angeblich die Gründer der Heimat Hawthorne's [sic], also Neu-Englands. Wie weit diese Angabe stimmt, wird zu beweisen sein" (p. iv). Contents: "Hauptteil A": "Neu-England und seine Tradition": I. "Die Geschichtliche Entwicklung Neu-Englands," II. "Die Entstehung und Entwicklung der Hauptformen des Englischen Protestantismus und seine Bedeutung für Neu-England," and III. "Die Besonderheiten der Dissidentischen Weltanschauung"; and "Hauptteil B": "Hawthorne als Mensch und Dichter innerhalb der Neu-Englandtradition": I. "Die Familie Hathorne in Neu-England," II. "Das Individualprinzip der Neu-Englandtradition bei Hawthorne," III. "Das Gemeinschaftprinzip der Neu-Englandtradition bei Hawthorne," and IV.

"Der Einfluss der Alten Welt auf Hawthorne's Neu-Englische Kunst"; and "Zusammenfassung,"

1935-9   Warner, Robert Austin. "The Indians of Southern New England to 1725: A Study in Culture Contact." Ph.D., Yale Univ. xiii, 366 leaves.

Narrates the decline of the Indians of southern New England through their contact with Europeans. Contents: I. "the aboriginal culture," II. "the effect of trade contact," III. "struggle for dominion," IV. "transition period, 1643-75," V. "missionary theory," VI. "laymen impose a social system," and VII. "loss of a way of life."

1935-10   Widenmann, Helene. "Neuengland in der erzählenden Literatur Amerikas." Dr. phil., Humboldt-Univ. zu Berlin (Germany).

Published under same title: Halle (Saale) : Max Neimeyer Verlag, 1935. -- xiv, 128 p. -- (Studien zur englischen Philologie ; Heft 86). Reprinted: Waluf bei Wiesbaden : M. Sändig, 1973. -- xiv, 128 p. -- (Studien zur   englischen Philologie ; Heft 86). Relevant chapters: A. "Einleitung: Das Problem 'Neuengland'": 1. "Neuengland von den Anfängen bis zum Bürgerkrieg,"   2. "Neuengland und die amerikanische Literatur," and 3. "Puritanismus und Neuengland"; B. "I Hauptteil. Die Auffassung Neuenglands bei den einzelnen Schriftstellern": "Das theokratische Neuengland" (including a section on "Hawthorne als Neuenglandpuritaner"); C. "II Hauptteil. Neuenglisches Leben, an der Hand der Erzählungen": 1. "Neuenglische Menschen," 2. "Sitten und Gebräuche in Neuengland," and 3. "Neuenglische Weltanschauung"; D. "Schluss. Zusammenfassung"; and E. "Anhang. Yankee, Angelsachsentum und Puritanismus."

1936-1   Bridenbaugh, Carl. "The Rise of the Colonial Towns, 1625- 1742." Ph.D., Harvard Univ. 3 vols. (x, 936 leaves).

Revision published as Cities in the Wilderness: The First Century of Urban Life in America, 1625-1742. -- New York : Ronald Press, 1938. -- xiv, 500 p. -- (Ronald Ser. in History). A 2nd ed. published: New York : Alfred A. Knopf, 1955. -- xiv, 500 p. Reprint of 2nd ed.: New York : Capricorn, 1964. -- xiv, 500 p. -- (Capricorn Giant ; 242). "Preface" (1955 ed.): "In these pages I have undertaken to describe the life of colonial America from 1625 to 1742 as it developed under urban conditions. In an attempt to secure a fully rounded treatment, the examination of this emerging society is concerned with its physical, economic, social and cultural aspects" (p. vii). Boston and Newport are two of the five representative towns selected for study. Contents: Part I. "The Planting of the Villages, 1625-1690": I. "The Village Physiognomy," II. "Economic Life in the Villages," III. "The Appearance of Urban Problems," IV. "Village Society," and "Conclusion"; Part II. "The Awakening of Civic Consciousness, 1690-1720": V. "The Expanding Scene," VI. "The Economic Pattern," VII. "Problems of a Growing Society," VIII. "Social Life in the Towns," and "Conclusions"; Part III. "Rounding Out the Century, 1720-1742": IX. "The Urban Setting," X. "Commercial

Rivalries," XI. "Resistant Problems of an Urban Society," XII. "Social Maturity," and "Conclusion"; and "Conclusion: One Hundred Years of Urban Growth."

1936-2   Cobbledick, Melville Robert. "The Status of Women in Puritan New England, 1630-1660: A Demographic Study." Ph.D., Yale Univ. 333 leaves.

    Abstract in DAI, vol. 31 (11), sec. A., p. 6173: "On the frontier the family was the unit of production and the members of each household raised and processed for themselves most of the necessities which they required. In the clear-cut division of labor between the sexes, women's duties were those of the home, men's, those outside it although closely connected with it." Contents: "Introduction," "Women in Relation to Economic Life," "Women in Relation to the Family Organization," "Women in Relation to Religion," "Women in Relation to Regulation," and "Notes on Certain Developmental Aspects of the Status of Women."

1936-3   Harvey, Shirley Wilcox. "Nathaniel Ward: His Life and Work, Together with an Edited Text of His Simple Cobler." Ph.D., Boston Univ. (Graduate School). ix, 450, xi-xxv leaves.

    Contents: I. "Early Life and Education," II. "Travels," III. "The Rector of Stondon," IV. "The American Divine," V. "The Lawgiver," VI. "The Discontented Exile," VII. "The Simple Cobler," VIII. "Ezekiel 10:14," IX. "Shenfield," X. "A Religious Demurrer," XI. "Apocrypha," and XII. "The Nathaniel Ward They Knew." Ward's biography is followed by the "Text of The Simple Cobler."

1936-4   Jaeger, Julius Peter. "An Introduction to Richard Baxter's A Holy Commonwealth." Ph.D., Univ. of Washington. 2 vols. (iv, 421 leaves).

    Contents: Vol. I: I. "Foreword," II. "Background of Baxter's Political Thought," III. "Sketch of Baxter's Life to 1642," IV. "Baxter's Relation to Public Affairs, 1642-59," V. "Authorship and Edition of A Holy Commonwealth," VI. "Date and Occasion of Writing and Publication," VII. "Leading Ideas of A Holy Commonwealth," and VIII. "Chronological Table"; vol. II: "Text of the Prefatory Matter of A Holy Commonwealth" and "Notes on the Prefatory Matter of A Holy Commonwealth." Appendices: I. "Baxter's Revocation of A Holy Commonwealth and Its Condemnation and Burning at Oxford" and II. "Notes on A Holy Commonwealth, chapter 13."

1936-5   Perrin, Porter Gale. "The Teaching of Rhetoric in the American Colleges Before 1750." Ph.D., Univ. of Chicago. iv, 225 leaves.

    "Preface": "This study is a chapter in the transfer of higher education to the American colonies, specifically treating the discipline of rhetoric at Harvard College, the College of William and

Mary, and Yale College from their foundings to about 1750. . . . This program in rhetoric of the first century of our colleges contains the seeds of the later ramifying growth of instruction in public speaking, written composition, and literature" (p. ii). Contents: I. "The First Three Colleges to 1750," II. "Rhetoric in the Curriculum," III. "Text and Reference Books in Rhetoric," IV. "Rhetorical Topics Before 1720," V. "Transition in Rhetoric, 1720-1730," VI. "The Process of Composition and Exercises of Rhetoric," and VII. "Other College Exercises." Appendices: A. "Theses Rhetoricae," B. "Jonathan Mitchell's Notes in Rhetoric, 1647," C. "Book Lists," D. "Cotton Mather on Style," and E. "Student Exercises."

1936-6   Piercy, Josephine Ketcham. "Studies in Literary Types in Seventeenth-Century America, with Particular Emphasis upon the Beginnings of the Essay (1607-1710)." Ph.D., Yale Univ. 529 leaves.

Revision published as Studies in Literary Types in Seventeenth-Century America (1607-1710). -- New Haven : Yale Univ. Press ; London: H. Milford, Oxford Univ. Press, 1939. -- xi, 360 p. -- (Yale Studies in English ; vol. XCI). A 2nd ed. published: Hamden, Conn. : Archon Books, 1969. -- xi, 368 p. Contents (1969 ed.): Part I. "Literary Types": "'The Times Opinionists,'" "'The Latest News,'" "The Almanac," "The Scientific Essay," "Personal Records," "Dedications, Prefaces, and Introductions," "Satire and Invective," "Meditations," "The Sermon and Religious Discourse," "The Beginnings of Biography," and "Cotton Mather"; Part II. "Influences": "Literary Forms," "Seventeenth-Century Prose Style," "The Classical Inheritance," "'The Times Opinionists' Answered," and "Poetry." Appendices: A. "Almanacs," B. "S[amuel] Danforth, An Astronomical Description of the Late Comet (1665)," and C. "Cotton Mather, Of Poetry and Style; Samuel Sewall, On Slavery; Thomas Thacher, A Brief Rule against Small Pocks."

1936-7   Preston, Richard Arthur. "The Colonial Schemes of Sir Ferdinando Gorges." Ph.D., Yale Univ. 383 leaves.

A "greatly enlarged" and "completely rewritten" version published as Gorges of Plymouth Fort: A Life of Sir Ferdinando Gorges, Captain of Plymouth Fort, Governor of New England, and Lord of the Province of Maine. -- Toronto : Univ. of Toronto Press in co-operation with the Royal Military College of Canada, 1953. -- vii, 495 p. "Preface" (1953 ed.): The "original thesis" of the diss., "namely that Gorges's career was equally important as a pre-natal stage in the development of royal administration for the colonies and as an early example of a colonial proprietary, has been maintained" in published version (p. v). Contents: I. "Introduction," II. "A Younger Son in a Gentle Family," III. "A Captain in Elizabeth's Expeditionary Forces," IV. "Plymouth Fort and St. Nicholas Island," V. "The Spanish Peril, 1595-1600," VI. "A Tragic Interlude: The Essex Revolt," VII. "Plymouth Fort in Time of Peace, 1603-19," VIII. "The Exploration of New England," IX. "The Opposition of the Virginia Company," X. "Fishing versus Plantation," XI. "The Council for New England in Operation, 1622-4," XII. "Plantation Deferred, 1624-9," XIII. "The Intrusion of the Puritans," XIV. "Laud's Policy of 'Thorough' in New England," and

XV. "The Province of Maine." Appendices: "Illustrations, Maps, and Tables."

1936-8   Records, Ralph Hyden. "Land as a Basis for Economic and
     Social Discontent in Maine and Massachusetts to 1776." Ph.D.,
     Univ. of Chicago. x, 379 leaves.

     "Introduction": "Since land was one of the three economic
mainstays of New England life, was it a basis of social discontent in
Maine and in Massachusetts and factor in the Revolution which ended in
the independence of the colonies? . . . In order to trace the course
of social discontent which arose from the varying phases of land
ownership, one must turn back to the earlier decades of the colonial
period to study the causes which may have been at work during several
generations. One has to note, on the one hand, the efforts to advance
their position by those upper classes which were endeavoring to
control the life of the colonies to their own advantage, and, on the
other, the demands made by the less fortunate elements for an increase
of power and the betterment of their position" (p. 2). Contents:
"Introduction"; I. "Commoners and Non-Commoners"; II. "Trespasses,
Encroachments, and Ejectments"; III. "Titles"; IV. "The King's Woods";
V. "Speculation": A. "The Seventeenth Century" and B. "The Eighteenth
Century to 1763"; VI. "Squatters"; VII. "Absentee Proprietors"; VIII.
"Taxation"; and IX. "Conclusions."

1936-9   Riley, Arthur Joseph. "Catholicism in Colonial New England:
     1620-1788." Ph.D., Catholic Univ. of America.

     Revison published as Catholicism in New England to 1788. --
Washington, D. C. : Catholic Univ. of America, 1936. -- ix, 479 p. --
(Catholic Univ. of America, Studies in American Church History ; vol.
XXIV). Contents (published version): I. "Introduction," II.
"Formation of the New England Colonial Mind with Regard to the
Catholic Church," III. "The New England Colonial Mind and the Catholic
Rule of Faith," IV. "Opposition of the New England Colonial Mind to
Catholic Worship," V. "The New England Colonial Mind and Catholic
History," VI. "Attitude of the New England Colonial Mind toward
Catholic Priests," VII. "Legal Restrictions against Catholics," VIII.
"Catholics in New England," and "Summary." Appendices: A. "The Anti-
Priest Laws of Massachusetts," B. "English Declarations, Test Oaths,
Oaths of Allegiance, Supremacy, and Abjuration," C. "Anti-Catholic and
Catholic Books in New England Colonial Libraries," D. "Extract from
New England Courant relating to death of Father [Sébastien Râle,
1724]," and E. "Tables relating to New England captives, converted to
Catholicism in Canada."

1936-10   Simpson, Claude Mitchell, Jr. "The English Speech of Early
     Rhode Island, 1636-1700." Ph.D., Harvard Univ. x, 314 leaves.

     "Preface": "The purpose of this study is to ascertain the
pronunciation current in Rhode Island before 1700, as far as it is
possible to do so by the use of naïve spellings. Besides establishing
a tentative phonology, I have commented rather briefly on certain

interesting aspects of inflection, syntax, and at some length have discussed the occurrence or usage of words peculiar to either the seventeenth or the twentieth century. Perhaps the chief value of the present investigation is in assembling and making available additional materials, useful for an ultimate definitive work in early American speech" (pp. iii-iv). Contents: I. "Introductory": 1. "The Settling of Rhode Island," 2. "The Sources of Rhode Island Speech," 3. "The Materials," and 4. "The Interpretation of Naïve Spellings"; II. "The Stressed Vowels"; III. "The Unstressed Vowels": "Unobscured Vowels," "Obscured Vowels," and "Adjacent Vowels"; IV. "The Consonants"; V. "Notes on Inflection and Syntax"; and VI. "Lexical Notes." Chapters I-IV of diss. appeared as Early Rhode Island Pronunciation, 1636-1700, as Reflected in Published Town Records. -- Washington, D. C. : American Documentation Institute, 1937. -- viii, 147 p. -- (American Documentation Institute ; Document 1013) (The American Dialect Society Microfilm Monographs ; no. 1).

1937-1   Bachelder, Joseph E., Jr. "The Relation of Social Change to the Development of Criminal Laws in Connecticut." Ph.D., Yale Univ. v, [426] leaves.

"Summary": "An examination was made of the criminal laws of Connecticut as they appeared in six codes, including the first one in 1650. . . . It was found that the reasons for changes in criminal law lie in the changing life-conditions, and that criminal law thus adjusts to such changes as does any other social device and institution" (p. iv). Relevant chapters: I. "Introduction," II. "The Code of 1670," III. "The Revision of 1784," VIII. "General Analysis," IX. "Analysis of Categories," and X. "Conclusion."

1937-2   Brockunier, Samuel Hugh. "Roger Williams: A Study of His Life and Career to 1657." Ph.D., Harvard Univ. 500, 31 leaves.

Expanded and revised version published as The Irrepressible Democrat, Roger Williams. -- New York : Ronald Press, 1940. -- xii, 305 p. -- (Ronald Ser. in History). Contents (1940 ed.): 1. "Portents," 2. "Cambridge and the Puritan Leaven," 3. "Frustration and Flight," 4. "Troubler in Israel," 5. "The Salem Rebellion," 6. "Oligarchy in the Judgment Seat," 7. "Wilderness Exile," 8. "Democracy on the Anvil," 9. "The Rhode Island Way," 10. "Insecurities and Alarums," 11. "Dickering for a Charter," 12. "Naboth's Vineyard," 13. "A More Perfect Union," 14. "Indian Trader and Frontier Peacemaker," 15. "Colonial Diplomat," 16. "President Williams," 17. "Liberty Without License," 18. "The Nemesis of Orthodoxy," 19. "The Narragansett Land Fever," 20. "Democracy on the Defensive," and 21. "Roger Williams and the American Tradition."

1937-3   Craig, Hardin, Jr. "The Geneva Bible as a Political Document." Ph.D., Harvard Univ. 301, viii leaves.

"Introduction": "The purpose of this study is two-fold: to examine the Geneva Bible and to form an estimate of what we call the biblical issue in the latter half of the 16th century. Roughly speaking, such a study may be confined to the reign of Elizabeth, 1558-1603, but it will also be necessary to go back a few years to the Marian Exiles and forward to 1611, the publication date of the Authorized Version" (p. 1). "The line between politics and religion was never harder to draw than in 16th century England, and anyone who has ever studied the works of Anglican and puritan controversialists knows how large a part the Bible plays in the religion of that time. Under an Establishment, where conformity is a state concern and where nonconformity is defiance of the government, the reasons for nonconformity become of political importance; it was the Bible which funded those reasons to a large group of Englishmen" (p. 3). Contents: Part I. "Introduction; The Marian Exiles and the Bible"; Part II. "Background of the Scriptural Controversy; Material of the Scriptural Controversy"; and Part III. "Conclusion of the Scriptural Controversy." Appendices: I. "Comparison of texts," II. "The Geneva Bible in the 17th century," and III. "A Puritan manifesto: Foxe's edition of Tyndale."

1937-4   Dawson, Edward Barker. "Nathaniel Hawthorne's Knowledge and Use of New England History: A Study of Sources." Ph.D., Vanderbilt Univ. iii, 305 leaves.

"Introduction": "In the following chapters I shall attempt to show the manner and the extent of Hawthorne's borrowings from his sources. Each of Hawthorne's historical works will be considered, sources will be pointed out or suggested, and we shall see if we can account for the mass of historical information that is found in his writings. There are, to be sure, great gaps in this information, and some of it is not quite accurate, but in the end, I think that we shall see that as far as New England history is concerned, Nathaniel Hawthorne is a historian of no mean order" (p. 20). Relevant chapters: "Introduction," I. "The works dealing with the period prior to 1642," II. "The Scarlet Letter: 1642-1649," III. "The works dealing with the period 1650-1691," IV. "Witchcraft: 1692," V. "The works dealing with the period 1693-1764," and "Conclusion." Chapter VI treats of the Revolutionary period.

1937-5   Farrell, John Thomas. "The Administration of Justice in Connecticut about the Middle of the Eighteenth Century." Ph.D., Yale Univ. 220 leaves.

"Summary" (loose leaf at end of diss.): "This dissertation is based for the most part upon the records and files of the Superior and County Courts of Connecticut at a point midway in the eighteenth century. Its purpose is to give a picture of the administration of justice in the colony at that time with detailed explanations of the court system, the framework of civil procedure, and the criminal law. Lawyers and judges come in for their share of attention. . . . The obvious conclusion is that English tradition was the force which most influenced the legal system of Connecticut in the middle of the eighteenth century." Contents: I. "Introduction," II. "The Court System," III. "Procedure and Civil Actions," IV. "Procedure and Criminal Cases," V. "The Criminal Business of the County Court," VI. "The Justice of the Peace," VII. "Attorneys and Judges," and VIII.

"Conclusion."   Diss. includes historical treatments of the administration of justice in the seventeenth and early eighteenth centuries as well.

1937-6   Longhorn, Milton. "The Rise of the Merchant Class in Rhode
     Island." Ph.D., Univ. of Wisconsin at Madison. 304, xiii leaves.

     "Foreword": "The present study is concerned with the history of the merchant class and commerce of Rhode Island which brought about the change from a colony in which agriculture was dominant to one in which commerce was the controlling interest" (p. 1). Contents: I. "The Course of Rhode Island Commerce, 1700-1755," II. "Methods and Mechanics of Rhode Island Commerce," III. "The Merchants versus the Farmers," IV. "Social Life of the Merchants," and V. "Conclusion."

1937-7   Moreland, Marion.   "Development of the Concept of
     Individualism with Reference to the Work of Roger Williams."
     Ph.D., Univ. of Toronto (Canada).

     Cited in CDI, vol. 36, p. 155; not in NUC, BMGC, OCLC, or DAI. Diss. may no longer be extant: not held by Univ. of Toronto or by National Library of Canada. Two addresses of the author were provided by the Univ. of Toronto Alumni Records Office, but letters sent to the author in February, 1982, inquiring about the diss. received no response.

1937-8   Reinhold, Heinz. "Puritanismus und Aristokratie." Dr. phil.,
     Univ. Leipzig (Germany).

     Revision published under same title: Berlin : Junker & Dünnhaupt, 1938.   -- (Neue Deutsche Forschungen ; Bd. 164) (Abteilung Englische Philologie ; Bd. 11). Contents (1938 ed.): 1. "Vorbemerkung," 2. "Die puritanische Theorie über das Verhältnis von Herrschern und Untertanen," 3. "Das aristokratische Lebensideal und die christliche Tugendlehre," 4. "Das Ideal der Demut," 5. "Die Askese," 6. "Puritanische Äusserungen allgemeiner Art über die Aristokratie,"   7.   "Die adlige Herkunft," 8. "Das Problem der Arbeit," 9. "Die Jagd," 10. "Allerlei Zeitvertreib," 11. "Lususäusserungen verschiedener Art," 12. "Die Kleidermoden," 13. "Die Haartracht, das Schminken und andere Modeeigentümlichkeiten," 14. "Das Fluchen," 15. "Kavalierstour und Duell," 16. "Liebesleben und Ehe," 17. "Soziale Misstände," 18. "Die Erziehung," 19. "Zusammenfassender Rückblick über die Entwicklung.--Cromwell und Milton.--Puritanische Aristokraten," 20. "Anti-aristokratische Tendenzen in Schriften, die nicht zur puritanischen Literatur im engeren Sinne gehören," and 21. "Die Folgen."

1938-1   Boaz, Roy Delp. "A Study of the Faith and Practice of the
     First Congregational Church of West Haven, Connecticut, 1719-
     1914." Ph.D., Yale Univ. ii, 402 leaves.

     "Abstract" (at beginning of diss.): "The First Church in West

Haven designed to fit into the structural framework of an ecclesiastical system of churches recognized and promoted by the Colonial Assembly in 1708." The church survived "the full impact of the Anglican invasion from 1720 to 1734." "Conclusion": "The petition of the West Side farmers in 1715 for ecclesiastical independence was prompted primarily by a desire for independent worship of God. The church, after its organization, was immediately committed to the provisions of the Saybrook Platform. By the provisions of this ecclesiastical constitution of faith and practice, the local church and similar churches in the Colony were bound by the Calvinistic faith as outlined in the Westminster Confession, and to a series of rules and regulations for their guidance, discipline, and protection" (p. 388). Relevant chapters: I. "The Establishment of the Parish" and II. "The Anglican Invasion": 1. "The First Pastor, Samuel Johnson, 1719-1722," and 2. "The Second Pastor, Jonathan Arnold, 1725-1734." Chapters III-X treat the later events.

1938-2   Ferguson, William W.   "The Development of Home-Made Governments in New England." Ph.D., Indiana Univ. iii, 207 leaves.

Contents: I. "The Development of Self-Government in Plymouth Colony," II. "Self-Government in Rhode Island," III. "The Development of Self-Government in Connecticut," IV. "The Development of Self-Government in New Haven," V. "Self-Government in New Hampshire and Maine," and VI. "Influence of Congregationalism on the Development of Self-Government in New England."

1938-3   Gambrell, Mary Latimer. "Ministerial Training in Eighteenth-Century New England." Ph.D., Columbia Univ. 171 leaves.

Published under same title: New York : Columbia Univ. Press ; London : P. S. King & Sons, 1937. -- 169 p. -- (Columbia Univ., Faculty of Political Science, Studies in History, Economics, and Public Law ; no. 428). Reprinted: New York : AMS Press, 1967. -- 169 p. Mainly concerned with period from 1740 to 1808, but first two chapters provide background: I. "Puritan Theories of Clerical Education" and II. "Ministerial Training in Early New England."

1938-4   Goldman, Irvin. "The Beginnings of Theories of Natural Ethics and Theology in Seventeenth-Century America." Ph.D., Univ. of Michigan. v, 427 leaves.

Diss. may no longer be extant. Cited in CDI, vol. 34, p. 678; not in DAI, NUC, or OCLC. In January, 1981, Univ. of Michigan Library supplied pagination and call number (Diss #1333), but on June 6, 1982, Library's Interlibrary Loans Department responded, "We do not own."

1938-5   Horner, George F. "A History of American Humor to 1765." Ph.D., Univ. of North Carolina. 2 vols. (iv, 916 leaves).

Includes material drawn from New England almanacs, the Boston

News Letter, the New England Courant, the New England Weekly Journal, and the writings of such New Englanders as Nathaniel Ames, William Bradford, Anne Bradstreet, Robert Calef, Benjamin Colman, Daniel Gookin, Sarah Kemble Knight, Cotton Mather, Thomas Morton, Benjamin Tompson, Nathaniel Ward, John Wise, and William Wood. Relevant chapters: One: "American Humor in the Light of Criticism," Two: "Laughter in the Provinces, 1607-1685," Three: "Laughter in the Transition Period, 1685-1720," and Four: "Laughter in the Colonies, 1720-1765." Chapters Five through Seven deal with later periods.

1938-6   McClure, William Harris. "English Public Opinion and the Colonies under the Restored Stuarts, Charles II and James II, 1660-1689." Ph.D., Univ. of Michigan. iii, 226 leaves.

Abstract in MA, vol. 1 (1), p. 15: "The years between 1660 and 1689 were important in the growth of England's colonial policy. Public opinion, particularly of interested groups, distinctly left its impression on the policy adopted. . . . New England produced more discussion than any other settlement, largely hostile, because of unsuitable climate, products competitive with England's and a population likely to rebel."

1938-7   Morrison, Elizabeth Knowles. "The History of Poor Relief in Maine." Ph.D., Univ. of Chicago. iii, 238 leaves.

Chapter I: "It is interesting to consider to what extent the motives that animated the earliest Maine settlers, so different from the motives of religious freedom and revolt against political autocracy which drove the pioneer settlers to Massachusetts, have influenced political and social thinking and institutions in Maine, giving the peoples' methods of meeting social needs a somewhat different form and feeling from the usual New England pattern" (p. 1). Relevant chapters: I. "The Political and Social Background of the Province and State of Maine," II. "Relief of the Poor in Maine in the Seventeenth Century," and III. "Care of the Poor in Maine under the Province Laws of Massachusetts, 1700-1780": "Summary of the Legislation in Force at the Beginning of the Eighteenth Century" and "Legal Regulations and Administration in Regard to Establishing the Right to Public Support, 1700-1780." Appended at beginning of Univ. of Chicago diss. copy (T17702) is a letter, dated August 27, 1969, "To Whom It May Concern," from Rachel B. Marks, Professor in the School of Social Service Administration, which states in part: "Elizabeth Morrison received her Doctoral Degree at the August, 1938, Convocation. At that time the plan was that the School would publish the dissertation as a monograph. . . . Miss Morrison died suddenly in March, 1939, before she had completed the revision of this study. . . . This copy of the dissertation is substantially as it was completed by Miss Morrison. It does not include her final revisions, and it has not been possible to find a copy of her bibliography, which was, doubtless, extensive."

1938-8   Schenck, Lewis Bevens. "The Significance of Infant Baptism in the Presbyterian Church in America." Ph.D., Yale Univ. 261 leaves.

Revision published as The Presbyterian Doctrine of Children in the Covenant: An Historical Study of the Significance of Infant Baptism in the Presbyterian Church in America. -- New Haven : Yale Univ. Press ; London : H. Milford, Oxford Univ. Press, 1940. -- 188 p. -- (Yale Studies in Religious Education ; XII). Relevant chapter (1940 ed.): I. "The Historic Doctrine of the Presbyterian Church concerning the Significance of Infant Baptism." Chapters II-V deal with the Great Awakening and later periods.

1938-9   Sharp, Morrison. "The New England Trainbands in the Seventeenth Century." Ph.D., Harvard Univ. 315 leaves.

Chapter V: "The New England system of defence was a people in arms, at times stupid, sleepy, and cowardly, but with enormous moral and physical reserves" (p. 289). Diss. discusses such matters as discipline, artillery, the troopers, frequency of training, equipment, the training field, and auxiliary services. Contents: I. "The English Militia, 1540-1640," II. "Leadership and Democracy in the Trainbands," III. "The Elite Companies," IV. "Activities of the Trainbands," and V. "The Militia and the System of Defence."

1939-1   Clyde, Walter Raymond, Jr. "The Development of American Presbyterian Theology, 1705-1823." Ph.D., Hartford Seminary Foundation. viii, 416 leaves.

Relevant chapters: I. "The Theology of the Founding Fathers" and II. "The Adopting Act of 1729." Subsequent chapters deal with later periods.

1939-2   Cole, Martin Lawrence. "The Rise of the Legislative Assembly in Provincial Massachusetts." Ph.D., Univ. of Iowa. ii, 233 leaves.

Chapter I: "The process by which the legislative assembly in provincial Massachusetts (1691-1774) rose gradually from a distinctly inferior position in relation to the royally appointed governor to one of comparative supremacy is both interesting and significant. This almost continuous conflict between the royal governor and the popular assembly throws light on the living forces of the period, and is the chief element in the political growth of the province" (p. 1). Contents: I. "Factors and Forces in Provincial Massachusetts," II. "The Charter of 1691," III. "The General Court in Action," IV. "Constitutional Conflict," and V. "The Control of Finance."

1939-3   McClurkin, Paul Theodore. "Presbyterianism in Colonial New England." Ph.D., Hartford Seminary Foundation. ix, 297 leaves.

"Preface": "The view is upheld in this thesis that the Scottish settlers from the North of Ireland were the backbone of the Presbyterian congregations and presbyteries which were organized in colonial New England. The English Puritans were willing to accept the slightly Presbyterianized Congregationalism of the Plymouth Colony" (p. ii). Relevant chapters: Part One: "The English and French Presbyterian Elements Blend with Congregationalism in Colonial New England": I. "Presbyterianism in Massachusetts Congregationalism," II. "Presbyterianism in Connecticut Congregationalism," and III. "The French Presbyterianism"; Part Two: "The Scotch-Irish Element Becomes the Leading Factor in the Establishment of Presbyterianism in Colonial New England": IV. "The Early Scotch-Irish Settlements." Chapters V-XI deal with later periods.

1939-4 · Plath, Raymond Arthur. "British Mercantilism and the British Colonial Land Policy in the Eighteenth Century." Ph.D., Univ. of Wisconsin at Madison. iii, 313 leaves.

Relevant chapters: I. "The Interest of the Merchants in the Land Policy," II. "The Naval Stores Industry and the Preservation of the Woods," and III. "Immigration and the Frontier Problem to 1763." Chapters IV-VIII deal with irrelevant colonial areas and/or later periods.

1940-1   Ballou, Richard Boyd. "The Grammar Schools in Seventeenth-Century Colonial America: A Study of the Grammar Schools in New England, New Amsterdam, New York, Pennsylvania, Virginia, and Maryland with Special Reference to the Ideas Which Led to Their Establishment and Influenced Their Early History." Ed.D., Harvard Univ. viii, 433 leaves.

"Abstract": "The investigation has sought to determine the ideas and ideals which were essentially responsible for the establishment of the Latin grammar schools in the American colonies in the 17th century. Although the New England colonies were most successful in founding and maintaining such schools, the Latin school was part of the heritage of all the colonies" (p. i). Relevant chapters: "Introduction," I. "European Antecedents," and II. "New England Grammar Schools in the 17th Century": "Concern of the Colony," "Action of the Towns," "The Nature of the Free Grammar School," "Scholars, Masters, and Schools," "In Quest of Their Ideal," "Cotton Mather and the Grammar Schools," and "Some New England Thoughts on Education." Relevant appendices: A. "Some New England Schoolmasters" and B. "The Commonwealth Educators: Puritan Progressives." Chapters III-VII treat of other colonies. CDI, vol. 33, p. 217, incorrectly gives the date of the diss. as 1950.

1940-2   Bennett, Walter Hartwell. "American Concept of Federalism from the Colonial Period to 1900." Ph.D., Duke Univ.

Revision published as American Theories of Federalism. -- University : Univ. of Alabama Press, 1964. -- 227 p. "Preface" (1964 ed.): "The present study . . . is an attempt to analyze in detail the different conceptions of federal union or federal government which

Americans have from time to time advanced and to indicate the importance which these conceptions have had in political controversy. . . . The study concentrates . . . on the legal aspects of federalism as these aspects have been viewed by American constitutional theorists" (pp. 9-10). Relevant chapter: 1. "The Federalized Empire," which includes information on the New England Confederation.

1940-3   Evans, Evan Alfred, Jr. "Literary References in New England Diaries and Other Personal Records, 1700-1730." Ph.D., Harvard Univ. 260 leaves.

"Conclusion": "In the preceding pages we have studied the reading of various men, in various walks of life. We have had some taste of the learning of the Boston ministers, and we have seen how the rural pastors, near and far, upheld the cultural level of the colonies. In the laymen we have observed a retardation of intellectual interest, though in many cases this meant a conservative clinging to the old religious books rather than a complete apathy towards reading in general. . . . Finally we noticed the influence of the colleges as instrumentalities of culture, and we saw the rise of a liberal attitude within academic walls" (p. 175). Contents: "Introduction," One: "Boston," Two: "Rural New England," Three: "The Collegiate Sphere," and "Conclusion." Appendices: A. "Book-stock of Michael Perry," B. "Commonplace Book of Joseph Hinde," and C. "Notes on the Reading of Women."

1940-4   Guthrie, Warren Alan. "The Development of Rhetorical Theory in America, 1635-1850." Ph.D., Northwestern Univ. vi, 260 leaves.

"Introduction": "The study is a history and analysis of the rhetorical theory of this period in terms of the prevailing rhetorical conceptions and trends in rhetorical doctrine" (p. ii). Relevant chapters: "Introduction" and I. "The Dominance of the Rhetoric of Style, 1635-1730." Later chapters treat of later developments.

1940-5   Singer, Gustav Helmut. "Das Verhältnis von Herrschaft und Diensbote im Puritanismus." Dr. phil., Univ. Leipzig (Germany).

Revision published as Puritan Masters and Servants: Ein Kapitel puritanischer Ethik. -- Engelsdorf-Leipzig : C. & E. Vogel, 1940. -- 103 p. "Einleitung" (published version): "Der puritanische Vater als Hausherr und Mensch, der puritanische Diensbote in seiner beruflichen Abhängigkeit, seiner persönlichen Freiheit und Würde, beider Rechte und Pflichten, die Wechselwirkung ihrer sozialen und menschlichen Beziehungen: das soll der Gegenstand dieser Untersuchung sein, die zu einer tieferen Erkenntnis des Ursprungs der noch heute Verständnis der bürgerlichen Ideale in England beitragen, ein besseres Verständnis der bürgerlichen Literatur des 16. bis 18. Jahrhunderts ermöglichen und endlich einen neuen Bewis für die These liefern soll, die die literarische Geschmacksentwicklung von gesellschaftlichen Verschiebungen abhängig Macht" (p. 12). Contents: I. "Einleitung," II. "Das Dienstverhältnis als soziologische Gebenheit," III. "Der gute Herr," IV. "Der gute Diener," and V. "Schluss."

1940-6   Wiley, Margaret Lenore. "Scepticism in the Writings of John
        Donne, Richard Baxter, Jeremy Taylor, Sir Thomas Brown, and
        Joseph Glanvill." Ph.D., Harvard Univ. (Radcliffe College).   199
        leaves.

     Revision published as The Subtle Knot: Creative Scepticism in
Seventeenth-Century England. -- Cambridge, Mass. : Harvard Univ.
Press ; London : Allen & Unwin, 1952. -- 303 p. Reprinted: New York :
Greenwood Press, 1968. -- 303 p. Chapter VI (1968 ed.):   "The
specific evils which Baxter laid at the door of religious controversy
serve to define the boundaries of his own intellectual system.   Over
against prefidence he set man's essential ignorance and his necessary
wrestling with his own doubts. Against what his opponents presented
as simple and direct truths, he offered the dualistic nature of man
and his world and therefore the paradoxical and oblique quality of
truth.   In place of their initial confidence, which was soon
dissipated, he proposed a terminal confidence built up gradually on
the principle that 'if any man will do his will, he shall know of the
doctrine.' . . . [Baxter] appears as an outstanding exponent of the
sceptical method put to the use of Christian apologetics" (pp. 164-
65).   Relevant chapters: I. "Prolegomena to the Definition of
Scepticism," II. "An Historical Definition of Scepticism," III.
"Seventeenth-Century Scepticism: The Knot," and VI. "Richard Baxter
and the Problem of Certainty."

1941-1   Barber, Laurence Luther, Jr.   "Modifications of Town
        Government in New England." Ph.D., Harvard Univ. 279 leaves.

     "Introduction":   "Town government in [more than five hundred New
England municipalities] has at one time or another failed to meet the
exact or the complete needs of local government.   As a result,
modifications or mutations have appeared" (p. 2). "Modifications do
not necessarily come thru [sic] territorial or functional changes.
Some towns have depended upon structural or organizational reforms to
produce needed modernization" (p. 5). Relevant chapters: I.
"Introduction," II. "The Unorganized Territory," III. "Plantations,"
and XII. "Conclusion." Chapters IV-XI treat of later events.

1941-2   Bash, Wendell Hubbard.   "Factors Influencing Family and
        Community Organization in a New England Town, 1730-1940." Ph.D.,
        Harvard Univ. viii, 320 leaves.

     Relevant chapters: I. "Family and Community in Sociological
Theory," II. "Southampton [Mass.]'s Two Centuries," III.   "Religious
Organization,"   IV. "Town Government and Community Organization,"   V.
"Economic Factors in Community History," VI. "Demographic Factors in
the Changing Community," VII. "The Great Family in Southampton," and
IX. "Conclusions." Chapter VIII deals with later events.

1941-3   Bever, Virginia Margaret.   "The Trade in East India
     Commodities to the American Colonies, 1690-1775." Ph.D., Univ.
     of Iowa. iv, 204 leaves.

     Contents: I. "Early Contacts of the East India Commodities with
the American Colonies," II. "The Madagascar Pirates," III. "Legal
Trade," IV. "The Trade in Prohibited Goods," V. "Illegal Trade," and
VI. "Tea."

1941-4   Brock, Leslie Van Horn.   "The Currency of the American
     Colonies, 1700-1764: A Study in Colonial Finance and Imperial
     Relations." Ph.D., Univ. of Michigan. v, 589 leaves.

     Published under same title, by photoreproduction, with new
preface and new title page: New York : Arno Press, 1975. -- ix, 601
p. -- (Dissertations in American Economic History).   New 1975
"Preface": Earlier students thought that "incontrovertable paper
currency was evil per se. . . ." But "such a simple, all-embracing
explanation did not fit the facts, . . . that paper currency issued in
anticipation of taxes was often a necessary instrument of government
finance, that issues on loan provided needed long-term private credit,
and that both provided a medium of exchange" (p. v).   Relevant
chapters: I. "The Currency of the American Colonies Before 1751: The
General Problem; Coin, Commodity Currency; Tobacco Rates," II. "Paper
Currency in the Colonies Before 1751: New England." IV. "Early
Attempts at Imperial Control of Colonial Currency: Coin," V. "Early
Attempts at Imperial Control of Colonial Currency: Bills of Credit.
The Currency Act of 1751," and X. "Conclusions." Relevant appendix:
Table II (Revised): Part B. "New England Bills of Credit Outstanding
[1703-51]."

1941-5   Crepeau, Henry Joseph. "Rhode Island: A History of Child
     Welfare Planning; Being an Analysis of Public Efforts to Make
     Legal Provisions for Children in Need of Special Care." Ph.D.,
     Catholic Univ. of America. 499 leaves.

     Published under same title: Washington, D.C. : Catholic Univ. of
America Press, 1941. -- xii, 340 p. "Introduction": "This study is
an attempt to present an analysis of three centuries of effort made by
the people of Rhode Island on behalf of children in need of special
care. It is primarily an account of a changing public opinion which
has succeeded or failed, from time to time, to bring about the
enactment of provisions intended to safeguard and protect the rights
of certain classes of children" (p. xi). Contents: "Introduction,"
I. "Child Welfare in Transition," II. "The Problem of Child
Dependency," III. "The Problem of Child Dependency (Continued)," IV.
"The Child of Unmarried Parents," V. "The Adopted Child," VI. "The
Child at Work," VII. "The Defective Child," VIII. "The Child
Offender," and IX. "Offenses Against Children." Relevant appendix:
I. "List of Laws of Rhode Island Relating to Children in Need of
Special Care."

1941-6   Vreeland, Herbert Harold, Jr. "Public Secondary Education in
          Connecticut in the Seventeenth and Eighteenth Centuries, with
          Special Reference to Its Support by Private Bequests and Gifts."
          Ph.D., Yale Univ. xi, 482 leaves.

    Contents: "Introduction": Part I. "The Transition of the Latin
Grammar School to New England": 1. "The Cultural Standards of Early
New England--With Special Reference to the College at Cambridge and
the Grammar Schools Tributary Thereto" and 2. "The Support of the
Latin Grammar Schools in the Colony of Massachusetts Bay Before 1645";
Part II. "Public Secondary Education in Connecticut--1636 to 1800":
3. "The Latin Grammar School in the New Haven and Connecticut Colonies
to the Adoption of the Code of 1672," 4. "Public Secondary Education
in Connecticut--1674 to 1690," and 5. "Public Secondary Education in
Connecticut--1690 to 1800"; and "Conclusion." Relevant appendix: IV.
"Regulations of the Hopkins Grammar School [in New Haven]--1684."

1942-1   De Jong, Peter Ymen. "The Covenant Idea in New England
          Theology, 1620-1847." Ph.D., Hartford Seminary Foundation. x,
          513 leaves.

    Revised and slightly condensed version published under same
title: Grand Rapids, Mich. : William B. Eerdmans, 1945. -- 264 p.
"Introduction" (1945 ed.): "This aims at being a study in the history
and development of some of the fundamental conceptions and theories
current in the New England churches respecting the doctrine of the
covenant. An attempt will be made to demonstrate in what way this
doctrine was modified, especially in its application to the practices
of the churches. Here indeed certain far-reaching changes were made
which contributed not a little towards preparing for the final
obscuring of this conception" (p. 11). Relevant chapters: Part One.
"Foundations": 1. "The Covenant Idea in the Reformed Churches" and 2.
"The Covenant Idea among the Anabaptists"; Part Two. "Development":
3. "The Early Puritan Conception of the Covenant," 4. "The Beginnings
of Change," 5. "The Synod of 1662: The Half-Way Covenant Adopted,"
and 6. "Stoddardeanism: The Half-Way Covenant Modified"; and Part
Three. "Evaluation": 10. "The Influence of the Covenant Idea upon New
England Religious Thought," 11. "The Weaknesses of the Covenant Idea
in New England Theology," and "New England Calvinism in the Light of
the Covenant Idea." Chapters 7-9 are concerned with a later period.

1942-2   Greene, Lorenzo Johnson. "The Negro in Colonial New
          England, 1620-1776." Ph.D., Columbia Univ.

    Published under same title: New York : Columbia Univ. Press ;
London : P. S. King & Staples, 1942. -- 404 p. -- (Columbia Univ.,
Faculty of Political Science, Studies in History, Economics, and
Public Law ; no. 494). Reprinted: Port Washington, N.Y. : Kennikat
Press, 1966. -- 404 p. Reprinted with a new preface by Benjamin
Quarles: New York : Atheneum, 1968. -- 404 p. -- (Studies in
American Negro Life). Contents (1968 ed.): I. "Black Merchandise,"
II. "Social Repercussions," III. "Negro Population," IV. "Slave
Occupations," V. "Machinery of Control," VI. "Crimes and Punishment,"
VII. "The Slave Before the Law," VIII. "The Slave Family," IX. "Master

and Slave," X. "Slavery and Conversion," XI. "The Free Negro," and XII. "Summary."

1942-3   Herge, Henry Curtis. "Colonial Long Island: A Collection of Historical Facts and Folk Material of Early Long Island." Ed.D., New York Univ. xi, 222 leaves.

"Preface": "In reading this book you will come to realize that we have inherited much from the three distinct cultures, Indians, Dutch, and English, which have fused after we became a nation. . . . This collection contains many stories, legends, customs, beliefs, superstitions and references to historical events of the colonial period of Long Island" (p. ix). Relevant chapters: I. "Our Indian Predecessors," II. "Indian Legends," III. "Colonial Life, Customs, and Folklore," IV. "Child Life in Colonial Days." V. "Family Customs," VI. "Colonial Courts and Justice," VII. "Watermills and Windmills," VIII. "Gentlemen of Fortune," IX. "The Whaling Industry on Long Island," X. "Superstitions," and XI. "Witchcraft." The stated audience for this work is "Long Island boys and girls."

1942-4   Knorr, Klaus Eugen. "British Colonial Theories: 1570-1850." Ph.D., Univ. of Chicago. 503 leaves.

Revision published with a foreword by H. A. Innes: Toronto : Univ. of Toronto Press, 1944. -- xix, 429 p. Reprinted: London : F. Cass, 1963. -- xix, 429 p. "Preface" (1963 ed.): Diss. intends "to present and examine significant British colonial theories on the advantages and disadvantages resulting to the mother country from the establishment and maintenance of overseas colonies. For what reasons was the building and the preservation of the Empire thought profitable or unprofitable to the British nation?" (p. xvii). Relevant chapters: Part I: I. "Introduction," II. "Colonial Theories, 1570-1660," III. "Colonial Theories, 1660-1776," and IV. "The Old Colonial System: Basic Objectives, Conceptions, Policies." Part II deals with the later colonial system.

1942-5   Kramer, Leonard John. "The Political Ethics of the American Presbyterian Clergy in the Eighteenth Century." Ph.D., Yale Univ. vi, 419 leaves.

"Introduction": "This study seeks to present the political ethics which the Presbyterian clergy taught their people in the period from the beginning of the eighteenth century to the close of the American Revolution. So far as is possible the attempt is also to account for the attitudes and tenets of the group in question by setting forth their social and theological sources, as well as the conditions under which they came to expression" (p. iii). Relevant chapters: "Introduction," I. "Old World Roots," II. "Settlement Beside Quaker and Anglican," and "Conclusion." Chapters III-X concern the period after 1730. Relevant appendices: A "Quotations" and B. "Bibliography of Presbyterian Writing on Political Ethics."

1942-6   McGown, Russell Miller. "The Congregational Way in Higher
    Education." Ph.D., Yale Univ. v, 796 leaves.

    "This study starts from the premise that a certain body of
principles in polity and administration has been so characteristic of
the Congregational Churches of America that it has been commonly
referred to as the Congregational Way. . . . This study discovers in
tracing the founding and early development of a succession of these
colleges across the country that they tended to follow the same
pattern the Congregationalists used in organizing their churches,
i.e., independence, fellowship, and a devotion to the religion
revealed by the Word" (p. ii). Relevant chapters: I. "What is the
Congregational Way?" II. "The Congregational Way Requires a Literate
Ministry," and "Epilogue." Chapters III-VII treat of later periods
and of colleges other than Harvard and Yale.

1942-7   Mills, Barriss. "Attitudes of Some Nineteenth-Century
    American Writers Toward Puritanism." Ph.D., Univ. of Wisconsin
    at Madison. 485 leaves.

    "Introduction": "This study is an attempt to survey and estimate
the attitude toward Puritanism of several leading authors of the
nineteenth century. . . . In addition to these major figures, a
number of American historians who dealt with Puritanism are included--
[George] Bancroft, [John Lothrop] Motley, [John Gorham] Palfrey,
[John] Fiske, [Van Wyck] Brooks, and Charles Francis Adams-- for the
light which their more or less erudite research may shed upon the less
scholarly views of their more purely literary contemporaries. And
finally the attitudes of representative writers of the eighteenth and
twentieth centuries have been brought in for the perspective they give
to the general picture" (pp. 1-2). Contents: I. "Introduction," II.
"1775-1836," III. "Hawthorne," IV. "Whittier," V. "Emerson," VI.
"Longfellow," VII. "[James Russell] Lowell," VIII. "[Oliver Wendell]
Holmes," IX. "Historians," X. "[George] Santayana," XI. "[H. L.]
Mencken, [Stuart P.] Sherman, [Van Wyck] Brooks," and XII.
"Conclusion."

1942-8   Morgan, Edmund Sears. "Religion and the Family in
    Seventeenth-Century New England." Ph.D., Harvard Univ. 323
    leaves.

    Revision published as The Puritan Family: Essays on Religion and
Domestic Relations in Seventeenth-Century New England. -- Boston :
Trustees of the Public Library, 1944. -- 118 p. A 2nd ed. published:
Boston : Trustees of the Public Library, 1956. -- 118 p. New ed.,
revised and enlarged, published as The Puritan Family: Religion and
Domestic Relations in Seventeenth-Century New England. -- New York :
Harper & Row, 1966. -- x, 196 p. -- (Harper Torchbooks. The Academy
Library). The 1966 ed. reprinted: Westport, Conn. : Greenwood Press,
1980. -- x, 196 p. Chapter I (1966 ed.): "The order of society . . .
consisted in certain dual relationships, most of them originating in
agreements between the persons related and all arranged in a pattern
of authority and subjection. . . . God, according to the Puritans,
. . . had assigned special and peculiar duties to each relationship."

This book "is confined . . . to the duties of husbands and wives, parents and children, masters and servants, and with the implications of these relationships in the society the Puritans founded in seventeenth-century New England" (p. 28). Contents: I. "Puritanism and Society," II. "Husbands and Wives," III. "Parents and Children," IV. "The Education of a Saint," V. "Masters and Servants," VI. "The Family in the Social Order," and VII. "Puritan Tribalism."

1942-9   Schulz, Louis. "Social Applications of the Gospel in Congregational Churches." S.T.D., Temple Univ. ix, 164 leaves.

"Introduction": "We plan to trace the development of the social applications of the Gospel among Congregational churches from the days of 'Separatism' to the creation of the Council for Social Action in 1934" (p. viii). Relevant chapters: I. "Introduction," II. "Social Backgrounds in England," and III. "A New World and a New Beginning." Later chapters deal with later periods.

1943-1   Brooks, Charles Burnell. "Puritanism in New England Fiction, 1820-1870." Ph.D., Princeton Univ. 237, iv leaves.

Abstract in DA, vol. 12 (3), p. 296: "The best known interpreter of Puritanism in American fiction is, of course, Hawthorne, but so great is his reputation that he is frequently looked upon as its only interpreter. This thesis is a treatment of Hawthorne's predecessors and contemporaries who also dealt with Puritanism, in many cases using the same themes and subjects that Hawthorne employed." Nathaniel Hawthorne and over a dozen other writers are discussed.

1943-2   Davies, D. Horton M. "The Worship of English Puritans During the Sixteenth, Seventeenth, and Early Eighteenth Centuries." D.Phil., Univ. of Oxford (U.K.).

Revision published as The Worship of the English Puritans. -- Westminster [London] : Dacre Press, 1948. -- 304 p. Contents (1948 ed.): I. "The Nature of English Puritanism," II. "The Theology of Reformed Worship," III. "The Transmission of the Reformed Heritage," IV. "Puritan Worship and the Continental Reformed Churches," V. "The Word of God as the Supreme Liturgical Criterion," VI. "Puritans and the Book of Common Prayer," VII. "The Worship of the English Separatists," VIII. "Set Forms or Extemporary Prayers?" IX. "Puritan Prayer-Books," X. "The Praises of the Puritans," XI. "Puritan Preaching," XII. "Puritan Administration of the Sacraments," XIII. "Puritan Ordinations," XIV. "Puritan Exercise of Ecclesiastical Discipline," and XV. "A Survey and Critique of Puritan Worship." Appendices: A. "A Comparative Analysis of Puritan Liturgies," B. "Art and Music in Puritan Worship," C. "The Puritan Attitude to the Creeds," and D. "Puritan Family Worship."

1943-3   Dean, Harold Lester. "The New England Courant, 1721-1726: A
          Chapter in the History of American Culture." Ph.D., Brown Univ.
          xi, 305 leaves.

     "Introduction": Diss. explores "the relation of the paper to the
social, political, and cultural background of Boston during the
1720's" (p. vi). "Though the experience of the Courant's publisher
[James Franklin] will reveal that the consciousness of the Puritan
theocracy still survived, the challenge to the ministers and the
magistrates was at least symptomatic of the new attitudes. As the
principal spokesman for the secular attitude, the Courant may
justifiably serve as the subject for an extended investigation, the
object of which is to show . . . how adequately it represented the
minds of the people it served as spokesman" (pp. x-xi). Contents: I.
"The Governor," II. "Social Ferment," III. "The Courant in the
Inoculation Controversy," IV. "The Courant Against the Magistrates,"
V. "Ties with England," and VI. "Literary Culture."

1943-4   Dorson, Richard Mercer. "New England Popular Tales and
          Legends." Ph.D., Harvard Univ. xi, 774 leaves.

     Revision published as Jonathan Draws the Long Bow. -- Cambridge,
Mass. : Harvard Univ. Press, 1946. -- viii, 274 p. Reprinted: New
York : Russell & Russell, 1970. -- viii, 274 p. Chapter 1 (1946 ed.):
"Elizabethan superstitions, frontier humor, rural character types,
outdoor occupations, Indian place histories, and geographical
landmarks have largely determined the content and flavor of American
homespun yarns, which grow from a people born in seventeenth century,
when . . . emigrants crossing the sea exchanged old associations for
new. Americans wove the fresh materials of their experiences and
livelihoods into story stuff dyed with Old World superstition and New
World extravagance, and by the devious routes of folklore channels,
stories passed into a popular currency, and crusted into a traditional
lore" (p. 3). Relevant chapters including seventeenth-century
stories/anecdotes: I. "New England Storytelling," II. "Supernatural
Stories," IV. "Tall Tales," V. "Local Legends," and VI. "Literary
Folktales."

1943-5   Hawkridge, Percy Bernard. "The Kingdom at the Threshold: A
          Study of the Apocalyptic Element in English Puritanism." Ph.D.,
          Univ. of London (Richmond College) (U.K.). 306 leaves.

     Chapter I: "'Apocalyptic' means literally an uncovering and thus
a revelation and may refer to the act of revealing or to the thing
revealed, or, by extension, to the book or literature in which the
revelation is recorded. It is usually associated with eschatology or
the revelation of last things" (p. 1). Contents: I. "The Meaning and
Value of Apocalyptic Studies," II. "The Ancestry of Puritan
Apocalyptic. Four Heresies of Identification," III. "Some Aspects of
the Apocalyptic Element in Elizabethan Puritanism. A Difference
Indicated," IV. "The Apocalyptic Element in some Puritan Conceptions,"
V. "The Apocalyptic Element in the Experience of Prominent Individuals
[i.e., Richard Baxter, John Bunyan, John Milton, Oliver Cromwell,
George Fox]," VI. "The Apocalyptic Element in the Puritan Sects," and

VII. "Some Conclusions."

1943-6   Kiefer, Monica Mary. "A History of the Changing Status of
         the American Child in the Colonial and Early National Periods as
         Revealed in Juvenile Literature." Ph.D., Univ. of Pennsylvania.

     Revision published as American Children Through Their Books,
1700-1835, with a foreword by Dorothy Canfield Fisher. -- Philadelphia
: Univ. of Pennsylvania Press, 1948. -- 248 p. "Introduction" (1948
ed.): "This study is an attempt to trace the changing status of the
American child in the colonial and early national periods as it is
revealed in juvenile literature. The general movement of a child's
escape from a submerged position in an adult setting at the beginning
of the eighteenth century advances slowly towards the recognition of
his rights as a distinct personality by 1835" (p. 1). Contents:
"Neutral Pabulum of Godly Children," "War with the Devil," "The Art of
Decent Behaviour," "Learning of Divers Sorts," "Young Victims of
Kitchen Physicks," "Snares of the Old Deluder," and "Summary."

1943-7   Levy, Babette May. "Preaching in the First Half Century of
         New England History." Ph.D., Columbia Univ.

     Published under same title: Hartford, Conn. : American Society
of Church History, 1945. -- vii, 215 p. -- (Studies in Church
History ; vol. VI). Reprinted: New York : Russell & Russell, 1967.
-- vii, 215 p. "Preface" (1967 ed.): "This study concerns itself
primarily with the Puritan preaching of New England's first fifty
years of settlement. During this period English-bred ministers were
in control of the village pulpits, but in the 1650's and 1660's the
first Harvard graduates began to take the places made vacant by the
deaths of the first pastors. I have not included men who reached
their preaching-prime in the last decades of the century" (p. v).
Contents: I. "The Background and Preparation of the Preachers," II.
"The Doctrine as It Was Preached," III. "Success: The Puritan High
Road to Damnation," IV. "Practical Teaching: Politics and War," V.
"The Form of the Sermons," VI. "Sermonic Similitudes: A Sidelight
upon the Puritan Mind," VII. "The Plain Style and Its Variations," and
VIII. "The Reception of the Sermons." Diss. was awarded biennial
prize of the Frank S. Brewer Fund by the American Society of Church
History.

1943-8   Loughrey, Mary Ellen. "France and Rhode Island, 1686-1800."
         Ph.D., Columbia Univ.

     Published under same title: New York : King's Crown Press, 1944.
-- vii, 186 p. "Preface" (1944 ed.): "In this study, I have
outlined, as a historical background, the various sojourns of
Frenchmen in Rhode Island during the seventeenth and eighteenth
centuries, and have placed in this setting the evidences of interest
in French culture which I have discovered to have existed. A chapter
of comments on Rhode Island, selected from the journals, memoirs and
diaries of French travellers and observers, seemed to be a fitting
conclusion to this picture" (pp. v-vi). Relevant chapters: I. "The

Huguenot Refugees," II. "Frenchmen in Rhode Island during the
Intercolonial Wars," VIII. "French Opinions of Rhode Island," and IX.
"Conclusion." Chapters III-VII deal with other matters and later
periods.

1943-9   Waterman, Margaret Barber. "Surnames of the Original
     Settlers in Watertown, Massachusetts." Ph.D., Univ. of Wisconsin
     at Madison. vii, 280 leaves.

     "Introduction": "The procedure followed in making this study has
fallen mainly into three parts: a study of the group chosen; i.e., the
origins (so far as they can be ascertained) of the settlers themselves
and of their names; an examination of the Watertown Records for
spelling variations, their significance, and their relation to the
development of the English language in America; and finally, an
examination of the 1790 Census Reports in an attempt to see to what
degree--in a century and a half--the names had become standardized in
spelling, and how wide the distribution of the Watertown names had
become" (p. 1). Original list of names of Watertown settlers is based
on George Frederick Robinson's Great Little Watertown (1930).
Contents: I. "Introduction," II. "Settlement of Watertown; its Early
History," III. "The Development of English Surnames," IV. "The
Watertown Surnames," and V. "Conclusions." Appendices: I.
"Derivations," II. "Genealogy," III. "Heads of Families in 1790 Census
Reports of Watertown, Waltham, and Weston," and IV. "A Sample Page from
the Watertown Records."

1944-1   Green, Samuel Magee. "An Introduction to the History of
     American Illustration from Its Beginning in the Late Seventeenth
     Century Until 1850." Ph.D., Harvard Univ. iii, 177 leaves.

     "Foreword": "In the process of investigating certain aspects of
American graphic art, it was discovered that practically nothing had
been published on American illustration as it had existed previous to
1850. . . . The purpose of this thesis is an attempt to increase the
slight knowledge thus available. . . . The thesis is presented in the
form of an introduction to the broader field of American illustration.
. . . The method of presentation divides the field into a discussion
of the material and a consideration of its artistic character" (pp. i-
ii). Relevant chapter: I. "From the Beginning Until the Revolution."

1944-2   Morgan, Irvonwy. "The Nonconformity of Richard Baxter."
     Ph.D., Univ. of London (Richmond College) (U.K.).

     Published under same title: London : Epworth Press, 1946. -- 266
p. Contents (1946 ed.): 1. "Puritan Purpose," 2. "'Church of England
and a Good Thing,'" 3. "A Reformed Pastor," 4. "A Pillar of the
Church" 5. "The Outcast," 6. "The Bishop of Nonconformity," 7.
"Baxter's Doctrine of the Church," 8. "The Ministry," 9. "The Word of
God," 10. "The Sacraments," 11. "Baxter and the Hierarchical
Conception," 12. "Things Indifferent," 13. "A Mere Nonconformity," and
14. "Some Aspects of Reunion Reconsidered." Appendix: "Puritan
Propaganda."

1944-3   Nuttall, Geoffrey Fillingham. "The Holy Spirit in Puritan
     Faith and Experience." D.D., Univ. of Oxford (U.K.).

     Revision published under same title: Oxford : Basil Blackwell,
1946. -- xii, 192 p. A 2nd ed. published: Oxford : Basil Blackwell,
1947. -- xii, 192 p. Contents (1947 ed.): "Historical Introduction,"
I. "The Spirit and the Word," II. "The Discerning of Spirits," III.
"The Witness of the Spirits," IV. "The Spirit of Prayer," V. "The
Spirit and Prophesying," VI. "The Spirit and the Ordinances," VII.
"The Liberty of the Spirit," VIII. "The Government of the Spirit," IX.
"The Life and Fellowship of the Spirit," and X. "The Spirit in Every
Man." Appendix: "The Holy Spirit in Puritanism and Quakerism."

1944-4   Shera, Jesse Hauk. "Foundations of the Public Library: The
     Origins of the Library Movement in New England, 1629-1855."
     Ph.D., Univ. of Chicago. 341 leaves.

     Revision published under same title: Chicago : Univ. of Chicago
Press, 1949. -- xv, 308 p. -- (The Univ. of Chicago Studies in Library
Science). Reprinted: Hamden, Conn. : Shoe String Press, 1965. -- xv,
308 p. "Introduction" (1965 ed.): "We are here concerned with those
elements in American life which contributed directly or indirectly to
the growth of the public library as a social agency and the character
of the environment from which it emerged. . . . [Much] of what is
said here with reference to New England is equally applicable
elsewhere. . . . But New England, because it is the cradle of
American librarianship and because its cultural records have been so
assiduously preserved, was the logical . . . place to begin" (p. v).
Relevant chapters: I. "New England Background," II. "Colonial
Beginnings," and "Conclusion." Relevant appendix: III. "The
Dispersion of Public and Quasi-Public Libraries throughout New
England, 1650-1850." Other chapters and appendices concern later
matters.

1945-1   Bernhard, Harold Ernest. "Charles Chauncy: Colonial
     Liberal, 1705-1787." Ph.D., Univ. of Chicago. v, 140 leaves.

     "Conclusion": "As minister of First Church, Boston, Chauncy held
a place of prominence in the religious life of New England. . . .
Representative of a liberal religious trend in the aristocratic
element of New England, his mind was susceptible to the
intellectualism and latitudinarianism of the eighteenth century" (p.
126). Relevant chapters: Part I. "The Man": I. "Family," II.
"Education," and III. "Ministry." Part II treats his later career.

1946-1   Brown, Robert Eldon. "The Road to Revolution in
     Massachusetts." Ph.D., Univ. of Wisconsin at Madison. ix, 548
     leaves.

     Considerably revised version published as Middle-Class Democracy
and the Revolution in Massachusetts, 1691-1780. -- Ithaca : Published

for the American Historical Assn. by Cornell Univ. Press, 1955. -- ix, 458 p. Reprinted: New York : Russell & Russell, 1968. -- ix, 458 p. Also reprinted: New York : Harper & Row, 1969. -- xiv, 458 p. -- (Harper Torchbooks). "Preface" (1968 ed.): "For the past fifty years or more a thesis has been current in the teaching and writing of American history, political science, and literature that the society which produced the American Revolution and the federal Constitution was not a democratic society. . . . In the following pages I have raised some questions about this accepted interpretation as it applies to one colony and state, Massachusetts from 1691 to 1780. Did an upper economic class control economic life in the colony? Were property qualifications for voting sufficiently high to exclude an important number of adult men from participation in politics?" (pp. v-vi). Relevant chapters: I. "Economic Democracy," II. "The Province Voting Franchise," III. "Political Democracy in Province Elections," IV. "Representation and Its Restriction," V. "Town-Meeting Democracy," VI. "Religion, Education, and Democracy," VII. "'Perpetual Discordance,' 1691-1755," and "Conclusion." Chapters VIII-XV treat of later events.

1946-2   Dawes, Norman Herbert. "Social Classes in Seventeenth-Century New England." Ph.D., Harvard Univ. 2 vols. (xvii, 503 leaves).

"Abstract" (at end of diss.): "Heritage, environment, determinants of social place, mobility, and methods of expressing social discrimination combined to produce an essentially class society of six major levels of varying clarity in outline and of varying compactness of personnel. A leading class, an embryonic or incipient professional class, a middle class, a free lower class, a quasi-class of servants, and a cast of slaves comprised the societal elements in the totality of the social structure. For each level a more or less distinct mode of existence obtained for its personnel. Both subjectively and objectively, or psychologically and materially, the individuals who made up the personnel of the several levels were distinguished by a group personality" (pp. 2-3). Contents: I. "New England's Social Heritage," II. "New Horizons," III. "Social Adjustment to Frontier Life," IV. "God and the Ordering of Society," V. "Religious Orthodoxy as a Determinant of Social Place," VI. "The Social Weight of Gold," VII. "Wealth as a Determinant of Social Place," VIII. "The Social Significance of the Family," IX. "New England Interfamilyship and Their Role as a Determinant of Social Place," X. "Contribution of Education and/or Trained Ability Toward Determining Social Place," XI. "Social Mobility--Ascent," XII. "Social Mobility--Descent," XIII. "Insignia of Social Honor," XIV. "Discriminations in According Social Honor and Precedence," and XV. "The Way of the Classes." Appendices: A. "Dudley-Winthrop-Saltonstall-Leverett-Cotton Interfamilyships," B. "Harvard Statistics," C. "Gentlemen in Seventeenth-Century New England," and D. "Seventeenth-Century New England Armigers." Diss. dated "1940-41"; degree granted 1946.

1946-3   Laird, James Herbert. "The Influence of John Cotton in the Massachusetts Bay Colony." Ph.D., Boston Univ. (Graduate School). iv, 181, vi ["Abstract"] leaves.

"Abstract": "The purpose of this dissertation is to determine exactly how much influence John Cotton actually had in the Massachusetts Bay Colony. This has been done by following the outcome of various proposals, recommendations, and projects behind which Cotton threw the weight of his influence, and by evaluating the publications that came from his pen" (p. i). "The influence of John Cotton was not so strong as has been maintained" (p. v). Contents: I. "Introduction," II. "John Cotton in England," III. "John Cotton in New England," IV. "Influence of Cotton in Religious Affairs," V. "Influence of Cotton in Church Affairs," VI. "The Antinomian Controversy," and VII. "Summary and Conclusions."

1946-4   Metz, William Dewitt. "Politics and Finance in Massachusetts, 1713-1741." Ph.D., Univ. of Wisconsin at Madison. ii, 543, [14] leaves.

Relevant chapters: I. "Massachusetts in 1713," II. "The Economic Problem," III. "The 1714 Bank Struggle," IV. "Revival of the Popular Party," V. "Challenging the Prerogative," VI. "Appeal to the Crown," VII. "Climax of the Salary Controversy," VIII. "[Gov. Jonathan] Belcher's First Years: The Popular Party Wins and Loses," and XI. "Politics and Finance in Massachusetts, 1713-1741." Chapters IX and X deal with events in the 1730's.

1946-5   Miller, Ralph Norman. "The Historians Discover America: A Study of American Historical Writing in the Eighteenth Century." Ph.D., Northwestern Univ. viii, 334, [15] leaves.

"The thesis of this study is that at the time of the Revolution the writing of history adopted new forms, new expressions, and new concepts in a very great degree because of a criticism levelled at America by Europe that denied everything to the new world but . . . essential inferiority" (p. iii). "I have attempted to show that in general the writing of history in the period before the controversy over the supposed deficiencies of the continent was provincial in other than merely political terms . . . , that they are not essentially histories of America, but are histories of a transplanted England" (p. v). Contents: "History-Writing of the pre-Revolutionary Period": I. "The Formal Histories," and II. "The Informal Histories"; and "History-Writing of the Revolutionary and post-Revolutionary Periods": III. "The Man of America," IV. "The American Scene," V. "The American Character," and VI. "The New History." Treats of some twenty eighteenth-century histories including substantial material on early New England.

1947-1   Chapman, Clayton Harding. "The Life and Influence of Reverend Benjamin Colman, D.D. (1673-1747)." Th.D., Boston Univ. (School of Theology). xvii, 322 leaves.

Contents: I. "Preparation for Life Work," II. "Benjamin Colman and the Communion of Churches," III. "Benjamin Colman and the Church of England," IV. "Benjamin Colman and the Colleges," V. "Benjamin Colman and the Mission to the Indians," VI. "Benjamin Colman and the United Ministers of Boston," VII. "Benjamin Colman and the Great Revival," VIII. "Benjamin Colman: His Writings and Theology," and IX. "Conclusion."

1947-2   Duffy, John. "A History of Epidemics in the American Colonies." Ph.D., Univ. of California at Los Angeles.   172 leaves.

Revision published as Epidemics in Colonial America. -- Baton Rouge : Louisiana State Univ. Press, 1953. -- xi, 274 p. Paperback reprint: Baton Rouge : Louisiana State Univ. Press, 1971. -- ix, 274 p. Reprinted: Port Washington, N.Y. : Kennikat Press, 1972. -- xi, 274 p. "Preface" (1971 ed.): "Epidemic sickness played a disastrous part in colonial life, and it has been my endeavor to determine which diseases were involved, to clarify them in order of importance, and to show both collectively and singly their effect upon colonial development. From a social and economic standpoint infectious disorders were evidently costly. Not so apparent was the influence upon the religious thinking of the omnipresent threat of death through recurring epidemics" (pp. vii-viii). Contents: I. "Introduction," II. "Smallpox" (including "Smallpox in New England"), III. "Diphtheria and Scarlet Fever," IV. "Yellow Fever," V. "Measles, Whooping Cough, and Mumps," VI. "Respiratory Diseases," VII. "Agues, Fluxes, and Poxes," and VIII. "Conclusion."

1947-3   Jensen, John Granville. "Settlement Pattern of the Providence Region as an Adjustment to Its Geography."   Ph.D., Clark Univ. 7 ["Abstract"], iv, 256, 13 ["Bibliography"] leaves.

"Abstract": "The settlement pattern of the Providence Region represents the aggregate of human adjustments to attributes of place inherent to the Providence Region. Location at the head of the bay, where commerce of land and sea could meet far inland, first laid the bases for modern industry and established part of the settlement pattern. Settlement avoided the rough lands, to center on level outwash plains, around the upper bay" (p. 1). Relevant chapters: Part One. "The Attributes of the Providence Region Derived from Natural Phenomena": I. "Locational Attributes of the Providence Region," II. "Influences of the Site on the Providence Conurbation," III. "Geomorphology of the Providence Region," IV. "The Climate of the Providence Region"; Part Two. "Development of the Settlement Pattern in the Providence Region": VI. "The Settlement Pattern" and IX. "Conclusion." Chapters VII and VIII treat of later events.

1947-4   Maclear, James F. "The Puritan Party, 1603-1643: A Study in a Lost Reformation." Ph.D., Univ. of Chicago. iii, 340 leaves.

"Introduction": "To a considerable extent, the Puritan aims can be summed up in the term 'reformation.' . . . [The] Puritans were principally, though not exclusively, concerned with religion. Throughout their period of growth and predominance, the Puritans were in a very real sense striving for that thorough reformation of the church which England has somehow missed in the middle of the sixteenth century. . . . [The] Puritans could not believe that Anglicanism was more than temporary and consequently they labored to terminate an incongruous ecclesiastical situation by forcing the government to establish some sort of consistently Protestant church, purged of all vestiges of Rome" (pp. 1-2). Contents: "Introduction," I. "Prologue: The Puritan Party under Elizabeth and James," II. "The New Puritan Party: The Laity and the Parliament," III. "The New Puritan Party: The Clergy and the Parliament," IV. "The Alliance with Buckingham," V. "The Long Night and the Dawn: 1629-1640," VI. "Sources of Party Strength: 1640-1642," VII. "Triumph of the Party: The Religious Revolution," VIII. "The Disintegration of Puritanism and the Puritan Party," and IX. "Epilogue: The Emergence of Lay Opposition."

1948-1   Fairchild, Byron. "The William Pepperrells, Merchants at Piscataqua." Ph.D., Princeton Univ. 323 leaves.

Abstract in DA, vol. 15 (4), p. 568. Revision published as Messrs. William Pepperrell: Merchants at Piscataqua. -- Ithaca : Published for the American Historical Assn. by Cornell Univ. Press ; London : Oxford Univ. Press, 1954. -- xi, 223 p. "Preface" (1954 ed.): "For William Pepperrell, and for many another, the end was to transplant to America the social pattern of the English country squire. Because in history, as in husbandry, man reaps what he sows regardless of the soil, the fact of a frontier in seventeenth- and eighteenth-century New England did not mean the rise of democracy. The story of the Pepperrells is thus a study of the growth of aristocracy" (p. v). Diss. is principally concerned with careers of the William Pepperrells who lived 1648-1734 and 1696-1759. Relevant chapters: I. "Piscataqua in New England," II. "The Coming of William Pepperrell," III. "Early Cargoes and the Course of Trade," IV. "The Postwar Pattern, 1713-1723," and V. "Shifting Winds, 1723-1733." Chapters VI-IX deal with later periods.

1948-2   Garvan, Anthony Nicholas Brady. "The Origin of Colonial Architecture and Town Planning in Connecticut: A Study in American Social History." Ph.D., Yale Univ. 233 leaves.

Revision published as Architecture and Town Planning in Colonial Connecticut. -- New Haven : Yale Univ. Press, 1951. -- xiv, 166 p. -- (Yale Historical Publications. History of Art ; 6). "Preface" (1951 ed.): The work was "an investigation of the relationship between domestic architecture and the demography and national origins of colonial Connecticut. . . . [The] colony's racial homogeneity failed to explain its architectural variety" (p. vii). Deals mainly with the seventeenth century. Contents: I. "The People," II. "The Towns," III. "The Lands," IV. "The Country Builder," V. "Wilderness Homes," VI. "Public Buildings," and "Conclusion."

1948-3   Hertz, Karl Herbert. "Bible Commonwealth and Holy
    Experiment: A Study of the Relation between Theology and Politics
    in the Puritan and Quaker Colonies." Ph.D., Univ. of Chicago.
    vi, 367 leaves.

"Preface":   Diss. is "intended to focus attention on one
important aspect of the colonial history of the United States, namely,
the attempt to establish communities that gave expression to the
theological convictions of their founders" (p. ii).   Relevant
chapters: I. "The English Civil War and the Settlement of America,"
II. "The Organization of the Puritan Migration," III. "Divine
Authority for the Community," IV. "A Visible People of God," V. "The
Holy Commonwealth Becomes the Status Quo," VI. "The Triumph of the
Visible World," and XII. "Theology and Politics."   Chapters VII-XI are
concerned with the Quakers and/or a later period.

1948-4   McKee, William Wakefield. "The Idea of Covenant in Early
    English Puritanism (1580-1643)." Ph.D., Yale Univ. 346 leaves.

"Introduction": "It is proposed in this thesis to inquire into
and describe the idea of covenant as set forth among English Puritans
from its infrequent use in the Elizabethan period, through its more
systematized expression, and down to the time of the English civil
war. Over this space of roughly sixty years 'covenant' was not only
employed to describe the relationship between God and man but also to
define most human relationships. The year 1643, when the Solemn
League and Covenant was adopted, has been chosen somewhat arbitrarily
as the terminal point of this study" (n.p.).   Contents:
"Introduction"; "The Covenant Between God and Man": I. "The
Development of the Covenant Idea on the Continent" and II. "The
English Covenant Preachers"; "The Covenant Between God and Man": III.
"The Covenant in Theology" and IV. "Some Implications of the
Theological Covenant"; "The Covenant Between Men": V. "The Covenant
and the Church" and VI. "The Covenant and Civil Societies"; and
"Conclusion."

1948-5   Olsson, Karl Arthur. "Theology and Rhetoric in the Writings
    of Thomas Shepard." Ph.D., Univ. of Chicago. ii, 144 leaves.

Diss. applies Aristotle's theories and Christian theology to
Shepard's writings. Contents: "Introduction," I. "Shepard's Writing
Considered as Conventional Rhetoric," II. "Shepard's Rhetorical
Procedure," III-V. "The Framework of Topics," and VI. "The Diction."

1948-6   Roddy, Clarence Stonelynn. "The Religious Thought of Roger
    Williams." Ph.D., New York Univ. iv, 306 leaves.

"Introduction": "It is the purpose of this study to analyze the
religious thought of Roger Williams in an effort to discover his
fundamental religious positions: 1. the extent to which his basic
position is Calvinistic or Lutheran in the two great historic
Protestant interpretations of Christianity; 2. whether he is to be
classed as a Separatist, or a Baptist or a Seeker with sceptical

tendencies toward revealed religion such as later characterized
Emersonian Transcendentalism; 3. whether his views on Church and
State were derived from his political philosophy or from his religious
views and experience" (p. 1). Contents: I. "Introduction," II.
"Roger Williams: A Brief Biography," III. "The Holy Scriptures," IV.
"The Idea of God," V. "Anthropology and Soteriology," VI. "The
Doctrine of the Church," VII. "The Doctrine of the Spiritual Life,"
VIII. "The Idea of Church and State," IX. "Origin of Williams' Ideas
on Church and State," and X. "Summary and Conclusion." The
bibliography includes "The Writings of Williams."

1948-7   Welles, Judith B. "John Cotton, 1584-1652: Churchman and
          Theologian," Ph.D., Univ. of Edinburgh (U.K.). iii, 324 leaves.

"Foreword": "My purpose in writing this thesis is two-fold:
first, to make a thorough study of John Cotton, his life and his work
... ; secondly, to indicated so far as is possible the extent of his
influence outside of the Massachusetts Bay Colony and particularly in
England, his native land. ... I have sought only to give an accurate
and full account of Cotton's life, and to examine the treatises which
he wrote and the ideas for which he stood, together with those who
opposed him" (pp. i-ii). Contents: I. "The Background"; II. "The Life
of John Cotton"; III. "The Theology": A. "The Structure of Cotton's
Doctrine" and B. "Attacks upon Cotton's Orthodoxy"; IV. "The Church
Polity": A. "The Growth of Cotton's Nonconformity," B. "The
Congregational Way," and C. "Support and Opposition"; V. "Church and
State"; and VI. "Cotton's Influence and Importance." Relevant
appendix: A. "The Writings of John Cotton."

1949-1   Abel, Aaron Darrel. "The Immortal Pilgrim: An Ethical
          Interpretation of Nathaniel Hawthorne's Fiction." Ph.D., Univ.
          of Michigan. 384 leaves.

Abstract in MA, vol. 9 (2), p. 116: "In general, Hawthorne
accepted Transcendentalist assumptions but criticized them from a
Calvinist point of view. He believed in an ideal world transcending
the real, but insisted that since human life was a pilgrimage through
the material world, man's immediate concerns were mundane
satisfactions and moral perils of his pilgrimage. He believed in
man's intuition of and aspiration toward the transcendent world, but
regarded man as being feeble in will and prone to evil. He pictured
man's life as a struggle to realize the best elements of his nature."

1949-2   Come, Donald Robert. "John Cotton, Guide of the Chosen
          People." Ph.D., Princeton Univ. 538, 4 ["Abstract"] leaves.

Abstract in DA, vol. 15 (4), p. 566: "The clergy in
Massachusetts [loomed] large in the making of major decisions and in
the forming of major policies in affairs political and economic as
well as religious. And John Cotton was rightfully recognized as being
the greatest and most influential of all the clergymen during his
residence in the Bay from 1633 to his death in 1652. . . . In
Massachusetts John Cotton led in bringing forth arguments and in

proposing political devices to secure authority in the hands of a
ruling oligarchy of ministers and magistrates. Cotton's opinions were
always authoritative and most often decisive."

1949-3   Covey, Cyclone. "Religion and Music in Colonial America."
      Ph.D., Stanford Univ., ix, 335 leaves.

      "Conclusion": "Everything in this study bears out its principal
presupposition: that, especially in the planting stage of American
civilization, a particular set of religious ideas would have far-
reaching directive consequences in a man's non-theological as well as
theological thought and activity. . . . The uniformly lethal effects
of the Calvinistic frame of mind on music" (p. 295) are also explored.
Relevant chapter: 1. "Calvinism and Music": a. "The Pilgrims and
Music," b. "The Puritans and Music," c. "The Independents and Music,"
and d. "The Presbyterians and Music." Chapters 2-7 deal with other
religious groups.

1949-4   Goodman, Avram Vossen. "American Overture: Jewish Rights in
      Colonial Times." Ph.D., Univ. of Texas at Austin.

      Published previously under same title: Philadelphia : The Jewish
Publication Society of America, 1947. -- xiv, 265 p. Univ. of Texas
at Austin Library "cop. 2" includes approval leaf and diss. title leaf
tipped in at beginning of published version and a two-leaf "Vita"
tipped in at end. "Preface" (1947 ed.): "My main consideration has
been the interaction of Jewish forces with the early American scene as
manifested in the expanding rights of the Jewish community and in the
growing recognition that Jews were men who might aspire to full civic
equality. This theme has tremendous meaning in the unfolding of
Jewish history and in the upbuilding of the democratic principle as we
know it today. It serves fittingly as an American overture" (p. vii).
Relevant chapters: I. "How a Thousand Men and Women Made History,"
II. "Jewish Rights in Puritan Canaan," and III. "Retreat from Roger
Williams." Chapters IV-XII treat of other colonies and/or later
periods.

1949-5   Hand, George Othell. "Changing Emphases in American
      Evangelism from Colonial Times to the Present." Th.D., Southern
      Baptist Theological Seminary. 214 leaves.

      "Preface": "The relative failure to Christianize the world is
not a reflection upon the efficacy of the Christian religion, but upon
the means of communicating its achievements and values--a reflection
upon evangelism" (p. iv). Relevant chapter: I. "The Era of
Revivalism": 1. "Revivalism as a Product of the Problems Confronting
Colonial Christianity": (1) "Problems associated with frontier life";
(2) "Marked religious decline in all the colonies": a. "Primary
factors in the decline," b. "Signs of the times," and c. "The half-
way covenant"; and (3) "Moral decline and attendant evils."

1949-6   Muse, Raymond. "William Douglass, Man of the American
         Enlightenment, 1691-1752." Ph.D., Stanford Univ. 278 leaves.

     Contents: "Introduction," I. "William Douglass: Doctor of
Medicine," II. "William Douglass: Oracle of the Anti-Paper Party,"
III. "William Douglass: Historian," and IV. "William Douglass:
Eighteenth-Century American Savant." Appendices: I. "Table of
Contents for Douglass's Summary" and II. "List of Printed Works
Referred to in Douglass's Summary."

1949-7   Reilly, Bartholomew Michael. "The Elizabethan Puritan's
         Conception of Nature and Destiny of Fallen Man." Ph.D., Catholic
         Univ. of America. 342 leaves.

     Contents: "Introduction," I. "The Origin and Meaning of
Puritanism," II. "The Nature of Fallen Man," III. "The Destiny of
Fallen Man: Predestination," IV. "Pilgrim in Progress," and
"Conclusion."

1949-8   Starkey, Lawrence Granville. "A Descriptive and Analytical
         Bibliography of the Cambridge, Massachusetts, Press from Its
         Beginnings to the Publication of Eliot's Indian Bible in 1663."
         Ph.D., Univ. of Virginia. xxxii, 415 leaves.

     Published under same title: Lexington : Univ. of Kentucky Press,
1955. -- 10 cards. -- (Kentucky Microcards. Ser. A. Modern Languages
Ser. ; no. 5). Contents: "Introduction," One: "The Beginnings of the
Cambridge Press, 1638-45," Two: "Routine Printing, 1646-48. The 1648
Book of the General Laws and Liberties," Three: "Samuel Green Begins
to Print, 1649-53," Four: "Subsidization by the Society for the
Propagation of the Gospel. [John] Eliot's First Printed Indian
Translations," and Five: "The Third Cambridge Printer. The
Collaboration Between Green and [Marmaduke] Johnson Which Produced
Eliot's Indian Bible." Appendices: A. "A Description of Every Item
Printed by the Cambridge Press, 1640-63, of Which at Least One Copy is
Extant," B. "Type-Ornaments, Initial Letters, Factotums and Fonts of
Type Used by the Cambridge Press from 1640-1663," C. "Watermarks Found
in Books Printed by the Cambridge Press from 1640-1663," and D.
"Miscellaneous Title Pages and Documents."

1950-1   Borough, Basil L. "Edward Randolph, Royal Agent of the
         Restoration." Ph.D., Stanford Univ. vii, 221 leaves.

     "Introduction": "Randolph was the most important royal official
to be intimately connected with the affairs of the colonies in New
England in the late seventeenth century. . . . It shall be my purpose
to look upon him as a royal agent and to judge him in this light being
as impartial as possible . . . [and] to sketch the broad outline of
his achievements" (pp. vi-vii). Contents: "Introduction," I.
"Randolph's First Mission to America," II. "Randolph in Conflict with
Massachusetts," III. "Randolph as Collector of Customs," IV.
"Randolph's Procedure Against the Massachusetts Church," V. "Randolph
as Assistant to Andros," VI. "Randolph and the New England

Revolution," and "Conclusion."

1950-2   Brown, Paul Edward. "The Principle of the Covenant in the
    Theology of Thomas Goodwin." Ph.D., Drew Univ. iv, 368, vi
    leaves.

    "Introduction": "An important phase of the Puritan development
with England is centered around the doctrinal expression that became
known as 'Federal Theology.' In fact among the great creeds of the
Reformed Churches we do not find, with the exception of the creed of
Westminster, a single reference to the 'Federal or Covenant Theology.'
. . . The individual whose writings form the basis of this
dissertation was a member of the Assembly of Westminster Divines.
[Goodwin's] theology is an expression of 'Federal Theology.' . . . We
shall therefore undertake . . . to examine and analyze his theological
system as set against the background of covenant theology in its
relationship to English Puritanism and Calvinism" (pp. 3-4). "Life":
"At one time during the proceedings of the Westminster Assembly, . . .
he almost accepted an invitation from [John] Cotton to go to New
England and actually placed part of his library on board ship before
friends prevailed upon him to remain" (p. 22). Contents:
"Introduction," "Life of Goodwin," I. "The Biblical Basis for a
Doctrine of the Covenant," II. "History of the Doctrine of the
Covenant," III. "The Covenant of Redemption," IV. "The Covenant of
Works," V. "The Covenant of Grace," VI. "The Doctrine of the Covenant
as the Basis for Church Polity," VII. "Criticism and Evaluation of the
Permanent Values in the Theology of Thomas Goodwin." Appendix A.
argues against Goodwin's authorship of a sermon attributed to him by
the editor of his Works; and B. reproduces an unsigned article from
the British Weekly of March 23, 1950, as evidence that the "influence
of Thomas Goodwin is still to be felt in the nonconformist life of
London." The diss. is not cited in CDI.

1950-3   Bryan, George Cochrane. "Concepts of Leadership in American
    Political Thought: The Puritan Period." Ph.D., Harvard Univ.
    vii, 260 leaves.

    "Conclusion": "From [the Puritans'] theories of religion and
government a theory of leadership was logically developed. Only a few
should rule and those few were those who were predestined by God for
eternal salvation. . . . The function of these rulers was to lead
their people much as a shepherd leads his flock of innocent and
sometimes misguided sheep. The civil and church leaders worked side by
side with but one thought in mind, living a perfect life in the eyes of
God and helping others do the same. The leaders of this little society
were 'chosen' by the freemen-church members, but this was looked upon
more as a ratification of God's will than out and out political
struggle for power" (p. 201). "Summary" (at end of diss.): "This
thesis represents an attempt to correlate one aspect of political
theory with political and social institutions and to analyze the varied
factors which undermined the theory and its institutions" (p. 1).
Contents: I. "Introduction," II. "Puritanism," III. "Institutional
Reflections and Leadership," IV. "The Challenges of Puritan Dominance,"
V. "Conclusion." Appendices: "The Charter of the Colony of

Massachusetts Bay in New England" and "Members of the General Court and the Court of Assistants of the Colony of Massachusetts Bay in New England, 1630-1641."

1950-4   Davis, Harold A. "An International Community on the St. Croix (1604-1930)." Ph.D., Columbia Univ.

Published under same title: Orono, Me. : Printed at the Univ. Press, 1950. -- xi, 412 p. -- (Univ. of Maine Studies ; 2nd ser., no. 64). A 2nd ed., with an Introduction by Alice R. Stewart, published: Orono, Me. : Univ. of Maine, 1974. -- xiv, 412 p. "Foreword" (1974 ed.): "The fact that the [St. Croix Valley of Maine and New Brunswick] is a border region . . . has affected the pattern of life there to a considerable degree" (p. xi). Relevant chapters: I. "The Place and Aborigines" and II. "Champlain, DeMonts, and the Acadians."

1950-5   Leach, Douglas Edward. "The Causes and Effects of King Philip's War." Ph.D., Harvard Univ. iii, 529 leaves.

Revision published as Flintlock and Tomahawk: New England in King Philip's War with an introduction by Samuel Eliot Morison. -- New York : Macmillan, 1958. -- x, 304 p. Reprinted: New York : W. W. Norton, 1966. -- x, 304 p. "Preface" (1966 ed.): "The Indians who fought the war and lost it left behind them no records to tell us their side of the story, a fact which makes a complete and impartial reconstruction of the events especially difficult for the modern historian. I set out to learn all I could about the war by carefully studying the scattered and sometimes fragmentary records which have survived, and by visiting most of the scenes of action" (p. vii). Contents: I. "The Land and the People," II. "Gathering Clouds," III. "The Outbreak of War," IV. "The July Campaign of 1675," V. "The War Spreads," VI. "Men, Materiel, and Money," VII. "The Campaign Against the Narragansetts," VIII. "The Problem of the 'Friendly Indians,'" IX. "A Time of Troubles (February-May, 1676)," X. "The Spirit of Zion," XI. "The Waning of Indian Strength," XII. "Philipus Exit," and XIII. "The Aftermath."

1950-6   Maurer, Maurer. "The Musical Life of Colonial America in the Eighteenth Century." Ph.D., Ohio State Univ. vi, 385 leaves.

"Preface": Diss. is mainly concerned with "the musical life of the American colonies in the later colonial period. . . .   Some general historical background has been included to show music in relation to the broader cultural environment" (p. iv). Relevant chapters: I. "English Background," VI. "In the Wilderness," and VIII. "Saints and Musicians." Other chapters deal with other groups in more southern colonies, or with later periods.

1950-7   McCarty, Fern Fitzpatrick. "The Attitude of the English Puritan Toward the Accumulation of Wealth, 1564-1688." Ph.D., Univ. of Colorado at Boulder. xx, 299 leaves.

"Introduction": "Many Puritan divines and laymen did uphold the accumulation and possession of money, as [Max Weber, Ernst Troeltsch, and J. W. Tawney] maintained. On the other hand, a much larger number held to the idea that the true Christian must regard material wealth with indifference, if not with antagonism. The former point of view has been found to obtain from 1603 to 1688 and to become strongest from 1640 to 1688. . . . It would seem . . . that the commercial order of the seventeenth century could not be attributed to specific Puritan admonition to acquire money" (p. vii). Contents: "Introduction," I. "Some Background Factors," II. "Puritan Objections to Worldly Prosperity from 1564-1603," III. "Elements in the Sixteenth Century Unfavorable to 'Other Worldliness,'" IV. "Puritan Opposition to Money in the Reigns of the Early Stuarts," V. "Evidences of Puritan Approval of Money from 1603-1640," VI. "The Traditional Attitude Toward Money-Making Upheld by Various Sects After 1640," VII. "The Worldly Non-Conformist, 1640-1688," VIII. "John Bunyan and Richard Baxter," and IX. "Conclusion."

1950-8   Roberts, J. E. "Richard Baxter's Influence on English Nonconformity in the 17th and 18th Centuries in Organisation and Theology." Ph.D., Univ. of Leeds (U.K.).

No abstract available. Cited in Jacobs (#4708) but not found in CDI, DAI, NUC, BNB, BMGC or OCLC. CRL (February 2, 1982): "The author's permission is required for a copy to be made; Leeds can trace no address for the author."

1950-9   Smith, Willard Wallace. "The Relations of College and State in Colonial America." Ph.D., Columbia Univ. 175 leaves.

Abstract in MA, vol. 10 (2), p. 97: "The purpose of this study is to trace the colonial development of the tradition that institutions of higher education are so essential to American life that the state must accept a responsibility in providing for them. . . . The study shows that Harvard, William and Mary, Yale, and Columbia were closely related to the state in colonial times. This was especially true of the first three named colleges because their purposes closely paralleled the guiding purposes of their colonies, they were under considerable state control, and they received significant amounts of public financial support."

1950-10   Zimmerman, Lester Fred. "Some Aspects of Milton's American Reputation to 1900." Ph.D., Univ. of Wisconsin at Madison. iii, 386 leaves.

Relevant chapters: I. "Milton's Reputation in America to 1800" and XI. "Conclusion." Includes information on the early reception of John Milton's poetry by the American Puritans.

1951-1   Carroll, Richard Sutcliffe. "Studies in the Background and Practice of Prose Style in New England, 1640-1750." Ph.D., Harvard Univ. 397 leaves.

"Summary" (at beginning of diss.): "This thesis will attempt by considering selected figures from four generations to combine or extend the techniques of previous studies [by Perry Miller, Babette M. Levy, and Kenneth B. Murdock]. . . . By examining individual figures it tries to show more concretely the influence of the general literary tradition on specific men, and in turn the manner in which their leading views affected the tradition" (p. 1). Relevant chapters: I. "The English Background," II. "John Cotton," III. "Thomas Shepard," IV. "Increase Mather," V. "Cotton Mather," and VII. "Conclusion." Chapter VI treats of two later figures.

1951-2   Gates, Warren J. "The Broad Arrow Policy in Colonial America: A Study of the Forest Utilization Program of the British Government." Ph.D., Univ. of Pennsylvania. ix, 338 leaves.

"Preface": "This study traces the development by the British government [between 1685 and 1776] of a forest utilization policy for the American colonies and its attempts to implement that policy in America. . . . Without minimizing the extra-American factors involved in the initiation and development of the utilization program, primary emphasis is placed on the influence of events in America on the program. The government developed an integrated program to encourage the exploitation of masts and naval stores from America, to direct the colonial exports of these commodities to the English market, and to conserve the American source of masts. . . . Since New England developed commercial exploitation of the woods more extensively than the other colonies, the program had greater impact there than in the other continental colonies. . . . The study takes its name from the 'Broad Arrow,' the traditional symbol of naval property. The 'Broad Arrow,' a mark like a crow's track made with three strokes of a marking hatchet, was cut into some of the finest pines of New England to signify that they were reserved for the King's use" (pp. iii-iv). Relevant chapters: I. "Competitors for the Forests," II. "The Approach of Control," III. "Legislative Encouragement and Trade Regulation," IV. "Forest Conservation Laws and the Provincial Courts," V. "Forest Conservation and the Vice-Admiralty Courts," VI. "The Surveyors of the Woods 1705-1743," and "Conclusions." Appendices: A. "Preamble to the [Bounty] Act of 1705," B. "Instructions to John Bridger [surveyor]," and C. "Tenure of Surveyors." Chapter VII treats later events.

1951-3   Haller, William, Jr. "The Puritan Frontier: Town-planting in New England Colonial Development, 1630-1660." Ph.D., Columbia Univ.

Published under same title: New York : Columbia Univ. Press, 1951. -- 119 p. -- (Columbia Univ., Faculty of Political Science, Studies in History, Economics, and Public Law ; no. 568). Reprinted: New York : AMS Press, 1968. -- 119 p. -- (Columbia Univ. Studies in the Social Sciences ; no. 568). "Foreword": Diss. is "an attempt to discover some of the relationships between the development of human ideas and that of economic institutions in a fairly narrow geographical and historical setting" (p. 7). Contents: Part I. "The Puritan Design for Frontier Development": I. "Introduction," II. "The

Colonies' Town-planting Policies," and III. "The Discovery of the Frontier"; and Part II. "Town-planting as a Technique of Frontier Development": IV. "Growth of the Towns," V. "Religious Diversity," VI. "Accommodation of Newcomers," VII. "Some Puritan Promoters," and VIII. "The New England Frontier."

1951-4   Hanna, Archibald, Jr. "New England Military Institutions, 1693-1750." Ph.D., Yale Univ. 316 leaves.

"Summary" (at beginning of diss.): "The New England colonies were from the beginning faced with the necessity of training and mobilizing large bodies of troops for their defense. Adapting the traditional English system of train bands to American conditions, they organized a militia in which every male of military age was enlisted and trained. . . . Although containing serious weaknesses, the New England military institutions performed with reasonable success the functions for which they were created" (n.p.). Contents: "Introduction," I. "The Militia and Military Training," II. "The Defense of the Frontier," III. "Expeditionary Forces," IV. "Control of the Armed Forces," V. "Command and Discipline in the Field Forces," VI. "The Pay of the Soldier," VII. "Supply of the Forces," and "Conclusion."

1951-5   Hughes, Paul Lester. "The Puritan Concept of Empire, 1650-1660." Ph.D., Univ. of Iowa. iii, 193 leaves.

Contents: "Introduction," I. "Oliver Cromwell's Concept of Empire," II. "Cromwellian Imperial Policy and the Merchants," III. "Cromwell's Foreign Policy and its Relationship to his Concept of Empire," IV. "New World Puritanism and its Relationship to Cromwell's Concept of Religious Imperialism," and V. "Cromwellian Imperial Thought and the Radical Sectarians."

1951-6   Legge, Garth Warren. "The Element of Christian Asceticism in English Puritanism and French Jansenism in the Seventeenth Century." Ph.D., Univ. of Edinburgh (New College) (U.K.). x, 399 leaves.

"Preface": "The writer welcomed the opportunity of investigating a persistent, though to the modern mind uncongenial, type of Christian piety about which such a variety of opinions are held; while the specific problem of why two contemporary movements should manifest marked ascetic tendencies was in itself stimulating, especially in the absorbing context of the seventeenth century" (p. v). Relevant chapters: Part One. I. "Christian Asceticism"; Part Two: II. "The Setting and Origins of Puritan Asceticism": A. "England: The Seventeenth Century Ethos," B. "English Puritanism: The Seventeenth Century," and C. "Puritan Asceticism: An Analysis of Formative Factors"; III. "The Puritan Character: The Spiritual Athlete": A. "Intra-Mundane Ascetic Rigorism," B. "Spiritual Disciplines," C. "Labour in Calling," D. "Bodily Mortifications," and E. "Qualities of the Ascetic Life"; IV. "Recreation and the Arts": A. "The Basic Principles," B. "Sabbatarianism and Recreations," C. "Sobriety and

Simplicity," D. "The Arts and Worship," and E. "The Emotions and Reason"; and V. "Aids to Godliness": A. "Spiritual Direction," B. "Church Discipline," and C. "Moral Legislation"; and Part Four: X. "Critical Conclusion." Part Three treats of Jansenism.

1951-7   Strandness, Theodore Benson. "Samuel Sewall: The Man and His Work." Ph.D., Michigan State Univ. xix, 517 leaves.

Abstract in DA, vol. 12 (3), p. 310. Revision published as Samuel Sewall: A Puritan Portrait. -- East Lansing : Michigan State Univ. Press, 1967. -- xiv, 234 p. "Preface" (1967 ed.): In "Sewall's own pages . . . we move in the honest realm of fact. I intend in this book to remain there. Sewall stands in no need of wings. If there be that about him that amuses and sometimes dismays us, there is more which wins affection and respect. If we lose the paragon, we gain a credible and interesting man. The loss in reverence for the gain in truth seems a fair exchange" (p. ix). Contents: One: "Background and Early Years," Two: "Harvard College and Intellectual Life," Three: "Merchant and Man of Property," Four: "Servant of Colony and Province," Five: "Writer," and Six: "Private Life and Last Years."

1951-8   Tufft, John R. "William Perkins (1558-1602), His Thought and Activity." Ph.D., Univ. of Edinburgh (U.K.). vii, 307 leaves.

"Preface": "The problem of this study is to define clearly the thought of William Perkins and to realize how it was applied to sixteenth- and seventeenth-century Christians" (p. iii). Contents: I. "Historical Background," II. "His Life," III. "As a Reformer," IV. "Theology--Dogmatics," V. "Theology--Ethics," VI. "The Word of the Spirit," VII. "As a Preacher," and VIII. "His Importance and Influence" (including a section on "His Influence in America").

1951-9   Tyack, Norman C. P. "Migration from East Anglia to New England before 1660." Ph.D., Univ. of London (U.K.). 2 vols. (ix, ii, 581, cxix, xx, xi leaves).

Between 1620 and 1660 about two thousand persons emigrated from Essex, Suffolk, and Norfolk owing to 1) the depression of 1629-32, 2) movement of population from cloth and textile centers, and 3) religious persecution by Archbishop William Laud. Contents: I. "The Movement of People," II. "The Economic and Social Background," III. "The Religious Background," and IV. "The Political Background." Appendices: I. "Emigrants from East Anglia to New England before 1660," II. "The Geographic Distribution of the Emigrants," and III. "The Occupational Structure of the Emigrants."

1951-10   Tyler, Glenn Edward. "The Influence of Calvinism on the Development of Early Modern Science in England and America." Ph.D., Univ. of Minnesota. 411 leaves.

Chapter I: "The enormous complex structure of modern science has been built up through the centuries by many individual investigators impelled by a variety of motives. If we ever hope to comprehend the processes which have created this most characteristic feature of our Western Civilization, . . . we must examine the theories and motives of those men who have labored in the past to add to man's understanding of the secrets of nature. . . . Therefore, in this study, an attempt will be made to see the earlier problems of science through the spectacles of the men who solved them, rather than through those in vogue at the present time" (p. 1). Contents: I. "The Medieval Crisis of Nature vs. Faith," II. "The Calvinistic Solution," III. "The Calvinistic Conquest of English Religion," IV. "The Calvinistic Conquest of English Science," V. and VI. "Calvinism and the Search for a 'New Philosophy,'" VII. "The Triumph of English Calvinism and Science," and VIII. "The Partial Eclipse of English Calvinism and Science."

1952-1   Beall, Otho Thompson, Jr. "Cotton Mather's Knowledge of Medicine." Ph.D., Univ. of Pennsylvania. 279 leaves.

Abstract in DA, vol. 13 (2), p. 220. Revision/collaboration published as Cotton Mather, the First Significant Figure in American Medicine, by Beall and Richard H. Shryock. -- American Antiquarian Society. -- Proceedings. -- Worcester, Mass. : The Society, 1953. -- Vol. 63 (Pt. 1), pp. [37]-274. Reprinted: Baltimore : Johns Hopkins Press, 1954. -- ix, 241 p. -- (Publications of the Institute of the History of Medicine, 1st Ser.: Monographs ; vol. 5). Also reprinted under title Cotton Mather. -- New York : Arno Press, 1979. -- ix, 241 p. -- (Johns Hopkins Univ. Press Reprints). Contents (1954 ed.): I. "On the Rediscovery of Cotton Mather," II. "Mather's Approach to Medicine," III. "The Medical Background," IV. "Mather's Medicine in Non-Medical Works," V. "History of 'The Angel of Bethesda,'" VI. "The Nature of 'The Angel,'" VII. "The Advent of Preventive Medicine: Boston, 1721," VIII. "Conclusions: Mather's Place in Medicine," and "Selected Sections from 'The Angel.'"

1952-2   Behen, Dorothy M. Forbis. "The Captivity Story in American Literature, 1577-1826: An Examination of Written Reports in English, Authentic and Fictitious, of the Experiences of White Men Captured by the Indians North of Mexico." Ph.D., Univ. of Chicago. 429 leaves.

Chapter I: "One of the most prominent themes recurring in . . . English-language reports of exploration and settlement was the Indian menace. For Englishmen, as for other Europeans attempting to conquer underdeveloped regions, one of the most common obstacles was the hostile opposition of the aboriginal inhabitants. . . . Given such circumstances, and given the high incidence of literacy which prevailed among English explorers and colonists, the development of the Indian captivity tale was virtually inevitable. . . . The earliest allusions to capitivity adventures were brief and merely treated captivity as one of the many hardships and dangers risked by explorers and pioneer settlers. Yet these fragments represent the initial stage in the development of the story of Indian captivity" (pp. 1-2). Relevant chapters: I. "The Evolution of the Indian

Captivity Genre," II. "Episodes of the Narratives of Captivity," IV. "Leading White Characters in Narratives of Captivity and in Novels Containing Captivity Episodes," V. "Indian Characters in Narratives of Captivity: Cruel Beasts and Virtuous Savages," and VII. "Other Concepts of Indian Nature Presented in Narratives of Captivity and in Novels Containing Captivity Episodes."   Chapters III, VI, and VIII are concerned with fictional works.

1952-3   Cook, George Allan.   "John Wise: Early American Democrat." Ph.D., Columbia Univ.

    Published under same title: New York : King's Crown Press, 1952. -- 246 p.   Reprinted: New York : Octagon Books, 1966. -- ix, 249 p. "Introduction" (1966 ed.):   "John Wise was, for the times, a democrat in both action and in thought.   Not only did he champion the right of the colonists to impose their own taxes but he also wrote two forceful and witty books in support of congregational autonomy in the New England churches" (p. 1).   Contents: I. "Ancestry and Early Life," II. "Years at Harvard," III. "Unsettled Years," IV. "For a Good God and a Good King," V. "Chaplain Against Quebec," VI. "'Storms of Witchcraft,'" VII. "Life at Chebacco," VIII. "The 'Popish Plot' in New England," IX. "The Churches Quarrel Espoused," X. "Wise's 'Small Treatise,'" XI. "Liberal Notions," and XII. "The Lamp Burned Out."

1952-4   Greeley, Priscilla Marguerite.   "The County in Massachusetts."   Ph.D., Harvard Univ. (Radcliffe College).   xix, 420, 4 ["Summary"] leaves.

    "Summary":   "This study is intended to be a comprehensive survey of the Massachusetts county considered both as an independent unit of government and as an administrative area. . . .   Part II traces the roots of Massachusetts colonial government back to Anglo-Saxon times and describes the transplanting of English institutions of local government to Massachusetts soil and the adaptation of these institutions" (p. 2).   Relevant chapter: Part II. "The Historical Development of the Massachusetts County."   Parts I, III-V treat of current events.

1952-5   Lindemann, Robert Alfred.   "Important Factors in the Colonial History of Rhode Island Influencing Her Participation in the Revolutionary Movement."   Ph.D., Indiana Univ.   iii, 170, xxviii leaves.

    "Preface":   "It is the purpose of this dissertation to present a study of some of the factors which finally influenced Rhode Island to break away completely from the mother country" (p. ii).   Relevant chapters: I. "Rhode Island's Charter and Efforts of the Mother Country to Have It Annulled," II. "Relations of Rhode Island with Other Colonies," III. "Some Political Controversies in Eighteenth-Century Rhode Island," and IV. "Rhode Island and the Old Colonial System, 1660-1763."   Chapter V treats of later events.

1952-6   Sanford, Charles Le Roy. "The Days of Jeremy Dummer,
     Colonial Agent." Ph.D., Harvard Univ. vi, 467 leaves.

     "Preface": "My biography of Jeremiah Dummer is intended as a
study of Anglo-American relations in the first half of the eighteenth
century and of the origins in colonial psychology of that East-West
conflict which has been so basic to the American experience.
Conceived in such terms, Dummer's life is more than an isolated
chapter in a neglected period of American history. His exodus to
England in 1708 conforms to a familiar pattern in the extrapatriation
of many American writers and intellectuals. . . . His role as
colonial agent was to mediate between the East and the West in a
period of rising tensions. He administered to every aspect of the
problem: religious, cultural, political and economic. His interest
in the northern wilderness of Maine and Nova Scotia was but his
response to the traditional lure of the West in its immense riches and
natural resources. . . . It is not too much to say that Dummer by his
spirited defense of colonial economic interests against the demands of
British mercantilism helped launch American free enterprise" (pp. iii-
iv). Contents: I. "Mammon and the Virgin Mary," II. "The Formative
Years," III. "A Backwoods Theologian," IV. "The Glorious Enterprise,"
V. "Post-Mortem on a Glorious Enterprise," VI. "The Colonial Agency,"
VII. "Cultural Ambassador to New England," VIII. "Private Bank and
Public Bank," IX. "Bonanza Fever," X. "Defense of the Colonial
Charter," and IX. "Epilogue." Appendix: "Genealogical Enclosure."

1952-7   Thompson, Luther Joe. "A Study of Roger Williams' Religious
     Thought, with Special Reference to His Conception of Religious
     Liberty." Ph.D., Univ. of Edinburgh (U.K.). x, 245 leaves.

     Chapter VII: "In conclusion, let us keep in mind that while
Roger Williams' writings are important and have become a significant
influence upon political and especially religious liberty, his
principal contribution lay in the realm of the practical and not the
theoretical and philosophical. . . . Williams was willing to wager
his life on the conviction that men, free both in the realm of
religion and politics, could live in peace and prosperity. The
generations that have followed have rejoiced in the assurance that has
come of his winning this wager" (p. 230). Contents: I. "A Definition
of Terms: What is Religious Liberty?" II. "A Brief Survey of the
History of the Development of the Idea of Religious Liberty Up to
Roger Williams," III. "Roger Williams' Developing Concept of Religious
Liberty as Revealed in His Life Story," IV. "The More General Elements
of Roger Williams' Religious Thought with Special Consideration of the
Basis of His Conception of Religious Liberty," V. "The Specific
Elements of Roger Williams' Conception of Religious Liberty," VI.
"Roger Williams' Concept of Religious and Political Liberty Compared
and Contrasted with That of John Milton," and VII. "An Evaluation of
Roger Williams' Contribution." Appendix: I. "An Account of the
Writings of Roger Williams."

1953-1   Abbott, Orville L. "A Study of the Verb Forms and Verb Uses in Certain American Writings of the Seventeenth Century." Ph.D., Michigan State Univ. 233 leaves.

Abstract in DA, vol. 14 (2), p. 361: "The purpose of this thesis is to examine the verb forms and verb uses in American English of the seventeenth century. . . . As a basis for this study samplings were made from the writings of the New England area from c. 1630 to c. 1700. The following types were considered: History and Narrative, writings on Religious subjects, Diaries, Letters, writings of a legal character, and Poetry." Contents: I. "Personal Endings," II. "Preterite and Past Participle of Strong and Weak Verbs," III. "The Formal Subjunctive," IV. "The Modals," and "Conclusion."

1953-2   Bailyn, Bernard. "The New England Merchants in the Seventeenth Century: A Study in the History of American Society." Ph.D., Harvard Univ. vi, 497 leaves.

Revision published under same title: Cambridge, Mass. : Harvard Univ. Press, 1955. -- viii, 249 p. Reprinted: New York : Harper & Row, 1964. -- viii, 245 p. -- (Harper Torchbooks. The Academy Library). Contents (1964 ed.): I. "Origins of Trade," II. "The Establishment of the Puritan Merchant," III. "Adjustments and Early Failures," IV. "The Legacy of the First Generation," V. "Introduction to Empire," VI. "Elements of Change," and VII. "The Merchant Group at the End of the Seventeenth Century." Diss. includes three appendices not in published versions: A. "Tax Assessments on Mercantile Wealth, Boston, 1687," B. "Tax Assessments on Real Estate, Boston, 1687," and C. "Total Tax Assessments, Boston, 1687."

1953-3   Calloway, James Edward. "Disallowance of Colonial Legislation, 1696-1737." Ph.D., Indiana Univ. x, 423 leaves.

Abstract in DA, vol. 13 (4), p. 542: "The first part of this thesis contains the definition and discussion of the different agencies of the British government that attempted control over the American colonies. . . . The second part contains a listing of all the laws that met with disallowance during the period. . . . The last part consists of a classification of the various reasons for such disallowance in so far as they were formally given or expressed in the arguments and discussions at the time." Includes separate chapters on New Hampshire, Massachusetts, Rhode Island, and Connecticut and on disallowance due to violation of political expediency, law affecting business enterprise, violation of property rights, and religion or religious influence."

1953-4   Curtis, Mark H. "Oxford and Cambridge in Transition: An Essay on the Changing Relationships Between the English Universities and English Society, 1558-1642." Ph.D., Yale Univ.

Considerably revised version published under same title: Oxford: Clarendon Press, 1959. -- vii, 314 p. The relevant chapter (1959 ed.), VIII. "The Universities and the Religious Movements of the Age," states: "Puritanism within the universities was pre-eminently a church-centred movement. The university Puritans, among whom Laurence Humphrey, John Rainolds, Henry Airey, and John Prideaux of Oxford and Thomas Cartwright, Laurence Chaderton, William Perkins, Samuel Ward, and John Preston of Cambridge, were some of the outstanding figures, were with few exceptions men who held tenaciously to the idea that the Church of England should be one body" (p. 189).

1953-5   Eusden, John Dykstra.   "English Puritan and Common Law
    Concepts of Political Authority, 1603-1630." Ph.D., Yale Univ.
    297, xxiv leaves.

    Revision published as Puritans, Lawyers, and Politics in Early
Seventeenth-Century England. -- New Haven : Yale Univ. Press, 1958. --
xii, 238 p. -- (Yale Studies in Religious Education ; vol. 23).
Reprinted: Hamden, Conn. : Archon Books, 1968. -- xii, 238 p.
"Preface" (1968 ed.): "This book grew out of the author's interest in
the relationship of religion and law. It was undertaken originally to
discover what influence, if any, Puritanism and common law had upon
each other in early seventeenth-century England. . . . It became
clear that the relationship of Puritanism and common law was one of
ideological parallelism. The divines and the barristers were joined
to one another by more than a personal association and a tactical
alliance against the Stuart crown. Both were legalists; the one group
spoke of divine sovereignty and the other of fundamental law; each
advocated a special kind of reason as requisite for understanding of
theology or law; both groups insisted on institutional independence;
and neither tolerated speculative systems of religious or political
thought" (pp. vii-viii). Contents: "Introduction," 1. "The Puritans:
Pests in Church and Commonwealth," 2. "The Common Lawyers: Meddlers
with the King's Prerogative," 3. "The Nature of Puritan and Common Law
Opposition," 4. "Puritan Divines versus Stuart Kings," 5. "Judges and
Lawyers against the Crown," 6. "Puritans and Lawyers on Political
Authority," 7. "Puritan and Common Law Influence on Parliament," and
8. "Sovereignty and the Stuff of Political History."

1953-6   Hinson, William J. "The Theological Thought of John Goodwin
    (1593-1665)." Ph.D., Univ. of Edinburgh (U.K.). 297 leaves.

    Contents: I. "Puritan Champions of Freedom," II. "Theological
Method," III. "Calvinism and Arminianism," IV. "Doctrine of the
Church," V. "Plea for Toleration," and VI. "Summary and Conclusion."

1953-7   Hunter, Richard Edward. "William Whittingham: A Study of
    His Life and Writings, with Especial Reference to the Geneva New
    Testament." Ph.D., Univ. of Pennsylvania. 315 leaves.

    Abstract in DA, vol. 13 (2), p. 233: "The purpose of this
dissertation is to establish William Whittingham's position in the
literary and religious history of England. . . . William Whittingham
(c. 1524-79), after studying at Oxford . . . , traveled in Edward VI's
reign on the continent, where he met John Calvin. He returned to

England about 1550, but shortly after Mary's accession he left England once more, an exile for religion . . . at Geneva . . . [where] he translated and annotated the Geneva Testament (1557) and helped to produce the Geneva Bible (1560)."

1953-8   Kelley, Darwin Newton. "Separation of Powers: The American Development of the Separation of Powers and the Use of the Principle in the Constitution of the United States, 1607-1789." Ph.D., Indiana Univ. iv, 281 leaves.

Abstract in DA, vol. 13 (6), p. 1173: "This study traces the development of the English continental colonies of separation of powers from the time of the first settlements to the drafting of the United States Constitution. The most notable sources are organic law, statutes, judicial decisions, and the writings of the men who wrestled with the problems of government."

1953-9   Rogers, George Calvin, Jr. "Sir Henry Vane, Junior: Spirit Mystic and Fanatic Democrat." Ph.D., Univ. of Chicago. xi, 451 leaves.

The first chapter, I. "The Young Puritan," treats of Vane's early life, including the 1635-37 period in Massachusetts Bay. The subsequent nine chapters are concerned with his later English career.

1953-10   Sloane, William. "England and American Children's Books of the Seventeenth Century: An Annotated Checklist, Together with the First Printed Catalogue of Children's Books." Ph.D., Columbia Univ. 139 leaves.

Revision published as Children's Books in England & America in the Seventeenth Century: A History and Checklist, Together with The Young Christian's Library, the First Printed Catalogue of Books for Children. -- New York : King's Crown Press, Columbia Univ., 1955. -- ix, 251 p. "Preface" (1955 ed.): "This book is . . . in two parts, the first a history of English and American children's books of the seventeenth century, and the second a chronological checklist of books [published between 1557 and 1710] with additional discussion of individual problems. In the appendix I have reprinted one of the Bodleian copies of The Young Christian's Library (1710), the first published catalogue of books recommended for children" (p. viii). Contents: One. "The History": 1. "The Little Victims Play," 2. "My Son, Hear the Instruction of Thy Father," 3. "Remember Now Thy Creator," 4. "Farewell, Rewards and Fairies," and 5. "A Sad Tale's Best for Winter"; Two. "The Checklist": 1. "What is Included," 2. "How the List is Organized," 3. "Symbols and Abbreviations," and 4. "The Checklist"; and Three. "The Young Christian's Library."

1953-11   Smith, Aleck Lewis. "Changing Conceptions of God in Colonial New England." Ph.D., Univ. of Iowa. iii, 286 leaves.

Abstract in DA, vol. 13 (6), p. 383: "This thesis deals with the genesis of the conception of God in the Reformed Church of Colonial New England. It traces the most important changes in the New Englander's attitude towards his God during the seventeenth and early eighteenth centuries. An analysis is made of certain fairly well defined conceptions of the deity that at one time or another had a wide appeal to him. The thesis attempts to show the relationship of each of these concepts to its social and cultural context." Contents: I. "The God of the Covenant," II. "The God of Wonderful Providences," III. "The God of Design," and IV. "The God of the Millennium."

1953-12   Stanford, Donald Elwin. "An Edition of the Complete Poetical Works of Edward Taylor." Ph.D., Stanford Univ. clxxxix, 632 leaves.

Abstract in DA, vol. 14 (3), p. 528. Revision published with a foreword by Louis L. Martz as Poems. -- New Haven : Yale Univ. Press, 1960. -- lxii, 543 p. A 2nd, abridged ed. published: New Haven : Yale Univ. Press, 1963. -- xxv, 369 p. -- (Yale Paperbound). Contents (1960 ed.): "Introduction," "Prologue," "Preparatory Meditations (first series)," "Preparatory Meditations (second series)," "God's Determinations," "Miscellaneous Poems," and "Glossary." Appendices: 1. "Editions" and 2. "Manuscripts."

1953-13   Trefz, Edward Kenneth. "A Study of Satan, with Particular Emphasis upon His Role in the Preaching of Certain New England Puritans." Th.D., Union Theological Seminary in the City of New York. [c.350] leaves.

Includes Benjamin Colman, John Cotton, John Davenport, Thomas Hooker, Cotton Mather, Increase Mather, Thomas Shepard, Solomon Stoddard, Benjamin Wadsworth, Nehemiah Walter, and Samuel Willard. Contents: I. "Satan in the Bible," II. "Satan Through the Christian Centuries," III. "Puritanism and Satan," IV. "Satan as the Prince of Evil," V. "Satan as a Polemical Instrument," VI. "Satan's Hand in History," VII. "Satan as a Witch's Confederate," VIII. "Satan as a Homiletical Instrument," and IX. "Satan's Use of the Puritans."

1954-1   Blake, John Ballard. "Public Health in the Town of Boston, 1630-1822." Ph.D., Harvard Univ. iv, 531 leaves.

Revision published under same title: Cambridge, Mass. : Harvard Univ. Press, 1959. -- x, 278 p. -- (Harvard Historical Studies ; 72). Relevant chapters (1959 ed.): I. "The Seventeenth Century," II. "Founding a Basic Policy, 1691-1720," III. "The Medical Profession and Public Health," IV. "The Inoculation Controversy, 1721-1722," V. "The Smallpox Era, 1722-1775," and VI. "Endemic Disease and Public Health, 1720-1775." Appendices: I. "The State of Smallpox Inoculation," II. "Population, Death, and Death Rates, Boston, 1701-1774," and III. "Notes on the History of Yellow Fever."

1954-2   Calamandrei, Mauro. "Theology and Political Thought of Roger Williams." Ph.D., Univ. of Chicago. vii, 378 leaves.

"Preface": "The present study is intended as a comprehensive interpretation of the nature and significance of Roger Williams' thought. . . . It is both the premise and the conclusion of this study that Roger Williams can be adequately understood only if interpreted in terms of the social and intellectual problems of his own age" (pp. ii-iii). Contents: Part I. "Introduction": I. "History and Myth of Roger Williams," II. "Roger Williams in England," and III. "Roger Williams in America"; Part II. "Theology": IV. "The Word and the Spirit," V. "God and Man," and VI. "Man and History"; Part III. "Ecclesiology": VII. "Introduction to the Doctrine of the Church," VIII. "The Church," IX. "The Ministry," and X. "Roger Williams and the Seeker Movement"; Part IV. "Political Theory": XI. "The Doctrine of the Two Kingdoms," XII. "Civil Government," and XIII. "Liberty of Conscience"; and "Conclusion." Appendix: "Roger Williams' Writings."

1954-3   Cunningham, Homer F. "The Effect of the Decline of the Puritan Oligarchy upon the Schools of Massachusetts Between 1664 and 1758." Ph.D., New York Univ. 2 vols. (vi, 340 leaves).

Abstract in DA, vol. 15 (2), p. 255: "Puritanism should be regarded as a living, changing, vital movement which played an important role in shaping American life. The Puritans established a holy commonwealth of their own in Massachusetts. Gradually, however, the oligarchy of ministers lost control over the colony and the character of life in the colony changed. During the decline of the Puritan oligarchy fundamental changes were concurrently taking place in the schools. The purpose of this thesis is to trace the decline of the oligarchy as well as the changes which were transpiring in the schools and to determine if a causal relation existed between these movements within the Puritan world."

1954-4   Hoyt, Joseph Bixby. "The Historical Geography of Berkshire County, Massachusetts: A Study of Man's Changing Evaluation of a Physical Setting." Ph.D., Clark Univ. vii, 438 leaves.

Abstract in DA, vol. 14 (10), p. 1677: "The influence exerted by the physical setting of Berkshire County, Massachusetts, upon the human occupation of the area is the central theme of this thesis. Both directly, through its elevation and degree of slope, and indirectly through its control over climate, vegetation, and soils, the topography has influenced man's use of the region. Other elements, such as, situation and minerals, have also effected [sic] human settlement. . . . Historical as well as geographical techniques are utilized in the study. Material has been organized and presented chronologically from 1722 to 1954. In addition the major elements are arranged systematically permitting the reader to trace developments in agriculture, industry, or population apart from other phases of the county's history. Separate chapters are also devoted to such aspects as political divisions, . . . mining and forestry, and transportation showing their relationship to topography and the whole physical setting."

1954-5   Hudson, Roy Fred.   "The Theory of Communication of Colonial
    New England Preachers, 1620-1670." Ph.D., Cornell Univ. vi, 248
    leaves.

"Preface": "The present study examines the preacher's own words
as contained in his various publications for the purpose of
reconstructing a theory of communication that will be representative
of the New England minister of the first half-century of New England
life. It reports the views of the period on ministerial training and
preparation for communication, the most appropriate channel for
conveying the Puritan message, the aid of logic and rhetoric in the
task, the psychology of audiences, and the effects of communication on
the auditors. Through such an examination, the understanding and
appreciation of this period in our history may be increased and light
thrown on the development of rhetorical theory in America" (p. v).
Contents: One. "Introduction," Two. "Minister," Three. "Sermon,"
Four. "Logic and Rhetoric," Five. "The Audience," and Six. "Conversion
and Edification."

1954-6   Kinney, Charles B., Jr.   "Church and State in New Hampshire."
    Ph.D., Columbia Univ.   272 leaves.

Revision published as Church & State: The Struggle for Separation
in New Hampshire, 1630-1900. -- New York : Teachers College, Columbia
Univ., 1955. -- vii, 198 p. -- (Teachers College Studies in Education).
"Introduction" (1955 ed.): "This study has been made in the hope that
it will furnish some historical perspective for the consideration of
. . . current issues. . . .   The study attempts to describe the
divergent historical traditions that are in existence in New Hampshire
and how these traditions collide head-on in the field of public
education" (p. 4). Relevant chapters: "An Introduction"; I.
"Development of the Puritan Theocracy: Establishment in the European
Tradition": "Settlement of the Four Original Towns," "Union with
Massachusetts," "Resumption of Direct English Control, 1679," "Struggle
Between Puritan and Anglican," and "Summary--The Seventeenth Century";
II. "The Eighteenth Century--Expansion of the Colony: Breaking Down
the European Tradition": "Beginning of the Breakdown" and "Expansion
into the Interior"; and V. "Church, State, and Public Education:
Conflict Between Two Traditions": "Education in the European
Tradition." Relevant appendices: A. "The Province and State of New
Hampshire": 1. "Provincial Executives" and 3. "The Provincial and
State Legislature: Terminology." Chapters III and IV treat of later
events.

1954-7   Morey, Verne D. "The Brownist Churches: A Study in English
    Separatism, 1553-1630." Ph.D., Harvard Univ. iii, 525 leaves.

Chapter IX: "The Brownist tragedy was that the government
interpreting the role of church and state in much the same manner as
they were [sic] forced to consider ecclesiastical deviation as a civil
offence, punishable as sedition. Neither believed in separation of
church and state and for authorities, loyalty to the commonwealth also
meant loyalty to the established religion. Neither separation from

nor violent denunciation of the Church of England could be tolerated: given a watchful authority and a people who were willing to separate from the establishment and voluntarily set up churches of their own at this period of English history, only exiles and martyrs could result" (p. 503). Contents: I. "Marian Separation," II. "Elizabethan Separatism Before 1580," III. "Robert Browne," IV. "London Separatism Under the Leadership of Henry Barrow and John Greenwood," V. "Martyrs and Exiles," VI. "The Brownists in Amsterdam, 1597-1606," VII. "Recruits and Secessions: John Smyth and John Robinson," VIII. "Schism and Final Fragmentation," and IX. "The Morphology of Brownism."

1954-8   Natunewicz, Henry. "Geopolitics of the Colony and State of Connecticut." Ph.D., Columbia Univ. iii, 225 leaves.

Abstract in DA, vol. 15 (2), p. 252: "This work is a politico-geographic analysis of the colony and state of Connecticut from its inception to the present. The principles and concomitant problems of legislative representation in the state's General Assembly constitute the general theme of study in this particular investigation. The main issue here revolves about the dilemma of unequal representation in the lower house. ... [Geographic] elements have played a vital role in the process of ecological and human interaction which resulted in the evolution of Connecticut's polity and sovereignty."

1954-9   Oberholzer, Emil, Jr. "Saints in Sin: A Study of the Disciplinary Action of the Congregational Churches of Massachusetts in the Colonial and Early National Periods." Ph.D., Columbia Univ. 468 leaves.

Revision published as Delinquent Saints: Disciplinary Action in the Early Congregational Churches of Massachusetts. New York : Columbia Univ. Press, 1956. -- x, 379 p. -- (Columbia Studies in the Social Sciences ; no. 590). Reprinted: New York : AMS Press, 1968. -- x, 379 p. Contents (published versions): "Introduction," I. "The Covenant Owned," II. "The Covenant Broken," III. "The First Table of the Law: Sins of Omission," IV. "The First Table of the Law: Sins of Commission," V. "'False Doctrine, Heresy, and Schism,'" VI. "Domestic and Marital Relations," VII. "Extramarital Relations," VIII. "'The Affected Bottle' and Its Consequences," IX. "The Sixth Commandment: Offenses against the Person," X. "Bearers of False Witness," XI. "Business Ethics and Property Rights," XII. "The Churches as Courts of Law," XIII. "The Churches and the State," XIV. "The Enjoyment of Time and Worldly Pleasures," and XV. "The Unattained Utopia."

1954-10 Packer, James Innell. "The Redemption and Restoration of Man in the Thought of Richard Baxter." D.Phil., Univ. of Oxford (U.K.). Leaves a-g ["Abstract"]; vi, 500 leaves.

"Abstract": "The object of this study is to furnish a full, sympathetic exposition of Richard Baxter's doctrine of man, created and fallen; of his redemption by Jesus Christ; and of the restoration of him in the image of God through the obedience of faith by the power

of the Holy Spirit. . . . The material has been arranged in such a
way as to reveal the relationship between the topics discussed in
Baxter's own theological system" (p. a). Contents: "Introduction";
Part I. "The Theologian"; Part II. "The Ruin of the Race": A.
"Doctrine: The Truth about Man" and B. "Use: The Strategy of
Evangelism"; Part III. "The Redemption of the World": A. "Doctrine:
The Rule of the Redeemer" and B. "Use: The Religion of the Redeemed";
Part IV. "The Restoration of the Elect": A. "Doctrine: New Creation"
and B. "Use: Heaven on Earth"; and "Conclusion." Includes an
appendix of "Corrections in the 'Aphorisms.'"

1954-11   Wasserman, Maurice Marc. "The American Indian as Seen by
     the Seventeenth-Century Chroniclers." Ph.D., Univ. of
     Pennsylvania. 2, 483 leaves.

     Abstract in DA, vol. 14 (5), p. 823: "In the New England area,
historians, diarists, and chroniclers were abundant. . . . The thesis
evaluates the reliability of the major chroniclers of the time,
considering their temperaments and their prejudices, according to the
following plan: first, geographically from the northern to the
southern colonies; and second, chronologically within each
geographical section." Contents: I. "Chronicles and Chroniclers,"
II. "Appearance," III. "Clothing," IV. "Language," V. "Dwellings and
Handicrafts," VI. "Character and Disposition," VII. "Family Life,"
VIII. "Work and Play," IX. "Food--Drink--Tobacco," X. "Medicine and
Mortuary Customs," XI. "Warfare and Weapons," XII. "Government and
Law," XIII. "Trade and Money," XIV. "Religion," XV. "Inter-racial
Relations," and XVI. "Origin."

1955-1   Amon, Marie Celine. "Influence of Political Philosophy on
     Education in Seventeenth-Century New England." Ph.D., St. Louis
     Univ. iv, 364 leaves.

     "Introduction": "It has been said that no factor is more
influential in molding educational theory and practice than that of
political philosophy. . . . It is to investigate the validity of this
assertion that political philosophy was chosen as the influential
factor. An attempt will be made to demonstrate to what extent it has
been instrumental in shaping the educational system of seventeenth-
century New England" (p. 15). Contents: I. "Introduction"; II.
"Education and Politics"; III. "Historical Antecedents": "Reformation
on the Continent," "Political Tenets of the Reformers," and "Subsequent
Reaction in England"; IV. "Political Philosophy of Early New England":
"Fourfold Causality," "Covenant Theory," "Relationship of Church and
State," "Nature of Authority," "Nature of Man," and "Summary"; V.
"Status of Education in Early New England": "Purpose of Education,"
"Number and Types of Schools," "Agency and Policy of Administration,"
"Contents of Curriculum," and "Financial Support of the Schools"; VI.
"Extent to Which Political Philosophy Influenced Education in
Seventeenth-Century New England"; and VII. "Summary, Conclusions, and
Suggestions for Further Research."

1955-2   Bohn, Ralph Paul. "The Controversy Between Puritans and
     Quakers to 1660." Ph.D., Univ. of Edinburgh (U.K.). viii, 384
     leaves.

     "Historical Introduction":   "While the main point of our
investigation begins with the year 1653, the previous years cannot be
ignored" (p. 11).   "The controlling interest throughout is
theological, and the attempt to analyze the controversy [is] in terms
of the theological issues involved. . . . Most of the historical
aspects of the struggle have been confined to the Introduction. This
approach is, of course, based on the premise that the controversy
between Puritans and Quakers was basically a theological one, and the
differences in politics and in manners and morals, etc., stemmed
ultimately from conflicting theologies" (p. 25). John Owen, Richard
Baxter, and John Bunyan are the principal spokesmen for the Puritan
point of view. Contents: "Historical Introduction," I. "Immediate
Revelation and the Indwelling Spirit," II. "The Light of Christ
Within," III. "The Doctrine of the Scriptures," IV. "Christological
and Eschatological Disputes," V. "Sin, Sanctification and Salvation,"
VI. "The Church and Ordinances," VII. "The Office of the Ministry,"
VIII. "The Church and the State," and "Critical Conclusion."

1955-3   Campbell, Philip Storer. "Cotton Mather." Ph.D., Brown
     Univ. v, 236 leaves.

     Abstract in DA, vol. 15 (8), p. 1296: "Cotton Mather had the
misfortune to live in a time of transition when the fundamental
assumptions of the old order in church and state were being more and
more called into question by men and events, yet when the new order
had not sufficiently revealed itself to give assurance to any but the
most disenchanted spirits. It was Mather's further misfortune to have
been committed from birth and by birth to the past. The shades of his
grandfathers, who had built the Puritan church upon a rock, were ever
with him; the substantial shadow of his father, who sought to hand on
the faith undiminished, fell upon him until the final years of his
life."

1955-4   Daniel, Ralph T. "The Anthem in New England before 1800."
     Ph.D., Harvard Univ. 930 leaves.

     Revison published under same title: Evanston, Ill. :
Northwestern Univ. Press, 1966. -- xvi, 282 p. -- (Pi Kappa Lambda
Studies in American Music). Reprinted: New York : Da Capo Press,
1979. -- xvi, 282 p. -- (Da Capo Press Music Reprint Ser.). Chapter I
(1979 ed.): "The history of church music in New England begins with
the psalmody of the Pilgrim colonists and, indeed, consists solely of
the practice and development of psalmody for more than one hundred
years" (p. 3). Relevant chapter: I. "Church Music in New England
before 1760."

1955-5   Dunn, Richard Slator. "John Winthrop, John Winthrop, Jr.,
    and the Problem of Colonial Dependency in New England, 1630-1676:
    A Study in Contrasts." Ph.D., Princeton Univ. 3, ix, 480
    leaves.

    Abstract in DA, vol. 16 (3), p. 522. Enlarged revision published
as Puritans and Yankees: The Winthrop Dynasty of New England, 1630-
1717. -- Princeton : Princeton Univ. Press, 1962. -- xi, 379 p.
Reprinted: New York : W. W. Norton, 1971. -- 376 p. Contents: Book
One: "John Winthrop, 1588-1649," Two: "John Winthrop, Jr., 1606-
1676," and Three: "Fitz Winthrop, 1638-1707; Wait Winthrop, 1642-
1717."

1955-6   Emerson, Everett Harvey. "Thomas Hooker and the Reformed
    Theology: The Relationship of Hooker's Conversion Preaching to
    Its Background." Ph.D., Louisiana State Univ. vi, 264 leaves.

    "Abstract": "Recent students of New England Puritanism have
argued that the theology of such writers as John Cotton, Thomas
Shepard, and Thomas Hooker is not to be confused with Calvinism, for it
differs in important ways: It is covenant theology, a later
development of the Reformed theology which put more emphasis on man's
spiritual ability and less on predestination. This dissertation
examines the teachings of the important Puritan divine Thomas Hooker
(1586-1647) on conversion, in the light of Calvin's teachings and
seventeenth-century Reformed and Puritan thought" (p. iv). Contents:
"Introduction," I. "Reformed Thought on Conversion before Hooker," II.
"The Puritan Background," III. "Thomas Hooker's Theology and Ethics,
and His Concept of the Role of Preaching," IV. "Hooker's Covenant
Theology, and the Sermon as the Means of Grace," V. "Additional
Preaching Techniques Used by Hooker," VI. "Shepard and Cotton in
Relation to Hooker," and "Conclusion."

1955-7   Farrell, Frank E. "Richard Sibbes: A Study in Early
    Seventeenth-Century English Puritanism." Ph.D., Univ. of
    Edinburgh (U.K.). v, 304 leaves.

    Contents: Part I. "Richard Sibbes: The Man in His Times": I.
"The Making of a Puritan," II. "Service of Distinction," III. "Times
of Testing," and IV. "Triumph of Faith"; and Part II. "Richard Sibbes'
Religious Thought": I. "The Knowledge of God," II. "The Word of God,"
III. "Grace Through the Covenant," and IV. "Christian Warfare."
Appendices: I. "List of the Separate Works of Richard Sibbes" and II.
"Commendatory Poem by Francis Quarles for The Soul's Conflict."

1955-8   Friedelbaum, Stanley Herman. "Bellomont: Imperial
    Administrator--Studies in Colonial Administration during the
    Seventeenth Century." Ph.D., Columbia Univ. 222 leaves.

    Abstract in DA, vol. 15 (8), p. 1379: "This study focuses
attention upon the Earl of Bellomont's (1636-1701) career as colonial
administrator and early British imperialist. Governor of New York and
New England from 1698 to 1701, the Earl undertook reforms necessary to

insure honesty in government and the success of the new imperial
policy embodied in the Navigation Act of 1696. Bellomont's
understanding of fiscal management, his realization of the need for a
sound personnel policy, and his proposals for the conservation of
natural resources placed him many decades in advance of colonial
practice and thought."

1955-9   Haffenden, Philip Spencer. "England's Colonial Policy and
    Administration in North America and the West Indies, 1681-88."
    Ph.D., Univ. of London (King's College) (U.K.). 479, [28]
    leaves.

    Relevant chapters: I. "The Machinery at the Centre and the Men
in Control"; II. "The Administration of Imperial Defence": 1.
"Regular forces of the Crown on Imperial stations and the Colonial
Militia," 2. "Ordnance Supply and Fortifications," and 3. "The Naval
Guardship and the Plantations"; III. "Piracy and Naval Measures": 2.
"Piracy in Bermuda and the Mainland colonies"; IV. "The Beginnings of
a Forward Policy": 1. "The Anglo-French Peace, 1681-88" and 3.
"Indian policy and the Frontier with New France"; V. "Anglicans as an
Instrument of Colonial Policy": 1. "The State of the overseas
Anglican Church," 2. "Supervision from England," and 3. "The attempt
to break fresh ground in Puritan New England"; VI. "The Movement
towards Imperial Centralisation in its Political Aspect": 1. "The
preliminary attack against Massachusetts and the fall of the Bermuda
charter," 2. "Achievements and Limitations under Charles II," and 3.
"Political reorganisation: the beginnings"; and VII. "The Extension
of Treasury Influence." Cf. Haffenden's New England in the English
Nation, 1689-1713 -- Oxford : Clarendon Press, 1974.

1955-10   Hammelef, John Christensen. "British and American Attempts
    to Coordinate the Defenses of the Continental Colonies to Meet
    French and Northern Indian Attacks, 1643-1754." Ph.D., Univ. of
    Michigan. ii, 255 leaves.

    Abstract in DA, vol. 15 (5), p. 807: "Successful defense of the
British colonies on the North American continent required military
cooperation between provinces. Leaders in the New World and at home
soon learned this, but since frontier settlements were widely
scattered and the colonies politically separate, joint activities were
difficult to arrange. . . . Between 1643 and 1748 united action was
tried repeatedly. The New England Confederacy was quite successful;
other methods of permanent, formally organized cooperation either
failed or were never tried."

1955-11   Highfill, William Lawrence. "Faith and Works in the Ethical
    Theory of Richard Baxter." Ph.D., Duke Univ. iv, 311 leaves.

    "Preface": "It is my province to clarify Baxter's treatment of
faith and works and to show how he relates them. The consideration of
this problem unveils the essence of his ethical system" (p. ii).
Contents: I. "The Seventeenth-Century Background," II. "The Man
Richard Baxter," III. "Faith and Works as 'Conditions' of

Justification," IV. "The Divine Life," V. "The Virtues of the Divine Life," VI. "Casuistry and the Problem of Faith and Works," and VII. "Conclusion."

1955-12   Miller, Dale, Jr. "Protestantism and Politics in Rhode Island, 1636-1657." Ph.D., Univ. of Chicago. iii, 177 leaves.

"Introduction": "The purpose and plan of the thesis can . . . be stated as follows: to rewrite the account of Rhode Island history from 1636 to 1657 . . . in order to study the relationship between Christian belief and political theories and events in that time--in the hope that such a study will enlighten our present day concern about the general relationship between religious thought and political consequences" (p. 7). Contents: "Introduction," I. "Origins in Massachusetts Bay," II. "1638-41: Emergence of Basic Rhode Island Concerns," III. "1641-47: Development of the Issues around [Samuel] Gorton," IV. "1647-51: Explosion of the Charter Union," V. "1651-54: Divided Rhode Island," VI. "1654-57: Roger Williams and Political Reality," and VII. "Summary and Conclusion."

1955-13   Perluck, Herbert A. "Puritan Expression and the Decline of Piety." Ph.D., Brown Univ. iv, 233 leaves.

Abstract in DA, vol. 15 (8), p. 1389: "The purpose of this dissertation is the explication of the Puritan 'drama of the spirit,' a metaphor introduced in the first chapter and used throughout to represent the idea that the course of development of Puritanism can best be understood as resulting from certain interior requirements and necessities. By an examination of the evolution of forms of expression in the Puritan literature (which are taken as reflecting this inner condition of the 'spirit'), the dissertation seeks to define 'organically' the circumstances which brought about the decline of Puritanism in America, seen here as a failure of the spirit, rather than as a defeat by outside forces. . . . Briefly stated, the central thesis is that the spiritual failure of Puritanism can in great part be attributed to a kind of 'failure of expression.' The logical, analytical forms of Puritan expression were inimical to the requirements of piety."

1955-14   Towner, Lawrence William. "A Good Master Well Served: A Social History of Servitude in Massachusetts, 1620-1750." Ph.D., Northwestern Univ. vii, 465 leaves.

Abstract in DA, vol. 15 (11), p. 2185: "Servitude before 1750 in what is now Massachusetts had two important and complementary functions: it helped supply the ever-growing need for labor, and it provided a means of control for social deviates whom the community could not at first afford to place in institutions of brick and mortar. As a consequence, the servant class was composed of many types and was drawn from varied domestic and foreign sources, their relative importance changing to meet the needs and opportunities of the settlers. But despite this diversity, the servants were a class with certain characteristics as important as those distinguishing them one from another."

1955-15   Vitelli, James Robert. "The Resurrection of the Puritan: A
    Study of an American Literary Symbol." Ph.D., Univ. of
    Pennsylvania. lii, 521 leaves.

    Abstract in DA, vol. 15 (5), p. 832: "During the first three
decades of the twentieth century, many American writers, seeking to
understand, to explain, and finally to recreate the American
experience, expressed their efforts with a symbol: the Puritan. This
dissertation is an account of how a collective symbol of the Puritan
appeared, took shape, and was put to use; how it served to develop an
American criticism; how it created an articulate consciousness about
America and American literature. . . . The dissertation aims at a
synthesis of the contributions of individual writers to the making of
the symbol, rather than at an analysis of it." The works of Irving
Babbitt, Randolph S. Bourne, Van Wyck Brooks, W. C. Brownell, H. L.
Mencken, Paul Elmer More, George Santayana, Stuart P. Sherman, and Joel
E. Spingarn are discussed in detail.

1955-16   Ziff, Larzer. "John Cotton: Congregationalist, Theocrat,
    Puritan." Ph.D., Univ. of Chicago. vii, 272 leaves.

    Revision published as The Career of John Cotton: Puritanism and
the American Experience. -- Princeton : Princeton Univ. Press, 1962.
-- x, 280 p. "Preface" (1962 ed.): Ziff attempts to "maintain a
constant cross reference between the great events in which Cotton took
part and the ideas of the nature of God and man he held. Moreover,
since he was an influential actor in important events--the migration to
America, the Antinomian controversy, the toleration controversy, and
others--I have again traced the circumstance of these familiar
occurrences" (p. vii). Contents: One. "Education for Puritanism
(1584-1612)," Two. "The First Boston (1612-1633)," Three. "The Second
Boston (1633-1636)," Four. "Pupil and Lesson on Trial (1636-1638),
Five. "The Teacher's Art and Attitude (1639)," Six. "The Time of the
Fifth Vial (1640-1644)," Seven. "The Middle Path (1645-1648)," Eight.
"The Late Howling Wilderness (1648-1652)," and "Afterword."

1956-1   Allen, Neal Woodside, Jr. "Court Records of York County,
    Maine, 1692-1711." Ph.D., Harvard Univ. 2 vols. (xclv, 695
    leaves).

    Revision published as The Court Records of York County, Maine,
Province of Massachusetts Bay, November, 1692-January, 1710/11. --
Portland : Maine Historical Society, 1958. -- 427 p. -- (Maine (Colony)
Province and Court Records of Maine ; vol. 4). Intended to continue
Maine Province and Court Records, vols. 1-3. -- Portland : Maine
Historical Society, 1928-1947, edited by Charles Thornton Libby and
(for 1947) Robert E. Moody, and continued by Allen's own vol. 5 (1964)
covering the period April, 1711-October, 1718. Contents of vol. 4:
"Introduction: The Courts; The Records; The Background; County Justice
During Wartime; The Offices of the Courts; Notes on Law and Procedure";

"Note of Editorial Practice"; "Court Records of York Co., November, 1692-April, 1699; from York Deeds, Book V, Part II, Pages 14-129"; "Court Records of York Co.: Records of the Inferior Court of Common Pleas, October, 1600-January, 1710/11; from Court Records, Vol. VI, Pages 116-166"; "Court Records of York Co.: Records of the Court of General Sessions of the Peace, October, 1699-January, 1710/11; from Court Records, Vol. VI, Pages 275-372." Appendices: A. "Family Connections of the York County Magistracy," B. "The Offices of the County, 1692-1711," and C. "Table of Cases."

1956-2   Brown, Earl Kent. "Richard Baxter's Contribution to the Comprehension Controversy: A Study in Projected Church Union." Ph.D., Boston Univ. (School of Theology). vi, 336 leaves.

Abstract in DA, vol. 16 (7), p. 1293: "This study is an investigation of the thought and activity of Richard Baxter in the area of church union and cooperation. Three things appeared: (1) a descriptive historical survey of Baxter's thought and activity in this area; (2) the changes in Anglican usage he deemed desirable to achieve comprehension--i.e., the inclusion of the Puritans in the Establishment; (3) the terms he deemed the minimum acceptable to achieve comprehension."

1956-3   Counts, Martha Louise. "The Political View of the Eighteenth-Century New England Clergy as Expressed in Their Election Sermons." Ph.D., Columbia Univ. ix, 282 leaves.

Abstract in DA, vol. 16 (7), p. 1245: "This study traced the changes in the New England clergy's political philosophy as revealed in the eighteenth-century election sermons. The most significant shift involved the clergy's concept of the role of the people. The way in which they viewed the people influenced their entire thinking on government. During the early years of the century the clergy expressed little faith in the people. Even though the ministers repudiated the doctrine of nonresistance and passive obedience, they remained skeptical about the masses' ability to ascertain when they were genuinely oppressed. The clergy preferred that the elite of society make decisions about delicate political matters. The people should continue to obey their rulers as long as the latter did not demand that they go counter to God's laws." Appendices: A. "A Brief History of the Election Sermon" and B. "Chronological list of ministers who preached the election sermons in Massachusetts, Connecticut, Vermont, and New Hampshire from 1710-1810."

1956-4   Crawford, John Oliver. "The Impact of Puritanism on Education." Ph.D., Univ. of Colorado at Boulder. 172 leaves.

Abstract in DA, vol. 17 (10), p. 2259: "Education was a recurrent topic in Puritan literature of the sixteenth and seventeenth centuries. The present study is an examination of this literature for the purpose of determining what influence Puritanism had on education during the period under investigation. Educational treatises, school legislation, poems, dramas, sermons, pamphlets, and miscellaneous prose were studied not only for the purpose of clarifying the state of English education in the sixteenth and seventeenth centuries but also for seeking out and discovering those Puritan tenets, beliefs, and opinions that were dynamic enough to bring about change in the kind and quality of education in the British Isles and New England. This study embraced the years 1500 to 1660. . . . In America, the Puritans established our public school system, began compulsory education, founded Harvard College, and began educating and Christianizing the Indians."

1956-5   Dawson, John L. "The Effect of the Discovery of the American Frontier on English Shipping, 1650-1688." Ph.D., Univ. of Edinburgh (U.K.). ix, 301 leaves.

"Preface": "The primary objective of this study is to present the facts indicating the effects of the discovery of the American frontier on English shipping. . . . A good deal of material on trade in general has been included in this study, for obviously it is difficult to make a clear cut distinction between trade and shipping" (p. iii). Relevant chapters: Part I: "The Trade of the Continental Colonies, 1650-1688": I. "Introduction"; IV. "New England Colonies": A. "Massachusetts, Maine, and New Hampshire," B. "Connecticut and Rhode Island," C. "Factors Affecting Trade," and D. "Effects of the Founding and Settlement of these Colonies on English Shipping"; Part II: "The West Indies Trade, 1650-1688": VIII. "The Frontier Requirement of Slaves and the Indirect Effects on English Shipping"; and Part III: "Conclusion": IX. "Conclusion." The other chapters deal with other colonies than those of New England or with irrelevant aspects of the West Indies trade.

1956-6   Donnelly, Marian Card. "New England Meeting Houses in the 17th Century." Ph.D., Yale Univ.

Revision published as The New England Meeting House of the Seventeenth Century. -- Middletown, Conn. : Wesleyan Univ. Press, 1968. -- x, 165 p. "Preface" (1968 ed.): "The present study has been made in order to provide at least an introduction to a more meticulous scrutiny of the New England meeting houses in relation to their English and Continental contemporaries. This preliminary investigation indicates that the meeting houses were apparently not linked to fashionable developments in the English Renaissance or to experimental Protestant architecture in northern Europe, but were derived naturally from late medieval English village traditions" (p. 3). Contents: One. "New England Meeting Houses of the Great Migration 1630-1642," Two. "Continental Protestant Architecture Before 1630," Three. "Reformation to Revolution: English Worship 1536-1643," Four. "Meeting Houses of the Middle Period: 1643-1660," Five. "Meeting Houses of the Late Period: 1660-1700," and Six. "The New England Meeting Houses as Puritan Architecture." Appendices; A. "Alphabetical List of Towns" and B. "Chronological List of Meeting Houses, 1631-1700."

1956-7   Hall, Michael Garibaldi. "Edward Randolph and the American Colonies, 1676-1703." Ph.D., Johns Hopkins Univ.

Revision published under same title: Chapel Hill : Published for the Institute of Early American History and Culture by the Univ. of North Carolina Press, 1960. -- xi, 241 p.   Reprinted: New York : W. W. Norton, 1969. -- 241 p. -- (Norton Library).   "Introduction" (1960 ed.):   "The development of an imperial structure, the theory and machinery for administering an empire, the growth of a body of colonial servants all came before British imperialism. ... Relatively minor figures [like Randolph took the place of] the great political figures of England" and shaped the empire (p. xi).   Contents: 1. "Background," 2. "The Issues Drawn, 1676-1679," 3. "Trouble in the Colonies, 1680-1683," 4. "Quo Warranto, 1683-1685," 5. "Failure of the Dominion, 1686-1689," 6. "Surveyor General, 1690-1695," 7. "A New Law and an Attack on the Proprietaries, 1695-1697," 8. "Surveyor General Again, 1698-1700," and 9. "End of a Career, 1700-1703."

1956-8   Malone, Joseph J.   "The British Naval Stores and Forests Policy in New England."   Ph.D., Univ. of London (U.K.).

Revision published as Pine Trees and Politics: The Naval Stores and Forest Policy in Colonial New England, 1691-1775. -- London : Longmans, 1964. -- 219 p.   Reprinted: Seattle : Univ. of Washington Press, 1965. -- xi, 219 p.   Also reprinted: New York : Arno Press, 1979. -- xi, 219 p. -- (The Development of Public Land Law in the U.S.).   "Preface" (American eds.):   "Two English policies will be considered in some detail.   The first visualized New England as a more useful unit of the colonial system through realizing its potential as a producer of naval stores.   The second sought to safeguard the supply of masts for the Royal Navy" (p. ix).   Relevant chapters: I. "Introduction," II. "A Policy Evolved, 1691-1705," III. "Naval Stores and New England Trade, 1705-75," IV. "The All-Important Mast Trade," V. "Guardian of the Forests, 1706-20," and VI. "The Woodland Rebellion, 1720-43."   The final chapter deals with a later period.   Appendices: A. "Royal Licenses and Mast Contracts," B. "Prices of Masts and Naval Stores," C. "A Royal Navy Masting Table," D. "'Informations & Directions for the Making of Tar & & [sic] the choice of trees for the same as in Finland,'" and E. "New England's Export Trade."

1956-9   Marcuse, William.   "Local Public Finance in Colonial Connecticut."   Ph.D., Columbia Univ.   xiii, 317 leaves.

Abstract in DA, vol. 16 (7), p. 1224:   "This dissertation describes local taxation and expenditure and examines the role played by local public finance in colonial Connecticut.   The purpose was not only to describe the system but also to present in quantitative terms the level of local taxation in relation to that of the colony.   Once quantitative estimates were available it was inevitable that some attempt be made to determine the tax burden and to briefly examine this burden, colonial and local, in comparison to that of pre-Revolutionary England."

1956-10   Pichierri, Louis.   "Music in New Hampshire, 1623-1800."   Ph.D., Syracuse Univ.   xiii, 358 leaves.

Abstract in DA, vol. 16 (6), p. 1150. Revision published under same title with a foreword by Otto Kinkeldey: New York : Columbia Univ. Press, 1960. -- 297 p. Relevant chapters (1960 ed.): I. "The Setting," II. "Instruments in New Hampshire," III. "Religious Music," IV. "Secular Music," and XVI, "Conclusion." Chapters V-XV are concerned with later periods.

1956-11   Poole, Harry Alexander. "The Unsettled Mr. Cotton." Ph.D., Univ. of Illinois at Urbana-Champaign. vi, 370 leaves.

Abstract in DA, vol. 16 (9), p. 1670: "This is a study of the theology of John Cotton, a divine who arrived in New England in 1633. He soon became involved in the Antinomian dispute, and his somewhat discreditable behavior brought upon him considerable opprobrium from English opponents of the Congregational Way. Despite Cotton's weak defence of his vacillating role in the Antinomian Trials, he went on to become one of the leading publicists for the New England Congregationalists during the English Civil Wars. . . . Seeking an explanation of Cotton's behavior I delved deeply into the theological writings of this divine."

1956-12   Powell, Summer Chilton. "The Formation of a New England Town: A Case Study of the English Background and Early Development of Sudbury, Watertown, and Marlborough, Massachusetts." Ph.D., Harvard Univ. [12], 178, [19] leaves.

Revision published as Puritan Village: The Formation of a New England Town. -- Middletown, Conn. -- Wesleyan Univ. Press, 1963. -- xx, 215 p. Paperback ed.: Garden City, N.Y. : Doubleday, 1965. -- xx, 258 p. -- (Anchor Books). In 1963 published version was awarded the Pulitzer Prize in History. "Introduction" (1965 ed.): "The best approach to a study either of the origins of a set of social institutions or the transition of these from England to New England is a careful examination of those emigrants who comprised and administered these institutions when they were living in England and again when they had gathered to form a new town" (p. xv). Contents: I. "The Web of Open-field Life," II. "Land Hunger, Borough Rights and the Power to Tax," III. "The Secrets of the Corporation of This Town of Sudbury," IV. "'It Is Ordered by the Court,'" V. "Watertown on the Charles," VI. "'It Is Ordered and Agreed by This Town,'" VII. "'All Liberties As Other Towns Have,'" VIII. "'We Shall Be Judged by Men of Our Own Choosing,'" IX. "'Interest in This Town of Marlborough,'" and X. "The Origin and Stability of a New England Town."

1956-13   Tjossem, Herbert Karl. "New England Pronunciation before 1700." Ph.D., Yale Univ. 256 leaves.

Abstract in DA, vol. 28 (7), p. 2669: "By applying the principles of historical phonology to the rhymes and spellings of early American poets it is possible to discover something about the pronunciation of colo-English in its relation to the language of seventeenth-century England and to later American speech. With some general exceptions, the linguistic situation in New England before 1700 . . . does not seem to have differed greatly from that of the present day."

1956-14   Toombs, Gordon Livingstone. "The Puritan Idea of the Holy
    Commonwealth with Special Reference to John Eliot and Richard
    Baxter." Ph.D., Univ. of Edinburgh (U.K.). 321, [15] leaves.

    "Conclusion": "We conclude that the political culmination of the
Puritan idea of the Holy Commonwealth was a democracy. In Eliot's
case, the dream was of a republic, and in Baxter's of a constitutional
monarchy. The foundation of the Puritan scheme was the congregation.
In Baxter's conception of Church Government the parish congregation or
congregations were the highest court in the Church. The local
officials were elected by and responsible to the congregation, although
they held their authority under Christ. Furthermore, it was the
Puritan desire for freedom of conscience which vindicated the principle
of popular rights and independence for minorities" (p. 308). Contents:
I. "Historical Introduction"; II. "John Eliot's Christian
Commonwealth; III. "Richard Baxter's Holy Commonwealth": i. "God's
Kingdom and the Earthly Kingdom," ii. "Sovereignty and Power," iii.
"Sovereign Perspectives, Obedience and Resistance," iv. "Church and
State," and v. "Theocracy"; and IV. "Criticism and Appraisal": i.
"Basic Assumptions," ii. "Political Ideas," and iii. "Conclusion."
Appendices: A. "Eliot's Communion of Churches," B. "Diagrammatic
Sketch of Eliot's Commonwealth," C. "Things Undetermined by Scripture,"
D. "Varieties of Christian Subjects," E. "Extract from [Baxter's]
'Catalogue of Errours,'" F. "Extract from [Baxter's] 'Catalogue of
Prescribed Doctrine,'" and G. "Diagrammatic Sketch of Baxter's
Commonwealth."

1956-15   Yetman, Charles Duncan. "The Hartford Public High School,
    1639-1865." Ph.D., Yale Univ. vii, 449 leaves.

    "Summary" (at beginning of diss.): "This history of the Hartford
foundation reveals certain unique qualities in the school itself and
suggests their significance for the development of the Connecticut
state educational system. . . . Deprived of the strong leadership
given education in the New Haven Colony but provided with funds from
the Hopkins and other legacies, the Hartford school early moved away
from the traditional Latin grammar pattern to become a Latin-English
town school. Its existence helped to inspire the Colony laws of 1690
and 1693 requiring grammar schools in the country towns" (n.p.).
Relevant chapters: "Introduction," I. "The Pioneer Period, 1639-1664,"
II. "The County Grammar School, 1665-1705," and III. "The Free School,
1705-1753." Relevant appendices: I. "The [Edward] Hopkins Will, March
7, 1657," II. "The [William] Goodwin-[John] Davenport Agreement with
the General Assembly on June 13, 1664," and VII. "List of Teachers,
1639-1798." Chapters IV-VIII deal with later developments.

1957-1   Cole, Norwood Marion. "The Origin and Development of Town-
    School Education in Colonial Massachusetts, 1635-1775." Ed.D.,
    Univ. of Washington. xii, 599 leaves.

    Abstract in DA, vol. 18 (4), p. 1328: "Three principal themes are characteristic of the educational history of Massachusetts, 1635-1775. The period is marked by the evolution of an educational system based on an English model to the formation of the common school. Within two decades after the settlement of the Bay colony eight (possibly nine) schools had been established. . . . In [the opinion of the Puritan leaders] education was essential also for good citizenship and worldly accomplishment. Upon this basic philosophy the Puritan educational system was based. . . . Local responsibility was a second characteristic of the Massachusetts school system. . . . Perhaps the most important development was the emergence of the free, tax-supported school."

1957-2   Collinson, Patrick. "The Puritan Classical Movement in the Reign of Elizabeth I." Ph.D., Univ. of London (Royal Holloway College) (U.K.). 3 vols. (xvi, 1339, [7] leaves).

Revised version published as The Elizabethan Puritan Movement. -- Berkeley and Los Angeles : Univ. of California Press ; London : Cape, 1967. -- 528 p. Reprinted: London ; New York : Methuen, 1982. -- 528 p. -- (Methuen Library Reprints). "Preface" (1967 ed.): "What I have written is no more than a history of the quest by the Elizabethan Puritans for what some of them called 'a further reformation,' the logical completion of the process of reconstituting the national Church, which in their view had been arrested halfway. Although the activities of the more extreme, presbyterian puritans, expecially in the 1580s, provide the justification of this study, I have set that episode in the wider context of Elizabethan church history" (p. 12). Contents: One: "Puritanism and the Elizabethan Church," Two: "The Breach Opens," Three: "The First Presbyterians," Four: "Moderate Courses," Five: "1584," Six: "The Grand Design," Seven: "Presbytery in Episcopacy," and Eight: "Discovery, Prosecution and Dissolution."

1957-3   Cross, Wilford Oakland. "The Role and Status of the Unregenerate in the Massachusetts Bay Colony, 1629-1729." Ph.D., Columbia Univ. vi, 495 leaves.

Abstract in DA, vol. 17 (10), p. 2326: "The purpose of this dissertation is to describe the role and status of the unregenerate inhabitants within the social and ecclesiastical commonwealth of Massachusetts Bay throughout the first one hundred years of the life of the Colony. . . . Throughout every effort is made to take account of the historical, political, economic, religious, and intellectual factors which conditioned and determined the changing status and role of the unregenerate."

1957-4   Henson, Robert Eston. "Sorry after a Godly Manner: A Study of the Puritan Funeral Elegy in New England, 1625-1722." Ph.D., Univ. of California at Los Angeles. vii, 314 leaves.

"Preface": "I have only made an attempt to hitch the elegies to their proper literary stars where before they have been herded together as 'belatedly metaphysical' or, worse, treated as wholly innocent of any literary connections. I have also attempted to show that they

constituted a thoughtful and deliberate social gesture and were not the
random product of minds too preoccupied with theology to be aware of
the efficiency and graciousness of poetry" (p. v). Contents: I. "The
Place of the Elegy in Puritan Life," II. "The Apology for Artlessness,"
III. "The Courtly Tradition," IV. "The Metaphysical Tradition," V. "The
Portrait-Exhortation," VI. "Neoclassical Experiments," and VII.
"Conclusion."

1957-5   Jellema, William W.   "The Christian Attitude to Death in
      Seventeenth-Century Puritanism."   Ph.D., Univ. of Edinburgh
      (U.K.). vi, 281 leaves.

    "Preface": "The intent of this study is to examine the subject of
death in seventeenth-century Puritanism from a theological point of
view. . . . The subject of death is a vantage point from which to
examine Puritan thought because death pervaded every sphere of that
thought. This thesis demonstrates how closely the Puritan's view of
life was tied to his view of death. It shows the relation between his
attitude to death and his attitude to heaven. It reveals something of
the Puritan's intimate personality by showing his primary concern with
his own death, his reaction to the death of loved ones, and his
lifelong struggle for a victorious death.   Because death is a
theological subject, an examination of it exposes the effect of
covenant theology on Puritanism and reveals much of Puritan thought in
general" (p. iii).   Contents: I. "Preparation for Death," II.
"Deviations from Calvin's Theology," III. "Death of Loved Ones," IV.
"The Intermediate State," V. "Fear and Desire," and VI. "Summary and
Critical Conclusion."

1957-6   Kleber, Brooks E.   "The Colonial Newspaper and the Emergence
      of an American Community." Ph.D., Univ. of Pennsylvania. xxiii,
      231 leaeves.

    Abstract in DA, vol. 17 (12), p. 2993: "The purpose of this study
is . . . to point out the various facets of intercolonial contact and
to show the part played in this far-reaching and important intercourse.
. . . Investigation was made in the press of Charleston, Williamsburg,
Philadelphia, New York, and Boston from the date of the earliest
journals until the meeting of the First Continental Congress."

1957-7   Kolling, Harold Earl.   "The New England Confederation of
      1643: Its Origin, Nature, and Foreign Relations, 1643-1652."
      Ph.D., Univ. of Chicago. v, 296 leaves.

    "Preface": "In 1643 four youthful colonies of New England, acting
like independent states, entered into an agreement forming a
confederation. . . . For two decades the union played an active role
in the life of the member colonies and in their relations with their
neighbors and mother country, although domestic conflicts revealed
inherent weaknesses. . . . [In 1684] the confederation came to a
permanent and inglorious end . . . when the royal government in Britain
imposed its own scheme of colonial unification in the form of the
Dominion of New England" (pp. ii-iii). Contents: I. "The Historical

Setting," II. "The Genesis," III. "The Covenant," IV. "Dealing with the Barbarous Natives," V. "Treating with the Papist French," VI. "Competing with the Dutch and Swedes," and VII. "In Retrospect."

1957-8   Levy, Alfred Jacob. "Nathaniel Hawthorne's Attitude toward Total Depravity and Evil." Ph.D., Univ. of Wisconsin at Madison. iv, 373 leaves.

Abstract in DA, vol. 17 (8), p. 1751: "Nathaniel Hawthorne was neither a believer in total depravity and absolute evil nor was he a transcendentalist; he was a Christian dualist, . . . who believe that man was made of 'marble and mud.' . . . Secondly, his use of nature reinforces this idea of light beyond darkness. . . . Thirdly, man's gift of free-will dignified him as a human and made him responsible for his actions. . . . Fourthly, Hawthorne thought man so constructed psychologically that he could do no wrong without intense, inward self-accusation and eventual confession. . . . Fifthly, Hawthorne believed in the possibility of the educative effect of sin. . . . Sixthly, Hawthorne repudiated the chief exponents of total depravity, the Puritans, calling their system 'sinister' to both mind and heart. . . . Lastly, Hawthorne's lifelong faithfulness to the ideals of the Jacksonian Democrats reinforces the idea that he was temperamentally incapable of believing in total depravity or the absoluteness of evil."

1957-9   Major, Minor Wallace. "Thomas Morton and His New English Canaan." Ph.D., Univ. of Colorado at Boulder. iv, 330 leaves.

Abstract in DA, vol. 18 (5), p. 1788: "Since the original text of the New English Canaan is hard to obtain and harder to read, a modernized, annotated edition is included with this study." The study includes a biography of Morton, highlighting his activities in Massachusetts and England between 1624 and 1647.

1958-1   Bass, William Ward. "Platonic Influences on Seventeenth-Century English Puritan Theology, as Expressed in the Thinking of John Owen, Richard Baxter, and John Howe." Ph.D., Univ. of Southern California. xii, 307 leaves.

"Introduction": "This study is designed to investigate the influence of Platonic philosophy and theology upon a segment of seventeenth-century English Puritan thought. The segment consists of the views of three of the leading thinkers of this time, place and association--John Owen, Richard Baxter, and John Howe. The central effort is an attempt to determine the extent and direction of Platonic influence upon each of these men. To do this adequately, the central problem is divided: (1) The immediate sources of their possible knowledge of and influence by Platonic thought must be considered. (2) The central viewpoint of each of the three men must be considered to help determine what place Platonism held in their thinking, if any" (p. vi). Contents: "Introduction"; Part I. "The Major Historical Developments Relevant to Puritan Platonism": I. "The Revival of Platonism," II. "The Cambridge Platonists," III. "The Historical Development of Puritanism," and IV. "The Formulation of Puritanism";

and Part II. "The Influence of Platonism on Puritan Theology": V. "The Scholastic Theology of John Owen," VI. "The Mediating Theology of Richard Baxter," VII. "The Cambridge Theology of John Howe," and VIII. "Summary, Conclusions, and Recommendations."

1958-2   Battis, Emery John. "Troublers in Israel: The Antinomian Controversy in the Massachusetts Bay Colony, 1636-1638." Ph.D., Columbia Univ. 2 vols. (xi, 594 leaves).

Abstract in DA, vol. 19 (2), p. 306. Revision published as Saints and Sectaries: Anne Hutchinson and the Antinomian Controversy in the Massachusetts Bay Colony. -- Chapel Hill : Published for the Institute of Early American History and Culture by the Univ. of North Carolina Press, 1962. -- xv, 379 p. "Preface" (1962 ed.): The work "offers an account of a specific religious movement and its leader and of the circumstances which gave rise to that movement" (p. vii). Contents: I. "Prologue: 'A Masterpiece of Woman's Wit,'" II. "Father and Husband," III. "Master Cotton and God's Free Grace," IV. "'A Faire and Easie Way to Heaven,'" V. "'Thine Eyes Shall See Thy Teachers,'" VI. "New England's Zion," VII. "'A Prophetesse Raised Up by God,'" VIII. "'Divers Jealousies,'" IX. "John Wheelwright," X. "'The Jarring Sound of Rattling Drums,'" XI. "'Behold the Bed That Is Solomon's,'" XII. "'Assembly of the Churches,'" XIII. "Winterset," XIV. "'Dux Foemina Facti,'" XV. "After Hagar and Ishmael," XVI. "'Withdraw Yourself as a Leper,'" XVII. "'Vile Sectaries,'" and XVIII. "Epilogue: Zion Preserved." Appendices: I. "Statistical Tables on the Hutchinson Movement," II. "Personnel in the Core Group," III. "Personnel in the Support Group," IV. "Personnel in the Peripheral Group," V. "Adult Male Population of Boston Circa 1637," VI. "Composition of the General Courts of May and November, 1637," and VII. "A Diagnosis of Mrs. Hutchinson's Behavior in Terms of Menopausal Symptoms."

1958-3   Evans, Eifion. "The Inspiration and Interpretation of Scripture in the Thought of Richard Baxter," Ph.D., Univ. of London (New College) (U.K.). a-b ["Abstract"], ii, 416 leaves.

"Abstract": "The object of this study is to determine Baxter's doctrine of Scripture, its nature, the principles and means of its interpretation. In order to attempt an evaluation of Baxter's contribution in this field, it has been necessary to survey the Reformed and Puritan conceptions regarding Scripture, and thus to point out the sources upon which Baxter drew, and the distinguishing features of his system" (p. a). Contents: "Introduction"; Part I. "A Historical and Contemporary Survey of the Doctrine of Scripture": I. "The Exact Standard" and II. "The Guide to Godliness"; Part II. "The Inspiration of Scripture": III. "The Book of God," IV. "The Work of the Spirit," and V. "The Rule of Faith"; Part III. "The Interpretation of Scripture": VI. "The Understanding of the Revelation" and VII. "The Proclamation of the Message"; and "Conclusion." Relevant appendix: II. "Bibliographical Notes on Some Seventeenth-Century Commentaries."

1958-4   Fink, Jerome Sanford. "The Purposes of the American Colonial Colleges." Ed.D., Stanford Univ. 224 leaves.

Abstract in DA, vol. 18 (4), p. 1328: "Despite the sparse population and frontier conditions of colonial America, nine colleges emerged between 1636 and 1776. ... The colonial colleges came into being as liberal arts colleges not as theological seminaries despite the assertions made by some writers. ... The colleges, to be sure, educated prospective ministers, but they also prepared future lawyers, teachers, physicians, and businessmen all from the same common intellectual source."

1958-5   Foster, Margery Somers. "Economic History of Harvard College in the Puritan Period (1636 to 1712)." Ph.D., Harvard Univ. (Radcliffe College). xxi, 469 leaves.

Revision published as "Out of Smalle Beginnings . . . ": An Economic History of Harvard College in the Puritan Period (1636 to 1712). -- Cambridge, Mass. : Belknap Press of Harvard Univ. Press, 1962. -- 243 p. Contents (1962 ed.): I. "The General Setting," II. "Harvard College Financial Records in the Seventeenth Century," III. "Economic Values in Puritan New England," IV. "Income from Students," V. "Government Aid," VI. "Income from Gifts, from Endowment, and Summary of All Income," VII. "Analysis of Disbursements," VIII. "Assets," and IX. "Overview." Appendices: A. "List of Presidents, Treasurers and Stewards," B. "Scholarships," and C. "Stewards' Accounts."

1958-6   Grabo, Norman Stanley. "Edward Taylor's Christographia Sermons: Edited from the Manuscript, with a Discussion of Their Relationship to His Sacramental Meditations." Ph.D., Univ. of California at Los Angeles.

Revision published as Christographia: New Haven: Yale Univ. Press, 1962. -- xlviii, 507 p. Edition of Taylor's sermons delivered between 1701 and 1703, each with a corresponding poetic meditation. Contents (1962 ed.): "Introduction," "Note of the Text," and "The Sermons." Appendices: "Taylor's Marginal Notes" and "Explanatory Notes."

1958-7   Johnson, Louis Richard. "American Preaching in the Seventeenth Century." Th.D., Northern Baptist Theological Seminary. ix, 217 leaves.

"Summary": "By far the most productive of preaching were the New England colonies where there was a galaxy of great preachers. The most outstanding were John Cotton, Richard Mather, John Eliot, John Davenport, Roger Williams, John Clarke, Henry Dunster, Increase Mather, and Cotton Mather. Other worthy men, not so prominent, include John Wilson, Thomas Hooker, Thomas Shepard, John Norton, Charles Chauncey [sic], and Michael Wigglesworth" (p. 208). Contents: I. "European Backgrounds of Seventeenth-Century Preaching": I. "The Reformation on the Continent" and II. "Seventeenth-Century England"; II. "Seventeenth-Century America": I. "Opening Up the New World," II. "Spain in America," and III. "The English in America"; III. "Seventeenth-Century

American Preachers"; IV. "Seventeenth-Century American Preaching":   I.
"Seventeenth-Century Preaching was Learned Preaching," II.
"Seventeenth-Century Preaching was Influential Preaching," III.
"Seventeenth-Century Preaching was Greatly Supplemented by Teaching,"
IV. "Seventeenth-Century Preaching was Associated with Statesmanship,"
V. "Seventeenth-Century Preaching was Biblical Preaching," VI.
"Seventeenth-Century Preaching was Homiletical Preaching," VII.
"Seventeenth-Century Preaching was Theological Preaching," VIII.
"Seventeenth-Century Preaching was Lengthy Preaching," IX.
"Seventeenth-Century Preaching was Plain-Spoken on Public and Social
Issues," and X. "Seventeenth-Century Preaching Waned in Effectiveness
as the Century Drew to a Close"; and "Summary."

1958-8   Manierre, William Reid, III. "Cotton Mather and the Plain
     Style." Ph.D., Univ. of Michigan. 292 leaves.

     Abstract in DA, vol. 19 (8), p. 2092: "Three closely related
purposes govern this study of the style of Cotton Mather's Magnalia
Christi Americana. The first two of these are to describe Mather's
style and to distinguish between it and that of other New England
writers of the seventeenth century. The third is to trace what is
distinctive in Mather's style to its ultimate source in the Puritan
'world picture'--to those intellectual and emotional currents which
define New England Puritanism. The method is descriptive and
comparative, characterized by frequent movements from matters stylistic
to matters more purely intellectual."

1958-9   Noble, Dorothy Louise. "Life of Francis Nicholson." Ph.D.,
     Columbia Univ. 2 vols. (vi, 816 leaves).

     Abstract in DA, vol. 19 (2), p. 348: "This biography of Francis
Nicholson presents him as a builder of the British Empire during the
years when the imperial policies of the Stuarts were being reoriented
under the leadership of William of Orange, Marlborough, and Parliament.
It attempts to prove that as a governmental advisor Nicholson
influenced the development of these policies and that as a governmental
official he implemented them with much success. . . . The introduction
and opening chapters of this study present a summary of policies and
problems, an account of the life of Nicholson, [and] a description of
his service in the Dominion of New England. . . . Membership in the
garrison at Tangier was followed by promotion and assignment to the
Dominion of New England in 1686. In 1688 he became lieutenant governor
there and represented [Sir Edmund] Andros in New York until he was
driven out by [Jacob] Leisler in 1689."

1958-10   Pellman, Hubert Ray. "Thomas Hooker: A Study in Puritan
     Ideals." Ph.D., Univ. of Pennsylvania. xxx, 246 leaves.

     Abstract in DA, vol. 18 (6), p. 2129: "Thomas Hooker's importance
for the student of early New England Puritanism is established by the
estimates of his contemporaries as well as by historians and scholars
from his day to the present. In many respects a paragon of Puritanism
in its pristine state, he was of sufficiently creative temper to differ

significantly from John Cotton, Governor Winthrop, and others who represent rigid Puritan orthodoxy. . . . Hooker was greatly concerned with the intricacies of the conversion process. . . . Hooker's otherworldliness did not exclude the secular. . . . Hooker was not democratic in the modern sense. . . . Hooker's literary theory, based on his theology, emphasized communication as the only worthy good."

1958-11   Phillips, James McJunkin. "Betweeen Conscience and the Law: The Ethics of Richard Baxter (1615-1691)." Ph.D., Princeton Univ. x, 371 leaves.

Abstract in DA, vol. 19 (12), p. 3390: "Although there has been a revival of interest in many phases of the life and work of Richard Baxter, English Puritan pastor and theologian, little attention has been paid to his ethics, an aspect of his thought for which he was justly famous in his own day. In an age which sought to reconcile the ideals of social stability and scientific progress, Baxter wanted to make the new dimensions of the moral categories of his time amenable to the traditional categories of Christian ethics."

1958-12   Portz, John Taylor. "Cotton Mather and Rationalism." Ph.D., Harvard Univ. 337 leaves.

"Preface": "My purpose was to offer a general estimate of one aspect of Mather's thought, rather than to shed new light on special problems. I have subordinated all else to a central discussion of rationalism and Enthusiasm. . . . My estimate of Mather's character . . . may seem waspish and harsh . . . ; for myself I can only see Mather as a man about whom there was very little that was attractive, and very much that was repellent. It would have gone against the grain to interpret his character in any other way" (n.p.). Contents: I. "The Cult of Reason," II. "Cotton Mather's Secular Philosophy," III. "The Limits of Reason," IV. "Reason in Practical Affairs: Toleration and Unity," and V. "The Turn to Enthusiasm."

1958-13   Roberts, William Iredell, III. "The Fur Trade of New England in the Seventeenth Century." Ph.D., Univ. of Pennsylvania. liii, 237 leaves.

Abstract in DA, vol. 19 (1), p. 126: "Fur was among the first of New England's products to attract the attention of English merchants and speculators. . . . The establishment of permanent settlements in New England was essential to the success of the fur trade because English promoters failed to comprehend the sophisticated Indian tastes in trade goods and the true financial requirements of the fur trade. . . . In the decade following King Philip's War the fur trade ceased to be significant in the New England economy."

1958-14   Stoeckel, Aletha Lucille. "Politics and Administration in the American Colonial Colleges." Ph.D., Univ. of Illinois at Urbana-Champaign. iv, 172 leaves.

Abstract in <u>DA</u>, vol. 19 (10), p. 2595: "The colonial college was not a unifying force in American intellectual life: it was regional in outlook and denominational in background. . . . The colonial college was easily reproduced: its organization was simple, its teaching staff small, its purpose limited. . . . This study traces the development of the colonial college from its beginnings in 1636 to the American Revolution."

1958-15   Taylor, John Golden.   "Hawthorne's Transmutations of Puritanism." Ph.D., Univ. of Utah. vi, 284 leaves.

Abstract in <u>DA</u>, vol. 19 (10), p. 2605: "It is the problem of the present study to determine in specific detail the nature of Hawthorne's artistic use of Puritan history and thought. I have limited the scope of this study to a consideration of only those sketches and stories by Hawthorne that deal centrally with New England Puritanism largely within the seventeenth century. . . . I give detailed consideration to the major literary works. My procedure is to identify the main elements of history and art in each of the tales considered and to summarize and draw conclusions on the relationships and divergencies that exist between historic Puritanism and Hawthorne's ostensible representations of Puritanism. . . . [As] an artist, Hawthorne quite freely and legitimately transmuted New England Puritanism, historically and philosophically, to meet his preconceived artistic designs. . . . Hawthorne approves some aspects of Puritanism and repudiated others. . . . Hawthorne's ambivalence toward Puritanism is based on the conflict between his filiopietistic attachment to Puritanism . . . and his enlightened nineteenth-century, democratic tolerance." A considerably condensed version of the diss. was published as <u>Hawthorne's Ambivalence Toward Puritanism</u>. -- Logan : Utah State Univ. Press, 1965, -- 69 p. -- (Utah State Univ. Monograph Ser. ; vol. 12, no. 1).

1959-1   Blawie, James Louis. "Fundamental Concepts in Considering Home Rule for New England Towns and Cities." Ph.D., Boston Univ. (Graduate School). 591 leaves.

Abstract in <u>DA</u>, vol. 20 (7), p. 2819: "This dissertation is basically a study of the nature of the state-local constitutional relationship and division of power in the various New England states, past, present and prospective. The problem with which it is concerned is the definition of the constitutional and legal status of the New England municipality in general, and the New England town in particular. The principal medium used to explore this relationship is the New England political or social myth-like concept of local independence. . . . This concept is traced from its historical origins in the independent actions of the independent New England towns. . . . The primary purpose is to examine the varying theories, rules of interpretation, and political and jurisprudential theories which continued assertion of the concept engendered. . . . The thesis is that this tradition of local independence . . . remains a fact of present day practical significance in New England."

1959-2   Bohi, Mary Janette. "Nathaniel Ward, Pastor Ingeniosus, 1580?-1652." Ph.D., Univ. of Illinois at Urbana-Champaign. xi, 372 leaves.

Abstract in DA, vol. 20 (5), p. 1751: "As one studies the life of Nathaniel Ward he becomes aware that he is meeting a Puritan of extraordinary ability and accomplishment. . . . He made significant contributions without pioneering, and what at first seems an innovation turns out to be a very natural manifestation of all that made up his life. It was so with his famous book, The Simple Cobler of Aggawam in America. . . . Ward deserves a biography not because he was a great man but because he is an example of many individuals whose contributions have been forgotten in our attempt to capture the celebrities of history."

1959-3   Carroll, Warren Hasty. "John Adams, Puritan Revolutionist: A Study of His Part in Making the American Revolution, 1764-1776." Ph.D., Columbia Univ. 3, v, 449 leaves.

Abstract in DA, vol. 20 (7), p. 2767: "The hypothesis is advanced that John Adams was primarily motivated in his support of the American Revolutionary movement by his admiration of the Puritan revolutionaries of the previous century and their concept of a special mission and destiny for America. As proof of this hypothesis evidence is presented indicating the persistence of the Puritan political tradition in eighteenth-century New England and Puritan influences in John Adams's own writings."

1959-4   Dietel, William Moore. "Puritanism vs. Anglicanism: A Study of Theological Controversy in Elizabethan England." Ph.D., Yale Univ. v, 345 leaves.

"Summary" (at beginning of diss.): "It has been assumed [by earlier studies] that Puritanism and Anglicanism during the reign of Elizabeth at least, did not differ over theological principals [sic], and therefore Puritanism has been defined and explained with little reference to its theological foundations. This dissertation is an effort to prove that Puritans and Anglicans did not hold common theological presuppositions, and, therefore, that any accurate definition of Puritanism must seriously consider the theological assumptions and doctrines of the two groups" (n.p.). Contents: I. "Elizabethan Puritanism and Its Interpreters," II. "Theological Controversy: [Peter] Baro and [Laurence] Chaderton, Cambridge, 1581," III. "The Development of Theological Differences Before 1581," IV. "Contemporary Theological Debate, 1581-1595," V. "The Puritan Doctrine of Authority," VI. "The Puritan Doctrine of God," VII. "The Puritan Doctrine of Man," and "Conclusion."

1959-5   Everson, Don Marvin. "The Puritan Theology of John Owen." Th.D., Southern Baptist Theological Seminary. xvi, 381 leaves.

Discusses in detail various aspects of the religious views of John Owen (1616-83). Contents: I. "Introduction," II. "The Doctrine of

God," III. "The Doctrine of Redemption," IV. "Salvation," and V. "The Church."

1959-6   Hook, Harold Phillip. "The Doctrine of the Kingdom in Covenant Premillennialism." Th.D., Dallas Theological Seminary. ix, 252 leaves.

"Summary": "Covenant Premillennialism was determined to be the combination of covenant theology with the belief that Christ will return before His literal earthly rule for one thousand years" (pp. 235-36). Contents: I. "Introduction and Defense of Terms," II. "The Resurgence of Premillennialism in Theological Thought" (including that of Increase Mather), III. "The Theological Approach to the Kingdom Idea in Covenant Premillennialism," IV. "The Old Testament Doctrine of the Kingdom According to Covenant Premillennialism," V. "The Kingdom Idea as Presented in the Gospel and Acts," VI. "The Kingdom Idea in Covenantal Ecclesiology," VII. "The Tribulation and the Return of Christ in Covenant Premillennialism," VIII. "The Doctrine of the Millennial Kingdom as It Is Presented by Covenant Premillennialism," and IX. "Summary and Conclusion."

1959-7   Maitland, David Johnson. "Three Puritan Attitudes toward Learning: An Examination of the Puritan Controversies over a Learned Ministry, 1640-1660, and the Consequences of This Struggle for Puritan Concern about the Reformation of Learning." Ph.D., Columbia Univ. iv, 279 leaves.

Abstract in DA, vol. 20 (2), p. 591: "While historians have made a variety of conflicting judgements regarding Puritan attitudes toward learning, it may be said with certainty of the English Puritans of the period 1640-1660 that they were supporters of learning. .... It is necessary both to distinguish between the forms of learning and to demonstrate what the 'parties' within Puritanism thought about the ends which learning should have served." The three "parties" are termed the "Conservatives," "Moderates," and the "Sectarians."

1959-8   Palmer, William R. "The Whaling Port of Sag Harbor." Ph.D., Columbia Univ. v, 327 leaves.

Abstract in DA, vol. 20 (2), p. 655: "Sag Harbor, New York, was one of America's oldest and most important whaling ports. This was natural because organized whaling began a few miles from the port and the eastern end of Long Island in 1644. For the next seventy years Long Island farmers made a tidy profit from shore whaling during the winter months." Sag Harbor began its history under the jurisdiction of New Haven Colony. The first chapter of the diss. is relevant.

1959-9   Quartermain, Peter Allan. "Nathaniel Hawthorne and Puritanism: A Study of Puritan Influences on Nineteenth-Century New England Literature." Ph.D., Univ. of Nottingham (U.K.). 396 leaves.

Published under same title in positive microfiche ed. (11 cards of typescript): East Ardsley, England : Micro Methods, Ltd., 1964. "Introduction": "Hawthorne's revolt . . . was primarily against historic Puritanism, against the narrow bigotry, the didacticism, the persecution, the intense seriousness, the lack of artistic perception, the lack of sympathy. He accepted, almost without reservation, certain tenets of the Puritan doctrine and theology, such as the innate sinfulness of man, the destructiveness of sin, the educational value of sin, the worthlessness of earthly vanities, the futility of ambition" (p. 18). Contents: "Introduction"; 1. "The Attitude of Puritanism"; Section One: "Hawthorne as Puritan": 2. "The Problem of Isolation," 3. "'Men's Infirmities and Evil Dispositions': The Concept of Sin," and 4. "The Progress of the Soul"; and Section Two: "The Puritan as Artist": 5. "The Symbolic Outlook," 6. "The Use of Symbol," and 7. "The Failure of Symbol"; and "By Way of Conclusion."

1959-10   Root, Robert Walter. "The Religious Ideas of Some Major Early Writers of America." Ph.D., Syracuse Univ. vii, 989 leaves.

Abstract in DA, vol. 20 (11), p. 4378: "This study was undertaken to relate to each other the religions of the chief early American writers, to discover the main streams of religious thought, and thus to improve our understanding of American literature and culture. . . . Their work was examined to learn whether they believed in God as terrible judge or merciful father; in man as inherently sinful or good; in salvation through faith or works; in God's transcendence or immanence; and other selected questions. . . . The Puritans established a theocratic religious pattern in American life on lines of orthodox Christianity--Pauline, Augustinian, or Calvinistic. Revolting against this were the first sectarians, Roger Williams, whose faith demanded freedom of conscience, and Anne Hutchinson, who believed God spoke to her mystically." Later New England writers discussed are Jonathan Edwards, John Adams, and Timothy Dwight.

1959-11   Rutman, Darrett Bruce. "A Militant New World, 1607-1640: American's First Generation: Its Martial Spirit, Its Tradition of Arms, Its Military Organization, Its Wars." Ph.D., Univ. of Virginia. 2 vols. (ix, 824 leaves).

Abstract in DA, vol. 20 (4), p. 1346:   Published by photoreproduction under same title: New York : Arno Press, 1979. -- ix, 824 p. -- (The American Military Experience). Contents: "Some Notes on the Notes," I. "Spirit and Substance," II. "The Militant Parent," III. "Bold New Venture," IV. "'The Quiet Primness of a Corpse,'" V. "'Blood Will Be the Seed of the Plantation,'" VI. "'The Struggling Plantations,'" VII. "Profit minded Puritans," VIII. and IX. "'The Soldiers of Christ,'" X. "Holy War," and XI. "A Militant New World." Appendices: A. "Powhatan's Indian Plantation," B. "Excerpted Entries from the Records of the Massachusetts Bay Colony Relative to the Formation and Shipment of a Military Company to Salem in the Spring of 1629," and C. "The Plymouth Military Code of 1658."

1959-12   Troutman, William Fife, Jr.   "Respecting the Establishment
    of Religion in Colonial America."   Ph.D., Duke Univ.   viii, 586
    leaves.

    Abstract in DA, vol. 20 (9), p. 3811:   "Congregationalists in
Puritan New England . . . insisted that religion and moral truths were
mediated by God through the Scriptures only to His elected saints in
the 'gathered church.'"   Diss. also treats of the views, regarding
established Christian churches, of the Anglicans; of the Baptists, who
"followed the lead of Roger Williams in emphasizing an acute dichotomy
between the church and state"; of John Wise, who, "in the early
eighteenth century, adapted the doctrines of the European rationalists
to New England Congregationalism"; and of the colonial Presbyterians
and Quakers.

1959-13   Van de Wetering, John Edward.   "Thomas Prince: Puritan
    Polemicist."   Ph.D., Univ. of Washington.   411 leaves.

    Abstract in DA, vol. 20 (1), p. 282: "Thomas Prince, co-pastor of
the Old South Church in Boston, spent forty years working as a
polemicist for the reestablishment of traditional Puritan leadership
and influence in New England society.   Puritan leadership had been
weakened with the advent of secular political control in Massachusetts
under the royal charter of 1691, and the growing secular spirit in the
community. . . .   Prince devoted his career to the reassertion of
Puritan influence in New England society by pietistic appeals for
conversion, and periodic insistence on the singular character of the
New England covenant society."

1959-14   Vassar, Rena Lee.   "Elementary and Latin Grammar School
    Education in the American Colonies, 1607-1700."   Ph.D., Univ. of
    California at Berkeley.   viii, 331 leaves.

    Relevant chapters: "Introduction," I. "Schools and Student Life
in England, 1550-1700"; Part I. "The Founding of Schools in America,
1607-1700":   II. "The New England Colonies to 1660"; Part II. "A
Maturing Society, 1660-1700": V. "Educational Developments in the New
England Colonies, 1660-1700"; Part III. "School Men of the Seventeenth
Century" and IX. "Conclusion: School Life in Early America."   Other
chapters deal with areas outside New England.

1959-15   Wilcox, William George.   "New England Covenant Theology:
    Its English Precursors and Early American Exponents."   Ph.D.,
    Duke Univ.   372 leaves.

    Abstract in DA, vol. 20 (10), p. 4195: "New England Covenant
Theology, as presented in the work of William Perkins, John Preston,
William Ames, John Cotton, Thomas Hooker, and Peter Bulkeley, was a
type of seventeenth-century Reformed Theology as conditioned by English
life and thought.   Although Cotton, Hooker, and Bulkeley immigrated to
the New World, while the others remained in the Old, there was a
general doctrinal similarity among them. . . .   Based on Biblical
exegesis, covenant theology attempted to make the inscrutable will of

God more understandable, to erect an orderly world view, and to form the framework for the life of man. . . . The church covenant proved to be the crucial doctrine and the focal point of controversy in New England."

1960-1   Dollar, George William. "The Life and Works of the Reverend Samuel Willard (1640-1707)." Ph.D., Boston Univ. (Graduate School). viii, 207 leaves.

Abstract in DA, vol. 21 (3), p. 603: "Reverend Samuel Willard stands as a representative figure of the colonial transition at the end of the seventeenth century, orthodox himself but broadly tolerant of those within his fellowship who were not. He was alert to the spiritual declension of his generation but, perhaps unconsciously, sowed the seeds of New England Liberalism. . . . In the midst of this ministry he produced one of the outstanding works of colonial Puritanism, The Body of Divinity."

1960-2   Hiten, Stephen Stegmann. "The Historical Background of the Election Sermon and a Rhetorical Analysis of Five Sermons Delivered in Massachusetts between 1754 and 1775." Ph.D., Univ. of Michigan. iv, 286 leaves.

Abstract in DA, vol. 20 (12), p. 4754: "Election sermons were delivered annually at the opening of the Massachusetts legislative year and immediately preceding the election of the Governor's Council. The custom apparently began in 1634 and was observed every year . . . until 1884. . . . This study investigated Massachussetts election sermons from two points of view. The first dealt with the origin and development of the sermons; the training, social status, and political interests of the preachers; the nature of the election day activities and ceremonies in Boston; and the type of audiences which normally attended election sermons." The other point of view is rhetorical and concerns a later period. Appendices: A. "Libraries Holding Election Sermons" and B. "Massachusetts Election Sermons."

1960-3   Jordan, Winthrop Donaldson. "White over Black: The Attitudes of the American Colonists Toward the Negro, to 1784." Ph.D., Brown Univ. iv, 378 leaves.

Abstract in DA, vol. 23 (5), p. 1672: Revision published as White over Black: American Attitudes Toward the Negro, 1550-1812. -- Chapel Hill : Published for the Institute of Early American History and Culture by the Univ. of North Carolina Press, 1968. -- xx, 651 p. Reprinted: Baltimore : Penguin Books, 1969. -- xx, 651 p. Also reprinted: New York : W. W. Norton, 1977. -- xx, 651 p. -- (Norton Library). "Preface" (1968 ed.): "This study attempts to answer a simple question: What were the attitudes of white men toward Negroes during the first two centuries of European and African settlement in what became the United States of America?" (p. vii). Relevant chapters: Part One. "Genesis 1550-1700": 1. "First Impressions: Initial English Confrontation with Africans" and 2. "Unthinking Decision: Enslavement of Negroes in America to 1700" (including 6. "Enslavement: New

England"); and Part Two. "Provincial Decades 1700-1755": III. "Anxious Oppressors: Freedom and Control in a Slave Society," IV. "Fruits of Passion: The Dynamics of Interracial Sex," V. "The Souls of Men: The Negro's Spiritual Nature," and VI. "The Bodies of Men: The Negro's Physical Nature." Cf. Jordan's The White Man's Burden: Historical Origins of Racism in the United States. -- New York : Oxford Univ. Press, 1974. -- xvi, 229 p.

1960-4   Kinloch, Hector Gilchrist Lusk MacTaggart. "Anglican Clergy in Connecticut, 1701-1785." Ph.D., Yale Univ. iv. 278 leaves.

"Abstract": "A study of the ministerial careers of [forty-five Anglican missionary clergy] together with some consideration of the influence of forty-seven other Church of England leaders closely associated with them, reveals the creation and molding of an essentially American religious denomination within the framework of disintegrating New England Calvinism" (p. 11). Relevant chapters: "Introduction," I. "Historical Background," II. "The Anglican Clergy in Connecticut, 1701-1785," III. "Analysis," IV. "The Yale Anglicans," and "Conclusion." Chapter V and VI deal with the latter part of the period.

1960-5   Kraus, Joe Walker. "Book Collections of Five Colonial College Libraries: A Subject Analysis." Ph.D., Univ. of Illinois at Urbana-Champaign. vi, 306 leaves.

Abstract in DA, vol. 20 (12), p. 4666: "This historical study of the libraries of five colleges established during the colonial period . . . is . . . concerned with the availability of books and the nature of the book collections. . . . It seeks to answer the following questions: What books were available in the colonial colleges? What were the predominant subjects in the book collections? and, What use was made of the books? The sources are . . . printed catalogs and . . . published lists of the principal donations of books to Harvard . . . [and] Yale."

1960-6   Larson, Robert Nelson. "The Governor's Council in New England." Ph.D., Boston Univ. (Graduate School). v, 248 leaves.

Abstract in DA, vol. 21 (4), p. 947: "This dissertation presents the thesis that the council [in Maine, New Hampshire, and Massachusetts] is an anachronism in modern state government. . . . The council, originating in the boards of directors of the early English trading companies which sent out the colonists to North America, served in colonial times as the upper house of legislature, as a judicial court, and as an advisory council to the governor in the administration of the colony. The councillors, originally called 'assistants,' and usually appointed by the Crown or by the governor, were drawn from the upper classes and exercised a markedly conservative influence in colonial government."

1960-7   Le, Van-Diem. "Puritan Idealism and the Transcendental
    Movement." Ph.D., Univ. of Minnesota. 205 leaves.

    Abstract in DA, vol. 21 (7), p. 1929: "This dissertation attempts
to validate a remark often made by historians . . . that New England
Puritanism . . . contained a vigorous strain of Renaissance Platonism.
By analyzing the sermons and writings of a few New England Puritans in
the first and second chapters, the author shows to what degree these
men participated in the Renaissance Platonism which preceded the modern
age of reason and became part of the rationalism of eighteenth- and
nineteenth-century New England. . . . In the next three chapters the
author shows how the Transcendentalism of the nineteenth-century is not
so discrepant in nature from Puritanism, but that the two are related
by sharing . . . in the Platonic trend. . . . The thesis concludes
with a study of Emerson and Hawthorne."

1960-8   Murphy, Geraldine Joanne. "Massachusetts Bay Colony: The
    Role of Government in Education." Ph.D., Harvard Univ.
    (Radcliffe College). ii, 417 leaves.

    "Introduction": "The 1647 Law [passed by the General Court]
obliged towns of certain sizes to 'keep' the kinds of schools that a
few towns had been maintaining for a decade . . . [but] the 1647 Law
did not succeed for forty-five years. . . . In 1692, the Law was
clarified, amended, and enforced by the Provincial government. . . .
From 1692 until the end of the seventeenth century and beyond, every
town subject to the terms of the Law complied with its requirements"
(p. 1). "At the close of the seventeenth century, the intent of the
Law . . . was 'shamefully betrayed.' The Provincial government had
been able to force only a 'faithful' practice of terms of the Law. It
was not able to stem or reverse the decline of Latin grammar
instruction. The central government wrote the Law and the courts
enforced it, but the towns translated it into practice and informed its
observance with a new intent. . . . This thesis attempts only to show
how the town-sponsored, town-supported, 'public' school for all studies
emerged from a practical reconciliation of the demands of the Law with
the desires and needs of the towns" (p. 3). Contents: "Introduction,"
"Glossary," i. "'The Smale Beginings': 1635-1642," II. "From Education
to Schooling: 1642-1647," III. "'A Further Order': 1647-1660," IV.
"'A Necessary Law Shamefully Neglected': 1660-1671," V. "Subversive
Compliance: 1672-1692," VI. "Model for a Town School: 1672-1692,"
VII. "'Constantly Provided for a Schoolmaster': 1692-1700," and VIII.
"A New Learning." Appendix consists of texts of laws relating to
education and some information on the population of various towns.

1960-9   Oedel, Howard Tredennick. "Portsmouth, New Hampshire: The
    Role of the Provincial Capital in the Development of the Colony
    (1700-1775)." Ph.D., Boston Univ. (Graduate School). 3 vols.
    (xxvi, 967 leaves).

    Abstract in DA, vol. 21 (5), p. 1169: "Throughout the colonial
period the town of Portsmouth directed the life and spirit of New
Hampshire. Not only was Portsmouth the major center of population, but
it controlled the political and economic activities of the colony. As

the provincial capital, Portsmouth also set the standards for the social and cultural patterns of life in New Hampshire. . . . It has been the intention of this writer to develop a 'portrait' of eighteenth-century Portsmouth in all its aspects: political, economic, social, religious, and cultural."

1960-10   Oki, Hideo. "Ethics in Seventeenth-Century English Puritanism: A Study of the Protestant Contribution to the Formation of Modern Democracy." Th.D., Union Theological Seminary in the City of New York. viii, 439 leaves.

Abstract in DA, vol. 21 (10), p. 3176: "How did the change take place from the Lutheran idea of religious 'personality' to the modern democratic man's self-consciousness in terms of 'Human Right'? How did the change occur from 'Status Society' to 'Contract Society'? How did a religious deepening of self in Protestantism become relevant to modern society? Above all, how did the shift take place from the mediaeval cosmo-ontological idea of Natural Law to the modern individual-personal idea of Natural Right? Fundamentally, what is the ethical meaning of Protestantism in relation to the formation of the modern world? These questions, stated in the Introduction, are answered by clarifying the ethics in 17th Century English Puritanism. This is a study done from the standpoint of the history of Christian ethics." Contents: "Introduction," I. "Theological Background of Puritan Ethics--Covenant Theology," II. "Puritan Casuistry, or Puritan Ethics before the Revolution," and III. "Revolutionary Puritan Ethics during the Civil War--History and Ethics."

1960-11   Shepherd, Emma Louise. "The Metaphysical Conceit in the Poetry of Edward Taylor (1644?-1729)." Ph.D., Univ. of North Carolina at Chapel Hill. iii, 214 leaves.

Abstract in DA, vol. 21 (7), p. 1942: "The purposes of this dissertation are to define the metaphysical conceit, to study Edward Taylor--an early American poet believed to have used the conceit--to show that he did use it, and to evaluate the way in which his conceits contribute to the unity of his poems. . . . Chapter I contains a survey of definitions of 'metaphysical conceit' from earliest English criticism to the present. . . . Chapter II is a general study of Taylor. . . . Chapter III describes conceits in Gods Determinations. . . . Chapter IV discusses the manner in which Taylor's conceits unify his poems. . . . Chapter V presents general evaluations of his poetry and of his role as a metaphysical poet."

1961-1   Buntin, Arthur Roy. "The Indian in American Literature, 1680-1760." Ph.D., Univ. of Washington. ix, 685 leaves.

Abstract in DA, vol. 21 (12), p. 3757: "To describe the emotions and patterns of experience communicated in literature born of this great Indian adventure is the goal of this study. Its purpose, also, is to demonstrate what works were available at a given point in time, and to suggest that captivity narratives, historical and travel narratives, sermons and essays, verse, and printed Indian treaties may have helped shape or confirm the thoughts of literate colonists about their Indian neighbors." Contents: I. "Indian Mancatchers and Masters," II. "The Indians of Historical Memory," III. "The Contemporary Indian," and IV. "The Indian Speaks."

1961-2   Bushman, Richard Lyman. "Government and Society in Connecticut, 1690-1760." Ph.D., Harvard Univ. xi, 431 leaves.

Revision published as From Puritan to Yankee: Character and Social Order in Connecticut, 1690-1765 with a foreword by Oscar Handlin. -- Cambridge, Mass. : Harvard Univ. Press, 1967. -- xiv, 343 p. -- (Publication of the Center for the Study of Liberty in America, Harvard Univ.). Reprinted: New York : W. W. Norton, 1970. -- ix, 343 p. -- (Norton Library). "Preface" (1970 ed.): "My thesis is that law and authority embodied in governing institutions gave way under the impact first of economic ambitions and later of the religious impulses of the Great Awakening. Restraint of ambition was a vulnerable spot among the interlocking institutions and beliefs that contained men through most of the seventeenth century, for Puritan preachers could not clearly distinguish laudable industry from reprehensible worldliness. As . . . merchants and farmers felt free to pursue wealth with an avidity dangerously close to avarice, the energies released exerted irresistible pressure against traditional bounds" (pp. iv-v). Contents: I. "Government and Society, 1690-1700," II. "Land, 1680-1740," III. "Money, 1710-1750," and IV. "Churches, to 1760."

1961-3   Chalker, William Houston. "Calvin and Some Seventeenth-Century English Calvinists--A Comparison of Their Thought Through an Examination of Their Doctrines of the Knowledge of God, Faith, and Assurance." Ph.D., Duke Univ. viii, 312 leaves.

Abstract in DA, vol. 22 (12), p. 4421: "In this dissertation the theological writings of Calvin and certain English Calvinists are examined for the purpose of discovering . . . differences. The English Calvinists included in the study are William Perkins, William Ames, Thomas Shepard, Elisha Coles, and John Howe. . . . The specific doctrines found to be crucial for this purpose are the doctrines of faith, the doctrine of the knowledge of God, the doctrine of knowledge of the self, and the doctrine of the assurance of salvation."

1961-4   Connors, Donald Francis. "Enchanted Wilderness: A Commentary on Thomas Morton's New English Canaan." Ph.D., Columbia Univ. 193 leaves.

Abstract in DA, vol. 22 (2), p. 562. Revision published as Thomas Morton. -- New York : Twayne Publishers, 1969. -- (Twayne's United States Authors Ser. ; 146). "Preface" (1969 ed.): The work intends "to evaluate Morton's place among the authors of seventeenth-century New England and to measure his influence upon American writers of more recent times. To this end, the information presented in the New English Canaan is compared with statements made by William Bradford, John Smith, William Wood, and other early reporters; his intentions as a writer are examined; the ideas, language, and form of his book are considered; and the legend of the May Lord in nineteenth- and twentieth-century American literature is explored" (p. 9). Contents: "Chronology," 1. "Morton of Merry Mount," 2. "An Abstract of New England," 3. "The Children of the Forest," 4. "Land of Milk and Honey," 5. "Revels of New Canaan," 6. "The Kingdom of the Separatists," and 7. "The Legend of the May Lord."

1961-5   Crichton, Robert Jocelyn. "Roger Williams on Church and State." Ed.D., Columbia Univ. (Teachers College). v, 200   leaves.

Chapter I: "The following study is presented in terms of the considerations which [Williams] himself expressed in writing. It attempts to show that Roger Williams had a prior concern for New Testament religion and God's right over His own kingdom. It also reveals that he had little interest in philosophies of government for the nations of this world. Such a view departs radically from the popularly accepted image of Roger Williams, but his own unadorned statement fully support the position taken. . . . The focus in this essay is on the long-continuing problem of church and state in America. We propose to examine the views of Roger Williams on the church and the relation of the state to its life in an effort to determine his motivating principles" (p. 2). Contents: I. "The Williams Legend in the Twentieth Century," II. "Roger Williams on the Church," III. "The Relation Between the Civil Order and God's Church," and IV. "Modernist, or Seventeenth-Century Sectary?" Relevant appendices: A: "Williams and [John] Cotton on The Parable of the Tares" and C. "Calvin and [Theodore] Beza on Church and State, quoted by Williams."

1961-6   Denholm, Andrew Thomas. "Thomas Hooker: Puritan Teacher, 1586-1647." Ph.D., Hartford Seminary Foundation. viii, 532 leaves.

Abstract in DA, vol. 25 (9), p. 5235: "The Preface defines the thesis as an attempt to describe and analyze the life, work and writing of Thomas Hooker, Puritan preacher, author and statesman.   . . . Part I is biographical. . . . Part II discusses Hooker's writings. . . The unusually large appendix consists mainly of documents not readily available: Hooker's personal note-book, Miscellanea; The Wolcott Diary; The Thanksgiving Sermon; The Twenty Propositions; and Inventory of the estates of Hooker and [Samuel] Stone."

1961-7   Ericson, Jon Meyer. "John Wise: Colonial Conservative." Ph.D., Stanford Univ. vi, 219 leaves.

Abstract in DA, vol. 22 (5), p. 1593: "This study focuses on the two polemics of John Wise: The Churches Quarrel Espoused (1713) and A Vindication of the Government of New-England Churches (1717). Attention centers on three questions: What were the issues that gave rise to Wise's polemics? What was the nature of Wise's 'democratic' philosophy? And, for what purpose were his writings published in 1772? . . . Lest Wise be misinterpreted, it should be understood that he spoke in his time as one who expressed a conservative view."

1961-8   Forbes, Henry Ashton Crosby. "A Study of Religious Melancholy and Seventeenth-Century English Puritan Dissent." Ph.D., Harvard Univ. xi, 422 leaves.

"Abstract" (at end of diss.): Diss. intends "to re-examine the much debated problems of the Puritan temperament and the Puritan conscience in the light of contemporary seventeenth-century views both of the Puritans and of their contemporaries. Far from being an illusion of the modern mind, the idea of the Puritan as melancholy and fearful was well established from the beginning." Diss. also intends "to investigate the total output of a representative number of Puritan writers for what they have said about melancholy" (p. 1). These writers are William Perkins, Richard Greenham, Richard Baxter, John Owen, John Howe, John Bunyan, and Philip Doddridge. Contents: I. "Religious Melancholy and the Seventeenth-Century English Puritan Dissent: A Preliminary View," II. "The Evolution of English Melancholy and Its Significance for Puritanism," III. "The Puritan Background: The Heritage of Intensity, Affliction and Consolation," IV. "The Carnal and the Precise: An Important Psychological Cleavage in Seventeenth-Century England," V. "Puritan Afflictions and the Theology of Calvinism: 'Doctrinals,'" VI. "Puritan Afflictions and the Cure of Souls: 'Practicals,'" and VII. "Religious Melancholy and Seventeenth-Century Puritan Dissent: A Concluding Estimate."

1961-9   Langdon, George Dorland, Jr. "New Plymouth: A History of the Old Colony." Ph.D., Yale Univ. 361 leaves.

Revision published as Pilgrim Colony: A History of New Plymouth, 1620-1691. -- New Haven : Yale Univ. Press, 1966. -- xi, 257 p. -- (Yale Publications in American Studies). "Preface" (1966 ed.): "I have tried only to tell the story of the colony as best I was able. . . . While I have no major thesis to propound, the more familiar I have become with seventeenth-century Plymouth . . . , one consideration stands out beyond all others. In the opportunities to hold office, to vote in elections, to gain church membership, and to obtain land, the people who settled before 1640 seem . . . to have enjoyed marked advantages over their successors" (p. x). Contents: 1. "'The Very Root and Rise of the Same,'" 2. "'A Place of Habitation,'" 3. "'This Way is No More,'" 4. "'Liberty to Go and Seek Out a Convenient Place or Two or Three,'" 5. "'A Due Course for the Suppressing of Error,'" 6. "'Signes of Gods Despleasure,'" 7. "'A Civil Body Politic,'" 8. "'The Same Spirit of Truth,'" 9. "'A Pious Orthadox Minnestry,'" 10. "'The Right Worship of God,'" 11. "'Much Imployment About the Things of This Life,'" 12. "'Mischiefe from the Indians,'" 13. "'The Greate Indian Warre,'" 14. "'Our Old and Indeed Imperfect Grant,'" 15. "'A New Booke of Lawes,'" 16. "'The State of Things as Now They Stand With Us,'" 17. "'This Poor Colony,'" and 18. "'The Government Over Us is Yet in the Hands of Saints.'"

1961-10   Middlekauff, Robert Lawrence. "Ancients and Axioms: A History of Secondary Education in Eighteenth-Century New England." Ph.D., Yale Univ. 323 leaves.

Revision published as <u>Ancients</u> <u>and</u> <u>Axioms:</u> <u>Secondary</u> <u>Education</u> <u>in</u>
<u>Eighteenth-Century</u> <u>New</u> <u>England.</u> -- New Haven : Yale Univ. Press, 1963.
-- viii, 218 p. -- (Yale Historical Publications. Miscellany ; 77).
Reprinted: New York : Arno Press, 1971. -- viii, 218 p. -- (American
Education: Its Men, Ideas, and Institutions. Ser. II). Relevant
chapters: "Introduction: Establishing an Educational Tradition"; Part
I. "The Persistence of the Puritan Tradition in Education, 1700-1783":
1. "School and Community: The Village Pattern," 2. "Variations in the
Village Pattern," 3. "City Schools: Boston and Newport," 4. "The
Development of Private Education," 5. "The Curriculum: Latin, Greek,
Rhetoric, and Logic," 6. "The Curriculum: Arithmetic, Mathematics,
Navigation, Surveying, Geography, and Astronomy," and 7. "The
Curriculum: The 'Female Branches' of Learning"; and Part III. "The
Fruit of the Tradition, 1700-1800": 12. "Masters and Scholars" and 13.
"Education as an Intellectual Force." Part II deals with the period
1784-1800. The diss. was awarded the George Washington Egleston Prize
at Yale.

1961-11   Swanhart, Harry Gerald. "Solomon Stoddard, Puritan
        Patriarch: A Biography." Ph.D., Boston Univ. (Graduate School).
        v, 392 leaves.

Abstract in <u>DA</u>, vol. 22 (4), p. 1280: "This dissertation presents
the biography of Solomon Stoddard, 1643-1729, and evaluates his
contribution to New England Puritanism. ... The form is narrative,
and the underlying thesis is to sustain or refute Puritan hagiography,
which has either ignored Stoddard or condemned him as a malefactor.
... Stoddard's life spanned a significant and critical period in the
development of Puritanism in New England. In a long and distinguished
career as minister of the Northampton Church and ecclesiastical
spokesman for the Connecticut Valley, he exerted an influence over
ecclesiastical affairs surpassed by none of his contemporaries."

1961-12   Wack, Thomas George. "The Imagery of Edward Taylor's
        <u>Preparatory</u> <u>Meditations.</u>" Ph.D., Univ. of Notre Dame. vii, 306
        leaves.

Abstract in <u>DA</u>, vol. 22 (7), p. 2389: "A classification of the
images in a representative number of Meditations reveals that Taylor
drew heavily on the learning of his day, especially the Biblical
learning. ... Gifted with a rich poetic imagination and an obvious
love for the art of language, he drew fully on every aspect of his
experience to construct a baroque poetry of devotion out of humble
materials."

1962-1   Bloom, Jeanne Gould. "Sir Edmund Andros: A Study in
        Seventeenth-Century Administration." Ph.D., Yale Univ. 359
        leaves.

Abstract in <u>DAI</u>, vol. 30 (6), sec. A, p. 2455: "The dissertation
deals with the career as an American colonial governor of Sir Edmund
Andros (1637-1714), one of first professional colonial servants of the
Crown in English history. ... The Introduction presents a brief

biography of Andros. . . . Part Two presents Andros' most important governorship--the Dominion of New England (1686-1689) which is studied in sections dealing with the removal of the Massachusetts charter, the organization and expansion of the Dominion, problems of religion and of the economy, and finally the overthrow of the Dominion, and the establishment of a new government to replace it. . . . The Conclusion attempts an evaluation of Sir Edmund Andros as a colonial governor."

1962-2   Botond-Blazek, Joseph Bela. "An Inquiry into the Legal Enforcement of Sexual Morality in 17th-Century Massachusetts." Ph.D., Univ. of California at Los Angeles. xi, 273 leaves.

"Preface": "This thesis will treat the efforts of the Puritans to enforce sexual morality by legal means. I will discuss their conception of the good life and the manner in which they put it into practice" (p. i). Contents: "Introduction," I. "The Puritan Goal," II. "Marriage and Its Problems," III. "Problems Outside of Marriage," IV. "Attitudes Toward Punishment," and "Conclusion." Appendices: A. "Federal Theology" and B. "Case Histories." Appendix B comprises 119 pages and 191 "case histories."

1962-3   Fender, Stephen A.   "Edward Taylor and the Sources of American Puritan Wit." Ph.D., Victoria Univ. of Manchester (U.K.). 268 leaves.

"Preface": "Taylor's collection of Puritan commentaries on the Bible" and "the influence of the English metaphysicals and the renaissance and sixteenth-century rhetorical techniques are suggested as the sources of Taylor's wit, and are also given as the reason why witty writing was more common among the American Puritans than has been supposed" (p. 3). Contents: One: "The Public Poems," Two: "The Nature of Christ," Three: "The Lord's Supper," Four: "Salvation, Sin and Meditation," Five: "Imagery and Rhetoric," and Six: "The American Puritan Context." Appendices: A: "The Organization of the Poetical Works," B: "The Covenant of Grace and the Doctrine of God's Attributes," and C: "The Tree of Life--Examples of Its Use in Anglo-Catholic and Puritan Poetry."

1962-4   Forston, Raymon Charles. "The Threat of Elizabethan Puritanism to the Existing Social Order." Ph.D., Indiana Univ. 237 leaves.

Abstract in DA, vol. 23 (6), p. 2239: "There was a Puritan ideology sufficiently distinct and formulated to permit its followers to be distinguished from Anglicans. Elizabethan Puritanism was incompatible with the prevailing social order. A belief in the unique and ostensibly complete authority of the Bible, a use of historical examples which added to their arguments and their contemptuous classification of traditions incompatible with God's word as historical relics, and a rationalism into which they were forced because of the practical inadequacy of the Bible and history, were the means by which the Puritans justified their utopia. . . . The Puritan utopia was a holy community in which all activities must be arranged and conducted

for the glory of God. ... The importance of the Puritan doctrines in
the history of social thought is that they were predicated on a new
authority or a new sanction for the determination of the good life.
That new authority, no longer in the state, lay ultimately in the
individual conscience."

1962-5   Johnson, Warren Bertram. "The Content of American Colonial
     Newspapers Relative to International Affairs, 1704-1763." Ph.D.,
     Univ. of Washington. viii, 485 leaves.

     Abstract in DA, vol. 23 (8), p. 2891: "Historical literature has
given very little recognition to the fact that the colonists of America
in the early eighteenth century were well-informed on international
relations. Much of this information came to them through their
newspapers, dating from 1704 when the first newspaper appeared in
Boston. . . . The introduction characterized the newspapers themselves
and presents them in their urban eighteenth-century American setting.
. . . Chapter I traces international affairs in the newspapers to the
Treaty of Seville in 1729. Chapter II deals with the period of the
1730's."

1962-6   Morris, Rita Mary L. "An Examination of Some Factors Related
     to the Rise and Decline of Geography as a Field of Study at
     Harvard, 1638-1948." Ed.D., Harvard Univ. viii, 282 leaves.

     "Abstract": "This thesis should be useful as a general
contribution to the history of geography as a field of collegiate study
and should make a contribution to the knowledge of the origin, course
of development and decline of geography as a field of study at Harvard
in particular. ... The specific aims of this thesis are (1) to trace
the rise and decline of geography as a field of study at Harvard and
(2) to determine the factors which may have some relation to the rise
and decline of the subject" (p. ii). Relevant chapters: I.
"Background of the Study," II. "An Over-view of the Development of
Collegiate Geography," III. "A History of Geography as a Part of the
Curriculum at Harvard from 1638 to 1948," IV. "Extra-Institutional
Factors Related to the Rise and Decline of Geography as a Field of
Study at Harvard," V. "Intra-Institutional Factors Which Influenced the
Development of Geography as a Field of Study at Harvard, Part I, 1638-
1869," and VIII. "Conclusion." Chapter VI deals with later events.
Appendix A: "Statistics Relevant to Collegiate Geography."

1962-7   Terris, Walter Franklin.   "The Right to Speak:
     Massachusetts, 1628-1685." Ph.D., Northwestern Univ. 359 leaves.

     Abstract in DA, vol. 23 (12), p. 4668: "The study seeks to define
the freedom of speech as it was viewed and practiced by the
Massachusetts Bay Colony during the seventeenth century. It was
discovered that the colony was aware of and used the common law
principles that were applicable to 'undesirable' religious dissent.
Nowhere did they punish more than the common law held punishable. The
use of the common laws against blasphemy, heresy, and the disruption of
church order . . . declined over the period. The most frequently used

principles were those of seditious libel and contempt. . . . The study concluded that the colony was never more restrictive of the freedom of speech than the common law of England."

1962-8   White, Ann Stanford. "The Poetry of Anne Bradstreet." Ph.D., Univ. of California at Los Angeles. vi, 285 leaves.

"Introduction": "I have attempted to look at Anne Bradstreet's work in relation to four areas. In the first place, her work is influenced by the ideas current in the time in which she lived. The ideas she reflects are most often generally current among all educated people of the late sixteenth and seventeenth centuries: Ideas of the nature of men and the universe and of politics that differ markedly from those that we hold today. Second, beyond those generally circulating ideas are the Puritan concepts with which she was thoroughly indoctrinated, concepts which gave her writing a certain structure and tension. . . . Third are the forms and genres which Anne Bradstreet inherited from the Elizabethans and which were being developed by the seventeenth-century writers, forms to which Anne Bradstreet was particularly sensitive. And finally, her work may be seen as the product of an intelligent, witty, and independent mind" (pp. 1-2). Contents: I. "Introduction"; Part I. "The Ipswich Poems": II. "The Ipswich Period," III. "The Elegies: The Great Past," IV. "The Poems to Her Husband: Puritan Love," V. "The Quaternions: Utility in Art," VI. "The Four Monarchies," VII. "Old England and New: The Political Climate," and VIII. "The Tenth Muse"; and Part II. "The Andover Poems": "Introduction: The Move to Andover," IX. "The Poems of Affliction and Thanksgiving," X. "The Spiritual Combat," XI. "Meditation and Contemplation," and XII. "The Weary Pilgrim."

1962-9   Whitney, Herbert Allen. "The Narragansett Region Concentrations of Population, 1635-1885." Ph.D., Univ. of Michigan. viii, 166 leaves.

Abstract in DA, vol. 23 (1), p. 199: "The study considers the problems of how the major concentration of population of the lands bordering Narragansett Bay in southern New England developed first at the entrance of the bay, how after a century and a half the location of the major center came to shift from the entrance to the head of the bay, and how the concentration of population at the head of the bay came to have an ever-increasing proportion of the total population of the region."

1962-10   Wiley, Elizabeth. "Sources of Imagery in the Poetry of Edward Taylor." Ph.D., Univ. of Pittsburgh. iii, 242 leaves.

Abstract in DA, vol. 23 (6), p. 2122: "The first two chapters introduce the subject and offer such biographical facts about Taylor as are pertinent to the study. Chapter three, the largest one, included my own classification of Taylor's images. . . . Chapter four introduces his known reading. . . . Chapter five investigates possible sources of imagery in the Bible and the other books that formed Taylor's library. . . . Chapter six reviews the criticism of Taylor, primarily as it is related to this imagery. It also states my thesis: that Taylor's reading of the Bible and other doctrinal and devotional prose works influenced his imagery and to some extent tied his works to the mainstream of poetry written by his contemporaries, who were also influenced by the same body of literature."

1962-11   Wilson, John Frederick. "Studies in Puritan Millenarianism under the Early Stuarts." Th.D., Union Theological Seminary in the City of New York. 296 leaves.

Expanded version of the diss.'s first "study," "The Sermons Preached before Commons to 1645," published as Pulpit in Parliament: Puritanism During the English Civil Wars, 1640-1648. -- Princeton : Princeton Univ. Press, 1969. -- x, 289 p. "Preface" (1969 ed.): The book is a study of "a series of sermons originally preached by invitation to members of the Long Parliament at periodic fasts and occasional thanksgivings" (p. viii). Contents: I. "Preaching in the Long Parliament," II. "The Genesis of the Commons Preaching Program," III. "The Program of Humiliations and Thanksgivings," IV. "Parliamentary Sponsors and Puritan Preachers," V. "The Plain Style and Puritan Texts," VI. "Puritan Piety for a Covenanted Nation," and VII. "Puritanism in the Time of Civil War." In the diss.'s second "study," "Millenarianism and Puritanism," the most relevant chapter is VI. "John Cotton and the Foreground in England and New England."

1962-12   Woodfield, Arthur John. "The Theory and Practice of Poetry among Puritans and Early Dissenters from Gosson to Watts." Ph.D., Univ. of London (King's College) (U.K.). 614 leaves.

"Abstract" (at beginning of diss.): "This thesis purports to give a critical and descriptive account of the poetry of English Puritanism. . . . Because the diatribes of Gosson and Stubbes have been largely responsible for the fiction of Puritan hostility to poetry, these writers are examined and shown to be neither Puritan nor fundamentally unreasonable. . . . The thesis briefly outlines traditional Christian teachings about literature and points out that Calvin's were such as to elevate esteem for sacred poetry. . . . The next section of the thesis examines the influence of Du Bartas in the first half of the seventeenth century, the theory and practice of certain Puritan approved poets, . . . and the Humanism of Puritan leaders of the period. . . . The final chapter deals with the post-Restoration period. . . . The conclusion estimates the character and importance of Puritan poetry" (n.p.). Contents: I. "'The Odious Name of Puritan,'" II. "The 'Puritanism' of Stephen Gosson and Philip Stubbes," III. "Reformed Religion and Poetry in the Later Sixteenth Century," IV. "[Guillaume] Du Bartas and Christian Humanism," V. "The First Four Decades of the Seventeenth Century," VI. "The Witty Poetry of Puritanism," VII. "Poets of Independency," VIII. "Pious Verse of the Second Half of the Seventeenth Century," IX. "The Revival of Incantation and Fervour," and X. "Conclusion."

1963-1   Ballowe, James C. "The Art and Criticism of Santayana's The Last Puritan. Ph.D., Univ. of Illinois at Urbana-Champaign. 219 leaves.

Abstract in DA, vol. 24 (1), p. 292: "This essay shows that George Santayana's novel The Last Puritan: A Memoir in the Form of a Novel serves as the crucible of his theories of fiction and as the dramatization for his cultural dialectic. . . . Each aspect of the novel is integrated toward the single purpose of dramatizing Santayana's concept of the ultimate puritan who is alien to a world his forebears have created. . . . The novel describes the incapacity of the atavistic puritan mind to cope with either of its twentieth-century precipitants, the American Will ('mechanical democracy') and the American Intellect ('genteel tradition')."

1963-2   Breward, Ian. "The Life and Theology of William Perkins, 1558-1602." Ph.D., Victoria Univ. of Manchester (U.K.). 326, lxxiii leaves.

Chapter 1: Diss. attempts "to relate particular aspects of his thought to the whole . . . [and to] see him in the continental perspective which both his sources and influence demand" (p. 5). "Conclusion": "Perkins was the first English theologian in the sixteenth century to be of more than local significance, as well as being the key figure in the systematization of 'puritan' thought and practice. . . . In New England his influence lasted until the end of the [seventeenth] century" (pp. 325-26). Contents: 1. "The Making of the Man," 2. "The Rule of Faith and Life," 3. "Not Lately Hatched at Home," 4. "The Reformed Catholike," 5. "In the Room of Christ," 6. "The Golden Chain," 7. "The Direction of Conscience," 8. "The Christian and His Calling," and 9. "Conclusion."

1963-3   Brightman, Anna. "Fabrics and Styles of Colonial Window Hangings as Revealed Through Boston and Salem, Massachusetts, Records, 1700-1760." Ph.D. Florida State Univ. viii, 219 leaves.

Abstract in DA, vol. 24 (1), p. 273: "As an aid to the student of colonial domestic and social life . . . , this research was undertaken to determine the nature of the fabrics and window treatments used in one area of the Massachusetts Bay Colony. Specifically, the purpose of the research was three fold: 1. To determine . . . the fabrics used. . . . 2. To determine to what extent window curtains and the specific fabrics were used; the frequency of occurrence; and their use in relation to economic level. 3. To assemble a written and photographic description of the fabrics and styles of window hangings, . . . and the degree of adherence to known English fashion of the time."

1963-4   Brodeur, David Dallin. "Geographic Consequences of the Location of Some New England Town Commons and Greens." Ph.D., Clark Univ. vii, 207 leaves.

Abstract in DA, vol. 24 (7), p. 2862: "The purpose of this study is to examine the function of the common and green as a centrally located open space in the urban and suburban landscape. The emphasis is primarily historical. . . . [Commons] and village greens originated in at least three different ways. The large majority stem from the original meeting house lot. Others originated as pieces of common grazing land, and a few, found chiefly in the Connecticut Valley, developed from broad survey highways. . . . The materials for this study were gathered from town records and town histories, as well as from site observations of forty-three commons, mostly in Massachusetts."

1963-5   Brumm, Ursula. "Die religiöse Typologie im amerikanischen Denken: Ihre Bedeutung für die amerikanische Literatur- und Geistes-geschichte." Dr. phil., Freie Univ. zu Berlin (West Germany).

Revision published under same title: Leiden : Brill, 1963. -- 195 p. -- (Studien zur amerikanischen Literatur und Geschichte ; 2). English translation by John Hooglund published as American Thought and Religious Typology. -- New Brunswick, N.J. : Rutgers Univ. Press, 1970. -- x, 265 p. Contents (1970 ed.): Part I. "Presuppositions": 1. "The Problem," 2. "Definitions," and 3. "Typology and Its Significance"; Part II. "The American Puritans: Their Forms of Thought and Their Way of Interpreting the World": 4. "Samuel and Cotton Mather," 5. "Edward Taylor's Meditations on the Lord's Supper," and 6. "Jonathan Edwards and Ralph Waldo Emerson"; and Part III. "The Heirs of the Puritans and Their Literary Works": 7. "Nathaniel Hawthorne," 8. "Herman Melville," and 9. "Christ and Adam as 'Figures' in American Literature."

1963-6   Cohen, Sheldon Samuel. "The Connecticut Colony Government and the Polity of the Congregational Churches, 1708-1760." Ph.D., New York Univ. vi, 300 leaves.

Abstract in DA, vol. 26 (3), p. 1611: "This dissertation is primarily an effort to study and to analyze the attempts of the Connecticut government to sustain its new ecclesiastical establishment through a large part of the eighteenth century. The first two chapters describe the background and the nature of this establishment. . . . Chapter III spans the years from 1710 to 1722. . . . Chapters IV and V survey the period from 1722 to 1740."

1963-7   Colacurcio, Michael Joseph, Jr. "The Progress of Piety: Hawthorne's Critique of the Puritan Spirit." Ph.D., Univ. of Illinois at Urbana-Champaign. v, 310 leaves.

Abstract in DA, vol. 24 (12), p. 5405: "I contend . . . that Hawthorne's best writing is seriously historical and that its most penetrating insights are into the 'distortions of the moral nature' which the Calvinism of the American Puritans produced. . . . Close analysis of Hawthorne's most frankly historical tales . . . discloses an ambivalent attitude towards the Puritans. . . . The conclusion, implied throughout, is that Hawthorne's moral vision was Christian but not Calvinist, and that his major fiction recreates and judges the moral vagaries of American Puritanism and of its progeny in America."

1963-8   Fritz, Robert Bradley. "The Seventeenth-Century Arts of New England: Their Role in Fine Arts Education." Ed.D., Columbia Univ. (Teachers College). iv, 119 leaves.

"Introduction": "The subject of this study is the potential role of the seventeenth-century arts of New England in Fine Arts education. . . . It is a study written primarily for the art educator. . . . Acquaintance with the artifacts of seventeenth-century New England immediately discloses their splendid qualities as works of art, their historical significance, and, related to these, their significance for us today" (p. 1). Contents: I. "Introduction," II. "Domestic Architecture," III. "The Decorative Arts," IV. "Silver," V. "The Meetinghouse," VI. "Community Planning," and VII. "Conclusions."

1963-9   Fulcher, John Rodney. "Puritan Piety in Early New England: A Study in Spiritual Regeneration from the Antinomian Controversy to the Cambridge Synod of 1648 in the Massachusetts Bay Colony." Ph.D., Princeton Univ. xviii, 311, xix leaves.

Abstract in DA, vol. 24 (7), p. 2998: "The dissertation attempts an analysis of the piety of the first generation in the Massachusetts Bay Colony, primarily during the decade bounded by the Antinomian controversy (1636-1638) and the Cambridge Synod (1646-1648), through a study of spiritual regeneration as understood by the leading Congregational divines [i.e., John Cotton, Thomas Hooker, Thomas Shepard]. The investigation sustains the argument presented in recent researches in Puritanism, reviewed in the introduction, that the dynamics of the movement must be accounted for in terms of its piety; moreover, this study seeks to demonstrate the centrality of conversion in the piety of early American Puritanism."

1963-10   Giles, Charles Burke. "Benjamin Colman: A Study of the Movement Toward Reasonable Religion in the 17th Century." Ph.D., Univ. of California at Los Angeles. xi, 248 leaves.

Abstract in DA, vol. 24 (12), p. 5356: "Benjamin Colman has long been considered an early exponent of the Enlightment in eighteenth-century Boston. Because his ministerial career reveals both English and American influences to a remarkable degree, he presents an ideal picture of the transition of religious thought from the dogmatic Puritanism to the broad principles of latitudinarianism. Those factors which shaped his religious philosophy are particularly interesting and provide the focal point for this study. The Bath Sermons, . . . 1698-99, have provided the key to his basic religious philosophy."

1963-11   Jacobson, Alf Edgar. "The Congregational Clergy in Eighteenth-Century New England." Ph.D., Harvard Univ. iii, 538 leaves.

"Preface": "My aim in writing this thesis has been to present an analysis of the role and place of the Congregational clergy in the

colonial society of eighteenth-century New England" (p. ii). Contents:
1. "The Seventeenth-Century Ministry," 2. "The Ministry in the
Eighteenth Century," 3. and 4. "The Congregational Theory of the
Ministry," 5. "The Ministerial Role in Preaching," 6. "The Ministerial
Role in the Administration of the Sacraments," and 7. "The Ministry and
Church Discipline."

1963-12   Junkins, Donald Arthur. "An Analytical Study of Edward
      Taylor's Preparatory Meditations." Ph.D., Boston Univ.
      (Graduate School). 415 leaves.

      Abstract in DA, vol. 24 (5), p. 2013: "The purpose of this
dissertation is to substantiate Edward Taylor's Puritanism.   Its
methodology is a close analysis of four aspects of his Preparatory
Meditations: his poetic theory as it is revealed in the attitudes he
expresses within the poems toward the poems; his meticulous revisions
of the manuscript; his images; and the comparison of fourteen of his
Meditations with their corresponding sermons.   The conclusions
demonstrate that Taylor was not an Anglo-Catholic in disguise, not a
heretical Calvinist, and not a dichotomized Puritan . . . , but that
the nature of his Puritanism is mystical as well as theological. . . .
Chapter I discusses the private nature of Taylor's Meditations and
their lived relationship to the tradition of mystical devotions in
Renaissance Europe. . . .   Chapter II discusses Taylor's attitude
toward his poems. . . .   Chapter III discusses Taylor's Meditations as
acts of devotion. . . . Chapter IV discusses the mystical nature of
Taylor's images. . . .   Chapter V compares fourteen of Taylor's
Meditations with their corresponding sermons (Christographia) and
demonstrates the unified nature of Taylor's religious and aesthetic
life as a testimony of his Puritanism."

1963-13   Little, David. "The Logic of Order: An Examination of the
      Sources of Puritan-Anglican Controversy and of their Relation to
      Prevailing Legal Conceptions of Corporation in the Late 16th and
      17th Century in England." Ph.D., Harvard Univ. v, 328 leaves.

      Revision published with a preface by Robert N. Bellah as Religion,
Order, and Law: A Study in Pre-Revolutionary England. -- New York :
Harper & Row, 1969. -- v, 269 p. -- (Harper Torchbooks) (The Library of
Religion and Culture). Reprinted: Oxford : Basil Blackwell, 1970. --
v, 269 p.   "Conclusion" (1969 ed.):   "Weber made an abiding
contribution not only to the systematic study of society, but to the
investigation of religious phenomena as well. The key concept of order
elaborated here provides an important link in relating religious-moral
language to the issues of social organization. It is hoped that this
book has helped to emphasize Weber's true significance and to
supplement and revise his work fruitfully" (p. 225). Contents: Part
I. "Introduction": 1. "The Problem" and 2. "Religion, Order, and Law
and the Thought of Max Weber"; Part II. "Theology and Conflict of
Order": 3. "The New Order of John Calvin," 4. "The Elite of the New
Order: The Puritans," and 5. "The Old English Order and Its Anglican
Defenders"; Part III. "Law and the Tensions of Society": 6. "Sir
Edward Coke and the Conflict in Law and Order." Appendices
(bibliographical essays): A. "Representative Literature Critical of

The Protestant Ethic," B. "The Question of Economic Regulation in Pre-Revolutionary England," C. "The Social Implications of Humanist Thought," and D. "Some Problems in the Interpretation of Puritanism."

1963-14   McCandlish, George Edward. "Annotations for a New Edition with a Definitive Text of Cotton Mather's Magnalia Christi Americana (1702), Books I and II." Ph.D., Harvard Univ. 204 leaves.

"Introduction": "Neither Mather nor his agent in London had oversight of the printing of the Magnalia, or a chance to correct the proofs. When, in the autumn of 1702, Mather had his first glimpse of the handsome folio volume, five years had elapsed since he had recorded in his Diary his thanks to the Lord for assisting him to finish his church-history. . . . No one would suggest retaining this text unchanged; but where to make the changes? which errors may we ascribe to the printer? which changes subject the editor to the charge of tampering with Mather's text? We can accept his own list of errata, but this is by no means complete. . . . For the most part I have refrained from emending the 1702 text without a compelling reason for the change" (pp. 3-5). Contents: 1. "Introduction," 2. "Textual Emendations," 3. "Footnotes," and 4. "Endnotes."

1963-15   Mignon, Charles William, Jr. "The American Puritan and Private Qualities of Edward Taylor, the Poet." Ph.D., Univ. of Connecticut. iv, 292 leaves.

Abstract in DA, vol. 24 (11), 4679: "My purpose is to show that Taylor's poetry must be seen in its private instead of its public character before final critical judgment is made about his reputation as a poet. Questions raised about Taylor's poetry and the main answers have been based on the assumption that he wrote for public intelligibility. . . . [The] poetry was not, in fact, for public consideration or publication. . . . My argument is briefly this: that several aspects of Taylor's theology and poetic and not unorthodoxy may account for Taylor's wish that his heirs never publish his works."

1963-16   New, John Frederick Hamilton. "Anglican and Puritan: The Basis of Their Opposition Reconsidered." Ph.D., Univ. of Toronto (Canada).

Revision published as Anglican and Puritan: The Basis of Their Opposition, 1558-1640. -- Stanford : Standford Univ. Press ; London : A. & C. Black, 1964. -- 140 p. "Introduction" (1964 ed.): "Subtle doctrinal differences existed from the outset and became more and more apparent over the years. These differences amounted to alien 'universes of discourse,' to use philosophers' jargon, from which shifting conflicts emerged and re-emerged, and it is these dogmatic bases of opposition that invite clear attention" (p. 4). Contents: 1. "Man," 2. "The Church," 3. "Sacraments and Eschatology," 4. "Doctrine and Ethics," and "Conclusion."

1963-17   Parkander, Dorothy Josephine. "Rhetorical Theory and
     Practice: The Sermons of the English Puritans from 1570-1644."
     Ph.D., Univ. of Chicago. iii, 213 leaves.

     Contents: I. "The Scriptural Basis for Puritan Rhetorical
Theory," II. "Puritan Theories of Sermon Rhetoric," III. "The Practice
of Non-Sectarian Puritan Preachers--Preaching as Preaching: The Plain
Style," IV. "The Practice of Non-Sectarian Puritan Preachers--
Preaching as Oratory," and V. "The Emergence of the Typical Puritan
Sermon."

1963-18   Pettit, Norman.   "The Image of the Heart in Early
     Puritanism: The Emergence in England and America of the Concept
     of Preparation for Grace." Ph.D., Yale Univ. 268 leaves.

     Revision published as The Heart Prepared: Grace and Conversion
in Puritan Spiritual Life. -- New Haven : Yale Univ. Press, 1966. --
ix, 252 p. -- (Yale Publications in American Studies ; 11). "Preface"
(1966 ed.): "This study of the interior life deals with the
conversion experience. It is concerned with the emergence and
development of a theological notion: the concept for preparation for
grace. In orthodox Reformed theology of the sixteenth century no
provision had been made for the biblical demand to prepare the heart
for righteousness. . . . Yet in Puritan thought the image of the
'heart prepared' came to have momentous import. . . . Our purpose
here is to discover the extent to which this notion altered original
Reformed convictions, as well as the degree to which it influenced the
intellectual life of New England" (p. vii). Contents: 1.
"Preparation and the Problem of the Heart," 2. "Continental Reformed
Theologians," 3. "The English Preparationists," 4. "The American
Preparationists," 5. "Early Criticism and the Antinomian Controversy,"
6. "Later Criticism: To the Halfway Covenant and Beyond," and
"Epilogue."

1963-19   Robinson, Lewis Milton.   "A History of the Half-Way
     Covenant." Ph.D., Univ. of Illinois at Urbana-Champaign. iv,
     327 leaves.

     Abstract in DA, vol. 25 (1), p. 440: "An attempt has been made
in this study to show how the Half-Way Covenant system was closely
interwoven with such major problems as terms of admission to church
membership, to infant Baptism and to the Lord's Supper. These issues
were involved in the Antinomian controversy, the Cambridge Synod, the
Assembly of 1657 and the Synods of 1662 and 1679. They were the cause
of much concern on the part of the General Courts of the various
colonies. Controversies over these issues in the first churches of
Hartford and Boston caused major convulsions involving the entire
colonies. . . . This study sets forth Solomon Stoddard as one who
pushed the theory of continuity in Covenant theology to its logical
conclusion and also shifted the basic orientation of New England
theology."

1963-20   Sprunger, Keith LaVerne. "The Learned Doctor Ames." Ph.D.,
      Univ. of Illinois at Urbana-Champaign. viii, 326 leaves.

      Abstract in DA, vol. 24 (12), p. 5370. Revision published as The
Learned Doctor William Ames: Dutch Backgrounds of English and
American Puritanism. -- Urbana : Univ. of Illinois Press, 1972. -- xi,
289 p. "Preface" (1972 ed.): "The pages that follow tell the story
of William Ames (1576-1633), the 'learned doctor' of Puritanism. . . .
This study attempts to place Ames into the stream of continental
theology, but the larger emphasis is to place him into English and
American Puritanism, where his heart most was" (p. ix). Contents:
Part I. "Puritanism's Learned Doctor": I. "Puritanism and William
Ames, 1576-1610," II. "Exile in the Netherlands," III. "The Synod of
Dort," IV. "The University of Franeker," and V. "A Puritan 'of the
Rigidest Sort'"; Part II. "The Theology of Living to God": VI.
"Technometria: Prolegomena to Theology," VII. "The Marrow of Ames'
Theology," VIII. "Puritan Ethics," and IX. "The Church"; and Part III.
"Puritanism Abroad": X. "Militant Puritanism in the Netherlands" and
XI. "Doctor Ames of Famous Memory."

1963-21   Van Dyken, Seymour. "Samuel Willard, 1640-1707: Preacher
      of Orthodoxy in an Era of Change." Th.D., Princeton Theological
      Seminary. 455 leaves.

      Abstract in DA, vol. 24 (6), 2598. Revision published under same
title: Grand Rapids, Mich. : William B. Eerdmans, 1972. -- 224 p.
"Preface" (1972 ed.): "Although Samuel Willard has been acknowledged
by both his contemporaries and by historians as one of the most
important preachers among the second generation of New England
Puritans, one who summarized the theological thought of seventeenth-
century American Puritanism, no extended study has been published on
either his life or his thought. As one of the chief propagators and
defenders of this inherited orthodoxy in an era of social, economic,
political and religious change, in a distinct sense he epitomized the
New England mind, and kept alive the orthodoxy which with
modifications was to become more efflorescent in the next generation"
(p. 7). Contents: 1. "The Formative Years," 2. "The Emergence of a
Champion," 3. "Church and State: Under the First Charter," 4. "Church
and State: Without a Charter" 5. "Church and State: Under a New
Charter," 6. "Arminianism," 7. "Antinomianism," 8. "The Baptists," 9.
"The Quakers," and 10. "History and the Judgments of God."

1963-22   Vose, Godfrey Noel. "Profile of a Puritan: John Owen,
      1616-1683." Ph.D., Univ. of Iowa. 365 leaves.

      Abstract in DA, vol. 24 (6), 2599: "The study is an analysis of
certain aspects of the theology of John Owen, . . . and is designed to
direct attention towards a significant but neglected seventeenth-
century English theologian. It is also . . . a contribution to the
understanding of puritanism. . . . Underlying this study have been
two basic assumptions: first, that John Owen is relatively unknown in
two important fields of research--that of historical theology and that
of English puritanism; secondly, that his life and thought are of

sufficient intrinsic and historical value to warrant fresh consideration."

1964-1   Blackmon, Dora Mae Eldredge. "The Care of the Mentally Ill
     in America, 1604-1812, in the Thirteen Original Colonies."
     Ph.D., Univ. of Washington. iv, 218 leaves.

Abstract in DA, vol. 25 (12), p. 7216: "This is a descriptive study of the care and treatment of the mentally ill in the thirteen original colonies during the seventeenth and eighteenth centuries. . . . The first three chapters are devoted to the theories of the function of the mind, the theories of mental illness, and the treatment of insanity. Before mental illness could be treated as a disease, it was necessary to separate the soul from the mind, and to do away with the idea that mental illness was the result of sin. The etiology of sin was advanced by Roger Williams and Cotton Mather."

1964-2   Blackmon, Joab Livingston, Jr. "Judge Samuel Sewall, 1652-
     1730: A Biography." Ph.D., Univ. of Washington. iii, 325
     leaves.

Abstract in DA, vol. 25 (5), p. 2836: "This is a biography of Samuel Sewall of Boston, Massachusetts, who was an important figure in the life of the colony. . . . Sewall was a second-generation Puritan who believed implicitly in the mission of the faithful to establish a Bible Commonwealth in the New World. He sought to stave off the downfall of Puritanism; but the enlightened New Englander of the eighteenth century could not be a Puritan. Sewall stands as a connecting link between the extreme Puritan Theocracy of John Cotton, Richard Mather, and John Winthrop and the enlightened world of the late eighteenth century in which Benjamin Franklin flourished."

1964-3   Burstein, Frances Brownell. "The Picture of New England
     Puritanism Presented in the Fiction of Henry James." Ph.D.,
     Boston Univ. (Graduate School). iii, 578 leaves.

Abstract in DA, vol. 25 (5), p. 2977: "This dissertation is primarily an extended critical analysis of Henry James's presentation and use of New England Puritanism in his fiction. . . . The [second] four chapters offer a chronologically structured presentation and analysis of James's portrait of New England Puritanism in his fiction, from early simplified images through increasingly complex portraits culminating in The Ambassadors. Consideration is given to both his artistic use of Puritanism, and his personal interest in the Puritan mind."

1964-4   Carson, David Melville. "A History of the Reformed
     Presbyterian Church in America to 1871." Ph.D., Univ. of
     Pennsylvania. xxvi, 255 leaves.

Abstract in DA, vol. 25 (4), p. 2469: "The Reformed Presbyterian Church began its separate existence in Scotland about 1680. . . . Its

adherents did not join the Church of Scotland as established in 1688.
. . . The migration from Ulster about 1720 brought some 'Covenanters'
to America, the first of many later immigrants. . . .   The
dissertation is a study of this institution, untypical of the American
scene in its distinctive features--of the mechanisms by which it
sought to maintain itself and the way in which it was itself
affected." Relevant chapters: I. "Before the Beginnings," II. "The
Transplanting to the Colonies," and "Epilogue." Chapters III-XIII
concern a later period.

1964-5   Cauger, Richard Edward. "The Concept of the Puritan in
     American Literary Criticism, 1890-1932." Ph.D., Northwestern
     Univ. ii, 238 leaves.

     Abstract in DA, vol. 25 (11), p. 6618: "This dissertation
purports to examine the uses of the term 'Puritan' in American
literary criticism from 1890 to 1932, in order to arrive at an
understanding of the meaning of the term, its applicability in
literary and social criticism, and the reasons for its usefulness.
The term is shown to be a fruitful rhetorical device in the critical
discussion of events and ideas of this period. . . . The dissertation
is organized chronologically, with the years 1890-1932 broken into
four periods, each with a distinctive character and particular
critical use for 'Puritan.'" Among those critics discussed are H. L.
Mencken, Van Wyck Brooks, and Irving Babbitt.

1964-6   Chatfield, Donald F. "The Congregationalism of New England
     and Its Repercussions in England and Scotland, 1641-1662."
     Ph.D., Univ. of Edinburgh (U.K.). vii, 347 leaves.

     "Preface": "The intention of this essay is an examination of the
conflict and interaction between the Presbyterian and Congregational
church polities, as seen in the colonial and apologetic material
published concerning the 'New England way' between 1641 and 1662. No
attempt is made to describe the historical influence of one polity on
the development of the other, except by the way; the aim is rather to
present a systematic view of the arguments actually used by each side
in attack and defence. In the works under survey, the attack was
largely made by the Presbyterian divines, the defence by the New
Englanders; as a result, the emphasis is on the Congregational system
under Presbyterian criticism, rather than vice versa" (p. iii).
Contents: "Introduction," I. "The Bible," II. "The Church: (1) The
Conflict," III. "The Church: (2) The Issues," IV. "The Covenant," V.
"The Keys," VI. "The Oligarchy," and "Conclusion." Appendices: A.
"New England Covenant Practice," B. "Was the New England Way
'Democraticall'?" C. "Congregational Officers [i.e., pastor, teacher,
Ruling Elder, Deacon]," D. "New England Worship," and E.
"Chronological List of Chief Works."

1964-7   Erikson, Kai T. "Wayward Puritans: A Study in the Sociology
     of Deviance." Ph.D., Univ. of Chicago. 268 leaves.

     Revision published under same title: New York : Wiley, 1966. --

xv, 228 p. "Preface": (1966 ed.): "The purpose of the following study is to use the Puritan community as a setting in which to examine several ideas about deviant behavior" (p. vii); "deviant forms of behavior are often a valuable resource in society, providing a kind of scope and dimension which is necessary for all social life" (p. viii). Contents: 1. "On the Sociology of Deviance"; 2. "The Puritans of Massachusetts Bay"; 3. "The Shapes of the Devil": "The Antinomian Controversy," "The Quaker Invasion," and "The Witches of Salem Village"; 4. "Stabilities and Instabilities in the Puritan Crime Rates"; and 5. "Puritanism and Deviancy." Appendices provide seventeenth-century statistics on criminal convictions and population estimates for Essex County.

1964-8   Hall, David Drisko. "The Faithful Shepherd: The Puritan Ministry in Old and New England, 1570-1600." Ph.D., Yale Univ. 278 leaves.

   Revision published as The Faithful Shepherd: A History of the New England Ministry in the Seventeenth Century. -- Chapel Hill : Published for the Institute of Early American History and Culture by the Univ. of North Carolina Press, 1972. -- xvi, 301 p. Reprinted: New York : W. W. Norton, 1974. -- xvi, 301 p. -- (Norton Library). "Preface" (1974 ed.): The work is "a history of the orthodox, official ministry" (p. xii). Contents: 1. "A Ministry of the Word," 2. "England and Reformed: Puritan Doctrines of the Church and Ministry," 3. "The Faithful Shepherd," 4. "The First Generation," 5. "To the Cambridge Platform," 6. "Church and State," 7. "Shepherds in the Wilderness," 8. "The Second Generation," 9. "Beyond the Cambridge Platform," 10. "Declension Politics," 11. "Beyond Conversionism," and 12. "Puritan and Provincial."

1964-9 Hasler, Richard Albert. "Thomas Shepard: Pastor-Evangelist (1605-1649): A Study in the New England Puritan Ministry." Ph.D., Hartford Seminary Foundation. xviii, 326 leaves.

   Abstract in DA, vol. 25 (12), p. 7400: "As a contribution to the contemporary investigation of the ministry in its historical development, this dissertation concentrates upon the early New England Puritan ministry and more specifically focuses upon Thomas Shepard of Cambridge. Since the concept of the Puritan minister as an evangelist has not been examined to any significant extent in previous historical studies, it is important to note the prominence of evangelism in Shepard's view of the minister. . . . Part One is a biographical sketch of Shepard's early life in England and his later life in the New England Commonwealth. . . . Part Two is an analysis of Shepard's covenant ecclesiology. . . . Part Three . . . is an exposition of the evangelical task of the ministry. . . . In the Conclusion, Shepard's view of the minister is described in the term 'pastor-evangelist.'" Appendices: A. "Shepard's Ms. 'Advertisements to the Reader,' Defence of the Answer" and B. "The Plain Style."

1964-10   Hays, Garry D. "The Idea of Union in Eighteenth-Century Colonial America." Ph.D., Univ. of Kansas. viii, 459 leaves.

Abstract in DA, vol. 26 (2), p. 1003: "The purpose of this work
. . . is to study comprehensively the idea of union within the social,
cultural, and political context of the eighteenth century up to the
first Continental Congress. . . . A background chapter on the
seventeenth century reviews the New England Confederation and the
Dominion of New England. Chapter three discusses the relation of
selected aspects of culture to the idea of union prior to 1740."
Chapters V and VI are concerned with later events.

1964-11   Loubser, Johannes Jacobus. "Puritanism and Religious
    Liberty: Change in the Normative Order in Massachusetts, 1630-
    1850." Ph.D., Harvard Univ. v, 416 leaves.

"Introduction": "It is here contended that . . . there is a
highly significant and vital link between Puritanism and religious
liberty even though few Puritans--mainly of the 'left-wing'--were
champions of the cause. This study is designed to explore the nature
of this link by focusing on Puritans right of center to determine its
generality and to analyze the ways in which it influenced the
development of religious liberty in America, more particularly in
Massachusetts" (n.p.). Contents: I. "Introduction"; Part I. "The
Pattern of Religious Autonomy": II. "The Divine-Human Relation," III.
"The Individual and the Church," IV. "The Individual and Society," and
V. "The Church in Relation to Society and Other Churches"; Part II.
"The Development of Religious Liberty": VI. "Institutionalized
Individualism," VII. "Religious Freedom," VIII. "Public Neutrality,"
IX. "Volunteerism," and X. "Denominational Pluralism"; and XI.
"Summary Analysis."

1964-12   Ludwig, Allan Ira. "Carved Stone-Markers in New England:
    1650-1815." Ph.D., Yale Univ.

Revision published as Graven Images: New England Stonecarving
and Its Symbols, 1650-1815. -- Middletown, Conn. : Wesleyan Univ.
Press, 1966. -- xxxi, 428 p. Paperback ed.: Wesleyan Univ. Press,
1975. -- xxxi, 428 p. "Introduction" (1966 ed.): "The image of
Puritanism has been badly distorted by history. . . . If we are going
to understand the meaning of Puritan art, we must have some clear-cut
notion about Puritan belief. If we are going to try to understand why
Puritans cut grave images of their tombs but would not allow the same
imagery into their meetinghouses we will have to know something more
about Puritanism than the story of the lamentable witch hunts of 1692.
If we are going to comprehend why an iconophobic culture
enthusiastically embraced the imagery of icons in stone we will have
to understand what the Puritans thought of symbols and idolatry" (p.
3). Contents: "Introduction": I. "The Puritan Background" and II.
"The Language of Religious Symbolism"; I. "Puritan Religion": "The
Function of Symbolism in Normative Puritan Theology," II. "Puritan
Symbolism in Religion until 1800," III. "Puritan Theology, Symbolism,
and Imagery," IV. "Symbolic Mediacy and Immediacy in New England:
Religion and Art," V. "Symbolic Stonecarving: A Study in Realized
Eschatology," VI. "English Burial Rituals," and VII. "Burial Rituals
in New England"; II. "Iconography": I. "New England Funerary Art,"

II. "The Repertory of Symbols," and III. "Modalities of Meaning"; III.
"Sources and Definitions of the Major New England Styles":   I.
"English Stonecarving: 1550-1850," II. "Engraving, Woodcuts, and
Emblem Books," III. "The Origins of the Provincial Baroque Style in
Massachusetts: 1647-1735," IV. "The Growth of the Provincial Baroque
Style in Massachusetts: 1722-1815," V. "The Provincial Baroque Style
in Rhode Island: 1690-1815," VI. "The Provincial and Baroque Style in
Connecticut in the 18th Century," VII. "The Origins and Development of
the Neoclassical Style in New England: 1769-1815," VIII. "The Origins
and Development of the Ornamental Styles in New England: 1668-1815,"
and IX. "Summary"; and "Conclusions":   I. "Puritanism and Puritan
Art," II. "The Vernacular and the Cultivated Traditions in Art," and
III. "American Art and New England Stonecarving."   Cf. Ludwig's
preliminary study (unpublished typescript in Library of Congress):
The Graven Images of Early New England: 1653-1800. -- [s.l., s.n.],
1959. -- ii, 150 leaves.

1964-13   Mixon, Harold Dean.   "The Artillery Election Sermon in New
      England, 1672-1774."   Ph.D., Florida State Univ.   iii, 224
      leaves.

      Abstract in DA, vol. 25 (12), p. 7420:   "An investigation of 47
artillery election sermons was conducted in terms of the occasion, the
audience, the speakers, and the speeches. Objectives of the study
were to provide a survey of artillery election sermons in general, and
to assess the role of those sermons in the development of
revolutionary sentiment. . . .   The sermons were delivered on
artillery election day,   an occasion which brought together a
distinguished audience, usually including government officials,
prominent clergymen and members of the general public."

1964-14   Nicolaisen, Peter.   "Die Bildlichkeit in Edward Taylors
      Preparatory Meditations."   Dr. phil., Christian-Albrechts-Univ.
      Kiel (West Germany).

      Revision published as Die Bildlichkeit in der Dichtung Edward
Taylors. -- Neumünster : Karl Wachholtz Verlag, 1966. -- 179 p. --
(Kieler Beiträge zur Anglistik und Amerikanistik ; Bd. 4). English-
language "Summary" (1966 ed.):   Taylor's "imagery is no doubt the most
important aspect of his poetry. It is closely related to the poet's
aims and at the same time it is determined by the limitations imposed
on him by his historical and theological background. My paper uses
this interrelationship as a starting-point for a new investigation of
Taylor's poetry. As the interdependence in the 'Preparatory
Meditations," this collection of poems provides the main material for
my study" (p. 175). Contents: I. "Einleitung," II. "Die 'Preparatory
Meditations' und die Möglichkeit religiöser Dichtung," III. "Die Bibel
als Quelle der Bildlichkeit in den 'Preparatory Meditations,'" IV.
"Die Verwendungsart der Bildlichkeit in den 'Preparatory
Meditations,'" V. "Die typologische Bildlichkeit in den 'Preparatory
Meditations,'" VI. "Die Bildlichkeit in 'God's Determinations,'" VII.
"Die Bildlichkeit in den Gelegenheitsgedichten," and "Zusammenfassung
in englischer Sprache."

1964-15   Rowlette, Edith Jeannine Hensley. "The Works of Anne
    Bradstreet." Ph.D., Boston Univ. (Graduate School). xlvii, 541
    leaves.

    Abstract in DA, vol. 25 (8), p. 4707: "Although she was not a
great poet, she was a significant minor poet, and she deserves to be
remembered for the aesthetic quality of her work. . . . To establish
a reliable text of her works is the purpose of this edition. . . . To
establish this text all available copies of the 1650 and the 1678
editions have been compared, by machine."

1964-16   Silverman, Kenneth Eugene. "Colonial American Poetry: An
    Anthology." Columbia Univ. ix, 837 leaves.

    Abstract in DA, vol. 26 (1), p. 359. Revised ed. with editor's
introduction published as Colonial American Poetry. -- New York :
Hafner Publishing Co., 1968. -- xv, 449 p. Includes a section of
"Puritan Verse": "The Puritan Elegy," "Edward Taylor," and "Later New
England Verse." About thirty relevant poets are included.

1964-17   Steele, Ian Kenneth. "The Board of Trade in Colonial
    Administration, 1696-1720." Ph.D., Univ. of London (King's
    College) (U.K.).

    Revision published as Politics of Colonial Policy: The Board of
Trade in Colonial Administration, 1696-1720. -- Oxford : Clarendon
Press, 1968. -- xvi, 217 p. "Introduction" (1968 ed.): "The real
role of the Board of Trade varied with the value of the reports
submitted, and also with the influence of the members upon the
Sovereign, the Privy Council, and the chief ministers. To study its
role in the administration, the Board should be viewed as a changing
group of individuals rather than as a bureaucratic institution; its
influence on Whitehall and the colonies was related to its membership,
the composition of the ministry, and the tasks being undertaken" (p.
xiii). Contents: Part I. "King William's Board of Trade": I.
"Background and Founding," II. "1696-7, Exploring an Office and its
Limitations," III. "1697-1700, The War on Piracy," and IV. "1700-2,
Resumption of Chartered Governments"; and Part II. "Queen Anne's Board
of Trade": V. "1702-6, War and the Ministers," VI. "1707-10, A Board
of Whigs," VII. "1711-14, A Board of Tories," and VIII. "Transition
and Retrospect."

1964-18   Vaughan, Alden True. "New England Puritans and the American
    Indian, 1620-1675." Ph.D., Columbia Univ. ix, 476 leaves.

    Revision published as New England Frontier: Puritans and
Indians, 1620-1675. -- Boston : Little, Brown, 1965. -- xvii, 430 p.
Revised ed.: New York : W. W. Norton, 1979. -- lviii, 430 p.
"Preface": "This book attempts to reconstruct [a] portion of
seventeenth-century New England history--a story of the Puritan and
the American Indian. In part it is a narrative of the significant
contacts between the native and New Englanders; in part it is an

examination of Puritan ideals and institutions and how they adjusted
to the practical exigencies of the Indian frontier; and finally, to a
lesser extent, it is an attempt to gauge the impact of Puritan
colonization on native society" (p. v--1965 ed.; p. xlvii--1979 ed.).
Contents: "Introduction" (1979 ed. only), I. "Antecedents," II. "The
Indians of New England," III. Pilgrim Precedents, 1620-1630," IV. "The
Expansion of New England," V. "The Pequot War, 1637," VI. "Puritan
Policy: Confederation and the Indians, 1638-1675," VII. "Puritan
Policy: Laws and Litigation, 1620-1675," VIII. "Commercial Relations,
1620-1675," IX. "Early Missionary Activity, 1620-1650," X. "Missionary
Efforts: Years of Growth, 1650-1665," XI. "Missionary Efforts: Years
of Harvest, 1665-1675," and XII. "Epilogue and Conclusion." Published
versions include seven appendices.

1964-19   Watkins, Harold Keith. "The Ecclesiastical Contributions of
    Increase Mather to Late Seventeenth- and Early Eighteenth-Century
    Puritan Thought." Th.D., Pacific School of Religion. iv, 425
    leaves.

    Abstract in DA, vol. 25 (6), p. 3721: "Increase Mather (1639-
1723) was one of the most significant figures during this half century
of debate and change. For fifty-nine years he was teacher of the
Second Church in Boston, also serving during much of that time as
president of Harvard College. For four years he represented colonial
interests in London and was largely responsible for the new charter
granted to the Massachusetts Bay Colony in 1691. . . . Book One
describes the New England Way which the second generation inherited
from the first-generation founders. Book Two takes up the debates
surrounding the Half-Way Covenant Synod of 1662 while Book Three
continues the exploration of developments relating to the synod's
major theme--the nature of the church and the meaning of membership.
Book Four considers the relationship between congregations and between
church and state."

1965-1   Bercovitch, Sacvan. "New England Epic: A Literary Study of
    Cotton Mather's Magnalia Christi Americana." Ph.D., Claremont
    Graduate School. iii, 416 leaves.

    Abstract in DA, vol. 28 (10), sec. A, p. 4117: "This
dissertation is a study of Cotton Mather's Magnalia Christi Americana
as a major work of imaginative literature, an American epic expressive
of the culture which its author inherited, reacted upon, and
transmitted to his Puritan and anti-Puritan successors. . . . In
order to emphasize the imaginative unity of the Magnalia as the key to
Mather's life and thought, the study is organized thematically. In
substance, it deals with: the epic themes and structure of the
Magnalia, its concept of America, the symbolic design of its learned
allusions, its dominant metaphors, its stylistic interplay between
image and idea, and typological meanings behind its portrayal of the
New England venture. In the process of this explication, I try to
fill in Mather's historical and ideological background to the end
. . . of revealing the Magnalia as a twofold achievement: at once
representative of an age which by 1700 was irrevocably lost, and a
germinal, if primitive, symbolic work of art."

1965-2   Bertrand, Arthur Louis.   "The Religious Motive in the
     Development of Education in Colonial Western Massachusetts."
     Ph.D., Univ. of Connecticut. vi, 201 leaves.

     Abstract in DA, vol. 26 (9), p. 5203: "The religious zeal of the
Puritans was a dynamic force in the shaping of the social and
political life of the early New England settlers. . . . The writer
proposes the hypothesis that the influence of religion in educational
matters in colonial Western Massachusetts was less significant than is
generally believed, and that education quite early became dominated by
secular rather than religious purposes. . . . Springfield,
Northampton, and Westfield were three of the earliest and most
important of the newer towns along the Connecticut River.   The
educational histories of these towns were examined to learn whether
the religious motives of the Puritan did, in fact, play a significant
role in the educational progress of each."

1965-3   Bumsted, John Michael.   "The Pilgrims' Progress: The
     Ecclesiastical History of the Old Colony, 1620-1775." Ph.D.,
     Brown Univ. 2 vols. (v, 478 leaves).

     Abstract in DA, vol. 26 (6), p. 3274: "The purpose of this
thesis is to supplement various studies of the 'New England Mind' with
an analysis of local institutions and dynamics, particularly as they
relate to ecclesiastical life.   The area chosen for detailed
investigation, the three-county area of southeastern Massachusetts,
was originally the Plymouth Colony before its merger into
Massachusetts Bay in 1691. Although Plymouth Colony was doctrinally
quite similar to Massachusetts Bay, in ecclesiastical practices it was
quite different. Plymouth only reluctantly institutionalized its
church establishment, and did so incompletely. It was far more
tolerant than was the Massachusetts Bay. . . . Plymouth, moreover,
did not in the seventeenth century adopt those major innovations of
American Puritanism: the Cambridge Platform, the halfway covenant,
the narrative of conversion experience. . . .   After 1691,
southeastern Massachusetts fully accepted the principle of territorial
churches."

1965-4   Epperson, William Russell.   "The Meditative Structure of
     Edward Taylor's 'Preparatory Meditations.'" Ph.D., Univ. of
     Kansas. 297 leaves.

     Abstract in DA, vol. 27 (3), sec. A, p. 770: "The present study
outlines the traditional meditative method, surveys the Puritan
apprehension of that method, and then examines Taylor's 'Preparatory
Meditations,' seeking to determine how their poetic structuring
relates to the structuring of the traditional meditations. . . . The
introduction to the study includes a review of research done on New
England's intellectual history and on Edward Taylor specifically.
Here also the basic meditative approach is examined. . . . The first
chapter deals with the writers who might have had a direct role in
forming Taylor's concept of meditation [e.g., Richard Baxter, John

Cotton, Thomas Hooker]. . . . The remaining chapters of the dissertation treat Taylor's poems as examples of Puritan meditation. The poems are examined chronologically and their varying subjects, their varying approaches to God and to self, indicate the progress of Taylor's mystical tendency."

1965-5   Gilsdorf, Aletha Joy Bourne.   "The Puritan Apocalypse: New England Eschatology in the Seventeenth Century." Ph.D., Yale Univ. ii, 232 leaves.

Abstract in DA, vol. 26 (4), p. 2160: "An expectation that the world would end soon was common during the Reformation. . . . By 1639, when two leading exponents of the New England Way, John Cotton and Thomas Goodwin, wrote commentaries on Revelation, the idea of an age within history during which the visible church would be virtually perfect was well established. Both men expected the millennium to arrive soon and thought of it as a thousand-year extension of the regenerate church order of New England. Other New England ministers, including John Davenport, Thomas Shepard, Thomas Parker, and John Eliot, shared these apocalyptic expectations. . . . Puritan missionary efforts among the Indians were directly related to their apocalyptic expectations--as was their conception of the wilderness itself. . . . Between them, Stoddard and the advent of the century of enlightenment marked the end of the New England Way."

1965-6   Greven, Philip Johannes.   "Four Generations: A Study of Family Structure, Inheritance, and Mobility in Andover, Massachusetts, 1630-1750." Ph.D., Harvard Univ. 2 vols. (xvii, 504 leaves).

Revision published as Four Generations: Population, Land and Family in Colonial Andover, Massachusetts. -- Ithaca : Cornell Univ. Press, 1970. -- xvi, 329 p. "Introduction" (1970 ed.): The work is "a case study in demographic, economic, and familial history which focuses upon certain central, but almost totally neglected, aspects of life in an early American community: the fundamental events of birth, marriage, and death as they affected both individual families and the population of the community as a whole; the relationship of families to the land, which is of crucial importance in shaping the character of family life in an agrarian society and of the basic importance for the character of the society as a whole as well; the relationships of fathers and sons in successive generations, particularly as they reflected the extent to which sons succeeded in establishing their own autonomy when they reached maturity; the structures of families and the variations in structure which resulted from the changing economic and demographic circumstances within the town in successive generations; and, finally, the extent to which families remained permanently rooted to this particular community or emigrated to other places" (p. 1). Contents: 1. "Introduction: Problems, Sources, and Methods"; Part I. "The First and Second Generations": 2. "Life and Death in a Wilderness Settlement," 3. "Land for Families: The Formative Decades," and 4. "Patriarchalism and the Family"; Part II. "The Second and Third Generations": 5. "The Expanding Population in a Farming Community" and 6. "Control and Autonomy: Families and the

Transmission of Land"; Part III. "The Third and Fourth Generations": 7. "Change and Decline: Population and Families in a Provincial Town" and 8. "Independence and Dependence in Mid-Eighteenth-Century Families"; and Part IV. "Conclusion": 9. "Historical Perspectives on the Family." Appendix: "General Demographic Data."

1965-7   Harling, Frederick Farnham. "A Biography of John Eliot, 1604-1690." Ph.D., Boston Univ. (Graduate School). iv, 281 leaves.

Abstract in DA, vol. 26 (5), p. 2709: "The objective of this dissertation is to recreate, as thoroughly as possible, the life of John Eliot, 1604-1690. To accomplish this end, the author has used an historical and descriptive method. . . . The author began by gathering all the available material he could find which had direct bearing on the preacher's life. These materials were then critically evaluated in the light of scholarly knowledge of New England Puritanism. The result is an essay designed to reveal in an organized manner the life of the 'Apostle to the Indians' and the 'Saint of the New England Way,' within his historic, political, and social setting." Contents: "Early Life," "The Theological Climate in Massachusetts," "Eliot as Teacher and Pastor," "Eliot's Efforts for the Indians," "Eliot's Other Labors," and "Eliot's Last Years."

1965-8   Kaledin, Arthur Daniel. "The Mind of John Leverett." Ph.D., Harvard Univ. iv, 331 leaves.

"Introduction": ""This study is an attempt to draw an intellectual portrait of John Leverett, President of Harvard College from 1708 to 1724, a time when that tiny Puritan institution . . . began slowly to adjust to the Enlightment. Despite the uproar caused by his Presidency, despite the uniform testimony of historians that his stewardship of the college was of great importance, and the fact that under him the college, after three decades of neglect, drift, adversity and contention, once again began to flourish, the man himself remains a mystery" (p. 1). "This thesis attempts to reconstruct the mind of John Leverett, to describe his response to various issues and tendencies of the Enlightenment, to point out the subtle way in which he served as a transitional figure even though he did not abandon any article of the orthodox creed" (p. 3). Contents: I. "Fundamentalist in the Age of Reason": 1. "The Excellence of Scripture," 2. "Miracles and Natural Philosophy," and 3. "Reason, Learning and the Bible"; II. "Orthodoxy in Early Eighteenth Century New England": 1. "From a Sovereign God to a Benevolent Deity," 2. "Grace and God Man," 3. "The Virtuous Life," and 4. "The Bases of Toleration: Leverett and the Brattle Church"; III. "Leverett and History as Religious Drama: The Puritan Idea of History and Society": 1. "Saints and Satan: History as Religious Drama" and 2. "Politics, Society, and the Idea of Ordained Order"; and "Conclusion." Appendix: "Leverett's Expositions of Scripture, Booklets 45 (2v) to 48, The Peopling of The New World."

1965-9   King, Harold Roger. "The Settlement of the Upper Connecticut
        River Valley to 1675." Ph.D. Vanderbilt Univ. iv, 306 leaves.

        Abstract in DA, vol. 26 (4), p. 2164: "Soon after arrival in New
England, the people of Massachusetts began to exploit the fertile farm
land and lucrative fur trade of the Connecticut River Valley. This
dissertation is an analysis of the development of the upper
Connecticut River Valley, an area dominated by the towns of
Springfield, Northampton, and Hadley, and is an attempt to determine
the extent to which there existed in that area a distinct frontier
society. The major sources used were the public records of the colony
and the individual towns, as well as personal manuscript records of
William and John Pynchon, the leaders of the seventeenth-century
Connecticut River Valley."

1965-10   Lockridge, Kenneth Alan. "Dedham, 1636-1736: The Anatomy
        of a Puritan Utopia." Ph.D., Princeton Univ. vi, 366 leaves.

        Abstract in DA, vol. 26 (10), p. 6000. Revision published as A
New England Town: The First Hundred Years, Dedham, Massachusetts,
1636-1736. -- New York : W. W. Norton, 1970. -- xv, 208 p. -- (Norton
Essays in American History). "Introduction" (1970 ed.): "The main
theme of the book is almost mystical in its scope. What was it like
in 'the world we have lost'? What was the essence of the pre-
industrial village within this American town? How was this lost part
of our national experience changing in the century after it began?
Intertwined with this theme is another, the theme of American
uniqueness" (p. xiv). Contents: I. "A Utopian Commune, 1636-1686":
1. "The Policies of Perfection: The Town," 2. "The Heart of
Perfection: The Church," 3. "The Pattern of Communal Politics," 4.
"The Pattern of Communal Society," and 5. "Decline"; II. "A Provincial
Town, 1686-1736": 6. "Toward a New Community," 7. "Toward a New
Politics," and 8. "Toward a New Society?"; and III. "Dedham and the
American Experience": 9. "Dedham and the American Experience."

1965-11   Marcus, Richard Henry. "The Militia of Colonial
        Connecticut, 1639-1775: An Institutional Study." Ph.D., Univ.
        of Colorado at Boulder. 381 leaves.

        Abstract in DA, vol. 27 (3), sec. A, p. 732: "This study is
drawn largely from manuscript collections relating to the militia and
colonial wars which form part of the Connecticut Archives. It seeks
to examine the militia of the colony both as an institution and as a
component of the defense system of the northern British American
colonies."

1965-12   Nitz, Donald Arthur. "Community Musical Societies in
        Massachusetts to 1840." D.M.A., Boston Univ. (Graduate School).
        ix, 413 leaves.

        Principally focused on musical societies, 1740-1840, but provides
some background information. Relevant chapters: I. "The Problem" and
II. "Music and the Puritans of Massachusetts": "The Holy

Commonwealth," "The Eighteenth-Century Enlightenment," and "The First Reform in Music."

1965-13   Radabaugh, Jack Sheldon. "The Military System of Colonial Massachusetts, 1690-1740." Ph.D., Univ. of Southern California. ix, 598 leaves.

Abstract in DA, vol. 26 (3), p. 1618: "The arrival of English settlers in the New World set the stage for a conflict with the aborigines. . . . The conflict, in its early stages, was complicated by the struggle for empire among European nations. . . . Etched in vivid lines of conflict on a colonial background of intermittent warfare is the story of the Massachusetts militia in its struggle with the men and officers of New France and their astute and determined allies, the Indians. The commitment of the New England rustic to the arts of Mars was not by his choice, but was forced by the circumstances he faced in the confrontation of a dual enemy, one fighting for the integrity of ancestral hunting grounds and the other struggling for the fruits of empire in an international war."

1965-14   Ricketson, William Fred, Jr. "A Puritan Approach to Manifest Destiny: Case Studies from Artillery Election Sermons." Ph.D., Univ. of Georgia. vi, 151 leaves.

Abstract in DA, vol. 26 (11), p. 6662: "This dissertation is an appraisal of the New England Puritans' contribution to American traditions in foreign affairs. There was much significant thought on foreign policy, especially manifest destiny--including policies on defensive warfare, isolation, arbitration and territorial expansion-- and a representative sampling of it is preserved in the annual artillery election sermons. . . . Of the fifteen concepts of manifest destiny, delineated by Albert Weinberg in his detailed work on the subject, six were brought from Europe to America by the Puritans."

1965-15   Sands, Alyce Enid. "John Saffin: Seventeenth-Century American Citizen and Poet." Ph.D., Pennsylvania State Univ. iii, 272 leaves.

Abstract in DA, vol. 26 (11), p. 6724: "This thesis offers the first full-length appraisal of John Saffin, a significant seventeenth-century New England poet. . . . He profited as a merchant, a trader of goods, slaves, and land, but also was one of the central figures in the long dispute over the Narragansett territory. As the century's most articulate spokesman for the prevailing pro-slavery opinion, he engaged Samuel Sewall in a notorious debate in published pamphlets. . . . Saffin was involved, too, in the legal business of the colony; for almost fifty years he served well in Massachusetts and Rhode Island as lawyer, judge, and ultimately Justice of the Superior Court. . . . He was one of our most productive early American poets, and surpassed every other poet in the exceptionally wide range of his subjects and poetic forms."

1965-16   Schlenther, Boyd S.   "The Presbytery as Organ of Church Life
    and Government in American Presbyterianism from 1706 to 1788."
    Ph.D., Univ. of Edinburgh (U.K.).   xii, 412 leaves.

"Preface": "There is a real problem in attempting to speak of
'Presbyterianism' in the colonies prior to the eighteenth century.
This stems from the difficulty in distinguishing between
Presbyterianism and Congregationalism at the level of the local
church.   It is evident that seventeenth-century Puritanism should be
classified as predominantly Congregationalist, since--a crucial
point--an authoritative area judicatory, a 'presbytery', was absent.
Without this, Presbyterianism could be nothing more than a tendency.
. . . But as the colonies entered the new century a monumental shift
took place in colonial life.   The center of British interest turned to
the 'Middle Colonies'. . . . It is here that we will devote the main
body of our study, for the eighteenth century was the truly formative
period of American Presbyterianism. . . . It is the story of the
development of polity within the 'higher' judicatories of the church
from 1706-1788."   Contents: One: "Conditions prior to the Formation
of the Original Presbytery," Two: "The Formation of the Original
Presbytery," Three: "The Authority of the Original Presbytery," Four:
"The Polity of the Synod of Philadelphia, 1717-1740," Five: "The Order
and Work of the Presbyteries, 1717-1740," and "Conclusion."   Chapters
Six through Nine deal with later periods.

1965-17   Shields, James Leroy.   "The Doctrine of Regeneration in
    English Puritan Theology, 1604-1689."   Ph.D., Southwestern
    Baptist Theological Seminary.   vii ["Abstract"], vii, 262 leaves.

"Abstract": "The purpose of this dissertation is to present the
doctrine of regeneration as it was understood and taught by the
English Puritan theologians of the seventeenth century.   Seven
representative theologians have been chosen.   They are William
Perkins, Richard Sibbes, Richard Baxter, John Owen, Thomas Goodwin,
Stephen Charnock, and John Howe" (p. ii).   "Regeneration was
considered synonymous with conversion, resurrection, sanctification,
and vocation or calling.   All of these terms later became distinct
parts in the order of salvation" (p. vii).   Contents: I.
"Introduction," II. "The Necessity for Regeneration," III. "The
Foundation of Regeneration," IV. "The Efficient Cause of
Regeneration," V. "The Means of Regeneration," VI. "The Nature and
Results of Regeneration," VII. "The Relation of Regeneration to the
Order of Salvation," and "Conclusion."   Appendices: A. "A Brief
History of the Concept of Regeneration Before the Puritan Era" and B.
"A Survey of the History of English Puritanism."

1965-18   Sidwell, Robert Tolbert.   "The Colonial American Almanacs:
    A Study in Non-Institutional Education."   Ed.D., Rutgers Univ.
    xix, 566 leaves.

Abstract in DA, vol. 27 (2), sec. A, p. 377: "This study is
concerned with an aspect of the educational history of colonial
America. . . . This study . . . is focused upon . . . the colonial
American almanac.   Through a detailed analysis of the content of these

almanacs of the seventeenth and eighteenth centuries, this study seeks to verify the contention that they were significant and valuable educative instruments throughout the colonial period of American history. . . . Next to the Bible, the almanac was the most widely read literary production in colonial America. . . . In the pages of these almanacs may be found an accurate reflection of the modification and development of the colonial American climate of opinion." Relevant chapters: I. "1646-1699," II. "1700-1729," and X. "Concluding Remarks and Some Implications for Further Research." The other chapters treat of later developments.

1965-19   Simmons, Richard Clive. "Studies in the Massachusetts Franchise, 1631-1691." Ph.D., Univ. of California at Berkeley. 226 leaves.

Abstract in DA, vol. 26 (12), p. 7287: "Chapter I considers the franchise in its relation to the Massachusetts Charter and to the religious views of the godly state. Roger Williams' criticisms are examined. The franchise was device which protected the state and the churches and also promoted the end of a goodly society. . . . Chapter II considers office-holding. . . . Chapters III and IV consider the franchise in its relation to political history. . . . In the Introduction, appendices and Conclusion historians' attitudes to the franchise are discussed and assessed."

1965-20   Wall, Robert Emmet, Jr. "The Membership of the Massachusetts General Court, 1634-1686." Ph.D., Yale Univ. vii, 740 leaves.

Abstract in DA, vol. 26 (4), p. 2172: Diss. "is a town by town analysis of the deputies to the general court during the period of the First Royal Charter. It investigates the political, family, and economic backgrounds of each of the 528 deputies to the general court, as well as the backgrounds of the governors, deputy governors, and assistants. It investigates the various legal qualifications for political office, as well as the extra legal qualifications."

1965-21   Wallace, Dewey D., Jr. "The Life and Thought of John Owen to 1660: A Study of the Significance of Calvinist Theology in English Puritanism." Ph.D., Princeton Univ. iii, 336 leaves.

Abstract in DA, vol. 26 (7), p. 4101: "Theologically, Puritanism was Calvinism. . . . This theological basis . . . must be given attention as the center from which Puritanism's special interests in reform, polity, preaching, and piety radiated. . . . John Owen (1616-1683), perhaps the leading Puritan dogmatician of the mid-seventeenth century, well illustrates how central this theological concern was. The greatest influence upon him was the Arminian controversy of the time, to which his life work was a reaction. . . . Leaving [Oxford], he had a ministry in Essex during the war years. At this time, under the influence of John Cotton's writings, he defined himself as an 'Independent.' . . . Through his theological writings and his leadership in the Savoy Synod, Owen stamped this group with

Calvinistic orthodoxy, in contrast to the group of 'Presbyterians' joining under [Richard] Baxter's leadership. This theological difference between the two leaders helps to explain the later theological differences between the two 'denominations.'" Cf. Wallace's Puritans and Predestination: Grace in English Protestant Theology, 1525-1695. -- Chapel Hill : Univ. of North Carolina Press, 1982. -- xiii, 289 p., especially chapters 3 and 4, which include material from the diss.

1965-22   Waters, John Joseph, Jr. "The Otis Family in Provincial and Revolutionary Massachusetts (1631-1780)." Ph.D., Columbia Univ. ix, 230 leaves.

Abstract in DA, vol. 30, sec. A, p. 642. Revision published as The Otis Family in Provincial and Revolutionary Massachusetts. -- Chapel Hill : Published for the Institute of Early American History and Culture by the Univ. of North Carolina Press, 1968. -- xi, 221 p. Reprinted with a new preface: New York : W. W. Norton, 1975. -- xv, 221 p. Contents (1968 ed.): I. "First Plantations," II. "Plymouth Roots," III. "The Barnstable Homestead," IV. "Barnstable Bailiwicks," and V. "James Otis, Sr., Colonial Politician." The principal Otises treated are John I (1581-1657), John II (1621-84), John III (1657-1727), John IV (1687-1758), and James, Sr. (1702-78).

1965-23   Webb, Stephen Saunders. "Officers and Governors: The Role of the British Army in Imperial Politics and the Administration of the American Colonies, 1689-1722." Ph.D., Univ. of Wisconsin at Madison. v, 388 leaves.

Abstract in DA, vol. 25 (12), p. 7233: "Part I of this work examines the nature of military experience in England, 1660-1722, defines its phases and its content as these relate to officers who became governors. The development of the Restoration army is described from its Cromwellian roots.... [Diss.] seeks to broadly outline the enormous and hitherto ignored political and administrative role of the British army in the development of the American empire." Relevant chapters: I. "Introduction," II. "The Restoration Army, Cavalier to Professional 1660-1688," III. "Professionalism and Politics: British Army 1689-1710," and IV. "Social Views of the Officer Class." Part II is devoted exclusively to events in Virginia. Cf. Webb's The Governors-General: The English Army and the Definition of the Empire, 1569-1681. -- Chapel Hill : Published for the Institute of Early American History and Culture by the Univ. of North Carolina Press, 1979.

1965-24   Williams, Ray S. "The American National Covenant, 1730-1800." Ph.D., Florida State Univ. viii, 158 leaves.

Abstract in DA, vol. 26 (12), p. 7302: "The concept of the national covenant originated in the theology of those Puritans who emigrated from England to Massachusetts Bay in the seventeenth century. According to their belief, God had made a covenant with them in which He promised temporal salvation to the community on the condition of righteousness among the people. This concept flowered during the seventeenth century, reaching a peak of importance during the 1690's and early years of the 1700's. Although the eighteenth century was a period of transition in which many Puritan beliefs gradually abated . . . , the idea of the national covenant persisted in importance through the greater part of the period. The persistence of this idea was a significant factor in strengthening the moral fiber of an American national character. The concept contributed measurably to a sense of purpose among the American people."

1966-1   Beebe, David Lewis. "The Seals of the Covenant: The Doctrine and Place of the Sacraments and Censures in the New England Puritan Theology underlying the Cambridge Platform of 1648." Th.D., Pacific School of Religion. x, 323 leaves.

Abstract in DA, vol. 27 (4), sec. A, p. 1100: "This dissertation discusses the worship of the New England . . . Puritans. Specifically, it examines the sacramental theology of the Congregational Puritans in and around the Massachusetts Bay Colony in the first two decades of its settlement. The study focuses upon the events and controversies which led to the Cambridge Synod of 1646-48. It compares the Cambridge Platform with preliminary drafts by Richard Mather and Ralph Partridge. Of the New English divines studied, the dissertation relies chiefly upon John Cotton, Thomas Hooker, Richard Mather, and John Norton. . . . The dissertation recognizes a division in New England Puritan thought and experience between an emphasis upon the sacraments as objective seals of grace and an opposite emphasis upon the inward experience of grace. The dissertation nevertheless concludes that the sacraments were central to the New English religious experience."

1966-2   Cassidy, Ivan. "The Calvinist Tradition in Education in France, Scotland and New England during the Sixteenth and Seventeenth Centuries. Ph.D., Queen's Univ. of Belfast (U.K.). 340 leaves.

"Introduction": Part One treats of "three aspects of Calvin's educational philosophy--its general tone, theoretical basis, and practical application" (n.p.). Chapter VIII: "It has always been recognised that 'the founding fathers' were the pioneers of American education: within less than thirty years they had established an educational system which 'served as a model for other kindred communities.' The purpose of these chapters is to show how and to what extent this important development was influenced by Calvin" (p. 204). Relevant chapters: Part One: "The Calvinist Tradition at its Source": I. "Calvin in the Making," II. "Calvin's Theology and its Educational Corollaries," and III. "Calvin as an Educational Administrator"; and Part Two: "The Calvinist Tradition in its Outflow": VIII. "The Founding of New England and the Beginnings of Higher Education in America," IX. "Cultural Aspects of Puritanism and their Reflection in the Early History of Harvard College," X. "Primary and Secondary Education in New England during the Seventeenth Century," and XI. "Conclusion." Remaining Parts are concerned with developments in France and Scotland.

1966-3   Clark, Charles Edwin. "The Eastern Parts: Northern New
    England, 1690-1760." Ph.D., Brown Univ. viii, 418 leaves.

    Abstract in DA, vol. 27 (11), sec. A, p. 3806. Revised, expanded
version published as The Eastern Frontier: The Settlement of Northern
New England, 1610-1763. -- New York : Alfred A. Knopf, 1970. -- xiii,
419, xvi p. "Preface" (1970 ed.): "I have aimed primarily at writing
a social . . . history--that is, a study of a people, their way of
living, their problems, their social organization, their cultural
accomplishments, and, so far as possible, their distinctive character
and ways of thought" (p. viii). Relevant chapters: Part One: I. "The
Sea and the Forest," II. "Our Main End Was to Catch Fish, 1610-1680,"
III. "The Puritan Conquest, 1638-1658," IV. "From Servants to
Oligarchs, 1635-1692," V. "Growing Pains, 1660-1713," VI. "The
Conquest Bears Fruit, 1660-1732," and VII. "The Oligarchy Prospers,
1700-1730"; and Part Two: VIII. "Expansion, 1713-1744," IX.
"Resettlement: The Massachusetts Colonial System, 1713-1750," X.
"Moses Pearson and Old Falmouth, 1727-1764," XI. "Into the Back Parts,
1719-1750," XII. "From Wilderness to Country Town, 1720-1760," XIII.
"The Country Town Takes Shape, 1725-1760," XIV. "Making Good, and
Three Who DID," and XV. "The Life of the Country Town, 1725-1763."
Part Three deals with a later period.

1966-4   Foote, William Alfred. "The American Independent Companies
    of the British Army, 1664-1764." Ph.D., Univ. of California at
    Los Angeles. xxvi, 564 leaves.

    Abstract in DA, vol. 27 (6), sec. A, p. 1734: "The independent
companies of the British Army, which formed most of the garrisons in
the period of the First British Empire, were integral and important
parts in the machinery of colonial government. . . . The following
specific questions required answers. First, were the companies
organized . . . in accordance with any fixed purpose or pattern?
Second, were these companies an integral part of the British Army, or
were they 'independent' as their name might imply? Third, did the
companies become an active part of colonial society, or were they
unassimilated? Fourth, did the companies serve to tie the colonies in
which they were stationed to England, or were they regarded as an
instrument of oppression? . . . Massachusetts . . . was a vigorous
supporter of imperial defense, and regarded the British ports of Nova
Scotia and Newfoundland as her northern frontiers." Relevant
chapters: "Introduction"; Part I. "The British Army and Its American
Companies": I. "The Eighteenth-Century British Army," II. "British
Army Administration in America," III. "The Independent Companies, the
Constitution, and the American Colonies," IV. "The Independent
Companies and the British Army," and V. "The Independent Companies on
the American Scene"; and Part II. "Unit Histories of the American
Companies": X. "The New England Companies." Chapters VI-IX treat of
other colonies. Appendices: A. "Abstract of the Daily Pay of Foot
Troops," B. "The American Half-Pay List of 1713," and C. "List of
Officers, the American Companies."

1966-5   Foster, Stephen.   "The Puritan Social Ethic: Class and
     Calling in the First Hundred Years of Settlement in New England."
     Ph.D., Yale Univ. xii, 415 leaves.

     Abstract in DA, vol. 27 (8), sec. A, p. 2475: Revision published
as Their Solitary Way: The Puritan Social Ethic in the First Century
of Settlement in New England. -- New Haven : Yale Univ. Press, 1971.
-- xxii, 214 p. -- (Yale Historical Publications. Miscellany ; 94).
"Preface" (1971 ed.):   "I have tried to get at the imperatives,
aspirations, and inhibitions which collectively comprised the way a
seventeenth-century New Englander thought he ought to act toward other
seventeenth-century New Englanders when they came together in an
organized civil society" (p. xi).   Contents: "Introduction," Part
One. "Foundations":   1. "Order" and 2. "Love"; Part Two. "Details":
3. "Government: The Character of a Good Ruler," 4. "Wealth: The
Calling, Capitalism, Commerce, and the Problem of Prosperity," and 5.
"Poverty: Affliction, Poor Relief, and Charity"; and Part Three: 6.
"Puritanism and Democracy: A Mixed Legacy."   Appendices: A. "The
Massachusetts Franchise in the Seventeenth Century," B. "The
Nomination of Massachusetts Magistrates under the Old Charter," C.
"The Merchants, the Moderates, and Edward Randolph," and D. "Family
Connections of Merchants, Ministers, and Magistrates."

1966-6   Mair, Nathaniel Harrington.   "Christian Sanctification and
     Individual Pastoral Care in Richard Baxter." Th.D., Union
     Theological Seminary in the City of New York.   vii, 303, 3
     leaves.

     Abstract in DA, vol. 28 (1), sec. A, p. 287: "Baxter's doctrine
of sanctification . . . shaped his pastoral care principles.   His
emphasis upon the teaching of doctrine; the individual yet impersonal
character of the pastor-parishioner relationship; the advocacy of
repression in the combat of sin; the insistence on duty; and the use
made of the signs of holiness all reflect the particular cast of his
doctrine of sanctification."

1966-7   McElroy, John Harmon.   "Images of the Seventeenth-Century
     Puritan in American Novels, 1823-1860." Ph.D., Duke Univ. ix,
     187 leaves.

     Abstract in DA, vol. 27 (11), sec. A. p. 3845: "During the
thirty-eight years before 1860 at least twenty-eight novels with
settings in seventeenth-century New England were published in the
United States. . . .   Three basic images of the Puritan reappear again
and again from the earliest novel about the historical Puritans. . . .
One of the consistently developed images is that of the 'Puritan
Fathers' who, refusing to submit to religious and political tyranny in
England, fled their homeland 'for conscience' sake' and brought the
seminal idea of freedom into 'the howling wilderness' of New England.
. . .   The dominant image in the novels of the period is a vivid,
reproachful picture of the persecuting or Procrustean Puritan who
tried to force all individuals in the community into the iron bed of
Puritan orthodoxy. . . .   A third image . . . can be termed the
imperialistic Puritan because it arises from the Puritans' treatment

of the Indians."

1966-8   Malefyt, Calvin Sterling DeWaal. "The Changing Concept of
          Pneumatology in New England Trinitarianism." Ph.D., Harvard
          Univ. 297 leaves.

    "This thesis is a genetic study of the changing concept of
Pneumatology among New England Trinitarians from 1635-1755. It begins
in 1635, when John Cotton, minister of the First Church in Boston,
asserted that the Holy Spirit . . . confirmed salvation by an
immediate revelation to the soul. . . . I wish to show what
intellectual, historical, and social antecedents modified the
traditional concept of the Spirit prior to [1755 in Jonathan] Mayhew's
redefinition of Pneumatology; I also wish to note other concepts of
the Spirit emerging concurrently" (p. 1). Contents: Part One: "An
Emerging Ideal, 1635-1652": I. "An Historical Perspective," II.
"Spiritualist Evangelicalism, 1635-1638," III. "Antinomian Enthusiasm,
1636-1638," IV. "Covenantal Formalism: Theology, 1639-1652," and V.
"Covenantal Formalism: Church and State, 1639-1652"; and Part Two:
"Fragmentization, 1644-1755": VI. "Revolutionary Enthusiasm, 1644-
1672," VII. "An Ideal Disintegrates, 1662-1684," and VIII.
"Sacramental Formalism, 1687-1729." The remaining chapters deal with
later developments.

1966-9   Murrin, John M. "Anglicizing an American Colony: The
          Transformation of Provincial Massachusetts." Ph.D., Yale Univ.
          vi, 320 leaves.

    Abstract in DA, vol. 27 (7), sec. A, p. 2121: "Between the
Glorious Revolution and the Stamp Act crisis, provincial Massachusetts
experienced a radical transformation. The colony slowly lost most of
the unique features which had characterized it throughout the
seventeenth century. In their place it imported British institutions
and British ideas. This pattern of Anglicization characterized the
religious life of New England, the movement from a militia towards a
local 'army,' the transformation of the court system, the rise of a
provincial bench and bar, and both the structure and conduct of
provincial politics." Contents: One. "A Problem in Search of Its
Context," Two. "The Fading of the Puritan Dream," Three. "The Colonial
Militia: A Medieval Response to a Wilderness Need," Four. "The Legal
Transformation: The Courts," Five. "The Legal Transformation: The
Bench and Bar," and Six.   "Conclusions and Suggestions:
Anglicization, the Revolution and After."

1966-10   Plotkin, Frederick Sheldon. "Sighs from Sion: A Study of
          Radical Puritan Eschatology in England, 1640-1660." Ph.D.,
          Columbia Univ. 247 leaves.

    Abstract in DA, vol. 28 (2), sec. A, p. 771: "The purpose of the
dissertation was to investigate the development of millenarian thought
in seventeenth-century England through a study of the writings of
radical puritan sectaries who were dominated by the idea of human and
historical perfectibility during the period of the Civil Wars and

Interregnum. The subjects covered were the exegetical methods of the puritan millenary, the form and function of the millennial New Sion, the Hebraic nature of Christ's millennial 'government,' and the covenant idea in millenarian thought."

1966-11   Ransome, Joyce Olson. "Cotton Mather and the Catholic Spirit." Ph.D., Univ. of California at Berkeley. 332 leaves.

Abstract in DAI, vol. 31 (4), sec. A, p. 1736: "I have tried to avoid the pitfall of 'presentism' by delineating Mather against the background of that widely used and much-applauded, though rather imprecise, contemporary term, a 'catholic spirit.' This was a term in general use on both sides of the Atlantic and so brings out the extent of Mather's concern for and contact with the wider community of Christendom. Indeed, the expansion of Mather's knowledge of his community and the influence this broad perspective exercised upon him is one of the major themes of the dissertation. The term catholic spirit also suggests the prevalent hope within that larger realm of Christendom that the bitterness and divisions . . . might at last give way to a more becoming spirit of love and brotherhood. . . . This dissertation . . . tries to suggest both the general concepts and specific circumstances that guided Cotton Mather's pursuit of that . . . ideal of a catholic spirit."

1966-12   Reed, John William. "The Rhetoric of a Colonial Controversy: Roger Williams versus the Massachusetts Bay Colony." Ph.D., Ohio State Univ. v, 199 leaves.

Abstract in DA, vol. 27 (7), sec. A, p. 2213: "Roger Williams stands at the beginning of the American tradition of radicalism and dissent. As America's first great dissenter he engaged the Massachusetts Bay Colony in the first 'great American debate.' Since the content of the real debate between Roger Williams and Thomas Hooker before the General Court of Massachusetts in 1635 was not recorded, the basic materials for the study became the extended pamphlet controversy between Roger Williams and the spokesman of the Massachusetts Bay Colony--John Cotton. . . . It became apparent in evaluating the rhetorical career of Roger Williams that his reputation is based on abilities other than preaching. . . . It is apparent that his great contribution to rhetorical study lies in his radicalism and dissent."

1966-13   Rosenmeier, Jesper. "The Image of Chirst: The Typology of John Cotton." Ph.D., Harvard Univ. 238 leaves.

Chapter I: "The Puritans' exodus from England to America was made to establish a plantation where the image of God would be renewed, and in the Old Testament types, figures, similitudes, and sacramental designs, they possessed the images and symbols in which they could speak their errand into the wilderness" (p. 18). Contents: I. "Heaven's Map," II. "Europe's Heavens" (treats Cotton's use of Tertullian, Augustine, Luther, Calvin, Matthias Flacius, William Ames, and William Perkins), III. "The Language of Canaan," IV. "Daniel's

Antitype," V. "A Shadow Vanished," and VI. "A Furious Trope."
Appendix: "Dating the Works of John Cotton."

1966-14   Scholz, Robert Francis. "'The Reverend Elders': Faith,
    Fellowship, and Politics in the Ministerial Community of
    Massachusetts Bay, 1630-1710." Ph.D., Univ. of Minnesota. vii,
    281 leaves.

    Abstract in DA, vol. 28 (8), sec. A, p. 3123: "The Reverend
Elders is an analysis of the formation, influence and decline of an
organized group of Congregational ministers in Massachusetts Bay. The
pluralistic background of the ministers and laymen in the Bay's
churches prompted frequent clerical gatherings to develop common
doctrines and procedures. Experiences of ministerial association in
seventeenth-century England and an appreciation of the Reformed church
order served as the rationale for this clerical matrix of
congregationalism known to the period as 'the Reverend Elders.'"

1966-15   Shea, Daniel Bartholomew, Jr. "Spiritual Autobiography in
    Early America." Ph.D., Stanford Univ. xiii, 296 leaves.

    Abstract in DA, vol. 27 (7), sec. A, p. 2135. Revision published
under same title: Princeton : Princeton Univ. Press, 1968. -- xvi,
280 p. "Preface" (1968 ed.): "The spiritual autobiographer is
primarily concerned with the question of grace: Whether or not the
individual has been accepted into divine life, an acceptance signified
by psychological and moral changes which the autobiographer comes to
discern in his past experience" (p. xi). Relevant chapters: Part
Two: "Puritan Spiritual Narratives": III. "Traditional Patterns in
Puritan Autobiography": "Edward Taylor's 'Spiritual Relation'" and
"John Winthrop's 'Christian Experience'"; IV. "Of Providence, for
Posterity": "Anne Bradstreet's 'Religious Experiences,'" "The Memoirs
of Roger Clap," "John Dane's Declaration of Remarkable Providences,"
and "Thomas Shepard's 'My Birth & Life'"; V. "The Mathers": "The
'Autobiography' of Increase Mather" and "The 'Paterna' of Cotton
Mather"; and "Conclusion": "The Quaker and Puritan Autobiographical
Modes: Thoreau, Whitman, [Emily] Dickinson, and [Henry] Adams."

1966-16   Shealy, William Ross, Jr. "The Power of the Present: The
    Pastoral Perspective of Richard Baxter, Puritan Divine: 1615-
    1691." Ph.D., Drew Univ. v, 427 leaves.

    Abstract in DA, vol. 27 (8), sec. A, p. 2607: "The basic
question of this study may be stated as follows: What was the
pastoral perspective which informed Richard Baxter's life of ministry?
. . . Baxter's pastoral perspective was found to be held dynamically
in a triplex framework of Universality, Institutionality and
Particularity. The Scriptures and the Essentials are . . . the
constants which ground and sanction this entire conception.
Universality involves those aspects of pastoral perspective which are
to be understood primarily with respect to the Universal church. . . .
Institutionality expresses the presence of Christ as the Lord of the
Kingdom of Redemption. . . . Particularity is the point towards which

all else converges. . . .   In the last analysis, the pastor-parishioner relationship is both the hub and the hope of history."

1966-17   Walton, Gary Max.   "A Quantitative Study of American
      Colonial Shipping." Ph.D., Univ. of Washington. ix, 181 leaves.

      Abstract in DA, vol. 27 (9), sec. A, p. 2712.   Revision in collaboration with James F. Shepherd published as Shipping, Maritime Trade, and the Economic Development of Colonial North America. -- Cambridge, England : Cambridge Univ. Press, 1972. -- ix, 255 p. Published ed. based on Walton's diss. and that of Shepherd, "A Balance of Payments for the Thirteen Colonies, 1768-72" (Ph.D., Univ. of Washington, 1966).   "Preface" (1972 ed.): "This study represents our attempt to view certain important aspects of the external economic relations of the British North American colonies as they can be pieced together from the voluminous evidence that has survived.   The central focus in upon the critical role that overseas trade and improvements in transportation played in the economic development of North America" (pp. vii-viii). Relevant chapters: 1. "Introduction," 2. "Colonial economic development: a suggested framework," 3. "Colonial economic development and trade: an overview," 4. "Colonial trade, distribution costs, and productivity change in shipping," 5. "Sources of productivity change in shipping and distribution," and 9. "Reinterpretations of issues in colonial shipping." Chapters 6-8 deal with the period 1768-72. Relevant appendices: I. "Data from the Naval Office Lists and estimates of trade with southern Europe and the West Indies for earlier years in the eighteenth century," II. "Official value and real values of English exports to the colonies," III. "Quantitative data related to shipping," and VI. "Foreign exchange earnings from the sale of ships to overseas buyers."

1966-18   Warden, Gerard Bryce.   "Boston Politics, 1692-1765." Ph.D.,
      Yale Univ.   308 leaves.

      Abstract in DA, vol. 27 (8), sec. A, p. 2490. Revision published as Boston, 1689-1776. -- Boston : Little, Brown, 1970. -- 404 p. Relevant chapters (1970 ed.): "Prologue," I. "The Eighteenth of April 1689," II. "The Town," III. "The Town, the Crown, and the Merchants," IV. "The Old Order: 1702-1715," V. "Innovation: 1715-1730," and "Epilogue." Chapters VI-XV deal with later events.

1966-19   Withers, Richard Eugene.   "Roger Williams and the Rhode
      Island Colony: A Study in Leadership Roles." Ph.D., Boston
      Univ. (Graduate School). x, 422 leaves.

      Abstract in DA, vol. 27 (5), sec. A, p. 1456: "The problem of the dissertation is a delineation of the leadership roles of Roger Williams in the Rhode Island Colony. Chief emphasis is given to the origin and functioning of Williams's roles within the context of Narragansett towns and colony. . . . The methodological approach of the study is the use of a framework of sociological theory for the interpretation of historical source materials pertaining to the origin and development of towns and Colony from 1636 to 1683. Social system theory, involving concepts of social structure, cultural structure, and processes of social control and anomie, is used to analyse the context of town and Colony."

1966-20   Wolverton, Byron Adams. "Keyboard Music and Musicians in the Colonies and United States of America before 1830." Ph.D., Indiana Univ. vii, 495 leaves.

Abstract in DA, vol. 27 (11), sec. A, p. 3899: "The purpose of this study is to investigate the earliest known uses of keyboard instruments . . . in the English colonies of North America and to trace the development of keyboard music and musicians from that point through 1830. . . . Three time periods (beginning to 1720, 1720-1790, 1790-1820) are used, and these in turn are subdivided according to cities and other locations." Developments in New England during the first two time periods are discussed.

1967-1   Banks, Linda Jo Samuels. "The Poems of Richard Baxter: A Critical Edition with Notes and Commentary." Ph.D., Emory Univ. cxxxviii, 822 leaves.

Abstract in DA, vol. 28 (10), sec. A, p. 4114: "Richard Baxter (1615-1691), remembered chiefly for his prose, wrote more lines of poetry than either George Herbert or John Donne. These poetical works, found in six different collections, have never been extensively commented upon or even published together. This dissertation, then, serves first to introduce and evaluate the poems (Chapters I-IV) and second, to make available the old-spelling texts. . . . Finally, there are three appendices: A) Substantive Changes, B) Books and Authors Recommended by Baxter, and C) Poems Written about Baxter."

1967-2   Barrow, Robert Mangum. "Newspaper Advertising in Colonial America, 1704-1775." Ph.D., Univ. of Virginia. x, 282 leaves.

Abstract in DA, vol. 28 (7), sec. A, p. 2618: "The present study attempts to [examine the subject of colonial newspaper advertising] . . . by focusing on such topics as development, audience, methods and techniques, uses, and economics. . . . The main concern of colonial advertisers was to capture as large a share of existing markets as possible . . . and the newspaper offered them the largest possible audience." Diss. included references to the Boston News-Letter (begun 1704), the Boston Gazette (begun 1719), and the New-England Courant (begun 1721).

1967-3   Benton, Robert Milton. "The American Puritan Sermon before 1700." Ph.D., Univ. of Colorado at Boulder. xiii, 290 leaves.

Abstract in DA, vol. 29 (2), sec. A, p. 559: "At least 175 volumes of sermons are known to have been published in New England before 1700. . . . A study of those sermons published in New England in the seventeenth century reveals that Puritan ministers became self-conscious prose stylists. . . . The Puritan sermons of seventeenth-century New England possess an earnestness, a vitality and an imaginative use of language which make them worthy of critical appraisal and literary consideration." Diss. ends with "A chronological listing of American Puritan sermons published in New England before 1700."

1967-4   Bothell, Larry Lee. "Cloak and Gown: A Study of Religion and Learning in the Early Career of Samuel Johnson of Connecticut." Ph.D., Princeton Univ. xix, 299 leaves.

Abstract in DA, vol. 28 (3), sec. A, p. 1122: "The early career of Samuel Johnson of Connecticut (1696-1772) illustrates the process by which New England Puritan intellectual and institutional systems were challenged during the first third of the eighteenth century. . . . Detailed discussion of Johnson's career during the twenty years that separate his entrance into the Collegiate School of Connecticut (Yale College) from the American visit (1729-1731) of George Berkeley highlights the religious and intellectual continuities that underlie the radical changes in Johnson's public life. The exchange of a Puritan cloak for an Anglican gown was Johnson's way of resolving controversial issues affecting religion and learning in a common Anglo-American culture."

1967-5   Burg, Barry Richard. "Richard Mather (1596-1669): The Life and Work of a Puritan Cleric in New England." Ph.D., Univ. of Colorado at Boulder. xi, 453 leaves.

Abstract in DA, vol. 29 (1), sec. A, p. 198. Revision published as Richard Mather of Dorchester. -- Lexington : Univ. Press of Kentucky, 1976. -- xiii, 207 p. "Preface" (1976 ed.): "Unlike the men who regularly become the subjects of historical investigation, Richard Mather never influenced the destiny of nations or determined the fate of even a small portion of mankind. . . . Yet it is this very obscurity that makes Mather's life valuable for the historian. . . . His life provides much that illuminates the careers and provides a broader understanding of the ordinary pastors and teachers in seventeenth-century Massachusetts Bay" (pp. xi-xii). Contents: I. "In England," II. "Settled," III. "Defense of the New England Way," IV. "The New England Preacher," V. "The Cambridge Platform," VI. "The Halfway Covenant," and "Epilogue."

1967-6   Burnette, Rand. "The Quest for Union in the American Colonies, 1689-1701." Ph.D., Indiana Univ. 216 leaves.

Abstract in DA, vol. 28 (11), sec. A, p. 4559: "This is a study of Anglo-American efforts at union in the reign of William III, specifically 1689-1701. The emphasis is on the northern colonies, and especially New York: This area was most exposed to enemy attack during King William's War. Despite the problems facing intercolonial cooperation, there was a growing interest in colonial union; this led to the creation of a military confederation in 1697, and contributed much to such success as was enjoyed by its governor the Earl of Bellomont." After 1697 Bellomont was joint-governor of New York,

Massachusetts, and New Hampshire and had "commissions over the militia of all northern colonies except Pennsylvania. . . . But regardless of Bellomont's abilities there was little possibility of a successful colonial union until the colonies became more responsive."

1967-7   Bush, Sargent, Jr. "The Relevance of Puritanism to Major Themes in Hawthorne's Fiction." Ph.D., Univ. of Iowa. xv, 266 leaves.

Abstract in DA, vol. 28 (7), sec. A, p. 2677: "The fictional themes in the works of Nathaniel Hawthorne reveal a preoccupation with many of the same subjects as concerned the American Puritans. Even more surprising is the very frequent similarity of his conclusions on particular subjects to those of the Puritans. His way of looking at and thinking about the universe is strikingly similar to theirs. . . . Hawthorne is no Puritan but there are more fundamental points of relevance than has usually be recognized."

1967-8   Cohen, Ronald Dennis. "Colonial Leviathan: New England Foreign Affairs in the Seventeenth Century." Ph.D., Univ. of Minnesota. vii, 496 leaves.

Abstract in DA, vol. 28 (12), sec. A, p. 4984: "In theory the Old Colonial System, one of England's responses to mercantilist tenets, made the colonies mere tools, functioning only at the mother country's discretion. Yet in practice such was not the case. [The New England colonies] were, in fact, able to establish virtually autonomous settlements. . . . Indeed, the New Englanders developed a native mercantilism which came into direct conflict with that of the mother country. . . . Each of the colonies . . . concentrated upon promoting its own economic status, and in the process competed with its neighboring colonies, whether English or foreign, and England alike."

1967-9   Engdahl, Bonnie Thoman. "Paradise in the New World: A Study of the Image of the Garden in the Literature of Colonial America." Ph.D., Univ. of California at Los Angeles. ix, 390 leaves.

Abstract in DA, vol. 28 (3), sec. A, p. 1073: "This study . . . focuses upon a certain broadly-defined and evolving image--the garden--and traces its uses as a representation of the American experience. It explores and discusses a wide range of primary materials: narratives of voyages and settlement, promotional literature, journals, histories, some sermons and tracts, topographical description, essays, and verse. . . . The New England Puritan did not idealize the land, but he wrote of the Garden Church and the garden of the soul. He also told the story of Canaan in his own way. New England, to the Puritan, was not the Land of Milk and Honey, but the Promised Land. . . . To the Puritan the garden is a symbol of redemption." Relevant chapters: "Introduction," I. "Paradise in the New World," II. "Canaan in New England," and III. "The New England Muse." Chapters IV-VIII do not concern the Puritans.

1967-10   Flaherty, David Harris. "Privacy in Colonial New England,
     1630-1776." Ph.D., Columbia Univ. 455 leaves.

     Abstract in DA, vol. 28 (5), sec. A, p. 1760. Revision published
as Privacy in Colonial New England. -- Charlottesville : Univ. Press
of Virginia, 1972. -- xii, 287 p. Contents (1972 ed.):
"Introduction"; Part One: "Privacy in Family Life": 1. "The Home,"
2. "The Family," and 3. "The Neighborhood and Community"; and Part
Two: "The Individual in Colonial Society": 4. "The Privacy of
Letters," 5. "The Church," 6. "Government and the Law," 7. "Law
Enforcers," and 8. "The Courts"; and "Epilogue."

1967-11   Foster, Mary Catherine. "Hampshire County, Massachusetts,
     1729-1754: A Covenant Society in Transition." Ph.D., Univ. of
     Michigan. iv, 331 leaves.

     Abstract in DA, vol. 28 (7), sec. A, p. 2621: "Hampshire County,
first settled in 1636, was, although on the Massachusetts frontier, a
matured society by 1729. It appears to have been less influenced by
secular changes than other parts of Massachusetts. Under the
leadership of Solomon Stoddard the Hampshire Ministerial Association
had been able, through its control of ordinations, to maintain the
orthodoxy upon which the covenant society was based. The great 'river
gods' recognized the spiritual authority of the ministry. . . .
During the years 1729 to 1754 important changes took place which
effectively undermined the existence of a covenant society."

1967-12   Gilman, Harvey. "From Sin to Song: Image Clusters and
     Patterns in Edward Taylor's Preparatory Meditations." Ph.D.,
     Pennsylvania State Univ. 213 leaves.

     Abstract in DA, vol. 28 (10), sec. A, p. 4126: "The principal
purposes of this study are to determine the nature and extent of
Edward Taylor's poetic development in the Preparatory Meditations and
to describe the shape of the Meditations as a single, unified work of
art. . . . Chapter I is devoted to the major critical controversies
surrounding Taylor's imagery and image criticism in general. . . .
Chapter II is a reading of the 49 meditations that make up Taylor's
First Series. . . . Chapter III is an examination of the first 56
poems in the Second Series: the group of 30 poems based on biblical
typology and the 'Christographic' meditations which follow. . . .
Chapter IV is a survey of the remaining meditations with special
emphasis on the series of poems based on texts from Canticles."

1967-13   Holsinger, John Calvin. "A Survey of the Major Arguments
     Used by English Promoters to Encourage Colonization and Interest
     in America by the Early Colonial Era." Ph.D., Temple Univ. v,
     121 leaves.

     Abstract in DA, vol. 29 (4), sec. A, p. 1192: "This monograph
has attempted to show--through a analysis of the major arguments used

in the writings of the late Tudor and early Stuart periods--how the
nation of England was made aware of the significance which America
might hold for their country. This was accomplished by an amazing
group of propagandists representing a broad spectrum of occupations
and social rank.   But though these men were diverse in their
perspective and interest in America their efforts helped establish in
the minds of their countrymen the idea of colonial expansion."
Contents: I. "The Groundwork Is Laid for an Empire," II. "American
Settlement Opposed in England," III. "Religion Promoted as a Reason
for Englishmen to be Interested in America," IV. "American Settlement
Promoted as a Solution of Relieving England's Domestic Problems," V.
"Interest in America Promoted as Having Economic Value to England,"
VI. "Interest in America Promoted as a Point of Patriotic Concerns,"
and VII. "Summary and Conclusion."

1967-14   Humphrey, Richard Alan.   "The Concept of Conversion in the
    Theology of Thomas Shepard (1605-1649)."   Ph.D., Drew Univ.
    viii, 255 leaves.

Abstract in DA, vol. 28 (5), sec. A, p. 1890: "In this thesis
Thomas Shepard is seen as a humanitarian, preacher, and theologian,
who dedicated his life, preaching and writing to a view of man's
conversion from sin and total depravity to an estate in which man, the
empty vessel, is filled with the Holy Spirit. . . . Chapter one gives
historical background and reviews the contradictory and confusing
modern evaluations of Shepard. . . . Shepard's life and times are
summarized in Chapter Two. . . . In Chapter Three the meaning of
man's fallen estate and his utter dependence upon the promise of God
as revealed in the nature and work of Jesus Christ are powerfully
described in Shepard's doctrines of God and man. . . . It is pointed
out in Chapter Four that it does man no harm to prepare for his
conversion. . . . In Chapter Five the conversion process and the work
of the Holy Spirit are analyzed in greater detail."

1967-15   Jackson, Frank Malcolm.   "An Application of the Principles
    of Aristotelean Rhetoric to Certain Early New England Prose."
    Ph.D., Univ. of Texas at Austin. v, 192 leaves.

Abstract in DA, vol. 28 (5), sec. A, p. 1788: "It is the
intention of this study to demonstrate that an application of the
principles of Aristotle's Rhetoric to the Puritan sermons, histories
and journals will produce more penetrating and relevant observations
than are commonly made about these texts. . . . The sermons discussed
include 'A True Sight of Sin' by Thomas Hooker [and] 'The Sovereign
Efficacy of Divine Providence' by Urian Oakes. . . . The histories
discussed are Wonder-Working Providence of Sion's Saviour in New
England by Edward Johnson, Of Plymouth Plantation by William Bradford
and Magnalia Christi Americana by Cotton Mather. . . . The journals
discussed include Narrative of the Captivity of Mrs. Mary Rowlandson,
Memoirs of Roger Clap, and The Autobiography of Increase Mather.
Through an analysis of the logic, structure and style of these
representative texts, the author concludes that whatever the cultural
aim of the Puritan texts, the textual aim is consistently persuasive."

1967-16   Lesser, Marvin Xavier. "'All for Profit': The Plain Style
    and the Massachusetts Election Sermons of the Seventeenth
    Century." Ph.D., Columbia Univ. vi, 224 leaves.

    Abstract in DA, vol. 28 (6), sec. A, p. 2253: "The first chapter
of the dissertation recounts the several theories generally offered
for the change in prose style in seventeenth-century England and
develops the Puritans' special concern with sermonic prose. The
second chapter is an attempt to define the plain style of the Puritans
in their own words, from the prefaces to their published works and the
handbooks on preaching they read, and to suggest stylistic
possibilities open to them. An intensive reading of the Massachusetts
election sermons makes up the third and fourth chapters, the longest
part of the dissertation. Here the attempt has been to detail the
prose style of the period and to relate it to the declension in New
England."

1967-17   Lewis, Theodore Burham, Jr. "Massachusetts and the Glorious
    Revolution, 1660-1692." Ph.D., Univ. of Wisconsin at Madison.
    ix, 455 leaves.

    Abstract in DA, vol. 28 (2), sec. A, p. 599: "A narrative and
analytical history of Massachusetts politics from 1660 to 1692; and a
brief discussion of the constitutional ideas of 1689 and their
relevance to the American Revolution. . . . Part I discusses the
politics of the Bay Colony from 1660 to the revocation of the charter
in 1684. Emphasis is placed on the growth of the moderate party, a
loose coalition of Congregationalists primarily from coastal towns who
sought accommodation with the crown. . . . Part II discusses the
administration of Sir Edmund Andros as governor of the Dominion of New
England. The author concludes that Andros was politically inept.
. . . [The] concluding chapter summarizes the negotiations in London
over the settlement of a government for Massachusetts. The author
then discusses the political and constitutional legacy of the
revolution. . . .   Appendix I argues that Robert Mason's title to New
Hampshire was defective. Appendix II provides new data on the
population of Massachusetts. Appendix III confirms the traditional
view that the suffrage was greatly restricted under the first charter.
 . . . Appendix IV contains biographical sketches of important
political figures."

1967-18   Lowance, Mason Ira, Jr. "Images and Shadows of Divine
    Things: Puritan Typology in New England from 1660-1750." Ph.D.,
    Emory Univ. iii, 242 leaves.

    Abstract in DA, vol. 28 (10), sec. A, p. 4255. Considerably
expanded and revised version published as The Language of Canaan:
Metaphor and Symbol in New England from the Puritans to the
Transcendentalists. -- Cambridge, Mass. : Harvard Univ. Press, 1980.
-- x, 335 p. "Preface" (1980 ed.): "The 'language of Canaan' is a
phrase that refers to the prophetic and metaphorical language used by
God's chosen people when they talk of the kingdom of God and its
realization in the last days. It was employed by the Puritans in the

sixteenth and seventeenth centuries to describe the language the
saints will use when the kingdom has been established" (p. vii).
"Much of this study is concerned with symbolic expression in its
peculiarly prophetic role, with particular emphasis placed on the
development of millennial and eschatological symbols derived from the
Biblical process of typological foreshadowing and antitypical
fulfillment" (p. ix). Contents: "Introduction," I. "The Beginnings
of Figural Expression," II. "Figuralism in Late Seventeenth Century
New England" (includes Samuel Mather and Edward Taylor), III.
"Recapitulative Typology and Eschatology" (includes Cotton Mather),
and IV. "Epistemology and the Biblical Symbol from the Great Awakening
to the American Renaissance."

1967-19   McAvoy, Muriel Gravelle. "Boston Sugar Merchants before the
     Civil War." Ph.D., Boston Univ. (Graduate School). xiii, 325
     leaves.

     Abstract in DA, vol. 28 (5), sec. A, p. 1768: "Boston's chief
source of sugar before the Civil War was the Caribbean, where she
could trade such traditional Yankee wares as lumber, barrel staves and
fish. . . . As early as the 1640's, she traded chiefly with the
British islands, and in the eighteenth largely with the French."

1967-20   Markham, Coleman Cain. "William Perkins' Understanding of
     the Function of Conscience." Ph.D., Vanderbilt Univ.   244
     leaves.

     Abstract in DAI, vol. 28 (10), sec. A, p. 4256: "The purpose of
this thesis is to show that conscience is the central factor in the
writings of William Perkins (1558-1602), the point at which
soteriology and ethics, faith and works, are held together. . . .
Since the emphasis in Perkins is practical rather than theoretical,
. . . the study is oriented toward the functional rather than the
ontological understanding of conscience. Searching of conscience for
indications of how to act and think with regard to faith and social
relations is a recurring theme in his writings. . . .   Since
conscience in its mediating function is always seen in relation to
something else, the study comprises two main aspects: (1) conscience
and faith, (2) conscience and the world. In the first section the
role that conscience plays in the receiving of faith and continuing in
faith is discussed, but the chief emphasis is placed on the assurance
of having faith. . . . The second part of the study focuses upon
conscience as the means for determining proper actions in particular
segments of society."

1967-21   Millar, David Richard. "The Militia, the Army, and
     Independency in Colonial Massachusetts." Ph.D., Cornell Univ.
     vii, 318 leaves.

     Abstract in DA, vol. 28 (7), sec. A, p. 2627: "The objectives of
this dissertation are several: to examine the origins of the colonial
militia, to describe the colonial military establishment as it existed
in law, and to evaluate its effectiveness from a colonial point of

view; to trace the development of colonial independency and its
influence on British colonial policy; to examine the decision to
maintain a standing army in North America, to determine whether the
threat of colonial independency influenced the decision, and to
examine its consequences."

1967-22   Muth, Philip Arthur. "The Ashursts: Friends of New
     England." Ph.D., Boston Univ. (Graduate School). vi, 343
     leaves.

     Abstract in DA, vol. 28 (6), sec. A, p. 2160: "The English
family of Ashurst performed valuable services in support of the New
England colonies in the late seventeenth and early eighteenth
centuries. . . . A clear and detailed description of the Ashurst
family and of the services which its members rendered to New England
indicates that the Ashursts were motivated by religious and political
sympathies toward the colonists. . . . The lives and services of
Alderman Henry Ashurst [agent for Plymouth and New Hampshire] and of
his two sons, Sir Henry [agent for Massachusetts and Connecticut] and
Sir William, are conspicuous."

1967-23   Perzel, Edward Spaulding. "The First Generation of
     Settlement in Colonial Ipswich, Massachusetts, 1633-1660."
     Ph.D., Rutgers Univ. x, 405 leaves.

     Abstract in DA, vol. 28 (5), sec. A, p. 1744: "John Winthrop,
Jr., son of the governor of Massachusetts Bay, led a small group of
men north of Boston to start a settlement at Agawam. This settlement
became Ipswich in Essex County. . . . Ipswich was an important town
in both the political and religious development of Massachusetts Bay.
. . . In order to thoroughly analyze the development of the first
generation inhabitants and to determine what forces were most
significant in shaping the institutions every adult male inhabitant of
the first generation has been thoroughly studied. Material as to
birth, death, migration, English origin, landholding, commoner status,
political status, occupation, and any other pertinent information has
been gathered on each individual."

1967-24   Pope, Robert Gardner. "The Half-Way Covenant: Church
     Membership in the Holy Commonwealth, 1648-1690." Ph.D., Yale
     Univ. x, 285 leaves.

     Abstract in DA, vol. 28 (10), p. 4101. Revison published as The
Half-Way Covenant: Church Membership in Puritan New England. --
Princeton : Princeton Univ. Press, 1969. -- xi, 321 p. Contents (1969
ed.): "Introduction: New England's Crisis," 1. "Hesitant Answers:
1646-1661," 2. "The Half-Way Synod," 3. "Connecticut Confronts the
Problem: 1664-1668," 4. "Connecticut's Resolution: 1667-1690," 5.
"Trials of Orthodoxy: Massachusetts Churches and the Half-Way
Covenant: 1662-1670," 6. "John Davenport and the Politics of the
Half-Way Covenant," 7. "The New Orthodoxy: 1676-1692," 8. "Their
Separate Ways: Four Churches and the Half-Way Covenant," 9. "The
Continuing Search: 1675-1692," and 10. "New England Churches and the

Half-Way Covenant." Appendix of eight graphs and four tables.

1967-25   Pratte, Richard Norman. "A History of Teacher Education in
      Connecticut from 1639 to 1939." Ph.D., Univ. of Connecticut.
      443 leaves.

    Abstract in DA, vol. 28 (9), sec. A, p. 3480: "This study traces
the background, origin, and development of teacher education in
Connecticut from 1639 to 1939. . . . Chapter II dealt with the social
and professional background of teachers during the colonial and early
American ending in 1800 [sic]."

1967-26   Priebe, Victor Lewis. "The Covenant Theology of William
      Perkins." Ph.D., Drew Univ. 286 leaves.

    Abstract in DA, vol. 28 (5), sec. A, p. 1893: "Recognizing the
extensive influence of William Perkins upon his own and subsequent
generations of Puritans, this thesis is predicated upon the assumption
that the reasons for Perkins' popularity and influence must be sought
primarily in the content and structure of his theology itself, rather
than in his ability merely to simplify and popularize theological
issues. . . . Perkins' idea of the covenant is not that of a
conditional-contractual type, but in reality affirms the priority and
primacy of the unconditional promise or testament in a manner most
nearly identical to Calvin."

1967-27   Reinitz, Richard Martin. "Symbolism and Freedom: The Use
      of Biblical Typology as an Argument for Religious Toleration in
      Seventeenth-Century England and America." Ph.D., Univ. of
      Rochester. viii, 398 leaves.

    Abstract in DA, vol. 28 (5), sec. A, p. 1773: "The literal
interpretation of the state-church of Israel provided the main
Biblical support for the use of civil power to maintain Christian
orthodoxy. Some separatists came to justify their break with the
established order by attacking the exercise of state power in
religious matters. Roger Williams, building upon the work of earlier
separatists, used typology to undermine the validity of the use of Old
Testament state-church relations as a literal precedent for those of
Christian states. . . . Puritans such as John Cotton who opposed the
idea of liberty of conscience also relied upon typology. An
examination of the debates between Williams and Cotton reveals the
differences in the way in which they interpreted the Bible and in
their attitudes toward liberty of conscience were derived from opposed
views of the nature of man."

1967-28   Spencley, Kenneth James. "The Rhetoric of Decay in New
      England Writing, 1665-1730." Ph.D., Univ. of Illinois at Urbana-
      Champaign. 191 leaves.

    Abstract in DA, vol. 27 (11), sec. A, p. 3851: "New England

Puritans . . . viewed the world as decaying, largely because of men's sins. . . . Not content with condemning sinful practices in direct discourse, Puritan preachers employed vivid, yeasty metaphorical language. . . . Their use of figurative language was governed by the belief that rhetoric, as an ornament of speech, was subordinate to grammar; metaphors and similes should be comprehensible to the least educated of men, for salvation of souls was dependent upon God's imparting grace during the preaching and reading of His word. . . . So great was their respect for the power of the word that Puritans active about 1730 continued to use metaphorical language coined by their grandfathers."

1967-29   Stover, Dale Arden. "The Pneumatology of John Owen: A Study of the Role of the Holy Spirit in Relation to the Shape of a Theology." Ph.D., McGill Univ. (Canada). ix, 315 leaves.

"Preface": "Because this study in theology with its historical focus in John Own operates with a specific approach, there has been an attempt to provide a check upon the critical viewpoint by looking at the larger historical context of the theological movements which impinge upon Owen. Therefore, the study has approached nearly every section of Owen's pneumatology with historical sketches which supply perspective depth and an orientation check upon the interpretive position. . . . The contribution of the study . . . to these larger areas--Calvin, Calvinism, Ramism, Augustinianism, Puritanism--comes by way of this study of Owen and from the force of its analysis of him" (pp. ii-iii). Contents: I. "Introduction: Pneumatology and John Owen," II. "The Holy Spirit and Knowledge of God: Rational Theology," III. "The Holy Spirit and Scripture: Authoritative Theology," IV. "The Holy Spirit and Jesus Christ: Systematic Theology," V. "The Holy Spirit and the Christian Man: Metaphysical Theology," VI. "The Holy Spirit and the Church: Individualistic Theology," and VII. "Conclusion: John Owen and Pneumatology."

1967-30   Strickland, William Jefferson. "John Goodwin as Seen through His Controversies of 1640-1660." Ph.D., Vanderbilt Univ. v, 264 leaves.

Abstract in DA, vol. 28 (10), sec. A, p. 4260: "The purpose of this study is twofold: (1) to show Goodwin's controversial writings in light of the broader significance of the changing times in which he lived, and (2) to place Goodwin in the historical and theological context of seventeenth-century English thought, particularly his relationship to Puritanism and Arminianism. For the most part, the order is historical and chronological. . . . Part One consists of two chapters and sets forth the biographical framework of Goodwin's career as a controversialist. . . . In part Two, there are three chapters which enlarge upon specific areas of controversy outlined in the first part."

1967-31   Taylor, Douglas Hanson. "John Wise and the Development of American Prose Style." Ph.D., Univ. of California at Davis. ii, 264 leaves.

Abstract in DA, vol. 28 (5), sec. A, p. 1796: "John Wise's two major treatises, The Churches Quarrel Espoused, 1713, and A Vindication of the Government of the New England Churches, 1717, are important to the history of American thought and the development of American prose style. Generally, American prose in the years from [Thomas] Hooker to [Benjamin] Franklin underwent a radical change, requiring greater clarity, plainness, and colloquial diction. Wise's writings are symptomatic of this change."

1967-32   Walsh, James Patrick. "The Pure Church in Eighteenth-Century Connecticut." Ph.D., Columbia Univ. vi, 283 leaves.

Abstract in DA, vol. 28 (5), sec. A, p. 1747: "The Puritans who settled New England . . . tried to create a pure church system, in which only regenerate persons would be allowed to partake of the Lord's Supper. At the same time, the Puritans expected to retain many of the features of an established church. The combination of a pure and an established church was basically unstable and began to break down even before the end of the seventeenth century. . . . In Connecticut, by the beginning of the eighteenth century, the pure church remained an ideal, but the actual practice of admissions to Communion had become much less restrictive. Solomon Stoddard finally attacked the ideal itself in his attempt to create in New England a 'national' church of which every Christian, regenerate or not, would be a member. Stoddard's out-right rejection of the pure church ideal was not so widely accepted in Connecticut as has been believed; Stoddardeanism encouraged a tendency toward less restrictive admission in practice, a tendency which even the Mathers, who believed in pure church theory, encouraged." Two appendices list twenty-three "Stoddardean Churches" and sixty-three "Pure Churches."

1967-33   Werge, Thomas Alan. "The Persistence of Adam: Puritan Concerns and Conflicts in Melville and Mark Twain." Ph.D., Cornell Univ. vi, 204 leaves.

Abstract in DA, vol. 28 (9), sec. A, p. 3653: "An important part of the Calvinist and Puritan inheritance in nineteenth-century America is the doctrine of original sin. A preoccupation with the fallen Adam--and with the corrupt state of human intellect and will as symbolized by Adam--is characteristic of Augustine, Calvin, the Puritans, and Jonathan Edwards. . . . This study explores the historical tensions in this traditional dialectic on the question of original sin. It then locates the influence on Melville and Twain of the Augustinian or Puritan conception of original sin as a corruption of 'nature.' . . . Melville and Twain cannot believe in traditional forms of 'salvation,' but they can believe only too well in man's fallen state. This Calvinistic emphasis on fallen human nature and on the total inadequacy of man's intellect and will illuminates the controlling ideas of Moby Dick and the philosophical themes of Mark Twain."

1967-34   Zemsky, Robert Michael. "The Massachusetts Assembly, 1730-1755." Ph.D., Yale Univ. iii, 329 leaves.

Abstract in DA, vol. 28 (1), sec. A, p. 186. Revision published as Merchants, Farmers, and River Gods: An Essay on Eighteenth-Century American Politics. -- Boston : Gambit, 1971. -- xiii, 361 p. "Preface" (1971 ed.): "The first question I asked of that time and place was simply, 'What did government in the eighteenth century do?' ... What precisely did politicians compete for when they sought personal power? How big was the budget? How large was the army? How extensive was the civil service? ... I next sought to learn something of the texture of the political fabric: how complex and intricate was its weave? ... How rigid were its rules and customs? Did young men grow old waiting their turn to exercise power? ... Drawing again on data supplied by the General Court, I next asked, 'Who were Massachusetts' leaders?' How extensive was their power? ... Finally, I sought to measure the impact non-officeholders had on public policy" (p. xiii). Relevant chapters: "Prologue: The Business of Government," 1. "The Legislative Task," 2. "The Social Prerequisites of Power," and 3. "The Professional Style." Chapters 4-11 deal with later matters. "Statistical Appendix": "A Method for Our Madness."

1967-35   Zimdars, Dale Everett. "John Goodwin and the Development of Rationalism in Seventeenth-Century England." Ph.D., Univ. of Chicago. ix, 203 leaves.

"Preface": "The task of this study is to discover the nature, extent, and development of [John Goodwin's] rationalism and compare his criteria for religious truth and resulting theological convictions with those of a more orthodox member of his party, Thomas Goodwin. This will be related also to contemporary interests and movements on the English scene. In this way it is hoped that the meaning of rationalism at that time may be more accurately demonstrated" (p. ii). Contents: I. "Rationalistic Tendencies in England in the Sixteenth and Seventeenth Centuries": "Liberal Theologians and Churchmen," "Rationalistic Theologians," "The Cambridge Platonists," and "Natural Law, Science, and Philosophy"; II. "Rationalism within Puritanism"; III. "Two Goodwins"; IV. "Scripture and Reason"; V. "Nature and Grace"; and VI. "Contrasts, Similarities, and Conclusions."

1967-36   Zuckerman, Michael Wolodin. "The Massachussetts Town in the Eighteenth Century." Ph.D., Harvard Univ. 2 vols. (341; 275 leaves).

Revision published as Peaceable Kingdoms: New England Towns in the Eighteenth Century. -- New York : Alfred A. Knopf, 1970. -- ix, 329 p. Reprinted: New York : Random House, 1972. -- ix, 329 p. -- (Vintage Books). Also reprinted: New York : W. W. Norton, 1978. -- ix, 329 p. "Preface" (1970 ed.): "The book is an attempt to comprehend the culture of provincial Massachusetts whole, to get at its values and its behavior. If, for all that, the final result is ultimately more a study of values than of behavior, the values examined are at least the values of ordinary, otherwise nameless men speaking the language and the assumptions of their everyday affairs" (p. vii). Contents: "Introduction," I. "The Context of Community: The Town and the Province," II. "Principles of Peace," III. "The Practice of Peace," IV. "Healing and Divisions," V. "The Sense of the Meeting," VI. "A Happy Mediocrity," and VII. "War and Peace." Includes ten appendices.

1968-1   Anderson, Marcia J. "Devils and Divines: The New England Puritan in American Drama." Ph.D., Brandeis Univ. 422 leaves.

Abstract in DA, vol. 29 (8), sec. A, p. 2665: "In a study of thirty-four American plays involving New England Puritans and Pilgrims as characters, I find a general tendency for the playwright to view the Puritans as villains, the Pilgrims as heroes. . . . The Salem witchcraft episode provides the basis for fourteen of the plays, and allows for the presentation of the Puritan at his most villainous. . . . Eleven of the plays deal with the Pilgrims. . . . The remaining nine plays present mixtures of villainy and heroism. Four involve Thomas Morton of Merry Mount. . . . The final five plays present characters martyred by the Puritans: Quakers, Anne Hutchinson, and Roger Williams."

1968-2   Breen, Timothy Hall. "The Character of the Good Ruler: A Study of Puritan Political Ideas in New England, 1630-1730." Ph.D., Yale Univ. viii, 412 leaves.

Abstract in DA, vol. 29 (7), sec. A, p. 3941. Revision published under same title: New Haven ; London : Yale Univ. Press, 1970. -- xx, 301. Reprinted: New York : W. W. Norton, 1970. -- xx, 301 p. "Introduction" (1970 ed.): The book "examines the transformation of political ideas in a society often regarded as a model of stability. The seemingly static quality of the seventeenth- and early eighteenth-century election sermons could easily lead one to conclude that political theory had changed very little during New England's first hundred years. . . . Despite their static appearance, Puritan political ideas were not an unchanging or uniform body of thought" (p. xi). Contents: 1. "The English Background: The 1620s," 2. "A Family Quarrel: 1630-1660," 3. "The Fruits of Diversity: 1660-1684," 4. "The Glorious Revolution: 1684-1691," 5. "The Politics of Property: 1691-1694," 6. "Two New Englands: 1695-1730," 7. "The Country Persuasion," and "Epilogue."

1968-3   Carroll, Peter Neil. "Puritanism and the Wilderness: The Intellectual Significance of the New England Frontier, 1629-1675." Ph.D., Northwestern Univ. 249 leaves.

Abstract in DA, vol. 29 (7), sec. A, p. 2172. Revised and expanded version published as Puritanism and the Wilderness: The Intellectual Significance of the New England Frontier, 1629-1700. -- New York ; London : Columbia Univ. Press, 1969. -- xi, 243 p. "Preface" (1969 ed.): The book intends "to examine the role of the wilderness in the thought of one group of colonists, the settlers of New England. It will analyze both the Puritan attitude toward the forest and the influence of the wilderness upon Puritan social thought" (p. vii). Contents: "Introduction," Part I: "Two Worlds," Part II: "The Symbolic Wilderness," Part III: "A Wilderness Society," and "Epilogue."

1968-4   Darrow, Diane Marilyn. "Thomas Hooker and the Puritan Art of Preaching." Ph.D., Univ. of California at San Diego. vi, 225 leaves.

Abstract in DA, vol. 29 (5), sec. A, p. 1535: "This study attempts a critical examination of Thomas Hooker's collection of sermons, The Application of Redemption, in the light of Renaissance theological and artistic concerns rather than from the narrower standpoint of colonial American intellectual history. . . . It is seldom acknowledged that his writings belong to the rhetorical traditions that shaped the art of the sermon from its classical origins to its seventeenth-century forms. . . . In The Application of Redemption, Hooker achieved an implicit 'poetic' of the sermon, explaining and embodying the spiritual artifice by which the Puritan preacher gave his religious doctrines the imaginative realization necessary for them to move the hearts and affections of the Puritan congregation."

1968-5   Davis, Delmer Ivan. "Critical Editions of Samuel Sewall's Phaenomena quaedam Apocalyptica and Proposals Touching the Accomplishment of Prophesies Humbly Offered." Ph.D., Univ. of Colorado at Boulder. c, 330 leaves.

Abstract in DA, vol. 29 (4), sec. A, p. 1205: "A concern with Biblical prophecy was more pervasive among American Puritans than has generally been recognized by scholars. . . . Samuel Sewall was not unusual in his composition of two treatises concerned with prophetic analysis. . . . Phaenomena quaedam Apocalyptica was written in answer to a short chapter authored by Joseph Mede, the English divine, who had suggested that America would be the source of Satan's last followers--those who would attempt to destroy the New Jerusalem after the millennium. Sewall not only attempted to refute Mede's hypothesis, but he maintained that America might well be the site of the New Jerusalem when it was established. . . . Proposals . . . was a supplement to Phaenomena . . . , and it merely reiterated the claim that America would eventually be the site of paradise. . . . The prophetic treatises are records of Sewall's limitations as a literary artist. . . . The text [of Phaenomena] represented here has been based on a comparison of several printed copies of both the 1697 and 1727 editions. . . . The text of Proposals . . . is based on the manuscript and the 1713 printed edition."

1968-6   Davis, Thomas M. "The Tradition of Puritan Typology." Ph.D., Univ. of Missouri at Columbia. 412 leaves.

Abstract in DA, vol. 29 (9), sec. A, p. 3094: "Although a number of critics have briefly commented on Puritan typology, none has recognized how extensively typological imagery appears in Puritan literature, nor how complex are the traditions of medieval art and literature which inform the Puritan use of the typical image. . . . The purpose of this study, then, is to trace the development of typological interpretations from New Testament authors to English and colonial Puritans, indicating how typological traditions culminate in Puritan literature. . . . Of New England artists, Edward Taylor was perhaps the most knowledgeable about typology and the most influenced by its traditions."

1968-7   Dinkin, Robert Joseph.   "Provincial Massachusetts: A
    Deferential or a Democratic Society?" Ph.D., Columbia Univ. 242
    leaves.

    Abstract in DAI, vol. 32 (1), sec. A, p. 336: "This dissertation attempts to disprove the Brown thesis on colonial democracy. In 1955, Professor Robert E. Brown . . . published an important monograph, Middle-Class Democracy and the Revolution in Massachusetts, 1691-1780 [see #1946-1, above]. In this work, Brown claims that . . . provincial Massachusetts contained a middle-class democratic society in which a large majority of people owned a substantial amount of property and possessed the right to vote. . . . This study maintains that provinicial Massachusetts was primarily a deferential, not a democratic, society. Despite the fact that a majority of adult males owned a considerable amount of property and possessed the franchise, the colony cannot be termed democratic in the modern sense. In the social and political spheres the inhabitants of the Bay deferred to the gentlemen of wealth and influence."

1968-8   Dunn, Edward Thomas.   "Tutor Henry Flynt of Harvard College,
    1675-1760." Ph.D., Univ. of Rochester. vii, 495 leaves.

    Abstract in DAI, vol. 30 (9), sec. A, p. 3882: "By birth, education, and position Henry Flynt was closely connected with influential individuals in colonial New England. . . . Flynt augmented his salary as tutor by investment in land, trade through his merchant relatives, speculation in silver and gold, and money lending. . . . His chief extra-personal concern was Harvard. Clerk of the Board of Overseers and active member of the Corporation, he sat on numerous committees on the college's policy and holdings."

1968-9   Finlayson, Michael George. "Independency in Old and New
    England, 1630-1660:   An Historiographical and Historical Study."
    Ph.D., Univ. of Toronto (Canada). ix, 352 leaves.

    Abstract in DAI, vol. 33 (1), sec. A, p. 250. "Almost all historians who have discussed Puritanism, before and during the Civil War, either in England or in Massachusetts, have . . . based their analyses on a dialectical logical model. . . . An alternative approach, that pays more respect to the complexity of the subject and to the attitude of contemporaries, is to base our analysis on the model of a spectrum. . . . Having abandoned the dialectic, the simplistic Presbyterian-Independent conflict becomes less relevant; rather it becomes necessary to distinguish between various sorts of

Presbyterians and Independents. Then . . . it soon becomes evident that English clerical Independency, that is, the Independency of the Dissenting Brethren which is quite different from lay Independency, affords us a much less striking contrast with the New England Way than has hitherto been suggested."

1968-10   Gibbs, Lee Wayland. "The Technometry of William Ames." Th.D., Harvard Univ. x, 617 leaves.

Revision published as Technometry by William Ames (1576-1633), a translation of Guilelmi Amesii Technometria, with an introduction and commentary by Gibbs. -- Philadelphia : Univ. of Pennsylvania Press, 1979. -- xii, 202 p. -- (The Twenty-Fourth Publication in the Haney Foundation Ser., Univ. of Pennsylvania). "Preface" (1979 ed.): "Those familiar with the period recognize the dominant influence exercised by Ames and his works in the history and development of Puritanism in England, the Netherlands, and especially New England. He has justifiably been called 'the spiritual father of the New England churches,' 'the favorite theologian of early New England,' and 'the father of American theology'" (p. vii). Contents: "Introduction": "The Life and Work of William Ames," "The Major Sources of Technometry," "The Definition, Structure, and Function of Technometry," "The Influence of Technometry," "Conclusion," and "Notes"; "Technometry"; and "Commentary."

1968-11   Gowen, James Anthony. "Some Puritan Characteristics of the Poetry of Edwin Arlington Robinson." Ph.D., Stanford Univ. iii, 213 leaves.

Abstract in DA, vol. 29 (5), sec. A, p. 1538: "The purpose of this study is to examine the relationship of the poetry of Edwin Arlington Robinson to the earliest native tradition, American Puritanism. . . . The thesis of this study is that Robinson's most important traditional ties are with Puritanism--or, more specifically, with the vestiges of that tradition as they survived in his home influence of Gardiner, Maine. . . . The study . . . focuses on the poetry itself, examining it in terms of fundamental puritan concepts-- sense of human depravity, predestination, grace, reprobation, election, and the Christian calling. These concepts and the related language pervade the poetry from beginning to end. . . . What some of his contemporaries called pessimism . . . stems from a Puritan sense of the absolute disparity between this world and the next and correspondingly between man's fallen condition and the harmony of the divinely ordered universe."

1968-12   Harris, Billy Laydon. "The New England Fast Sermon, 1639-1763." Ph.D., Florida State Univ. iii, 202 leaves.

Abstract in DA, vol. 29 (5), sec. A, p. 1612: "The New England colonists believed that God intervened directly in men's affairs. Abundant harvests, a military debacle, a home ravished by fire--all were interpreted as God's pleasure or displeasure with his people, and whether it warned or rewarded, God's voice should be acknowledged.

Regular sabbath services were not adequate for this purpose because God had sent a special sign; thus, special days were needed. Fast days were created to satisfy this need. The purpose of this study was to analyze thirty-two fast sermons delivered on these fast days. . . . The data was arranged into six chapters: (1) Introduction, (2) The Historical Setting, (3) The Speakers, (4) Arrangement and Themes, (5) Modes of Proof, and (6) Evaluation of Effectiveness."

1968-13   Henretta, James Aloysious. "The Duke of Newcastle, English Politics, and the Administration of the American Colonies, 1724-1754." Ph.D., Harvard Univ. 458 leaves.

Revision published as "Salutary Neglect": Colonial Administration under the Duke of Newcastle. -- Princeton : Princeton Univ. Press, 1972. -- xii, 381 p. "Preface" (1972 ed.): "In the end, this study has become less an individual biography [of Thomas Pelham-Holles, Duke of Newcastle] than a group portrait, less a discussion of 'Anglo-American' patronage and politics than an analysis, from a colonial perspective, of the developing political and administrative system of the mother country during the first half of the eighteenth century. . . . Events which took place in the new world are introduced into the narrative only in so far as they impinged upon or reflected developments in London" (pp. vii-ix). Relevant chapters: 1. "The Structure and Politics of Colonial Administration, 1721-1730," 2. "The Movement for Reform," and 3. "The Beginnings of the Newcastle Era." Chapters 4-7 treat of events from 1737-54.

1968-14   Howard, Alan Blair. "The Web in the Loom: An Introduction to the Puritan Historians of New England." Ph.D., Stanford Univ. xii, 422 leaves.

Abstract in DA, vol. 29 (7), sec. A, p. 2214: "This study represents the first extended introduction to Puritan historical thought and method, as well as a tentative functional description of the histories of the period, of the diverse ways in which they exemplify attempts to define . . . both the New England way and the 'errand into the wilderness.' . . . [This] dissertation attempts to demonstrate that Puritan historical writing was as complex, as diverse in its virtues and defects, aims and accomplishments, as the historians themselves. . . . The 'Introduction' presents a brief essay on modern views of Puritan historical writing, from those of Moses Coit Tyler to those of Peter Gay. . . . Chapter I attempts to reconstruct the providential interpretation of history. . . . Chapter II discusses the Puritan's conception of the 'craft of the historian,' the definitions of the proper goals of history, the varieties of historical writing, and the subjects, styles, and methods of selection appropriate to each particular kind. . . . The third chapter focuses upon the Puritans' attempts to locate New England's own history within the larger providential plan. . . . Chapters IV and V present detailed essays on individual Puritan histories, William Bradford's Of Plymouth Plantation and John Winthrop's Journal." Diss. ends with a "Conclusion."

1968-15   Johnson, James Turner. "A Society Ordained by God: A Study
    of English Puritan Marriage Doctrine in the First Half of the
    Seventeenth Century." Ph.D., Princeton Univ. vii, 286 leaves.

        Abstract in DA, vol. 29 (8), sec. A, p. 2788. Revision published
as A Society Ordained by God: English Puritan Marriage Doctrine in
the First Half of the Seventeenth Century. -- Nashville : Abingdon
Press, 1970. -- 219 p. -- (Studies in Christian Ethics Ser.).
"Preface" (1970 ed.): "This book is not intended to be a refutation
of popular misconceptions of Puritanism; in particular it does not
take up and refute twentieth-century notions of what the Puritan sex
ethic was. What it does do is explore how certain Puritan writers in
the first half of the seventeenth century conceived of the
relationship of marriage, that is, what they said marriage should be
ideally and what grounds they allowed for ending it when it fell short
of the ideal" (pp. 5-6). Relevant chapters: "Introduction," I. "The
Covenant Idea and the Puritan Doctrine of Marriage," II. "Early
Statements of the Puritan Marriage Doctrine," III. "Dutiful
Companionship: The Crystallization of Puritan Marriage Doctrine," and
VI. "Conclusions." Chapters IV and V deal with John Milton's views of
marriage. Appendices: A. "Two Polemical Authors on Marriage: Edmund
Bunny and John Rainolds" and B. "Topics from Ramist Logic."

1968-16   Johnson, Thomas E., Jr. "American Puritan Poetic Voices:
    Essays on Anne Bradstreet, Edward Taylor, Roger Williams, and
    Philip Pain." Ph.D., Ohio Univ. 164 leaves.

        Abstract in DA, vol. 29 (9), sec. A, p. 3141: "The purpose of
the dissertation is to identify some of the distinctive, Puritanesque
qualities which are in the poetry of Anne Bradstreet, Edward Taylor,
Roger Williams, and Philip Pain. The voices of these poets
demonstrate degrees of variety, unity, and individuality found in
selected poetry of four American Puritan poets. . . . The essays in
this work dealt with the poetry of Roger Williams, in A Key to the
American Language (London, 1643); Philip Pain, in Daily Meditations
(Cambridge, Mass., 1668); Anne Bradstreet, in Several Poems (Boston,
1678); and Edward Taylor, in Poems (New Haven, 1960)."

1968-17   Kawashima, Yasuhide. "Indians and the Law in Colonial
    Massachusetts, 1689-1763." Ph.D., Univ. of California at Santa
    Barbara. xiii, 423 leaves.

        "Abstract" (at beginning of diss.): "Through an examination of
the legal aspect of the Indian-white relations in colonial
Massachusetts, attempts will be made to see . . . what the colonial
authorities were trying to do with the natives, . . . and to grasp
. . . the entire field of colonial law in Massachusetts more clearly"
(p. ix). Contents: I. "Massachusetts Relations with the Indians,
1630-1763," II. "Massachusetts Judicial System and the Indians," III.
"Jurisdiction of the Colonial Courts over the Indians," IV. "Indian
Land Policy," V. "Legal Nature of Massachusetts Indian Reservations,"
VI. "Indian Trade Regulations," VII. "Crime and Punishment of the
Indians," VIII. "The Indians and Civil Cases," IX. "Special Laws and
Regulations Concerning the Indians," X. "The Indians and the

Massachusetts Court Procedure," and XI. "Legal Position of the Indians
in Colonial Society." Announced but not yet published as this
bibliography was in preparation: Kawashima's Puritan Justice and the
Indian: White Man's Law in Massachusetts, 1630-1763. -- Middletown,
Conn. : Wesleyan Univ. Press, [1983?].

1968-18 King, Irving Henry. "The S.P.G. in New England, 1701-1784."
    Ph.D., Univ. of Maine. 322 leaves.

    Abstract in DA, vol. 29 (6), sec. A, p. 1835: While "the role of
the Anglican Church in New England was not as significant as that of
the Congregational, it certainly was not trivial.... The history
of the Anglican Church organization, the Society for the Propagation
of the Gospel in Foreign Parts, was more complex than old traditions
have made it out to be. The characterization of the S.P.G. by text
book writers as a very insignificant and ineffective organization in
New England is not at all accurate. The S.P.G. was a forceful
organization in the period before the American Revolution. It was
increasing the influence, economic stability, and membership of the
Anglican Church in the years between 1701 and 1774." Relevant
chapters: I. "First Thrusts and Parries," II. "Genesis of the
S.P.G.," III. "Conversion of the Indians Policy," IV. "First
Proceedings in New England," V. "First Proceedings Protested," VI.
"Revolution in Higher Education," VII. "The Case of John Checkley,"
VIII. "Years of Growth and Wealth," and IX. "Puritanism Penetrated."
Chapters X-XVII deal with later events.

1968-19   Kubrin, David Charles. "Providence and the Mechanical
    Philosophy: The Creation and Dissolution of the World in
    Newtonian Thought. A Study of the Relations of Science and
    Religion in Seventeenth-Century England." Ph.D., Cornell Univ.
    xii, 387 leaves.

    Abstract in DA, vol. 29 (6), sec. A, p. 1835: "This study
centers around a cosmogonical tradition existing in England at the
time of Newton, a tradition sharing a common interest in questions
regarding the past Creation and future conflagration of the earth.
The theories of the 'world-makers' were reactions, at the same time,
to two contemporary religious heterodoxies: the first, that the world
is eternal, having neither Creation nor dissolution, and the contrary
belief that the world, far from being immortal, is so very mortal that
its end is quite close at hand. This last belief belonged to various
millennial sects of the seventeenth century, sects whose millennial
theories were given social, political, and even military expression in
the Civil War and Restoration.... This study tries to demonstrate
the strength of the cosmogonical tradition before it died out, and to
show the central role it played in the evolution of Newtonian
metaphysics and in the relations science and religion had in
seventeenth-century England."

1968-20   Lewis, Norma. "English Missionary Interest in the Indians
    of North America." Ph.D., Univ. of Washington. viii, 493
    leaves.

     Abstract in DA, vol. 29 (10), sec. A, p. 3560: "The seventeenth-
century English missionary idea which focuses on the Indians of North
America was . . . the product of a peculiar combination of factors.
. . . Methods in missionary work varied considerably. Geographical
isolation, theological difference, and variations in local environment
produced notable differences in the work of such men as . . . Roger
Williams in Rhode Island, John Eliot near Boston, and the Thomas
Mayhews on Nantucket Island. Means employed included preaching,
training and educating native children, direct legislation, Indian
self-help with missionaries as advisors, and construction of
settlements with totally new social and religious norms for the
settlers. . . . Though missionary successes were small in terms of
proposed goals, the work formed a significant element in relations
between the white and Indian races during the colonial period."

1968-21   Lovelace, Richard Franz. "Christian Experience in the
     Theology of Cotton Mather." Th.D., Princeton Theological
     Seminary. v, 534 leaves.

     Abstract in DA, vol. 29 (8), sec. A, p. 2791. Revision published
as The American Pietism of Cotton Mather. -- Grand Rapids, Mich. :
Christian Univ. Press ; W. B. Eerdmans [distributor], 1979. -- x, 350
p. Contents: One: "Reinterpreting Mather: An Introduction," Two:
"The Sources and Structure of Mather's Theology," Three: "The
Experience of Rebirth," Four: "The Machinery of Piety," Five: "The
Godly Life," Six: "The Ministry of Doing Good," Seven: "The Unity of
the Godly," and "Epilogue."

1968-22   McCune, Marjorie Wolfe. "The Danforths: Puritan Poets."
     Ph.D., Pennsylvania State Univ. 332 leaves.

     Abstract in DA, vol. 29 (12), sec. A, p. 4498: "All of the
extant poetry of Samuel Danforth and his sons John and Samuel II,
three Puritan clergymen of the Massachusetts Bay colony in the
seventeenth and early eighteenth centuries, is presented for the first
time in one edition. . . . The text is preceded by a general
discussion of the history of the verse, an account of the Danforths'
place in early New England life and letters, a critical examination of
the poetry in the perspective of Puritan and English colonial
aesthetic with a discussion of the genres involved, and, finally, a
note on editorial policy. The edition of the poetry has explanatory
footnotes. Following the text are textual notes and a bibliography of
the Danforths' writings. . . . The Danforths' verse reflects the
impelling conviction that in conquering and peopling the new world
Puritans were participating in a moment of divine history for which
the eloquence of poetry was aesthetically appropriate."

1968-23   Nuckols, Thomas Wheeler. "A Holy Commonwealth: The
     Political Thought of Richard Baxter." Ph.D., Duke Univ. xi, 261
     leaves.

     Abstract in DA, vol. 29 (8), sec. A, p. 2792: "The purpose of this study is a critical exposition of the political thought of Richard Baxter (1615-1691). Since Baxter's writings were occasional writings which cannot be understood apart from the historical context and events, an historical study of the period and Baxter's relationships and activities has been prefixed to the exposition of his thought. An assessment of his relationship to the emerging liberal democratic state and its early spokesman, John Locke, concludes the study. . . . He was perhaps the ablest spokesman for the conservative Puritans at the time that Puritan movement reached the peak of its influence and began to disintegrate as a cohesive force."

1968-24   Potter, Robert Atkinson. "Church, Converts, and Children: Implications for Christian Education in the Doctrine of the Church Held by Seventeenth-Century New England Puritans as Particularly Exemplified in John Norton's The Answer." Ed.R.D., Hartford Seminary Foundation. ix, 234 leaves.

Abstract in DAI, vol. 30 (2), sec. A, p. 800: "Chapter I gives an exposition of The Answer. . . . Chapter II discusses several central issues in the doctrine of the church which are directly related to the task of Christian education. . . . The purpose of chapter III is to illustrate the ways in which the institutional church tried to meet the educational demands of a particular era. . . . Chapter IV focuses on the educational leadership of two later Puritans, namely Isaac Watts and Horace Bushnell. . . . Chapter V presents several major implications for present-day Christian education."

1968-25   Ruth, John Landis. "English Hymn-Writing in America, 1640-1800." Ph.D., Harvard Univ. iv, 331 leaves.

"Preface": "Now that Americans have begun to interrogate curiously every aspect of their national heritage, I have felt justified in tracking to its source our earliest protohymnody, and asking certain non-literary questions about its most interesting examples. Limiting myself to those written in English before 1800, I have asked: Why was this or that hymn written? What did it mean to its author? What was it really 'about' in terms of the author's dialogue with his community, his culture, his self, his God? Beginning with such questions demands, of course, a recognition that the story of hymnody is always a chapter in a larger story. It has been my attempt to let these hymns tell a part of the story of their time and culture" (pp. ii-iii). Relevant chapters: I. "'Psalms and Hymns and Spiritual Songs' in New England (1630-1700)," II. "From Psalm to Hymn with Isaac Watts (1700-1740)," and VII. "Retrospect (1640-1800)." Chapters III-VI treat of later developments.

1968-26   Seig, Louis. "Concepts of Change and the Historical Method in Geography: The Case of Springfield, Massachusetts." Ph.D., Univ. of Minnesota. xi, 299 leaves.

Abstract in DA, vol. 29 (10), sec. B, p. 3785: "Although

historical explanation is a necessary adjunct to any geographical study, it is entirely proper to accomplish geographic analysis from an historical point of view to gain a thorough understanding of change. . . . To illustrate the theoretical concepts, a case study of the Springfield, Massachusetts, area from 1636 to 1880 is presented. . . . From the time of the first settlement in 1636 until 1685, Springfield changed from a frontier town to a well ordered functioning place on the Connecticut River. Although it was started as a trading enterprise, most of the inhabitants were engaged in agriculture. . . . In 1685, Springfield was established as a town within set bounds. It had a theocratic form of government and was a closed agricultural society. During the transitional period from 1690 to 1820, many changes took place."

1968-27   Shumway, Floyd Mallory.   "Early New Haven and Its Leadership." Ph.D., Columbia Univ. xviii, 436 leaves.

Abstract in DAI, vol. 30 (2), sec. A, p. 667: "This dissertation described the development of New Haven's early elite and offers evidence that the descendents of this group were able to dominate the business, professional, and political life of the community until the Federalist Party fell from power in Connecticut. . . . A small oligarchy consisting of wealthy merchants planned and founded New Haven in 1638 and provided its leadership during the first generation. . . . By 1665, when their ill-fated undertaking collapsed and was absorbed into Connecticut, the oligarchs had become generally discredited in the eyes of their neighbors, and a new elite was beginning to emerge, made up of practical, previously undistinguished men who possessed the qualities needed for frontier existence. . . . The members of the rising elite prospered during the next two generations and increased their participation in public life, meanwhile uniting in marriage with the relatively few surviving descendants of the original oligarchy to create a new hybrid type enjoying aristocatic status."

1968-28   Strother, Bonnie Lew. "The Imagery in the Sermons of Thomas Shepard." Ph.D., Univ. of Tennessee. iii, 344 leaves.

Abstract in DAI, vol. 29 (5), sec. A, p. 1548: "Among the stylistic qualities of the American Puritan sermon which have received insufficient attention is imagery. For this reason the work of Thomas Shepard, one of the most significant preachers of the early New England colony, has been selected for study. First has been given a brief biographical sketch of Shepard indicating something of his importance to the Massachusetts Bay settlement. This is followed by a discussion of the style of seventeenth-century Puritan sermons in general and of Shepard's in particular. Finally, the greatest space is devoted to the images themselves, including form, source, and kind."

1968-29   Tichi, Cecelia Louise Halbert.   "The Art of the Lords Remembrancers: A Study of New England Puritan Histories." Ph.D., Univ. of California at Davis. vi, 210 leaves.

Abstract in DAI, vol. 29 (7), sec. A, p. 2211: "When Puritan descendant Thomas Prince decided in 1728 to compile a history of New England, he had available to him the writings of Puritan historians dating back nearly one century. The 'Lords Remembrancers,' a term applied by Puritan minister Urian Oakes to historians recording God's mercies in New England, had been most active since 1630 in writing accounts of the New England Israel in an American wilderness. . . . The major Puritan historians, from William Bradford to Cotton Mather, were unique in seventeenth-century literature in adapting the formulaic genre of spiritual biography to the New English Israel in its journey toward salvation. Their phraseology is often typical of that genre where figures are connotatively fraught to emphasize Christian unity of experience. . . . The historians' rhetorical response to a cluster of tribal temptations indicates the spiritually biographic strain in New England Puritan history, and provides a new basis on which to evaluate the art of the 'Lords Remembrancers.'"

1968-30   Trimpey, John Eccles. "The Poetry of Four American Puritans: Edward Johnson, Peter Bulkeley II, Nicholas Noyes, and John Danforth." Ph.D., Ohio Univ. xvii, 310 leaves.

Abstract in DAI, vol. 29 (9), sec. A, p. 3112: "This . . . is the purpose and method of this study: to recognize four neglected poets according to their merit by regarding their poetry as the unique expression of an individual. This study arrives at no generalized result. . . . Not all of them wrote pedestrian poetry all the time, nor were all of them fully representative of the abstract conception of a Puritan. One finds in the verse personalities and skills that have often been overlooked."

1968-31   Warch, Richard. "Yale College: 1701-1740." Ph.D., Yale Univ. xiii, 388 leaves.

Abstract in DAI, vol. 30 (2), sec. A, p. 563. Revision published as School of the Prophets: Yale College, 1701-1740. -- New Haven : Yale Univ. Press, 1973. -- xii, 339 p. -- (The Yale Scene: Univ. Ser. ; 2). "Preface" (1973 ed.): "Previous works on early Yale have, in the main, told the institutional history of the school faithfully. They have not, it seems to me, given the intellectual, social, and religious dimensions of the college their due. The first forty years of the eighteenth century were ones of intellectual and religious transition and tension in the colonies, prior to the so-called American Enlightenment on the one hand and the divisive impact of the evangelical revivals on the other" (p. ix). Contents: 1. "'Liberty to Erect a Collegiate School,'" 2. "'A Thing, Which They Call a College,'" 3. "'Declining and Unhappy Circumstances,'" 4. "'A Most Grevous Rout and Hurle-Burle,'" 5. "'A Repairer of the Breach,'" 6. "'Ballance in Favour of the College,'" 7. "'A Most Valuable Man,'" 8. "'Wherein Youth May Be Instructed in the Arts & Sciences,'" 9. "'Their Establishment in the Principles of the Christian Protestant Religion,'" 10. "'A Succession of Learned & Orthodox Men,'" 11. "'The Liberal, & Relligious Education of Suitable Youth,'" and 12. "'School of the Prophets.'"

1968-32   Wright, Paul Orrin. "Roger Williams: God's Swordsman in Searching Times." Th.D., Dallas Theological Seminary. 3 ["Abstract"], viii, 285 leaves.

"Abstract": "The aim of this dissertation is two-fold: to present an exposition of the quality of religious belief found in the writing of Roger Williams and to demonstrate that it is his conception of himself as a prophet of the Lord defending the pure church against the antichrists of the seventeenth century which leads to his promulgation of religious toleration and the separation of church and state" (p. 1). Contents: "Chronology"; Part I. "In These Searching Times": I. "The Protestant Experience," II. "The Puritan Experience," and III. "The Colonial Experience"; and Part II. "The Swordsman of the Lord": I. "The Swordsman and His Satanic Foe," II. "Christ's Two-Edged Sword," III. "The Sword Unsheathed," IV. "The Razor's Edge," and V. "The Blunted Blade."

1969-1   Affleck, Bert, Jr.   "The Theology of Richard Sibbes, 1577-1635." Ph.D., Drew Univ. 415 leaves.

Abstract in DAI, vol. 30 (5), sec. A, p. 2120: "A popular Puritan preacher of seventeenth-century England, Richard Sibbes proclaimed an experiential theology relevant to men of every age and condition. The central thesis of Sibbes's theological interpretation of life affirms that the work of the Spirit is a thorough-going Christocentric reality. The Holy Spirit motif unites Sibbes's theology, but an experiential Christology acts as the life-giving Spirit to be the meaning of our history. Christ is the Lord of history who has shown that meaning in history is to be found in the suffering love of God revealed in the Servanthood of Christ. . . . On the basis of this Christological foundation Sibbes conceives of God, the Word, man, faith, freedom, Church, and the Christian life as doctrines truly relevant to historical experience. . . . The possibility of new life becomes reality . . . only in the life of faith."

1969-2   Anania, Pasquale. "Adult Age and the Educating of Adults in Colonial America." Ph.D., Univ. of California at Berkeley. v, 460 leaves.

Abstract in DAI, vol. 30 (10), sec. A, p. 4247: "This dissertation is an historical study of the educating of adults in colonial America. It is a report on documentary research into the nature of adulthood in England and America from c. 1607-1776 and a report on how colonial adults were educated. . . . Chapter One reviews scholarly literature relevant to the thesis. . . . Chapter Two supplies proof that colonial views of age are misconstrued because English practices from which they are derived are misunderstood, especially civil ideas, customs, and legal processes. . . . Chapter Three provides evidence that the English conception of maturation was transferred to America [and] . . . also demonstrates the age distributions of Harvard and Yale students throughout the seventeenth

and eighteenth centuries with particular reference to adult age. . . .
Chapter Four describes how these and other forms of informal, formal,
and quasi-formal education were developed and operated in the American
colonies during the seventeenth century. . . . Chapter Five does the
same with the progress of adult education in the eighteenth century.
. . . Chapter Six provides a summary of the educating of adults and
considerations raised by this study. . . . Appendix I provides a
lengthy series of documentary extracts proving that adult age and age
of discretion were equivalent and that females entered adult age at
twelve and males at fourteen. . . . Appendix II supplies a list of
over fifty personal and 'public' libraries in the colonies. . . .
Appendix III provides a list of evening schools."

1969-3   Batinski, Michael Clement.   "Jonathan Belcher of
     Massachusetts, 1682-1741." Ph.D., Northwestern Univ. v, 345
     leaves.

     Abstract in DAI, vol. 30 (7), sec. A, p. 2666:   "This
dissertation is a biography of Jonathan Belcher, Governor of
Massachusetts and New Hampshire from 1730 to 1741. . . . The first
two chapters cover Belcher's life from his birth in 1682 to 1730. The
first discusses his father's ambitions that he assume the role of
gentleman, the problems of acquiring the trappings of gentility in a
frontier society, the importance of a Harvard education, and his
travels to London and the courts of Europe to fulfill this role.
. . . The second chapter treats with the problems of being a
politician in a society where ultimate political authority lay beyond
the grasp of most local elites and in the hands of London politicians.
Belcher was partially able to bridge this gap by cultivating friends
and patrons in England who became the key to his political success and
who also afforded him the opportunity to protect New England's
interests. . . . The third chapter discusses Belcher's political
philosophy." The remaining chapters deal with Belcher's later career.

1969-4 Bell, Michael Davitt. "Hawthorne and the Romantic Treatment
     of Puritanism: Seventeenth-Century New England in American
     Fiction, 1820-1850." Ph.D., Harvard Univ. iii, 412 leaves.

     Revision published as Hawthorne and the Historical Romance of New
England. -- Princeton : Princeton Univ. Press, 1971. -- xii, 253 p.
"Preface" (1971 ed.): "The present inquiry is directed toward the
treatment of the Puritan past in Hawthorne's fiction. . . . I am
concerned with Hawthorne's historical themes as they inform his tales
and novels of seventeenth-century New England" (p. viii). Contents:
"Introduction: The Treatment of the Past," One: "The Founding
Fathers," Two: "Tyrants and Rebels: Conventional Treatments of
Intolerance," Three: "A Home in the Wilderness," Four: "Fathers and
Daughters," and "Epilogue: Past and Present."

1969-5 Birkner, Gerd. "Heilsgewissheit und Literatur: Metapher,
     Allegorie und Autobiographie im Puritanismus." Dr. phil., Univ.
     Konstanz (West Germany).

Published under same title: München : Wilhelm Fink, 1972. -- 183 p. -- (Theorie und Geschichte der Literatur und der schönen Künste: Texte und Abhandlungen ; Bd. 18). Works by William Perkins, Richard Sibbes, John Preston, and others are discussed; references to events in New England are included. Contents: I. "Heilsnot und Prädestination," II. "Puritanische Metaphorik," III. "Puritanische Allegorie," and IV. "Spiritual Autobiography."

1969-6   Cuddigan, John D. "Three Puritan Peers: Their Religious Beliefs and Activities in the Puritan Revolution." Ph.D., Univ. of Minnesota. 317 leaves.

    Abstract in DAI, vol. 31 (3), sec. A, p. 1184: "This dissertation consists mainly of an analysis of the beliefs and activities of three early seventeenth-century Puritan noblemen: William Fiennes, first Viscount Saye and Sele, Robert Greville, second Baron Brooke, and Denzil Holles, first Baron Holles of Ifield. . . . Historians have too often attributed the conflict between the Anglicans and the Puritans to such secondary religious issues as liturgy or episcopacy. This thesis attempts from the writings of three Puritan laymen to expose the vital, theological beliefs which were the real source of conflict between the two religious groups. . . . The five main sources of religious controversy to be found in the writings of these three Puritan noblemen revolve around their beliefs cocncerning the nature of man and his relationship with God, the nature of the church and episcopacy, the nature of worship and the sacraments, the relationship between the church and the state, and the question of religious toleration." Fiennes (1582-1662) and, to a lesser extent, Greville (1608-1643) were active in Puritan colonial activities in New England during the 1630's.

1969-7   Danner, Dan Gordon. "The Theology of the Geneva Bible of 1560: A Study in English Protestantism." Ph.D., Univ. of Iowa. v, 216 leaves.

    Abstract in DAI, vol. 30 (7), sec. A, p. 3085: "The Geneva Bible of 1560 is one of the most important documents in the story of the English Bible. . . . [The] popularity of the Geneva Bible of 1560 may be accounted for by examining the prefaces, 'Arguments,' and annotations which were appended to the text. Even after the Authorized Version came out in 1611, the Geneva Bible continued to be the most popular Bible among the Puritans and Nonconformists. . . . This study is an examination of all the annotations of the Geneva Bible of 1560. The examination has uncovered the basic theological presuppositions and tendencies of the translators. Their doctrine of God, doctrine of man, views of salvation, ethics, and the church and history and the state have, for the first time, been clearly brought out into the open."

1969-8   Ehalt, David Russel. "The Development of Early Congregational Theory of the Church, with Special Reference to the Five 'Dissenting Brethren' at the Westminster Assembly." Ph.D., Claremont Graduate School. ix, 312 leaves.

Abstract in <u>DAI</u>, vol. 30 (3), sec. A, p. 1227: "The purpose of this study is the characterization of the theory and practice of classical Independency as it developed in sixteenth- and seventeenth-century England, with special reference to the important work of definition carried out by the five 'Dissenting Brethren' at the Westminster Assembly--William Bridge, Jeremiah Burroughs, Thomas Goodwin, Philip Nye, and Sidrach Simpson-- . . . [who in 1643/4] gave normative shape to the Separatist-Independent-Congregational movement which had been evolving since at least the days of Elizabeth." Contents: I. "Introduction: The Separatist Congregational Puritans as Covenant Theologians: A Basis for Churchmanship," II. "The Dissenting Brethren in Historical and Theological Context," III. "The Thought of the Dissenting Brethren on the Church: Covenantal Congregationalism and Divinely-Ordained Polity," IV. "The Dissenting Brethren and Their Allies," and V. "Conclusion."

1969-9   Ellis, Joseph John-Michael, III. "The Puritan Mind in Transition: The American Samuel Johnson (1696-1772)." Ph.D., Yale Univ. viii, 246 leaves.

Abstract in <u>DAI</u>, vol. 31 (3), sec. A, p. 1186. Revision published as <u>The New England Mind in Transition: Samuel Johnson of Connecticut, 1696-1772</u>. -- New Haven ; London : Yale Univ. Press, 1973. -- xii, 292 p. -- (Yale Historical Publications. Miscellany ; 98). "Preface" (1973 ed.): "The central theme of this book is the way certain habits of thought were challenged and, in some cases, changed. . . . The title of the book, then, is meant to refer not only to Johnson and his mental development, but also to the intellectual alteration that orthodox Puritans made in response to Johnson. . . . Another theme that runs throughout the following chapters is the slow and surreptitious nature of the intellectual change in eighteenth-century New England. So much of Puritan theology and polity was a matter of subtle emphasis that a slight shift in perspective was capable of producing fundamental religious change" (p. ix). Relevant chapters: 1. "Tradition and Turmoil: School and Churches," 2. "Curricular and Universal Order," 3. "The New Learning," and 4. "Anglicization." Johnson's conversion to the Church of England occurred in 1722; chapter 5-12 deal with his later life and mental development.

1969-10   Fiering, Norman Sanford. "Moral Philosophy in America, 1700 to 1750, and Its British Context." Ph.D., Columbia Univ. xiii, 392 leaves.

Abstract in <u>DAI</u>, vol. 33 (1), sec. A, p. 250: "This dissertation attempts to do several things: 1) to describe and comment upon the moral philosophy written by Americans in the first half of the eighteenth century . . . ; 2) to describe and comment on ethical works by non-American authors that were influential in the American colonies . . . ; 3) to propound certain theories about the relationship between earlier religious thought and the character of much moral philosophy in the eighteenth century; 4) to discuss the changes in psychological theory . . . which followed from certain schools of ethical thought in the seventeenth and eighteenth centuries; and 5) to describe the process by which moral philosophy grew from a rather suspect component of the curriculum of Protestant education in the seventeenth century to a position of near domination in the eighteenth century. . . . The so-called 'sentimentalist' school of ethics had a particular vogue in America, exemplified by the use of texts by Francis Hutcheson and David Fordyce at Harvard for the major part of the eighteenth century. . . . The American Samuel Johnson had a special interest in the curriculum and the interrelationships of the different parts of learning. In his early writings Johnson followed the system of William Ames, which denied the independence of ethics from theology." Cf. Fiering's Moral Philosophy at Seventeenth-Century Harvard: A Discipline in Transition. -- Chapel Hill : Published for the Institute of Early American History and Culture by the Univ. of North Carolina Press, 1981. -- x, 323 p.

1969-11   Fortin, Roger Antonio. "The Decline of Royal Authority in
           Colonial Massachusetts." Ph.D., Lehigh Univ. iv, 270 leaves.

        Abstract in DAI, vol. 30 (9), sec. A, p. 3883: "The purpose of this study is two-fold: to describe the royal instruments of authority in eighteenth-century Massachusetts and to examine the decline of royal rule in the province before the American Revolution. Royal authority in Massachusetts, based on the 1692 charter and the Crown's commission and instructions to the governor, sought to tighten the bond between England and the colony. In practice, however, these three instruments conflicted. Both popular leaders and the governor, by turning to the charter and the governor's commission and instructions respectively created constitutional or political skirmishes which generated popular interest and weakened connections between Massachusetts and England. . . . During the eighteenth century local rule gradually supplanted royal prerogative."

1969-12   Goldenberg, Joseph Abraham. "The Shipbuilding Industry in
           Colonial America." Ph.D., Univ. of North Carolina at Chapel
           Hill. 414 leaves.

        Abstract in DAI, vol 31. (1), sec. A, p. 338. Revision published as Shipbuilding in Colonial America. -- Charlottesville : Published for the Mariners Museum, Newport News, Virginia, by the Univ. Press of Virginia, 1976. -- xiii, 306 p. -- (Museum Publication--Mariners Museum ; no. 33). Relevant chapters (1976 ed.): I. "Ships and Shipbuilding in the First Colonial Settlements," II. "Shipbuilding Patterns in Seventeenth-Century America," III. "The Early Eighteenth-Century Expansion of Colonial Shipbuilding," IV. "Colonial Shipwrights," V. "Ship Construction in Eighteenth-Century America," and IX. "Conclusion." Chapters VI-VIII treat later periods. Relevant appendix: "Shipping Tables": Tables 1-4: "Massachusetts shipping register, 1697-1714."

1969-13   Leverenz, Langmuir David. "A Psychoanalysis of American
           Literature." Ph.D., Univ. of California at Berkeley. 692 leaves.

Abstract in DAI, vol. 31 (2), sec. A, p. 793. A considerable revision of this "far more grandiose dissertation" published as The Language of Puritan Feeling: An Exploration in Literature, Psychology, and Social History. -- New Brunswick, N. J. : Rutgers Univ. Press, 1980. -- xi, 346 p. "Preface" (1980 ed.): "My focus is on male and female styles and fantasies, against a background of changing work and family roles, first in England and then in New England" (p. x). Contents: "Introduction," One. "Why Did Puritans Hate Stage Plays?" Two. "Ambivalence in an Age of Dislocation," Three. "Mixed Expectations: Tender Mothers and Grave Governors," Four. "Obsessive Dependence," Five. "Breasts of God, Whores of the Heart," Six. "New England Styles: Diverse Fathers" (e.g., Thomas Hooker, John Cotton, and Thomas Shepard), Seven. "New England Styles: Divergent Sons" (Increase Mather and Samuel Willard), Eight. "[Benjamin] Franklin and [Jonathan] Edwards," and Nine. "Freud and the American Puritan Tradition."

1969-14   Mitchell, Robert M.   "The Weber Thesis as Tested by the Writing of John Calvin and the English Puritans of the Sixteenth and Seventeenth Centuries." Ph.D., Michigan State Univ. iv, 303 leaves.

Abstract in DAI, vol. 30 (6), sec. A, p. 2465. Revision published as Calvin's and the Puritan's View of the Protestant Ethic. -- Washington, D.C. : Univ. Press of America, 1979. -- ix, 79 p. "Introduction" (1979 ed.): "The main purpose of this book is to examine the writing of John Calvin and a number of English Puritan fathers to see how they fit into the pattern formulated by Weber in The Protestant Ethic and the Spirit of Capitalism. It will be necessary to: first, set forth Weber's thesis as succinctly and lucidly as is possible; secondly, to look at the economic and social views of John Calvin, the man whom Weber considers to be the father of that branch of Protestantism responsible for the development of capitalism. It will also be essential to glance at certain aspects of Calvin's theology. The final task will be to search the writings of the English Puritans to see how well they substantiate the contentions of Weber" (p. ix). Contents: I. "Max Weber's Thesis"; II. "Some Theological Views of John Calvin as They Relate to the Weber Thesis": A. "Scripture as the Basis of Calvin's Teachings," B. "Predestination," C. "Calling," and D. "Asceticism"; III. "The Bible and Christian Religion as the Basis of Calvin's Social and Economic Views": A. "The Life of a Christian Man: Social Views," B. "Economic Views of John Calvin: Usury," C. "Wealth and Poverty," and D. "Work and Wages"; IV. "The Spirit of English Protestantism: Religious Aspects": A. "Origin of the Name 'Puritan,'" B. "The Bible as the Basis of Puritan Teachings," C. "The Puritan Concept of God and the Doctrine of Election," D. "Calling," E. "Asceticism and Labor as They Relate to the Calling," F. "Fruits of Labor in a Calling as a Sign of God's Blessing," and G. "Signs of Salvation Are Spiritual"; V. "The Bible and Christian Religion as the Basis of the Puritan's Social and Economic Views"; and VI. "Concluding Remarks."

1969-15   Roddey, Gloria J.   "The Metaphor of Counsel: A Shift from
    Objective Realism to Psychological Subjectivism in the Conceptual
    Cosmology of Puritanism." Ph.D., Univ. of Kentucky.   225 leaves.

Abstract in DAI, vol. 31 (1), sec. A, p. 367: "This study deals
with the Puritan method of concretizing its ideology and explores the
thesis that Puritan metaphor shifted from a traditional Position [sic]
of objective and moderate realism (reality of mind and phenomenal
world) to a concept more closely approximating the genus of idealism
and, in more exact terms, subjective psychological realism.   It
explores the proposition that this shift was due primarily to the
effective force of the Puritan doctrine of election. . . . The
specific Puritan treatments of metaphor discussed include the
pertinent writings of [John] Foxe, [Thomas] Cartwright, [William]
Prynne, [John] Milton, [John] Bunyan, [Richard] Baxter, William
Bradford, Increase and Cotton Mather, [Anne] Bradstreet, [Edward]
Taylor, and [Jonathan] Edwards. . . . The study culminates with a
treatment of [Nathaniel] Hawthorne, and contends that those of
Hawthorne's writings cast in the Puritan milieu give a viable
illustration of the ultimate change in Puritan ideology and hence of
the shift proposed by the thesis."

1969-16   Scheick, William Joseph.   "The Will and the Word: The
    Experience of Conversion in the Poetry of Edward Taylor." Ph.D.,
    Univ. of Illinois at Urbana-Champaign.   211 leaves.

Abstract in DAI, vol. 30 (7), sec. A, p. 2979.   Revision
published as The Will and the Word: The Poetry of Edward Taylor. --
Athens : Univ. of Georgia Press, 1974. -- xvi, 181 p. "Introduction"
(1974 ed.): "It was particularly the relation between the will and
its words which became the main focus of Taylor's poetic meditations"
(p. x). Contents: "Introduction"; Part One: "Will": I. "Reason and
Nature," II. "The Human Body," and III. "The Will"; and Part Two:
"Word":   IV. "The Word as Piety," V. "The Poetic Word," and VI. "The
Poetic Self."

1969-17   Schnucker, Robert Victor.   "Views of Selected Puritans,
    1560-1630, on Marriage and Human Sexuality." Ph.D., Univ. of
    Iowa. 2 vols. (v, 698 leaves).

Abstract in DAI, vol. 30 (2), sec. A, p. 802: "It has been
frequently asserted that puritans held a prudish attitude toward
marriage and human sexuality. The purpose of this dissertation . . .
was to describe attitudes toward marriage and human sexuality prior to
1630 among selected and representative puritans, and thus to provide a
basis for further studies that might be able to verify or deny the
assertion--puritans were prudes. . . . The method used to accomplish
this purpose was to examine the writings of selected and
representative puritans. . . . The topics used ranged from
contraception to aphrodisiacs, to labor pain, to coital positions, to
abnormal sexual experiences, and the theological rationale that
supported the institution of marriage. . . . The results revealed
that puritan attitudes were shaped by the intellectual environment of
the time, and by puritan adherence to Scripture as the source and norm

of their positions." Contents: I. "Introduction," II. "Puritan Attitudes Toward Marriage," III. "Puritan Attitudes Toward Courtship and the Marriage Ceremony," IV. "Puritan Attitudes Toward the Sexual Aspects of Marriage," V. "Puritan Attitudes Toward Some Aspects of Sexual Deviation and Other Selected Topics," and VI. "Conclusion."

1969-18   Sharp, Royal Chesla. "Aspects of Syntactic Change in American Utilitarian Prose Between 1630 to 1765." Ph.D., Univ. of Wisconsin at Madison. 207 leaves.

Abstract in DAI, vol. 31 (1), sec. A, p. 379: "This thesis is a study of some syntactic changes in American utilitarian prose between 1630 and 1765. The study is made within the framework of generative-transformational grammar as outlined by Noam Chomsky in 1962 and focuses on non-stylistic and potentially stylistic changes. . . . The data for the non-stylistic changes consist of three tracts, a sermon, and a treatise from the Colonial Period and three tracts, a sermon, a letter, and a treatise from the Revolutionary Period. The data for the potentially stylistic change is limited to 360 sentences taken from the works and is grouped into primary and secondary data to allow for a genre comparison within utilitarian prose."

1969-19   Shively, Charles Allen. "A History of the Conception of Death in America, 1650-1860." Ph.D., Harvard Univ. 394 leaves.

"Summary" (at end of diss.): "The study of the Puritan conception of death begins with the founders, whose stoical vision of heaven and hell hardly resembled that of their descendants. The impact upon the early vision was analyzed by tracing the effects of a growing materialism, individualism, and emotionalism on early beliefs; an attempt was made to demonstrate the effects of these changes both on the more philosophical and more practical approaches to death. Most remarkable was the discovery that the early Puritans had virtually no funeral services at all and that the subsequent elaborate funerals and memorials developed by Cotton Mather's time had no precedent in his grandfather's generation" (p. 2). Relevant chapters: Part One: "New England Approach to Death, 1650-1750": I. "Early Thought and Offices of Death," II. "Intellectual Impact of Materialism, Emotionalism, and Individualism," III. "Changes in the Offices of Death," and IV. "Strains in the Eighteenth-Century Puritan Ideas of Death."

1969-20 Smith, Roy Harold. "A Study of the Platonic Heritage of Love in the Poetry of Edward Taylor." Ph.D., Bowling Green State Univ. 193 leaves.

Abstract in DAI, vol. 30 (10), sec. A, p. 4466: "An examination of the influence of Platonic love in the poetry of Edward Taylor, this study provided an expanded cultural framework for explaining Taylor's 'unusualness' as a Puritan. Taylor's Platonic inheritance was surveyed by comparing ideas and images of love from the Platonic dialogues, the Enneads, and The Courtier. The continuing influence of Platonism within a complex tradition of Christian love was evident in

Taylor's poetry through his expansive view of man and in a vitality and vividness of imagery.... [Love] in Taylor's devotional poetry was shown to be dependent upon the reality of an intellectual vision. It was a love moved by sensual delight but guided by understanding, and it satisfied the intellectual demands of Platonism by joining the desire for beauty with a love of soul for what may also be known as good."

1969-21   Van Deventer, David Earl. "The Emergence of Provincial New Hampshire, 1623-1741." Ph.D., Case Western Reserve Univ. x, 487 leaves.

Abstract in DAI, vol. 30 (9), sec. A, p. 3896. Revision published under same title: Baltimore : Johns Hopkins Univ. Press, 1976. -- xviii, 302 p. "Preface" (1976 ed.): "This monograph analyzes the development of society in colonial New Hampshire through a detailed examination of its creation and its changing characteristics in the seventeenth and early eighteenth centuries. It is my hope that this intensive study of a small frontier colony's societal development can serve as a model for understanding social development in the larger, more complex colonies" (p. xv). Contents: Part I. "Beginnings": I. "A Frontier for England and Massachusetts Bay Colony"; Part II. "The Promise of the Land": II. "The Promise of the Land: Utilization of Basic Resources," III. "Threats to Utilization of the Land: The Proprietary Controversy," and IV. "Threats to Utilization of the Land: Indian Wars and Lesser Irritants"; Part III. "The Ascendancy of Trade": V. "Opportunities and Directions," VI. "Internal Threats to Mercantile Enterprise," and VII. "External Threats and Trade Developments"; and Part IV. "The Transformation of Society": VIII. "The Emergence of a Provincial Society." Includes three maps and thirty-four tables.

1969-22   Webber, Robert E. "The Controversy Provoked by William Perkins' Reformed Catholike: A Study in Protestant-Roman Catholic Relations in the First Quarter of the Seventeenth Century in England." Th.D., Concordia Seminary. 276 leaves.

"Introduction": "The controversy provoked by William Perkins' Reformed Catholike [1597] reflects the general social, political, and theological setting of recusant history and literature. Although the actual controversy occurred between 1598 and 1614 ... , the concern of the literature reflected the broader history of English Catholicism from 1559 to 1625. . . . The purpose of this thesis is to present an objective investigation of source material, previously unexamined . . . [that] will permit the writers to speak their minds on the theological and political-ecclesiastical issues of the day" (p. 19). Contents: Part I: "The First Phase of the Controversy: General Theology": I. "Introduction," II. "Opening the Controversy," III. "Rome is Babylon and the Pope is Antichrist," IV. "The Issue: General Theology," V. "Atheism," and VI. "An Advertisement"; and Part II: "The Second Phase of the Controversy": VII. "Introduction," VIII. "Of Popes and Kings," IX. "Of Laws and Recusants," X. "The True Ancient Roman Catholic Church: A Protestant View," XI. "The True Ancient Roman Catholic Church: A Roman View," and XII. "Conclusion."

1969-23   Wilkinson, Ronald Sterne. "John Winthrop, Jr., and the
     Origins of American Chemistry." Ph.D., Michigan State Univ.   vi,
     475 leaves.

     Abstract in DAI, vol. 30 (4), sec. A, p. 1486: "John Winthrop,
Jr., was the first scientist of importance in the English colonies.
. . . Winthrop became a charter member of the Royal Society of
London, contributing papers both to its meetings and the Philosophical
Transactions. . . . Winthrop's main scientific activity was in the
various areas of chemistry. . . . Little is actually known about his
alchemical experiments except that he conducted them over some time.
There is, however, good evidence that he was the original author of an
important group of alchemical treatises eventually published under the
pseudonym of 'Eirenaeus Philalethes.' . . . To fulfill the needs of
New England's settlers, Winthrop gave much attention to the practical
applications of chemistry."

1969-24   Worrall, Arthur John. "New England Quakerism, 1656-1830."
     Ph.D., Indiana Univ. x, 234 leaves.

     Abstract in DAI, vol. 30 (5), sec. A, p. 1972. Revision
published as Quakers in the Colonial Northeast. -- Hanover, N.H. ;
London : Univ. Press of New England, 1980. -- viii, 238 p. "Preface"
(1980 ed.): The work's intent is "to explore the Quaker experience in
the Northeast from the time Quaker missionaries first appeared in 1656
until 1790" (p. vii). Relevant chapters: Part I. "From Heretics to
Dissenters" (1656-1731): 1. "The Quaker Invasion," 2. "Schism,
Persecution, and Politics," and 3. "Decline of the Quaker Menace."
The remainder of the book deals with later periods.

1970-1   Akin, M. Barbara. "The Standing Order: Congregationalism in
     Connecticut, 1708-1818." Ph.D., Univ. of Chicago.   iv, 264
     leaves.

     "Introduction": "The connection between church and state was
closer in Connecticut than in any other American colony during the
colonial period. . . . Even in colonial times, the nexus was
recognized and contemporaries termed the close relationship between
the Congregational church and the civil authorities of Connecticut,
the 'Standing Order.' Until the middle years of the eighteenth
century, close ties with the state were thought to be necessary for
the survival of the church; also they were in accordance with
Congregational theory as accepted in New England at the time. . . .
It is the purpose of this study to discuss the reasons for such a
connection and to trace the causes of its ultimate collapse" (p. 1).
Relevant chapters: "Introduction," I. "The Search for Unity: The
Saybrook Platform," II. "The Salvation of Individuals: The Great
Awakening" (includes background information of relevance), and
"Conclusions." Appendices: A. "Alphabetical Listing of Churches in
Connecticut, 1630-1818" and B. "Chronological Listing of Churches in
Connecticut, 1630-1818."

1970-2   Alliman, Kirk Gilbert. "The Incorporation of Massachusetts
    Congregational Churches, 1692-1833: The Preservation of
    Religious Autonomy." Ph.D., Univ. of Iowa. ix, 319 leaves.

Abstract in DAI, vol. 31 (9), sec. A, p. 4661: "This
dissertation examines the development of ecclesiastic corporations as
a means of discharging the temporal responsibilities and defining the
legal existence of eighteenth-century Massachusetts Standing Order
churches. . . . Chapter I documents the extent to which early
eighteenth-century standing churches were independent of ecclesiastic
and civil authorities outside the local congregation and precinct
provide for the public worship of God, jurisdiction over
administrative detail, temporal responsibilities, and matters of
doctrine and discipline remained with local officials. The religious
homogeneity of most local communities was sufficiently extensive to
enable church members to rely on precincts for their churches' legal
standing."

1970-3   Ball, Bryan W. "A Study of Eschatological Thought in English
    Protestant Theology, 1640-1662, with Special Reference to the
    Second Coming of Christ and the End of the Age." Ph.D., Univ. of
    London (New College) (U.K.).

Revision published as A Great Expectation: Eschatological
Thought in English Protestantism to 1660. -- Leiden : Brill, 1975. --
x, 281 p. -- (Studies in the History of Christian Thought ; vol. 12).
Provides a great deal of background material relating to Puritan
eschatology. Contents (1975 ed.): "Introduction," I. "The World of
God and the Second Coming of Christ," II. "Apocalyptic Interpretation
and the End of the Age," III. "Signs of the Times and the Time of the
End," IV. "The Kingdoms of the World and the Kingdom of God," V. "Last
Events and the Millennial Rule of Jesus," and VI. "The End of Faith
and the Godly Life."

1970-4   Bates, George Edward, Jr. "The Emergence of a Modern Mind in
    Colonial America, 1700-1760." Ph.D., Univ. of Illinois at
    Urbana-Champaign. vii, 227 leaves.

Abstract in DAI, vol. 31 (12), sec. A, p. 6507: "From the dawn
of western civilization the material and spiritual worlds had been
intimately interconnected through the dualistic synthesis. The
synthesis had been woven into men's lives through a series of
transcendental linkages that provided the determinant interpretive
framework for the natural world. . . . At the turn of the eighteenth
century, Americans embraced the dualistic synthesis; there was no
alternative. Indeed, Cotton Mather's scholarship represents the
colonial flowering of dualistic knowledge. . . . The emergence of a
modern mind created the foundations for a profound change. As dualism
declined, theology's development turned inward, and theologians denied
their formerly catholic approaches and views. . . . Finally, when
men's attentions, values, and affections were redirected from the
synthesis to an autonomous natural world, a genuine secular and
materialistic spirit developed which had far-reaching social and

political implications."

1970-5   Carroll, Charles Francis. "The Forest Civilization of New
    England: Timber, Trade, and Society in the Age of Wood, 1600-
    1688." Ph.D., Brown Univ. 2 vols. (xiv, 645 leaves).

    Abstract in DAI, vol. 31 (12), sec. A, p. 6509. Revision
published as The Timber Economy of Puritan New England. -- Providence,
R.I. : Brown Univ. Press, 1974. -- xiii, 221 p. "Preface" (1974 ed.):
The work relates "the story of the settlers' reactions to the forest
and efforts to exploit its resources" (p. xii). Contents: 1. "The
Timber Shortage in England," 2. "The Presettlement Forests of New
England," 3. "English Exploration and Settlement, 1602-1628," 4. "The
Great Migration, 1630-1640," 5. "The Timber Trade, 1640-1688," 6.
"Timber Imperialism, 1632-1692," and 7. "The Wilderness Transformed."
Appendices: A. "Shipping Tonnage and the Timber Trade" and B.,
consisting of six Tables.

1970-6   Chartier, Richard Gerard.   "King Philip's War in
    Representative American Literary Works of the Period 1820-1860."
    Ed.D., Ball State Univ. 187 leaves.

    Abstract in DAI, vol. 31 (10), sec. A, p. 5354: "This study
examined the literary treatment of the Indians in the works of five
representative writers who, between 1820 and 1860, used the materials
of King Philip's War as their narrative focus. The works are James
Eastburn and Robert Sands' Yamoyden (1820), a verse romance, John
Augustus Stone's Metamora (1829), a stage melodrama, James Fenimore
Cooper's The Wept of Wish-ton-Wish (1828), G. H. Hollister's Mount
Hope (1851), and D. P. Thompson's The Dismal Chief (1860), all prose
romances."

1970-7   Clark, James William, Jr. "The Tradition of Salem Witchcraft
    in American Literature: 1820-1870." Ph.D., Duke Univ. v, 203
    leaves.

    Abstract in DAI, vol. 31 (10), sec. A, p. 5355: "An
investigation of the literary interest in the subject of Salem
witchcraft reveals that about 1820 . . . native writers began
exploiting the accounts of the delusion of 1692 in imaginative
literary works. . . . To this summary can be added four conclusions.
. . . First, the artists whose meditations upon colonial history gave
birth to this series of literary works were natives of the Northern
states. . . . Second, these artists expressed the results of their
contemplation . . . in both poetry and prose, for the stage as well as
for the book stalls. Third, the initial items in the series were
called into being by the urgent demands for various pictures of
peculiarly American experience. . . . [And, fourth,] out of the
period of fifty years comes a generally severe censure of Cotton
Mather." Works by John Neal, Whittier, Hawthorne, Cornelius Mathews,
John W. DeForest, and Longfellow, among others, are discussed.

1970-8   Conley, Patrick Thomas. "Rhode Island Constitutional
     Development, 1636-1841: Prologue to the Dorr Rebellion." Ph.D.,
     Univ. of Notre Dame. viii, 299 leaves.

     Abstract in DAI, vol. 31 (10), sec. A, p. 5312: "The work
surveys Rhode Island constitutional history from the founding of the
colony in 1636 by Roger Williams to the edge of the 'great divide' in
the state's constitutional history, the Dorr Rebellion of 1842. . . .
Roger Williams's basic principles of religious liberty and separation
of church and state were incorporated into the royal charter of 1663,
a basic law which granted to the Rhode Islanders a greater degree of
civil and religious autonomy than existed anywhere in the British
Empire. During the colonial era the freemen of the colony developed a
passionate attachment to the charter and stoutly defended it against
attempted encroachment by the Mother Country." Relevant chapters:
One: "Roger Williams and His 'Lively Experiment'" and Two: "The
Munificent Charter." The final three chapters treat of later events.

1970-9   Corkran, David Hudson, III. "The New England Colonists'
     English Image, 1550-1714." Ph.D., Univ. of California at
     Berkeley. 210 leaves.

     Abstract in DAI, vol. 31 (7), sec. A, p. 3463: "New England
colonists inherited an ambivalent image of England from their
Elizabethan Puritan forebears. English Puritans had depicted England
as God's elect nation, thus advancing a positive concept of England.
Since elect nations might fall into corruption and lose God's favor
there was also a strong Puritan tendency to emphasize England's sins
and advocate her reformation, with the result that England was often
portrayed as a den of iniquity. Which aspect of the English image
Puritans stressed depended upon whether or not the nation seemed to be
adopting the Puritan reform program."

1970-10   Daniels, Bruce Colin. "Large Town Power Structures in
     Eighteenth-Century Connecticut: An Analysis of Political
     Leadership in Hartford, Norwich, and Fairfield." Ph.D., Univ. of
     Connecticut. v, 241 leaves.

     Abstract in DAI, vol. 31 (12), sec. A, p. 6511: "This
dissertation analyzes the power structures between 1700 and 1784 in
three of Connecticut's largest towns, Hartford, Norwich, and
Fairfield. Before investigating the towns individually, a short
introduction reviews the historical literature on politics and society
in the eighteenth century and a beginning chapter analyzes the role of
town government in relation to colony government. Basically, the
dissertation is seeking to see whether these towns' political power
structures correspond to the elite model of colonial political bodies
or if they correspond to Robert Brown's democratic model in
Massachusetts [see #1946-1, above]. The power structures are analyzed
as they existed prior to the Great Awakening. . . . The method
employed is basically a statistical one. Leadership points are
assigned to major offices on a sliding scale and in this way the
political leadership is measured quantitatively. . . . The
dissertation concludes that the power structures . . . were elite and

were based primarily on great wealth and family connections associated with the town's early settlement."

1970-11   Davis, Edwin Vance.   "Christian Understandings of the Legislator and His Responsibility in Puritan Massachusetts Bay (1630-1700) and Quaker Pennsylvania (1680-1750)." Ph.D., Drew Univ. viii, 374 leaves.

Abstract in DAI, vol. 31 (6), sec. A, p. 3016: "The Puritans of early Massachusetts Bay and the Quakers of early Pennsylvania provide two illustrations of colonial Christian thinking about the legislator and his responsibility. . . . John Winthrop and John Cotton are representative of the orthodox view of the legislative vocation. . . . Thomas Hooker . . . exemplifies a variation upon the way the legislator relates to the constituents. Roger Williams presented a greater challenge to Puritan orthodoxy by secularizing the legislative vocation. Thomas Shepard, Nathaniel Ward, and Thomas Cobbett corroborate the witness of Winthrop and Cotton. . . . The second and third generations of Puritans repeated many of the ideas of the founders but with less zeal and less depth. The election sermon saw legislative responsibility largely in terms of the duty to reform a declining Puritan way. Cotton Mather reduced the legislator's role almost exclusively to that of moral reformer. By the early eighteenth century the covenant idea of Puritanism was secularized and with it went the original understanding of legislative duty."

1970-12   Davis, Thomas Robert.   "Sport and Exercise in the Lives of Selected Colonial Americans: Massachusetts and Virginia, 1700-1775." Ph.D., Univ. of Maryland. ix, 216 leaves.

Abstract in DAI, vol. 31 (8), sec. A, p. 3930: "This research examined the role that sport and exercise played in colonial life and the difference in this role between northern and southern colonists. . . . Diaries and other writings of selected individuals who lived in or visited [Massachusetts and Virginia] were examined. . . . In addition to the diaries of subjects, other areas examined included selected studies relative to colonial sport, histories of specific sports, and journals of individuals other than those under consideration. . . . Contrary to the belief of some historians, sport was permitted in colonial Massachusetts, and in some cases even encouraged. Because some sports were legislated against, or because all sport was discouraged on Sundays, those historians appeared to conclude that Puritans were against sport. . . . Evidence from this study indicated that eighteenth-century colonists believed that a physically fit body was instrumental in life, and that exercise was vital to fitness."

1970-13   Decker, Robert Owen.   "The New London Merchants: 1645-1909: The Rise and Decline of a Connecticut Port." Ph.D., Univ. of Connecticut. vi, 354 leaves.

Abstract in DAI, vol. 31 (12), sec. A, p. 6496. Considerably revised and expanded version published as The Whaling City: A History of <u>New London</u>. -- Chester, Conn. : Published for the New London County Historical Society by the Pequot Press, 1976. -- xv, 415 p. Relevant chapter (1976 ed.): I. "Settlement and Merchant Beginnings 1645-1774": "The Area and Its Settlement," "The Winthrop Family," "Maritime Activities," and "Merchant Families."

1970-14   Ellzey, Diana Seifert. "Edward Taylor's <u>Christographia</u>: The Poems and the Sermons." Ph.D., Univ. of Michigan. 178 leaves.

Abstract in <u>DAI</u>, vol. 31 (12), sec. A, p. 6545: "An examination of the <u>Preparatory Meditations</u> which were written in conjunction with the fourteen <u>Christographia</u> sermons reveals several interesting principles of Edward Taylor's poetic method. Taylor, who wrote his poems as a religious duty whenever he composed a Sacrament Day Sermon, had a standard method of composition. The poem was structured to parallel, thematically and often imagistically, the movement of the sermon. . . . This standardized method is found to result in mediocre poetry. . . . Taylor's meditations are successful only when he deviates from his usual pattern and unifies either the theme or the imagery."

1970-15   Erickson, Nancy Lou. "The Early Colonial Humorist." Ph.D., Univ. of North Carolina at Chapel Hill. ix, 392 leaves.

Abstract in <u>DAI</u>, vol. 31 (5), sec. A, p. 2283: "There was a good deal of humor in early American writing, but in the one hundred years before Benjamin Franklin began his literary career there were only eight American writers who used comic means so intentionally and so consistently that they could properly be called humorists. These included: Thomas Morton, Nathaniel Ward, . . . Peter Folger, Benjamin Thompson [sic], and Sarah Kemble Knight. . . . Following an introductory chapter which presents some definitions of the terms wit and humor as they were used in the seventeenth century, along with a variety of examples of humor in American writing at that time, attention is turned to Thomas Morton. . . . Each of the other major humorists is then taken up in turn, and following a biographical sketch and character analysis, an attempt is made to determine his intentions in using humor, the specific comic means he employed, the extent to which he accomplished his immediate purpose, and his long-range significance in history and literature."

1970-16   Freeman, William Glen. "Homiletical Theory of Cotton Mather." Ph.D., Univ. of Iowa. iv, 243 leaves.

Abstract in <u>DAI</u>, vol. 31 (9), sec. A, p. 4930: "This study is concerned with a well-known third-generation American Colonial preacher, Cotton Mather (1662-1728). His ideas have been collected from a selected sample of his works in order to construct his homiletical theory. The principal works consulted were biographies of ministers, ordination sermons, funeral sermons for preachers, and treatises on theology and the nature of man. . . . The primary purpose of this study is to fill a gap in our understanding of

Colonial homiletic theory in the transitional period just before and just after the beginning of the eighteenth century with an analysis of the homiletic theories of one of the leading religious theoreticians of the time. . . . The study is divided into five chapters. The first chapter explains the rationale and method of the study. Chapter two is a brief look at some of the major formative influences and events in Mather's life. The third chapter is a discussion of . . . William Perkins's Art of Prophycying and William Ames's Marrow of Theology. . . . Chapter four contains the ideas of homiletics extracted from the writings of Cotton Mather. The final chapter contains a summary of Mather's homiletic theory and a discussion of its place and importance."

1970-17   Gallagher, Edward Joseph. "A Critical Study of Edward Johnson's Wonder-Working Providence of Sions Saviour in New England." Ph.D., Univ. of Notre Dame. 222 leaves.

Abstract in DAI, vol. 31 (9), sec. A, p. 4712: "Edward Johnson's Wonder-Working Providence was the first general history of New England to be published, but it has always been overshadowed by the famous 'first generation' histories of William Bradford and John Winthrop. The purpose of this dissertation is to provide sound criteria for understanding and appraising the Wonder-Working Providence as a document of literary history and as a work of art, thereby establishing its considerable significance for students of American culture and literature. . . . The dissertation begins with a brief chapter devoted to the use, knowledge, and critical opinion of the Wonder-Working Providence since its publication. The core of the dissertation, however, begins with a chapter devoted to an extensive examination of the milieu out of which this history was written. After a chapter which provides an overview of the Wonder-Working Providence and which establishes its general connection with the cultural moment, three chapters deal with the specific literary devices and structural principles which make the Wonder-Working Providence a unique representative of that cultural moment. The brief concluding chapter delineates Johnson's work, in form and in content, from all other first generation New England historical writing, and appendices provide evidence that Johnson also wrote Good News from New England (1648), and provide a list of biblical references in the Wonder-Working Providence."

1970-18   Gueguen, John A., Jr. "Political Order and Religious Liberty: A Puritan Controversy." Ph.D., Univ. of Chicago. xvi, 339 leaves.

"Preface": "The body of the present study introduces, elucidates, and compares the arguments and conclusions of [Roger] Williams and [John] Cotton in the course of their exchanges of views. . . . They can be said to represent classical types because their orientations to the whole question of the relationship between order and liberty proceed from fundamentally opposed theories about the relations between politics and religion" (p. x). Contents: I. "Introduction": A. "The Problem of Order and Liberty in Political Philosophy" and B. "The Problem of Method in Political Controversy";

II. "Background": A. "The Historical Context of the Williams-Cotton Controversy" and B. "The Biographical Context of the Controversy"; III. "The Puritan Heritage: Convergent Elements": A. "Dogmatic and Moral Theology," B. "Historical World View," and C. "Political Thought"; IV. "The Puritan Heritage: Divergent Elements": A. "The Conceptual Frame of Reference," B. "The Sources of Political Knowledge," and C. "Doctrinal Conclusions"; V. "Religious and Political Fundamentals": A. "The Relations of Religion to the Civil State" and B. "Consequences for Political Philosophy"; VI. "Religious Liberty and Political Order": A. "Liberty of Conscience and Religious Liberty" and B. "The Impact of Religious Expression on the Civil Order"; and VII. "Conclusion."

1970-19   Hibler, David Joseph. "Sexual Rhetoric in Seventeenth-Century American Literature." Ph.D., Univ. of Notre Dame. iv, 181 leaves.

Abstract in DAI, vol. 31 (8), sec. A, p. 4121: "The subject of this dissertation is the use of sexual rhetoric in the writings of seventeenth-century New England. . . . The first section consists of a general discussion of the ways in which the Puritans used sexual rhetoric in both a positive and a negative fashion--that is, for the propagation of virtue and the suppression of vice. Chapter 1 focalizes on the positive usage, discussing such rhetoric in relation to the Puritan ideal of human and divine love. Chapter 2 concentrates on the negative usage, with specific discussion of the rhetoric employed in castigating the sins of onanism, fornication, adultery, homosexuality and bestiality.... The second section consists of a listing of the different usages of sexual rhetoric to achieve certain social, political or religious ends. Chapter 3 discusses such rhetoric in relation to the Indians, treating of the Puritans' dual attitude of both curiosity and fear. Chapter 4 centers on the use of such rhetoric as a means of attack against heretical forces in the Church and State, especially against Anne Hutchinson, the Quakers and Thomas Morton. Chapter 5 treats of the general cultural change taking place at the end of the seventeenth century, and of the more hysterical tone which enters into the sexual rhetoric."

1970-20   Holifield, Elmer Brooks. "The Covenant Sealed: The Development of Puritan Sacramental Theology in Old and New England, 1570-1720." Ph.D., Yale Univ. x, 437 leaves.

Abstract in DAI, vol. 31 (12), sec. A, p. 6702. Revision published under same title: New Haven ; London : Yale Univ. Press, 1974. -- xi, 248 p. "Preface" (1974 ed.): "In its initial form, my study traced a doctrinal development. In the process of revising the manuscript for publication, I became increasingly aware that sacramental dimensions revealed some of the enduring and fundamental presuppositions of Puritan thought. Implicit in the debates and the devotional manuals were crucial assumptions about finitude and infinity, spirit and flesh, reason and the senses. With each revision, my doctrinal history gradually transformed itself into an expanded discourse on Puritan piety and intellect, though the sacramental focus remains" (p. x). Contents: 1. "The Continental

Background," 2. "The Sacramental Doctrine of the Early Puritans," 3. "Baptismal Debate in England," 4. "The Lord's Supper: Debate and Devotion," 5. "New England: Ambivalence and Affirmation," 6. "The New Baptismal Piety," 7. "The Sacramental Renaissance," and "Epilogue."

1970-21   Hunsaker, Orvil Glade. "Calvinistic Election and Arminian Reparation: A Striking Contrast in the Works of Roger Williams and John Milton." Ph.D., Univ. of Illinois at Urbana-Champaign. xiv, 206 leaves.

Abstract in DAI, vol. 31 (12), sec. A, p. 6553: "A significant philosophical divergence between Roger Williams and John Milton caused them to champion religious and civil liberty for quite different reasons. While both men were principally concerned with God's plan for regenerating man's fallen nature and while they approached each of the major issues of the day in terms of its relationships to that eternal plan, Williams' thinking was dominated by his belief in Calvinistic election, and Milton's views were the result of ... his belief in Arminian reparation.... This study of the philosophical divergence between Williams and Milton clarifies the views they took on the major issues of the period and explains their willingness to sustain great personal sacrifice in the cause of religious and civil liberty."

1970-22   Israel, Calvin. "American Puritan Literary Theory: 1620-1660." Ph.D., Univ. of California at Davis. ix, 253 leaves.

Abstract in DAI, vol. 31 (12), sec. A, p. 6553: "Although the early American Puritans denied any artistry in their writings, and although the majority of modern critics deny the presence of an aesthetic theory in the literature, this dissertation maintains that such a literary theory exists and is implicit in their work. . . . Everywhere in his writing, the early American Puritan praises a 'plain' style and rejects an aesthetic viewpoint or artistry in his work, but the gulf is wide between these explicit, theoretical criteria and the literary practice. . . . In both prose and poetry the early American Puritans demonstrate a strong drive toward artistic unity, and exhibit everywhere examples of conscious artistry. . . . Virtually all rhetorical figures and devices are present in early American Puritan literature, especially alliteration and assonance, and often the writers seem to prefer rhetorical 'vices.' . . . Upon close study and careful examination, early American Puritan prose and poetry reveals [sic] the aesthetic impulses of conscious artists fully engaged in the delight of creating literature, and bending every effort inventively and imaginatively toward achieving standards of literary grace."

1970-23   Jones, James William, III. "The Beginnings of American Theology: John Cotton, Thomas Hooker, Thomas Shepard, and Peter Bulkeley." Ph.D., Brown Univ. vii, 346 leaves.

Abstract in DAI, vol. 31 (12), sec. A, p. 6703: "The basis of

this dissertation is that all these men can best be understood by
means of a scale of decreasing Christocentrism. All of these men saw
Christianity as the union of the believer with Christ. In this union
a tension existed between the role of the believer and the role of
Christ. To the extent that Christ predominated over the believer in
this union a position is termed Christocentric. Moving along this
scale means more than a decreased Christocentrism. It means an
increased potency given to the law . . . [and] an increased power
attributed to man's will and more emphasis on the believer's
sanctification. . . . The final chapter sets this scale within a
typology of theocentrism . . . , Christocentrism . . . , and
anthropocentrism. . . . This typology implies that it was the
Christocentrism of this theology and not preparation or the covenant
which moved American Puritanism from Christocentrism to
'anthropocentrism.'"

1970-24   Lichtenthal, Jack. "Eschatology and the Political Life: An
    Analysis of Seventeenth-Century Origins in Puritan New England."
    Ph.D., New School for Social Research. 245 leaves.

Abstract in DAI, vol. 31 (10), sec. A, p. 5481: "This
dissertation is intended to contribute to a new evaluation and
understanding of the political life and the genesis of political
theory in seventeenth-century New England by a re-examination of
Puritan eschatology. . . . The religious and political meaning of
eschatology is discussed in the Introduction and in the first chapter,
'The Genre-Political in Eschatology and History.' In the following
chapter, a distinction is made in the eschatological importance given
to 'The City of Refuge in New England' by the Puritan clergy from the
meaning found in the Old Testament. This study concentrates on the
eschatological literature extant in the writings of the New England
clergy during the seventeenth century: however in some writers, the
published sources lead into the first two decades of the eighteenth
century."

1970-25   Lucas, Paul Robert. "Valley of Discord: The Struggle for
    Power in the Puritan Churches of the Connecticut Valley, 1636-
    1720." Ph.D., Univ. of Minnesota. xiv, 358 leaves.

Abstract in DAI, vol. 31 (5), sec. A, p. 2314. Revision
published as Valley of Discord: Church and Society along the
Connecticut River, 1636-1725. -- Hanover, N.H. : Univ. Press of New
England, 1976. -- xiv, 275 p. "Preface" (1976 ed.): "My analysis of
the church system's evolution proceeds on separate yet related levels.
On one level I dissect the system to find the mechanism or mechanisms
inducing change. On a second level I show how the evolving church
system both molded and reflected a changing society. . . . The
evidence revealed that the system evolved through conflict. The
actors, while not clearly differentiated at first, gradually separated
into distinct groups: Brethren and clergy. The issues between them
were of paramount importance: the nature of the church and,
especially, the locus of authority" (pp. xiii-xiv). Contents:
"Introduction," One. "'The Disciplyne of the Churches,' 1636-1650,"
Two. "Contention and Separation," Three. "A Widening Chasm," Four.

"Church, Town, and the Half-Way Covenant," Five. "'The Right Way to Escape Deserved Ruine,' 1670-1700," Six. "The Search for a New Moral Order, 1665-1700," Seven. "The Politics of Ecclesiastical Disruption," Eight. "The [Solomon] Stoddard-[Increase and Cotton] Mather Debate," Nine. "From the Saybrook Platform to the Great Awakening," and "Conclusion."

1970-26 McCusker, John James, Jr. "The Rum Trade and the Balance of Payments of the Thirteen Continental Colonies, 1650-1775." Ph.D., Univ. of Pittsburgh. xxviii, 1377 leaves.

Abstract in DAI, vol. 31 (5), sec. A, p. 1978: "The English colonists on the North American Continent shared with their modern counterparts a concern over their balance of payments. How they organized themselves to meet their obligations, particularly their debts owed to Great Britain, reveals much about the strength and sophistication of the Colonial American economy. Recent research has indicated some of this; a study of the trade of a pair of related commodities adds still another dimension." Contents: I. "Introduction: The Context of the Rum Trade"; Pars Prima. "The Debt Column: Molasses and Rum Exported into the Continental Colonies": II. "Sugar and Rum in the New World: Origins and Directions," III. "The Sugar Industry of the Spanish and Portuguese Colonies," IV. "The Sugar Industry of the British West Indies," V. "The Sugar Industry of the French, Dutch and Danish Caribbean Colonies," and VI. "The Importation of Rum and Molasses into the Continental Colonies: An Accounting"; Pars Secunda. "The Credit Column: Molasses and Rum Exported from the Continental Colonies": VII. "Molasses in the Continental Colonies: Its Importation, Consumption, Distillation and Re-Exportation," VIII. "Rum in the Continental Colonies: Its Origins, Internal Trade, Consumption and Exportation," and IX. "The Exportation of Rum and Molasses from the Continental Colonies: An Accounting"; and Pars Tertia. "The Importance of the Rum Trade and the Continental Colonies: Beyond the Balance Sheet." Appendices: A. "The Political Geography of the Caribbean Region, 1650-1775," B. "Population Estimates for the British Isles and the Western Hemisphere, 1650-1775," C. "Weights, Measures, and Casks," D. "Sugar, Molasses, and Rum Imported into and Re-Exported from England, Scotland and Ireland, 1683-1775," E. "Currency, Exchange Rates, and the Price of Rum, Molasses, and Sugar," and F. "The Current Value of English Exports to the Continental Colonies, 1697-1800."

1970-27   McCutcheon, Henry Richard. "Town Formation in Eastern Massachusetts, 1630-1802: A Case Study in Political Areal Organization." Ph.D., Clark Univ. viii, 157 leaves.

Abstract in DAI, vol. 31 (12), sec. B, p. 7365: "The purpose of this study is to examine the evolution of the areal organization of a network of political units, to determine the principles involved in the settlement process. . . . The primary factor in the development of the structure was distance to meeting houses. In a central place context, the meeting houses approached a uniform distribution, with town boundaries drawn on the basis of distance to neighboring meeting

houses. Political competition for space operated in a manner similar
to economic competition in the organization of space. At the time
they were delimited, the political unit areas corresponded to economic
and social areas."

1970-28   Meyer, Richard E. "Colonial Values and the Development of
      the American Nation as Expressed in Almanacs, 1700-1790." Ph.D.,
      Univ. of Kansas. vii, 314 leaves.

Abstract in DAI, vol. 31 (6), sec. A, p. 2852: "Commentary in
eighteenth-century almanacs serves as a valuable source of information
for the study of colonial values and the development of American
nationalism. These annual publications reveal what many Americans
thought about human nature, government, religion, education, and
society. . . . This study examines these topics as reflected in
almanac commentary. . . . One purpose of this dissertation is
evaluating the role played by almanacs in colonial life. . . .
Differing connotations of the word 'country' are also considered.
. . . The concluding chapters of this study examine the almanac
commentary which suggests the nature of the relationship between
Britain and the mainland colonies." Relevant chapters: I. "A
Faithful Servant," II. "Competition and Conflict," III. "Religion,
Education, and Government," IV. "Virtue," and V. "A Working Society."
Chapters VI-VIII are exclusively concerned with later events.

1970-29   Miller, Eleanor Aileen. "The Christian Philosophy in the
      New England Novels of Harriet Beecher Stowe." Ph.D., Univ. of
      Nevada at Reno. 199 leaves.

Abstract in DAI, vol. 32 (1), sec. A, p. 445: "This study deals
with Harriet Beecher Stowe's four New England novels: The Minister's
Wooing (1859), The Pearl of Orr's Island (1862), Oldtown Folks (1869),
and Poganuc People (1878). The unity of these four novels lies in
Stowe's minute examination of the New England mind affected by
Puritanism. Because of her love for her native region, she could not
endorse the Puritan doctrines and practices that in her opinion harmed
its inhabitants. Stowe respected the early Puritans to America [sic]
for their courage and fortitude in conquering the hostile New England
land, but she could not subscribe to their doctrine of the innate
depravity of man."

1970-30   Morgans, John Ivor. "The National and International Aspects
      of Puritan Eschatology, 1640-1660: A Comparative Study." Ph.D.,
      Hartford Seminary Foundation. 351 leaves.

Abstract in DAI, vol. 31 (11), sec. A, p. 6149: "The purpose of
this thesis is to examine the eschatological thought which is common
to Seventeenth-Century Puritanism. Part A of this thesis deals with
those aspects which are typical of the whole of Puritanism, i.e., its
certainty that the End of the World was at hand (Chapter One); the
identification of the Antichrist particularly with the papacy, but
also with episcopacy, sectarianism, and the Turks (Chapter Two); and
the Puritan concern to discover evidence from history which would

illustrate the imminence of the End. This meant that the Puritan created a common interpretation of history through the retention of medieval norms (Chapter Three). . . . Part B of the thesis shows how the eschatological aspects of Puritan thought were interpreted within the different national and geographical settings (England in Chapters Four and Five . . . and New England in Chapter Eight)."

1970-31   Runyan, Michael Gracen. "The Poetry of William Bradford: An Annotated Edition with Essays Introductory to the Poems." Ph.D., Univ. of California at Los Angeles. 395 leaves.

Revision published as Bradford's The Collected Verse. -- St. Paul, Minn. : John Colet Press, 1974. -- xv, 276 p. -- (The John Colet Archive of American Literature, 1620-1920 ; no. 1, Spring, 1974). Contents (1974 ed.): "General Introduction"; "On John Robinson," "On the Various Heresies," "A Word to New Plymouth," "A Word to New England" and "Of Boston in New England," "Some Observations," and "Epitaphium Meum"; "Notes to the Introduction," "Textual Commentary," and "Subject Index to the Verse."

1970-32   Schmitt, Dale Joseph. "The Response to Social Problems in Seventeenth-Century Connecticut." Ph.D., Univ. of Kansas. vii, 306 leaves.

Abstract in DAI, vol. 31 (11), sec. A, p. 5969: "It is the purpose of the present study, by a careful examination of one colony, to explore the interaction between Puritan social thought and the problems of frontier existence. Connecticut, which during the Seventeenth Century was small, homogeneous, and free of direct British interference, provided a perfect setting for a true experiment in Puritan government. . . . The primary material of this study is the great body of local and colonial laws and regulations. . . . Chapter I, introductory in nature, discusses the general context of Connecticut society. . . . Chapter II explains how the town became the most important unit in Puritan government and shows some of its major duties. Chapter III deals with the family and the duties and responsibilities of parents. Puritan attitudes towards commerce, business, and labor are discussed in Chapters IV and V. Chapter VI analyzes the Puritan dilemma concerning moral legislation and the attempted assimilation of the Indian population. The last chapter goes into greater detail with specific social problems: Veterans' benefits, public education, disease prevention, and poverty programs."

1970-33   Searl, Stanford Jay, Jr. "The Symbolic Imagination of American Puritanism: Metaphors for the Invisible World." Ph.D., Syracuse Univ. iii, 205 leaves.

Abstract in DAI, vol. 32 (1), sec. A, p. 399: "This dissertation analyzes language in selected works of 17th Century American Puritans and some later American writers. In the opening two chapters, the dissertation identifies the method and the style through which American Puritans make the world meaningful. Because of their religious beliefs and because of the impact of the American environment upon these beliefs, the dissertation shows how the American Puritan writer operates within a symbolic process called the 'plain stile.' This 'plain stile' describes how various early American writers make the connections of relationships between themselves and God. . . . After rather full critical analysis of the symbolic structures and the internal designs of both Bradford's and Winthrop's histories, the dissertation examines the sermons of Thomas Hooker. . . . The final chapter explores later versions of the 'plain stile' in American writings"--e.g., Jonathan Edwards, Emerson, Thoreau, and Whitman.

1970-34   Short, Kenneth Richard MacDonald.   "The Educational Foundations of Elizabethan Puritanism: with Special Reference to Richard Greenham (1535?-1594)."   Ed.D., Univ. of Rochester. xviii, 251 leaves.

Abstract in DAI, vol. 31 (7), sec. A, p. 3311: "Richard Greenham (1535?-1594) was a leading representative of the so-called moderate element of Elizabethan puritanism. . . . An analysis of his posthumously published works indicates that universal lay education was an essential element of his program for the continued reformation of English society. . . . The major task of this thesis is to document the means by which universal religious education was to have been imposed upon English society in the projections of moderate puritans like Richard Greenham. A secondary contribution is to point out the stress laid by Greenham and William Perkins on education as a part of the process of salvation." Contents: I. "Background for Puritan Education," II. "The Indelible Stampe of Geneva," III. "The Reformation of the Parish," IV. "The Educational Task of the Family," V. "The School-day of the Sabbath," VI. "Evolution Through Religious Education," and VII. "From the Frying Pan into the Fire."

1970-35   Slater, Peter Gregg.   "Views of Children and of Child Rearing during the Early National Period: A Study in the New England Intellect."   Ph.D., Univ. of California at Berkeley.   xi, 323 leaves.

Abstract in DAI, vol. 31 (12), sec. A, p. 6532.   Revision published as Children in the New England Mind: In Death and in Life. -- Hamden, Conn. : Archon Books, 1977. -- 248 p. "Preface" (1977 ed.): "In the not too distant American past, the death of a child was a common event. The reactions of parents to this loss were complicated in Puritan culture by the notion of infant damnation. The first essay examines the resulting patterns of Puritan bereavement, relying in part on the techniques of psychohistory" (p. 11). Relevant chapters: Part One. "The Dead Child": I. "'From the Cradle to the Coffin': Parental Bereavement and the Shadow of Infant Damnation in Puritan Society" and "Coda: From the Puritans to Bushnell."

1970-36   Stark, Bruce Purinton.   "Lebanon, Connecticut: A Study of Society and Politics in the Eighteenth Century."   Ph.D., Univ. of Connecticut.   ix, 511 leaves.

Abstract in <u>DAI</u>, vol. 31 (12), sec. A, p. 6532: "Lebanon, an eastern Connecticut hill town, was New Light in religion and radical in politics. . . . Economically, Lebonon was a subsistence, middle-class, agricultural community with no substantial wealthy or permanent lower class. . . . Freemanship was widely distributed, and neither the property nor non-property qualifications served as significant barriers to freemanship. . . . One quality that characterized life in Lebanon was widespread popular participation in the decisionmaking process, when important issues were involved." Relevant chapters: "Introduction," I. "The Early Years," II. "The Religious Persuasion," and III. "The Great Awakening," Most of Chapter III and all of IV-X treat of later periods.

1970-37   Stoever, William Kenneth Bristow. "The Covenant of Works in Puritan Theology: The Antinomian Crisis in New England." Ph.D., Yale Univ. viii, 268 leaves.

Abstract in <u>DAI</u>, vol. 32 (1), sec. A, p. 530. Revision published as <u>A Faire and Easie Way to Heaven: Covenant Theology and Antinomianism in Early Massachusetts.</u> -- Middletown, Conn. : Wesleyan Univ. Press, 1978. -- xi, 251 p. "Preface" (1978 ed.): "The following essay seeks to examine the substance of the ministerial debate in Massachusetts in relation to elements of its contemporary theological, controversial, and sectarian context, and to clarify the issues in dispute and the way in which the participants seem to have apprehended them" (pp. x-xi). Contents: 1. "The Dialectic of Nature and Grace," 2. "The New England Controversy," 3. "The Preeminence of the Spirit: John Cotton," 4. "The Objectivity of Regenerating Grace: Thomas Shepard and Peter Bulkeley," 5-6. "The Doctrine of the Two Covenants," 7. "The Order of Redemption and the Ground of Assurance," 8. "The Quest for Assurance: Radical Solutions and Puritan Dialectics," 9. "The Nature of New England Antinomianism," and "Epilogue." Appendix: "Preparation for Salvation."

1970-38   Stuart, Robert Lee. "The Table and the Desk: Conversion in the Writings Published by Solomon Stoddard and Jonathan Edwards during Their Northampton Ministries, 1672-1751." Ph.D., Stanford Univ. vii, 266 leaves.

Abstract in <u>DAI</u>, vol. 31 (5), sec. A, p. 2356: "The Half-Way Covenant of 1662 merely postponed New England's reckoning with a crucial inconsistency in logic and a central complication of practice. In the preaching and writing of Solomon Stoddard the issue was joined; subsequently the practice of requiring a relation of personal, regenerative religious experience was abandoned throughout most of New England's Puritan churches. . . . For Stoddard the Supper as the Word dramatized was coordinated in function with the proclamation of the gospel from the desk. It was therefore appropriate to invite regenerate and unregenerate alike . . . to the table. . . . The chief purpose of the dissertation is to view the attempt of both [Stoddard and Edwards] to keep in tension the inclusiveness and exclusiveness of the Christian community: to keep open the doors of the church wide enough to encourage hope of redemption, but not so wide as to foster indiscriminate communion."

1970-39   Swedlund, Alan Charles.   "The Genetic Structure of an
     Historical Population: A Study of Marriage and Fertility in Old
     Deerfield, Massachusetts."   Ph.D., Univ. of Colorado at Boulder.
     x, 86 leaves.

     Abstract in DAI, vol. 31 (9), sec. B, p. 5137:   Revision
published under same title: Prescott, Ariz. : Center for Man and
Environment, Prescott College, 1971. -- v, 78 p. -- (Univ. of
Massachusetts, Department of Anthropology, Research Reports ; no. 7).
Chapter I (1971 ed.): "Data for the present study are derived from
vital statistics and genealogical records of the town of Deerfield,
Massachusetts.   Fieldwork . . . consisted primarily of library
research in the Deerfield area, and re-recording the information for
computer use.   The period of time covered by these records is between
1680 and 1850, or, 170 years" (p. 1).   Contents: I. "Background of
the Study": "Introduction," "Description of Deerfield," "Demographic
Background," and "The Problem"; II. "Population Numbers":
"Introduction," "Effective Population Size," and "Coefficient of
Inbreeding"; III. "Migration": "Introduction," "Migration in Time,"
and "Migration over Space"; IV. "Selection": "Introduction,"
"Selection Intensity," and "Differential Fertility"; and V. "Summary
and Conclusions": "Introduction," "Population Numbers," "Migration,"
and "Selection."   Includes thirteen tables, eight figures.

1970-40   Van de Wetering, Maxine Schorr.   "The New England Clergy and
     the Development of Scientific Professionalism."   Ph.D., Univ. of
     Washington.   xii, 223 leaves.

     Abstract in DAI, vol. 31 (10), sec. A, p. 5342:   "The period from
the 1720's to the 1750's . . . was a period of great searching for a
reconciliation between professional science and religion. . . .
Ministers grappled with problems concerning God's specific role in the
physical universe, the nature of disease, the nature of physical
catastrophe, and the right of clergymen to practice as well as preach
science. . . .   The most influential of the scientist-ministers during
the three decades . . . were Cotton Mather, Thomas Prince, John
Barnard, Benjamin Colman, Thomas Paine, Increase Mather, [and] Thomas
Foxcroft. . . .   These clerics wrote, preached, and lectured on
scientific topics throughout their productive lives. . . .   Three
natural catastrophes, all of enormous scope and devastation, provide
the focus of this study.   One was the smallpox epidemic of 1721 . . .;
the second and third were two earthquakes, one in 1727 and the other
in 1755."

1970-41   Warner, Frederic William.   "Some Aspects of Connecticut
     Indian Culture History."   Ph.D., Hartford Seminary Foundation.
     v, 179 leaves.

     Abstract in DAI, vol. 31 (11), sec. B, p. 6396:   "The purpose of
this thesis is to provide a critical assessment of archaeological and
ethnographical material to reconstruct the culture history of the
Connecticut Indians, with special reference to data concerning pottery

and food patterns. . . . Most of the archaeology section is devoted to the ceramics of the Woodland stage. . . . The evidence suggests the most important food items were vegetable products, followed by fish, shellfish, and mammals."

1970-42   Westby, Selmer Neville. "The Puritan Sermon in Seventeenth-Century England." Ph.D., Univ. of Southern California. ii, 233 leaves.

Abstract in DAI, vol. 31 (11), sec. A, p. 6076: "This work is an investigation of certain aspects of the Puritan funeral sermon in seventeenth-century England, its changing structure, the uses of the dedicatory epistle which frequently accompanied the printed versions, the commonly recurring themes, and the chief characteristics of the eulogy."

1970-43   Worthley, Harold Field. "The Lay Offices of the Particular (Congregational) Churches of Massachusetts, 1650-1755: An Investigation of Practice and Theory." Ph.D., Harvard Univ. 4 vols.: vols. 1 and 2 (vii, 824 leaves); vols. 3 and 4 (xiv, 716 leaves).

"Summary" (at end of vol. 2 of diss.): The diss.'s intention is "to investigate the powers exercised and the functions fulfilled by lay officers, i.e., the ruling elders and the deacons, of the particular (congregational) churches of Massachusetts between 1620 and 1755. The lay offices themselves are considered in several different contexts: (1) that of their employment in the fugitive English congregational churches of the early seventeenth century; (2) that of their place in the changing structure of such of those churches as migrated to or were gathered in what is today the Commonwealth of Massachusetts; and (3) that of the place of those churches and their officers in the total society of Massachusetts, a society in which both ecclesiological theory and churchly practice had vital parts to play. Internal to the particular church, the thesis pays special attention to the shifting relationships among the teaching elders (the pastor and the teacher) the ruling elders, the deacons, and the brethren" (p. 1). Contents: I. "Introduction," II. "The Pilgrim Experience," III. "The Non-Separatist Congregational Tradition," IV. "The Churches of Plymouth and the Bay, 1648-1691," V. "The Churches of the Province of Massachusetts, 1692-1755," and VI. "Conclusion." Vols. 3 and 4 of diss., a "bibliographical appendage" of the thesis, published in a photo-offset copy as An Inventory of the Records of the Particular (Congregational) Churches of Massachusetts Gathered 1620-1805. -- Cambridge, Mass. : Harvard Univ. Press, 1970. -- xiv, 716 p. -- (Harvard Theological Studies ; 25). "Introduction": "As far as can be determined, every particular (congregational) church gathered before 1806 within the present-day borders of the Commonwealth of Massachusetts is represented in the following inventory. Churches which were only briefly congregational and which later affiliated with another tradition (such as the Baptist), as well as churches which had their origins in non-congregational traditions (such as the Presbyterian) and later became congregational, are included" (p. iii).

1970-44   Youngs, John William Theodore, Jr. "God's Messengers:
           Religious Leadership in Colonial New England, 1700-1750." Ph.D.,
           Univ. of California at Berkeley. vii, 504 leaves.

Abstract in DAI, vol. 31 (12), sec. A, p. 6535. Revision
published under same title: Baltimore ; London : Johns Hopkins Univ.
Press, 1976. -- xi, 176 p. "Preface" (1976 ed.): "The history of the
Congregational clergy in provincial New England is the story of mortal
men entrusted with a divine mission. The pastors nurtured the
spiritual life of a community that had become, in their eyes,
shamelessly secular. But even in seeking to arouse religious
sentiments among their people, they had difficulty in transcending
their own material interests. . . . [During] the first half of the
eighteenth century, many pastors appeared to care more for the
prestige of their profession than for the well-being of their
congregations. This development . . . can be termed 'Congregational
clericism'" (p. ix). Contents: I. "The Ministers and Their Times,"
II. "The Minister's Calling," III. "The Minister's Work," IV.
"Congregational Clericism," V. "The Failure of Clericism," VI.
"Revivalism," and "Epilogue." Most of chapter VI and all of chapter
VII deal with later events. Appendix: "Length of Ministerial
Settlement." This work was awarded the Frank S. and Elizabeth D.
Brewer Prize of the American Society of Church History.

1971-1   Aiken, Samuel Robert. "The New-Found-Land Perceived: An
          Exploration of Environmental Attitudes in Colonial British
          America." Ph.D., Pennsylvania State Univ. iii, 319 leaves.

Abstract in DAI, vol. 33 (1), sec. B, p. 261: "The major purpose
of the dissertation is to demonstrate that attitudes toward nature
during the American colonial period varied within both their spatial
and temporal domains. . . . From the initial core areas of settlement
along the Atlantic Seaboard . . . the colonies of Massachusetts,
Pennsylvania and Virginia were chosen for detailed study. Chapter II
. . . provides a discussion of the social, cultural and economic
background of these three colonies. . . . In this work a heavy
reliance is placed on the poetry, prose and travel literature of the
colonial era. From an examination of these sources four central
themes are isolated and discussed in Chapter III . . . [:] The
Wilderness Motif, The Paradise Myth, Aestheticism, Utilitarianism.
. . . Chapter IV provides a discussion of the spatial and temporal
variations in people's attitudes toward nature in the colonial period.
. . . The final chapter demonstrates that the themes discussed in
Chapters III and IV are still important in present-day American
thinking."

1971-2   Barry, Peter Ralph. "The New Hampshire Merchant Interest,
          1609-1725." Ph.D., Univ. of Wisconsin at Madison. xi, 374
          leaves.

Abstract in DAI, vol. 32 (6), sec. A, p. 3192: "This study
examines the origin and development of economic and political activity
in the Piscataqua River Basin. The Piscataqua, which forms the

boundary between the states of Maine and New Hampshire, was the scene of some of the earliest English commercial ventures in New England. During the 115 years after it was first settled in 1609 the area developed into a small but significant province on the northern New England frontier. . . . This history describes the growth of the maritime economy and analyzes the role which the merchants played in the development of political institutions. The study is divided into three parts using the years 1680 and 1702 as political milestones."

1971-3   Beales, Ross Worn, Jr. "Cares for the Rising Generation: Youth and Religion in Colonial New England." Ph.D., Univ. of California at Davis. xiii, 246 leaves.

Abstract in DAI, vol. 32 (9), sec. A, p. 5139: "By focusing on the problem of the transmission of Puritanism between generations, this study examines the evolution of Puritanism in the New World and the place of young persons in New England society. . . . Much that we think we know about young persons in Puritan culture is derived from the notion that Puritan children were 'miniature adults.' Chapter One . . . examines the idea of miniature adulthood and suggests that adult status . . . was achieved at a late age. . . . In the 1630's, most New England churches began to require that prospective communicants . . . give a 'relation' of their conversion experience. . . . Because of their membership requirements, the churches continuously faced the problem of bringing the 'rising generation' into communion or at least under their control. Chapter Three examines the adoption and use of the half-way covenant by the First Church of Dorchester, Massachusetts." Chapters Four-Six deal with developments during the Great Awakening.

1971-4   Bernhard, Virginia Purington. "'Essays to Do Good': A Puritan Gospel of Wealth, 1690-1740." Ph.D., Rice Univ. ii, 161 leaves.

Abstract in DAI, vol. 32 (4), sec. A, p. 2010: "Although the Puritans believed in a traditional hierarchical social structure which contained 'some rich and some poor,' they found it difficult to deal with riches and poverty in their society. . . . By the beginning of the eighteenth century the Massachusetts clergy, like the rest of society, seemed to be infected by a desire for worldly property. . . . What Puritan society needed was a way to justify such pursuit for the good of the holy community. . . . By 1710, when Cotton Mather's Essays to Do Good appeared, a new formula for success had been established in many sermons and tracts: The pursuit of wealth could be justified by the doing of good. More important, works of charity were the means by which 'small men' could rise to 'estates undreamed of.' Instead of urging upon men the traditional resignation to fixed social status, the idea of Do-Good offered unlimited opportunity for advancement, both spiritual and material, to the doer of good."

1971-5   Bradley, Michael Raymond. "The Puritans of Virginia: Their Influence on the Religious Life of the Old Dominion, 1607-1659." Ph.D., Vanderbilt Univ. iii, 216 leaves.

Abstract in <u>DAI</u>, vol. 32 (7), sec. A, p. 4094: "The purpose of this dissertation is to show that there was an influential group of Puritans in Virginia during the period 1607-1659. This group helped shape and direct the religious life of the Old Dominion in a way generally overlooked by historians. . . . The Virginia Company of London included many Puritans in its membership. . . . Puritanism was well represented among the early settlers of Virginia. . . . In the colony the presence and influence of the Virginia Puritans is readily observed. . . . The religious opinions of these men also colored the laws of the colony, especially in the areas of personal conduct and Sabbath observance. . . . The life of the Anglican Church in early Virginia shows the same Puritan influence as do the laws of the colony. . . . Even after the accession of Governor [William] Berkeley the Puritan group continued its growth and influence."

1971-6   Brewer, Robert Sidney. "The Convention Sermon in Boston, 1722-1773." Ph.D., Louisiana State Univ. viii, 239 leaves.

Abstract in <u>DAI</u>, vol. 32 (7), sec. A, p. 4147: "One of Boston's three special preaching events in late spring, the Massachusetts Convention of Congregational Ministers, is analyzed in this study to determine the nature of the discourses, speakers, audiences, and occasions for this annual ministerium between 1722 and 1773. Particular attention is given to the way in which the messages reflected religious ideas and attitudes of the times. . . . Convention speakers concentrated their remarks on the topics of a minister's qualifications and responsibilities and the trials and triumphs of the ministry. They preached that an ideal minister was knowledgeable, prayerful, and pious and his primary duty was preaching. The annual messages were customarily replete with homiletical advice regarding the preparation and delivery of sermons."

1971-7   Clifton, Ronald Dillard. "Forms and Patterns: Room Specialization in Maryland, Massachusetts, and Pennsylvania, Family Dwellings, 1725-1834." Ph.D., Univ. of Pennsylvania. xcix, 342 leaves.

Abstract in <u>DAI</u>, vol. 32 (4), sec. A, p. 1733: "This dissertation tests the working hypothesis that there is a measurable association between the use of interior architectural space in family dwellings and (1) wealth, (2) occupation, (3) size of family, (4) location relative to the urban center, (5) time of living in the dwelling, and (6) home ownership. It determines the incidences, measures the change, and isolates the variables associated with dwellings having specialized rooms. . . . Data taken from nine simple random samples (3 from each area) totalling 1,125 sets of wills and inventories taken in ten-year groups, (1725-35 [sic]; 1775-84; 1825-34)."

1971-8   Gefvert, Constance Joanna. "Edward Taylor: An Annotated Bibliography." Ph.D., Univ. of Minnesota. 159 leaves.

Abstract in <u>DAI</u>, vol. 32 (8), sec. A, p. 4562. Revision published as <u>Edward Taylor: An Annotated Bibliography, 1668-1970</u>. -- Kent, Ohio : Kent State Univ. Press, 1971. -- xxxiii, 83 p. -- (The Serif ser.: Bibliographical Checklists ; no. 19). Contents (published version): "Introduction: Taylor Scholarship, 1937-1970"; I. "Primary Sources": A. "Editions of Taylor's Works," B. "Letters," C. "First Publication of Poems in Works Not by Taylor," D. "First Publication of Other Works," and E. "Manuscripts"; and II. "Secondary Sources": F. "Bibliographies," G. "Biographies and Genealogies," H. "Critical Books," I. "Critical Articles in Books," J. "Critical Articles in Periodicals," and K. "Dissertations and Theses."

1971-9   Gildrie, Richard Peter. "Salem, 1626-1668: History of a Covenant Community." Ph.D., Univ. of Virginia. 395 leaves.

Abstract in <u>DAI</u>, vol. 32 (8), sec. A, p. 4526. Expanded revision published as <u>Salem, Massachusetts, 1626-1683: A Covenant Community</u>. -- Charlottesville : Univ. Press of Virginia, 1975. -- x, 187 p. "Preface" (1975 ed.): "Salem [was] a coastal village that developed into a commercial town. ... Its transition took over three decades and was painful as its citizens tried to reconcile the organicism of Puritan ideals with the atomization encouraged by economic growth. Salem, like other Puritan communities, attempted to create an orderly, mutually dependent society. But its hopes were frustrated by conflicts between older settlers and newcomers and by both mercantile and agricultural expansion. This study explores Salem's original character and its transformation in order to illuminate this part of the spectrum and the town's significant role in many of the Bay Colony's political and religious controversies" (p. ix). Contents: I. "Origins of the Implicit Covenant, 1626-1630," II. "The Crisis of the Implicit Covenant, 1630-1636," III. "Institution of the Explicit Covenant, 1636-1638," IV. "The Social Structure of Salem, 1636-1650," V. "Communal Society and Patterns of Dissent, 1638-1650," VI. "Communal Identity: Salem in Colonial Politics, 1636-1647," VII. "The Transformation of Salem, 1647-1668," VIII. "The Collapse of Communal Unity, 1650-1668," IX. "Forging a New Order, 1650-1668," X. "Commercial Salem, 1668-1685," and XI. "The Salem Symbols."

1971-10   Goulding, James A. "The Controversy between Solomon Stoddard and the Mathers: Western versus Eastern Massachusetts Congregationalism." Ph.D., Claremont Graduate School. 2 vols. (vi, 830 leaves).

Abstract in <u>DAI</u>, vol. 32 (5), sec. A, p. 2784: "In 1677 Solomon Stoddard (1643-1729), pastor of the church in Northampton, Massachusetts, began to break with some of the basic tenets of New England Congregationalism. These principles had been followed since the earliest settlement of Massachusetts and had been set down in a systematic manner in the Cambridge Platform of 1648. This challenge soon resulted in a dispute with Increase Mather (1639-1723) and his son Cotton (1663-1728) and their followers in Boston, which continued until 1710. They attacked each other and defended their positions through sermons, books and a few personal encounters. The purpose of this dissertation was to discuss and analyze the controversy between

Solomon Stoddard and the Mathers historically and theologically in the context of late seventeenth and early eighteenth century New England Puritan Congregationalism. . . . The major theological issues of the controversy were six: attitude toward Scripture, church tradition, and the early American Puritan divines; understanding of covenant; theology of conversion and preparation; view of church membership; interpretation of the function of the Lord's Supper; and church polity. Each of these views are [sic] discussed in separate chapters."

1971-11   Hardman, Keith Jordan. "Jonathan Dickinson and the Course of American Presbyterianism, 1717-1747." Univ. of Pennsylvania. xxvi, 352 leaves.

Abstract in DAI, vol. 32 (8), sec. A, p. 4703: "A New England Congregationalist by birth and education, Dickinson became pastor of the Dissenter church of Elizabethtown, New Jersey, in 1709, and steered the church toward the Presbyterian fold. The fact that the Presbyterian Church received, in its formative stages, the New England element, of which Dickinson was the acknowledged leader, was to have enormous repercussions felt even today. . . . The general conclusion of the dissertation is that Dickinson was the key leader in the first half of the eighteenth century in determining the future of Prebyterianism in America."

1971-12 Kelly, Richard Edward. "A Study of the Schoolmasters of Seventeenth-Century Newbury, Massachusetts." Ph.D., Michigan State Univ. v, 358 leaves.

Abstract in DAI, vol. 32 (6), sec. A, p. 3069: "The purpose of this work was to provide a study of the schoolmasters of seventeenth-century Newbury, Massachusetts. Although some of the more noted schoolmasters have been studied extensively, comparatively little is known about the more typical pedagogues. The selection of Newbury as a town with representative rather than exceptional schoolmasters enabled the completion of much more extensive research than would have been possible in a more general study. . . . Throughout the seventeenth century, it was the Puritan clergy that was principally responsible for making education available to the town. Through providing an intellectually virile tradition in the training of men who would be pious Puritans as well as gentleman and scholars, Newbury's minister-schoolmasters left to succeeding generations an impressive educational legacy."

1971-13   Krugler, John David. "Puritan and Papist: Politics and Religion in Massachusetts and Maryland before the Restoration of Charles II." Ph.D., Univ. of Illinois at Urbana-Champaign. ix, 344 leaves.

Abstract in DAI, vol. 32 (2), sec. A, p. 888: "This dissertation is an analysis of what happened with regard to religion and politics, and why it happened, in two English colonies founded within a few years of each other by groups which were not in favor with the

established English government, ecclesiastical or civil. And while
the primary concern is a reassessment of the relationship between
religion and politics in early Maryland, the dissertation examines how
the founders of Maryland and Massachusetts defined their approaches to
religion and politics, how well they followed their intentions and how
circumstances . . . forced alterations in their intentions. . . .
The study concludes . . . that only in the area of toleration was
there a marked difference in these two colonies."

1971-14 Lewis, Stephen C. "Edward Taylor as a Covenant Theologian."
    Ph.D., New York Univ. 219 leaves.

Abstract in DAI, vol. 32 (7), sec. A, p. 3956: Taylor's "poetry
can be most fully comprehended as it relates to Covenant Theology.
. . . In 'Gods Determinations Concerning His Elect,' Taylor presents
his picture of conversion. . . . In such poems as 'Huswifery,' and
'He Is a New Creature,' Taylor describes how the saint, through God's
grace, is enabled to lead a morally sound life as a result of
sanctification. . . . Taylor's poetic Meditations express the doubts
and tensions of a Puritan saint who realizes that conversion is a
gradual process, and that sanctification is imperfect. Moreover,
Taylor employs his poetry to state his gratitude to God and his desire
to serve his savior through his art."

1971-15   Lowrie, Ernest Benson.   "A Complete Body of Puritan
    Divinity: An Exposition of Samuel Willard's Systematic Theology."
    Ph.D., Yale Univ.   ii, 263 leaves.

Abstract in DAI, vol. 32 (5), sec. A, p. 2787. Revision
published as The Shape of the Puritan Mind: The Thought of Samuel
Willard. -- New Haven : Yale Univ. Press, 1974. -- xi, 253 p.
"Introduction" (1974 ed.): "A careful reading of Willard's
'Systematic Divinity' is the primary intention of this study. The
analytic task of unpacking his technical language is balanced by the
synthesizing task of showing the play of various distinctions and
concepts in the fabric of his thought. Broadly speaking, the
exposition moves from Willard's metaphysical beliefs to his ethical
theory, to his Christian reflections on the human situation in the
light of the cardinal mysteries of the Puritan creed. . . . [This]
study is also intended as a guide to the mentality of Puritan America,
for the movement shared a rich common language and mode of thought"
(p. 6).   Contents: "Introduction," 1. "Teacher of a Church in
Boston," 2. "Willard's 'Systematic Divinity,'" 3. "God the Master
Workman," 4. "The Created and Governed World," 5. "Man the Reasonable
Creature," 6. "The Natural Moral Law," 7. "The Rebel," 8. "The
Creation and Fall of Adam," 9. "The Covenant of Grace," 10. "The Life
of Faith, Love, and Hope," 11. "Jesus Christ: The God-Man Mediator,"
and "Epilogue." Appendix: "Publications by Samuel Willard."

1971-16   Malone, Patrick Mitchell. "Indian and English Military
    Systems in New England in the Seventeenth Century." Ph.D., Brown
    Univ. vi, 337 leaves.

Abstract in <u>DAI</u>, vol. 32 (9), sec. A, p. 5155: "Two cultures, each with its own military system, existed in southern New England in the seventeenth century.   A military system is much more than soldiers, weapons, and methods of fighting; it includes everything which contributes to the preparation for or conduct of warfare.   Both Indians and English colonists realized that readiness for combat was a necessity for survival.   Colonist feared attack by Indians or by other colonial powers; red men lived with the almost constant threat of intertribal war or the possibility of armed conflict with the English. Soldiers from the Puritan colonies, assisted by Indian allies, fought two wars against local tribes: the Pequot War of 1637 and King Philip's War from 1675 through 1676.   This study compares the military system of the red men with that of the colonists and examines the ways in which each affected the other before 1677."

1971-17   McDowell, Marion De Nonie Barber. "Early American Almanacs: The History of a Neglected Literary Genre."   Ph.D., Florida State Univ. v, 327 leaves.

Abstract in <u>DAI</u>, vol. 35 (2), sec. A, p. 1054: "For over half a century (before the advent of newspapers), the almanac had no competition as reading matter for the common man.   In addition to its importance today as cultural history, the almanac, in its own time, was influential in disseminating knowledge about science, literature, history and current events, manners and morality, heavenly portents and warnings, the weather, and the tides.   It also served a useful purpose as a medium for propaganda. . . .   This study is divided into two main sections dealing generally with the history and development of the almanac and specifically with its literary content.   Chapter I begins with the origin of the American almanac and traces its development from its issue as a first book from the American press in 1639, through the eighteenth century.   The Puritans of early New England produced an excellent astronomical almanac at Cambridge and laid the foundations for the more versatile and comprehensive eighteenth-century almanac. . . .   Chapter II includes discussion, with examples, of almanac prose and verse, presented chronologically in relation to subject matter, or function."

1971-18   McGee, James Sears. "The Rhetoric of Suffering in England, 1630-1670:   An Inquiry into Fundamental Anglican-Puritan Differences." Ph.D., Yale Univ. 370 leaves.

Abstract in <u>DAI</u>, vol. 32 (12), sec. A, p. 6900. Revision published as <u>The Godly Man in Stuart England: Anglicans, Puritans, and the Two Tables, 1620-1670</u>. -- New Haven : Yale Univ. Press, 1976. -- xviii, 299 p. -- (Yale Historical Publications. Miscellany ; 110). "Preface" (1976 ed.):   "This is a study of two ideal types of individual Christian man, one Anglican and the other Puritan, and of the way in which interpretors of the duties of the Two Tables [i.e., Commandments I-IV and V-X] serve as trustworthy guides to the important points of difference between the two models in the period before, during, and immediately after the Revolution itself" (p. x). Contents: 1. "The English Protestant Minds"; 2. "The Rhetoric of Suffering":   "The Cause," "The Message," "The Use," and "The Cure"; 3.

"The Two Tables": "Puritans and the First Table" and "Anglicans and the Second Table"; 4. "The Fruits of Conversion: Obedience and Peace": "The Puritan Imperatives" and "The Anglican Imperatives"; 5. "The Fruits of Conversion: Fellowship and Charity": "Puritans and the 'Idol of our Godly Brethren'" and "Anglicans and the 'Constellation of Gospel Graces'"; and 6. "The True Israelite."

1971-19   Miller, Glenn Thomas. "The Rise of Evangelical Calvinism: A Study in Jonathan Edwards and the Puritan Tradition." Th.D., Union Theological Seminary in the City of New York. vi, 520, 22 leaves.

Abstract in DAI, vol. 32 (3), sec. A, p. 1614: "The thesis of this dissertation is that the Evangelical Calvinism of Jonathan Edwards was a development of the preparationist-Stoddardean tradition. . . . The thesis is developed in three parts." Part I. "The Seventeenth Century in New England" is relevant; the final two parts treat of Edwards. Part I "is concerned with the role of the doctrine of conversion in the life of New England during the seventeenth century. The part begins with a general delineation of English Puritanism in the light of Puritanism's self-understanding and moves from there to a consideration of the particular case of the New England colonies. The doctrine of conversion in its preparationist form was the basis of the form of church government known as the New England Way which stressed the idea that church membership should be restricted to the Visible Saints. . . . In the last quarter of the seventeenth century, New England passed through an intellectual crisis associated with the gradual erosion of the covenant theology. . . . Solomon Stoddard of Northampton . . . developed a theology in which the conversion of the individual soul was seen as the central end or purpose of all of God's work ad extra. He associated two new ecclesiastical forms with this evangelical theology: open communion and the 'harvest' or revival."

1971-20   Munson, Charles Robert. "William Perkins, Theologian of Transition." Ph.D. Case Western Reserve Univ. vi, 257 leaves.

Abstract in DAI, vol. 32 (3), sec. A, p. 1614: "William Perkins . . . is the theologian of Tudor Puritanism who brought far-reaching modifications to high Calvinism through his use of the idea of the covenant. The argument of this dissertation is that William Perkins was the transitional theologian between scholastic high Calvinism and the later Federal Theology. . . . This study shows that predestination was the organizing principle of Perkins' theology. It illustrates from his own major works how carefully he was dominated by the double decrees of election and reprobation. The study then demonstrates how he used the covenant in a subordinate role as the instrument of election. . . . With [a] study of Perkins' high view of preaching, and his own influence as a preacher promoting his theology of transition, this dissertation closes."

1971-21   Rankin, Samuel Harrison, Jr. "Conservatism and the Problem
          of Change in the Congregational Churches of Connecticut, 1660-
          1760." Ph.D., Kent State Univ. ix, 358 leaves.

Abstract in DAI, vol. 32 (9), sec. A, p. 5162: "The purpose of
this thesis is to supplement various studies of Puritanism in New
England with an analysis of the institutions and dynamics of change in
Connecticut's established churches. The institutions and rationale of
Congregationalism in Connecticut assumed from the beginning that local
parishes would have a degree of autonomy in seeking solutions to the
problems of a rapidly expanding society. . . . The adoption of the
Saybrook Platform in 1708 was the result of a desire on the part of
religious leadership in the colony to provide a permanent system of
county councils to oversee the affairs of local churches. . . . Not
only did the Platform fail to provide a highly structured religious
establishment in terms of ecclesiastical practices, but its system of
county consociations and associations was also ill-suited to reverse
the trend toward factionalism within the colony's parishes in the
eighteenth century."

1971-22   Requa, Kenneth Alan. "Public and Private Voices in the
          Poetry of Anne Bradstreet, Michael Wigglesworth, and Edward
          Taylor." Ph.D., Indiana Univ. 162 leaves.

Abstract in DAI, vol. 32 (10), sec. A, p. 5802: "Committed to
the public mission in New England and yet aware that their primary
covenant was between the individual and God, the American Puritan
poets wrote both public and private poems. . . . Anne Bradstreet,
Michael Wigglesworth, and Edward Taylor wrote the same kinds of poetry
as their contemporaries, but each of these three wrote several kinds
of poetry, both public and private. . . . The poetry of Anne
Bradstreet reveals the situation of the Puritan woman. . . . [She] is
ill at ease with the public role of elegist and historian. . . . But
private poetry was close enough to her sense of domestic vocation that
she could create original, well constructed lyrics. . . . The poetry
of Michael Wigglesworth presents a situation almost the opposite of
Anne Bradstreet's poetry. . . . His private poetry . . . reveals the
self-examination through which Michael Wigglesworth could be assured
that he was not hypocritical. But his best work was his public
poetry, in which he is heard as the poet-preacher. . . . Edward
Taylor was known among his contemporaries as a minister, not a poet.
. . . The way in which he used metaphors distinguishes his private
from his public voice."

1971-23   Rosenmeier, Rosamond Rauch. "The Evidence of Things Not
          Seen: Perspectives on History in the Writing of Anne
          Bradstreet, Thoreau, and Wallace Stevens." Ph.D., Harvard Univ.
          iv, 332 leaves.

"Introduction": "The three writers I have concerned myself with
in this study are preoccupied, each in a different way, with the
advent of an era of rebirth in the world, and with the role of the
poet and the relationship of literature to the process they so eagerly
describe" (p. 2). Relevant chapters: I. "Introduction" and II.

"Hidden Manna: Method and Truth in the Art of Anne Bradstreet."   The
final three chapters treat of the other writers.

1971-24   Roth,   David Morris.   "Jonathan Trumbull,   1710-1785:
    Connecticut's   Puritan Patriot."   Ph.D.,   Clark Univ.   4,   iii,   376
    leaves.

    Abstract in DAI, vol. 32 (3), sec. A, p. 1423:   "This study
examines the ostensibly paradoxical character and career of a major
figure in eighteenth-century Connecticut. . . . Trumbull's conduct
was rooted in the values of early eighteenth-century Connecticut
Puritanism.   That faith . . . preached the importance of earthly
striving as a means both to bring glory to God and to demonstrate the
fruits of the regenerative experience. . . . Puritan society was
convinced of its chosen state in the eyes of God.   The Puritans saw
themselves as the agents in a Covenant with God to complete the
Reformation by bringing forth a unique society in which the practices
of early Christianity were to be actualized.   It was Trumbull's
adherence to this sense of mission which enabled him to assume his
responsibilities as Connecticut's Governor in the Revolutionary era
with the absolute conviction that his duties were a part of the
theologically necessary task of preserving the purity of America in
face of the corrupting influences of a decadent Britain."   Cf. Roth's
Connecticut's War Governor: Jonathan Trumbull. -- Chester, Conn. :
Published by Pequot Press for the American Bicentennial Commission of
Connecticut, 1974. -- 99 p. -- (Connecticut Bicentennial Ser. ; IX).

1971-25   Rowe, Karen Elizabeth.   "Puritan Typology and Allegory as
    Metaphor and Conceit in Edward Taylor's Preparatory Meditations."
    Ph.D., Indiana Univ.   ix, 262 leaves.

    Abstract in DAI, vol. 32 (8), sec. A, p. 4578:   "This study
suggests that narrowly delineated principles for Puritan exegesis of
biblical types and allegory condition Taylor's choice of subjects and
images and formulation of metaphors and conceits in the second series
of Preparatory Meditations.   The thesis attempts to determine Taylor's
dependence on seventeenth-century Puritan typological treatises or
expositions of the allegorical Canticles, to assess his original
contributions as he adapts these inheritances to suit powerful
spiritual needs,   and to propose an esthetic for Taylor which
acknowledges the union of Puritan inspiration and discipline with
poetic creativity. . . .   The first chapter defines typology and
summarizes exegetical developments from New Testament writings and
works of the Church Fathers to Protestant and Puritan treatises of
seventeenth-century England and America. . . . Chapter II establishes
Taylor's orthodoxy as a Puritan typologist and contrasts his private
poetic search for faith and understanding of Christ with the public
motivations of prose exegetes. . . .   The following three chapters
analyze Taylor's dominant themes and the integration of exegetical
with poetic techniques in the three major segments of the second
series of meditations. . . .   Chapter VI proposes a view of Taylor's
esthetic which affirms the influence of Puritan discipline and
inspiration on poetic technique."

1971-26   Rushing, Stanley Ballard.   "The Recovery of New England
    Puritanism: A Historiographical Investigation." Th.D., New
    Orleans Baptist Theological Seminary. v, 165 leaves.

    Contents: "Introduction"; I. "The Historiography of New England
Puritanism from 1880-1930": "Puritan Defenders" (church historians:
Leonard Bacon, Henry Martyn Dexter, and Williston Walker; literary
historians: Moses Coit Tyler, Barrett Wendell, and Thomas Goddard
Wright), "Puritan Detractors" ("gentlemen" historians: Brooks Adams
and Charles Francis Adams, Jr.; "progressive" historians: James
Truslow Adams and Vernon Louis Parrington), and "Summary"; II. "The
Reappraisal of New England Puritanism from 1930 to 1940": "Prominent
Early Leaders" (Kenneth Ballard Murdock, Samuel Eliot Morison, and
Clifford K. Shipton) and "Perry Miller's Role"; III. "The Extension
and Refinement of New England Puritanism: Studies from 1940 to the
Present": "Perry Miller's Role," "Other Secular Historians," and
"Church Historians"; and "Summary and Conclusions."

1971-27   Russell, Bernie Eugene.   "Dialectical and Phonetic Features
    of Edward Taylor's Rhymes: A Brief Study Based upon a Computer
    Concordance of His Poems." Ph.D., Univ. of Wisconsin at Madison.
    6 vols. (2426 leaves).

    Abstract in DAI, vol. 31 (12), sec. A, p. 6567: "I . . . made a
concordance on the computer of Taylor's Preparatory Meditations, God's
Determinations, and several miscellaneous poems in the standard Taylor
text, The Poems of Edward Taylor, edited by Donald Stanford [see
#1953-12, above]. There were a total of 13,178 lines of poetry fed
into the computer, and 79,948 listings were produced for the
concordance. . . . On the basis of the concordance I was able to list
the usage of unusual rhyme words and study them.   There are two
important conclusions I reached: First, Taylor's unusual rhymes can
often be accounted for by the fact that he was using dialect
(Leicestershire) rhymes. . . . Second, Taylor was not as unsystematic
as we might have thought with respect to his off-rhymes." The
concordance portion of the diss. was published, with an introductory
essay on "The Words of Edward Taylor" by Karl Keller, as A Concordance
to the Poems of Edward Taylor. -- Washington, D.C., : Microcard
Editions, 1973. -- xxiv, 413 p.

1971-28   Searles, Joan Carolyn. "The Worlds of Roger Williams."
    Ph.D., Pennsylvania State Univ.   216 leaves.

    Abstract in DAI, vol. 32 (11), sec. A, p. 6394: "This study of
the writings of Roger Williams views them as the literary expression
of a personality. It describes the public and private worlds in which
Williams moved, the concerns and the metaphors that ruled his mind,
and the power that lies behind his work.   It goes beyond the
intellectual superstructure and literary conventions of the
seventeenth century to recreate the matrix of feelings that gives his
writings their vitality. . . . Although prolix and rambling,
tenacious and immoderate, he is yet a complex combination of skillful
politician, effective writer and intense Christian."

1971-29   Snell, Ronald Kingman.   "The County Magistracy in
    Eighteenth-Century Massachusetts: 1692-1750." Ph.D., Princeton
    Univ. ix, 384 leaves.

Abstract in DAI, vol. 32 (3), sec. A, p. 1457: "The dissertation
addresses itself to a number of subjects related to the county
government and magistracy of eighteenth-century Massachusetts: the
seventeenth-century origins of the county; the legal establishment of
county government after the grant of the charter of 1691; the legal
duties and the functions of the individual justice of the peace and
county agencies made up of justices; the method by which justices were
chosen; and the social and political role of the magistracy within a
county. ... The magistracy in other counties has not been explored
to the extent that that in Hampshire has been. If the same
circumstances obtain in other counties, it will appear . . . that
eighteenth-century Massachusetts was an increasingly stratified
society, and that county government provided a focus for an
increasingly powerful elite."

1971-30   Straub, Carl Benton. "Providential Ecology: Puritan
    Envisagement of Their Wilderness Environment." Ph.D., Harvard
    Univ. v, 353 leaves.

"Introduction": "There are two levels of interest in this study.
The first is historical research of a moment in a Christian people's
journey into the American landscape. This interest focuses on a
decisive problem . . . [which] is the existential tension between the
Puritans' intellectual and belief-full assent to the logological
necessities of their theological/ethical tradition and their
experiential openness to and inevitable sensuous relationship with the
environing wilderness. Our historical research involves study of
selected writings from Puritan divines of the Massachusetts Bay Colony
and Province through the first generation (1630-ca. 1740). . . . We
want to see what such literature tells us about the Puritans' struggle
to reconcile their cultural/religious ethos with their ecological
situation. . . . [The] second level of interest . . . is an ethical
one. It is a commitment to the Christian ethical task of coming to
understand the lineaments of contemporary man's envisagement of his
natural environment as a prelude to designing a contemporary ethics of
dominion" (pp. 1-2). Contents: "Introduction: Justification of the
Study and Statement of the Thesis," I. "Theoretical Inscape: Toward a
Model of Envisagement," II. "The English Garden: Cultivation of the
Puritan Mood," III. "The American Wilderness: Blessings and Curses of
Covenant Keeping," IV. "The American Garden: Harvests of Piety and
Science in a Settled Land," V. "Toward a Contemporary Ethics of
Dominion: Uses of 'Providential' Ecology," and "Conclusion."

1971-31   Swaim, Gary Dale.   "Edward Taylor: Toward Union with God--
    Studies in the Preparatory Meditations." Ph.D., Univ. of
    Redlands. iii, 108 leaves.

"Introduction"": "It is the aim of this study to examine the mystic's effort toward union with God or the One and the impact of this idea upon Taylor's Preparatory Meditations. Successive chapters . . . treat the aims and methodologies . . . of the mystic, the role of language in regard to mysticism, and the manner in which Taylor's Preparatory Meditations are informed conceptually, structurally, and metaphorically by Christian mysticism." Contents: "Introduction"; I. "The Tradition of Union": "Language and Mysticism"; II. "Taylor and the Problem of Union": "Structure in the Preparatory Meditations," "The Meditations: Purgation and Illumination," and "The Dramatis Personae"; III. "Taylor and the Metaphor of Union": "The Guest at the Feast: Union in the Ingestive Metaphor" and "The Betrothed at the Feast: Union in the Sexual Metaphor"; and IV. "Taylor and the Glories of Union": "Again and Again: 'The Experience,'" "A Perennial Glory," and "Conclusion."

1971-32   Turner, Maxine Thompson. "A History of the Bay Psalm Book." Ph.D., Auburn Univ. vi, 117 leaves.

Abstract in DAI, vol. 32 (3), sec. A, p. 1424: "Metrical psalmody is a method whereby the psalms of the Old Testament are set to meter so that they may be sung in worship services. . . . Among the most famous of the metrical versions was the Bay Psalm Book, published in Cambridge, Massachusetts, in 1640. . . . A work characteristic of Puritan literature of the time, the Bay Psalm Book was used in Massachusetts until 1651 when a decision was made to revise it. . . . Three attempts were made in New England in the eighteenth century to adapt the Bay Psalm Book to the newer literary standards while preserving a traditional fidelity to the biblical text. . . . Their revisions were never widely used, and the Bay Psalm Book passed out of use in New England by the time of the Revolution."

1971-33   Twomey, Rosemary Katherine. "For Pure Church to Pure Nation: Massachusetts Bay, 1630-1692." Ph.D., Univ. of Rochester. vi, 292 leaves.

Abstract in DAI, vol. 32 (7), sec. A, p. 3939: "Intellectually, the history of theology and ecclesiology in Massachusetts Bay from 1630 to 1692 underwent a change whereby the original theory of the pure church in a sanctified state was abandoned in favor of a theory of Massachusetts as a 'chosen Nation' in covenant with God to perform His work through a 'new history' in the 'new world.' Approached in the most abstract terms, the contrast between time and space defined the response of the first generation of clergy to apocalyptic hopes and fears and the second generation's acceptance of New England as a 'place' and eventually as the promised land itself."

1971-34   Van Til, L. John. "Liberty of Conscience: The History of a Puritan Idea." Ph.D., Michigan State Univ. iv, 246 leaves.

Abstract in DAI, vol. 32 (6), sec. A, p. 3232. Revision published under same title: Nutley, N.J.: Craig Press, 1972. -- vi, 192 p. "Introduction" (1972 ed.): "Tracing the emergence of liberty of conscience from the days of William Perkins to the First Amendment has been particularly appealing for several reasons. First, it provided an opportunity to span several decades that are usually dealt with in a truncated fashion. . . . Second, this study has found its appeal in providing another clue to the problem of the definition of Puritanism. The difference between the Massachusetts Bay leaders' attitude toward conscience and that of their brethren in Old England may be helpful in understanding the genuine peculiarity or originality of the Massachusetts Bay Colony's experiment. Finally, it may be argued that there is a tendency among moderns to look back only as far as the eighteenth century to find ideas that inform institutions and climates of opinion in the present age" (p. 3). Contents: "Introduction," I. "Toleration and Liberty of Conscience in Elizabethan England," II. "Toleration and Liberty in Old England: 1600-1640," III. "Conscience and the Builders of the Bay Colony: 1630-1640," IV. "Liberty of Conscience in Old England: 1640-1660," V. "The Failure of Liberty of Conscience in Restoration England," VI. "The Acceptance of Liberty of Conscience in America: 1630-1770," VII. "Liberty of Conscience in the American Revolution," and VIII. "Conclusion."

1971-35   Vartanian, Pershing. "The Puritan as a Symbol in American Thought: A Study of the New England Societies, 1820-1920." Ph.D., Univ. of Michigan. vi, 323 leaves.

Abstract in DAI, vol. 32 (7), sec. A, p. 3939: "The American Puritans, who flourished in New England for less than a century, left behind a remarkable intellectual, religious, social and political legacy which ever since has inspired scholarly study and popular discourse about them. As a result, the Puritans have acquired metaphorical qualities, and the Puritan has become a national symbol. This study has focused upon the history of the Puritan symbol as it was displayed by New Englanders living in other sections of the country. In their rhetoric the Puritan symbol changed from a primarily regional and religious figure to a national and secular one."

1971-36   Young, Ralph F. "Good News from New England: The Influence of the New England Way of Church Polity on Old England, 1635-1660." Ph.D., Michigan State Univ. iv, 196 leaves.

Abstract in DAI, vol. 32 (6), sec. A, p. 3236: "The American colonies have for many years been studied either in isolation or as the offspring of England, dependent in most respects on English institutions, traditions, and ideas. However, there is abundant evidence which indicates that the infant colonies actually exerted a powerful influence on the mother country as early as the first three decades of settlement, especially in the realm of religious ideas. The introduction of these colonial ideas into England at this time, and their subsequent influence there is the subject of this dissertation. . . . The major research for this project fell into distinct categories: Firstly I examined the theological writings of New England ministers who returned during the civil wars to England (e.g., Thomas Weld, Samuel Eaton, Isaac Chauncy, Hugh Peter) and also those of the New England divines . . . whose sermons, letters, and pamphlets were read by their brethren in England (e.g., Thomas Hooker, John Cotton, and Richard Mather). Secondly, I studied the writings of the English ministers who . . . read the works of their colonial brethren (e.g., John Owen, Thomas Edwards, Robert Baillie, Richard Baxter, Thomas Goodwin, and John Goodwin). Finally, I explored the extant records of non-conformist churches in Great Britain (primarily in London and East Anglia) in an effort to determine whether or not the New England Way was actually adopted there. The findings of the study suggest that this was indeed the case."

1971-37   Zabierek, Henry Carl. "Puritans and Americans: An Inquiry into the Nature of English Settlement in New England." D.A., Carnegie-Mellon Univ. 436 leaves.

Abstract in DAI, vol. 32 (8), sec. A, p. 4547: "A senior high school American history course should consist of selected topics that seem particularly relevant to teen age students rather than an attempt to touch on all the major developments in the nation's past. . . . The dissertation itself analyzes the challenge of social historians to the Perry Miller school of Puritanism, a bibliography, and an account of the trial of the unit in the schools. Both the student materials and the lesson plans appear as appendixes to the dissertation."

1972-1   Anderson, Deyrol Ewald. "The Massachusetts Election Sermon: A Critical Analysis of a Social and Polemical Phenomenon." Ph.D., Univ. of Denver. 312 leaves.

Abstract in DAI, vol. 33 (10), sec. A, p. 5860: "The Massachusetts election sermon, delivered annually in Boston between 1634 and 1884, is one of the oldest traditions in American rhetoric and perhaps the most consistent speech occasion of early America. These sermons evidence the close bond that existed between church and state prior to the American Revolution. Further, they evidence the clerical attitudes toward personal freedom, religious toleration, and local political control which can be traced through the sermons from the earliest colonial days to and beyond the Revolutionary period. . . . The speech occasion and the nature of the audience afforded the election preacher a singular opportunity to put forth strong political views. . . . This study is an investigation of the political rhetoric and views of the election preacher as he each year over two hundred fifty years presents himself to the General Court and the gathered assemblage."

1972-2   Anderson, Terry Lee. "The Economic Growth of Seventeenth-Century New England: A Measurement of Regional Income." Ph.D., Univ. of Washington. ix, 160 leaves.

Abstract in DAI, vol. 33 (5), sec. A, p. 1956. Revision published under same title: New York : Arno Press, 1975. -- viii, 160 p. -- (Dissertations in American Economic History). "Abstract" (1975 ed.): "Measuring the progress of the American economy is a first step toward understanding the process of economic growth. . . . The purpose of this dissertation is to provide such a study for seventeenth-century New England. The complexity of the economy of these northern colonies combined with the lack of quantitative evidence makes the task of measuring their economic performance most difficult. To overcome this it was necessary to develop an analytical framework which described the sectors of the economy and their relationship to one another and to research new and useful data for measuring the region's income" (n.p.).   Contents: I. "The Seventeenth-Century New England Economy"; II. "Analytical Framework": "Agriculture and Resources, 1620-1640" and "Rise of Commerce, 1640-1709"; III. "Population, Labor Force and Payments to Labor"; IV. "Wealth and Its Composition"; and V. "New England's Regional Income from 1650-1709." Appendices: A. "Stable Population Model Applied," B. "Average Size of Completed Family in Massachusetts, by Decade and Town," C. "Sampling the Probates Estate Inventories," D. "Wealth, Land, and Capital by Estate Size," E. "The Commodity Price Index," and F. "Possible Sources of Bias."

1972-3   Aubin, George Francis. "A Historical Phonology of Narragansett." Ph.D., Brown Univ. iv, 91 leaves.

Abstract in DAI, vol. 33 (8), sec. A, p. 4379: "This thesis sketches in some detail the historical phonology of Narragansett as best we may determine it from a careful analysis of the Williams materials. The hypothesis that Roger Williams' recordings of Narragansett are substantially accurate in all cases is tested with some measure of success. . . . Following an extended discussion of Williams' transcription system, 197 Proto-Algonquian--Narragansett cognates are listed. The vowel, glide, single consonant, and consonant cluster correspondences are established from an analysis of these cognate sets."

1972-4   Barber, Eddice Belle. "Cotton Mather's Literary Reputation in America." Ph.D., Univ. of Minnesota. ii, 281 leaves.

Abstract in DAI, vol. 33 (4), sec. A, p. 1673: "Although Cotton Mather published 444 works, writing was not his profession. The prominence of piety through his writings was to him a duty as a minister of God. Because he was a learned man with wide interests, his writings exceeded that single purpose, and his best works show by their style and content that Mather merits a greater literary reputation than he has had." Barber reviews responses to Mather's writings from Benjamin Franklin to "the research of G. L. Kittredge, Kenneth B. Murdock, Julius H. Tuttle, Thomas J. Holmes, and David Levin [which] resulted in a knowledge of Mather and his works that makes possible a just placement of him in the intellectual and literary history of America."

1972-5   Barton, Bonnie. "New England Settlement: An Inquiry into the Comparability of Geographic Methodologies." Ph.D., Univ. of Michigan. vi, 214 leaves.

Abstract in DAI, vol. 34 (4), sec. B, p. 1578. Revision published as The Comparability of Geographic Methodologies: A Study of <u>New England Settlement</u>. -- Ann Arbor : Department of Geography, Univ. of Michigan, 1977. -- xxiii, 161 p. -- (Michigan Geographical Publications ; no. 20). "Abstract" (1977 ed.): "Explanation of the spatial aspects of human activities may be characterized as resulting from two distinctive and common geographical approaches. Some feel that the proper spatial explanation comes from seeing locational characteristics as outcomes of human behavior which is goal-oriented and purposive. Others feel that a truly scientific explanation of spatial distributions is had only from the consideration of space-filling processes. . . . It is felt that each approach has a legitimate place in geographic research and represents an entirely self-contained explanatory scheme. . . . The settlement of New England [1600-1800] is examined from each of these vantage points, termed the spatial perspective and the social-historical perspective" (p. iii). Contents: "Introduction"; I. "Philosophical Background"; II. "Spatial Perspective"; III. "Historical Perspective": 1. "Questions appropriate to social-historical analysis," 2. "Religious ideals as motivations for new settlement," 3. "Indian relationships and the establishment of settlements," 4. "Land pressure as a force for settlement," 5. "Economic opportunity as a motivation for settlement, 6. "Land granting policies as context of settlement," and 7. "Summary"; and IV. "The Two Methodologies." Appendices: I. "Reference Maps" and II. "Expansion of Settlement."

1972-6   Boston, Walter M., Jr. "A Study of Presbyterianism in Colonial New England." Ph.D., Michigan State Univ. viii, 232 leaves.

Abstract in <u>DAI</u>, vol. 33 (11), sec. A, p. 6265: "The purpose of this study is twofold: First, to show that the New England Churches and their leaders indicated strong tendencies toward Presbyterianism and this enabled them to adopt some presbyterian procedures such as synods and councils similar to those used by English Presbyterians; second, to show New England was the source of the ready acceptance of Presbyterians from Scotland, Ireland, and France in the late 17th Century and the result was the development of a homegrown variety of Presbyterianism in the 18th Century. Church records, both primary and secondary, of New England Congregational and Presbyterian Churches were used in this study."

1972-7 Bremer, Francis John. "Puritan Crisis: New England and the English Civil Wars, 1630-1670." Columbia Univ. x, 373 leaves.

Abstract in <u>DAI</u>, vol. 36 (5), sec. A, p. 3032: "This is the story of the roots, nature, and effect of the New England Puritan response to the Puritan Revolution and its aftermath in England. The author's thesis is that the colonists saw the Revolution as the outcome of their prayers and example--a major turning point in the struggle which they saw themselves waging against Antichrist--and that they fully committed themselves to supporting their brethren in England. . . . When the Civil War broke out in England, New Englanders claimed the credit for that Puritan revolt. . . . Many colonists left New England to aid the cause by their direct participation. . . . Another form of assistance tendered the English rebels was advice. . . . New England supported the Protector, and Cromwell reciprocated by aiding the colonists. . . . The Restoration dashed not only the hopes of the New Englanders but the interpretation of history which had motivated them."

1972-8   Bross, James Beverly. "Puritan v. Anglican: An Attempt to Define a Difference." Ph.D., Univ. of Iowa. v, 218 leaves.

Abstract in DAI, vol. 33 (12), sec. A, p. 7011: "This study of typical Puritan-Nonconformists and Anglicans aids in defining differences between the groups. John Walker's list of Anglican ministers sequestered between 1640 and 1660 and Edmund Calamy III's list of Nonconformist ministers ejected after the Restoration of Charles II were used as sources for randomly selecting twenty-one American ministers and twenty-one Nonconformist ministers for comparison. It was assumed that similarities between Puritans and Nonconformists out-weighed the differences. . . . The results of coding for the two groups were then compared. . . . Differences were accepted as significant at the 5% level. The results revealed the Nonconformist as placing more emphasis on typologies of God, self, and eschatology while the Anglicans were revealed as placing more emphasis on typologies of authority, church, and state. . . . For the most part, differences between the two groups appeared to be matters of degree of emphasis rather than opposition of opinion. The Nonconformists appear to be more introspective and idealistic while the Anglicans appear to be more pragmatic."

1972-9   Clark, Edward William. "A Modernized Text and a Critical Text of John Williams, The Redeemed Captive Returning to Zion (1707)." Ph.D., Univ. of Wisconsin at Madison. 240 leaves.

Abstract in DAI, vol. 33 (7), sec. A, p. 3578: "No scholarly text of John Williams' The Redeemed Captive Returning to Zion exists. . . . Therefore, a modernized text and a rectified, critical text have been evolved. . . . The first three editions were collated and the first edition established as the copy-text. . . . The critical text, an emended version of the copy-text, is included after the modernized text. A textual introduction precedes the critical text. Following the critical text are the appendixes, which contain discussions of the accidental and substantive variants of the first three editions, an explanation of editorial emendations, and a list of the end-of-line hyphenated compound words." The modernized text published as The Redeemed Captive. -- Amherst : Univ. of Massachusetts Press, 1976. -- 137 p.   Contents: "Introduction," "Textual Introduction," "Note on the Modernized Text," "Sample Pages from the Critical Text," The Redeemed Captive, and "Map of the Route to Canada." A "slightly modified version" of 1976 ed. reprinted in Puritans among the Indians: Accounts of Captivity and Redemption, 1676-1724. -- Cambridge, Mass. : Harvard Univ. Press, 1981. -- Pp. 167-226.

1972-10   Cook, Edward Marks, Jr.   "The Fathers of the Towns:
Leadership and Community Structure in Eighteenth-Century New
England." Ph.D., Johns Hopkins Univ.

Revision published under same title: Baltimore ; London : Johns
Hopkins Univ. Press, 1976. -- xvii, 273 p. -- (Johns Hopkins Univ.
Studies in Historical and Political Science ; 94th ser., no. 2).
"Preface" (1976 ed.): The work attempts to provide a "conceptual
framework for explaining how the experience of one town might relate
to that of another" (pp. xi-xii). Contents: 1. "The Choice of the
Town Meeting," 2. "The Townspeople and Their Leaders," 3. "The
Economics of Leadership," 4. "The Influence of the Family," 5. "Town
and Church," 6. "The Provincial Hierarchies," 7. "The Typology of
Towns," and 8. "Epilogue." Appendices: I. "The Population of Towns"
and II. "Comparative Data on All New England Towns."

1972-11   Daly, Robert James.   "God's Altar: A Study of Puritan
Poetry." Ph.D., Cornell Univ. 3, v, 280 leaves.

Abstract in DAI, vol. 33 (9), sec. A, p. 5168. Revision
published as God's Altar: The World and the Flesh in Puritan Poetry.
-- Berkeley : Univ. of California Press, 1978. -- ix, 253 p. Contents
(1978 ed.): "Introduction: Puritanism and Poetry," I. "The World's
Body," II. "Ars Poetica," III. "Anne Bradstreet and the Practice of
Weaned Affections," IV. "Gnostics and Naturalists" (Michael
Wigglesworth, Philip Pain, Nathaniel Ward, Edward Johnson, Samuel
Danforth, Richard Steere, Urian Oakes, Benjamin Tompson, and Roger
Williams), and V. "Edward Taylor: Christ's Creation and the
Dissatisfactions of the Metaphor." Appendix: "In Critics' Hands: A
Bibliographical Essay."

1972-12   Daub, Oscar Carl.   "Ramist Logic and Rhetoric in Edward
Taylor's Preparatory Meditations." Ph.D., Univ. of Georgia.
iv, 204 leaves.

Abstract in DAI, vol. 33 (9), sec. A, p. 5168: "The logical and
rhetorical system of Peter Ramus exerted great influence on
seventeenth-century American expression. . . . Analysis of the
Preparatory Meditations reveals that Taylor . . . followed the
dictates of Ramism. He employed the various Ramist arguments when
analyzing the Biblical texts affixed to his meditations as well as
when writing his poems, and he used rhetorical figures as mere
embellishment of logically validated ideas. Furthermore, a Ramist
study of the poems demonstrates that, despite their ostensibly
affective function, Taylor first developed the logical bases of the
poem and then elaborated the ideas rhetorically. Consequently, the
affective function of the poem does not reside in the rhetorical
devices. Rather, the affective purpose was achieved through the
poems' participation in the tradition of religious meditation."

1972-13   Dethlefsen, Edwin Stewart.   "Life and Death in Colonial New
England." Ph.D., Harvard Univ. v, 202 leaves.

Relevant contents: I. "The Anthropological Role of Demography; Rationale for an Anthropological Study of the Demography of Colonial New England; The Problem," II. "Mortality Records and Paleo-demography; Problems of Describing Archaeological Populations; Methodological Approaches to the Mortality Data," III. "The Data; Subject Matter of the Data: Gravestones, Vital Records, and Census Figures; Work to Date on Colonial American Demography; Towns to be Treated in this Study," IV. "The Life Tables," V. "The Towns: Plympton, Kingston, Cohasset, Scituate, Plymouth, Hanover," and VI. "The Life Tables; Population Composition According to Census Data; Life Table Population Composition Compared with Census Population Composition; Discussion and Conclusions; Population Composition; Life Expectance."

1972-14   Diebold, Robert Kent. "A Critical Edition of Mrs. Mary Rowlandson's Captivity Narrative." Ph.D., Yale Univ. cciv, 160 leaves.

Abstract in DAI, vol. 33 (5), sec. A, p. 2368. Diebold's edition of Mary White Rowlandson's work published as The Narrative of the Captivity and Restoration of Mrs. Mary Rowlandson: First Printed in 1682 at Cambridge, Massachusetts, & London, England, Whereunto Are Annexed a Map of Her Removes & Biographical & Historical Notes. -- The National Bicentennial ed. -- Lancaster, Mass. : [Lancaster Bicentennial Commission], 1975. -- ix, 96 p. Contents (1975 ed.): "Introduction," "Narrative," and "Notes."

1972-15   Diemer, Carl John, Jr. "A Historical Study of Roger Williams in the Light of the Quaker Controversy." Th.D., Southwestern Baptist Theological Seminary. vii ["Abstract"], v, 220 leaves.

"Abstract": "The purpose of this dissertation is to examine the controversy between Roger Williams and the Quakers in Rhode Island Colony between 1672 and 1679 and to show that in this critical test of Williams' position under fire he did not compromise his basic convictions about religious liberty" (p. 2). Contents: "Introduction," I. "A Historiography of Williams," II. "A Biographical Sketch of Williams," III. "Williams the Controversialist," IV. "The Quaker Controversy," V. "Polemical Literature of Roger Williams Against the Quakers," VI. "Polemical Literature of the Quakers Against Roger Williams," and VII. "Conclusion."

1972-16   Douglas, Walter Benjamin Theophilus. "Richard Baxter and the Savoy Conference of 1661." Ph.D., McMaster Univ. (Canada). x, 206 leaves.

"Abstract": "The object of this study is to call into question the well established assumption that Baxter was entirely responsible for the failure of the Savoy Conference and that his combativeness and 'overdoing' kept the non-conformists out of the Church" (p. iii). Contents: Part I. "The Man and His Times": I. "A Historical Survey of the Life and Times of Richard Baxter" and II. "'Politics and Divinity'

in the Thought of Baxter: Implications for the Savoy Conference";
Part II. "Problems of Church and State": III. "Presbyterians and
Independents: Ideas in Conflict" and IV. "Charles II and the
Presbyterians"; and Part III. "The Savoy Conference: A Re-
Interpretation in the Light of Recent Discovery":   V. "The Worcester
House Declaration 1660 and the King's Warrant 1661," VI. "The Savoy
Conference: Proceedings," and VII. "Conclusion."

1972-17 Du Priest, Travis Talmadge, Jr. "The Liturgies of Jeremy
     Taylor and Richard Baxter: A Study of Structure, Language, and
     Rhythm." Ph.D., Univ. of Kentucky. iv, 263 leaves.

     Abstract in DAI, vol. 33 (5), sec. A, p. 2323: "Coming as they
do at the end of the Interregnum, Taylor's Collection of Offices
[1658] and Baxter's Reformed Liturgy [1661] climax long and diverging
traditions of the liturgical genre in the seventeenth century. Hence,
the value of comparing and contrasting the liturgies of these two
minister-writers, Taylor an Anglican and Baxter an Anglo-Presbyterian,
is clear." Contents: I. "Introduction," II. "The Nature of Liturgy,"
III. "The Liturgies of Taylor and Baxter: Occasions and Theories,"
IV. "Stylistic Elements of the Treatises on Liturgy," V. "A Comparison
of the Patterns of Structure of the Two Liturgies," VI. "A Comparison
of the Styles of the Two Liturgies," and VII. "Conclusion."

1972-18   Elliott, Emory Bernard, Jr. "Generations in Crisis: The
     Imaginative Power of Puritan Writing, 1660-1700." Ph.D., Univ.
     of Illinois at Urbana-Champaign. iv, 253 leaves.

     Abstract in DAI, vol. 33 (10), sec. A, p. 5675.   Revision
published as Power and the Pulpit in Puritan New England. -- Princeton
: Princeton Univ. Press, 1975. -- xi, 240 p. "Preface" (1975 ed.):
The work's intention is "to show how the Puritan sermons provided
myths and metaphors that helped the people express their deepest
feelings, emotions created by their peculiar cultural situation and
aroused by crucial social events of the seventeenth century" (p.
viii). Contents: "Introduction," I. "Building the Patriarchy," II.
"Shaping the Puritan Unconscious," III. "Storms of God's Wrath," IV.
"Clogging Mists and Obscuring Clouds," V. "The Dawning of That Day,"
and "Epilogue."

1972-19   Goldstein, Steven. "The Act of Vision in Edward Taylor's
     Preparatory Meditations." Ph.D., Tufts Univ. 186 leaves.

     Abstract in DAI, vol. 34 (2), sec. A, p. 726: "This is a study
of Edward Taylor's treatment of the visual process in his Preparatory
Meditations, as a metaphor for religious experience and as actual
sight of the divine presence. As investigation of the poems will
show, this latter vision is always described in the past tense, for
the mystical illumination that it represents is the constant and
unrealized goal of the Meditations' spiritual struggle. . . . The
changing nature of the visual act, as it reflects the stages of that
struggle, determines the organization of this study. Chapter I and II
discuss the first stage, Taylor's recognition of his sins . . . and

his longing for lost grace. . . . Typology was . . . of great
importance to Taylor, as Chapter III illustrates with its analysis of
how the personal content in his typology poems is intensified by his
selection of Old Testament events. . . . The last two chapters,
concerning two visions of Christ inspired by Taylor's typological
reading of the Song of Solomon, are devoted to his anticipation of the
journey's end--the sight of Christ in his soul and ultimately in
heaven."

1972-20 Hamilton, Frank S. "The Origins and Development of the
     Presbytery and Its Role and Function in the Contemporary Church."
     S.T.D., San Francisco Theological Seminary. iii, 239 leaves.

     "Abstract": "The American church . . . was strongly influenced
by Scotch and Scotch-Irish emigrants in the Eighteenth century, who
were used to authoritarian polity structures within the Presbyterian
system of polity. However, it also had roots in the more democratic
tradition of English Presbyterians and was continually being
democratized by the American social milieu itself" (pp. i-ii).
Relevant chapters: I. "Introduction," II. "Early Origins," III.
"Calvin and Geneva," IV. "France," V. "Scotland and Ulster," VI.
"England," VII. "American Origins," and VIII. "The Synod and the
Subscription Controversy." Chapters IX-XV treat of later events.

1972-21 Hoffmann, John Maynard. "Commonwealth College: The
     Governance of Harvard in the Puritan Period." Ph.D., Harvard
     Univ. 2 vols. (xxiii, 815 leaves).

     Diss. is an institutional history of Harvard College from the
presidency of Nathaniel Eaton (1638-39) to that of Benjamin Wadsworth
(1725-36/37). "The thesis is designed to describe and analyze the
structure and operation of the primary educational endeavor of early
New England. Although the first half of the century is considered
somewhat more fully than the second fifty years, the entire account is
focused on governmental aspects of the institution--the constitution
of the College, the policies of its two boards, and the connections
between Harvard and the General Court and churches of colonial
Massachusetts. It is a political, legal, and administrative history
of an important enterprise of a society dedicated to Puritan ideals"
(p. ii). Contents: Part One: "The First Half Century": 1.
"Context," 2. "The General Court and the Support of Harvard," 3.
"Governmental Origins," 4. "Harvard under [Henry] Dunster and
[Charles] Chauncy," and 5. "From [Leonard] Hoar to [Increase]
Mather,"; and Part Two: "The Second Half Century": 6. "Mather's
Ascendancy," 7. "The College in Transition," 8. "The Gathering Storm,"
9. "The [Nicholas] Sever Controversy," and 10. "Equilibrium."
Appendices: A. "Constitutional Documents," B. "Trust, Corporation and
the Legality of the Charter," C. "Corporation Membership, 1650-72," D.
"The Relation of Early Yale to Harvard, 1701-22," and E. "Early
Sources: College Books."

1972-22   Johnson, Richard Rigby.   "Adjustment to Empire: War, New
England, and British Colonial Policy in the Late Seventeenth
Century."   Ph.D., Univ. of California at Berkeley.

Revision published as Adjustment to Empire: The New England
Colonies, 1675-1715. -- New Brunswick, N.J. : Rutgers Univ. Press,
1981. -- xx, 470 p.   "Preface" (1981 ed.):   "The study of religious
and social development . . . does not provide the necessary key for
understanding the most significant changes through which New England
passed during the era of the Glorious Revolution.   Rather, such an
understanding can best be obtained through analysis of the region's
relatively neglected political and institutional history, especially
as it focuses upon the colonies' dealings with one another and with
the outside world. . . .   Those who shaped events and attitudes within
New England during these years were as much seasoned and often far-
sighted politicans and participants in the Atlantic community as they
were men with their eyes fixed upon village life or the hereafter--or
the one in preparation for the other" (p. x).   Contents: I.
"Prologue: Expansion and Confrontation, 1675-1685," II. "'A Wolfe by
the Ears':   Dominion, Revolution, and Settlement, 1686-1689," III.
"'New England's Sad Condition':   Transatlantic Interaction and the
Fruits of Compromise," V. "Exploiting a Settlement: Confusion and
Conflict, 1692-1698,"   VI. "Agents and Office Seekers: The Evolution
of Transatlantic Politics, 1692-1715," and VII. "Conclusion:
Resurgence and Synthesis, 1698-1715."

1972-23   MacPhail, William Alasdair Boyd.   "Land Hunger and Closed-
Field Husbandry on the New England Frontier, 1630-1665:   The
First Generation of Settlement in Watertown, Massachusetts."
Ph.D., Brown Univ.   340 leaves.

Abstract in DAI, vol. 42 (6), sec. A, p. 2804:   "This
dissertation presents and develops the hypothesis that the settlers
did not share a unitary agricultural past when they came to
Massachusetts in the 1630's and '40's and that the colonial
authorities were fully aware of the conflict of interests which might
arise between closed-field East Anglian farmers and common or open-
field Midland husbandmen.   An eclectic plan for the frontier society
had therefore been devised in keeping with the ideological aspirations
articulated during the Great Migration. . . .   Preconceived in advance
of emigration, this plan proved in the long run to be ill-suited to
the colonization of an area where land was plentiful and its produce
marketable. . . .   Although a pattern of settlement modeled after the
extended and loosely-structured villages of East Anglia was judged to
be detrimental to the settlers' religious and social integrity, it
rapidly spread throughout the colony. . . .   The alleged 'declension'
of the Bible Commonwealth . . . was the unavoidable by-product of an
evolution from a relatively primitive type of husbandry to a more
profitable utilization of the land and labor force."

1972-24   Main, Gloria Lund. "Personal Wealth in Colonial America: Explorations in the Use of Probate Records from Maryland and Massachusetts, 1650-1720." Ph.D., Columbia Univ. xi, 342 leaves.

Abstract in DAI, 34 (1), sec. A, p. 250: "Based on the inventories and accounts of over five thousand estates found in the probate records of Suffolk and Hampshire Counties in Massachusetts and six counties of Maryland, this quantitative study pursues three distinct goals: first, analysis of the types of information to be gained from these records and the degree to which they represent the personal wealth holdings of the living population from which they are drawn; second, progress in the development of universal statistical measures for the comparative study of mass economic behavior; and third, exploration of the contents of the records organized by date, residence, and type of asset. . . . The final chapter of the dissertation summarized the findings on 'Maryland,' 'Rural Massachusetts,' and Boston and compares the three on the level, distribution and composition of wealth over time."

1972-25   North, Gary Kilgore. "The Concept of Property in Puritan New England, 1630-1720." Ph.D., Univ. of California at Riverside. xiii, 466 leaves.

Abstract in DAI, 34 (10), sec. A, p. 6571: "John Winthrop's band of Puritan refugees . . . assumed that the inherited intellectual framework of scholastic economic thought was in conformity with the natural law of God. . . . They enacted just prices and just wages--wage and price controls--sumptuary legislation, community controls on the use and distribution of land, export and import controls, and maximum rates of interest. . . . The last great flurry of such legislation was in 1675-76, during King Philip's War; open market competition steadily replaced the medieval framework after this time. . . . The clergy could no longer find any specific laws that would transform a formal legal code into an all-encompassing Christian framework. . . . The world of business, the laws of political economy, the standards of dress were all severed from any explicit Christian law-order. By 1720, the ground of [Benjamin] Franklin's later aphorisms was established. He could adopt Puritan conclusions regarding moderation, careful accounting, charity, and productivity, but abandon the theological foundations of the Holy Commonwealth. The realm of business and property had been secularized long before."

1972-26   Nutting, Parker Bradley. "Charter and Crown: Relations of Connecticut with the British Government, 1662-1776." Ph.D., Univ. of North Carolina at Chapel Hill. xii, 522 leaves.

Abstract in DAI, 33 (8), sec. A, p. 4317: "Since Connecticut's corporate Charter enabled considerable autonomy within the empire, historians have tended to assume the colony's relationship with Great Britain was negligible. However, the Crown had considerable influence on the lives of the colonists. This paper concentrates on five major imperial problems--colonial boundaries, maritime trade, war, judicial appeals, and religion."

1972-27   Parker, David Lowell. "The Application of Humiliation:
           Ramist Logic and the Rise of Preparationism in New England."
           Ph.D., Univ. of Pennsylvania. xix, 278 leaves.

Abstract in DAI, 33 (4), sec. A, p. 1825: "Chapter One of this
study highlights . . . similarities in the theories of reason
described by Calvin and [Petrus] Ramus that seem to account for the
demonstrable attractiveness of the Ramist logic to followers of
Calvin. Chapter Two identifies the Ramist principles used by [Thomas]
Hooker and [Thomas] Shepard to justify the divergence of their
'preparationist' conversion program from Calvin's positions on
election and regeneration. Chapter Three traces the effect of the
Ramist conditioned preparationist conversion process on the evolution
of church polity in New England; while Chapter Four describes the
impact of both the Ramist logic and the related preparationist ideals
on the work of Edward Taylor, the most impressive of America's Puritan
poets. . . . This study, then, investigates the nature of the
relationship between the Ramist logic and the preparationist movement
in America."

1972-28   Phelan, Joan D'Arcy.   "Puritan Tradition and Emily
           Dickinson's Poetic Practice." Ph.D., Bryn Mawr College.   207
           leaves.

Abstract in DAI, 33 (9), sec. A, p. 5136: "Dickinson's relation
to an orthodox tradition is evident in the affinities she shares with
Puritan poets of the past, particularly Anne Bradstreet and Edward
Taylor. Her own letters, however, are the most useful source of
information for illustrating how Puritanism determines Dickinson's
choice of subject matter and even influences the formulation of
aesthetic theories about her art. Emily Dickinson's corpus develops
as a reaction to Puritan norms which she can neither accept, nor
wholly reject--only subvert. . . . Mindful of the traditional Puritan
concepts of conversion, election, and the need for seeking salvation,
and equipped with the vocabulary, symbolism and Biblical principles of
her heritage, if not its metaphysic, Dickinson strives to endow her
poetic vision with a religious significance. But the vision is
personal, not absolute, and Dickinson is left in doubt about her
reading of the world, doubt about the meaning of life, and doubt about
. . . whether the human mind can survive the extinction of the body."

1972-29   Pierpont, Phillip Edward. "'Oh! Angells Stand Agastard at
           My Song': Edward Taylor's Meditations on Canticles." Ph.D.,
           Southern Illinois Univ. at Carbondale. 387 leaves.

Abstract in DAI, 33 (9), sec. A, p. 5194: "The primary purpose
of this study is to provide an extended reading of Edward Taylor's
meditations on Canticles--especially the thirty-nine consecutive poems
written between 1713 and 1719. . . . Every poem which is specifically
based on a text from Canticles has been discussed, at least in
passing; . . . the emphasis has been upon primary source explication
rather than the illustration of one central thesis. . . .   Chapter I

establishes Taylor's intimate knowledge and use of the imagery of Canticles . . . [and] illustrates the manner in which he used the commentaries. Chapter II examines Gods Determinations. . . . Chapter III examines all the meditations on Canticles before 1713. . . . Chapter IV deals with all the poems written after 1713."

1972-30   Salisbury, Neal Emerson. "Conquest of the 'Savage': Puritans, Puritan Missionaries, and Indians, 1620-1680." Ph.D., Univ. of California at Los Angeles. ix, 298 leaves.

Abstract in DAI, 32 (12), sec. A, p. 6905: "The earliest Puritan settlers considered conversion of the Indians among the highest priorities of their 'errand into the wilderness.' Yet, during the first sixty years of settlement, the culture and much of the population of southern New England Algonquians disappeared under the impact of Puritan colonization. In order to understand how and why the natives were destroyed rather than saved, this study examines Puritan attitudes toward the Indians in the wider context of Puritan thinking and experience, and the effect of English settlement on the Indians." Cf. Salisbury's Manitou and Providence: Indians, Europeans, and the Making of New England, 1500-1643. -- New York : Oxford Univ. Press, 1982. -- xii, 316 p.

1972-31   Scheer, Thomas Frederick. "'The Spectacles of God's Word': Spiritual Vision and Salvation in Seventeenth- and Eighteenth-Century Puritan History and Allegory." Ph.D., Univ. of Notre Dame. iv, 211 leaves.

Abstract in DAI, 33 (4), sec. A, p. 1695: "Richard Baxter's The Saints' Everlasting Rest is an important and representative document which demonstrates the Puritans' continual concern to verify their salvation. . . . One reason for [the appeal of this book] was the existence of an already developed tradition of Puritan history and allegory which sought similar ends of spiritual assurance, and which used similar methods to produce this assurance. . . . John Foxe [in his Actes and Monuments], John Bunyan [in The Holy War], Edward Johnson [in The Wonder-Working Providence], Cotton Mather [in the Magnalia Christi Americana], Samuel Sewall [in his Phaenomena quaedam Apocalyptica], and Joseph Morgan [in The History of the Kingdom of Basaruah] are all representative writers in the tradition of spiritual vision and allegory."

1972-32   Sheehan, Patrick Michael. "Harvard Alumni in Colonial America: Demographic, Theological and Political Perspectives." Ph.D., Case Western Reserve Univ. ix, 227 leaves.

Abstract in DAI, 32 (12), sec. A, p. 6792: "This study concerns the function of Harvard alumni 1642-1760 in colonial society and thought. Demographically, the alumni seem to reflect the high point, the decline and the fall of Puritan strength and influence in colonial New England and the consequent shift from a theological power base to a socio-economic one. The theological and political ideas of those alumni who published are also indicative of this change. . . . From demographic, theological and political perspectives, the decline and fall of Puritan power and influence among these Harvard alumni was seemingly as complete as was the concept of the covenant people upon which it rested."

1972-33   Shelly, Harold Patton. "Richard Sibbes: Early Stuart Preacher of Piety." Ph.D., Temple Univ. 269 leaves.

Abstract in DAI, 33 (11), sec. A, p. 6443: "This study surveys the historical, political, and theological background and then focuses in on the mystical and experiential dimensions in the warmhearted divinity of Richard Sibbes (1577-1635), lecturer at George's Inn, London, and Master of St. Catherine's Hall, Cambridge. For him, persuasive preaching was a means of curing the malignant Church of God in England, but perhaps more importantly this was God's chief means for conveying the soul to glory, the primary means of grace which the spirit uses to sanctify the believing soul on his pilgrimage. By his warmhearted divinity he intended to appeal to the understanding and the will and to move men to give Christ the marrow of their best affections, not merely to accept approved dogmatic propositions."

1972-34   Sherman, Arnold Alan. "Commerce, Colonies, and Competition: Special Interest Groups and English Commercial and Colonial Policy, 1660-1673." Ph.D., Yale Univ. 273 leaves.

Abstract in DAI, vol. 34 (1), sec. A, p. 258: "This study is an attempt to re-examine certain aspects of the commercial and colonial history of Restoration England. . . . The last chapter attempts to show how this commercial rivalry between the English and the Dutch affected England's relations with its own colonies, particularly in America. The 'Navigation Acts' and the regulations they imposed on colonial trade are examined from two vantage points: the needs of English merchants, and the feelings of English politicians, particularly in the House of Commons. . . . The acts represented, in part, Parliament's desire to do something to strike back at the Dutch in the only area of the world where Parliament could, in the American colonies. In this way, legislation that was designed to sever the commercial ties between the New World colonies and the Dutch, was caused by Dutch commercial rivalry and aggression in other parts of the world."

1972-35   Shuffleton, Frank Charles. "Light of the Western Churches: The Career of Thomas Hooker, 1586-1647." Ph.D., Stanford Univ. viii, 367 leaves.

Abstract in DAI, vol. 33 (5), sec. A, p. 2395. Revision published as Thomas Hooker, 1586-1647. -- Princeton : Princeton Univ. Press, 1977. -- xii, 324 p. "Preface" (1977 ed.): "I began this study in an attempt to discover in Hooker's sermons reason for his emigration, and what I discovered there has importance for Puritan and American life on a much wider scale. His concern for men's troubled minds, for civil harmony, and for the practice of a meditative, intensive piety has reappeared throughout our history, although I have confined myself to a consideration of his significance for the Puritan experience" (p. x). Contents: One: "Education and Conversion," Two: "Pastoral Beginnings," Three: "The English Preaching Career," Four: "The Netherlands Experiment," Five: "Massachusetts," Six: "Connecticut," Seven: "The New England Way," and Eight: "Heritage."

1972-36   Skaggs, Donald. "Roger Williams in History: His Image in the American Mind." Ph.D., Univ. of Southern California. iii, 258 leaves.

Abstract in DAI, vol. 33 (4), sec. A, p. 1661: "With few exceptions, Roger Williams' interpreters before the middle of the twentieth century misrepresented him, and some grossly. . . . Recent scholars, however, have attempted to understand Williams in the context of the seventeenth cenetury. As a result, they returned to a realistic view . . . that Williams was motivated by strong religious passions. While they differ in details, nearly all agree that he had a burning desire to be an instrument in accomplishing God's designs and purposes." Skaggs surveys the views held of Williams by his contemporaries, Baptist writers, Rhode Island writers, Massachusetts writers, and writers "who used Williams to lecture on Americanism."

1972-37   Steger, Thomas Theodore. "Conservatism and Radicalism: Richard Hooker's Dispute with the Puritans." Ph.D. Columbia Univ. 291 leaves.

Abstract in DAI, vol. 35 (10), sec. A, p. 6780: "As the first systematic defender of conservative constitutionalism and skepticism, [Richard Hooker] incorporated English thought on common law and tradition into a world view supported by a philosophy of reason and revelation. . . . Fundamental to the Puritan world view was a distrust of any ordering of human affairs not explicitly subject to divine direction. This distrust extended most explicitly to Church order, but it also embraced the concepts of custom and tradition. . . . The Puritan questioner, a stranger in his contemporary world and freed from old allegiances, felt justified in seeking a new order. Hooker's conservatism is an explicit answer to the Puritan radicalism of thought and feeling."

1972-38   Stevens, David Mark. "John Cotton and Thomas Hooker: The Rhetoric of the Holy Spirit." Ph.D., Univ. of California at Berkeley. xiii, 209 leaves.

Abstract in DAI, vol. 33 (7), sec. A, p. 3602: "John Cotton (1584-1652) and Thomas Hooker (1586-1647) were very sanguine about the purpose of rhetoric--they employed a speculum of style artistically designed as the rhetoric of spiritual witness to lead saints to glorification and to persuade members of congregations of the validity of Puritan spiritual experience. . . . It was their intention to use the plain-style in an artful, aesthetic way to persuade convinced Puritan saints of the validity of the Puritan vision. They felt their dynamic literary form conveyed an apprehension of reality gnostically perceived, rhetorically expressed and experientially approved. Their sermons stand as active types of discourse whose source for them was the Spirit of God."

1972-39   Tipson, Lynn Baird, Jr.   "The Development of a Puritan Understanding of Conversion." Ph.D., Yale Univ. v, 364 leaves.

Abstract in DAI, vol. 33 (7), sec. A, p. 3767: "The dissertation examines the development of the understanding of religious conversion eventually held by William Perkins, and leading Puritan theologian of Elizabethan England, and his best-known Puritan contemporaries. . . . It conceives conversion broadly as the whole process by which God was understood to draw sinful man back to Himself and His service, by which men turned from resistance to active participation in God's design for the world." Contents: "Introduction," I. "The Augustinian Background," II. "The Continental Reformed Tradition," III. "The English Reformation before William Perkins," IV. "The Impact of Perkins's Understanding of Conversion," and "Conclusion."

1972-40   Wasinger, Stephen Francis.   "Politics and the Full Persuasion: An Inquiry into the Source of the Puritan Project." Ph.D., Univ. of Notre Dame.   261 leaves.

Abstract in DAI, vol. 33 (4), sec. A, p. 1801:   "This dissertation attempts to identify the source of the Puritan critique of the Elizabethan English regime. . . . The source of this Puritan political project is the claim that only Scripture can order Christian action and, more importantly, that when Scripture absolutely orders action the visible church of Christ can become the true spiritual church of Christ. Puritan discipline serves this end by enforcing the rule of Scripture, correcting sin by excommunication and execution. . . . The end of the Puritan political project, then, is the self-salvation of some men by eliminating all men or things which testify to the questionableness of that project."

1972-41   Whitaker, Albert Henry Keith, Jr.   "The Integration of Social Ideals and Economic Reality in Early Settlement Massachusetts, 1628-1648." Ph.D., Boston Univ. (Graduate School). vi, 531 leaves.

Abstract in DAI, vol. 33 (4), sec. A, p. 1625: "This dissertation investigates the economy of Massachusetts Bay during the first two decades of settlement. While its focus is upon the progress, type and rate of development, as well as the obstructions overcome, consideration is also given to the relationship between public authority and private enterprise in the creation of a viable economy. The tangency and compatibility of socio-religious priorities and economic requirements also are opened to question. . . . Among the findings has been that of a strong mutuality between social, religious, and economic aspirations. A 'common-wealth ideal' which brought the interests of the individual and the community more closely together in the pursuit of both 'goodly' and 'Godly' lives, colored much of the economic decision-making."

1972-42   Whitlock, Maria Nevampaa. "Voluntary Associations in Salem, Massachusetts, before 1800." Ph.D., Ohio State Univ. iv, 309 leaves.

Abstract in DAI, vol. 33 (2), sec. A, p. 683: "This paper attempts to discover the origins of the voluntary association in one colonial community, Salem, Massachusetts, and the uses of association in the eighteenth-century town. For the purposes of this study, Arnold Rose's definition of voluntary association will be used: 'A small group of people, finding they have a certain interest (or purpose) in common, agree to meet and act together in order to satisfy that interest or achieve that purpose.'" Relevant chapters: "Introduction"; Part I. "Antecedents to Voluntary Associations in Salem": I. "Role of Governmental Community in Fostering Voluntary Associations," II. "The Church as a Model for Voluntary Association," III. "Role of Business Organizations in Fostering Voluntary Associations," and IV. "Ideological Beliefs and Norms of Association"; and Part II. "Growth and Development of Voluntary Associations in Salem": V. "Chronological Development of Voluntary Associations." Chapters VI-VIII deal with later periods.

1972-43   Wood, Gary Alan. "The 'Festival Frame': The Influence of the Tradition of Right Receiving on the Preparatory Meditations of Edward Taylor." Ph.D., Univ. of Pittsburgh. 275 leaves.

Abstract in DAI, vol. 33 (8), sec. A, p. 4372: "Chapter I questions the validity of reading the poems as spontaneous outpourings of Taylor's soul. . . . [A] sequence of specific activities, including examination of the soul for grace, meditation on Christ's sacrifical actions, and fervent prayer, came to be required of the communicant for proper reception of the sacrament. This sequence of actions, called the duties of right receiving, is suggested as a primary influence on the structure, themes, and imagery of the Preparatory Meditations. Chapter II offers a brief historical survey of works on right receiving in order to establish the existence of such a tradition and to show the development of an increasingly complex structure of duties to be observed before, during, and after the Supper is received. . . . Chapter III examines Taylor's Treatise Concerning the Last Supper. . . . Chapters IV-VIII examine selected poems from the standpoint of the influence of the tradition of right receiving."

1972-44   Yarbrough, Slayden A. "Henry Jacob, a Moderate Separatist, and His Influence on Early English Congregationalism." Ph.D., Baylor Univ. ix, 204 leaves.

Abstract in DAI, vol. 33 (9), sec. A, p. 5284: "During the last two decades of the sixteenth century a Christian movement emphasizing congregational polity appeared in England. . . . The less radical dissenters concluded that the individual English churches were true churches and encouraged limited religious communion with all true New Testament churches. . . . A major proponent of the latter position was Henry Jacob. Since no thorough study of this man or his

ecclesiological position has been made, this dissertation is dedicated
to the rectifying of this long-overdue deficiency.... Chapter 4
is an extensive examination of the influence of Henry Jacob on John
Robinson in the period 1610-1616. .... Chapters 5 and 6 assess the
direct and indirect ecclesiological influence of Jacob on early
English Independency or Congregationalism in England, Holland, and New
England. The conclusion is that seventeenth-century Congregationalism
was an outgrowth of English moderate Separatism which had as its chief
spokesman and practitioner, Henry Jacob."

1973-1   Baldwin, Lewis Morse, II. "Moses and Mannerism: An
    Aesthetic for the Poetry of Colonial New England." Ph.D.,
    Syracuse Univ. 150 leaves.

Abstract in DAI, vol. 35 (2), sec. A, p. 1035: "This thesis
contributes to a broader and deeper understanding of the aesthetic
that informs the major poetry of Colonial New England. It argues that
this aesthetic is metaphysical, and further that the stylistic and
philosophic origins of that style can be traced to John Calvin's
theories of absolute depravity and predeterminism. Thus one can see
evidence of the metaphysical style wherever the theories of Calvin and
Petrus Ramus, who applied Calvinist principles to logic and rhetoric,
had any significant impact. In Colonial New England, the influence of
Calvinism was both important and long lasting." The poetry of Anne
Bradstreet, Edward Taylor, and Michael Wigglesworth is considered in
light of Baldwin's thesis.

1973-2   Bissell, Linda Auwers. "Family, Friends, and Neighbors:
    Social Interaction in Seventeenth-Century Windsor, Connecticut."
    Ph.D., Brandeis Univ. vi, 246 leaves.

Abstract in DAI, vol. 34 (7), sec. A, p. 4137: Diss. "discusses
social interactions in a seventeenth-century New England community.
. . . Background chapters discuss the founding of Windsor,
demography, and economics. Four varieties of social interaction are
then analyzed: generational, sexual, spatial, and class. . . .
Research utilized quantitative techniques to help answer questions in
social history. .... [The diss.] concludes that the early years in
Windsor were ones of great flux, best characterized by the
dramatically high rates of geographic and economic mobility.
Residents soon established a highly structured system of social
interaction. The status network was a miniature model . . . of that
found in England."

1973-3   Burton, Royce Edwin. "Nathaniel Ward's The Simple Cobler of
    Aggawam in America: A Collation of the Five London Editions of
    1647, with Annotations." Ph.D., Univ. of Texas at Austin. viii,
    205 leaves.

Abstract in DAI, vol. 34 (5), sec. A, p. 2549: "The first and
second London editions of Nathaniel Ward's The Simple Cobler of
Aggawam in America . . . are collated using a copy of the first
edition as the basis for comparison. Author's additions and

emendations, as well as printer's variants, are arranged as sidenotes
to a facsimile text of the first edition. Comprehensive text notes
... make the meaning of the text and the extent of Ward's wordplay
available to the modern reader. Two introductory chapters provide:
(1) a biographical sketch of Nathaniel Ward, and (2) an identification
of each of the five London editions. ... A Table of pagination,
catchwords, and signatures of the five editions is included."

1973-4 Davidson, James West. "Eschatology in New England: 1700-
        1763." Ph.D., Yale Univ. iv, 285 leaves.

        Abstract in DAI, vol. 34 (11), sec. A, p. 7146. Revision
published as The Logic of Millennial Thought: Eighteenth-Century New
England. -- New Haven : Yale Univ. Press, 1977. -- xii, 308 p. --
(Yale Historical Publications. Miscellany ; 112). "Preface" (1977
ed.) poses these questions: "Granting the New Englander's strange
interest in prophecies, how did eschatology influence the way they
looked at the rest of the world? Did the Revelation and the tradition
of interpretation growing out of it have a logic of their own which
disposed people to think or act in certain consistent ways?" Relevant
chapters: Part 1: "Unraveling the Logic": 1. "Revelation," 2.
"Chronology," 3. "Judgment," and 4. "Conversion"; and Part 2:
"Applying the Logic": 7. "The End--and the Means." Chapters 5 and 6
treat of later periods.

1973-5   Davis, Leroy Alton. "A Comparative Investigation of Certain
        Similarities of Educational Concern between New England
        Puritanism and the Proposals for National Systems of Education in
        the Eighteenth Century." Ph.D., Ohio Univ. x, 331 leaves.

        Abstract in DAI, vol. 34 (5), sec. A, p. 2350: "The purpose of
this study is to indicate the extent to which certain similarities of
educational concern existed between New England Puritanism, which
maintained a strong religious component, and the proposals for
national systems of education in the late Eighteenth Century, which
were predominantly based upon secular considerations. ... It is
concluded that similarities of educational concern existed between the
proposals and Puritanism in terms of social themes taught, scientific
approaches, and an emphasis upon practicality in education. It is
further concluded that both approaches were posited upon highly
rational bases."

1973-6   Erickson, John H. "Emerson and the Transcendentalists:
        Their Attitudes toward Puritanism." Ph.D., Univ. of Chicago.
        ii, 235 leaves.

        Contents: I. "From Calvinism to Unitarianism to
Transcendentalism," II. "[William Ellery] Channing's Attitude toward
Puritanism," III. "[Theodore] Parker's Attitude toward Puritanism,"
IV. "Emerson's Attitude toward Calvinism," V. "Thoreau's Attitude
toward Puritanism," VI. "[George] Bancroft's Attitude toward
Puritanism," VII. "Emerson's Attitude toward the Puritans," and VIII.
"The Minor Transcendentalists: [Margaret] Fuller, [Bronson] Alcott,

[Orestes A.] Brownson, [Jones] Very."

1973-7   Gatta, John Joseph, Jr. "Dogma with Wit in the Poetry of
    Edward Taylor." Ph.D., Cornell Univ. v, 244 leaves.

        Abstract in DAI, vol. 34 (11), sec. A, p. 7231: "The thesis
studies the relation between the particular content of Taylor's
Puritan beliefs--his 'dogma'--and the ways in which he gave poetic
life to such beliefs through his varied application of 'wit.' This
Colonial poet's use of the Metaphysical conceit reflects only one
aspect of his 'wittiness.' For at his best he is, I believe, a highly
comic and playful poet--though this quality is not ordinarily
attributed to him, and though his 'comedy' is not entirely of the sort
that provokes laughter. To a large degree, this comic wit can be
explained with reference to Taylor's theological assumptions and
pastoral goals." Contents: "Introduction," I. "Edward Taylor's
Controversy with Solomon Stoddard: A Reassessment," II. "The New
England Mind of a Poet," III. "The Anatomy of Wit and the Diagnosis of
Melancholy," IV. "Wit and 'A Festival Frame of Spirit' in the Shorter
Poems," and V. "The Comic Design of Gods Determinations Touching His
Elect."

1973-8   Hart, Sidney. "The American Sense of Mission, 1783-1810:
    Puritan Historical Myths in Post-Revolutionary New England."
    Ph.D., Clark Univ. ix, 427 leaves.

        Abstract in DAI, vol. 34 (4), sec. A, p. 1824: "The aim of this
study is to determine the extent to which the Puritan tradition was
instrumental in forming the mission and sense of identity within post-
Revolutionary New England and the nation at large. . . . The
dissertation can be divided into two parts. The first two chapters
define Puritanism as a civic religion in post-Revolutionary New
England. . . . The dominant concerns and issues in a new republic
were political, of course, but it was Puritanism which still supplied
the underlying unity and context in post-Revolutionary New England.
. . . The remaining six chapters deal with the latter-day Puritan
historians of New England: Jeremy Belknap, Samuel Williams, George
Richards Minot, Jedediah Morse, Benjamin Trumbull, and Mercy Otis
Warren. What these writers shared in common was the Puritan 'Myth'
that still prevailed in post-Revolutionary New England."

1973-9   Jones, Janice Sue. "Metaphor and Poetic Structure in the
    Preparatory Meditations by Edward Taylor." Ph.D., Northwestern
    Univ. vi, 224 leaves.

        Abstract in DAI, vol. 34 (9), sec. A, p. 5916: "Within the frame
of seventeenth-century rhetoric and poetic, in this study a close
analysis is conducted of the function of metaphor in poems from Edward
Taylor's Preparatory Meditations. The poems chosen for analysis
exemplify various roles of metaphor in the structures of the
meditations: complementing the arrangement of incidents by
contrasting past and present, revealing aspects of the speaker's
psychological disposition, relating the type with the antitype in the

typological poems, reinforcing logical arguments, and maintaining decorum. . . . The poems present a range of metaphorical developments extending from simple one-word metaphorical replacement to conceits which are elaborated throughout a single poem."

1973-10   Jones, Phyllis Marian. "A Literary Study of the Sermons of the First-Generation Preachers of New England." Ph.D., Harvard Univ. 257 leaves.

"Introduction": Diss. "describes the literary and imaginative strengths of the sermons of the first-generation preachers of New England. The published sermons of the ministers Thomas Hooker, John Cotton, Thomas Shepard, John Davenport, Peter Bulkeley, Charles Chauncy, John Allen, and William Hooke, and of the lay preachers John Winthrop and Roger Cushman comprise some thirty series of sermons and twenty-two sermons" (p. 1). Diss. also "presents generalizations that imply these sermons influence later American expression and thought" (p. 12). Contents: "Introduction," One: "Presuppositions," Two: "Tropes, Figures, and Images," and Three: "Conventions." Appendices: "The Lives of the Preachers" and "Sermons and Sermon Series of the First-Generation Preachers."

1973-11   Kalu, Ogbu Uke. "The Jacobean Church and Essex Puritans: A Regional Study of the Enforcement of Church Discipline and on the Survival of Puritan Nonconformity, 1603-1628." Ph.D., Univ. of Toronto (Canada). [12], 510, xxxvi, [15] leaves.

Abstract in DAI, vol. 35 (9), sec. A, p. 6064: "Primarily, this dissertation sets out to probe into the fate of puritans after the Hampton Court Conference and the Convocation of 1604. Since the church used her courts as the administrative machinery, we have argued that a detailed analysis of the operation of these courts in the specific geographical unit constitutes the best approach to the problem. Therefore, the dissertation is a double-barrelled study of puritans and the enforcement of religious discipline in Essex from 1603-1628. . . . On the whole, puritans survived the aftermath of the Jacobean religious settlement because of the laxity of official enforcement and because of their own propaganda technique." Contents: Part I. "Prologue"; Part II. "Enforcement of the Religious Settlement": I. "Puritans and the Archdeacon's Court"; Part III. "Enforcement of the Jacobean Settlement": II. "Puritans and the Bishops"; and Part IV. "God's Cause: Aspects of Jacobean Puritanism in Essex." Appendices: 1. "Puritans and Patrons in Jacobean Essex, 1603-28," 2. "Analysis of Patrons of Puritan Clerics, 1603-28," 3. "Lecturers in Essex, 1603-28," 4. "Separatists in Jacobean Essex, 1603-28," and 5. "Who Is a Puritan?"

1973-12   Lewis, Guy Loran. "Daniel Gookin, Superintendent and Historian of the New England Indians: A Historiographical Study." Ph.D., Univ. of Illinois at Urbana-Champaign. iv, 240 leaves.

Abstract in DAI, vol. 34 (9), sec. A, p. 5876: "Daniel Gookin, one of the magistrates and Superintendent of the Indians for the Massachusetts Bay Colony during the period of Charter government, wrote two treatises concerning the red man of New England. This dissertation evaluates the significance of the office of Superintendent and the historiographical importance of Daniel Gookin's treatises for New England's historiography and for our understanding of Puritan attitudes toward the Indian. . . . Gookin's acquaintanceship with the Indians led him to write his 'Historical Collections' in 1674. . . . Gookin's second work, his 'Historical Account,' was occasioned by King Philip's War. . . . While Daniel Gookin's personal insights were partially hindered by some aspects of his faith, that same Puritanism impelled him to achieve perhaps the best understanding of the aborigines of New England to be reached by any white man of his day."

1973-13   Lystra, Karen Anne. "Perry Miller and American Puritan Studies: A Case Study in Scholarly Community." Ph.D., Case Western Reserve Univ. xiv, 413 leaves.

Abstract in DAI, vol. 34 (11), sec. A, p. 7135: "This inquiry is a 'community' study in American historical scholarship. . . . [It] focuses on the work of Perry Miller--and critical responses to that work in American Puritan studies--as a case study in the structures and functions of one scholarly community. . . . Working on the basic assumption that scholarship flourishes not in isolation but in community, it looks at historical work on the New England Puritans as a distinctly social enterprise, and develops methods for studying scholarship in this fashion. . . . The opening chapter uses the book review to get at modes of communication and social control in historical scholarship, using a population of some 112 critical responses to Perry Miller's books as its empirical base. . . . The second chapter focuses on Darrett Rutman and his response to the work of Miller, using Kai Erikson's social concept of 'boundary defense' as a device for getting at Rutman's role in the Puritan Studies community. The third chapter focuses on transactions between Perry Miller and his critics as centered on Miller's most notable work, The New England Mind: From Colony to Province (1953). . . . Finally, the last chapter investigates the 'core' community of demographic historians whose recent work in social history is alleged to have replaced the earlier intellectual history framework of Miller."

1973-14   Malmsheimer, Lonna Myers. "New England Funeral Sermons and Changing Attitudes toward Woman, 1672-1792." Ph.D., Univ. of Minnesota. 213 leaves.

Abstract in DAI, vol. 34 (7), sec. A, p. 4161: "The hypothesis behind the research was that some basic change in attitudes toward women had to precede their emergence into public spheres of activity in the early nineteenth century. . . . Changes in attitudes toward women are apparent within the funeral sermon. The seventeenth-century myth of woman was closely identified with negative attitudes toward Eve . . . [and] argued for the subjugation of women because of her weaker moral and religious nature. . . . [By] the late eighteenth century women were thought to be superior to men in one very important respect: they were more sensitive to religious and moral matters."

1973-15   Melchert, Dennis Don. "Experimenting on the Neighbors: Inoculation of Smallpox in Boston in the Context of Eighteenth-Century Medicine." Ph.D., Univ. of Iowa. vii, 281 leaves.

Abstract in DAI, vol. 35 (1), sec. A, p. 375: Traditionally "the introduction of inoculation of smallpox by Cotton Mather in Boston in 1721 . . . has been treated . . . [as] a 'good thing,' and [Mather and] Zabdiel Boylston, the practitioner who actually used the new method, became heroes of medical innovation; at the same time those who opposed the new treatment, especially Dr. William Douglass, the leader of the medically based opposition, have been villains. . . . This thesis attempts to avoid the bias in favor of inoculation and its promoters by carefully examining the traditions and content of medicine prior to 1721. . . . After establishing the dangerousness and rashness of inoculation in 1721, a major portion of the thesis is devoted to an identification of those 133 Boston individuals who became inoculees."

1973-16   Minor, Dennis Earl. "The Evolution of Puritanism into the Mass Culture of Early Nineteenth-Century America." Ph.D., Texas A&M Univ. x, 166 leaves.

Abstract in DAI, vol. 34 (12), sec. A, p. 7714: "Puritanism assumed an all-powerful God and that man fell through original sin. Man is therefore doomed in God's eyes, and might gain salvation either through God's arbitrary predestination or through God's agreeing to grant salvation on some condition. The Puritans in America believed that God would grant grace in return for man's faith or belief. The fatalism of predestination was not taught without some qualification. The Puritans also believed that good works were a necessary expression of the religious life but were not alone sufficient for salvation. Education is also one of the emphases of Puritanism. . . . After the decline of Puritan theology in America these same emphases were first brought to non-Puritan times through . . . [Michael Wigglesworth's] Day of Doom and the New England Primer. . . . Between the Primer and [Noah Webster's] Spelling Book the Puritan emphases were taught to millions of children. . . . There is, then, a Puritan heritage that became a part of the mass culture or heritage of the early nineteenth-century American." Contents: I. "Introduction," II. "The Theological Background, 1536-1623," III. "Puritan Theology in America, 1636-1741," IV. "Puritanism for the Masses, 1662-1783," V. "Puritan Emphases, 1783-1829," and VI. "Summary and Conclusion."

1973-17   O'Toole, Dennis Allen. "Exiles, Refugees, and Rogues: The Quest for Civil Order in the Towns and Colony of Providence Plantations, 1636-1654." Ph.D., Brown Univ. 575 leaves.

Abstract in DAI, vol. 34 (10), sec. A, p. 6572: "This dissertation is a narrative history of the early years of the towns of Providence, Portsmouth, Newport, and Warwick and of the colony, Providence Plantations, which the inhabitants of the four towns

founded in 1647. It attempts to describe the differing courses
community development took in the four towns, to identify the chief
factors in such development, and to trace the reciprocal relationship
events within the towns and the colony had upon each other. The
narrative concludes with the year in which the colony was reunited
after three years of division and political chaos. . . . Providence
Plantations survived, in part, by becoming the most libertarian and
the most loyal and legally traditional of the New England colonies."

1973-18   Percy, David Oran.   "The Anglican Interest in Early
    Eighteenth-Century New England: A Political Analysis."   Ph.D.,
    Univ. of Nebraska at Lincoln.   238 leaves.

Abstract in DAI, vol. 34 (12), sec. A, p. 7687: "The insistence
of colonial Episcopalians, known as Churchmen, on equal political
protection and support threatened the Congregational hegemony in
Massachusetts and Connecticut, which relied on their churches for
control of piety and morals.   Churchmen antagonized the
Congregationalists by using the ecclesiastical policies of the
imperial government to force changes in colonial policies. . . .
Without the decrees of religious toleration promulgated in the late
seventeenth century by the imperial government, the colonial Church of
England would not have been successful in obtaining equality with
other religious bodies."

1973-19   Polf, William Andrew.   "Puritan Gentlemen: The Dudleys of
    Massachusetts, 1576-1686."   Ph.D., Syracuse Univ.   xvii, 302
    leaves.

Abstract   in DAI, vol. 35 (2), sec. A, p. 1025: "Few families
had a greater impact upon New England society than the Dudleys of
Massachusetts. . . . The two most important members of the family,
Thomas Dudley and his son, Joseph, have attained historical
reputations for being representatives of the worst characteristics of
their respective generations. . . . This study concentrates upon the
Dudley family in order to attain insights into the development of New
England society generally. Concepts of rank, power, and religion are
examined as they related to the Dudleys and to New Englanders as a
whole. Joseph Dudley adapted the social, political, and religious
principles of his father to the peculiar circumstances of the second
generation; and, in doing so, managed to retain much of the substance
of first generation puritanism. . . . Continuity rather than change
characterized succeeding generations of Dudleys."

1973-20 Poteet, James Mark. "Preserving the Old Ways: Connecticut,
    1690-1740." Ph.D., Univ. of Virginia. 2 vols. (xiv, 465 leaves).

Abstract in DAI, vol. 34 (2), sec. A, p. 710: In "the eighteenth
century . . . [the] Christian Commonwealth of the founders, valuing
harmony, order and unity, ultimately gave way and was replaced by a
society characterized by competitiveness and diversity.   The
transformation from Puritan to Yankee has been closely observed in the
case of Massachusetts Bay. The character of the transformation

becomes even clearer by viewing the same process in the neighboring colony of Connecticut. In Connecticut, Puritan social values demonstrated remarkable vitality, surviving until at least half way through the eighteenth century. The greater continuity of Connecticut's colonial history is explained in part by the isolation of a small, agricultural colony and in part by the corporate nature of the colony which guaranteed an unusual degree of autonomy within the British empire. The colony's commitment to order and unity is, however, also explained by the purposeful actions of a group of leaders, influenced by events in the 1690's, who fixed the colony on a course of orthodoxy." The influence of such men as James Fitch, Fitz John Winthrop, and Gurdon Saltonstall is emphasized.

1973-21   Putre, John Walter. "Town and Province in Early Eighteenth-Century Massachusetts: A Study in Institutional Interaction, 1692-1736." Ph.D., State Univ. of New York at Stony Brook. x, 242 leaves.

Abstract in DAI, vol. 34 (5), sec. A, p. 2530: "The present study assesses the political relationship between the Massachusetts towns and central government in the years between the receipt of the 1691 charter and the Great Awakening. It interprets that relationship first by analyzing the efforts made by the central government to control affairs within the towns, and second by discerning the extent to which the provincial towns complied with the General Court's wishes. . . . Although for different reasons, the Massachusetts towns and the lives of the men and women within them remained in the eighteenth century, as they had been in the seventeenth, bound to Boston."

1973-22   Schmotter, James W. "Provincial Professionalism: The New England Ministry, 1692-1745." Ph.D., Northwestern Univ. i, 362 leaves.

Abstract in DAI, vol. 34 (9), sec. A, p. 5884: "As the seventeenth century ended, Congregational ministers in New England viewed their profession's future with anxiety. Their status, prestige, and effectiveness seemed to be decreasing. . . . In response to this perceived decline ministers began in the 1690's and 1700's to shift their attention away from theology and toward the problems of their callings. . . . This shift created a new professionalism among the Congregational ministers. . . . Yet this new professionalism proved counterproductive. A quantitative examination of the career expectancies of Congregational ministers between 1700 and 1740 shows that opportunities decreased and friction between pastors and parishioners rose. . . . [The] Awakening saw the end of the ministry's internal concensus on professionalism. . . . The fears of earlier ministers had come true, not because pastors had paid too little attention to their profession, but because they had paid too much."

1973-23   Scott, William Butler, "Every Man under His Own Vine and Fig
    Tree: American Conceptions of Property from the Puritans to Henry
    George." Ph.D., Univ. of Wisconsin at Madison. iv, 240 leaves.

Abstract in DAI, vol. 35 (1), sec. A, p. 384: "In this
dissertation I examined the ideas of a diverse group of Americans on
private ownership and the relationship of those ideas to their
conception of a good society. In the first chapters I briefly
examined the western intellectual foundations of American conceptions
of ownership. In subsequent chapters I focused on colonial New
England, colonial policy assumptions, property and the American
Revolution, property and the law, property as land, property as wages,
property as slaves, and, finally, property as corporate stock. The
first four chapters are organized chronologically, while the final
five chapters treat topically the variety of meanings Americans in the
nineteenth century attached to the word 'property.'"

1973-24   Smith, Daniel Scott. "Population, Family, and Society in
    Hingham, Massachusetts, 1635-1880." Ph.D., Univ. of California
    at Berkeley, xx, 387 leaves.

Abstract in DAI, vol. 36 (4), sec. A, p. 2382: "This study
employs quantitative and sociological methods to analyze the
historical transformation in demographic behavior, family structure
and social stratification in one New England town over a quarter
millennium. The period encompasses the demographic transition from
fertility which was high by contemporary western European standards in
the seventeenth and eighteenth centuries to near modern levels
attained by the mid-nineteenth century. Mortality, on the other hand,
showed no secular change. After subjecting the records to historical
and demographic criticism for inadequacies, the technique of family
reconstruction and linkage of other records organized the data for
analysis. . . . The centrality of the family of orientation was the
central characteristic of the 'traditional' period of the seventeenth
and first half of the eighteenth century."

1973-25   Sorensen, Charles William. "Response to Crisis: An
    Analysis of New Haven, 1638-1665." Ph.D., Michigan State Univ.
    viii, 191 leaves.

Abstract in DAI, vol. 34 (3), sec. A, p. 1226: "There are three
general parts to the dissertation. The first, encompassing Chapter I
and II, deals with the motivation of settlement, the failure of the
leadership to construct a viable port city, and the nature of the
authority that governed the everyday lives of the people in New Haven.
Chapters III and IV focus on dissidents within the town and the
repressive measures taken by the civil and religious leaders to quiet
their challenges to authority. The last two chapters analyze the
impact of that repression on the political structure within the town.
Special attention is given to the office of townsmen and growth of its
political power."

1973-26   Turner, Eldon Ray. "Law and Political Culture: A
    Functional Study of the Relation of Theology to Jurisprudence,
    Political Values and Legal Activity in Colonial Suffolk County,
    Massachusetts, 1671-1680." Ph.D., Univ. of Kansas. 2 vols.
    (vii, 465 leaves).

    Abstract in DAI, vol. 34 (6), sec. A, p. 3276: "Usually, legal
historians have accepted a jurisprudential examination of American law
from the perspective of equality. . . . During the Puritan era in
American history law supported inequality. . . . This dissertation
presents therefore an alternative model which is specific for Puritan
New England but which raises questions for legal history in general.
. . . Part One of this dissertation is an explanation of . . .
theoretical bases. The thesis is that law of Puritan New England,
viewed from a systems or cultural perspective, was a dominant social
item and that legal behavior should reveal a functional relation among
theology, political values, political and legal structure and legal
behavior. . . . Part Two of this study is an examination of the
theology and the administration of the Church and state. . . . Part
Three . . . is an extended examination into how law behaved in Puritan
political/legal institutions, specifically the county courts. . . .
Data in Part Four show marked patterns of behavioral reaction to
political stress, suggesting that law was an active element in Puritan
culture. . . . This study, then, reveals a legal system in which
inequality was a positive value and contributed to the legal process."

1973-27   Woolley, Bruce Chapman. "Reverend Thomas Shepard's
    Cambridge Church Members, 1636-1649: A Socio-Economic Analysis."
    Ph.D., Univ. of Rochester. v, 221 leaves.

    Abstract in DAI, vol. 34 (6), sec. A, p. 3330: "A primary
function of this dissertation is to present a major Shepard document
transcribed for the first time from Elizabethan script and rendered
with modern spelling and punctuation. The manuscript, entitled by its
author, 'The Confessions of Diverse Propounded to Be Received and Were
Entertayned,' contains the relations of faith of fifty person who
applied for membership in the church at Cambridge, Massachusetts,
circa 1638-1645. The transcribed work comprises Part II of this
paper. . . . Part I of this dissertation is designed as a guide to a
fuller understanding and appreciation of the doctrine contained in
Part II. Accordingly, a threefold examination is undertaken to:
review Puritan covenant theology with particular attention to the
views of Thomas Shepard; uncover the identity and backgrounds of those
persons making their confession of faith to the church at Cambridge;
establish unifying concerns among these fifty persons' confessions."
Cf. Thomas Shepard's Confessions. -- Ed. by George Selement and Bruce
C. Woolley. -- Boston : Colonial Society of Massachusetts, 1981. --
xii, 222 p. -- (Publications of the Colonial Society of Massachusetts.
Collections ; vol. LVII). Cf. #1974-27, below.

1973-28   Yackel, Peter Garrett. "The Original Criminal Jurisdiction
    of the Superior Courts of Judicature of Colonial Maryland, New
    York, and Massachusetts." Ph.D., Ohio State Univ. vi, 361
    leaves.

Abstract in DAI, vol. 34 (2), sec. A, p. 716: "This dissertation is a history of the authorization and criminal jurisdiction of the superior courts of Maryland, New York, and Massachusetts. It addresses the problems of (1) what factors influenced the growth of these judicatures, (2) the manifestation of that influence, (3) the sources of law that conditioned their development, and (4) their adoption and incorporation of jurisdictional principles and of criminal procedures. It describes and compares the processes by which these institutions evolved. ... The author of this study concludes that the superior courts in the colonies studied were the agents by which the proprietors exercised their chartered prerogative to administer provincial justice." Relevant chapters: "Introduction," I. "Superior Court of English Common Law: King's Bench Criminal Jurisdiction," IV. "Superior Court in Massachusetts, 1629-1776," and V. "Summary and Conclusions." Chapters II and III deal with Maryland and New York developments.

1974-1   Allen, David Grayson. "In English Ways: The Movement of Societies and the Transferal of English Local Law and Custom to Massachusetts Bay, 1600-1690." Ph.D., Univ. of Wisconsin at Madison. 2 vols. (xv, 591 leaves).

Abstract in DAI, vol. 35 (11), sec. A, p. 7214. Revision published as In English Ways: The Movement of Societies and the Transferal of English Local Law and Custom to Massachusetts Bay in the Seventeenth Century. -- Chapel Hill : Published for the Institute of Early American History and Culture by the Univ. of North Carolina Press, 1981. -- xxi, 312 p. "Preface" (1981 ed.): "This book is about the fundamentally English form and style of New England local institutions in the early seventeenth century. It demonstrates the remarkable extent to which diversity in New England local institutions was directly imitative of regional differences in the mother country. The first Massachusetts colonists, in other words, simply attempted to sustain their Old World ways in the New World. ... In the second and shorter part of the book, I have explored the causes of the migration of people from various English regions of New England. A brief concluding section examines the transformation of New England town life in the later seventeenth and eighteenth centuries when a variety of social, economic, political, and legal conditions made the old English ways unsuitable and impractical" (p. xv). Contents: 1. "Introduction: People, Land and Custom," 2. "'Those Drowsy Corners of the North,'" 3. "A Tale of Two Towns," 4. "'A Mixt Multitude,'" 5. "'Men of Good Ranke and Quality,'" 6. "The Migration of Societies," 7. "A Contrapuntal Life," and 8. "Epilogue: An Eighteenth-Century Perspective." Appendices: 1. "English Origins of the Landholders of Rowley, Massachusetts," 2. "English Origins of Pre-1640 Hingham, Massachusetts, Settlers," 3. "English Origins of Ninety-One Original Proprietors of Newbury, Massachusetts," 4. "English Origins of Ipswich, Massachusetts, Commoners," and 5. "English Origins of the Grantees of the First Division of Land, Watertown, Massachusetts." This book was the winner of the Jamestown Manuscript Prize for 1976.

1974-2   Alpert, Helle M. "Robert Keayne: Notes of Sermons by John
     Cotton and Proceedings of the First Church of Boston from 23
     November 1639 to 1 June 1640." Ph.D., Tufts Univ. 426 leaves.

     Abstract in DAI, vol. 35 (6), sec. A, p. 3667: "Robert Keayne
(1588-1656), a pious Puritan and ambitious merchant, settled in
Boston, Massachusetts, in 1635. Already while in England Keayne had
made it his habit to take sermon notes from the mouths of the Puritan
preachers he sought out. He carried his habit to America, producing
three volumes of sermons and proceedings of the First Church of Boston
between 1638 and 1646. . . . The dissertation presents a
transcription of the first one hundred and ninety-four pages of
Keayne's third (American) sermon book. . . . The five hundred and
eighty-four pages of the entire volume are a record of sermons by John
Cotton and Proceedings of the First Church of Boston from 1639 to
1642. The text of the excerpt offered here begins on 23 November 1639
and ends on 1 June 1640. . . . The introduction to the Keayne
manuscript excerpt contains, first, background material, describing
the Puritan custom of note-taking at sermons, the order of the sabbath
service in the First Church of Boston, and the Antinomian Crisis
(1636-1638). Section two discusses . . . four themes in Cotton's
sermon works relevant to his concerns in 1639-1642. Section three
deals with Cotton's preaching style. Section four outlines the
judicial procedure in the First Church. . . . The note on the text
describes the manuscript and the editor's policies. . . . Appendix A
has two parts: separate biographical sketches of John Cotton and
Robert Keayne. Appendix B identifies English immigrants mentioned in
the manuscript excerpt."

1974-3   Batson, Trenton Wayne. "Arminianism in New England: A
     Reading of the Published Sermons of Benjamin Colman, 1673-1747."
     Ph.D., George Washington Univ. iii, 177 leaves.

     Abstract in DAI, vol. 35 (4), sec. A, p. 2377: "Colman, minister
of Brattle Street Church from 1699 to 1747, demonstrated an affinity
with the spirit of Arminianism in his published sermons which
indicates that, by the beginning of the eighteenth century, religious
thought in New England was moving toward Arminianism. . . . Colman
adopted English latitudinarian features in his sermons but never
openly offended even the most orthodox in New England because his
latitudinarianism was more implicit than explicit. . . . Colman, by
his manner and method, compromised the force of Calvinist thinking in
New England. . . . [In] the Colman sermons, divine sovereignty seems
weakened at the expense of human responsibility. In this way, Colman
helped to move New England religion toward Arminianism."

1974-4   Coyle, Edward Wallace. "From Sinner to Saint: A Study of
     the Critical Reputation of Roger Williams with an Annotated
     Bibliography of Writings about Him." Ph.D., Univ. of
     Massachusetts. xi, 210 leaves.

     Abstract in DAI, vol. 35 (9), sec. A, p. 6133: "This study
examines the most important writings of the last three hundred years
on Roger Williams and his times to determine the ways in which the

critics have understood or misunderstood Williams. Since most of the over one hundred works dealing with Williams written before this century have approached him from the historical or biographical point of view, the focus in the earlier chapters is on these areas. The twentieth century has produced several studies that open new areas of investigation about Williams from a philosophical, typological, rhetorical, political, and even sociological viewpoint. . . . Finally this study concludes with an annotated bibliography of 326 writings about Roger Williams divided by century." A revised and expanded version of the bibliographic portion of the diss. was published as Roger Williams: A Reference Guide. -- Boston : G. K. Hall, 1977. -- xiii, 102 p. -- (Reference Guides in Literature). "Introduction": "I have included all works on Williams through 1974" (p. xi); over four hundred monographs and articles are cited.

1974-5   Crow, Steven Douglas. "'Left at Libertie': The Effects of the English Civil War and Interregnum on the American Colonies, 1640-1660." Ph.D., Univ. of Wisconsin at Madison. vi, 349 leaves.

Abstract in DAI, vol. 35 (5), sec. A, p. 2894: "The history of the American colonies between 1640 and 1660 must be placed against the backdrop of the Civil War and Interregnum in England. . . . Colonists could not escape being affected by such developments. . . . In each colony representatives in local assemblies . . . sought more power. . . . The unique character of each colony changed, too, as a result of the troubles in England. . . . New Englanders, particularly the Bay colonists, frightened by the religious excesses of independent congregations in tolerant England rushed to institutionalize the New England Way through the Platform for Church-Discipline. They also strengthened the alliance between the clergy and the civil leadership. Reverence for the new institutions rather than religious zeal became the measure of orthodoxy; willingness to protect the church and charter from any changes became the measure of civil leadership."

1974-6   Doggett, JoElla Ann Osborn. "Roger Wolcott's Poetical Meditations: A Critical Edition and Appraisal." Univ. of Texas at Austin. vi, 330 leaves.

Abstract in DAI, vol. 35 (8), sec. A, p. 5340: "This dissertation provides an interpretative explanation as well as a complete edition of a 1725 American publication, Roger Wolcott's Poetical Meditations, Being the Improvement of Some Vacant Hours, with Rev. John Bulkley's Preface. Wolcott's poetry . . . offers some interesting aesthetic touches. Even more surprising is a unifying political purpose in this book which . . . actually constitutes a factional argument in the land controversy hotly contested in early eighteenth-century Connecticut. This political application is not merely disguised by the title, the religious poems, and the epic of Connecticut's early history but actually aided by these literary appearances." The publication was subsidized by Joseph Dewey, one of the parties to the controversy.

1974-7   Faber, Eli. "The Evil That Men Do: Crime and Transgression
     in Colonial Massachusetts." Ph.D., Columbia Univ. ix, 440
     leaves.

     Abstract in <u>DAI</u>, vol. 38 (2), sec. A, p. 969: "Colonists in
Massachusetts defined crime as sin. . . . Equating crime with sin
encouraged prosecution for religious and moral transgressions, in
addition to crimes damaging to person and property. The courts also
punished culprits for activities thought to imperil order within the
commonwealth and within the family, notably during the seventeenth
century. Prosecutions for these offenses declined during the
eighteenth century, as well as for a number of moral and religious
errors. But despite the increasing significance of secular values in
the eighteenth century, the courts did continue to discipline certain
religious and moral offenders, while they also acquired greater
responsibilities for the crimes of riot, counterfeiting, or slander."

1974-8   Fienberg, Stanley P. "Thomas Goodwin, Puritan Pastor and
     Independent Divine." Ph.D., Univ. of Chicago. v, 378 leaves.

     "Preface": "This is the story of Thomas Goodwin, one of the most
important Puritan divines of the seventeenth century. Such a study
can be justified in terms of Goodwin's three-fold pre-eminence as a
Puritan pastor, a leader of Independency during the Civil War and
Interregnum period and a principal architect of the Cromwellian
domestic settlement. This focus of the discussion is not
biographical. Rather, this study centres on Goodwin's religious ideas
and their significance for Puritanism, independency and English
history during one of its most turbulent periods" (p. ii). Contents:
Part I. "Thomas Goodwin, Puritan Pastor": "Introduction," I. "Man's
Natural Condition and God's Work before Faith," II. "Justification,"
III. "Sanctification," and IV. "Social Ethics"; Part II. "Thomas
Goodwin and the Independent-Presbyterian Controversy":
"Introduction," V. "Biblicism," VI. "Eschatology," VII. "The
Progressive Interpretation of Truth," and VIII. "Ecclesiology"; and
Part III. "Thomas Goodwin, Puritan in Power": "Introduction," IX.
"The Oxford Visitation," X. "Church and State," XI. "Jewish Re-
Admission," XII. "The Savoy Conference," and XIII. "Restoration and
Conclusion." Appendices: I. "An Unpublished Letter by Thomas
Goodwin, Trier" and II. "Works and Editions by Thomas Goodwin."

1974-9   Gadt, Jeanette Carter. "Women and Protestant Culture: The
     Quaker Dissent from Puritanism." Ph.D., Univ. of California at
     Los Angeles. x, 336 leaves.

     Abstract in <u>DAI</u>, vol. 35 (3), sec. A, p. 1591: "This thesis is a
study of the relationship between two Protestant ideologies and women
in England and America during the seventeenth and eighteenth
centuries. Its specific focus rests on Quakerism, whose unique
position concerning women in theology and organization is illuminated
by its controversy with Puritanism. Opposition between Quakers and
Puritans originated from differing solutions offered to the social and
cultural problems of the seventeenth century which were experienced as
obedience vs. rebellion, order vs. anarchy, and rational, external

authority vs. spontaneous inward assurance. Puritans in nearly every instance favored the first element in each pair of opposites." Contents: "Introduction," One: "Eve and Domesticity: English Puritan Attitudes Toward Women," Two: "Seventeenth-Century Protestant Reform: The Quaker Alternative and Its Feminine Component," Three: "Attitude Toward Women in the New World: The Opposites of Quaker and Puritan," Four: "The Spirit of Unity: Love and Quaker Theology," Five: "The Spirit of Unity: The Human Will and Quaker Theology," and "Conclusion."

1974-10   Garber, Norman Bruce. "Norman Mailer: The Evolution of a Puritan-Existentialist Vision." Ph.D., Univ. of California at Santa Barbara. 280 leaves.

Abstract in DAI, vol. 35 (11), sec. A, p. 7303: "In . . . the first formulation of Mailer's American existentialist epistemology he calls for a willingness to 'accept the terms of death,' 'exist without roots,' and seek growth through the 'uncharted journey with the rebellious imperatives of the self.' In this 'dialectical conception of existence,' violence and creativity are seen to be inextricably locked together. This radically subjective epistemology is accompanied by an ontological conception of a divided universe and an embattled, existentialist God whose fate is 'flesh and blood' with ours. Thus Mailer's ideological and esthetic perceptual frame, his vision, may properly be termed Puritan-existential. . . . Through Mailer's first four novels can be traced the evolution of this vision."

1974-11   Gilmore, Michael Timo. "The Middle Way: Puritanism and Ideology in American Literature." Ph.D., Harvard Univ. 567 leaves.

Revision published as The Middle Way: Puritanism and Ideology in American Romantic Fiction. -- New Brunswick, N.J. : Rutgers Univ. Press, 1977. -- x, 220 p. "Preface" (1977 ed.): "This study seeks to trace some of the connections between the Puritan mind of the colonial era and the great flowering of American literature in the nineteenth century. It presents the thesis that the Puritan ideal of inner-worldly sainthood--the ideal of the middle way--decisively influenced the formal and thematic concerns of the prose romance. . . . I portray the romancers as social and political critics who carry on the Puritan spirit and who call attention to the gap between the promise of America and its achievement" (p. ix).   Contents: I. "Introduction," II. "The Puritans," III. "Cotton Mather and Benjamin Franklin," IV. "Hawthorne," V. "Melville," VI. "Henry James," and "Afterword." The diss. version also included chapters on "[M.-G. J. de] Crèvecoeur and [Charles Brockden] Brown" and "[George] Bancroft."

1974-12   Gilpin, William Clark. "The Way to Lost Zion: Millenarian Piety and Religious Controversy in the Career of Roger Williams." Ph.D., Univ. of Chicago. iii, 242 leaves.

Revision published as The Millenarian Piety of Roger Williams. --

Chicago : Univ. of Chicago Press, 1979. -- viii, 214 p. "Preface" (1979 ed.): "First, what were the relations, if any, between Williams's social and theological opinions about the Indians and his more famous views on liberty of conscience, the church, and the state? Second, what factors in Williams's own development or in his historical context led him to view the Indians as he did . . . ? Thus the continuing concern of this study has been to examine the development and varied dimensions of Williams's thought in their interrelationships and in relation to their historical setting" (p. vii). Contents: One: "Religious Experience and Religious Vocation," Two: "Ministry and Reformation in Massachusetts," Three: "Pilgrimage toward the Millennium, 1636-43," Four: "Christian Vocation for a Revolutionary Age," Five: "The Liberty of the Witnesses and the Restoration of the Church," Six: "Spiritual Ministry, 1645-1654," and Seven: "Controversy with the Quakers."

1974-13   Goodman, Robert Lord. "Newbury, Massachusetts, 1635-1685: The Social Foundations of Harmony and Conflict." Ph.D., Michigan State Univ. viii, 294 leaves.

Abstract in DAI, vol. 35 (9), sec. A, p. 6057: "This study endeavors to explore the interaction of specific social relationships and the social goals of harmony, peace, and cohesion in seventeenth-century Massachusetts. Using Newbury, Massachusetts, as their base, these essays examine the influence of kinship and friendship differentiation upon the development of the social structure and the emergence of contention in the town between 1635 and 1685. The spirit of this inquiry is inter-disciplinary, employing themes and perspectives developed by both historians and other social scientists. . . . In particular, the kinship and friendship structure of the town is determined according to network techniques hitherto employed largely in the social sciences, and the sociometric network, in turn, is used to analyze the interpersonal pattern of alignment which lay behind both harmony and contention in the town."

1974-14   Holdsworth, William K. "Law and Society in Colonial Connecticut, 1636-1672." Ph.D., Claremont Graduate School. xviii, 739 leaves.

Abstract in DAI, vol. 36 (2), sec. A, p. 1045: "This study seeks, through analysis of published and unpublished court records, letters, sermons, and other writings, to define the relationship between the political, social, and religious ideals of Connecticut's Puritan leaders and the adoption and enforcement of law in the colony during its formative years. Because the New Haven Colony was for many years an independent jurisdiction with its own laws and institutions, and because it became an integral part of Connecticut in the 1660's, the dissertation examines that colony from the same perspective. In doing so, it focuses mainly on criminal law and procedure."

1974-15   Jodziewicz, Thomas Walter. "Dual Localism in Seventeenth-
    Century Connecticut: Relations between the General Court and the
    Towns, 1636-1691." Ph.D., College of William and Mary. xi, 353
    leaves.

    Abstract in DAI, vol. 35 (4), sec. A, p. 2155: "The purpose of
this study is to define and to describe seventeenth-century
Connecticut's dual localism, i.e., the working-out of colony and town
interests within the structure of Connecticut's respective political
institutions: the General Court and the town meeting. The principal
method of research was to calendar all General Court orders and all
available town meeting records of nine representative towns--Hartford,
Windsor, Wethersfield, Farmington, Middletown, Fairfield, Norwalk, New
London, and Stonington--and then to correlate the results in order to
reconstruct the interaction of Court and town. . . . The study
concludes that while the General Court held ultimate sovereignty in
the colony the Court was moderate in its exercise of such authority.
. . . Connecticut's fundamental stability rested upon an essential
consensus within the colony on political means and ends, as well as on
a general acceptance of the institutional structure of dual localism."

1974-16   Keeble, N. H. "Some Literary and Religious Aspects of the
    Works of Richard Baxter." D.Phil., Univ. of Oxford (U.K.). viii
    ["Abstract"], vi, 380 leaves.

    Revision published as Richard Baxter: Puritan Man of Letters. --
Oxford : Clarendon Press, 1982. -- x, 217 p. -- (Oxford English
Monographs). "Preface" (1982 ed.): "This study outlines the course
of Richard Baxter's literary career, examines his attitude to the
profession of letters and his thinking on prose style, discusses the
aims and techniques of his works, and suggests something of their
significance for literary history" (p. v). Contents: 1. "A Pen in
God's Hand," 2. "A Puritan Bookman," 3. "The Puritan Style," 4. "The
Pastor and Practical Divine," 5. "Earth and Heaven," 6. "Cain and
Abel," and 7. "A Record of Christian Experience." Appendix: "A
Baxter Bibliography." Diss. includes two appendices: I. "Baxter's
Sermons: A Checklist" and II. "Bibliographical Sketch of Baxter's
Defense of 'The Protestant and Puritan, That Is, The Christian
Doctrine of Justification.'"

1974-17   Konig, David Thomas. "Social Conflict and Community
    Tensions in Essex County, Massachusetts, 1672-1692." Ph.D.,
    Harvard Univ. vii, 353 leaves.

    Revised, expanded version published as Law and Society in Puritan
Massachusetts: Essex County, 1629-1692. -- Chapel Hill : Univ. of
North Carolina Press, 1979. -- xxi, 215 p. -- (Studies in Legal
History). "Preface" (1979 ed.): "Scholars trained as historians have
been remiss in asking questions of legal records as they pertain to
the writing of history. Specifically, how did the legal system affect
the lives of individuals in seventeenth-century New England? How did
people in general--not just judges and lawyers--view the law, and what
role did they assign to it in their society? Conversely, how was the
law, like other institutions in early New England, affected by social,

economic, and political change?" (p. xi). Contents: 1. "English Law and Puritan Society: The Legal and Social Foundations of Order, 1629-1640," 2. "Real Property Litigation: The Social and Economic Backgrounds of Legal Change," 3. "Outsiders and Subgroups: The Cooperative Function of the Court," 4. "From Communalism to Litigation: The Elevation of Law and Legal Forms," 5. "The Court and the Community: Law in a Postrevolutionary Puritan Society," 6. "Challenges to the Law: The Conflict of Legal and Extralegal Methods of Social Control," 7. "Law, Magic, and Disorder: The Crisis of the Interregnum, 1684-1692," and 8. "Epilogue: 'A Contentious and Well-Ordered People.'"

1974-18   Luoma, John Kenneth Reynold. "The Primitive Church as a Normative Principle in the Theology of the Sixteenth Century: The Anglican-Puritan Debate over Church Polity as Represented by Richard Hooker and Thomas Cartwright." Ph.D., Hartford Seminary Foundation. iv, 224 leaves.

Abstract in DAI, vol. 35 (12), sec. A, p. 8011: "This dissertation examines the debate between Richard Hooker and Thomas Cartwright concerning the role of the primitive church as a norm in determining church polity. It is in essence a debate over the nature of church history. . . . The dissertation is distinctive in its examination of Hooker as a historian and his debate with the Puritans as a historical one. This study proves that there is a logical structure to Cartwright's argument, and it is this argument for restitution of the primitive church to which Hooker responds. This dissertation demonstrates that at every level Hooker is responding to Cartwright and that one can thoroughly understand Hooker only in relation to Cartwright."

1974-19   McIver, Isaiah. "Black Puritanism: Puritanical Parallels in Afro-American Educational Thought." Ph.D., Loyola Univ. of Chicago. 697 leaves.

Abstract in DAI, vol. 35 (2), sec. A, p. 943: "This study investigates the nature of African, European, and Afro-American Puritanism. It is concerned with the nature of the educational training obtained by Afro-Americans in the United States, their reaction to this education, with particular emphasis to the period 1619-1970. Included in the study is an account of the ideas, philosophies, and ideologies of secular leaders, spiritual leaders, educational leaders, political leaders, slaves, and freedmen without any claim to fame or prestige. . . . Spiritual Puritanism was the initial cultural encounter experienced by slaves. . . . Religion furnished for education its dynamic motive, the curriculum content at all levels was profoundly influenced by religious objectives, and ecclesiastical leaders directly controlled education."

1974-20   Menning, Viiu. "Mystery and Idea: An Examination of Anglican and Puritan Styles." Ph.D., Harvard Univ. ii, 227 leaves.

"Introduction": "Fundamental habits of thought radiate from an individual's conception of himself within the order of reality. During the English Renaissance such conceptions necessarily involved the individual's relation to God, the disposer of reality. Anglican and Puritan expression indicates radical divergence in these conceptions. . . . The five authors chosen for discussion [Richard Hooker, Lancelot Andrewes, John Milton, John Bunyan, and Richard Baxter] reveal the general pattern formed by Anglican and Puritan confrontation. . . . The several styles of the five authors express their differences" (pp. 1-3). Relevant chapters: "Introduction"; I. "Two Approaches to Discourse": i. "The Two Schools of Rhetoric" and ii. "Anglican and Puritan Practice"; II. "Style and Faith": i. "The Controversy over Style"; III. "Style and Reason": i. "Puritan and Anglican Attitudes to the Bible"; IV. "Worship and Language"; and V. "Conclusion."

1974-21   Moran, Gerald Francis. "The Puritan Saint: Religious Experience, Church Membership, and Piety in Connecticut, 1636-1776." Ph.D., Rutgers Univ. xii, 456 leaves.

Abstract in DAI, vol. 35 (6), sec. A, p. 3647: "This study brings together disparate types of local records, including church membership roles, vital statistics, and tax lists, and literary evidence to bear upon the social context of the religious history of colonial Connecticut. Three aspects of that history are studied in particular: individual experience up to and through religious conversion and admission as a full member into the church, general patterns of full membership over time, and expressions of piety among individual converts and the clergy. A long-range study of the pattern of admissions in those churches with extant records is combined here with an in-depth analysis of the circumstances accompanying conversion in ten parishes: Windsor First, Milford First, New London First, Stoughton First, Woodbury First, Preston First, Canterbury First, Suffield First, North Stonington, and Stonington East."

1974-22   Morrison, Alvin Hamblen. "Dawnland Decisions: Seventeenth-Century Wabanaki Leaders and Their Response to the Differential Contact Stimuli in the Overlap Area of New France and New England." Ph.D., State Univ. of New York at Buffalo. v, 163 leaves.

Abstract in DAI, vol. 35 (10), sec. A, p. 6291: "Wabanaki ('Dawnlanders') is the collective name of the historic Algonkian Amerinds of sub-St. Lawrence Canada and northern New England. . . . The modern names of the Wabanaki peoples are from east to west, Micmac, Maliseet, Passamaquoddy, Penobscot, Abnaki, and (now extinct) Pennacook. . . . This study first delineates three seventeenth-century Wabanaki clusters (Micmac, Etchemin, and Abnaki-Pennacook), then describes the forms of Wabanaki sociopolitical affairs in their far-from-absolute, yet fundamentally-authoritative leaders called sagamores. After a chapter analyzing the status and role of the Wabanaki sagamore, the differential nature and effects of first French, then English, contacts with the Wabanaki are considered, in a chapter on each. . . . In the last chapter of this study, the decisions known by us to have been made by various Wabanaki sagamores during the 1600s are analyzed to trace the effects they had on the integrity and adaptation of the Dawnlanders."

1974-23   Owen, Dennis Edward. "Satan's Fiery Darts: Explorations in the Experience and Concept of the Demonic in Seventeenth-Century New England." Ph.D., Princeton Univ. vi, 316 leaves.

Abstract in DAI, vol. 35 (9), sec. A, p. 6233: "The dissertation is a study of Puritan beliefs in the demonic, and of the ways in which these beliefs were expressed in actual experience. The dissertation is comprised of three main sections, each of which deals with one particular aspect of the problem. . . . The first section discusses the Puritan 'demonology,' placing it in the larger context of Puritan theology. . . . Section two covers Puritan-Indian relationships during the seventeenth century, arguing that the Indians were perceived as demonic figures, and that this perception was used to legitimate what amounted to a process of gradual extermination. . . . The third section deals with the outbreak of witchcraft accusations at Salem Village in 1692, applying methodologies drawn from recent studies of African witchcraft."

1974-24   Peyer, Jean B. "Jamaica, Long Island, 1656-1776: A Study of the Roots of American Urbanism." Ph.D., City Univ. of New York. x, 390 leaves.

Abstract in DAI, vol. 35 (3), sec. A, p. 1601: "An examination of the early history of Jamaica, New York, . . . provides an opportunity not only for a case study of a single town in colonial New York, but it also offers material for comparing local community development on Long Island with that of New England." Chapter I: "Jamaica, like neighboring towns, was a product of New England's dispersal, and its settlement was in varying degrees a reflection of the Puritans' sense of community, their quest for religious and political autonomy, and their search for more and better land" (p. 10). Contents: I. "The Formation of One Middle-Atlantic Community," II. "Government: Jamaica under Dutch and English Rule," III. "Town Government: Active to Passive Attitude," IV. "The Economy and Economic Class," V. "Land: Distribution, Ownership, Speculation, and Controversy," VI. "Religion: Denominations and Conflicts," VII. "Class Structure and Social Mobility," and "Jamaica in Perspective."

1974-25   Reed, Michael Duffy. "Edward Taylor: The Poetry of Defiance." Ph.D., Univ. of Oregon. 247 leaves.

Abstract in DAI, vol. 35 (8), sec. A, p. 5359: "In my thesis . . . , using theological and psychoanalytical approaches, I have examined the problem of orthodoxy in Edward Taylor's Preparatory Meditations, and have demonstrated that these poems are theologically orthodox and express the same psychological content as the Federal Covenantal theology which Taylor believed and practiced. Because the Federal covenantal theology is distinctively American, Edward Taylor's Preparatory Meditations are the expression and beginning of a uniquely

American tradition in literature. ... Chapter One: 'Sailing with Angels,' poses the question of the seeming conflict between the orthodoxy of Taylor's life and the apparent heresy contained in his poetry. ...   Chapter Two: 'The Blinks and Blisses of God's Love,' is a psychoanalytic examination of the Puritan Federal covenantal theology. ...   Chapter Three: 'The Telltale Tongue,' examines the orthodoxy of Meditation 8, first series. ...   Chapter Four: 'The Golden Poet,' is an examination of how Taylor's conception of metaphor functions as a defensive structure against the central Oedipal fantasy. ...   Chapter Five: 'Heavenly Sparks of Holy Fire,' demonstrates that the meditative form of Taylor's Preparatory Meditations is ... closely related to the meditative form advocated by Richard Baxter in his book, The Saints' Everlasting Rest."

1974-26   Sadowy, Chester P. "Benjamin Colman (1673-1747) as Literary
     Artist." Ph.D., Univ. of Pennsylvania. xli, 221 leaves.

     Abstract in DAI, vol. 35 (8), sec. A, p. 5361: "This dissertation is an examination of Colman from a literary standpoint, an attempt to examine this minister as a prose stylist and poet. . . . The first chapter, 'A Brief Life of Benjamin Colman,' is ... merely an attempt to place Colman in the context of his age and to examine the predominant ideas he expressed through his lifetime. ... The second chapter, 'The Prose Style and Sermonic Practice of Benjamin Colman,' explores and tries to define and isolate Colman's prose style. It is also an examination of the changes he tried to effect in the sermonic form. ... The third chapter, 'The Major Works of Benjamin Colman,' is a close study of nine of his most popular and influential works. ... The fourth chapter, 'The Funeral Sermons of Benjamin Colman,' is a study of the structure, content, and character sketches of Colman's funeral discourses. ... The fifth chapter, 'The Poetry of Benjamin Colman,' is an examination of Colman's poetic theory and of his poetry. ... All of Colman's poems are printed in this chapter."

1974-27   Selement, George Joseph. "The Means of Grace: A Study of
     Conversion in Early New England." Ph.D., Univ. of New Hampshire.
     401 leaves.

     Abstract in DAI, vol. 38 (2), sec. A, p. 981: "This dissertation consists of a fully annotated transcription of Thomas Shepard's 'The Confessions of Diverse Propounded To Be Received & Were Entertayned As Members,' a series of fifty-one confessions that Shepard's parishioners gave before the Cambridge congregation between 1638 and 1645 in order to be admitted into the church as members. The introduction to the 'Confessions' contains a series of essays on the community of Cambridge, the soteriology of Thomas Shepard, the soteriology of his fifty-one parishioners, and the psychology of conversion." Cf. Thomas Shepard's Confessions. -- Ed. by George Selement and Bruce C. Woolley. -- Boston : Colonial Society of Massachusetts, 1981. -- xii, 222 p. -- (Publications of the Colonial Society of Massachusetts. Collections ; vol. LVII). Cf. #1973-27, above.

1974-28   Seward, Rudy Ray. "The American Family: A Study of
    Structural Trends from the Colonial Period to the Present."
    Ph.D., Southern Illinois Univ. at Carbondale. vi, 311 leaves.

    Abstract in DAI, vol. 36 (2), sec. A, p. 1118. Revision
published as The American Family: A Demographic History, with a
foreword by Herman R. Lantz. -- Beverley Hills, Calif. : Sage
Publications, 1978. -- 223 p. -- (Sage Library of Social Research ;
vol. 70). Relevant chapters: 1. "Introduction" and 2. "The Colonial
American Family: A Recent Documentation of Its Structure."

1974-29   Signett, Roland Dale. "The Image of Christ and Symbolism of
    Atonement among the Puritan Clergy: Theology, Personality and
    the Social Order, 1600-1745." Ph.D., Univ. of Washington. iii,
    218 leaves.

    Abstract in DAI, vol. 35 (8), sec. A, p. 5267: "The emphasis of
this study is upon the examination of atonement in three periods of
Puritan thought between 1600 and 1745. The study was undertaken in an
effort to understand the Puritan's response, both psychological and
social, to the world in which he lived, a response in large part
precipitated, directed, and given meaning by the theological symbols
for Christ and His atoning work." Contents: I. "Introduction:
Symbol and Response," II. "Puritan England," III. "New England, 1640-
1670," IV. "Social Background," V. "Theological Developments," and VI.
"The New England Clergy and the Doctrine of the Atonement: 1700-1745."

1974-30   Skemp, Sheila Lynn. "A Social and Cultural History of
    Newport, Rhode Island, 1720-1765." Ph.D., Univ. of Iowa. ii,
    478 leaves.

    Abstract in DAI, vol. 35 (12), sec. A, p. 7823: "Newport, Rhode
Island, as it existed between 1720 and 1765, represents a unique era
in American History. In this period, the historian may trace the rise
and decline of merchant capitalism in an almost classic fashion. . . .
Newport's commercial leaders developed their power and influence
against terrific odds. They suffered from a chronic specie shortage,
a severely limited hinterland from which to draw marketable
commodities, and faced competition from the larger commercial center
of Boston. Yet, through a combination of skill, ingenuity and illegal
activity they managed to hold on to their mercantile empire in times
of war and peace, and the period between 1720 and 1740 proved to be
profitable for many merchants."

1974-31   Stout, Harry S., III. "Remigration and Revival: Two Case
    Studies in the Social and Intellectual History of New England,
    1630-1745." Ph.D., Kent State Univ. viii, 418 leaves.

    Abstract in DAI, vol. 35 (9), sec. A, p. 6081:   "This
dissertation represents an investigation of the interrelationship of
New England Puritanism and modernization that specifies Max Weber's
classical association of Calvinism and the 'spirit of capitalism.' Of

focal interest in this analysis are selected groups of educated elites
in New England who, through their collective biographies, reflect the
shifting currents of colonial thought and social structure. The
explicit concern of the dissertation is with . . . the specific
application of theological beliefs to the development and
institutionalization of social doctrine. In this task, I have taken
as my point of departure Ernst Troeltsch's and Max Weber's 'church-
sect' typology. . . . I have applied the 'revised' theory to two case
studies: the remigration of New England university men to England
between 1640 and 1660; and Old and New Light clergy at the time of the
Great Awakening."

1974-32   Sullivan, Jonathan Gray. "Perry Miller's The New England
    Mind: From Colony to Province: An Historiographical Study."
    Ph.D., Emory Univ. vi, 252 leaves.

Abstract in DAI, vol. 35 (11), sec. A, p. 7209: "This
dissertation asserts that historians can perceive the past only
through particular forms of inquiry. Around 1967 American
historiography started to shift from the study of various scholars'
descriptions of objective reality to the study of 'reality' in
historians' mental pictures. This transformation is analyzed in the
writing of three prominent American historiographers, John Higham,
David Levin and Gene Wise. . . . I propose a theory of metaphor
[that] asserts that historians use certain words so as to control the
meaning of other words. This hierarchy of words describes the
historians' structure of explanation. . . . Perry Miller's The New
England Mind: From Colony to Province (1953) is intensely analyzed by
the theory of metaphor." Contents: "Introduction," I. "Recent
American Historiography," II. "The Theory of Metaphor in
Historiography," III. "Perry Miller's Language in Colony," IV. "The
'New England Mind''s Component of Expression," V. "The 'New England
Mind''s Component of Psychology," VI. "The 'New England Mind''s
Component of Perception," and "Conclusion."

1974-33   Veninga, James Frank. "Covenant Theology and Ethics in the
    Thought of John Calvin and John Preston." Ph.D., Rice Univ. 2
    vols. (v, 387 leaves).

Abstract in DAI, vol. 35 (4), sec. A, p. 2392: Twentieth-century
"scholarship of the early Reformed tradition has had a tendency to
argue that there existed fundamental differences between Calvin and
the seventeenth-century Puritans. Since the basic difference brought
out in this scholarship centers in the priority given to the covenant
idea, this dissertation seeks to investigate the employment of the
covenant concept in the theology of John Calvin and a representataive
Puritan theologian of the early seventeenth century, John Preston.
The study seeks to demonstrate that the type of agreement that exists
between Calvin and Preston is far more significant than recent
scholarship would indicate."

1974-34   Ward, Churchill England. "The English Conception of
    America, 1550-1700." Ph.D., Case Western Reserve Univ. xi, 207
    leaves.

    Abstract in DAI, vol. 35 (5), sec. A, p. 2922: "Prior to the
eighteenth century, Englishmen interpreted America from within a
context that was essentially Graeco-Roman and Judeo-Christian. . . .
[As] Englishmen became aware of the existence of America, their
traditional classical and Christian assumptions about the world and
human nature seemed to be corroborated. . . . However, Englishmen
from within a traditional classical and Christian context--but in
opposition to this context--sometimes betrayed a quest for innocence,
and further, revealed an emerging Utopian consciousness which, if not
caused by the discovery of America, may have been heightened by an
awareness of this recently discovered land. . . . [Though] such an
ideal was derived from a Graeco-Roman and Judeo-Christian tradition
and was seemingly plausible as Englishmen became aware of the
unprecedented natural plenty of America, it was an ideal that also
conflicted with this resilient tradition and with the reality of an
uncivilized America."

1974-35   Wells, Michael Vernon. "Sex and the Law in Colonial New
    England." Ph.D., Ohio State Univ. iv, 202 leaves.

    Abstract in DAI, vol. 35 (8), sec. A, p. 5269:   "This
dissertation is a preliminary study of sex and the laws concerning it
in colonial New England. . . . Primarily using [William] Blackstone,
this dissertation first establishes the English background for the
Puritan court cases and laws concerning sexual offenses. The
dissertation then moves into a description of Puritan theories on
marriage, divorce, sex, and courtship. The influence of the Puritan
religion, church, and the Bible is also looked into. Finally, using
the early Puritan codifications, several county records and the
records of the Court of Assets of Massachusetts, the various sexual
crimes that plagued the Puritan communities are discussed. These
include rape, fornication, adultery, incest, sodomy, and buggery."

1975-1   Black, Barbara Aronstein. "The Judicial Power and the
    General Court in Early Massachusetts (1634-1686)." Ph.D.,
    Yale Univ. vii, 373 leaves.

    Abstract in DAI, vol. 36 (12), sec. A, p. 8227: "The General
Court was the highest judicial tribunal of the Massachusetts Bay
Colony under its first charter. Little has hitherto been said of the
extent and character of adjudication by this Court, beyond its actions
in such spectacular matters as the Antinomian affair and the trial of
John Winthrop. The primary aim of the present study is an
understanding of this adjudicative role. Chapter III contains a
descriptive and analytic account of twenty-two selected years of
adjudication in the General Court."

1975-2   Bosco, Ronald Angelo. "An Edition of Paterna, Cotton
    Mather's Previously Unpublished Autobiography, Complete, with
    Introduction and Notes." Ph.D., Univ. of Maryland.

    Abstract in DAI, vol. 36 (6), sec. A, p. 3708. Slightly revised
ed. published as Mather's Paterna: The Autobiography of Cotton
Mather. -- Delmar, N.Y. : Scholars' Facsimiles & Reprints, 1976. --
lxvii, 432 p. "Preface" (1976 ed.): "The edition of Paterna that
follows is the first public offering of the complete text of Cotton
Mather's autobiography. However, ... specificity concerning major
events during his life is not a prominent feature of . . . Paterna.
. . . I have attempted to compensate for Mather's unwillingness to
keep his reader informed of significant dates and events in his life
in both the chronological chart of Mather's life . . . and the
detailed annotation which accompanies the text of Paterna" (p. iii).
Contents: "A Chronological Chart of Significant Events in the Life
of Cotton Mather"; "Introduction": I. "The Dates of Composition and
History of Cotton Mather's Paterna," II. "Mather's Motives in
Paterna," III. "Mather's Literary Method in Paterna," and IV.
"Conclusions"; "Notes on the Text and Statement of Editorial
Principles"; and "Paterna." Appendices: A. "Chronological Summary
and Record of Diary Sources for Paterna," B. "A Record of Passages in
Paterna Which Have Been Located in Mather's Works Other Than the
Diary," C. "Biblical Texts Used by Mather in Paterna," D., "William
Perkins's Outline of the Conversion Experience," E. "Alternatives in
the Manuscript," and F. "Word-Division." Work is certified as "An
Approved Text" by the Center for Editions of American Authors of the
Modern Language Association of America.

1975-3   Carmical, Oline, Jr. "Plans of Union, 1634-1783: A Study
    and Reappraisal of Projects for Uniting the English Colonies in
    North America." Ph.D., Univ. of Kentucky. viii, 254 leaves.

    Abstract in DAI, vol. 36 (12), sec. A, p. 8228: "During the
century and a half preceding the 1783 Treaty of Paris, no less than
sixty-seven plans for uniting the English North American colonies were
offered by American provincials and Englishmen at home. The plans'
pragmatic authors set forth their projects at different times, under
multifarious conditions, and for various, often distinct motives. For
the planners, union was no abstraction: each of them promoted the
establishment of an intercolonial agency to attain some desired
objective or objectives beyond the capacities of any single colony.
. . . Only three of the plans were ever put into operation. The
first, the United Colonies of New England (commonly known as the New
England Confederation), was a decentralized, regional, military union.
. . . The English Crown's revocation of the Massachusetts Bay
Colony's charter in 1684 . . . led to the creation of the Dominion of
New England, the second of the three realized unions. . . . The third
union of the colonies, the short-lived (1697-1701), military
arrangement under the Earl of Bellomont, . . . terminated (with
Bellomont's death) before its usefulness could be tested."

1975-4   Cole, Ronald Fred. "Music in Portland, Maine, from Colonial
     Times through the Nineteenth Century." Ph.D., Indiana Univ.
     vii, 396 leaves.

     Abstract in DAI, vol. 36 (8), sec. A, p. 4836: "The first
references to music are in connection with the First Parish Church
(founded 1725). Financial records of that church . . . allude to
psalm books."

1975-5   Crandall, Ralph James. "New England's Haven Port:
     Charlestown and Her Restless People. A Study of Colonial
     Migration 1629-1775." Ph.D., Univ. of Southern California. vii,
     300 leaves.

     Abstract in DAI, vol. 37 (4), sec. A, p. 2380: "This study
recreates the life of Charlestown before [its destruction in] 1775 and
follows the migration of five important families to other New England
towns. It examines through five generations the lives, fortunes, and
movements of such original Charlestown families as the Spragues,
Frothinghams, Sweetsers, Whittemores, and Russells. Their story
becomes Charlestown's and their migrations in and out of Charlestown
reveal the town's viability as a haven from the long European voyage
and as a place for prospective settlement and community."

1975-6   Daigle, Jean. "Nos Amis les ennemis: Relations commerciales
     de l'Acadie avec le Massachusetts, 1670-1711." Ph.D., Univ. of
     Maine. 221 leaves.

     Abstract in DAI, vol. 37 (2), sec. A, p. 1141: "This study was
centred on the Acadian merchants of the Bay of Fundy who, from 1670 to
1711, maintained commercial relations with the English colonists of
Massachusetts. An effort has been made to identify those
entrepreneurs and to explain their motivation and behaviour. . . . It
was possible to explain the course of action followed by the Acadian
entrepreneurs who, even in time of war, continued to trade with their
enemies of Massachusetts. The main objective of the French traders
was to follow a path of accommodation with the Massachusetts colony.
This attitude enables them to continue in their role of intermediaries
between the two colonies." Text of diss. is in French.

1975-7   Earley, Lawrence Stephen. "Endangered Innocent, Arrogant
     Queen: Images of New England in Controversies over Puritan
     Persecution, 1630-1730." Ph.D., Univ. of North Carolina at Chapel
     Hill. ix, 297 leaves.

     Abstract in DAI, vol. 36 (10), sec. A, p. 6893: "In the
controversies between 1630 and 1730 over New England's intolerance,
two images of New England competed for attention. One was celebrated
by the Puritan Congregationalists themselves. Among all Christians,
the Puritans said, they were unique. Their church ordinances were
purer than others, their lives were distinguished by extraordinary
holiness. In their relations with others they described themselves as
innocent pilgrims beset by the minions of Satan. To preserve the

purity of these Christian innocents, New England's magistrates were empowered to suppress heresy wherever it arose. . . . The objects of the magistrates' vigilance, the sectarians who had come to the New World for religious freedom, held an entirely different idea of New England. To Baptists, Quakers and other suppressed dissidents, New England was a persecuting nation. In their tracts they exposed the fraudulence of New England's self-image and suggested one more in keeping with its cruelty and arrogance. . . . The irony of New England history was that a people fleeing persecution themselves became the worst of persecutors."

1975-8   Erler, Donald, J., Jr. "The Political Teaching of John Wise's Second Treatise on Ecclesiastical Government." Ph.D., Univ. of Dallas. vi, 211 leaves.

Abstract in DAI, vol. 36 (2), sec. A, p. 1061: "The majority of scholars who have examined the American political mind have concluded that John Wise (1652-1725) was the earliest and most articulate spokesman for liberal democracy in pre-revolutionary America. . . . The present study is the first book length analysis of the Vindication [of the Government of New-England Churches], and it represents an effort to eliminate the considerable scholarly confusion surrounding John Wise. . . . The present study contends that Wise attempted to persuade certain New Englanders that the theory of the social contract should subsume the teaching of covenant theology. Indeed, it is the central contention of this study that John Wise ought properly to be regarded as the principal American conduit through which the principles of Hobbesian political science entered colonial New England."

1975-9   Felsen, Karl Edwin. "Toward a Redefinition of Metaphysical Poetry: Donne, Herbert, Crashaw, and Edward Taylor." Ph.D., State Univ. of New York at Albany. 225 leaves.

Abstract in DAI, vol. 36 (3), sec. A, p. 1525: "This study, in reviewing and synthesizing past scholarship on metaphysical poetry, provides a more complete . . . definition of the metaphysical poets. The metaphysical poets were those poets of the seventeenth century who responded directly to the political, social, and religious turmoil of the times. . . . Understanding Taylor's use of meditations and how it is closely linked to the structure of his sermons makes the inner structure of his poems easily discernible. . . . Finally, including Taylor in this study . . . provides a touchstone . . . with which we can confirm the truth of the hypothesis we initially proposed concerning metaphysical poetry."

1975-10   Gates, Stewart Lewis. "Disorder and Social Organization: The Militia in Connecticut Public Life, 1660-1860." Ph.D., Univ. of Connecticut. 282 leaves.

Abstract in DAI, vol. 36 (7), sec. A, p. 4709: "This study surveyed the Connecticut militia in relation to maintenance of social cohesion from 1660 to 1860. It examined the militia both as an instrument used to suppress popular disorder, and as a social institution that reflected the nature of social cohesion and the forces of social dissolution. . . . The colonial militia existed solely to train men to defend the colony. The infrequency and public character of popular violence limited the role of the early militia to colonial defense."

1975-11   Goehring, Walter R.   "Henry Jacob (1563-1624) and the Separatists." Ph.D., New York Univ.   299 leaves.

Abstract in DAI, vol. 36 (7), sec. A, p. 4575:   "Henry Jacob, a Church of England clergyman, commonly considered to have been of Puritan persuasion, is recognized as an important figure for the understanding of Congregational origins. He is a representative of a group known variously as non-separating Congregationalists and Congregational Puritans." Contents: I. "Historical Background," II. "Henry Jacob: Biographical Notes," III. "Controversy with Thomas Bilson," IV. "Controversy with Francis Johnson," V. and VI. "Other Published Writings of Henry Jacob," VII. "Henry Jacob's Petition to the King," VIII. "Henry Jacob's Catechism," IX. "Henry Jacob and John Robinson," and X. "Significance and Contemporary Relevance." Appendix: "Jacob's Will."

1975-12   Goldman, Maureen. "American Women and the Puritan Heritage: Anne Hutchinson to Harriet Beecher Stowe." Ph.D., Boston Univ. (Graduate School). ix, 169 leaves.

Abstract in DAI, vol. 36 (3), sec. A, p. 1503:   "From the period of colonization to approximately mid-nineteenth century, women of Puritan background contributed to the cultural life of America. . . . This study examines the lives of some of these women with a view to appraising the role of Puritanism in their accomplishments. . . . The first two chapters define important elements of the Puritan impact on women by examining the lives of Anne Hutchinson and Anne Bradstreet. Chapter three is a study of four women: Jane Turell, Katherine Mather, Mary Rowlandson, and Esther Burr--all of whom held Puritan religious beliefs. This chapter shows how Puritan values evolve over a period of time and also how environment conditions a woman's response to Puritanism. The last three chapters trace these themes through the early nineteenth century by considering the lives and writings of the three most prominent women of the Puritan heritage: Abigail Adams, Mercy Otis Warren, and Harriet Beecher Stowe."

1975-13   Jones, Douglas Lamar. "Geographic Mobility and Society in Eighteenth-Century Essex County, Massachusetts." Ph.D., Brandeis Univ. xiii, 261 leaves.

Abstract in DAI, vol. 36 (1), sec. A, p. 482. Revision published as Village and Seaport: Migration and Society in Eighteenth-Century Massachusetts. -- Hanover, N.H. ; London : Published for Tufts Univ. by the Univ. Press of New England, 1981. -- xx, 167 p. "Preface" (1981 ed.): "Once I began to piece together the evidence, I concluded that the eighteenth-century New England experience represented the beginning of a transitional place in the history of migration, anticipating the even more fluid and mobile American society of the nineteenth and twentieth centuries. . . . This book is about the eighteenth-century origins of that migration transition, and it focuses on the people of a farming village, Wenham, and of a small seaport, Beverly. The evidence presented here centers on colonial Massachusetts, one of the largest and most populated of the American colonies and one whose people felt most directly the effects of both population growth and migration" (p. xiv). Contents: 1. "Economy and Society," 2. "Sources of Population Growth," 3. "Population Turnover and Economic Prospects," 4. "Economic Mobility," 5. "Family Formation and Migration," 6. "Inheritance," and 7. "Conclusion." Appendix: "The Calculation of Population Turnover in Eighteenth-Century Beverly and Wenham." Book includes nine figures and thirty-nine tables.

1975-14 Libster, Garry. "Puritan Specters and the Treatment of Those
         Who Are Different." Ed.D., Columbia Univ. (Teachers College).
         347 leaves.

    Abstract in DAI, vol. 36 (10), sec. A, p. 6602: "An analysis of the moralistic overtones often used to describe handicapped persons is examined historically by tracing the perception and treatment of 'deviant' individuals during the early years of the Massachusetts Bay Colony and by examining Puritan concepts of persons who were different. . . . The sociological and historical analyses of deviance suggest . . . that Puritan concepts of existence and morality are identifiable in contemporary practices of classifying and responding behaviorally toward deviant individuals."

1975-15   Lloyd, Peter. "The Emergence of a Racial Prejudice towards
          the Indians in Seventeenth-Century New England: Some Notes on an
          Explanation." Ph.D., Ohio State Univ. 229 leaves.

    Abstract in DAI, vol. 36 (6), sec. A, p. 3930: "This study asks a simple question: What attitudes did the first Englishmen to settle in New England form of the Indians? A simple answer would be that North Americans were viewed in racial terms as a people different and inferior. The attempt was made not simply to record these attitudes as they were expressed in the promotional tracts, journals, diaries, histories, and colonial legislation; but to explain how they were arrived at. Seventeenth-century descriptions of the Indians were found to be heavily biased. Throughout the century white opinion became more and more extreme on this subject."

1975-16   Mager, Gerald Marvin. "Zabdiel Boylston: Medical Pioneer
          of Colonial Boston." Ph.D., Univ. of Illinois at Urbana-
          Champaign. iv, 246 leaves.

    Abstract in DAI, vol. 36 (9), sec. A, p. 6270: "Dr. Zabdiel Boylston's name appears in many histories of colonial New England, but these works, almost without exception, merely state that at Cotton Mather's urging, Boylston introduced the practice of inoculation for smallpox to America in 1721. Indeed, Boylston has eluded historical

study in depth because most of the cloth of his story is gone. The
biographer must piece together the loose threads and widely scattered
scraps of his life. . . . [Because] of his pioneering efforts in
surgery and his monumental contribution to preventive medicine,
Zabdiel Boylston has a justifiable claim to the label of the first
significant figure of American medicine."

1975-17 Mank, Russell Walter, Jr. "Family Structure in Northampton,
     Massachusetts, 1654-1729." Ph.D., Univ. of Denver. xix, 232, 4
     leaves.

     Abstract in DAI, vol. 36 (10), sec. A, p. 6896: "This study of
Northampton examines the demographic, economic, and familial
circumstances affecting the lives of colonists living in a western
Massachusetts community in the seventeenth and early eighteenth
centuries. In this town, the family, land, and population were
interrelated, just as they were in other colonial communities. The
early settlers who established Northampton in 1654 created a viable
community; foremost in its development was a significant institution--
the family. . . . Over 100 families and more than 2400 individuals
bearing these family names lived in Northampton during this seventy-
five year period. . . . In addition to reconstructing the individual
families, the study also contains a description of the social setting
of the community in which the families lived."

1975-18   Marks, Michael Colton. "The Literature of Power:
     Pamphleteering in the Age of Mather and Franklin, 1689-1765."
     Ph.D., Indiana Univ. 484 leaves.

     Abstract in DAI, vol. 36 (11), sec. A, p. 7423: "Initially the
American pamphlet had been almost exclusively a vehicle for
theological disputation, but such controversies as the Andros affair
in 1689 [and] the Massachusetts currency debate of 1719-21 . . .
broadened the range of the pamphleteers' interests. . . . By
providing a focus for public debate on these issues, pamphleteering
directly reflected the development and expansion of American cultural
interests in a way unmatched by any other literary form. When this
growing cultural dialogue is considered together with the increasing
literary abilities of the pamphleteers, it becomes evident that the
pamphlet played a major role in formulating change and giving voice to
that change as it occurred."

1975-19   Morrison, Kenneth M. "The People of the Dawn: The Abnaki
     and Their Relations with New England and New France, 1600-1727."
     Ph.D., Univ. of Maine. 489 leaves.

     Abstract in DAI, vol. 36 (10), sec. A, p. 6854: Diss. "outlines
a narrative history of Abnaki relations with French and English
peoples to 1727. Particular emphasis is given to the developing
political connections between the three peoples and, consequently, to
the extraordinary effect the imperial conflict between the English and
the French had in shaping those relationships. It also estimates
Abnaki recognition of, and response to, the issues of the post-contact

world. Finally the study re-evaluates the mutual impact of the Abnaki, French, and English on each other and those factors which relegated northeastern Algonkian peoples to an increasingly marginal existence in a White dominated world."

1975-20   Mott, Wesley Theodore. "Emerson and Thoreau as Heirs to the Tradition of New England Puritanism." Ph.D., Boston Univ. (Graduate School). viii, 243 leaves.

Abstract in DAI, vol. 36 (12), sec. A, p. 7916: "Emerson and Thoreau exhibit ambivalence toward the Puritan past. They denounce what is outworn in nineteenth-century institutions; but they inevitably appeal to their Puritan forebears for models of tough virtue and community purpose. . . . One must treat Emerson and Thoreau as heirs to Puritanism in order to dispel the cliché that Emerson is the seer, Thoreau the Doer. Their differences are matters not of kind but of degree. Emerson and Thoreau both try to restore the balance between 'piety' and 'moralism,' emotion and reason, personal ecstasy and social responsibility. . . . They do not represent . . . the 'metaphysical' and 'passional' halves of the Puritan tradition; rather, they represent the Antinomian and experiential tendencies within a movement that reconstitutes much of the dialectic of orthodox New England Puritanism."

1975-21   Murray, Seán Collins. "The Reverend Samuel Johnson, 1696-1772: Anglican Protagonist in Colonial America." Ph.D., State Univ. of New York at Buffalo. iv, 499 leaves.

Abstract in DAI, vol. 36 (10), sec. A, p. 6898: "The Reverend Samuel Johnson was born in Guilford, Connecticut, in 1696 and . . . grew up in a staunch Puritan household. . . . Johnson received his B.A. and M.A. from the colony's collegiate school, later known as Yale College, and he subsequently returned to his alma mater as a tutor. From Yale he went on the become pastor of the Congregational Church in West Haven, Connecticut. In 1722 Johnson along with three friends . . . announced their intention of become Anglican priests, thus antagonizing Connecticut's Standing Order." Diss. is a biography of Johnson.

1975-22   O'Malley, Patricia Trainor. "Rowley, Massachusett, 1639-1730: Dissent and Delimitation in a Colonial Town." Ph.D., Boston College. iii, 287 leaves.

Abstract in DAI, vol. 36 (5), sec. A, p. 3073: "The study of Rowley combines narrative description and quantitative analysis to reveal the patterns of social networks existing in a colonial town. Early commentators, noting the town's textile industry and great size, considered Rowley a place of promise. In less than a hundred years from its founding, Rowley was reduced to half its size, agriculture had become the primary occupation and the promise had been replaced by tradition and conservatism. . . . Research into the causes of this change followed two lines. The first, a search into traditional historical sources, uncovered a story of community division during the

1670s and 1680s that was fully detailed in Church and court records. . . . The second line of inquiry involved the reconstruction of all Rowley families appearing from the town's founding up to 1730."

1975-23   Osowski, Edward John.   "The Writings of Michael Wigglesworth: The Rhetoric of Debate, Propaganda, and Typology." Ph.D., Rice Univ. 160 leaves.

Abstract in DAI, vol. 36 (4), sec. A, p. 2201: "Throughout his career, Wigglesworth strove to convince his reader of the reasonableness of assuming an other-world orientation--of the wisdom of regarding this world as the landscape in which to prepare for eternity. The form which best provided the opportunity for the exchange of ideas and the logical demonstration of the superiority of one statement over another is debate and dialogue. Through the use of typology the Puritan writer led his reader through the intricacies of rational propaganda and invited him to imitate the actions of notable types."

1975-24   Piersen, William Dillon.   "Afro-American Culture in Eighteenth-Century New England: A Comparative Examination." Ph.D., Indiana Univ. xix, 337 leaves.

Abstract in DAI, vol. 36 (8), sec. A, p. 5474: "This study examines the Afro-American culture of eighteenth-century New England with particular attention to the process of Americanization. The distinctive contribution small-scale New England family slavery made toward assimilation is developed in comparative perspective which illustrates interrelationships among Afro-American cultures. Focus is centered on the lives of New England blacks rather than on the regulations and culture which enslaved and exploited them." Relevant chapters: Part I. "The Americanization of Black Immigrants": I. "The Origins of New England's Slaves," II. "Acculturation and Americanization," III. "The Family System of Slavery," IV. "Slave Marriage and Family Arrangements," and V. "Religious Acculturation"; and Part II. "Studies in the Development of Afro-American Culture": VI. "Afro-American Religion and Belief," VII. "The Institution of Black Government," and X. "Conclusion." Chapters VIII and IX treat of later events.

1975-25   Polizzotto, Carolyn Mary. "Types and Typology: A Study in Puritan Hermeneutics." Ph.D., Univ. of London (New College) (U.K.). 298 leaves.

"Abstract": "Puritan writings were permeated with complex and colourful biblical images. Relying on the audiences' familiarity with this imagery, Puritan authors used it as a means of communicating their ideas. . . . From their writings it is evident that they looked upon the experiences of the Israelites as a divinely-ordained pattern for their own actions, which they strove to understand and to follow as closely as possible. . . . It is the contention of the present study that the Puritans' use of Israel's experiences as a guide to their times rested on a typological interpretation of the Old

Testament.... This thesis argues that many of the biblical images
in Puritan writings were regarded as types, and that an understanding
of this fact greatly illuminates them" (p. 2). Relevant chapters:
"Introduction"; Part I: "The Typological Significance of Puritan
Biblical Imagery, 1560-1660": 1: "'Old names and antient
resemblances': Typology as an Approach to Puritan Hermeneutics," 2:
"The Gainsaying of Korah: A Type of Antichristian Rebellion," and 3:
"Escape from Sodom, Egypt and Babylon: A Type of Godly Separation";
and "Conclusion." Part II treats of the role of typology in the
English Puritan debates on liberty of conscience, 1644-53.

1975-26   Prioli, Carmine Andrew. "Emblems, Blind Emblems, and the
           Visual Imagery of Edward Taylor." Ph.D., State Univ. of New York
           at Stony Brook. xii, 196 leaves.

    Abstract in DAI, vol. 36 (5), sec. A, p. 2791: "The purpose of
this dissertation is largely two-fold: to consider, first, the
evolution in England of the blind emblem, and, second, the utilization
of this convention in the verses of Edward Taylor." Contents: I.
"The Emblem Book: From Art to Artifice," II. "The English Emblem Book
and the Tradition of the Blind Emblem," III. "Zion's Inquisitive
Pilgrims: The Kindred Spirits of John Bunyan and Edward Taylor," IV.
"Heaven's Looking-Glass: The Visual Imagery of Edward Taylor," and V.
"'The Curious Needlework of Providence': Edward Taylor's Poetic
Tapestry."

1975-27   St. John, Raymond Alvin. "Biblical Quotation in Edward
           Taylor's Preparatory Meditations." Ph.D., Univ. of North
           Carolina at Chapel Hill.   240 leaves.

    Abstract in DAI, vol. 36 (10), sec. A, p. 6690: "The
indebtedness of Edward Taylor's Preparatory Meditations to the King
James Version, the poet's sole English Bible, has been all too often
neglected or misunderstood by critics. The nature of Taylor's
indebtedness is most evident in his Biblical quotation, both the
flagrant (that functioning epigraphically: i.e., the texts) and the
embedded (that assimilated into the fabric of the meditation). The
texts not only are the primary stimulus upon Taylor's imagination but
also reveal the variety of deliberately conceived meditative patterns.
. . . At the heart of Taylor's poetic method in the Preparatory
Meditations is a creative dependence upon Biblical materials."

1975-28   Schmeltekopf, Donald D. "Puritan Thought and the Formation
           of the Early American Political Tradition, 1630-1787." Ph.D.,
           Drew Univ. 338 leaves.

    Abstract in DAI, vol. 36 (5), sec. A, p. 2924: "This
dissertation is a study in early American political thought, in
particular the relationship between Puritan political ideas and those
of the Founding Fathers. The thesis is advanced as follows: that the
early American political tradition . . . was significantly influenced
by certain strands of Calvinist thought; that this influence was due
primarily to a heritage of theo-political ideas . . . of colonial

Puritans; and that, though secularized and transformed, enduring elements of this heritage had currency in the intellectual climate of the Constitutional period, thereby affecting the shape of the early American political tradition. . . . For the development of this thesis, the dissertation focusses on several figures: of the Puritans, John Winthrop, John Cotton, Roger Williams, Thomas Hooker, Increase Mather, and Jonathan Mayhew; of the Founding Fathers, John Adams, James Madison, and Alexander Hamilton.   The political thought of each is presented, together with a synopsis of his life.   The purpose of these studies is to reveal not only the contours of the thought of each thinker, but also to discern some possible links between the two traditions."

1975-29   Smith, Burley Gene.   "Edward Taylor and the Lord's Supper: The Controversy with Solomon Stoddard."   Ph.D., Kent State Univ. iv, 204 leaves.

Abstract in DAI, vol. 37 (1), sec. A, p. 278:   "This study investigates the ecclesiastical controversy surrounding the differing views of Edward Taylor and Solomon Stoddard regarding the Lord's Supper, the central ritual of seventeenth-century New England Puritans. . . . The dissertation is divided into four major segments. The first part, Chapter Two, provides the background of the controversy, including . . . Taylor's early defense of orthodoxy, and Stoddard's growing inclination toward a more flexible interpretation of Puritan doctrine.   Chapter three discusses Taylor-Stoddard manuscripts which . . . underscore Taylor's orthodox reaction to Stoddard's proposals regarding church membership and admission to the Lord's Supper.   The public phase of the controversy is analyzed in Chapter Four. . . .   Chapter Five continues the discussion of the Stoddard-[Increase and Cotton] Mather interchange and examines Taylor's response to the public controversy. . . .   The most significant contribution of the controversy surrounding the Lord's Supper is the manner in which it clarifies Taylor's poetry."

1975-30   Smith, Paul Joseph.   "The Debates on Church Government at the Westminster Assembly."   Ph.D., Boston Univ. (Graduate School).   xvi, 606 leaves.

Abstract in DAI, vol. 35 (12), sec. A, p. 7849:   "The purpose of this dissertation is to analyze the debates on church government at the Westminster Assembly of Divines, 1643-1646. . . .   This is a historical, descriptive, and critical study. . . .   The Westminster Assembly was summoned to advise the Long Parliament on reforming the doctrine, liturgy, and government of the Church of England.   For more than a year the ministers struggled to devise the best form of church government--one that would conform both to the Bible and to the practice of other Reformed churches.   Their recommendations were supposed to provide the basis for parliamentary legislation on the church. . . .   The overwhelming majority of assembly members favored a presbyterian polity. . . .   Their goal was to establish . . . jure divino presbyterianism in England. . . .   They failed to achieve their goal, however, because of the opposition of independents in the assembly and erastians in parliament."

1975-31   Stannard, David Edward. "The Puritan Way of Death: A Study
     in Religion, Culture, and Social Change." Ph.D., Yale Univ. xi,
     301 leaves.

     Abstract in DAI, vol. 36 (6), sec. A, p. 3941. Revision
published under same title: New York : Oxford Univ. Press, 1977. --
xii, 236 p. "Preface" (1977 ed.): "The Puritans of New England lived
life and, as this book attempts to show, faced death with an intensity
virtually unknown in American life. As a result, I believe that much
of importance in subsequent American history can be better understood
by closely examining the ideas and actions of the Puritans; . . . and
I believe that by focusing on a single thread of the culture--in this
case, the problem of death--'other threads . . . will become visible,
one by one'" (p. ix). Contents: I. "Introduction"; 1. "Death in the
Western Tradition"; II. "The Puritan Way of Death": 2. "The World of
the Puritans," 3. "Death and Childhood," 4. "Death and Dying," 5.
"Death and Burial," and 6. "Death and Decline"; and III. "Epilogue":
7. "Toward an American Way of Death."

1975-32   Ward, James Frederick. "Consciousness and Community:
     American Idealist Social Thought from Puritanism to Social
     Science." Ph.D., Harvard Univ. 500 leaves.

     "Introduction": "The present work is an exploration and
interpretation of a tradition of American social thought indebted to
and informed by modern philosophical idealism. . . . The thinkers
whose teachings I investigate sought an understanding of American
society as something more than a collection of atomistic individuals.
The idealist tradition in American social thought, however, must be
recovered rather than simply explicated, for its nature has been
obscure" (pp. 1-2). "New England Puritanism is the terminus a quo for
our account because it established an intellectual and cultural matrix
receptive to idealist philosophy. Puritan social theory depended upon
a psychological model of Christian conversion which required the
individual to surrender his isolated subjectivity and to become a
member of a community of believers. The symbolism of the covenant,
which pervaded Puritan thinking about the relations of men to God as
well as to other men, stressed the conscious, free and rational
attributes of God and men. Moreover, the process of conversion and
the operation of the covenant were presented as intelligible which
meant that piety and philosophy interpenetrated and sustained each
other. The freedom of an active mind or consciousness was contrasted
with the purely natural mind or extrinsic determinism that
characterized man when he was subservient to his empirical and
individual nature. The psychology of conversion survived Puritanism
and furnishes one of the central concepts for this study" (pp. 8-9).
Relevant chapters: "Introduction," One. "The Idealist Matrix: New
England Puritanism and Jonathan Edwards," and "Conclusion."

1975-33   Wenska, Walter Paul, Jr. "A Restless Temper: Toward a
     Definition of the 'Puritan Tradition' in American Literature."
     Ph.D., Stanford Univ. vi, 270 leaves.

Abstract in DAI, vol. 36 (5), sec. A, p. 2830: "This study suggests a way of regarding Puritans and Puritanism that would link more firmly the writings of seventeenth-century New England with those of a later America. ... It begins by sketching the backgrounds of the search--in the twentieth century--for an American literary history. . . . Chapters II and III examine [Perry] Miller's description of Puritanism and the Puritan aesthetic, as well as the recent objections and emendations to these descriptions. Particularly in their emphasis on Puritan emotionality and anxiety, these objections have allowed me, in Chapter IV, to suggest ways of approaching Puritan writings that would place them paradigmatically at the beginning of our literary history. ... Chapter V applies these formulations to William Bradford's history of Plymouth Plantation, and argues that his work functions as a paradigm of American historical and literary experience. The Epilogue briefly explores the relevance of Bradford's history to later American writings, and indicates the ways in which the issues raised in his history have persisted in the works of . . . later writers."

1975-34   White, Paula Kopacz. "Hawthorne's Use of the Puritan Theory of History." Ph.D., Columbia Univ. 371 leaves.

Abstract in DAI, vol. 38 (7), sec. A, p. 4144: "This thesis attempts to prove that Hawthorne used Puritan theories of history throughout his career. Works set in the seventeenth century, as well as those set in Revolutionary America and in Hawthorne's own time, can be seen to rely in structure and theme on the historical theories Hawthorne learned from his reading of such works as [John] Winthrop's Journal, [Nathaniel] Morton's New-Englands Memoriall, Increase Mather's Remarkable Providences, and Cotton Mather's Magnalia Christi Americana."

1976-1   Adams, Howard Crossett. "Benjamin Colman: A Critical Biography." Ph.D., Pennsylvania State Univ. 759 leaves.

Abstract in DAI, vol. 37 (7), sec. A, p. 4349: "Benjamin Colman was a central figure in New England during the first half of the eighteenth century, both as pastor of one of the most influential Boston churches and as the second most prolific writer in the colonies. ... Colman was indeed a man of his age, and to know his works is to take a significant step toward understanding early eighteenth-century New England." Diss. is both a biography and a study of Colman's works.

1976-2   Burton, William John. "Hellish Fiends and Brutish Men: Amerindian-Euroamerican Interaction in Southern New England; An Interdisciplinary Analysis, 1600-1750." Ph.D., Kent State Univ. iv, 385 leaves.

DAI, vol. 37 (11), sec. A, p. 7246: "Abstract not available." "Introduction": "I shall examine Amerindian-Euroamerican interaction in southern New England between the years 1600 and 1750. It is more than a story of Indian victimization by White oppression. . . . The Amerindians reacted to English culture and acted toward Puritan society in a complex, sophisticated manner" (pp. 16-17). Contents: "Introduction"; Part I. "'So Inclined to Freedom . . .': First Impressions, 1600-1643": I. "First Contacts and Indian Reactions," II. "Native American Cultural Adjustment to European Colonization: First Phase," and III. "Politics of the Pequot War"; Part II. "'I Doe But Right My Owne Quarrell': Acculturation without Assimilation, 1643-1678": IV. "Native American Cultural Adjustment to White Pressure: Missionaries, 1630-1675, " V. "Native American Cultural Adjustment to English Settlement: Conditions and Change," VI. "Native American Politics and Motivation to 1672," and VII. "King Philip's War: 'We Will Not Fight without They Fight Us First'"; Part III. "'They Thought Their Way Was Good': De-Culturalization and Tribalism: Persistence Through Adopted Traits, 1678-1750": VIII. "Settler Attitudes toward Native Americans," IX. "Native American Cultural Adjustment to Euroamerican Domination: Traditional Indian Politics within White Forms," and X. "Native American Cultural Adjustment to Euroamerican Domination: Indians in a Settler Economy and Society."

1976-3 Candee, Richard McAlpin. "Wooden Buildings in Early Maine and New Hampshire: A Technological and Cultural History, 1600-1720." Ph.D., Univ. of Pennsylvania. lviii, 396 leaves.

Abstract in DAI, vol. 37 (4), sec. A, p. 2267: "The small number of surviving structures from the early seventeenth and early eighteenth centuries in the two most northern New England Colonies have never been the subject of serious scholarly investigation. Six original towns on either side of the Piscataqua River . . . were the population center of both colonies during the first century of settlement. All the known structures traditionally dated before 1720 were located in this region. The diversity of construction methods, especially the adoption of walling materials uncommon or unknown in English timber-framing is their most significant feature. . . . The development of a commercial timber economy, through investment in waterpowered sawmill technology, offered economic incentives for the use of alternatives to traditional construction methods."

1976-4 Christianson, Eric Howard. "Individuals in the Healing Arts and the Emergence of a Medical Community in Massachusetts, 1700-1792: A Collective Biography." Ph.D., Univ. of Southern California. vi, 229 leaves.

Abstract in DAI, vol. 38 (10), sec. A, p. 6269: "This study identifies those local conditions which inspired the establishment of the medical profession and places them within the context of contemporary society. These perceptions of organizational needs were taken primarily from the observations of medical leaders of the period. . . . The medical profession of Massachusetts was founded on fragile personal relationships and uncertain institutions."

1976-5   Coffman, Ralph John, Jr. "Gardens in the Wilderness: Stuart
     Puritan Records and the Diversity of New England Puritanism,
     1604-1650." Ph.D., Harvard Univ. viii, 346 leaves.

"Preface": "The study investigates the origins of non-separating
Puritans in England, the transplantation of non-separating reforms to
New England, the diversity of ideas and practical implementations of
these reforms, the emergence of a functional orthodoxy and the defense
of this orthodoxy in a series of Anglo-American debates between 1635-
1660" (p. 1).   Contents: "Introduction," 1. "Localism in Stuart
England," 2. "The Puritan Collective Conscience: Antidote to
Localism," 3. "The [Thomas] Hooker-[John] Cotton Controversy and Its
Aftermath," and 4. "Functional Orthodoxy: Antidote to Localism in New
England."

1976-6   Dawson, Jan Carletta. "Changing Conceptions of Puritanism in
     America, 1830-1910." Ph.D., Univ. of Washington. 365 leaves.

Abstract in DAI, vol. 37 (5), sec. A, p. 3125: Diss. "examines
the ways in which thoughtful Americans viewed Puritanism and its role
in the development of American institutions and culture in terms of
three basic questions. First, how did Americans assess the nation's
debt to Puritanism during the same period in which foreign observers
from [Alexis de] Tocqueville to Guglielmo Ferrero diagnosed Puritan
influence as a dominant feature of American distinctiveness? Second,
what was the tradition of thinking about Puritanism inherited by such
critics as Van Wyck Brooks, [George] Santayana, and [H. L.] Mencken in
the second and third decades of the twentieth century? And third,
what do these changing conceptions disclose about the persistence of
ideas characteristic of the life and mind of colonial Puritanism?"

1976-7   Frankel, Gusti Wiesenfeld. "Between Parent and Child in
     Colonial New England: An Analysis of the Religious Child-
     Oriented Literature and Selected Children's Works." Ph.D., Univ.
     of Minnesota. ii, 275 leaves.

Abstract in DAI, vol. 38 (3), sec. A, p. 1572: "In recent years,
the history of the family and childhood have become topics for
innovative research. . . . There is a need . . . for description and
interpretation of the values and attitudes which shaped and gave
meaning to behavior. For colonial New England there is a body of
child-oriented materials consisting of sermons, treatises, Fifth
Commandment expositions, guides, addresses, lectures, and children's
stories.   The general purpose of this dissertation was to
systematically examine this literature within the context of the
changing colonial culture. . . .   In the first three chapters,
assumptions about childhood and attitudes toward children were
described in terms of the evolution of New England society from colony
to province. . . .   In the last two chapters, an attempt was made to
interpret certain aspects of the colonial child's life within the
context of the Puritan world-view."

1976-8   Geddes, Gordon Eldon. "Welcome Joy: Death in Puritan New
     England, 1630-1730." Ph.D., Univ. of California at Riverside.
     viii, 372 leaves.

     Abstract in DAI, vol. 37 (12), sec. A, p. 7919.   Revision
published as Welcome Joy: Death in Puritan New England. -- Ann Arbor,
Mich. : UMI Research Press, 1981. -- 262 p. -- (Studies in American
History and Culture ; no. 28).   "Introduction" (1981 ed.):
"Preparation for death was a major part of the Christian life in
seventeenth-century Christendom. A fearful fascination with death and
decay which had marked the late medieval and renaissance periods
lingered on in seventeenth-century New England. Death was a monster
of frightful mien, and a lifetime of preparation for dying, Cotton
Mather insisted, was scarcely sufficient. In part this anxiety
concerning death was countered by a well-established ritual of dying.
. . . This was the goal of Puritan spirituality, the prescribed
preparation for death" (p. 1). Contents: "Introduction," 1. "Ideas
of Death," 2. "Harbingers of Death," 3. "Holy Dying," 4. "Unholy
Dying," 5. and 6. "The Funeral," 7. "The Mourners' Cordial," and 8.
"Boundaries of Death."

1976-9   Goodman, Dana Richard. "Edward Taylor's 'Brightest Gem': A
     Religio-Aesthetic Explication of Gods Determinations." Ed.D.,
     Ball State Univ. iii, 249 leaves.

     Abstract in DAI, vol. 37 (10), sec. A, p. 6484: "This study
examines intensively Edward Taylor's Gods Determinations. . . . This
poetic history was probably written immediately prior to one of
Taylor's spiritual unions with God. . . . It is the work of a man
sure of himself and of his salvation. For Taylor the task was clear:
he must explain and justify to his parishioners the revelations from
God which he had so regularly and recently experienced during the
sacrament of communion. . . . The heart of this study is that Edward
Taylor the faithful Puritan minister was a serious poet who revised
and edited his poems. . . .   He controlled his material. Yet his
poetic devices were always harnassed to theological ideas. Thus
Taylor's poetic style is best viewed as religio-aesthetic, a
combination of spiritual and sensual realms."

1976-10   Greve, Lionel. "Freedom and Discipline in the Theology of
     John Calvin, William Perkins and John Wesley: An Examination of
     the Origin and Nature of Pietism." Ph.D., Hartford Seminary
     Foundation. iii, 293 leaves.

     Abstract in DAI, vol. 37 (1), sec. A, p. 405: "The purpose of
this dissertation is to define and delineate the nature of piety, by
answering the following problems: Who is to be considered a pietist
and for what reasons? What is the difference between a pietist and a
non-pietist? To what degree is pietism a legitimate expression and
interpretation of Christian faith? . . . By exploring the paradigm of
freedom and discipline, this dissertation attempts to discover the key
theological ingredients which constitute all forms of Christian piety.
. . . Broadly speaking [Calvin, Perkins, and Wesley] define piety in
terms of correlation, namely, as man's response to God's grace. . . .

William Perkins . . . goes beyond Calvin in his understanding of
piety, and defines it as the correlation between covenant and
conscience."

1976-11   Gross, Robert Allan. "Population, Economy, and Society in
    Concord, Massachusetts, 1720-1800." Ph.D., Columbia Univ.

    Abstract in DAI, vol. 38 (10), sec. A, p. 6272: "This is a
community study of the town of Concord, Massachusetts, during the era
of the American Revolution. It brings together two previously
separate lines of inquiry; first, the new social history of colonial
communities, which emphasizes long-term social, economic, and
demographic change; and second, the long-standing interest of
historians in the causes and consequences of the Revolution. . . .
Founded in 1635 as Massachusetts's first frontier, by the mid-
eighteenth century Concord had become a thickly settled community of
about 1500 people. And it was caught up in the disturbing consequence
of having too many young people and not enough land for all. . . .
The problems of population pressure on land began in the 1720s and
intensified in mid-century." A revision of the diss., The Minutemen
and Their World (New York : Hill & Wang, 1976), is concerned only with
events after the 1730's.

1976-12   Judson, Allan Brasier. "Some Characteristics of the Bay
    Colony Founders' Early Thinking about Their Dealings with the
    Physical Environment in New England." Ph.D., Harvard Univ.   429
    leaves.

    "Introduction": "The chapters that follow attempt to show that,
while the founders had some comparatively clear and definite ideas
with respect to various general religious, philosophical, and legal
considerations bearing upon dealings with the physical environment,
nonetheless their expectations as to the character of the New England
environment and as to the prospects of successfully establishing
familiar forms of resource exploitation there, despite their having
considerable foundation, were to prove not to be well-founded in
certain important respects. Similarly, what follows seeks to
demonstrate that during the early stages of the founding of the
plantation, virtually every other aspect of their thinking about their
dealing with the environment was indefinite and, with respect to most
matters, became defined only gradually" (pp. 5-6). Diss. has untitled
chapters.

1976-13   Kendall, R. T. "The Nature of Saving Faith from William
    Perkins (d. 1602) to the Westminster Assembly (1643-1649)."
    D.Phil., Univ. of Oxford (U.K.).

    Revision published as Calvin and English Calvinism to 1649. --
Oxford : Oxford Univ. Press, 1979. -- xii, 238 p. -- (Oxford
Theological Monographs). "Preface" (1979 ed.): "This book traces the
doctrine of saving faith from Calvin to Perkins to the Westminster
Assembly in order to discuss in what sense Westminster theology may be
regarded as the theological legacy of Calvin and/or Perkins" (p.

viii). "Conclusion": "Westminster theology hardly deserves to be
called Calvinistic. . . . Perkins may not have been the first to
assume that he upheld 'the Calvinist doctrine', . . . but the time is
surely overdue that historical theology present a more accurate
picture of what really happened between Calvin's era and that which
witnessed the emergence of Westminster theology" (pp. 212-13).
Contents: "Introduction": Part One. "The Reformers": 1. "John
Calvin's Doctrine of Faith," 2. "Theodore Beza and the Heidelberg
Theologians," and 3. "Some English Procursors of Perkins"; Part Two.
"William Perkins's Doctrine of Faith": 4. "William Perkins's Doctrine
of Faith" and 5. "William Perkins's Doctrine of Temporary Faith"; Part
Three. "The Experimental Predestinarian Tradition": 6. "Some
Contemporaries of William Perkins," 7. "Paul Baynes and Richard
Sibbes," 8. "John Cotton (to c. 1632) and John Preston," and 9.
"Thomas Hooker"; Part Four. "The Contribution from Holland": 10.
"Jacobus Arminius" and 11. "William Ames"; Part Five. "The Westminster
Assembly of Divines": 12. "John Cotton and the Antinomian Controversy
in America (1636-1638)," 13. "The Westminister Divines and their
Theological Unity," and 14. "The Nature of Saving Faith in the
Westminster Assembly Documents"; and "Conclusion."

1976-14   Kern, John. "The Politics of Violence: Colonial American
     Rebellions, Protests, and Riots, 1676-1747." Ph.D., Univ. of
     Wisconsin at Madison. v, 359 leaves.

     Abstract in DAI, vol. 37 (7), sec. A, p. 4563: "Colonial
Americans used the power of violent political opposition to challenge
the authorities of established government and to force changes in
political institutions, policies, practices, and attitudes. . . .
They generally resorted to violent political opposition after
unsuccessful peaceful protest against either a loss of prosperity or a
loss of political influence. Colonists also tended to become militant
during times of political instability and controversy over the
jurisdiction of colonial executive authority. Finally, they seem to
have drawn an inspiration for and a justification of violent political
opposition from instances of it elsewhere in the colonies and in the
British Isles." Relevant chapters: I. "Introduction" and II.B. "The
Glorious Revolution in America."

1976-15   Lord, Gary Thomas. "The Politics and Social Structure of
     Seventeenth-Century Portsmouth, New Hampshire." Ph.D., Univ. of
     Virginia. viii, 330 leaves.

     Abstract in DAI, vol. 37 (5), sec. A, p. 3130: "This study
offers a description and analysis of the politics and social structure
of Portsmouth, New Hampshire, from the time of the establishment of
the first permanent settlement in 1630 to the end of the century.
. . . The first section of this work takes a fresh look at the
activities of the Laconia Company in the Piscataqua Region in the
decade of the 1630s. . . . Next, the process by which Portsmouth was
annexed by Massachusetts in 1641 is detailed. . . . During the 1650s
a power struggle developed between the Old Planter and Puritan
factions. . . . In the 1670s Portsmouth became a Puritan community.
. . . During the 1680s Great Islanders began to develop a strong

sense of their own communal identity. . . . The partition of Portsmouth in 1693 was only the beginning of a process of fragmentation of the town and parish. . . . The final portion of this work reveals that the social structure of Portsmouth prior to 1660 was fluid and unstratified. During the 1660s, however, Portsmouth rapidly emerged as a commercial center and society began to follow lines of development similar to those found in Boston."

1976-16 Mappen, Marc Alfred. "Anatomy of a Schism: Anglican Dissent in the New England Community of Newtown, Connecticut, 1708-1765." Ph.D., Rutgers Univ. x, 207 leaves.

Abstract in DAI, vol. 37 (10), sec. A, p. 6705: "Religious schism occurred in many New England towns in the eighteenth century. This dissertation is a case study of one such schism in Newtown, Connecticut. . . . A Congregational church of the Standing Order, embracing all the inhabitants of the community, was established in Newtown in 1714, shortly after the establishment of the town. Eighteen years later, in 1732, the town minister and a small number of his parishioners broke with this church and formed an Anglican parish."

1976-17 Reid, John Graham. "Acadia, Maine, and New Scotland: Marginal Colonies in the Seventeenth Century." Ph.D., Univ. of New Brunswick (Canada). xi, 608 leaves.

Abstract in DAI, vol. 37 (11), sec. A, p. 7252. Revision published under same title with a foreword by Alfred G. Bailey: Toronto ; Buffalo : Published in association with Huronia Historical Parks, Ontario Ministry of Culture and Recreation, 1981. -- xviii, 293 p. "Preface" (1981 ed.): "This is a study in comparative North American colonial history. As such, it has two aspects. In the first place, it is an examination of three colonies--Acadia, Maine, and New Scotland--which originated from three different European countries-- France, England, and Scotland. Secondly, it is an account of the interaction of Europeans with the native peoples and physical environment of a region of North America" (p. xi). "Colonization in the seventeenth century was not a simple, clean, or inevitable process; it was complex, bloody, and unpredictable. The northeastern maritime region was one part of America where the Europeans did not carry all before them, and this study focuses on the reason why" (pp. xv-xvi). Content: Part I. "Introduction": 1. "Beginnings, to 1630"; Part II. "The Formative Years, 1630-1650": 2. "Relationships with Europe," 3. "Relationships with Native Peoples," 4. "Relationships with Other Colonies," and 5. "Internal Relationships"; Part III. "The Interplay of Forces, 1650-1690": 6. "Euroamerican Adjustment, 1650-1660," 7. "European Reassertion, 1660-1675," and 8. "Violent Dissolution, 1675-1690"; and "Conclusion." This work was the winner of the Sainte-Marie Prize for History, 1976.

1976-18 Schiavo, Bartholomew Peter. "The Dissenter Connection: English Dissenters and Massachusetts Political Culture, 1630-1774." Ph.D., Brandeis Univ. 647 leaves.

Abstract in DAI, vol. 37 (5), sec. A, p. 3096:   "The Massachusetts clergy and the English civil and religious leaders of Congregationalism they left behind formed the nucleus of a Connection which affected the foundations of the colony and influenced the development of the colony's religious and political culture during the colonial period. From the period of the practical application of the Puritan church-state model in Massachusetts until the independence necessitated its hiatus, the Connection fluctuated in importance and intensity and its nature and personnel changed, but its maintenance remained a prime concern for the New Englanders. . . . An analysis of the lives, sermons, pamphlets and letters of leading English Dissenters and their Massachusetts friends and correspondents throws light on the momentous nature of this Connection."

1976-19   Stone, Alan Noyes. "Nature's Fountain: Samuel Sewall's Gathering of a Pragmatic Literary Heritage during New England's Second Generation." Ph.D, Syracuse Univ. xix, 242 leaves.

Abstract in DAI, vol. 38 (5), sec. A, p. 2796: "The literary result of Sewall's course of life is a Diary which is a fountain of New England information. Its plain style reflects Puritan taste, while its understatement of controversial issues reflects a mind aware of civil exigencies. The Selling of Joseph, the first anti-slavery tract written in America displays an enlightment ahead of its time. . . . 'Talitha Cumi' . . . displays the spirit of the twentieth-century's women's liberation movement in its effort to be fair to the sexes. The New Heaven and New Earth [i.e., Phaenomena quaedam Apocalyptica] is a culmination of Sewall's interest in apocalyptic studies. In it he envisions New England as a kind of preparatory school where Christians are first made worthy of their Christian inheritance, an inheritance which presumably is the New Jerusalem as America-at-large."

1976-20   Storlie, Erik Fraser. "Grace and Works, Englightment and Practice: Paradox and Piety in John Cotton, Jonathan Edwards, and Dogen Zenji." Ph.D., Univ. of Minnesota. vi, 159 leaves.

Abstract in DAI, vol. 37 (6), sec. A, p. 3599: "I attempt to illuminate John Cotton's and Jonathan Edwards' resolutions of the paradox of grace and works by examining the parallel Buddhist paradox of enlightenment and practice. For the Buddhist materials, I use primarily writings of the Zen Master Dogen Zenji (1200-1253). . . . Cotton, Edwards, and Dogen express the union of man's finite works or practice with infinite grace or enlightenment in logical (and at times purposefully a-logical) discourse and in metaphors of unity derived from the natural universe. . . . Cotton, Edwards, and Dogen recognize language as a synthesis of ratiocination and metaphor which stands separate from experienced reality, but they nevertheless use both logic and poetry to convey their felt experiences of 'inexpressible' infinity."

1976-21   Stuart, Robert Orkney. "The Breaking of the Elizabethan
     Settlement of Religion: Puritan Spiritual Experience and the
     Theological Division of the English Church." Ph.D., Yale Univ.
     xvi, 265 leaves.

     Abstract in DAI, vol. 37 (7), sec. A, p. 4433: "The dissertation
examines the emergence of clear theological differences between
Puritan and Established Protestants in the Elizabethan Church. It is
an effort to increase our understanding of the forces which
permanently altered the religious life and social structure of England
and which eventuated in the first truly social revolution in the
western world." Contents: "Introduction," I. "Spirit and Structure
in the Elizabethan Religious Establishment," II. "The Puritan Presence
in the Elizabethan Church," III. "The Anatomy of Puritan Theology,"
Part One: "The Perception of Faith in the Thought of William
Perkins," IV. "The Anatomy of Puritan Theology," Part Two: "William
Perkins's Understanding of Conscience," V. "The Emergence of
Theological Division in the English Church," and VI. "The Anatomy of
Moderate Theology: The Perception of Faith in the Thought of [Peter]
Baro, [John] Overall, [Lancelot] Andrewes and [Richard] Hooker."

1976-22   Tyler, Richard. "The Children of Disobedience: The Social
     Composition of Emmanuel College, Cambridge, 1596-1645." Ph.D.,
     Univ. of California at Berkeley. 358 leaves.

     Abstract in DAI, vol. 37 (9), sec. A, p. 6015: "Before 1645, 130
university-educated Englishmen migrated to New England. Of this
number, thirty-five, including John Cotton, Thomas Hooker and Thomas
Shepard, attended Emmanuel College, Cambridge, in the half-century
following 1596. . . . Under its first two masters, Laurence Chaderton
(1584-1622) and John Preston (1622-1628), Emmanuel established a
tradition of nonconformity among contemporaries which later scholars
have made a commonplace. A statistical analysis of 2,606 members of
that society in comparison with the 4,433 from [Jesus, King's, and St.
John's Colleges] indicated that divinity alone did not distinguish
them from other Cantabrigians. . . . Confronted with the radical
changes in the Church and State espoused by the first Stuarts and
their episcopal hierarchy, the local gentry and clergy brought up in
an earlier orthodoxy at Emmanuel became 'the Children of Disobedience'
by attempting to form a new society in America and by restructuring
the old one in England."

1976-23   Wharton, Donald P. "Novus Homo: The Life of Richard Steere
     (1643-1721), to Which Is Added, an Edition of His Complete Poetry
     and Major Prose." Ph.D., Pennsylvania State Univ. 397 leaves.

     Abstract in DAI, vol. 37 (7), sec. A, p. 4379. Revision of
biographical portion published as Richard Steere: Colonial Merchant
Poet. -- University Park : Pennsylvania State Univ. Press, 1979. -- x,
87 p. -- (The Pennsylvania State Univ. Studies ; no. 44). "Preface"
(1979 ed.): "A poet of unusual versatility for his time and place,
Richard Steere adds breadth and complexity to the established canons
of seventeenth-century American poetry. . . . Of course, the poetry
by itself tells us a good deal about the man, but a greater knowledge

of the man will do much to increase our understanding of the poems"
(p. vii). Contents: "Introduction," "Citizen of London, 1643-1683,"
"New London, 1684-1710," "Earth's Felicities, 1711-1721," "Prose Works
in Defense of Liberty of Conscience," "Notes to Text," and "Notes to
the Prose Works."

1976-24   White, Peter Lewis. "A Critical Edition of the Poetry of
      Benjamin Tompson, Seventeenth-Century American Poet." Ph.D.,
      Pennsylvania State Univ. 299 leaves.

     Abstract in DAI, vol. 37 (11), sec. A, p. 7134. Revision
published as Benjamin Tompson, Colonial Bard: A Critical Edition. --
University Park : Pennsylvania State Univ. Press, 1980. -- xi, 218 p.
"Preface" (1980 ed.): "My hope is that this edition belatedly bestows
upon William Tompson, an insanely zealous minister victimized by the
pressures of the wilderness, and Benjamin Tompson, the discouraged
schoolteacher turned spokesman for his colony, some of the recognition
they so earnestly sought. In their lives and work, we have a
microcosmic model of American frontier, intellectual, and artistic
life" (pp. ix-x). Contents: I. "William Tompson: First-Generation
American Puritan," II. "Benjamin Tompson: Colonial Bard," III. "The
Achievement of Benjamin Tompson," IV. "The Historical Tompson:
Textual and Critical Commentary," and V. "Editorial Principles"; and
"An Edition of the Poetry by Benjamin Tompson." Appendices: A.
"Poems Probably by Tompson," B. "The Letters of Benjamin Tompson," and
C. "A Latin Salutatory Oration of 1662."

1976-25   Wilson, Robert John. "Poetics of the Sublime Poem in
      America, 1650-1860." Ph.D., Univ. of California at Berkeley. i,
      299 leaves.

     Abstract in DAI, vol. 37 (9), sec. A, p. 5835: "A documented
survey of American poetic theory and practice from [Anne] Bradstreet's
The Tenth Muse Lately Sprung Up in America (1650) to Whitman's Leaves
of Grass . . . reveals the continuity, in critical consciousness and
poetic usage, of the sublime poem, a style or form of poetry early and
increasingly valued in America on the affective or Common Sense
criterion of 'transport.' . . .   In such poems as Bradstreet's
'Contemplations' (1662), the poet withdraws to a natural grotto of
sacred presence and power, the better to present the 'feeling
knowledge' or sensations of transport and the desired union with place
and God."

1976-26   Zilboorg, Caroline Crawford. "The Speaking Self in American
      Puritan Literature: A Study in Genre and Rhetorical
      Continuities." Ph.D., Univ. of Wisconsin at Madison. ii, 340
      leaves.

     Abstract in DAI, vol. 37 (6), sec. A, p. 3632: "A significant
issue in American Puritan writing between 1620 and 1760 is the
definition and assertion of the self through the speaking voices which
various genres allow. The Puritans' conception of fallen man and
their consequent attitudes towards reason and emotion work against the

development of a speaker who interprets his material on the basis of individual and artistic perceptions. Works in which such interpretation is possible I call 'intimate,' for at their core is the writer's vision of his material. My discussion moves from examples of the least intimate mode (history) through progressively more intimate modes (diary, journal, autobiography, biography, and mixed genres) to the most intimate works which I call 'poetic.' . . . My approach is descriptive, for I explore in detail the rhetoric which prevents or allows self-assertion in examples from the various genres."

1977-1   Benensohn-Sager, Karen Maury. "American Abrahams: Some Antinomian Themes in American Literature." Ph.D., Northwestern Univ.   260 leaves.

Abstract in DAI, vol. 38 (11), sec. A, p. 6719: "This study explores some literary examples of an American cultural myth that might be called the 'American Abraham.' . . . Beneath the stories of various Abraham-like figures in American literature lies the problem of 'antinomianism,' the belief that one is above the law (literally, 'against the law'). What begins as a Reformation heresy, the belief that a person under certain circumstances of divine grace and direct, personal, divine revelation is beyond the law (religious and/or secular), becomes the accepted norm . . . of modern man according to existentialist ethics. . . .   Characters in American literature frequently find themselves in situations in which they must choose between the voice of isolated personal conscience . . . and the laws of conventional society. . . . The trial of Anne Hutchinson first brought together the concepts of antinomianism and Abrahamic dilemma: Hutchinson was convicted of the antinomian heresy because she identified herself with Abraham who received direct relevation from God."

1977-2   Bernstein, Mashey Maurice. "The Individual as a Work of Art: Jewish and Puritan Values in the Fiction of Norman Mailer and Edward Lewis Wallant." Ph.D., Univ. of California at Santa Barbara.   225 leaves.

Abstract in DAI, vol. 38 (6), sec. A, p. 3494: "Chapter One examines the writings of the Hinnuk, Moses Maimonides, and [Abraham Joshua] Heschel in relationship to the idea of mitzvah. It goes on to show how Puritan writers from [John] Cotton and [John] Winthrop to [George] Santayana owe a debt to the Hebraic frame of mind. The chapter concludes with an investigation into Jewish and Puritan attitudes to language and art. . . . Chapter Two applies Jewish and Puritan theology to the fiction of Hawthorne and [Henry] James. . . . Chapter Three examines all the fiction of Mailer from The Naked and the Dead to Armies of the Night to show how his novels follow in a Puritan tradition, relying on individual and subjective perceptions for their comprehension of truth. . . . Chapter Four continues the discussion by dealing with all the novels of Wallant from the same perspective."

1977-3   Bykerk, Loree Gerdes. "Representation by Delegate in the
    Early American Colonies." Ph.D., Columbia Univ. 240 leaves.

    Abstract in DAI, vol. 38 (1), sec. A, p. 451: "The early
American colonists' thoughts on representation have not been
adequately dealt with by scholars to date. No one has focused upon
the early colonial development of ideas and customs of representation
which later were revealed to be very different from those in England.
This inquiry is prefaced by a brief discussion of the logical
components of representation in an effort to assure a theoretically
clear approach to the complex interrelationships involved."

1977-4   Carden, Mark Allen. "The Ministry and the Word: The Clergy,
    the Bible, and Biblical Themes in Five Massachusetts Towns, 1630-
    1700." Ph.D., Univ. of California at Irvine. xii, 322 leaves.

    Abstract in DAI, vol. 38 (11), sec. A, p. 6891: "This study was
undertaken to examine in detail the seventeenth-century Puritan
clergy's dependence on the Bible as the final rule of faith and
practice, supreme in their minds even over reason and logic. By
studying the structure and content of the extant sermons and other
theological writings of the clergy in the five communities of Boston,
Cambridge, Dedham, Dorchester, and Roxbury prior to 1700, the clergy's
Biblical dependence is clearly evident. It also becomes clear . . .
that the great majority of the sermons could be categorized according
to five broad Biblical themes, based on the principal doctrine of each
sermon: (1) the person and work of Christ, (2) the problem of sin,
(3) the call to salvation, (4) the responsibilities of holy living,
and (5) the family of God in church and home. Each of these themes is
explored in detail in an attempt to more fully understand the
ingredients of Puritan theology throughout the seventeenth century."

1977-5   Carr, James Vincent. "Solomon Stoddard: An American Way of
    Religion." Ph.D., Hartford Seminary Foundation. x, 377 leaves.

    Abstract in DAI, vol. 39 (2), sec. A, p. 932: "Solomon Stoddard
. . . is one of a group of New England pastors whose theological and
ministerial careers have deeply influenced American religious history
and, in a derivative way, broader socio-political trends. The second
generation in New England of which Stoddard was a part, had the task
of combining an inherited form of individualized religious experience
with the continued settlement of the wilderness. . . . Stoddard's
role in New England's history has not received substantial treatment
yet. . . . In unfolding and analyzing Stoddard's major work, The
Safety of Appearing in the Righteousness of Christ, it is proposed to
give Stoddard his due."

1977-6   Chard, Donald F. "The Impact of Ile Royale on New England,
    1713-1763." Ph.D., Univ. of Ottawa (Canada). xix, 339, 4
    leaves.

    "Introduction": "By sheer volume and monetary value, New
England's recorded trade with Louisbourg was only occasionally as

important to New England as was that region's trade with the West Indies. . . . Nevertheless, Louisbourg had a significant impact on New England when both direct and indirect effects are considered. . . . Louisbourg's relationship to New England is significant in that it reveals much about the ways in which some members of the New England merchant community dealt with some of their major preoccupations" (p. vi). Relevant chapters: "Introduction," I. "Canso, 1710-1721: Focal Point of New England-Ile Royale Rivalry," II. "Patterns of Trade, 1720-1744," and "Conclusion." Chapters III-X deal with later periods.

1977-7   Clark, Michael Philip. "The Crucified Phrase: Puritan Semiology and Its Development in Colonial America." Ph.D., Univ. of California at Irvine. vii, 237 leaves.

Abstract in DAI, vol. 38 (9), sec. A, p. 5473: "I have examined the growth of Puritan semiology in Colonial America in the light of the discoveries of Reformation hermeneutics and the major voices of English Puritanism in the sixteenth century. . . . William Ames, William Perkins, and John Wilkins adapted [Luther's and Calvin's] exegetical methods and goals into a coherent semiology that became the basis for the linguistic and scientific systems of the Colonial Puritans, so . . . I trace the persistence and mutation of its Scripturalism in Puritan hermeneutics. In Chapter Two I watch the semiologies of Samuel Willard and Urian Oakes gradually depart from those of the Royal Society over the question of analogical correspondence between texts and their significance, and, in Chapter Three, Ames, Thomas Hooker, and John Cotton build the faculty psychology of their time into a description of man's ability to use signs to move his physical sight into spiritual vision. The Puritans' use of those signs becomes, in the fourth and concluding chapter, their way back to the Edenic union between the human and the divine that Calvin denied them, and as they carefully replace the revelation of the Incarnation with the significance of the Crucifixion, they convert the failures of the communication between man and God into the faith of their community."

1977-8   Cowell, Pattie Lee. "Women Poets in Pre-Revolutionary America, 1650-1775." Ph.D., Univ. of Massachusetts. xi, 347 leaves.

Abstract in DAI, vol. 38 (8), sec. A, p. 4824. Revision published as Women Poets in Pre-Revolutionary America, 1650-1775: An Anthology. -- Troy, N.Y. : Whitstone Publishing Co., 1981. -- x, 404 p. "Introduction" (1981 ed.): The book "makes accessible many long out-of-print or unpublished poems in a collected edition. Certainly all the poets considered here were minor figures, with few exceptions obscure even in their own day. None were so professional as Anne Bradstreet, the earliest of them for whom we have existing poems and herself a minor figure in American poetry. Yet taken together, these lesser poets have a greater statement to make than any of them can make individually. Examining who they were, what and why they wrote, may more fully develop our partial view of America's literary achievement" (p. 2). Relevant chapters: "Introduction"; "A Note on the Selection and Presentation of the Texts"; Part One. "Prolific Poets" (e.g., Anne Bradstreet and Jane Colman Turrell); Part Two. "Infrequent Poets" (e.g., Sarah Goodhue, Anna Tompson Hayden, Mary English, Sarah Kemble Knight, Mary French, Mercy Wheeler, Susanna Rogers, and Grace Smith); and "Checklist of Poetry by Women in Pre-Revolutionary America."

1977-9   Davis, Gerald Nelson. "Massachusetts Blacks and the Quest for Education: 1638 to 1860." Ed.D., Univ. of Massachusetts. xxiii, 291 leaves.

    Abstract in DAI, vol. 38 (6), sec. A, p. 3332: "The purpose of this study is to provide a comprehensive narrative and analysis of black educational opportunities in Massachusetts from the colonial era to the Civil War. In the absence of a definitive history of blacks in Massachusetts . . . , this study offers a general overview of the colonial and antebellum black society, its problems, institutions, and leadership as they relate to black educational opportunities. Furthermore, it explores the efforts of both blacks and whites, individuals and groups, to provide education for blacks."

1977-10   Ehle, Carl Frederick, Jr. "Prolegomena to Christian Zionism in America: The Views of Increase Mather and William E. Blackstone concerning the Doctrine of the Restoration of Israel." Ph.D., New York Univ. xvi, 375 leaves.

    Abstract in DAI, vol. 38 (12), sec. A, p. 7389: "The first salient school of thought in American history that advocated a national restoration of the Jews to Palestine was resident in the first native-born generation at the close of the seventeenth century in which Increase Mather played a dominant role. The men who held this view were Puritans, central figures in the Congregational movement. From that time on the doctrine of restoration may be said to have become endemic to American culture. . . . Mather was a premillennialist, holding that the millennium would follow upon the return of Christ. He foresaw two precursors to this event: the fall of the Antichrist (i.e., the papacy) and the restoration of the Jews to Palestine. The restoration and salvation of Israel would signal the latter-day glory of the church on earth."

1977-11   Hall, Dean Gaylord. "Edward Taylor: The Evolution of a Poet." Ph.D., Kent State Univ. xiv, 288 leaves.

    Abstract in DAI, vol. 38 (9), sec. A, p. 5477: "This study focuses on Edward Taylor's evolution as a poet by analyzing his early apprentice verse and the initial poems of his maturity. Such a study indicates that Taylor clearly changes as a poet . . . , and that his mature verse is substantially indebted to the apprentice verse. . . . Chapter One deals with the poems written in England. . . . Chapter Two investigates the elegiac poems Taylor wrote after he arrived in the New World. . . . When Taylor moves to Westfield in 1671, he assumes new responsibilities which modify the kind of poetry he writes. Chapter Three investigates the transitional nature of the

poetry of this period. . . . Chapter Four and Five examine <u>Gods</u>
<u>Determinations</u> from differing perspectives. . . . The dissertation
established . . . that Taylor moves through three distinct stages in
his evolution as a poet: he begins as a conventional versifier
reacting to specific events which demand a formalized response; he
moves to be a writer of personal poetry where his emphasis is on
events with which he is personally involved; and finally, he becomes a
private poet concerned chiefly with the state of his soul with God as
his audience."

1977-12   Heyrman, Christine Leigh. "A Model of Christian Charity:
    The Rich and the Poor in New England, 1630-1730." Ph.D., Yale
    Univ. v, 280 leaves.

    Abstract in <u>DAI</u>, vol. 38 (6), sec. A, p. 3681: "Sermons,
diaries, letters and church records reflect changing attitudes toward
poverty and charity during the first century of settlement in New
England. The first generation of American Puritans held that poverty
was neither a punishment for sin nor an indication of moral or
spiritual deficiencies; they regarded the poor as full-fledged,
indispensable members of the community. By contrast, third generation
New Englanders were more disposed to associate poverty with
wickedness, to condemn the poor for their idleness and 'vicious'
lives, and to regard them as marginal men, parasites on the social
body."

1977-13   Innes, Stephen Chandler. "A Patriarchal Society: Economic
    Dependency and Social Order in Springfield, Massachusetts, 1636-
    1702." Ph.D., Northwestern Univ. 247 leaves.

    Abstract in <u>DAI</u>, vol. 38 (11), sec. A, p. 6894: "This is not a
community study; neither is it a biography of the dominant family in
that community, the Pynchons. Rather it is an examination of the
patterns of interaction between elites and economic dependents in one
seventeenth-century town. The study focuses on the distribution of
goods and services, occupations, credit, indebtedness, prices, land
tenancy, labor patterns, mortgages, and foreclosures. It attempts to
reveal the rhythms of day-to-day existence and illuminate the economic
decisions made by all members of the community by tracing the economic
careers of approximately 200 male residents during the years 1636-
1702."

1977-14   Kelly, John Thomas. "Practical Astronomy during the
    Seventeenth Century: A Study of Almanac-Makers in America and
    England." Ph.D., Harvard Univ. vii, 319 leaves.

    Chapter I: "In America during the seventeenth century, astronomy
was the major area of scientific activity. . . . The seventeenth-
century almanacs provide valuable information about early American
astronomy. Numerous historians have studied almanacs from the
perspective of intellectual history. However, historians have not
assessed almanacs in terms of mathematical aspects of astronomy. . . .
This dissertation will analyze the almanacs from a mathematical point

of view to describe the early development of computational astronomy in America" (p. 2). Contents: 1. "The Prominence of Almanacs in the History of Astronomy in Colonial America," 2. "Computational Astronomy in England, 1500-1600: A Study of the Role of Almanacs and Their Authors," 3. "American Almanac-Makers During the Seventeenth Century: A Technical Assessment," 4. "The Influence of Universities on the Development of Computational Astronomy in England and America: A Study of Practical Astronomy at the University of Cambridge, the University of Oxford, and Harvard College," and 5. "Comparison of the Development of Computational Astronomy in Continental Europe, England, and America, 1500-1800: An Overview." Diss. includes nineteen appendices.

1977-15   Kibbey, Ann Marilyn. "The Language of the Spirit: Typology in John Cotton and William Whitaker." Ph.D., Univ. of Pennsylvania. 279 leaves.

Abstract in DAI, vol. 38 (3), sec. A, p. 1389: "This thesis focuses on two aspects of John Cotton's career, the antinomian crisis which exposed major theological differences between Cotton and other New England ministers, and Cotton's own radical change of views on church polity in the 1630's. . . . I examine his beliefs from the perspective of Elizabethan Protestant orthodoxy, chiefly as it is articulated by William Whitaker in his Disputation on Holy Scripture. In giving full consideration to Cotton's theory of history, typology, I show that Cotton's beliefs about individual faith and nonseparation conflict with his defense of Congregationalism."

1977-16   Kupperman, Karen Ordahl. "British Attitudes toward the American Indian, 1580-1640." Ph.D., Univ. of Cambridge (U.K.).

Revision published as Settling with the Indians: The Meeting of English and Indian Cultures in America, 1580-1640. -- London : J. M. Dent ; Totowa, N.J. : Rowman and Littlefield, 1980. -- x, 224 p. "Preface" (1980 ed.): "How do we describe people from a culture different from our own? How do we choose from among the hundreds of cues we see and hear those which tell us what is centrally important about other people? These questions were very important to me as I read and analyzed descriptions of America written for English readers in the early years of colonization. It very quickly became clear that not only was there a very great interest in the American natives, but also general agreement on what constituted a good description. There were felt to be clear and definite traits or patterns to be looked for when describing people from another culture, and societies were classified on the basis of the presence or absence of these traits and patterns. Thus in reading descriptions of the American Indians, we can learn a great deal about what English people thought were the essential elements of a society or culture worthy of the name" (p. vii). Contents: Part I. "English Writers Describe the Indians": 1. "The Scene and the Participants," 2. "Indian Appearance," 3. "Indian Society and Government," 4. "Indian Religion," and 5. "Indian Technology"; and Part II. "English Culture Confronts Indian Culture": 6. "Were the Indians Aliens?" 7. "English Social Ideals and Indian Culture," 8. "England's Special Relationship with North America," and

9. "The Nature of the Relationship." Appendix: "Profiles of the Writers."

1977-17 Landon, Esther Abrams. "Seventeenth- and Eighteenth-Century English and Colonial American Music Texts: An Analysis of Instructional Content." Ph.D., Univ. of California at Los Angeles. ix, 288 leaves.

Abstract in DAI, vol. 38 (11), sec. A, p. 6389: "This study traces the development of beginning music instruction in seventeenth- and eighteenth-century England and England Colonial America. . . . The particular need for a method of teaching sufficient music reading skills to sing psalm-tunes evolved from the social and political events of these times, and the relationship of historical events to the method has therefore been examined."

1977-18 Lockyer, Timothy John. "Religion and Good Literature: Puritan Devotional Poetry." Ph.D., Pennsylvania State Univ. 280 leaves.

Abstract in DAI, vol. 38 (12), sec. A, p. 7334: "This thesis is an attempt to locate the place of poetry in early American Puritan culture, and to determine the nature of that verse. Beginning with a brief historiography of the study of Puritan writings, it examines the many impedances [sic] to a fair view of seventeenth-century American literature, in particular the basic error: the assumption of the antipathy between Puritanism and poetry. Theories of Puritan verse . . . are refuted as insufficient to explain non-didactic verse. . . . A cultural framework which includes poetry as an integral part, and which agrees with the bibliographic facts as we now know them, is needed to replace that built by past critics. . . . Considering the amount of religious verse produced in seventeenth-century New England, and what the Puritans themselves had to say about poetry, it is reasonable to hypothesize that poetry, too, was a form of devotion or a mode of prayer--devotional poetry."

1977-19 Mann, Bruce Hartling. "Parishes, Law, and Community in Connecticut, 1700-1760." Ph.D., Yale Univ. viii, 224 leaves.

Abstract in DAI, vol. 39 (3), sec. A, p. 1787: "This dissertation is a study of changes in the meaning of community in eighteenth-century Connecticut. Its focus is on the towns of New Haven and Guilford, with some reference to the rest of New Haven county and to the colony as a whole. It examines the emergence and transformation of a new community known as the parish. It treats local litigation and the parish as two aspects of community and traces their development toward greater legal and administrative rationalization. Local litigation grew more formal and less tolerant of minor variations in individual disputes as population expanded and economic relations became more complex. Laws had to become more uniform, more predictable, to allow people to deal with one another across community boundaries. . . . Chapter One is an institutional and procedural description of the legal system. Chapter Two examines the nature and degree to which debt, property, and slander litigation and arbitration became rationalized. . . . Chapter Three describes how . . . the parish assumed from the town certain responsibilities. . . . I argue in Chapter Four [that] the . . . poll parish renewed the notion of a community defined by the people and was an essential step toward the eventual separation of church and state."

1977-20   Morrison, Malcolm Fleming. "The Political Relations between the English Dissenters and the New England Colonies, 1700-1750." Ph.D., Univ. of Southampton (U.K.). ii, 467 leaves.

"Abstract" (at beginning of diss.): "The thesis investigates the political aspects of the transatlantic religious link. In assesses the working of the Dissenting interest in Anglo-American politics and compares it with other similar groups, particularly Anglicans and Quakers" (n.p.). Contents: "Introduction," I. "The Early Years" (includes discussion of Sir Henry Ashurst), II. "The Political Relationship, 1710-1750," III. "The Intellectual Context I: The Concept of the United Brethren and the Unity among Dissenters," IV. "The Intellectual Context II: Relations with the Church of England and the Church of Scotland" (Chapters III and IV include much material from writings of Cotton Mather), V. "Testing the Relationship: Samuel Shute, a Dissenting Governor, 1716-1730," VI. "The Struggle for the Massachusetts Governorship, 1730-1741," VII. "The Anglican Challenge, 1720-1750," "Conclusion," and "Epilogue."

1977-21   Norris, Robert M. "The Thirty-Nine Articles at the Westminster Assembly: An Edition with Introduction and Analysis of the Debates of the Westminster Assembly on the Revision of the Thirty-Nine Articles of the Church of England." Ph.D., Univ. of St. Andrews (U.K.). lxxiv, 415 leaves.

Contents: I. "Introduction": (a) "Parliamentary activity leading to the calling of the Westminster Assembly of Divines," (b) "Composition of the Assembly," (c) "Regulations concerning the procedures of the Assembly," (d) "England and Scotland," (e) "Debates on the Thirty-Nine Articles," (f) "Methods of editing," and (g) "Footnotes on (a) to (e)"; II. "Analysis of the Debates--Sessions 45-74 of the Westminster Assembly of Divines"; and III. "Appendices": (a) "Appendix 1--Articles," (b) "Appendix 2--Continental Sources Cited," and (c) "Appendix 3--Participants in Debates."

1977-22   Pfeil, Gerd-Horst. "Die historische Entwicklung der Einkommensbesteuerung in Massachusetts (1619-1916)." Dr.phil., Johannes-Gutenberg-Univ. zu Mainz (West Germany). x, 399 leaves.

"Vorwort": "Die vorliegende Arbeit verfolgt den Zweck, dem Leser eine Vorstellung von den politischen, wirtschaftlichen und sozialen Strömungen zu   vermitteln, die über den Zeitraum von nahezu 300 Jahren die Entwicklung der Einkommensbesteuerung in dem amerikanischen Staate Massachusetts geprägt haben. Dar über hinaus will sie dazu beitragen, das Interesse an den historischen Begebenheiten

aufrechtzuerhalten, die in den freien Ländern der westlichen Welt eine
gemeinsame Kultur und sittliche Vorstellung von dem
Persönlichkeitswert des menschlichen Wesen begründet haben" (p. 1).
Relevant chapters: A. "Die Vorläufer der modernen Einkommensteuer":
"Die Einkommensbesteuerung in der Kolonie Massachusetts (1619-1692)":
1) "Steuerhoheit und Besteuerung," 2) "Die Einkommensbesteuerung im
Rahmen der Besteuerung," 3) "Die Einfluss der englischen
Steuergesetzgebung auf die Einkommensbesteuerung in Massachusetts,"
and 4) "Die Entwicklung des Einkommenssteuergedankens in
Massachusetts"; and II. "Die Einkommensbesteuerung in der Provinz
Massachusetts (1692-1775)":   1) "Die Experimentalperiode (1692-1699)"
and 2) "Das reguläre, klassifizierte Steuersystem (1700-1775)."

1977-23   Richardson, Philip Arthur.   "Commercial Growth and the
    Development of Private Law in Early Massachusetts: A Study of
    the Relationship between Economic and Legal Development."   Ph.D.,
    Univ. of Pennsylvania.   v, 242 leaves.

Abstract in DAI, vol. 38 (11), sec. A, p. 6952: "The purpose of
the present study is to contribute to existing theory and research
about the role of law in the economic order by examining the
interaction between economic and legal change in a specific society.
The society chosen for the study was the Massachusetts Bay Colony
between 1630 . . . and 1686. The assumption underlying the study is
that, by focusing on the legal history of a specific society and
period, it will be possible to draw conclusions about the relationship
between economic and legal change in general. A main objective of the
study is to illuminate and apply the hypotheses advanced by [Max]
Weber, Marx, and [Karl] Renner about the relationship between
commercial growth and the formulation of law."

1977-24   Rindler, Edward Paul.   "The Migration from the New Haven
    Colony to Newark, East New Jersey: A Study of Puritan Values and
    Behavior, 1630-1720."   Ph.D., Univ. of Pennsylvania.   xix, 448
    leaves.

Abstract in DAI, vol. 38 (11), sec. A, p. 6792: "Unlike prior
community studies, which have attempted to ascertain the relationship
between Puritan values and behavior by focusing on the social and
institutional development of a single isolated community, this
dissertation attempts to ascertain that relationship by examining the
transmission of Puritan culture from one community to another as the
New England frontier expanded in the seventeenth century.
Specifically, this dissertation analyzes the elastic but definable
groups of English emigres who founded the ultra-conservative New Haven
Colony in the 1640's only to abandon it for Newark, East New Jersey,
shortly after 1665 when the New Haven Colony was absorbed by
Connecticut. . . . The first stage [of the study] examines the
diversity of the Old and New World origins and cultural patterns of
the New Haven Colony's founders and explores the reasons for the
colony's settlement. . . . The second stage . . . centers in New
Haven Colony and focuses on the establishment and ecclesiastical
institutions of the Colony and its communities. . . . Finally, the
development of Newark from its founding in 1667 through 1720 is

examined in an attempt to determine the extent to which the community's founders had transplanted the cultural patterns of the extinct New Haven Colony in a non-Puritan environment."

1977-25   Rivers, Cheryl. "Cotton Mather's Biblia Americana Psalms and the Nature of Puritan Scholarship." Ph.D., Columbia Univ. 459 leaves.

Abstract in DAI, vol. 38 (1), sec. A, p. 267: "The nature of Mather's scholarship . . . has not been carefully examined by students of the colonial period. . . . An understanding of Mather's scholarly interests and achievements is best obtained, I believe, through a close examination of a section of the Biblia Americana, the culmination of Mather's scholarly career. . . . I have divided my study of Mather's work into the following chapters: The Biblia Americana: Its Cultural Context; Cotton Mather and the Puritan Exegetical Tradition; Cotton Mather's Psalm Exegesis; and Mather's Sources in the Biblia Americana Psalms. A transcription of the first thirty psalms from the Biblia Americana is at the end, with annotations and a separate bibliography."

1977-26   Salerno, Anthony Christopher. "The Character of Emigration from Wiltshire to the American Colonies, 1630-1660." Ph.D., Univ. of Virginia. vi, 264 leaves.

Abstract in DAI, vol. 38 (7), sec. A, p. 4315: "The dissertation's general purpose is to answer two obvious questions: who were the emigrants? and why did they leave? The chosen area of study, Wiltshire, permits a test of various emigration theses based exclusively on the East Anglian experience. The chosen period of study, 1630-1660, allows a comparison of two important migratory movements--that of the 1630's to New England, and that of the 1650's to Virginia and the West Indies. . . . The first section outlines 314 Wiltshire emigrants' general characteristics--i.e., age, sex, family and marital status, geographic origin, and socio-economic standing. . . . Section II deals with motivation."

1977-27   Schneider, Helen Margaret. "Three Views of Toleration: John Milton, Roger Williams, and Sir Henry Vane the Younger." Ph.D., State Univ. of New York at Albany. 206 leaves.

Abstract in DAI, vol. 38 (11), sec. A, p. 6750: "John Milton, Roger Williams, and Henry Vane as proponents of the Independent point of view were all in conflict with the majority viewpoint, first Anglican and then Presbyterian, that insisted upon orthodoxy of belief and tried to restrict free expression of ideas. . . . When Milton's Areopagitica is compared to Williams' Bloody Tenent of Persecution and Vane's Brief Answer to a Certain Declaration, Milton's rhetorical skill and his relationship to other Independent thinkers are brought into sharp focus. Vane's later work, The Retired Man's Meditations (1655), provides an even greater contrast to Milton's carefully executed strategy and sharply focused argument. . . . The prose of Williams . . . and Vane . . . is disorganized, digressive, and heavily

scriptural. . . . [The] differing religious attitudes of Milton, on
the one hand, and Williams and Vane, on the other, are also
significant."

1977-28   Sehr, Timothy Jerome.   "Colony and Commonwealth:
    Massachusetts Bay, 1649-1660." Ph.D., Indiana Univ. vi, 313
    leaves.

    Abstract in DAI, vol. 38 (8), sec. A, p. 5010: "During the first
thirty years of its existence the colony oscillated between . . . two
self-images. At various times Bay leaders emphasized the missionary
aspect of the colony which required contact with the homeland while at
other times they preferred isolation from England to protect the
colony's special relationship with God. This dissertation examines
one oscillation during the 1650's. . . . With the Restoration the
proper relationship with England became a divisive issue in colonial
politics. Different political factions represented the two self-
images, and this tendency accentuated the cleavages within colonial
society. Oscillations between the two images gave way to bitter
disputes about the true meaning of the Puritan enterprise in the
American wilderness."

1977-29   Shute, Michael Nathaniel.   "Earthquakes and Early American
    Imagination: Decline and Renewal in Eighteenth-Century Puritan
    Culture." Ph.D., Univ. of California at Berkeley. iii, 250
    leaves.

    Abstract in DAI, vol. 38 (8), sec. A, p. 5010: "This
dissertation traces aspects of decline and renewal in Puritan culture
around Boston during the eighteenth century. . . . Discussions in
1727 and 1755 about natural disruption, specifically earthquakes,
crystallized issues of relevance to the culture as a whole,
particularly in regard to connections between imagination and theology
and science. . . . Chapter I, a background essay, is entitled
'Imagination: Perceptions of Earthquakes in Western Culture.' . . .
Chapter II, 'Healing the Rift?: Cotton Mather, 1727,' discusses the
impact of the 1727 Boston earthquake. . . . Chapter III, 'The
Theology of Rupture: Thomas Prince, 1727,' evaluates Prince's
reaction to the dislocation in 1727. . . . Chapter III also discusses
ministers Benjamin Colman and John Barnard. . . . A brief conclusion
touches on nineteenth-century culture and Melville, through links from
the earthquake controversy itself. This statement deals with the
'split' between science and literature in America."

1977-30   Skillern, Harriet Miller. "A Socio-Legal Analysis of the
    Massachusetts Stubborn Child Law." Ph.D., Brandeis Univ. 265
    leaves.

    Abstract in DAI, vol. 38 (5), sec. A, p. 3067: "Massachusetts
has had a law relating to the disposition of 'stubborn children' since
the earliest colonial times (1646). In essence this law has provided
a means by which the parents of 'problem children' could petition the

court, i.e., the state, for assistance in handling said problem children. . . . The objectives of the dissertation are as follows: 1) To document the use of the Massachusetts stubborn child law from its beginnings in the 17th century to the present (1977). 2) To document the accompanying social changes. 3) To analyze and explain how the use and scope of the law evolved through changing administration of the law. . . . Beginning in the 17th century . . . the law was enacted as a part of a set of ideals designed to support legitimate authority as a scare tactic in the sense that children learned about the existence of the law as a capital crime. However, during this time the law was rarely invoked in formal court proceedings."

1977-31   Smith, Robert Gerard. "Toward a System of Law: Law Revision and Codification in Colonial America." Ph.D., Cornell Univ. vi, 338 leaves.

Abstract in DAI, vol. 38 (8), sec. A, p. 5011: "During the colonial period, the formation of a code of law was often a politically sensitive undertaking. To examine the revision and codification of early American law is to learn a good deal that is useful concerning the growth and maturity of American legal institutions, the role people expected statute law to play in creating and maintaining order and justice, and the legal and political relationship between England and the American colonies. . . . Five colonies--Massachusetts, Connecticut, New York, Maryland, and North Carolina--were selected for study. . . . [This] dissertation has been based almost entirely on original public records and private correspondence. . . . They revealed both similarities and differences among the colonies as each attempted to revise their [sic] laws."

1977-32   Stender, Thomas William. "Edward Taylor in Westfield." Ph.D., State Univ. of New York at Buffalo. 211 leaves.

Abstract in DAI, vol. 38 (3), sec. A, p. 1396: "Edward Taylor's experiences and ecclesiastical conditions in the Connecticut Valley conspired to clarify and accentuate the importance of the Lord's Supper in his vocation and his poetry. Taylor's poetry responded directly to those same forces. By focusing on the issues and events that most particularly motivated Taylor's poetry, this study shows that his work was not merely a private poetry of tragic inability, that instead it struggled to interpret God's will and that it played an integral role in maintaining the vitality of his ministry in Westfield. While this study necessarily takes Gods Determinations . . . as its central text, it also provides a reading of the Preparatory Meditations." Taylor's controversy with Solomon Stoddard is discussed at some length.

1977-33   Thompson, Marvin Gardner. "Litchfield, Connecticut, and an Analysis of Its Political Leadership, 1719-1784." Ph.D., Univ. of Connecticut. 3, v, 187 leaves.

Abstract in DAI, vol. 38 (8), sec. A, p. 5013: "This study of

Litchfield, Connecticut, from 1719 to 1784 is intended to show how one community was founded and developed during the colonial and Revolutionary periods within the context of Connecticut's political system. This is done by describing the major local events and concluding what they reveal about the nature of the town's local government. Also it is intended to analyze in detail the characteristics of the political leaders and what, if anything, set them apart from their fellow citizens."

1977-34   Towery, Allen Dan. "The Puritan Tradition in the Novels of Robert Herrick." Ph.D., Univ. of Mississippi. iv, 228 leaves.

Abstract in DAI, vol. 38 (3), sec. A, p. 1397: "Robert Herrick has been classified as a realist and a social historian of Chicago society in the decades just before and after the turn of the twentieth century. More accurately, however, he used Chicago as a symbol of urban America, and he analyzed it in terms of his New England Puritan background. . . . Chapter One deals with Herrick's treatment of the commercial instinct for fast material rewards at the expense of spiritual values. . . . Herrick's Puritan background demanded a code of ethics in every area of life, especially in business, and a sense of moral reponsibility on the part of every man. . . . Chapter Two is a consideration of the women in Herrick's novels. Only a limited number of them uphold the necessary Puritan virtues of moral support of one's husband and a devotion to the ideal of togetherness. . . . Chapter Three examines the Puritan emphasis on the importance of the will in overcoming the sensual appetites and the vitiating influences inherent in a commercial society. . . . The final chapter is an analysis of Herrick's attempts to point the way to salvation."

1977-35   Weisman, Richard Mark. "Witchcraft in Seventeenth-Century Massachusetts: The Construction of a Category of Deviance." Ph.D., Univ. of California at Berkeley. iv, 432 leaves.

Abstract in DAI, vol. 39 (2), sec. A, p. 1150: "This dissertation demonstrates how witchcraft was produced as a category of deviance in 17th century Massachusetts Bay. Specifically, it makes explicit the unacknowledged social processes in terms of which believers participated in the definition, imputation, and legitimation of imputations of witchcraft. . . . In the first part of the investigation, it is pointed out that European witchcraft incorporated two different belief systems consisting . . . of a secular emphasis upon witchcraft as malefic magic and . . . of a theological stress upon witchcraft as primarily an alliance with Satan. . . . In chapter 2, it is noted that these popular and theological definitions were . . . mutually inhibiting in England and New England. . . . In chapters 3-5, the interrelationship between these two definitions is explored further in the context of Massachusetts Bay. . . . In chapters 6 through 10, two periods of legal action are distinguished in terms of the interactional relationships entailed in the production witches [sic]. . . . A comprehensive appendix includes all legal actions against witchcraft in Massachusetts Bay."

1978-1   Brachlow, Stephen.   "Puritan Theology and Radical Churchmen
         in Pre-Revolutionary England: with Special Reference to Henry
         Jacob and John Robinson."   D.Phil., Univ. of Oxford (U.K.).
         v, 367 leaves.

"Abstract" (at beginning of diss.): "The thesis examines the
churchmanship of radical puritans and separatists during the
Elizabethan and Jacobean era. The study maintains that while radical
puritans and separatists were often locked in heated controversies
with one another, they nevertheless shared a similar approach to and
understanding of the nature and structure of the church. . . . While
ecclesiastically Robinson and Jacob found themselves ultimately on
opposing sides of the puritan/separatist divide, any significant
ecclesiological difference between the two is imperceptible. In this
way, their writings form a microcosm of the ecclesiological
compatibility of pre-revolutionary radical puritans and separatists"
(n.p.).   Contents: "Introduction," I. "Elizabethan Radical
Puritans," II. "Jacobean Radical Puritans," III. "English Separatism
and Anabaptism," IV. "Henry Jacob," V. "John Robinson," and
"Conclusion." Each chapter includes sections entitled "Ecclesiology
and Soteriology," "History and the Future," "Church Membership and
Saving Faith," "Government of the Gathered Church: Democracy and
Aristocracy," "Autonomy and Uniformity," and "Church and Moderate."

1978-2   Chu, Jonathan Moseley.   "Madmen and Friends: Quakers and the
         Puritan Adjustment to Religious Heterodoxy in Massachusetts Bay
         during the Seventeenth Century."   Ph.D., Univ. of Washington.   v,
         233 leaves.

Abstract in DAI, vol. 39 (6), sec. A, p. 3769: "By examining the
experience of Quakers in Massachusetts during the second half of the
seventeenth century, this study draws together three aspects of
colonial American history: the specific details of the development of
religious toleration, the maintenance of public order by the courts of
Massachusetts Bay and the relations between central and local
government. Quakerism in the Bay Colony provides a particularly
useful means of examining these issues not only because of its obvious
challenge to religious orthodoxy, but also because the Puritans
believed that the sect was inimical to order in general and because
Puritan authorities had to depend upon a dispersed, localized
mechanism of suppression. . . . Ultimately, the adjustments that
Puritans made to Quakerism in the last half of the seventeenth century
suggest that the Puritan impulse was tempered by a larger concern for
social cohesion and political accommodation."

1978-3   Coughtry, Jay Alan.   "The Notorious Triangle: Rhode Island
         and the African Slave Trade, 1700-1807."   Ph.D., Univ. of
         Wisconsin at Madison. 2 vols. (iii, 684 leaves).

Abstract in DAI, vol. 40 (5), sec. A, p. 2835. Revision
published under same title: Philadelphia : Temple Univ. Press, 1981.
-- xiii, 361 leaves. "Acknowledgments" (1981 ed.): "If it cannot be
determined that Rhode Island had a significant, sustained slave
commerce, the debate over the existence of a serious American slave

trade is permanently closed. I present that case herein, arguing that, with one exception (the question of the total American vessels in the trade), the Rhode Island slave trade and the American slave trade are virtually synonymous" (p. xi). Contents: "Introduction: The Rhode Island Slave Trade in Local, National, and International Perspective," 1. "The Rhode Island Slave Trade: An Accounting," 2. "Little Brigs, Brave Tars, and Fiery Rum: Pre-Voyage Planning and Preparations," 3. "Elmina, Accra, and Anomabu: Rhode Island Slavers on the African Coast," 4. "The Middle Passage," 5. "The West Indian Connection: Marketing Slaves in the New World," and "Epilogue." Chapter 6 deals with events of a later period.

1978-4   Creelan, Paul G. "Puritanism and the Rise of American Psychology." Ph.D., Univ. of Chicago. ii, 231 leaves.

Abstract in DAI, vol. 39 (1), sec. A, p. 474: "This study attempts to show the influence of developments within the tradition of Puritan religion upon the emergence and particular directions of scientific psychology. . . . As the mainstream Puritan piety, ascetic Puritanism gave rise to modern secularism in two major ways. First, its negative rationalistic emphasis diminished the positive experience of transcendence and focused human effort upon the domination of material Nature. Secondly, this negative emphasis bred a reactive recovery of Nature through naturalistic rebellions and ultimately through the interest in science. The emergence of modern science is understood as both a reaction against and a contribution of the distanced, controlled attitude of the ascetic Puritan. . . . Three case studies show the relation between this ambivalent reaction to ascetic Puritanism on the part of G. Stanley Hall, John Broadus Watson and George Herbert Mead."

1978-5   Durr, Jimmie Carol Still. "Anne Bradstreet in the Tradition of English Women Writers." Ph.D., Univ. of Mississippi. iv, 244 leaves.

Abstract in DAI, vol. 39 (6), sec. A, p. 3577: "Anne Bradstreet . . . deserves . . . acclaim as the first English woman to create a work of enduring aesthetic value. Although thirty-one English ladies had published before The Tenth Muse appeared in 1650 and three more began publishing shortly afterward, none of them managed to surmount the particular difficulties facing women as writers. . . . The first chapter contains a history of the English woman before 1650. . . . Chapter two deals with the woman writer in the Middle Ages. . . . The third chapter consists of a study of the women who published during the early Renaissance, 1500-1600. . . . The fourth chapter is an analysis of the role women played in the literary history of the early seventeenth century. . . . The fifth chapter is a consideration of the English women writers contemporary with Anne Bradstreet: Anne Collins, Katherine Philips, and Margaret Cavendish. . . . The sixth chapter contains an evaluation of Anne Bradstreet as the first women of English letters. In her prose and poetry she successfully combined the traditional feminine role with the still revolutionary one of woman as writer."

1978-6   Graham, John Kendell. "'Independent' and 'Presbyterian': A
    Study of Religious and Political Language and the Politics of
    Words during the English Civil War, c. 1640-1646." Ph.D.,
    Washington Univ. 2 vols. (1081 leaves).

    Abstract in DAI, vol. 39 (8), sec. A, p. 5094: "The history of
the words Independent and Presbyterian is both a history of the
doctrines spoken about the form and content of the New Jerusalem that
was envisaged for England and a history of the speech acts by which
the various ecclesiastical models were promoted and opposed during the
Civil War. . . .   To describe and explain the ways both words
interacted with these two histories close attention has been given to
the language of disputation and to the conditions of multivalence,
ambiguity, and abusiveness that were noticed to attend the words used
and called to account for much of what happened to the subjects
debated."

1978-7   Hornstein, Jacqueline. "Literary History of New England
    Women Writers: 1600-1800." Ph.D., New York Univ. 2 vols. (4,
    iii, 615 leaves).

    Abstract in DAI, vol. 39 (12), sec. A, p. 7347:   "The
dissertation discusses how Puritanism, life in the American wilderness
and events in eighteenth-century Boston encouraged women to write
about their beliefs and emotions, and it shows the characteristics of
the literature that emerged from this unique encouragement. . . .
Chapter one illustrates the Puritan religious and social beliefs which
particularly encouraged women as writers. . . . Chapters two and three
discuss the poetry and prose by New England women from 1630 to 1770.
. . .   The fourth chapter contains biographical sketches and critical
analyses of the works of Anne Bradstreet . . . , Anne Hayden, Jane
Turell . . . , Mary Rowlandson . . . , Sarah Knight, Elizabeth White,
[and] Sarah Fiske. . . .   Chapter six reviews New England women's
literature from 1630 to 1800, and discusses a continuum of subjects
and themes into the nineteenth century."

1978-8   Hubbard, Claude.   "English and American Puritan
    Autobiographies in the Seventeenth Century." Ph.D., Univ. of
    Chicago. 291 leaves.

    Contents: I. "Preliminary Problems of Definition, Criticism, and
Classification," II. "Literary Problems of Representing Religious
Experience," III. "The Two Worlds of Spiritual Autobiography: Some
Approaches to the Problem,"   IV. "Backgrounds of Spiritual
Autobiography in Seventeenth-Century England," V. "Spiritual
Autobiography in Puritan New England," VI. "John Winthrop's 'Christian
Experience,'" VII. "Thomas Shepard's Autobiography," VIII. "Another
Dimension: Roger Clap, John Dane, Elizabeth White, Anne Bradstreet,
and Michael Wigglesworth," IX. "The Forging of a Puritan Myth:
Biographies of John Cotton," and X. "The Autobiographies of Increase
Mather."

1978-9   Jamieson, John Franklin. "Jonathan Edwards and the Renewal
    of the Stoddardean Controversy." Ph.D., Univ. of Chicago. ii,
    422 leaves.

    Chapter I: "When Jonathan Edwards was ordained and installed as
assistant to his aged grandfather Solomon Stoddard at Northampton in
1727, he not only assumed the major pastoral responsibility for the
largest congregation in western Massachusetts, but he also became co-
administrator of the system of church polity which had prevailed at
Northampton and throughout the Connecticut River valley for some
thirty years. This system was generally referred to as
'Stoddardeanism'; for even though Solomon Stoddard did not originate
the theory, he became its most systematic, persistent, and influential
proponent in New England. Edwards was familiar with Stoddard's views
from the start of his ministry at Northampton, and despite the
misgivings he entertained about 'lax' polity, he was able to conform
to the practice without controversy for the next two decades" (p. 1).
Relevant chapters: I. "The Stoddardean Heritage": "The Development
of Stoddardeanism," "The Stoddardean Controversy," "Major Texts," and
"Stoddardeanism in Perspective: A Continuing Legacy" and II.
"Jonathan Edwards' Change of Position with Regard to Stoddardeanism."

1978-10   Jeske, Jeffrey Michael. "The Origins and Development of the
    Puritan Idea of Nature." Ph.D., Kent State Univ. iii, 264
    leaves.

    Abstract in DAI, vol. 39 (9), sec. A, p. 5513: "This study
charts the . . . evolution of Puritan nature philosophy . . . ,
which culminates in the abandonment of traditional modes for the
deist-oriented new learning of the eighteenth century. . . . Rather
than being a minor provincial reflection of the English and
Continental theological controversies of the sixteenth and seventeenth
centuries, New England Puritanism represents an important stage of
intellectual history, particularly with regard to nature philosophy."
Contents: "Introduction," I. "The Beginnings of Two Traditions," II.
"From Origen to Augustine: The Triumph of Mystico-Sacramentalism,"
III. "Thomas Aquinas: The Consolidation of Philosophical This-
Worldliness," IV. "The Continuation of the Two Traditions," V.
"Puritan Images of Nature," VI. "The Advent of Mechanism."

1978-11   Kempainen, Michael David. "The Salem Witch Trials and the
    Occult." Th.D., Dallas Theological Seminary. 229 leaves.

    "Abstract" (at beginning of diss.): "The aim of this study is to
present an acceptable case for the understanding of demon involvement
in the Salem witch trials of 1692. It is not the intention of this
study to support the original conception at Salem that witchcraft per
se was the cause of the afflictions of the young girls involved. It
is not the intention of this study, either, to support any of the more
modern rationalistic explanations for Salem 'witchcraft' that rule out
the supernatural completely. A reasonable case is made for
understanding the cause of the Salem outbreak to be that of demon
possession--not on the part of the accused, but on the part of the
accusers, the 'afflicted children' of Salem." Contents: I.

"Introduction"; II. "The Actual Happenings at Salem"; III. "The Interpretations of Salem by Historians": "Psychological Explanations," "Sociological Explanations," "Theological Explanations," and "Medical Explanations"; IV. "Occult Involvement at Salem": "The Reality of Demon Possession," "Examples of Demon Possession Contemporary with Salem," "Contact of the Salem Girls with the Occult," and "The Actions of the Instigators"; and V. "Conclusion."

1978-12   Lake, Peter Geoffrey. "Laurence Chaderton and the Cambridge
    Moderate Puritan Tradition, 1570-1604." Ph.D., Univ. of
    Cambridge (U.K.). 332 leaves.

Revison published as Moderate Puritans and the Elizabethan Church. -- Cambridge, England : Cambridge Univ. Press, 1982. -- viii, 357 p. "Preface" (1982 ed.): "When conformists sought to make continuance in the ministry conditioned on acceptance of what puritans took to be the corrupt elements in the structure of the English church, puritan ministers were forced to confront a choice between their puritan principles, the public, polemical commitments that their vision of the true religion had led them to make, and their practical capacity to pursue those same edificational, evangelical aims as ministers of the word. . . . This study seeks to examine how a certain group of divines sought to negotiate that choice and still retain both their self-image as 'puritans', . . . and the active role within the established church. These men, in fact, hoped to have the best of both worlds. The present study is intended to demonstrate the extent to which they succeeded in achieving that aim and the practical and ideological means they used to achieve it" (pp. 3-4). Contents: 1. "Introduction: Laurence Chaderton and the problem of puritans," 2. "Moderate beginnings: the case of Edward Dering," 3. "Chaderton's puritanism," 4. "The moderate puritan divine as anti-papal polemicist," 5. "Thomas Cartwright: the search for the centre and the threat of separation," 6. "William Whitaker's position as refracted through his anti-papal polemic," 7. "Theory into practice: puritan practical divinity in the 1580s and 1590s," 8. "William Whitaker at St. John's: the puritan scholar as administrator," 9. "The theological disputes of the 1590s" (includes Peter Baro), 10. "Conformity: Chaderton's response to the Hampton Court Conference," 11. "William Bradshaw: moderation in extremity," and 12. "Conclusion."

1978-13   Lee, Charles Richard. "'This Poor People': Poverty,
    Relief, and Correction in Massachusetts, 1620-1715." Ph.D.,
    State Univ. of New York at Buffalo. viii, 314 leaves.

Abstract in DAI, vol. 39 (3), sec. A, p. 1785: "Attitudes about the public responses to poverty in seventeenth-century New England were shaped by English precedents, the founders' social ideals, and actual conditions in the New World. From 1619 through 1630 the business of promoting colonization, organizing emigration, and establishing planned communities in New England was managed by men who believed that English society could be redeemed in the wilderness. . . . [This] redemptive vision imposed rigorous demands upon Plymouth,

Salem, and the cluster of Bay Colony towns established in 1630. From 1630 to 1660 colony and town officials repeatedly tried to make these fledgling settlements conform to their ideal. By screening inhabitants, regulating economic pursuits, caring for the orderly poor, and correcting the disorderly poor, officials believed the basis of a truly communitarian society could be established. . . . From 1675-1715 many Massachusetts towns were forced to adapt their relief and correction mechanisms to social, economic, and political change. . . . Instead of serving the interests of a particular kind of social order, the response to poverty devised by provincial Massachusetts served social order."

1978-14   Lewis, Thomas Reed, Jr.   "From Suffield to Saybrook: An Historical Geography of the Connecticut River Valley in Connecticut before 1800." Ph.D., Rutgers Univ. xi, 225 leaves.

Abstract in DAI, vol. 39 (7), sec. A, p. 4497: "This study in cultural historical geography deals with the impact of people on the landscape of the Connecticut River Valley before 1800. . . . Low open land including Indian old fields and a river with few rapids and no waterfalls attracted settlement. . . . By 1640 settlement nuclei had been established at Hartford, Windsor, and Wethersfield and at Saybrook. After 1640 settlement diffused from the earliest river towns to the last of the river meadows and terraces, and to land in eastern and western Connecticut. . . . The towns established in the Connecticut River Valley were large. . . . Mid-eighteenth-century farming practices were far different from the forest grazing of cattle and hogs which typified agriculture during the valley's frontier phase. . . . The predominantly English Protestant colonial settlers in the Connecticut valley built four basic house types. . . . Numerous structures dominated the cultural landscape." Cf. Lewis's Near the Long Tidal River: Readings in the Historical Geography of Central Connecticut. -- Washington, D.C. : Univ. Press of America, 1981. -- viii, 147 p.; which "includes excerpts from my doctoral dissertation" (p. vii).

1978-15   MacDonald, Ruth K.   "Literature for Children in England, 1659-1774." Ph.D., Rutgers Univ. v, 162 leaves.

Abstract in DAI, vol. 38 (11), sec. A, p. 6744. Revision published as Literature for Children in England and America from 1646 to 1774. -- Troy, N.Y. : Whitston Publishing Co., 1982. -- vii, 204 p. "Preface" (1982 ed.): "In most histories of children's literature, the late seventeenth and eighteenth centuries receive little notice. . . . This survey intends to fill that void in the history of children's literature in England and America. . . . Literature for children from 1646 to 1774 is particularly valuable for investigation because it is the basis for the literature which follows in later centuries, and because there are so many 'firsts' during this period. The opening date marks the publication of John Cotton's Milk for Babes, the first work for children in the American colonies" (p. v). Relevant chapters: I. "Introduction," II. "Religious Works," III. "Schools and Schoolbooks," IV. "Works of Good Advice," V. "Fables by Aesop and Others," and VI. "Fairy Tales, Nursery Rhymes, and Arabian

Nights." Chapter VII treats of events after 1730.

1978-16   Marquit, Doris Grieser. "Thomas Shepard: The Formation of
           a Puritan Identity." Ph.D., Univ. of Minnesota. iii, 368
           leaves.

     Abstract in DAI, vol. 39 (2), sec. A, p. 887: "This dissertation
is a study of the early cultural life, the works, and the reputation
of Thomas Shepard (1605-1649). Of all the Englishmen who came on the
errand into the wilderness in the second quarter of the seventeenth
century, none is a more representative leader. A product of Emmanuel
College at Cambridge University, the holder of a town lectureship in
Essex, and 'silenced minister' after a confrontation with [Archbishop
William] Laud, he was driven underground for a time before he took the
Lord's 'door of escape' to New England. There he became minister in
Cambridge, Massachusetts. He soon established a wide reputation as a
speaker and thinker, and remained a prominent leader of the society
until his death, witnessing little of the 'decline' of the New England
Way."

1978-17   Murphy, Susan. "In Remembrance of Me: Sacramental Theology
           and Practice in Colonial New England." Ph.D., Univ. of
           Washington. vii, 159 leaves.

     Abstract in DAI, vol. 39 (5), sec. A, p. 2942: "From one
principal doctrine, that of the covenant, hangs the whole system of
early New England theology. The idea of the covenant pervaded the New
England mind: It determined each man's relation to God, to the
church, and to the community. . . . In summary, New England reformed
sacramental theology followed a circular movement. From the
continental reformers who opposed medieval doctrine, through the
English Reformers who repudiated Anglicanism, to the belief and
practice that prevailed in seventeenth- and eighteenth-century New
England, one can trace a narrow line of development that finally went
back to its beginning."

1978-18   Nordbeck, Elizabeth Currier. "The New England Diaspora: A
           Study of the Religious Culture of Maine and New Hampshire, 1613-
           1763." Ph.D., Harvard Univ. xiii, 409 leaves.

     "Introduction": "This study is concerned with the religious
developments in northern New England during the 150 years that
intervened between the first French attempts to Christianize the
'barbarians' in Maine. During this time, slow but steady emigration
north from Massachusetts, and directly westward across the Atlantic
from Great Britain, created a characteristic religious climate in the
northernmost towns of New England. Initially this climate differed in
two significant respects from that of the Massachusetts Bay and
Connecticut colonies: it was marked by heterogeneity; and it was,
comparatively speaking, lukewarm" (p. i). Relevant chapters: I. "The
Early Settlement of New England," II. "The Massachusetts Takeover,
1633-1658," III. "The Massachusetts System, 1642-1680," IV. "Three
Decades of War, 1680-1713," V. "Expansion and Growth of the Churches,

1713-1741," VI. "Faith and Practice, 1700-1740," and VII. "Awakening, 1727-1748." Chapter VIII deals with a later period.

1978-19   Ogburn, Floyd, Jr.   "Style as Structure and Meaning: William Bradford's Of Plymouth Plantation." Ph.D., Univ. of Cincinnati. iv, 194 leaves.

Abstract in DAI, vol. 39 (9), sec. A, p. 5514. Revision published under same title: Washington, D.C. : Univ. Press of America, 1981. -- iii, 163 p. "Introduction" (1981 ed.): This "study argues that Bradford's history is tightly unified and structured in a unique manner. By combining a number of traditional literary and stylistic methods with two stylistic tools, foregrounding and collocation, I hope to present a new approach to the history--an approach that should prove helpful in my attempt to account for a unified and coherent structure" (p. 2). Contents: "Introduction," 1. "The Foregrounded Passages and the Intrasentence Description," 2. "The Intersentence Description of Stylistic Relationships," 3. "Collocation," 4. "A Discussion of Other Paragraphs," and "Conclusion."

1978-20   Osterhout, Paul Ragatz.   "Music in Northampton, Massachusetts, to 1820." Ph.D., Univ. of Michigan. vii, 398 leaves.

Abstract in DAI, vol. 39 (6), sec. A, p. 3215: Much "of the most significant musical activity in early New England took place in small towns and villages--interior settlements separated geographically, economically and culturally from Boston and the Atlantic seaboard. One such town was Northampton, Massachusetts, founded in 1654 on the Connecticut River. . . . In singling out Northampton for detailed study, I have attempted to put into sharper focus the history of early musical activity . . . in early New England. . . . In Part I, while a single chapter is devoted to secular musical activities--instruments, military music, singing, dancing and theater music--emphasis centers on sacred music in the Northampton area." Part II deals with the late eighteenth-century music publishing industry in Northampton.

1978-21   Pacy, Ronald William.   "Spiritual Combat: The Life and Personality of Hugh Peters, a Puritan Minister." Ph.D., State Univ. of New York at Buffalo. xi, 420 leaves.

Abstract in DAI, vol. 39 (3), sec. A, p. 1775: "This study brings into focus the emotional, irrational, human side of Puritanism. It examines Puritans caught in the shock waves of change, and records the fight of one man, Hugh Peters, who waged a war with his fellow Puritans against change. This biography looks at the behavior of men caught in the snare of their religiosity, to understand their motives, and to see how Puritanism worked its will upon its believers. In this context the biography centers on Peters' involvement in the development of religious imperialism--warfare Puritanism--which served as a means of resolving religious tensions and uncertainty and his search for religious meaning in a secularized world and on Peters' quest to create a new society that would establish religious certainty."

1978-22   Pencak, William Andrew. "Massachusetts Politics in War and Peace, 1676-1776." Ph.D., Columbia Univ. 478 leaves.

Abstract in DAI, vol. 39 (4), sec. A, p. 2489. Revision published as War, Politics, & Revolution in Provincial Massachusetts. -- Boston : Northeastern Univ. Press, 1981. -- xvi, 314 p. "Preface" (1981 ed.): "Massachusetts provincial politics consisted of the major issues debated by the General Court. These can be ascertained by reading the legislative journals and the correspondence of governors and other political notables. For the most part, Massachusetts' lawmakers argued over defense in wartime and constitutional and currency disputes in peacetime. . . . I examine how controversy started, and altered its nature over time. Chapter one advances the thesis that only the pressure of events and problems themselves can adequately account for political change in Massachusetts. . . . After laying this groundwork, I spend most of the book discussing the General Court's behavior" (p. xiii). Relevant chapters: I. "Introduction," II. "The End of Puritan Politics: 1676-1694," III. "Forging Provincial Unity: 1694-1713," and IV. "Paralysis: 1713-1730." The remaining chapters deal with later events.

1978-23   Schneiderman, Howard Gary. "The Antinomian Founding of Rhode Island and the Spirit of Factionalism." Ph.D., Univ. of Pennsylvania. iv, 221 leaves.

Abstract in DAI, vol. 39 (3), sec. A, p. 1878: "Rhode Island was founded by religious sectarians best characterized as antinomians, whose extreme individualism and distrust of all authority made colonial leadership difficult. From its beginning in 1636 the colony was torn by intense factional strife grounded in the antinomian and individualistic religious convictions of its founders. . . . Rhode Island was characterized by extremes in individualism, localism, sectarianism, factionalism, and plutocracy, as well as by a heterogeneous and centrifugal culture deeply imbued with antinomianism and producing anomic results. This dissertation is an attempt to explain Rhode Island's opposition to the Constitution in terms of the history of its centrifugal tendencies." Schneiderman treats in detail Roger Williams, founder of Providence; Anne Hutchinson, founder of Portsmouth and Newport; and Samuel Gorton, founder of Warwick.

1978-24   Stam, David Harry. "England's Calvin: A Study of the Publication of John Calvin's Works in Tudor England." Ph.D., Northwestern Univ. viii, 284 leaves.

Abstract in DAI, vol. 39 (8), sec. A, p. 5085: "Among the works of all the continental reformers, those of John Calvin were the most frequently translated into English during the Tudor period. . . . England's Calvin explores the history of the production of Calvin's works in England between 1548 and 1634, relating their appearances to political, religious, and social conditions of the late Tudor age.

. . . The central chapters contain a narrative description of the 126 editions of Calvin's works published in England during the later Tudor and early Stuart periods, analyzing the roles of translators and editors, printers and publishers, and the reciprocity of dedication to these works. . . . A concluding chapter discusses a number of issues related to Calvin's translators. . . . In sum, the study shows the propriety, the wide public, and the official esteem and sanction which Calvin's works enjoyed in Elizabethan England."

1978-25   Tomlinson, Caroline D. "The Search for God: Aspects of Mystical Insight in Some North American Poets." Ph.D., Univ. of Essex (U.K.). iv, 339 leaves.

"Preface": "It is the purpose of this dissertation . . . to show what mysticism is and how it falls into two categories, sacred and profane, and to examine the nature of each type as it manifests itself in the relatively narrow field of North American poetry. . . . The poetry of North America is significant in this context because the American society is founded on the austere precepts of a Puritan religion which originally informed every aspect of life in the same way as does that perception of Reality obtained by mystical insight. The Puritan approach with its heavy emphasis on an examination of the phenomenal aspects of existence is friendly to mystical perception in certain respects. This was originally part of the search for clues indicative of individual salvation and understanding of Reality, and although now largely transmuted into something more superficial, it has persisted in varying guises throughout the centuries" (p. ii). Relevant chapters: One. "The Origins of the Argument," Two. "Puritans and Transcendentalists" (Edward Taylor represents the Puritans), and Six. "Conclusions."

1978-26   Wagner, Hans-Peter. "Puritan Attitudes Towards Recreation in Seventeenth-Century New England. With Particular Consideration of Physical Recreation." Dr.phil., Univ. des Saarlandes (West Germany). 359 leaves.

Published under same title: Frankfurt am Main ; Bern : Verlag Peter Lang, 1982. -- 267 p. -- (Mainzer Studien zur Amerikanistik ; Bd. 17). "Introduction" (1982 ed.): "The colonies under survey will be primarily Massachusetts and Plymouth, with an occasional look at Connecticut and Rhode Island, while the historical period covered is the first one hundred years of New England's development. . . . [The word 'recreation'] was chosen in this study, since for the Puritan it meant intellectual and physical recreation as well as recreational activities which do not fit into either of these categories, such as games requiring no physical exercise (cards and board games), convivial gatherings, and some social events" (pp. 2-3). "New England Puritan life, seen from the recreational viewpoint, will be studied in the light of the Puritan ideas and ideals in order to ascertain how and to what degree everyday reality corresponded with or deviated from the Puritan theory. It will also be important to single out and--as far as possible--explain the causes of deviation, if deviation there was" (p. 4). Contents: "Introduction," I. "A Discussion of the Critical Literature on Puritan Recreation in Early New England," II.

"The Function of Recreation," III. "Puritan Theology and Recreation in New England," IV. "Recreation as an Issue in the Puritan Legislation," V. "The New England Puritan Leaders and the Issue of Recreation," VI. "The Attitude of the Average Church Members Towards Recreation," and "Conclusion."

1978-27   Wood, Joseph Sutherland. "The Origin of the New England Village." Ph.D., Pennsylvania State Univ. xii, 341 leaves.

Abstract in DAI, vol. 39 (8), sec. A, p. 5008: "The origin of the New England village lies deeply rooted in the material culture of New England. Most contemporary villages arose as commercial centers in the nineteenth century, not as colonial agricultural villages. Nevertheless, these commercial villages represent an elaboration of a persistent settlement pattern first set in the seventeenth century. . . . Unlike Europe, little land in New England could support the dense agricultural population of an agricultural village. Most New Englanders lived dispersed upon their farms from the 1630s onwards. Compact settlements of the period were largely coastal and commercial places. Only about twenty agricultural villages were found in New England, largely on the intervales of the Connecticut River Valley. . . . While farmers lived dispersed upon their farms in the colonial period, they still met regularly at a meetinghouse at town-center. . . . The geographical consequence of hiving was the creation across New England of a mosaic of uniformly sized towns and parishes, each with its own central meetinghouse."

1978-28   Young, Christine Alice.   "Peace as a River: Salem, Massachusetts, from 'Good Order' to Glorious Revolution, 1628-1689." Ph.D., Univ. of Pennsylvania. vi, 384 leaves.

Abstract in DAI, vol. 39 (10), sec. A, p. 6302. Revision published as From "Good Order" to Glorious Revolution: Salem, Massachusetts, 1628-1689. -- Ann Arbor, Mich. : UMI Research Press, 1980. -- 263 p. -- (Studies in American History and Culture ; no. 19). "Introduction" (1980 ed.): "At the risk of contributing to a further 'balkanization' of early American history, this study is proffered as an explicit attempt to explore the definition and principles of community in seventeenth-century New England through an analysis of the actual operations of the institutions of Massachusetts Bay's earliest town and the interactions of its inhabitants throughout the charter period. This exploration has been guided by Robert Redfield's contributions to the definition of community" (p. 6). Contents: One. "Introduction: Salem as a Social Unit," Two. "The Process of Accommodation: The Land to 1637," Three.   "The Limits of Accommodation: 1637-1650," Four. "The First Generation of Local Government," Five. "The Establishment of the Church," Six. "Beyond the Limits of Accommodation," Seven. "The Hegemony of the Merchants," Eight. "The Context of Leadership in Colonial Salem," Nine. "The Divisibility of Status in the Second Generation," Ten. "The Consequences of Dispersion and Differentiation, 1668-1684:   The Church," Eleven. "The Consequences of Dispersion and Differentiation, 1668-1684: The Town, " Twelve. "The Glorious Revolution: Salem in 1689." Appendices: A: "Occupations of Salem Heads of Household," B:

"Maps," and C: "Tables."

1979-1   Anderson, Philip James. "Presbyterianism and the Gathered
          Churches in Old and New England, 1640-1662: The Struggle for
          Church Government in Theory and Practice." D.Phil., Univ. of
          Oxford (U.K.). 6 ["Abstract"], vii, 324 leaves.

     "Abstract": "This thesis examines the issue of church government
as it pertained to Presbyterians and Independents during the Civil
Wars and Interregnum, as well as to New England from 1629 to the
Cambridge Synod and Platform of 1646-8. Special attention is given to
the aspects of power and authority in their respective polities, and
to the nature of their interchurch relations" (p. 1).   Contents:
"Introduction,"   1. "New Opportunities for Puritan Ecclesiology 1640-
1643"; 2. "New England Church Structures and Ministerial Authority
1630-1648":   "Transatlantic Scrutiny," "The New England Presbytery
Independent," "Consociation and Ministerial Organization," and "The
Cambridge Synod"; 3. "Presbyterian-Independent Debates and the Quest
for a Reformed National Church 1643-1646"; 4. "Ecclesiological
Experiments in Practice 1647-1654:   The Presbyterians"; 5.
"Ecclesiological Experiments in Practice 1640-1658:   The
Independents"; 6. "Accommodation, Variation, and Decline 1654-1662";
and "Conclusion."

1979-2   Barbour, Dennis Howard. "Edward Taylor's Treatment of
          Hexameral Themes in Gods Determinations." Ph.D., Auburn Univ.
          vi, 146 leaves.

     Abstract in DAI, vol. 40 (10), sec. A, p. 5441: "Edward Taylor's
Gods Determinations is a poem showing the influence of various
literary traditions and genres. ... The influence of the hexameral
literature, prose and poetic works on Genesis, has not been examined.
The purpose of the paper was to examine Taylor's treatment of
hexameral themes in Gods Determinations in order to determine what
part hexameral literature played in the poem. ... In writing Gods
Determinations during the 1680's, he treated the common themes of
hexameral literature: the Creation of the Earth, the temptation and
fall of Adam and Eve, and Satan's role in the fall of mankind. ...
Next, the doctrinal basis of the poem was studied, showing that Taylor
based his comments on hexameral themes on John Calvin's Institutes,
the basic interpretation of the Bible for Puritans. ...   Finally
Gods Determinations was compared to hexameral works by [Guillaume] Du
Bartas, [William] Alexander, [Thomas] Peyton, and Milton to determine
similarities and differences. ... He used hexameral themes to make
a statement of religious faith in the Calvinist system."

1979-3   Breitwieser, Mitchell Robert. "Plastic Economy: The Painful
          Birth of New Vision in the Writings of Cotton Mather and Walt
          Whitman." Ph.D., State Univ. of New York at Buffalo.   227
          leaves.

     Abstract in DAI, vol. 40 (9), sec. A, p. 5053: "There is a
certain plastic economy intrinsic to plants, Cotton Mather argued,

that enables them to preserve the species characteristic order of parts while simultaneously allowing the vegetable population to prosper in new and alien circumstances. His theory of plant growth is analogical to other transplantations which interested him, most notably the relocation of European culture to American soil. Walt Whitman--who admired 'feudal' exfoliations of British literature but concluded they were incommensurable with American experiences--also concerned himself with the problem of at once preserving and improving. The thesis of this dissertation is that a desire to provoke the originality of American letters despite felt risks is the central motive informing the writings of Cotton Mather and Walt Whitman."

1979-4   Butler, Charles James. "Religious Liberty and Covenant Theology." Ph.D., Temple Univ. vii, 324 leaves.

Abstract in DAI, vol. 40 (5), sec. A, p. 2574: "Because Reformed thought between 1530 and 1660 came to be dominated by Covenant Theology and because the theory of religious liberty developed during the same period, this dissertation proposes that the variations in the developing system of Covenant Theology produced a variety of positions on religious liberty. . . . To prove this thesis and to isolate the covenantal elements which led to intolerance, tolerance, or religious liberty, a historical framework was prepared for the development of 'Covenant Theology' and the general usage of each covenant suggested. Representative covenant systems were selected and analyzed. . . . In each of the thirteen covenant systems examined, the system did determine the position assumed on religious liberty. The key factor was the connection found for the Abrahamic Covenant of Grace. It it were connected to a National Religious Covenant, intolerance resulted; if to the covenant of a civil or religious subunit, tolerance appeared; if to the individual, religious liberty was asserted."

1979-5   Caldwell, Patricia Lee. "A Literary Study of Puritan Testimonies of Religious Experience from the 1630s to the 1660s, including a Critical Edition of Thomas Shepard's Manuscript, 'The Confessions of diverse propounded to be received & were entertayned as members,' from the First Church of Cambridge, Massachusetts, 1637-1645." Ph.D., Harvard Univ. iv, 554 leaves.

"Acknowledgments": "This study attempts to explore a body of materials that has not usually figured in considerations of our literary heritage: the testimonies of spiritual experience that Puritans delivered in the gathered churches of Old and New England between the 1630s and the Restoration, in order to qualify for church membership. Few of these 'relations' of religious conversion have survived, and on the American side there is only one large and significant body of so-called conversion narratives. This is a collection of fifty-one 'Confessions' given at the First Church of Cambridge, Massachusetts, between 1637 and 1645, and recorded in a small private notebook by the minister of the church, Thomas Shepard" (p. iii). Contents: "Introduction: Mrs. Elizabeth White and the Problem of Early American Literature"; Part I: 1. "Origins" and 2. "Controversy"; Part II: 3. "Disappointment," 4. "The Problem of

Expression," 5. "The American Morphology of Conversion," and 6. "The End." Appendices: 1. "The Confessions of Fifty-one Members of the First Church of Cambridge, Massachusetts, Delivered from 1637 to 1645 and Recorded by the Reverend Thomas Shepard" and 2. "Comparative Tables of the Use of the Bible in Conversion Narratives by the Shepard and Walker Congregations." Announced but not yet published as this bibliography was in preparation: Caldwell's The Puritan Conversion Narrative: The Beginnings of American Expression. -- Cambridge, England : Cambridge Univ. Press, [1983?]. -- (Cambridge Studies in American Literature and Culture).

1979-6   Cass, Edward Charles. "A Town Comes of Age: Pownalborough, Maine, 1720-1785." Ph.D., Univ. of Maine. vi, 230 leaves.

Abstract in DAI, vol. 40 (8), sec. A, p. 4713: "This study was designed to investigate the development of a Maine town during the eighteenth century. The goal was to determine the factors which influenced the growth of the town and its social, economic, and political systems. Town records, and private and public manuscript collections as well as published materials were examined with this end in view. A computer program, the Statistical Package for the Social Sciences . . . was utilized to correlate basic data on births, marriages, deaths, and economic status. . . . Pownalborough shared many characteristics with towns within the boundaries of Massachusetts proper."

1979-7   Churchill, Edwin Arnold. "Too Great the Challenge: The Birth and Death of Falmouth, Maine, 1624-1676." Ph.D., Univ. of Maine. vii, 463 leaves.

Abstract in DAI, vol. 40 (10), sec. A, p. 5557: "This study examines selected economic, political and social developmental aspects of Falmouth, Maine, from the founding of the first trading post in 1624 to the settlement's destruction by Indians in 1676. This particular frontier community was selected as a representative example of the small coastal plantation north of the Merrimack River. It was also the site of the only fishing station along the early American coast for which the business records are still extant. A major feature of the study is its comparison of actual conditions with commonly accepted views of northern New England frontier communities, i.e., as societies similar to those of eastern Massachusetts, or as rowdy camps of fishermen-fur traders."

1979-8   Eschenbrenner, Carl F. "The Role of the Minister in the Theology of Thomas Hooker." D.Min., Eden Theological Seminary. ii, 95 leaves.

"Introduction": "The center of the study deals with Hooker's preparationist theology, which was the heart of his practical ministry. This involved his theory of conversion, principally informed by his own conversion experience, and the process of redemption. His preaching career formed a systematic approach to this subject and those sermons collected and published, some posthumously, are the main source for the discussion in chapters three and four. . . . Because Hooker's theology was so intensely experimental and energized by his own experience, a brief biographical discussion is required to set the stage for the theological presentation. . . . It is the judgment of this writer that Thomas Hooker is one who was a principle [sic] formulator of civil and religious institutions in the New World" (pp. 2-3). Contents: I. "Introduction," II. "Historical Background," III. "Preparationist Theology," IV. "Pastoral Theology," V. "Direction for Contemporary Ministry," and VI. "Conclusion."

1979-9   Ferguson, Sinclair Buchanan. "The Doctrine of the Christian Life in the Teaching of Dr. John Owen (1616-83), Chaplain to Oliver Cromwell and sometime Vice-Chancellor of the University of Oxford." Ph.D., Univ. of Aberdeen (U.K.). vi, 530 leaves.

"Summary": "This study arose out of an obvious hiatus in the history of the development of reformed theology. Studies of the doctrine of the Christian life in Calvin's thought have already been made. But no such study seems to have existed of a major English Puritan's view of this extensive area of dogmatic and pastoral theology" (p. 5). Contents: "Introduction and Summary," I. "John Owen and His Christian Life," II. "The Plan of Salvation," III. "The Inauguration of the Reign of Grace," IV. "Fellowship of God," V. "Conflict in Sin," VI. "Fellowship with the Saints--The Church," VII. "The Ordinances of Grace" (i.e., scripture, sacraments, prayer, ministry), VIII. "Persevering to the End," and IX. "Conclusions." Appendix: "The Sermons of Owen in Manuscript."

1979-10   Fithian, Rosemary. "The Influence of the Psalm Tradition on the Meditative Poetry of Edward Taylor." Ph.D., Kent State Univ. v, 285 leaves.

Abstract in DAI, vol. 40 (8), sec. A, p. 4594: "Several traditions inform Edward Taylor's verse. Some critics have connected his poems with the major devotional and literary movements of the sixteenth and seventeenth centuries. Yet of these traditions, only the Book of Psalms combines religion and poetry, and also informs the meditative, baroque, metaphysical, biblical, and typological traditions all identified as influential on Taylor's Preparatory Meditations. . . . By defining the psalmic influences on his work, particularly in the light of the New England psalm tradition, one may regard Taylor as consciously attempting to become the 'new David,' offering up his own Psalms in the American wilderness."

1979-11   Folbre, Nancy Russell. "Patriarchy and Capitalism in New England, 1620-1900." Ph.D., Univ. of Massachusetts. xi, 207 leaves.

Abstract in DAI, vol. 40 (3), sec. A, p. 1621: "In this thesis I present a theoretical analysis of the relationship between capitalism and patriarchy that serves as a foundation for an historical study of the transition to capitalism in New England before 1900. The arguments presented here can be summarized in four propositions: 1)

Relations of exploitation are a subset of a larger category of relations of political control, or domination. 2) Patriarchal control over private means of production intensifies the motives and the means for control over children and is associated with an intensification of relations of domination governing childbearing and childrearing. 3) The growth of capitalism leads to a weakening of patriarchal control over children and a decrease in desired family size. It sets in motion a process of ideological change and political struggle which gradually diminishes the force of some forms of patriarchal control over women. 4) A number of aspects of the process of capital accumulation are significantly affected by the interaction between patriarchal and capitalist relations of domination."

1979-12   Galenson, David Walter. "The Indenture System and the Colonial Labor Market: An Economic History of White Servitude in British America." Ph.D., Harvard Univ. xx, 458 leaves.

Revision published as White Servitude in Colonial America: An Economic Analysis. -- Cambridge, England : Cambridge Univ. Press, 1981. -- xii, 291 p. "Preface" (1981 ed.): "White servitude was one of the major institutions in the economy and society of colonial British America. Indentured English men and women constituted the principal labor supply of many of the early British settlements in the New World, and their successors continued to make up an important part of the white immigration to the British colonies in America throughout the seventeenth and eighteenth centuries.... This book provides a description of the evolution of the economic functions of white servitude in colonial America based on an example of detailed evidence about the population of bound immigrants, and analyzes the sources of this process through the use of an explanatory framework designed to provide an understanding of the determinants of the major changes that occurred over time in the composition of the colonial labor forces" (p. ix). Contents: Part I. "Introduction": 1. "The significance and origins of the colonial indenture system"; Part II. "Characteristics of the servant population": 2. "The age and sex distributions of the indentured servants," 3. "The occupations of the indentured servants in the seventeenth century," 4. "Occupations in the eighteenth century," and 5. "Literacy and the occupations of the indentured servants"; Part III. "Migration and the transatlantic market for indentured servants": 6. "Patterns of servant migration from England to America" and 7. "The market for indentured servants"; Part IV. "White servitude in the colonial labor market": 8. "The role of the indenture system in the colonial labor market" and 9. "The indenture system and the colonial labor market: an overview"; and Part V. "Indentured servitude in American history." Includes nine appendices. Diss. won the David A. Wells Prize for 1979-80, awarded by the Department of Economics of Harvard Univ.

1979-13   George, Timothy Francis. "The Role of John Robinson in the English Separatist Tradition." D.D., Harvard Univ. viii, 427 leaves.

Revision published as John Robinson and the English Separatist Tradition. -- Macon, Ga. : Mercer Univ. Press, 1982. -- ix, 263 p. --

(National Assn. of Baptist Professors of Religion, Dissertation Ser. ;
1). "Preface" (1982 ed.): "The purpose of this study is to examine
in the writings of Robinson that interpretation of the gospel and
doctrine of the Church which characterized the early Separatist
existence. The underlying thesis is that the Separatist phenomenon
was not merely the most radicalized form of Puritan protest against
the Church of England, but also a distinctive quest for a new sense of
Christian community at odds on crucial points with both Anglican and
Puritan models. This is not to deny that Separatists were also
Puritans in the larger sense, nor that there were wide areas of
agreement--and, in the case of Robinson, even a measure of Christian
fellowship between the Separatists and their brethren who remained
loyal to . . . the national Church" (pp. vii-viii). Contents: I.
"Introduction: The Struggle for the Separatist Past," II. "The
English Separatist Tradition," III. "John Robinson, 1575-1625," IV.
"The Justification of Separation," V. "The Mystery of Election," VI.
"Conclusion: Yet More Light and Truth." Appendix: Robinson's
"Admonitio I.R. Ad Lectorem S V O Suorumque Nomine" (1616).

1979-14   Goodwin, Everett Carlton. "The Magistracy Recovered: The
     Development of a Specific, Independent Process of Adjudication in
     Connecticut, 1636-1818." Ph.D., Brown Univ. iv, 244 leaves.

     Abstract in DAI, vol. 40 (11), sec. A, p. 5976. Revision
published as The Magistracy Rediscovered: Connecticut, 1636-1818. --
Ann Arbor, Mich. : UMI Research Press, 1981. -- viii, 181 p. --
(Studies in American History and Culture ; no. 24). "Preface" (1981
ed.): "It is the purpose of this work to demonstrate . . . [a]
revolution in the law of Connecticut. A process of change occurred
that was far-reaching in its implications, for it involved the
transfer of authority for the law's interpretation and articulated a
separation of powers involved in the activity of legal application.
Specifically, Connecticut began its corporate life with a single,
undifferentiated, governing body in which all authority and power was
vested. That body, the General Court, perceived its major task to be
legal adjudication. . . . By 1818, however, that single unity of
legal authority no longer existed. Legislation had been defined as
separate from adjudication, and adjudication had been delegated to
specific courts" (pp. vii-viii). Relevant chapters: "Introduction";
1. "The Puritan Purpose in Law": "Covenant," "Discipline," and
"Magistrates"; 2. "Toward a Concept of Court": "Developing the
Particular Function of Adjudication," "The Adjudication of County and
Superior Courts," and "The Adjudication of the General Court"; and 3.
"The Refinement of the Basic Concept of Court": "The Legal
Profession" and "Managing the Process of Appeal." The remaining
chapters treat of later events.

1979-15   Hammond, Jeffrey Alan. "Songs from the Garden: Edward Taylor
     and the Canticles." Ph.D., Kent State Univ. iv, 352 leaves.

     Abstract in DAI, vol. 40 (8), sec. A, 4595: "Edward Taylor based
more of his Preparatory Meditations on the Canticles, or Song of
Songs, than on any other scriptural text. The lush imagery of the
Song permeates his work, from the sermons and early poetry to the

final Meditations. On a literal level, the Song consists of a series of love lyrics celebrating the marriage of Solomon to the beautiful Shulamite. Taylor, however, shared in an exegetical tradition in which the text was read as an allegory of the spiritual love and union between Christ and the individual believer or the Church as a whole. The purpose of this study is to investigate Taylor's use of the exegetical tradition and to demonstrate the special appropriateness of the Canticles to his thematic and artistic concerns."

1979-16   Holley, Larry Jackson. "The Divines of the Westminster Assembly: A Study of Puritanism and Parliament." Ph.D., Yale Univ. 387 leaves.

Abstract in DAI, vol. 40 (6), sec. A, 3462: "This study examines three distinct yet intricately connected phenomena: the Long Parliament's options and actions on Church reform from November 1640 to July 1643; the constituting and convening of the Westminster Assembly; and the lives and careers of the Divines themselves up to July 1643. By exploring the reciprocal influences of these phenomena upon one another, we achieve a more balanced picture of both Puritanism and Parliament. . . . A set of eighteen appendices gives a statistical breakdown of the Divines' livings, academic credentials, ages, proximity to London and parliamentary boroughs, lectureships, and capacities in which they served. Appendix XIX is a bibliography of the Divines' writings. . . . Appendix XX contains a biographical dictionary of the clergymen whom the Long Parliament nominated to their Assembly of Divines prior to 1 July 1643."

1979-17   Kantrow, Alan Mitchell. "Jacob's Ladder: Anglican Traditionalism in the New England Mind." Ph.D., Harvard Univ. vi, 288 leaves.

"Preface": "In its simplest form, the central line of argument can be summarized thusly: the ecclesiastical contention over the proper form of worship, the proper nature of the ministerial office, and the proper mode of clerical ordination reveals a profound disparity between Anglican and Puritan casts of mind--a disparity best spoken of as a fundamental disagreement over the effective locus of intellectual authority in 18th century New England. Puritans treated appeal to the existential experience of religion as determinant. For Anglicans, the locus of authority consisted not in experience so construed, but in tradition--in the legitimating power of dense, continuous, historically sequential, and cumulative practice and precedent" (p. iv). Relevant chapters: I. "The Sin of Jeroboam: Fathers and Sons--The Traditions of Men--The Customary Mind," II. "The Sin of Korah: The Sources of Ministerial Legitimacy--Historical Knowledge, Historical Knowing--Ministerial Ordination--The Power of the Laity," and III. "Turtles All the Way Down: The Covenant and the Problem of Continuity--The Doctrine of Succession--A Succession of Their Own--Sensible Evidence--Visible Saints and Living Stones--The Premises of Order." The final chapter is not relevant.

1979-18   Lind, Mary Jane.   "They Summoned Death to Challenge Dread:
    The Function of Parable in the Poetry of Herman Melville, Emily
    Dickinson and Their Puritan Antecedents." Ph.D., Univ. of
    Washington. ii, 307 leaves.

Abstract in DAI, vol. 40 (2), sec. A, p. 853: "Both Herman
Melville in his verse narrative Clarel: A Poem and Pilgrimage in the
Holy Land and Emily Dickinson in numerous lyrics manifest an obsession
with death. Viewed in reference to the puritan inheritance both poets
honor and criticize, this reaction clearly prompts their use of
parable.   In this dissertation I explore the manner in which Melville
and Dickinson use the parabolic mode of religious language as a bridge
toward transcendence within anxiety. . . .   According to biblical
scholarship, reviewed in Chapter I, the narrative parable is an
extended metaphor . . . whose enigmatic application provokes thought.
. . . Chapter II, 'Puritanism and the Parable,' holds that parable
solicits a choice which expresses ultimate 'Being' or spiritual
identity. . . .   For the Puritan, parable become an exercise in
knowing death, a decision to comprehend the spiritual implications of
mortality. . . .   Chapter II treats sermons on 'The Ten Virgins' by
Thomas Shepard and Benjamin Colman and Michael Wigglesworth's The Day
of Doom--all of which confirm the specific appeal of the parable to
the Puritan. The poet Edward Taylor is viewed as an original
parabolist. . . .   Chapter III analyzes the parabolic character of
Herman Melville's Clarel. . . .   Chapter IV examines [Dickinson's] use
of 'counterfeit' morals."

1979-19   Nellis, Eric Guest. "Communities of Workers: Free Labor in
    Provincial Massachusetts." Ph.D., Univ. of British Columbia
    (Canada). ix, 319 leaves.

Abstract in DAI, vol. 40 (4), sec. A, p. 2229:   "The particular
forms of work in provincial Massachusetts influenced and were
reflected in the structure of that society to an extent previously
ignored by social historians. While this study presents a description
of individual practices and collective patterns of work it addresses
itself to the broader framework of provincial society. As the
analysis proceeds, it tests the conclusions of a large number of
recent historians who have found significant changes in the social
structure of Massachusetts in the decades prior to 1765. . . .
[Recent] theories of social change in pre-Revolutionary Massachusetts
drawn from concepts of crowding, stratification and conflict, must be
reconsidered or modified in light of the stability and durability of
communal society as revealed in the conditions and aims of provincial
labor."

1979-20   Olive, Barbara Ann. "The Eighteenth-Century Family and
    Puritan Domestic Literature: A Study of the Origin and
    Development of Fictional Domestic Themes." Ph.D., Southern
    Illinois Univ. at Carbondale. v, 305 leaves.

Abstract in DAI, vol. 40 (8), sec. A, p. 4610:   "Puritan
domestic conduct manuals, one genre of the mass of Puritan literature
that inundated sixteenth- and seventeenth-century England, had

established a definable form and content by the early seventeenth century that served as a model for domestic instruction until the latter part of the eighteenth century. These manuals prescribed the reciprocal duties in the major familial relationships between husband and wife, parent and child, and master and servant. They also contained other familiar concepts, such as the close connections among the various domestic duties and reward and punishment attached to their performance." The diss. traces the influence of these manuals on the early English novel.

1979-21   Ranson, Leonard Buckland. "The Vocational Basis for the Founding of Harvard College: An Alternative to Samuel Morison and Winthrop Hudson." Ph.D., Univ. of Iowa. v, 170 leaves.

Abstract in DAI, vol. 40 (5), sec. A, p. 2515:   "In this dissertation the writer analyzes two major theories concerning the purpose for the founding and early development of Harvard College. These two positions held by Samuel Morison and Winthrop Hudson identify the reason for Harvard's founding to have been either for the 'liberal' education of Massachusetts Bay colonists, Morison; or for the preparation of young men for the Christian ministry, Hudson. The problem discussed in the dissertation was the possibility of an alternative reason for the establishment of [Harvard]. . . . The writer concludes that Harvard College was founded as a result of the vocational commitment of the Massachusetts Bay colonists and was intended to prepare young men to fulfill their calling in the service of God and the Colony. This conclusion provides a motive for Samuel Morison's hypothesis that the College was founded to 'liberally' educate young men . . . and broadens Winthrop Hudson's thesis that the College was founded solely for the preparation of young men for the ministry."

1979-22   Ralph, Rebecca Seward. "Emmanuel College, Cambridge, and the Puritan Movements of Old and New England." Ph.D., Univ. of Southern California. iv, 394 leaves.

Abstract in DAI, vol. 40 (4), sec. A, p. 2202:   Emmanuel College's "most obvious contribution to Puritanism lay in the number and calibre of its graduates. . . . Emmanuel sent more emigrants to New England than did any other college, including John Harvard, lawgiver Nathaniel Ward, Governor Simon Bradstreet, preachers John Cotton of Boston, Thomas Shepard of Cambridge, and Thomas Hooker, founder of Hartford, as well as schoolteacher Ezechiel [sic] Cheever. Harvard was founded on the assumption that 'New England must have a new Emmanuel.'" The work of the college's first two Masters, Laurence Chaderton and John Preston, is discussed.

1979-23   Temkin-Greener, Helena. "Fertility Transition and Patterns of Family Formation: Connecticut River Valley Communities during the Eighteenth and Nineteenth Centuries." Ph.D., Univ. of Massachusetts. xviii, 293 leaves.

Abstract in DAI, vol. 40 (3), sec. A, p. 1577:   "The focus of this research is upon demographic change, particularly fertility transition in predominantly rural communities of the Connecticut River Valley during the eighteenth and nineteenth centuries. Demographic change is examined both as a potential response to social and economic conditions and as a variable capable of creating conditions to which various alternative strategies, including demographic ones, are possible responses. The purpose of this study is to determine the causes of fertility behavior under the assumption that human behavior is ... an adaptive response necessitated by the changing forces in the total milieu. ... This study documents the emergence of early family limitation practices in an agricultural community."

1979-24   Tomas, Martha Mary. "The Concept of Christian Liberty in the Christographia of Edward Taylor." Ph.D., St. Louis Univ. 185 leaves.

Abstract in DAI, vol. 40 (11), sec. A, p. 5868:   "The study begins by tracing the concept of liberty as the English Puritan understood it and by pointing out the historical, political, social and educational influences in Taylor's search for authentic Christianity that led to apparent nonconformism. Through an analysis of the Christographia sermons . . . this study highlights Taylor's Christocentric theology while it traces the legacy of Christian liberty in Taylor's Puritan heritage, through Augustine and its roots in Scripture and the person of Jesus Christ. The study further reveals that the Christographia . . . is a portrait of Taylor's Christ as both free and liberating."

1979-25   Tucker, Edward Bruce. "The Founders Remembered: The Anglicization of the Puritan Tradition in New England." Ph.D., Brown Univ. viii, 234 leaves.

Abstract in DAI, vol. 40 (11), sec. A, p. 5983:   "Historians have traditionally described the provincial period of New England history as a time of religious decline. This study, however, presents evidence of a vibrant and innovative religious culture which profoundly altered the shape of religious life in eighteenth-century New England. Because New England assumed a more dependent relationship with England after 1689, ministers had to create a new sense of cultural identification. They could not simply jettison their Puritan heritage for the genteel tones of English rationalism. Between 1700 and 1740 they experimented with the ideas of the English physio-theologians and with Lockean epistemology. They assimilated English conceptions of political and religious authority which developed in the wake of the Glorious Revolution as part of their task to legitimize the new shape and direction of provincial society. Although they did not compromise the essential doctrines of Calvinist theology, they transformed their intellectual heritage from a revolutionary one to one of accommodation."

1979-26   Tyree, Wade. "Puritan in the Drawing-Room: The Puritan Aspects of Edith Wharton and Her Novels." Ph.D., Princeton Univ. iii, 318 leaves.

Abstract in <u>DAI</u>, vol. 40 (7), sec. A, p. 4047:   "While Edith Wharton is widely regarded as the chronicler of New York aristocracy and its <u>nouveaux riches</u> successors, there is a significant strain of Puritanism in her works, her background, and the woman herself.   Her novels are concerned with the struggle of man for his soul and depict the decline of Puritanism in American society.   Thus to deem Wharton merely a novelist of manners is to miss the deeply moral basis of her work.   This dissertation explores the evidence of Puritanism in the author and a selection of her works."

1979-27   Van Hof, Charles Lee. "The Theory of Sermon Rhetoric in Puritan New England: Its Origins and Expression." Ph.D., Loyola Univ. of Chicago. v, 495 leaves.

Abstract in <u>DAI</u>, vol. 40 (6), sec. A, p. 3304:   "The theory of sermon rhetoric of the first generation of New England preachers was based on a tradition of preaching rhetoric that extends far beyond the rhetoric of English Puritan plain style, the immediate source of New England sermon rhetoric. There was a genre of writing about sermon rhetoric in which New England preachers participated, and which helped to shape their rhetorical theory." Among those in the line of this tradition are Augustine, Wyclif, Luther, Calvin, William Tyndale, John Cotton, Thomas Hooker, and Thomas Shepard.

1979-28   Wall, Margaret Eleanor Rosson. "Puritanism in Education: An Analysis of the Transition from Religiosity to Secular Morality as Seen in Primary Reading Materials, 1620-1775."   Ph.D., Washington Univ. iv, 358 leaves.

Abstract in <u>DAI</u>, vol. 40 (7), sec. A, p. 3831:   Diss. "traces the changes in Puritan religious belief from a Theocracy to American secular morality as seen in various books to teach reading to primary children between 1620 and 1775. . . . A survey of social, political and educational events in England and New England provide a background for this analysis with the changes in the general society examined in relation to their effects upon children's reading materials. . . . The New England Primer and other primers, spellers, catechisms and religious materials known to have been used for primary reading instruction are examined."

1979-29   Watters, David Harper.   "'With Bodilie Eyes': Eschatological Themes in the Literature and Funerary Art of Early New England." Ph.D., Brown Univ. iv, 338 leaves.

Abstract in <u>DAI</u>, vol. 40 (11), sec. A, p. 5869.   Revision published as <u>"With Bodilie Eyes"</u>: <u>Eschatological Themes in Puritan Literature and Gravestone Art</u>. -- Ann Arbor, Mich. : UMI Research Press, 1981. -- xii, 255 p. -- (Studies in the Fine Arts: Iconography ; no. 3). "Introduction" (1981 ed.): "This study treats the aesthetics of New England Puritan literature and gravestone carving. In discussing Increase Mather's term, 'bodilie eyes,' I propose that Puritan literature and art were profoundly affected by the anticipation of the moment during the Resurrection when saintly humans would see, with human but glorified eyes, the beauties of Christ and the Millennium. The expectation of this apocalyptic moment sent ripples throughout the Puritan imagination, influencing thinking about literature and art at all levels of New England culture" (p. 1). Relevant chapters: "Introduction," 1. "Puritan Eschatology: The Evidence of Things Not Seen," 2. "Seeing is Believing: Puritan Strategies for Visualizing Divine Things," 3. "Increase Mather and the Prophecy of Perfection," 4. "The Prophetic Design of Early New England Carving," 5. "Edward Taylor and the Metaphors of Perfection," and 6. "Edward Taylor's 'Life Metaphoricall.'" Chapter 7 concerns the Great Awakening period.

1979-30   Willis, Mary Sue. "'United Essential Harmony': The Puritan Perception of Edward Taylor." Ph.D., Univ. of North Carolina at Greensboro. v, 255 leaves.

Abstract in DAI, vol. 40 (11), sec. A, p. 5869: "Contrary to much modern opinion, the American Puritans, in the words of Edward Taylor, expected their doctrine to yield 'United Essential Harmony.' This study is an attempt to find the harmony of which Taylor spoke in terms of some of his more prominent metaphors. An exploration into Taylor's figures appears appropriate, since he himself claimed the 'Metaphoricall' mode of Scripture as his own 'truth Speaking form.' The five chief figures to be examined here are called in this study the hygienic, the erotic, the organic, the domestic and the forensic. The first four can be found more definitely in Taylor's Preparatory Meditations and Taylor's occasional poetry, and the last in Taylor's long poem, Gods Determinations."

1980-1   Albers, Grover. "The Heart Divided, or John Cotton's Spatial Epistemology of the Knowledge of Christ." Ph.D., St. John's Univ. 3 ["Abstract"], xxxvii, 368 leaves.

"Preface": "The primary focus of this study is John Cotton's understanding of the epistemological problem of how a person knows God. This is a key religious problem for a Protestant. In addition, because of the nature of this religious knowledge, Protestants have difficulty justifying the existence of the Church. Cotton resolves this problem in brilliant fashion. Therefore, a secondary concern of the study is Cotton's concept of Church. Finally, as a result of the epistemological analysis, a basis for defining Puritanism emerged" (p. iii). Contents: Chapter I: Part I. "Augustinian Epistemology--Time," II. "Calvin's Epistemology--Space," and III. "The Protestant Faith and Church Dilemma"; Chapter II. "[William] Perkins' Epistemology--The Object and the Faculties"; Chapter III: Part I. "The Historical Setting for Discouragement" and II. "[Richard] Sibbes' Epistemology--The Object"; Chapter IV. "Cotton's Epistemology--The Object in Space or the Heart Divided"; V. "The Antinomian Controversy--The Object Misunderstood"; VI. "Cotton's Congregationalism--The Divided Heart Enlarged"; and VII. "Conclusion: Anglican and Puritan--Certain Knowledge and the Object."

1980-2 Baron, William R. "Tempests, Freshets and Mackerel Skies: Climatological Data from Diaries Using Content Analysis." Ph.D., Univ. of Maine. 649 leaves.

Abstract in DAI, vol. 41 (9), sec. A, p. 4139: "In order to study climate change and its implications, detailed records must be reconstructed for the longest possible time spans. . . . Eighteenth-century New England had a number of diarists who kept daily qualitative weather entries. Many of them belonged to a group of amateur scientists encouraged by the Royal Society of London to observe New World natural phenomena. . . . The qualitative weather diaries produced by these Harvard graduates were similar in many respects, employing the same organizational principles and descriptive vocabularies. . . . Results from the content analysis of a number of diaries from the Boston area, along with other diary materials and a few climate studies completed previously, were combined to reconstruct a climate record for eastern Massachusetts between the years 1700 and 1819."

1980-3   Beasley, James Roland. "The Success of the Cambridge Platform: Interchurch Communion in Early Massachusetts." Ph.D., Tufts Univ. 274 leaves.

Abstract in DAI, vol. 41 (3), sec. A, p. 1184: "This dissertation examined interchurch communion in Massachusetts between 1630 and 1815. The analysis centered on the theory of conciliar consociationism set out in the Cambridge Platform in 1648 and its evolution through the first two hundred years of Massachusetts history. . . . Chapter I studies the theories of interchurch communion espoused by the first generation of Bay Colony clergymen. . . . Chapter II discussed three types of interchurch communion in seventeenth-century Massachusetts: clerical consociationism, synodical consociationism, and conciliar consociationism. . . . Chapter III investigated the attempted use of consociationism to stem the tide of perceived declension in the Massachusetts churches. The Cambridge Proposals of 1705 and the Northhampton [sic] Proposals of 1714 were the culminations of efforts in eastern and western Massachusetts respectively to offset religious declension by instituting more Presbyterian-type polity. In the defeat of the calls for standing councils, the Cambridge Platform polity withstood its first major contest." The final three chapters deal with later events.

1980-4   Breed, James Lincoln. "Sanctification in the Theology of Cotton Mather." Ph.D., Aquinas Institute of Theology. 356 leaves.

Abstract in DAI, vol. 43 (1), sec. A, p. 190: "This thesis is an attempt to analyze Cotton Mather's theology of sanctification and his practice of the disciplines of piety--study of the Word of God, meditation, self-examination and prayer--to determine how this particular aspect of Christian doctrine took shape at the end of the 'theocratic era' (c. 1700) in New England. The first part of the thesis is an analysis of Cotton Mather's own spirituality in terms of his cultural identity, the reigning New England Puritan theology of his day, and the history of his life and ministry. The second part of this thesis attempts to compare and contrast Mather's spirituality with the doctrine of sanctification found in the Westminster Confession of Faith; in John Calvin's Institutes of the Christian Religion; in the writings of four key Puritan divines--William Perkins, John Preston, Richard Baxter and Samuel Willard; in the theology of the German Pietists of the eighteenth century, especially August Hermann Francke; and in certain Patristic, medieval, and counter-Reformation Catholic contemplative traditions."

1980-5   Hagglund, Carol. "Disowned without Just Cause: Quakers in Rochester, Massachusetts, during the Eighteenth Century." Ph.D., Univ. of Massachusetts. xi, 290 leaves.

Abstract in DAI, vol. 40 (12), sec. A, p. 6391: "This study explores the place of Quakers in Rochester, Massachusetts, during the eighteenth century, analyzing their activities in the context both of the community and of the Society of Friends. Present in Rochester from the earliest days of settlement in the late seventeenth century, these Quakers forged a unique lifestyle based on compromises between the values of the community and the religious teaching of the Friends. During the early eighteenth century, Rochester's Quakers both held powerful positions within the town's political structure and also won from the town exemptions from religious taxation. . . . Included are two maps of the Rochester area and sixteen tables, some in appendices, which allow analysis of the composition and activities of Rochester's Quaker group."

1980-6   Hambrick-Stowe, Charles Edwin. "The Practice of Piety: Puritan Devotional Disciplines in Seventeenth-Century New England." Ph.D., Boston Univ. (Graduate School). ix, 538 leaves.

Abstract in DAI, vol. 40 (12), sec. A, p. 6332. Revision published under same title: Chapel Hill : Published for the Institute of Early American History and Culture by the Univ. of North Carolina Press, 1982. -- x, 298 p. "Preface" (1982 ed.): "This book seeks to supplement certain commonly held ideas about New England religion in the seventeenth century and to correct others. Puritanism was as affective as it was rational, and Puritans were as wont to withdraw into contemplative solitude as they were to be active in the marketplace. Indeed, the particular forms of public worship and the characteristic private devotional exercises were what made a Puritan a Puritan" (p. viii). Contents: Part I. "Puritanism Considered as a Devotional Movement": 1. "New England Devotional Practice: Four Vignettes" (of Roger Clap, Thomas Shepard, Samuel Sewall, and Anne Bradstreet), 2. "'The Better Part: Heart Religion,'" and 3. "Puritan as Pilgrim"; Part II. "'The Way of Godly Conversation'": 4. "The Ordinances of Public Worship," 5. "Private Devotion: Neighborhood, Family, Conference," and 6. "Private Devotion: Secret Exercises"; and Part III. "'Constant Preparation for Glory'": 7. "Pilgrimage as Preparation," 8. "'The Travelling Interest of Christ in this Wilderness': The Devotional Crisis of the Second Generation," and 9.

"The Puritan Contemplative."

1980-7   Karlberg, Mark Walter. "The Mosaic Covenant and the Concept
          of Works in Reformed Hermeneutics: A Historical-Critical
          Analysis with Particular Attention to Early Covenant
          Eschatology." Th.D., Westminster Theological Seminary. vii, 353
          leaves.

        Abstract in DAI, vol. 41 (5), sec. A, p. 2169: "Our study of
early federalism up to the adoption of the Westminster Standards of
1648 directs itself to two questions. Is the concept of works (law
vs. grace) foreign to the theology of such men as [Heinrich] Bullinger
and Calvin? And more specifically, what shape did the biblical
interpretations of the Mosaic law covenant take during the course of
the Reformation? . . . Chapter one introduces the reader to the
predominant critical assessments of federalism, both Continental and
English. Chapter two surveys the background of the covenant idea in
early and medieval theology. . . . In the third chapter we consider
the teachings of the leading sixteenth-century federalists. . . .
Chapter four continues with a consideration of the early seventeenth-
century exponents, culminating with the work of the Westminster
divines. Included here are such related matters as the rise of
preparationism and the establishment of the Puritan theocracies of Old
and New England."

1980-8   Karlsen, Carol Frances. "The Devil in the Shape of a Woman:
          The Witch in Seventeenth-Century New England." Ph.D., Yale Univ.
          xvi, 412 leaves.

        Abstract in DAI, vol. 41 (11), sec. A, p. 4812: "This thesis is
a study of witchcraft in seventeenth-century New England as a process
through which Puritans reconciled beliefs about women with the
material experiences of a society in which those beliefs took shape.
. . . I argue that Puritanism contained within it, as a worldview, a
violent contradiction of ideas about women--ideas which eventuated in
the simultaneous celebration of the godly helpmeet and condemnation of
the witch. . . . Chapter One lays out the central ideas of the
witchcraft belief system. . . . Chapters Two, Three, and Four isolate
the characteristics of witches, both those ascribed to witches and
those which more objectively describe the women's lives. . . . [The
characteristics] divide roughly into demographic, economic, religious
and sexual features. . . . Chapter Five examines Puritan ideas about
women in general, particularly Puritan efforts to form an ideology of
womanhood more suitable to the world they were attempting to remake,
and suggest the connections between beliefs and feelings about women
and beliefs and feelings about witches. Chapter Six relates these
various beliefs to the actual structuring of New England society."

1980-9   Kulik, Gary B. "The Beginnings of the Industrial Revolution
          in America: Pawtucket, Rhode Island, 1672-1829." Ph.D., Brown
          Univ. vii, 397 leaves.

        Abstract in DAI, vol. 41 (12), sec. A, p. 5221: "The industrial revolution, that period in the history of the Atlantic economies from roughly 1750 to 1850, marks the most sweeping and important change in recorded human history." Pawtucket in 1790 is described as "a village with artisan and farming traders stretching back over a century." The early history of Pawtucket is briefly outlined.

1980-10   Lang, Amy Schrager. "The Antinomian Strain in American Culture." Ph.D., Columbia Univ. 221 leaves.

Abstract in DAI, vol. 41 (2), sec. A, p. 673: "The names by which a culture designates its heretics are telling. In the United States, antinomianism--literally, disregard for law--is one such name. First used in this country by the Massachusetts Bay colonists to describe the errors of Anne Hutchinson, the designation remained current as a term of social disapprobation well into the nineteenth century. The persistence of the term suggests that antinomianism defines a crucial cultural limit, but where exactly that limit lies has been difficult for Americans to describe. The other side of the disregard for the authority of the law is assertion of the authority of the self. In a culture where self-creation is highly valued, where . . . enormous authority accrues to the self, separating authority from the dominant ideology of individualism is problematic. This study examines four efforts to draw this distinction." The four efforts are those of Anne Hutchinson, Jonathan Edwards and Charles Chauncy, Emerson, and Melville.

1980-11   McCarron, Robert Louis. "Some Considerations of Style and Rhetoric in the Writings of Roger Williams." Ph.D., Indiana Univ. 149 leaves.

Abstract in DAI, vol. 41 (1), sec. A, p. 253: "In studying his eleven published books and tracts I have discovered Williams to be a highly competent and sophisticated writer who is not merely a polemicist, but adapts his style to fit various kinds of expression. . . . In the first chapter Williams' background and education are considered to determine their influence on Williams the artist. . . . In the following three chapters I have divided Williams' writings into three distinct functional types--the instructional, the controversial, and the devotional. I have then examined the individual works to determine how each of the three styles differs by concentrating on structure, point of view, tone, sentence structure, sentence types and lengths, diction, and such literary devices as oxymorons, parenthesis, allusions, personification, verbal wit, and metaphor. . . . When one considers all of Williams' works he must conclude that he is a serious, self-conscious, versatile, and sophisticated writer whose work deserves a more secure place in American letters than it now enjoys."

1980-12   McKim, Donald Keith. "Ramism in William Perkins." Ph.D., Univ. of Pittsburgh. 2 vols. (xiv, 526 leaves).

Abstract in DAI, vol. 41 (12), sec. A, p. 5139: "No complete study has been made of Perkins' collected Works to ascertain to what extent Ramism might be present in William Perkins. This dissertation seeks to accomplish that task. . . . The study examines Perkins' works to see how they were constructed methodologically. Since the hallmark of Ramism was its teachings on 'method,' evidence of Ramism is apparent when Ramus' procedure has been used. . . . The results of the study indicated that Perkins' debt to Ramus was substantial. With few exceptions . . . , all of Perkins' works were constructed Ramistically. Perkins followed Ramist method throughout his career. He used it as the means of presenting his theological subjects from systematic theology to cases of conscience."

1980-13   O'Donnell, James Paul. "Thomas Shepard's The Sincere Convert: A Critical Edition." Ph.D., Univ. of South Carolina. xiv, 488 leaves.

Abstract in DAI, vol. 41 (7), sec. A, p. 3109: "This edition of Thomas Shepard's The Sincere Convert (1640) presents a critical, unnormalized edition. The commentary includes historical and textual introductions, a discussion of adopted readings, list of emendations of the copy-text, a record of line end hyphenations, and a historical collation. . . . The textual introduction presents the rationale for the choice of the fifth edition as the copy-text. The historical introduction contains a biographical sketch of Shepard, a discussion of the printers and publications of the first six editions, and an explanation of how these sermons fit in with Shepard's preparationist theology."

1980-14   Peacock, John Hunt, Jr. "The Breach of Such a Covenant: Individualism and American Community." Ph.D., Columbia Univ. i, 133 leaves.

Abstract in DAI, vol. 43 (12), sec. A, p. 3912: "'A Model of Christian Charity,' John Winthrop's Arbella sermon to the men and women who were about to land on the shores of Massachusetts Bay in 1630, prescribed how commerce and charity, self-interest and social responsibility, were to be reconciled according to God's covenant with his chosen people to build a 'city upon a hill' in New England. 'A Model' also instilled fear of the 'breach of such a covenant,' which subsequent jeremiads said God punished with hurricanes, crop failures, Indian wars, epidemics, and other catastrophes. Ironically, evidence that a breach had occurred was often seen in the burgeoning pride of a community that had been so successful in channeling individualism in socially constructive ways." The remainder of the diss. traces the "covenant idea" as interpreted and transformed by Jonathan Edwards, James Madison, Thoreau, Emerson, and Melville. Contents: "Introduction," 1. "Arguments for the Plantation of New England," 2. "Anticipating both Madison and Thoreau: Jonathan Edwards For and Against the Constitution," 3. "Culture as Covenant, Civil Society as Breach: Emerson's Affiliated and Disaffiliated Individual," and 4. "Breach or Covenant?: Melville's Question About Science, Philanthropy, and Law."

1980-15   Pinkham, Harold Arthur, Jr.   "The Transplantation and Transformation of the English Shire in America: Essex County, Massachusetts, 1630-1768." Ph.D., Univ. of New Hampshire.   xii, 210 leaves.

Abstract in DAI, vol. 42 (3), sec. A, p. 1285: "In order to detail all twenty-one localities over 130 years, it is necessary to limit the characteristics studied to the political, economic, transportation, and marital and the period sampled to 1653-1655, 1679-1681, 1719-1721, and 1763-1765. By measuring the internal development and external contacts of each town for each of the characteristics and periods above, a locality can be ranked by the complexity of its internal institutions and positioned in a network of interconnections among the communities. . . . To the extent that political, road, trade, shipbuilding, and marriage links represent significant intracounty communal ties, Essex underwent regional integration and to the extent that particular towns expanded their services and functions, while increasing their outside contacts, they made important contributions to integration. . . . The expanding complexities of Salem, Newburyport, and Ipswich were crucial to the transition of Essex from a collection in 1643 of diverse plantations . . . to a relatively interdependent group of 'American' towns by 1768."

1980-16   Pope, Alan Howard. "Petrus Ramus and Michael Wigglesworth: The Logic of Poetic Structure." Ph.D., Univ. of New Mexico.   vi, 239 leaves.

"Preface": "The Dialectic of Petrus Ramus influenced the Diary and poetry of Michael Wigglesworth. While a student at Harvard, Wigglesworth studied Ramus's logic and wrote his Master's 'Synopsis' on the Dialectic. The Diary Wigglesworth kept while a tutor at Harvard records his intense interest in Ramus's logic. In The Day of Doom Wigglesworth uses syllogism to organize the poem. Meat Out of the Eater reveals a pattern of organization distinctly Ramean. . . . This study, divided into three sections, begins with an examination of the life and logic of Petrus Ramus. The second section analyzes the writing of Michael Wigglesworth, and the final section presents a translation of Ramus's Dialectic" (p. iv). Contents: "Introduction"; Section I. "Pierre de La Ramée": I. "The Life and Educational Reforms of Pierre de La Ramée" and II. "Synopsis and Discussion of the Dialectic, 1555"; Section II. "Michael Wigglesworth": III. "Secondary Criticism," IV. "Wigglesworth at Harvard," V. "The Day of Doom," and VI. "Meat Out of the Eater"; Section III. "Translation of Dialectic": VII. "Translator's Preface" and VIII. "Dialectic"; and "Conclusion."

1980-17   Rosenberg, Gary Leon. "Family and Society in the Early Seventeenth-Century Massachusetts Bay Area." Ph.D., State Univ. of New York at Buffalo.   ii, 281 leaves.

Abstract in DAI, vol. 41 (2), sec. A, p. 774: "This work is a demographic study of those men and women who left England between 1630 and 1649 and sailed for the Massachusetts Bay area. . . . Initially, the hopes and expectations of the men and women who sailed with John

Winthrop in 1630 and what happened to those colonists during their first years in the Massachusetts Bay area are examined in detail. The experiences of settlers who arrived after the Winthrop fleet are the studied and compared with the experiences of the Winthrop fleet members. ... In the final analysis, this work is a general history of the family in the seventeenth-century Massachusetts Bay area. ... A lengthy, detailed comparative analysis of the demographic data found in James Savage's Genealogical Dictionary is made with data independently collected from two New England towns, Dorchester, Massachusetts, and Windsor, Connecticut. ... [This] study demonstrates that the New England family was faced with a subtle, but nevertheless, persistent and real demographic crisis."

1980-18   Toulouse, Teresa Andrea. "The Aesthetic of Persuasion: Plain Style and Audience in John Cotton, Benjamin Colman, and William Ellery Channing." Ph.D., Harvard Univ. v, 168 leaves.

"Introduction": "The chapters that follow explore the baffling question of the so-called 'plain' style in three American preachers: John Cotton, Benjamin Colman, and William Ellery Channing. ... I started reading Puritan theories of style with their emphasis on 'literal' fidelity to the Word and ended up exploring these theories in light of Classical conceptions of the use and function of rhetoric. ... As I began to look at rhetorical theory, my focus broadened from a consideration of style to a consideration of audience. Questions of audience led, in turn, to general questions about the continuing importance of a plain style to American preachers. Did preachers retain similar attitudes about the form? about the audience for whom they preached? ... Each chapter, then, focuses on three interrelated factors: what contextual assumptions could have informed these preachers' attitudes toward preaching; what kind of audience is implied by their writings; and finally, what kinds of structures they used to construct their varying 'plain' style." Relevant chapters: "Introduction," I. "The Aesthetic of Election: John Cotton and the Complexities of 'Plain Style,'" and II. "The Aesthetic of Distance: Benjamin Colman and Eighteenth-Century Transformations of 'Plain Style.'"

1980-19   Ulrich, Laurel Thatcher. "Good Wives: A Study in Role Definition in Northern New England, 1650-1750." Ph.D., Univ. of New Hampshire. x, 538 leaves.

Abstract in DAI, vol. 41 (6), sec. A, p. 2741. Revision published as Good Wives: Image and Reality in the Lives of Women in Northern New England, 1650-1750. -- New York : Alfred A. Knopf, 1982. -- xv, 296 p. "Preface" (1982 ed.): "My emphasis on good wives betrays a propensity to search for normative elements in a history which from the time of Hawthorne has been dominated by outcasts and witches. Readers will find much about housekeeping, childbearing, and ordinary churchgoing, about small conflicts experienced by forgotten women, and about little triumphs that history has not recorded.... Good Wives is a study in role definition, an extended description constructed from a series of vignettes" (p. xiii). Contents: "Introduction"; Part One. "Bathsheba": 1. "The Ways of Her Household,"

2. "Deputy Husbands," 3. "A Friendly Neighbor," and 4. "Pretty Gentlewomen"; Part Two. "Eve": 5. "The Serpent Beguiled Me," 6. "Consort," 7. "Travail," and 8. "Mother of All Living"; Part Three. "Jael": 9. "Blessed Above Women," 10. "Viragoes," 11. "Captives," and 12. "Daughters of Zion"; and "Afterword."

1980-20   Verduin, Kathleen.   "Religious and Sexual Love in American Protestant Literature: Puritan Patterns in Hawthorne and John Updike." Ph.D., Indiana Univ. 410 leaves.

Abstract in DAI, vol. 41 (3), sec. A, p. 1059: "A complex of attitudes towrd religion and sexuality, established in seventeenth-century Puritan literature, reappears in the works of Nathaniel Hawthorne and John Updike, two authors who in their respective centuries express an affinity for a Protestant and specifically a Calvinist tradition.... Following the death of Jonathan Edwards, American Protestantism is split and sexualized: Puritan Calvinism becomes more and more patriarchal, while the opposing Unitarian religion gains increasingly feminine associations. Hawthorne in his fiction pits the 'feminized' culture of the nineteenth century . . . against a seventeenth-century tradition that is seen as patriarchal and anti-natural in emphasis. . . . In the fiction of John Updike the distance between patriarchal, Calvinist values and 'feminized' Unitarian ones, adumbrated in Hawthorne, is dominant and often dramatized as a conflict between husband and wife. . . . In these two authors who in some way ally themselves with a Puritan heritage, the profound importance of American religious history for American literature is demonstrated."

1980-21   Wetherell, Charles Wheeler. "Brokers of the Word: An Essay in the Social History of the Early American Press, 1639-1793." Ph.D., Univ. of New Hampshire. 236 leaves.

Abstract in DAI, vol. 42 (3), sec. A, p. 1287:   "This dissertation explores the social context of printing and publishing from 1639 to 1783 through an analysis of the complete extant record of colonial printing, and a collective biography of the printers, publishers and booksellers who comprised the press. Two general areas are explored. The first involves the size, stability and growth of the press, the second, the structure of the trade at large."

1980-22   Wilson, Robert John, III. "Ebenezer Gay: New England's Arminian Patriarch, 1696-1787." Ph.D., Univ. of Massachusetts. xix, 595 leaves.

Abstract in DAI, vol. 40 (12), sec. A, p. 6395: "The three high priests of New England Arminianism were Charles Chauncy, Jonathan Mayhew, and Ebenezer Gay. This dissertation has been written for the purpose of bringing the last member of this trio out of the shadows. . . . This study also analyzes the three major sources of Gay's Arminianism-- (1) The empirical spirit which he assimilated during his years at John Leverett's Harvard (1710-1717). (2) The works of the English liberal theologians such as Samuel Clarke and John Taylor. (3)

The interaction between Gay and the social forces that were transforming Hingham, the town in which he ministered for sixty-nine years."

1980-23   Wright, Conrad Edick. "Christian Compassion and Corporate Beneficence: The Institutionalization of Charity in New England, 1720-1810." Ph.D., Brown Univ. iv, 416 leaves.

Abstract in DAI, vol. 41 (12), sec. A, p. 5225: "Between the 1720's and 1810 charity as New Englanders thought about and practiced it changed in a number of respects. This dissertation seeks both to describe the transformations of beneficence that took place between the early eighteenth century and the beginning of the nineteenth century, and to portray the metamorphosis of charitable thought that practical changes produced. . . . The central, shaping element in the transformation of charity . . . was the institutionalization of beneficence, a process only dimly visible in the early eighteenth century. . . . In the 1720's when New Englanders thought of charity or practiced it they understood the virtue in private, personal terms. Their descriptions of charity emphasized each individual's own caritative responsibilities, as well as the bonds of compassion that joined him to his fellow man."

1980-24   Yentsch, Anne Elizabeth. "Expressions of Cultural Diversity and Social Reality in Seventeenth-Century New England." Ph.D., Brown Univ. 249 leaves.

Abstract in DAI, vol. 41 (12), sec. A, p. 5152: "The research presented in this dissertation is a synchronic study of seventeenth-century New England communities. The objective was to determine if the customs and values that English people brought with them were an important element in their adaptation to New England. Specifically, the effects of English regional cultures were traced. New England regions associated with different English regions were selected for study: Watertown, Rowley, Weymouth, Scituate, and the province of Maine. . . . I sought to trace the ways people differed from one another and to see whether these differences provided them with regionally based social identities. The focus was systems of customary precedence within the groups as revealed in people's behavior, commonplace events, and material culture."

1981-1   Bell, Susan Cherry. "History and Artistry in Cotton Mather's Magnalia Christi Americana." Ph.D., State Univ. of New York at Binghamton. 298 leaves.

Abstract in DAI, vol. 42 (2), sec. A, p. 701: "This study presents a fresh understanding of the Magnalia Christi Americana by attending to its rhetorical medium as the expression of a complex and sophisticated sensibility. It argues that a cluster of derogatory assumptions about the man . . . has coloured even the most distinguished reading of the work lending a special urgency to the problem of hearing Mather aright. This account eschews a straightforward chronological reading to engage more immediately the dynamics of each book (every one of which provides a different focus upon the whole of New England history from the beginnings to the present), and the pressure of its shaping voice."

1981-2   Butts, Francis Tiffany. "Perry Miller and the Ordeal of American Freedom." Ph.D., Queen's Univ. at Kingston (Canada).

Abstract in DAI, vol. 42 (4), sec. A, p. 1759: "This study challenges the conventional interpretation of [the work of Perry] Miller.   It contends that Miller's scholarship represents an expression of modern secular existentialism. The common themes of existentialism--alienation, human finitude, dread, bad faith, the paradoxes of the will, and metaphysical rebellion--pervade Miller's history. . . . Miller's existentialism disposed him to see in the history of America a symbol of man's spiritual wrestling with the consequences of his Promethean ambition."

1981-3   Dalton, John Vasmar. "Ministers, Metaphors, and the New England Wilderness, 1650-1700." Ph.D., Univ. of New Hampshire. vii, 219 leaves.

Abstract in DAI, vol. 42 (12), sec. A, p. 5219: "This study focuses upon ministerial perceptions of the New England wilderness, as seen in sermons preached between 1650-1700. The 'wilderness' is understood both in its metaphorical and Biblical sense. . . . This study concludes that, contrary to ministerial claims that the New England saints were increasingly degenerate and less pious than their ancestors, religious fervor did not wane. Noticeable religious fervor existed, evident in the success both of Solomon Stoddard and the Brattle Street Church, in 1700. This fervor, paradoxically, stemmed from the New England ministers' constant references to dependence upon the Spirit for guidance and clarification of the saints' mission in New England."

1981-4   Damerall, David Odell. "The Modernization of Massachusetts: The Transformation of Public Attitudes and Institutions, 1689 to 1715." Ph.D., Univ. of Texas at Austin. xxxiv, 290 leaves.

Abstract in DAI, vol. 42 (7), sec. A, p. 3272: "It is the intention of this study to examine the history of Massachusetts between 1689 and 1715 as a means of placing the events of those years into a new historical perspective. Rather than try to treat the period as an age of moral decline or as a seedtime for the Revolution, this essay will try to show how the Charter of 1691, the stress of prolonged intercolonial warfare, and regulatory pressure from imperial England caused a pluralistic society to emerge in Massachusetts which was based on property ownership and a balance of political power rather than on religious orthodoxy and consensual agreement. Within that institutional framework, Bay colonists developed a new set of attitudes about executive leadership, the function of the legislature, the purpose of the courts, and the proper role of the church in provincial affairs. The colonists' growing intolerance of the Indians was the only inconsistent feature of a period in which public institutions became more responsive to the heterogeneous interests of residents than at any previous time in the history of Massachusetts."

1981-5   Eckert, Richard Scott. "'The Gentlemen of the Profession': The Emergence of Lawyers in Massachusetts, 1630-1810." Ph.D., Univ. of Southern California. iv, 556 leaves.

Abstract in DAI, vol. 42 (1), sec. A, p. 346: "The emergence of the lawyer class in Massachusetts resulted from the evolution of an increasingly complex system of law and its adoption by the courts during the eighteenth century. The absence of trained lawyers prior to 1700 is best understood in terms of the colonists' reliance on simplified laws, exemplified by the codification movement of the 1640s, and judicial procedure. Their subsequent appearance paralleled the introduction of common law case law and procedure into provincial courts. Self-taught attorneys . . . possessed scant knowledge of the common law, yet they proved adequate as long as an understanding of the law administered by the courts remained within their grasp. Simplified procedures also encouraged litigants to argue their own causes."

1981-6   Ellsworth, Mary Ellen Tressel. "Two New England Writers: Harriet Beecher Stowe and Mary Wilkins Freeman." Ph.D., Columbia Univ. 233 leaves.

Abstract in DAI, vol. 42 (6), sec. A, p. 2674: "Harriet Beecher Stowe and Mary Wilkins Freeman contributed a number of classic novels and short stories to nineteenth-century American literature. Themselves women of the New England village, they recorded the impact of village life on women formed by its Puritan religious tradition and its intellectual and social heritage. . . . This dissertation examines Stowe's and Freeman's fiction as it falls into three major categories: one, the individual and her relationship to God; two, the individual as she is influenced by the church and its minister; and three, the individual in her social and community roles. . . . Calvinism in Stowe's fiction is a strong force: its severities may scar, but it is a faith which validates life. . . . In Freeman's fiction, vestigial Calvinism remains, coloring life, and causing worry and concern."

1981-7   Grayson, Robert Calvin. "History and the Imaginary in Hawthorne's Early Tales and Sketches." Ph.D., Univ. of Missouri at Columbia. 305 leaves.

Abstract in DAI, vol. 43 (1), sec. A, p. 168: "Responding to critics who called for an American literature like the Waverley Novels, Hawthorne fused history and the imaginary in a number of works published before 1836. In 'Seven Tales' history is only background: in four biographical sketches it is subject matter; however, in 'Provincial Tales' and the others, Hawthorne intermingled the imaginary with history in order to interpret key issues in New England's history. . . . In the seven other historical tales published between 1831 and 1836, Hawthorne implicitly criticized historians who rationalized New England's persecuting spirit and advocates of a Scott-like literature who wanted embarrassing episodes in Puritan history suppressed. . . . In these tales Hawthorne used extensively New England's histories that he withdrew from the Salem Athenaeum between 1826 and 1835. . . . The tales published between 1831 and 1836 not only blend history and the imaginary but demonstrate also that the imaginary concepts are an important component of history."

1981-8   Haims, Lynn Maria. "The American Puritan Aesthetic: Iconography in Seventeenth-Century Poetry and Tombstone Art." Ph.D., New York Univ. 227 leaves.

Abstract in DAI, vol. 42 (2), sec. A, p. 702: "This study explores some of the distinctive iconographic features of tombstone carving and poetry in Puritan New England in light of the biblical prohibitions against the making of 'graven images.' . . . The thesis is advanced that the Puritans, denied artistic channels for self-expression, . . . consciously sought representation through Bible-based imagery and unconsciously embellished them to approximate idolatrous forms. The need for art, coupled with the fear of idolatry, produced ambivalent designs that were, on the one hand, schematic, geometrical, rigid; and, on the other, passionate, witty, and imaginative. . . . A first chapter presents the backgrounds of European and English iconoclasm. . . . Chapter Two considers the phenomenon of stone icons, which appeared overtly to violate the Commandment. . . . Chapter Three discusses anthropomorphism in American Puritan poetry and sermon literature, emphasizing the bodily and facial images of Christ in Edward Taylor's Preparatory Meditations. . . . Chapter Four turns to the ambivalent stances American and English Puritans took to disguise their aesthetic motives in light of their fear of the imagination and of creating verbal images. . . . The fifth chapter considers the aesthetic features of Taylor's Gods Determinations."

1981-9   Hassler, Gregory Lyn. "Portrait of a Puritan Self: Increase Mather's Literature of Death." Ph.D., Emory Univ. 250 leaves.

Abstract in DAI, vol. 43 (2), sec. A, p. 445: "Because Increase Mather represents a significant literary figure of the second-generation Puritan preachers, and since the motif of death dominates his published pulpit prose, his literature of death--execution and funeral sermons, meditations on death--contains a portrait that is useful in deepening an understanding of the complexities confronting one particular preacher. . . . This dissertation argues that Mather's portrait of the self is that of an entity embraced by three interdependent spatial contexts. These spatial contexts include the depiction of hell as a prison, earth as a place of hellish elements, and heaven as a house. These metaphorical representations are found to have the persistent motifs of enclosure, bondage, and confinement."

1981-10   Jimenez, Mary Ann. "Changing Faces of Madness: Insanity in
     Massachusetts, 1700-1850." Ph.D., Brandeis Univ. 706 leaves.

     Abstract in DAI, vol. 42 (1), sec. A, p. 346: "This is an
historical study of the conceptions of insanity and the treatment of
the insane in early America. The changing responses to madness in
Massachusetts from 1700 to 1850 are described and linked to the
evolution of New England society in the same period. The central
argument of the study is that the shape of the material and cultural
realities of this society determined its response to madness. The
dissertation is historical in its methodology. . . . In colonial New
England madness was viewed as the manifestation of a personal struggle
between man and the supernatural. The mad were generally tolerated
and there were few efforts to cure or control them."

1981-11   Lynn, Catherine Willis. "Wallpaper in America: From the
     Seventeenth Century to World War I." Ph.D., Yale Univ.

     Revision published under same title with a "Foreword" by Charles
van Ravenswaay: New York : W. W. Norton, 1980. -- 533 p. -- (A Barra
Foundation/Cooper-Hewitt Museum Book). Chapter 1 (1980 ed.):
"Although a great deal is known about the colonists' chairs, tables,
and chests, there is less evidence about what they used to furnish
interior walls. . . . However, scattered bits of evidence in colonial
trading records and advertisements, as well as in eighteenth-century
correspondence and journals support the conclusion that the colonists
closely imitated English styles in wall coverings, as they did in
everything else" (p. 17).   Relevant chapters: "Introduction"; Part
One. "The Seventeenth and Eighteenth Centuries": 1. "The Earliest
American Wall Hangings": "English Precedents," "The First Wallpapers
in America," and "Wallpaper Styles of the Seventeenth and Early
Eighteenth Centuries"; and 2. "How Wallpaper Was Made."

1981-12   O'Bryan, Daniel Walker. "Law versus Discipline: An
     Examination of Episcopal and Congregational Modes in Richard
     Hooker's Of the Laws of Ecclesiastical Polity and Thomas Hooker's
     A Survey of the Sum of Church Discipline." Ph.D., Univ. of
     Washington. iii, 345 leaves.

     Abstract in DAI, vol. 42 (4), sec. A, p. 1638: "The church
polity of the sixteenth and seventeenth centuries provides an
excellent means of tracing subtle changes in the development of
Reformation doctrine. This dissertation takes two definitive church
polities . . . and develops characteristic and consistent modes of
thought typical of each. . . . In the first chapter, the criticism on
Richard Hooker's Laws is reviewed, Hooker is placed in a long
tradition of religious controversy stretching back to [William]
Tyndale, and the highly public nature of Hooker's episcopacy is
explored. . . . The second chapter moves from Episcopal to
Congregational polity and examines the life and early work of Thomas
Hooker to provide a basis for a careful analysis of Hooker's
Congregationalism. . . . [Thomas Hooker's Survey is] systematically
analyzed in chapter three both in isolation and in context. . . .
Hooker's Survey is solidly Ramist in structure and this fact permits,

in chapter four, an extended consideration of the influence of Ramus on a particular work. . . . In the final chapter the central Reformation concept of the individual seeking salvation without mediator is applied as a measurement of the success or failure of the polities of Richard Hooker and Thomas Hooker."

1981-13   Parmer, Phill Warren. "'Like Little Paul in Person, Voice, and Grace': A Comparative Study of Edward Taylor and St. Paul." Ph.D., Louisiana State Univ. vii, 265 leaves.

Abstract in DAI, vol. 42 (6), sec. A, p. 2678: "This study examines correlations between the writings of Edward Taylor and St. Paul to understand more precisely the influence that Taylor's particular theology exercised upon his poetry. . . . Chapter I is an introduction to Taylor and the Puritan debt to Paulism. . . . Chapter II, 'Old Adam and the Old Covenant,' explores St. Paul's and Taylor's concepts of Creation, Man's Fall in Adam, Original Sin, the Covenant of Works, Natural Revelation, Scripture, and God's wrath. . . . Chapter III, 'The Person and Work of Christ,' examines the Christology of both writers. . . . Chapter IV, 'The New Adam and the New Covenant,' examines Taylor's Calvinist doctrine of election with St. Paul's doctrine of election and inclusion 'in Christ.' Chapter V climaxes the study by arguing that the Pauline paradigm (Sin-Grace-Hope) functions as a structural and conceptual model for Gods Determinations and for sixty-five of the Preparatory Meditations. . . . Chapter VI summarizes the argument and suggests ripe areas for additional research."

1981-14   Scott, Sarah Moore. "A Thematic Study of the Writings of Puritan Women from the Time of the Original Settlers to 1770." Ph.D., Southern Illinois Univ. at Carbondale. v, 232 leaves.

Abstract in DAI, vol. 42 (5), sec. A, p. 2133: "The purpose of this dissertation has been two-fold: first, to find as much literature by Puritan women as I could . . . ; second, to come to an understanding and offer a systematic review of the themes in these writings. . . . I also present a bibliography of fifty-nine Puritan women writers as an appendix." Contents: One. "The Hidden Ones," Two. "Superwoman!" Three. "Concern of the World. Family, Friends, Home," Four. "Worldly Concerns. Business, Social Consciousness, Politics, Indians, Witchcraft, Nature," Five. "Concerns of the Soul," and "Conclusion. Contexts for Literary Criticism."

1981-15   Shaw, Mark Randolph. "The Marrow of Practical Divinity: A Study in the Theology of William Perkins." Th.D., Westminster Theological Seminary. iii, 327 leaves.

Abstract in DAI, vol. 42 (5), sec. A, p. 2253: "William Perkins and his place in the formation of the Puritan movement has been neglected in contemporary Puritan studies. The thesis of this study is that Perkins was an influential Puritan theologian whose practical writings reveal a faithfulness to the Reformation theologically; an integrated world view combining social, political, economic, theological and ecclesiastical concerns; and a commitment to serve the cause of English nationalism."

1981-16   Todd, Margo Fraizer.   "Christian Humanism and the Puritan
    Social Order." Ph.D., Washington Univ.   414 leaves.

    Abstract in DAI, vol. 42 (8), sec. A, p. 3714: "An analysis of the impact of Christian humanist ideas on Puritan social theory in the sixteenth and early seventeenth centuries reveals that it was the reformist precepts of Erasmianism, rather than Protestant theology, which modeled the Puritan conceptions of social order. Puritans were, in fact, part of a sixteenth-century consensus derived from humanist social theory. . . . The process by which humanist ideas were transmitted to Puritans is revealed in publication figures for humanist works to ca. 1660, the presence of humanist writings in Puritan library catalogues, references to Erasmian social ideas in commonplace books, and, most importantly, the humanist university training of Protestant divines."

1981-17   Van Keuren, M. Luise.   "American Indian Responses and
    Reactions to the Colonists as Recorded in Seventeenth- and
    Eighteenth-Century American Literature." Ph.D., Univ. of
    Delaware.   iv, 220 leaves.

    Abstract in DAI, vol. 41 (11), sec. A, p. 4715: "Although the American aboriginal peoples lived in preliterate societies during the colonial period, their reaction to the European colonists is captured in the writings of the era, especially in works by persons with considerable experience with Indians, such as interpreters, surveyors, traders, missionaries, officials, captives, promoters, historians, travelers, and others. A broad survey of Indian responses in works from northern, middle, and southern colonies between 1600 and 1775 shows the colonists in a special and refreshing perspective. Colonists appear vulnerable, inexperienced, acquisitive, and ethnocentric. . . . The responses illustrate the Indians' perception, wit, caution, strong sense of propriety and dignity, psychological acumen, and their keen power of observation. . . . [Colonial] literature is characterized by an intense interest in the Indian . . . and by a portrait exceptional in its breadth and diversity."

1981-18   Vickers, Daniel Frederick.   "Maritime Labor in Colonial
    Massachusetts: A Case Study of the Essex County Cod Fishery and
    the Whaling Industry of Nantucket, 1630-1775." Ph.D., Princeton
    Univ.   364 leaves.

    Abstract in DAI, vol. 42 (9), sec. A, p. 4122: "In the New World of the seventeenth century, the New England economy was a significant anomaly for it flourished without having to depend on formally bound labor. The case of the whale and cod fisheries, organized from the outset for export and profit, is a special peculiarity in light of their continuous demand for low-priced help. To explain how such export industries could develop in New England without a system of legally coerced labor is the focus of this study. . . . Two developments initiated the transformation of the maritime labor market. First, the surge of population in seaboard Massachusetts began to generate by the end of the seventeenth century a growing pool of landless and mobile young men, prepared to sell their services to others. Second, the easing of the Puritan utopian vision . . . weakened Puritan prejudice enough to facilitate the freer movement of men into and around the colony. The market in fishing and whaling labor was liberated primarily by economic scarcity."

1981-19   Weiss, Rona Stephanie. "The Development of the Market Economy in Colonial Massachusetts." Ph.D., Univ. of Massachusetts. 218 leaves.

     Abstract in DAI, vol. 41 (12), sec. A, p. 5194: "This dissertation employs a theoretically rigorous class analysis . . . in an overall attempt to explain the basis for the origins of capitalism in Massachusetts by 1800. The study covers the period 1620-1800, a span of time which encompasses the early settlements by 'Pilgrims' and 'Puritans' through the birth of the North American nation. . . . The first chapter defines and explains the key concepts and methodological approach of the dissertation. The second chapter . . . defines the variety of non-capitalist class relations present in early 17th Century Massachusetts. . . . The third and fourth chapters deal with the interactions between these classes 1640-1800. . . . [The] development of new classes, new economic structures can be seen as a complex process of structural growth and change rather than a series of external intrusions or the blossoming of inherent human propensities."

1981-20   Wilbur, Raymond Bernard. "Diary of the Damned: A Study in Theocentric Anxiety in Pre-Awakening New England." Ph.D., Univ. of New Hampshire. xi, 382 leaves.

     Abstract in DAI, vol. 43 (7), sec. A, p. 2429: "The diary of Joseph Moody, the subject of this dissertation, hidden behind a coded Latin text for 240 years, reveals the intensity with which some New England Puritans pursued the preparationist-predestinarian discipline propounded by Thomas Shepard and others among New England's founding fathers. Such was the 'preacher's gift' of Samuel Moody to his son Joseph, in the preparationist tradition of Shepard, that the son became convinced that God had passed him by and that he was irretrievably lost and damned forever. The diary is young Moody's record of his futile quest for signs of his election and salvation."

1981-21   Williams, Lloyd Glyn. "'Digitus Dei': God and Nation in the Thought of John Owen: A Study in English Puritanism and Nonconformity, 1653-1683." Ph.D., Drew Univ. xix, 367 leaves.

     Abstract in DAI, vol. 42 (3), sec. A, p. 1204: "During a large part of [the seventeenth century], John Owen (1616-83) was one of the most prestigious and politically involved Puritans in England. . . . In the Protectorate he was happy to advocate the greatest possible religious diversity. . . . In the Restoration years he was content to devote the largest proportion of his time to gaining liberty for, and the edification of, the Nonconformist (especially Congregational) churches. . . . Owen . . . , using the categories of the collective theology of Puritanism, helped produce in England . . . a kind of pluralism: a loose union of different religious, political and cultural groups within a progressive Protestant nation."

1981-22   Wisse, Alice Suzzane. "The Christology of Edward Taylor in Christographia with Reference to His Poetry." Ph.D., New York Univ. 358 leaves.

Abstract in DAI, vol. 42 (2), sec. A, p. 707: "The Christographia sermons reveal that Taylor faithfully subscribed to the catechism, creeds and doctrinal standards of the Calvinistic teachings prevalent in the seventeenth century. Taylor treats Christ's natures, personal union, qualifications, and works with meticulous precision to prove that Christ, completely prepared, is able to atone for man by his perfect obedience and death. The [Preparatory Meditations] contain the same theological distinctions as the sermons, but without reference to the sermons the full impact of this material remains unnoticed or unintelligible. The sermons elaborate and explain points of doctrine that the meditations may conceal with a seemingly insignificant phrase or a unique image."

Author Index

Short-Title Index

The Life and Thought of John Owen
[Wallace], 1965-21
The Life and Works of Increase
Mather [Murdock], 1923-6
The Life and Works of the
Reverend Samuel Willard
[Dollar], 1960-1
Life of Francis Nicholson
[Noble], 1958-9
Light of the Western Churches
[Shuffleton], 1972-35
"Like Little Paul in Person,
Voice, and Grace" [Parmer],
1981-13
Litchfield, Connecticut
[Thompson], 1977-33
Literary Culture in Early New
England [Wright], 1917-3
Literary History of New England
Women Writers [Hornstein],
1978-7
Literary Influences in Colonial
Newspapers [Cook], 1912-1
Literary References in New
England Diaries [Evans], 1940-3
A Literary Study of Puritan
Testimonies [Caldwell], 1979-5
A Literary Study of the Sermons
of the First-Generation
Preachers [Jones], 1973-10
Literature for Children in
England and America
[MacDonald], 1978-15
The Literature of Natural and
Physical Science [Tilley],
1933-5
The Literature of Power [Marks],
1975-18
The Liturgies of Jeremy Taylor
and Richard Baxter [DuPriest],
1972-17
Local Public Finance in Colonial
Connecticut [Marcuse], 1956-9
The Logic of Millennial Thought
[Davidson], 1973-4
The Logic of Order [Little],
1963-13

Madmen and Friends [Chu], 1978-2
The Magistracy Recovered
[Goodwin], 1979-14
The Magistracy Rediscovered
[Goodwin], 1979-14
Maine, Charles II, and

Massachusetts [Reid], 1976-17
The Maine Frontier [Moody], 1933-
3
Maine Province and Court Records
[Allen], 1956-1
Manitou and Providence
[Salisbury], 1972-30
Maritime Labor in Colonial
Massachusetts [Vickers], 1981-
18
The Marrow of Practical Divinity
[Shaw], 1981-15
Massachusetts and the Glorious
Revolution [Lewis], 1967-17
The Massachusetts Assembly
[Zemsky], 1967-34
Massachusetts Bay Colony
[Murphy], 1960-8
Massachusetts Blacks and the
Quest for Education [Davis],
1977-9
The Massachusetts Colonial Agents
in England [Ferrell], 1923-5
The Massachusetts Election Sermon
[Anderson], 1972-1
Massachusetts Politics in War and
Peace [Pencak], 1978-22
The Massachusetts Town in the
Eighteenth Century [Zuckerman],
1967-36
The Means to Grace [Selement],
1974-27
The Meditative Structure of
Edward Taylor's "Preparatory
Meditations" [Epperson], 1965-4
The Membership of the
Massachusetts General Court
[Wall], 1965-20
Merchants, Farmers, and River
Gods [Zemsky], 1967-34
Messrs. William Pepperell
[Fairchild], 1948-1
Metaphor and Poetic Structure in
the Preparatory Meditations
[Jones], 1973-9
The Metaphor of Counsel [Roddey],
1969-15
The Metaphysical Conceit in the
Poetry of Edward Taylor
[Shepherd], 1960-11
Middle-Class Democracy and the
Revolution in Massachusetts
[Brown], 1946-1
The Middle Way [Gilmore], 1974-11
Migration from East Anglia to New

1947-3

The Settlement of the Upper
Connecticut River Valley
[King], 1965-9

Settling with the Indians
[Kupperman], 1977-16

Seventeenth- and Eighteenth-
Century English and Colonial
American Music Texts [Landon],
1977-17

The Seventeenth-Century Arts of
New England [Fritz], 1963-8

Sex and the Law in Colonial New
England [Wells], 1974-35

Sexual Rhetoric in Seventeenth-
Century American Literature
[Hibler], 1970-19

The Shape of the Puritan Mind
[Lowrie], 1971-15

Shipbuilding in Colonial America
[Goldenberg], 1969-12

Shipping, Maritime Trade, and the
Economic Development of
Colonial North America
[Walton], 1966-17

Sibley's Harvard Graduates
[Shipton], 1933-4

Sighs from Sion [Plotkin], 1966-
10

The Significance of Infant Baptism
in the Presbyterian Church
[Schenck], 1938-8

Significance of the English and
the American Almanacs [Perrine],
1917-2

Sir Edmund Andros [Bloom], 1962-1

Sir Henry Vane, Junior [Rogers],
1953-9

A Social and Cultural History of
Newport, Rhode Island [Skemp],
1974-30

Social Applications of the Gospel
in Congregational Churches
[Schulz], 1942-9

Social Classes in Seventeenth-
Century New England [Dawes],
1946-2

Social Conflict and Community
Tensions [Konig], 1974-17

The Social Ideals and
Institutions of the Church-
State of Plymouth [Behan],
1899-1

A Society Ordained by God
[Johnson], 1968-15

A Socio-Legal Analysis of the
Massachusetts Stubborn Child
Law [Skillern], 1977-30

Solomon Stoddard: An American
Way of Religion [Carr], 1977-5

Solomon Stoddard, Puritan
Patriarch [Swanhart], 1961-11

Some Aspects of Connecticut
Indian Culture History
[Warner], 1970-41

Some Aspects of Milton's American
Reputation [Zimmerman], 1950-10

Some Characteristics of the Bay
Colony Founders' Early Thinking
[Judson], 1976-12

Some Considerations of Style and
Rhetoric [McCarron], 1980-11

Some Influences of Environment in
Massachusetts [Keir], 1917-1

Some Literary and Religious
Aspects of the Works of Richard
Baxter [Keeble], 1974-16

Some Puritan Characteristics of
the Poetry of Edwin Arlington
Robinson [Gowen], 1968-11

"Some Responses to Environment in
Massachusetts" [Keir], 1917-1

Songs from the Garden [Hammond],
1979-15

Sorry after a Godly Manner
[Henson], 1957-4

Sources of Imagery in the Poetry
of Edward Taylor [Wiley], 1962-
10

Soziologische Studien zur
neuenglischen Syntax
[Volckmar], 1930-4

The Speaking Self in American
Puritan Literature [Zilboorg],
1976-26

"The Spectacles of God's Word"
[Scheer], 1972-31

Spiritual Autobiography in Early
America [Shea], 1966-15

Spiritual Combat [Pacy], 1978-21

Sport and Exercise in the Lives
of Selected Colonial Americans
[Davis], 1970-12

The Standing Order [Akin], 1970-
1

The Status of Women in Puritan
New England [Cobbledick], 1936-
2

The Strenuous Puritan [Stearns],
1934-8

Institution Index

Concordia Seminary, 1969-22 (1)

Cornell University, 1927-6, 1934-9, 1954-5, 1967-21, 1967-33, 1968-19, 1972-11, 1973-7, 1977-31 (9)

Dallas Theological Seminary, 1959-6, 1968-32, 1978-11 (3)

Drew University, 1950-2, 1966-16, 1967-14, 1967-26, 1969-1, 1970-11, 1975-28, 1981-21 (8)

Duke University, 1940-2, 1955-11, 1959-12, 1955-15, 1961-3, 1966-7, 1968-23, 1970-7 (8)

Eden Theological Seminary, 1979-8 (1)

Emory University, 1967-1, 1967-18, 1974-32, 1981-9 (4)

Florida State University, 1963-3, 1964-13, 1965-24, 1968-12, 1971-17 (5)

George Peabody College For Teachers, 1934-7 (1)

George Washington University, 1974-3 (1)

Hartford Seminary Foundation, 1928-4, 1939-1, 1939-3, 1942-1, 1961-6, 1964-9, 1968-24, 1970-30, 1970-41, 1974-18, 1976-10, 1977-5 (12)

Harvard University, 1893-2, 1897-1, 1904-3, 1906-2, 1916-1, 1923-6, 1925-1, 1926-3, 1927-3, 1929-3, 1931-3, 1933-2, 1933-4, 1934-1, 1934-8, 1936-1, 1936-10, 1937-2, 1937-3, 1938-9, 1940-1, 1940-3, 1940-6, 1941-1, 1941-2, 1942-8, 1943-4, 1944-1, 1946-2, 1950-3, 1950-5, 1951-1, 1952-4, 1952-6, 1953-2, 1954-1, 1954-7, 1955-4, 1956-1, 1956-12, 1958-5, 1958-12, 1960-8, 1961-2, 1961-8, 1962-6, 1963-11, 1963-13, 1963-14, 1964-11, 1965-6, 1965-8, 1966-8, 1966-13, 1967-36, 1968-10,

1968-13, 1968-25, 1969-4, 1969-19, 1970-43, 1971-23, 1971-30, 1972-13, 1972-21, 1973-10, 1974-11, 1974-17, 1974-20, 1975-32, 1976-5, 1976-12, 1977-14, 1978-18, 1979-5, 1979-12, 1979-13, 1979-17, 1980-18 (79)

Indiana University, 1938-2, 1952-5, 1953-3, 1953-8, 1962-4, 1966-20, 1967-6, 1969-24, 1971-22, 1971-25, 1975-4, 1975-18, 1975-24, 1977-28, 1980-11, 1980-20 (16)

Johns Hopkins University, 1886-1, 1887-1, 1889-1, 1890-1, 1892-2, 1893-3, 1896-1, 1896-2, 1956-7, 1972-10 (10)

Kent State University, 1971-21, 1974-31, 1975-29, 1976-2, 1977-11, 1978-10, 1979-10, 1979-15 (8)

Lehigh University, 1969-11 (1)

Louisiana State University, 1955-6, 1971-6, 1981-13 (3)

Loyola University of Chicago, 1974-19, 1979-27 (2)

Michigan State University, 1951-7, 1953-1, 1969-14, 1969-23, 1971-12, 1971-34, 1971-36, 1972-6, 1973-25, 1974-13 (10)

New Orleans Baptist Theological Seminary, 1971-26 (1)

New School for Social Research, 1970-24 (1)

New York University, 1904-1, 1905-4, 1908-3, 1917-2, 1935-5, 1942-3, 1948-6, 1954-3, 1963-6, 1971-14, 1975-11, 1977-10, 1978-7, 1981-8, 1981-22 (15)

Northern Baptist Theological Seminary, 1958-7 (1)

Northwestern University, 1940-4, 1946-5, 1955-14, 1962-7, 1964-

5, 1968-3, 1969-3, 1973-9,
1973-22, 1977-1, 1977-13,
1978-24, (12)

Ohio State University, 1950-6,
1966-12, 1972-42, 1973-28,
1974-35, 1975-15 (6)

Ohio University, 1968-16, 1968-
30, 1973-5 (3)

Pacific School of Religion, 1964-
19, 1966-1 (2)

Pennsylvania State University,
1965-15, 1967-12, 1968-22,
1971-1, 1971-28, 1976-1, 1976-
23, 1976-24, 1977-18, 1978-27
(10)

Princeton Theological Seminary,
1963-21, 1968-21 (2)

Princeton University, 1943-1,
1948-1, 1949-2, 1955-5, 1958-
11, 1963-9, 1965-10, 1965-21,
1967-4, 1968-15, 1971-29, 1974-
23, 1979-26, 1981-18 (14)

Radcliffe College
See Harvard University

Rice University, 1971-4, 1974-33,
1975-23 (3)

Rutgers University, 1965-18,
1967-23, 1974-21, 1976-16,
1978-14, 1978-15 (6)

St. John's University, 1980-1 (1)

St. Louis University, 1931-2,
1955-1, 1979-24 (3)

San Francisco Theological
Seminary, 1972-20 (1)

Southern Baptist Theological
Seminary, 1949-5, 1959-5 (2)

Southern Illinois University-
Carbondale, 1972-29, 1974-28,
1979-20, 1981-14 (4)

Southwestern Baptist Theological
Seminary, 1965-17, 1972-15 (2)

Stanford University, 1949-3,
1949-6, 1950-1, 1953-12, 1958-
4, 1961-7, 1966-15, 1968-11,
1968-14, 1970-38, 1972-35,
1975-33 (12)

State University of New York-
Albany, 1975-9, 1977-27 (2)

State University of New York-
Binghamton, 1981-1 (1)

State University of New York-
Buffalo, 1974-22, 1975-21,
1977-32, 1978-13, 1978-21,
1979-3, 1980-17 (7)

State University of New York-
Stony Brook, 1973-21, 1975-26
(2)

Syracuse University, 1956-10,
1959-10, 1970-33, 1973-1, 1973-
19, 1976-19 (6)

Temple University, 1912-2, 1935-
2, 1942-9, 1967-13, 1972-33,
1979-4 (6)

Texas A&M University, 1973-16 (1)

Tufts University, 1910-2, 1972-
19, 1974-2, 1980-3 (4)

Union Theological Seminary in the
City of New York, 1953-13,
1960-10, 1962-11, 1966-6, 1971-
19 (5)

University of California-
Berkeley, 1959-14, 1965-19,
1966-11, 1969-2, 1969-13, 1970-
9, 1970-35, 1970-44, 1972-22,
1972-38, 1973-24, 1976-22,
1976-25, 1977-29, 1977-35 (15)

University of California-
Davis, 1967-31, 1968-29, 1970-
22, 1971-3 (4)

University of California-
Irvine, 1977-4, 1977-7, (2)

University of California-
Los Angeles, 1947-2, 1957-4,
1958-6, 1962-2, 1962-8, 1963-

Subject Index

Abnaki, 1974-22, 1975-19
Acadia. See New France
Acts of Trade. See Navigation
  Acts
Adams, Abigail (1744-1818), and
  Puritanism, 1975-12
Adams, Brooks (1848-1927), on
  Puritanism, 1971-26
Adams, Charles Francis (1807-86),
  on Puritanism, 1942-7, 1971-26
Adams, Henry (1838-1918), and
  Puritanism, 1966-15
Adams, James Truslow (1879-1949),
  on Puritanism, 1971-26
Adams, John (1735-1826), and
  Puritanism, 1959-3, 1959-10,
  1975-28
Admiralty Court, and R.I., 1928-1
administration of justice. See
  courts
adult age: in American colonies,
  1969-2; in New England, 1971-3
advertising, in colonial
  newspapers, 1967-2
aesthetics, Puritanism on, 1970-
  22, 1973-1, 1975-33
Afro-Americans. See blacks
Ag(g)awam, Mass. See Ipswich,
  Mass.; Springfield, Mass
agents, colonial. See colonial
  agents
agriculture: in Conn., 1931-1;
  literature of, in American
  colonies, 1933-5; in Mass.,
  1917-1, 1922-1, 1954-4, 1972-
  1963-20, 1969-10; on faith,

23; in New England, 1941-1,
  1972-2, 1978-27; in New Haven
  Colony, 1929-1; in R.I., 1937-6
alchemy. See chemistry
alcohol abuse, Congregationalism
  on, 1954-9
Alcott, Amos Bronson (1799-1888),
  on Puritanism, 1973-6
Alexander, William (Earl of
  Stirling, c.1567-1640),
  hexameral works by, 1979-2
Algonquins. See native
  Americans; names of individual
  tribes
allegory. See metaphor
Allen (or Allin), John (1597-
  1671), sermons of, 1973-10
almanacs, 1917-2, 1936-6, 1970-
  28, 1971-17; astronomy in,
  1971-17, 1977-14; and
  education, 1965-18; humor in,
  1938-5. See also newspapers;
  periodicals
America, English conception of,
  1974-34
American colonies. See New
  England; names of individual
  colonies and provinces
Amerindians. See native
  Americans
Ames, Nathaniel (1708-64), humor
  in almanacs of, 1938-5
Ames, William (1576-1633): and
  John Calvin, 1961-3; on the
  church, 1963-20; on ethics,
aristocracy, Puritanism and,

geography at, 1962-6; teaching
of rhetoric at, 1936-5;
teaching of science at, 1933-5;
and Yale, early relations of,
1972-21. See also names of
individual alumni and officials
Harvard, John (1607-38), library
of, 1917-3
Hawthorne, Nathaniel (1804-64):
on evil, 1957-8; knowledge and
use of New England history,
1937-4, 1943-1, 1969-4, 1975-
34, 1981-7; and Puritan
Platonism, 1960-7; and
Puritanism, 1935-8, 1935-10
1942-7, 1949-1, 1958-15, 1959-
9, 1963-7, 1967-7, 1969-15,
1974-11, 1977-2, 1980-20; on
Salem witchcraft, 1970-7; and
typology, 1963-5
Hayden, Anna Tompson (1648-
c.1720), poetry of, 1977-8,
1978-7
Herrick, Robert (1869-1938), and
Puritanism, 1977-34
hexameral literature, Edward
Taylor and, 1979-2
high schools. See education,
secondary
highways, in Mass., 1927-3
Hinde, Joseph, commonplace book
of, 1940-2
Hingham, Mass.: demography,
1972-13, 1973-24; settlers of,
1974-1
history: in colonial almanacs,
1917-2, 1971-17; writing of, by
New England Puritans, 1968-14,
1968-29, 1971-23, 1976-26;
writing on American, in 18th-
century America, 1946-5, 1973-
8; writing on American, in
19th-century America, 1973-8.
See also names of individual
historians
Hobbes, Thomas (1588-1679),
influence in New England,
1975-8
Hollister, Gideon Hiram (1817-
81), on King Philip's War,
1970-6
Holmes, Oliver Wendell (1809-94),
on Puritanism, 1942-7
Holy Spirit: Richard Baxter on,
1958-3; John Owen on, 1967-29;

William Perkins on, 1951-8;
Puritanism on, 1944-3, 1955-2,
1966-8; Thomas Shepard on,
1967-14; Richard Sibbes on,
1969-1; Roger Williams on,
1954-2. See also Trinity
homiletics. See sermons
Hooke, William (1601-78), sermons
of, 1973-10
Hooker, Richard (c.1554-1600):
vs. Thomas Cartwright, 1974-
18; on church history, 1974-18;
on faith, 1976-21; vs.
Puritanism, 1972-37; Of the
Laws of Ecclesiastical Polity
(1594-1613), 1981-12
Hooker, Thomas (1586-1647), 1958-
10, 1961-6, 1972-35; and
Cambridge Platform, 1966-1; on
church discipline, 1981-12; on
conversion, 1955-6; vs. John
Cotton, 1955-6, 1976-5; on
ethics, 1955-6; on faith, 1976-
13; as father-figure, 1969-13;
influence of Calvin on, 1972-
27; influence in England, 1971-
36; influence of Petrus Ramus
on, 1972-27, 1981-12; on
meditation, 1965-4; on
ministers, 1979-8; political
thought of, 1970-11, 1975-28,
on preparationism, 1972-27,
1979-8; rhetoric of, 1958-10,
1967-15, 1968-4, 1970-33, 1972-
38, 1973-10, 1979-27; on Satan,
1953-13; sermons of, 1953-13,
1955-6, 1958-7, 1967-15, 1968-
4, 1973-10, 1979-29; vs.
Thomas Shepard, 1955-6; on
signs, 1977-7; on spiritual
regeneration, 1963-9; theology
of, 1955-6, 1959-15, 1970-23;
use of word "self" by, 1932-4;
The Application of Redemption
(1657), 1968-4; A Survey of the
Summe of Church-Discipline
(1648), 1981-12; "A True Sight
of Sin" (1657), 1967-15
Hopkins, Edward (1600-57): and
Hopkins grammar school, 1933-6;
will of, 1956-15
Howe, John (1630-1705):
influence of Calvin on, 1961-3;
influence of Plato on, 1958-1;
on melancholy, 1961-8; on

See also newspapers; <u>names of</u>
<u>individual printers</u>
privacy, in New England, 1967-10
promoters, arguments of English,
to encourage colonization,
1967-13
pronunciation: in Conn., 1933-1;
in Mass., 1927-7; in New
England, 1956-13; in R.I.,
1936-10; Edward Taylor's, 1971-
27
property: in Mass., 1910-1; in
New England, 1936-8, 1972-25,
1973-23; Puritanism on, 1954-9,
1973-23. <u>See also</u> land; wealth
proprietors, town, in New
England, 1923-1
Providence, R.I., 1973-17;
founding of, 1978-23;
geography, 1947-3; population
of, 1962-9; settlement of,
1947-3
Providence Plantations (1644-63),
1973-17. <u>See also</u> Rhode Island
provincial.... <u>See</u> colonial...
Prynne, William (1600-69),
metaphors used by, 1969-15
Psalms: Cotton Mather on, 1977-
25; singing of (see hymns and
hymnody; music); and Edward
Taylor's poetry, 1979-10
psychoanalysis. <u>See</u> Freud,
Sigmund
psychology, Puritanism and
American, 1978-4. <u>See also</u>
mentally ill; mind
public health: in Boston, Mass.,
1954-1; in Conn., 1970-32
public speaking, in Mass., 1935-6
punishment. <u>See</u> church
discipline; courts; law; law,
criminal
Puritan-Anglican controversies,
1947-4, 1957-2, 1959-4, 1963-
16, 1969-6, 1972-8, 1976-21,
1979-17; on Bible, 1937-3,
1962-4, 1972-40, 1974-20; at
Cambridge Univ., 1953-4, 1978-
12; on church history, 1974-18;
on church polity, 1935-7, 1981-
12; on divorce, 1916-2; on
episcopacy, 1932-1; on ethics,
1971-18; on liturgy, 1972-17;
on man, 1971-18; on marriage,
1916-2; on rhetoric, 1974-20;

on religious knowledge, 1980-1;
on social organization, 1935-7,
1962-4, 1963-13, 1972-40; on
Ten Commandments, 1971-18. <u>See</u>
<u>also</u> Anglicans; Puritanism;
<u>names</u> of individual
controversialists
Puritan-Quaker controversies,
1955-2; on women, 1974-9. <u>See</u>
<u>also</u> Quakers
Puritan-Roman Catholic
controversies, 1963-2, 1969-22.
<u>See also</u> Catholics
Puritan-Separatist controversies,
1978-1. <u>See also</u> Separatism;
<u>names</u> of <u>individual</u>
controversialists
Puritanism: 18th-century views
of, 1916-1, 1946-6, 1973-8 (<u>see</u>
<u>also</u> names of individual
writers); 19th-century views
of, 1942-7, 1943-1, 1964-5,
1966-7, 1971-26, 1971-35, 1973-
8, 1976-6 (see also names of
individual writers); 20th-
century views of, 1942-7, 1955-
15, 1964-5, 1971-26, 1971-35,
1971-37, 1973-13, 1976-6 (see
also names of individual
writers); on aesthetics, 1970-
22, 1975-33; and aristocracy,
1937-8, 1969-6; on asceticism,
1937-8, 1951-6; on Atonement,
1974-29; and Augustine of
Hippo, 1972-39; on authority,
1953-5, 1955-1, 1959-4; on
Bible, 1955-2, 1974-20; and
Buddhism, 1976-20; and children
(see children; children's
books); Christian humanism and,
1962-12, 1981-16; on the
church, 1955-2, 1963-16; on
clothing, 1937-8; on
conversion, 1971-19, 1972-39;
on covenants, 1948-4, 1955-1,
1960-10, 1964-6, 1980-7; on
covenants (church), 1928-4,
1942-1, 1959-15, 1964-6, 1971-
33; on covenants (national),
1962-11, 1965-24; on creeds,
1943-2; on curses, 1937-8; on
death, 1957-4, 1957-5, 1969-19,
1970-35, 1975-31, 1976-8, 1979-
18, 1979-29; and democracy,
1966-5; on divorce, 1916-2,

race. See blacks; native
Americans
Rainolds, John (1549-1607), on
marriage, 1968-15
Râle, Sébastien (1654-1724),
death reported, 1936-9
Ramus, Petrus (1515-72), logic
of: Thomas Hooker and, 1972-
27, 1981-13; and marriage,
1968-15; William Perkins and,
1980-12; and poetry in colonial
New England, 1973-1; and
preparationism, 1972-27;
Thomas Shepard and, 1972-27;
Edward Taylor and, 1972-12,
1972-27; Michael Wigglesworth
and, 1980-16. See also next
main entry
Ramus, Petrus (1515-72), rhetoric
of: and poetry in colonial New
England, 1973-1; Edward Taylor
and, 1972-12
Randolph, Edward (1532-1703),
1950-1, 1956-7, 1966-5
rationalism. See reason
reading (for information, culture,
etc.). See books and reading
reading: teaching of, in New
Haven, 1934-6; texts, 1973-16,
1979-28
realism, objective (psychology),
shift from, in Puritanism,
1969-15
reason: John Calvin on, 1972-27;
John Goodwin on, 1967-35;
Thomas Goodwin on, 1967-35;
Cotton Mather on, 1958-12;
Puritanism on, 1951-6, 1967-35;
Samuel Willard on, 1971-15
recreation, Puritanism on, 1927-
1, 1937-8, 1951-6, 1970-12,
1978-26
redemption: Richard Baxter on,
1954-10; John Owen on, 1959-5
regeneration: Puritanism on,
1965-17; spiritual, in Mass.,
1963-9
religion: in Me. and N.H., 1978-
18. See also names of
individual doctrines, sects,
and sectarians
religious diversity, in New
England, 1951-3, 1976-5. See
also religious liberty; names

of individual sects
religious education. See
education and religion
religious knowledge: Richard
Baxter on, 1940-6; John Cotton
on, 1980-1; John Owen on, 1967-
29; Puritanism on, 1961-3,
1980-1; Richard Sibbes on,
1955-7, 1980-1; and typology,
1967-18
religious liberty: in Conn.,
1895-1; John Cotton on, 1967-
27, 1970-18; in Dominion of New
England, 1919-1; John Goodwin
on, 1953-6; in Mass., 1931-4,
1935-6, 1964-11, 1971-13;
Cotton Mather on, 1958-12; in
New England, 1892-2, 1936-9,
1975-7; Puritanism on, 1964-11,
1971-34, 1979-4; Richard Steere
on, 1976-23; and typology,
1967-27, 1975-25; Sir Henry
Vane, Jr., on, 1977-27; Roger
Williams on, 1952-7, 1954-2,
1967-27, 1968-32, 1970-18,
1970-21, 1974-12, 1977-27. See
also church and state
religious melancholy, Puritanism
on, 1961-8
religious persecution. See
religious liberty
remigration, to England from New
England, 1972-7, 1974-31
Renner, Karl (1870-1950), ideas
of, applied, 1977-23
representation: in American
colonies, 1977-3; in Conn.,
1954-8; in Mass., 1893-3, 1946-
1. See also elections,
political; suffrage
revivalism, background of
colonial, 1949-5
rhetoric: of Richard Baxter,
1974-20; books on, 1936-5; of
William Bradford, 1970-22,
1978-19; of John Cotton, 1951-
1, 1966-12; of Cotton Mather,
1951-1, 1958-8; of Increase
Mather, 1951-1; prose, in New
England, 1951-1, 1955-13, 1967-
15, 1967-28, 1967-31, 1970-22;
Puritanism on, 1974-20; sexual,
in New England, 1970-19; of
Thomas Shepard, 1948-5, 1951-1;
of suffering, 1971-18; and

John Owen on, 1979-9;
Puritanism on, 1943-2; 1963-16,
1966-1, 1970-20, 1978-17. See
also baptism; Lord's Supper
Saffin, John (1632-1710), 1965-15
Sag Harbor, N.Y., whaling
industry, 1959-8
sagamores, 1974-22
St. Croix River Valley (Me.),
1950-4
Salem, Mass., 1908-2, 1971-9,
1978-28, 1980-15; education in,
1908-4; voluntary associations
in, 1972-42; witchcraft (see
witchcraft, Salem, Mass.)
Saltonstall, Gurdon (1666-1724),
1973-20
Saltonstall family (Mass. and
Conn.), 1946-2
salvation: John Owen on, 1959-5,
1979-9; Puritanism on, 1914-1,
1955-2, 1961-3, 1965-17, 1972-
31, 1977-4; Thomas Shepard on,
1974-27; Roger Williams on,
1948-6
sanctification: Richard Baxter
on, 1966-6, 1980-4; Cotton
Mather on, 1980-4; Puritanism
on, 1955-2, 1980-4
Sands, Robert Charles (1799-1832),
on King Philip's War, 1970-6
Santayana, George (1863-1952), on
Puritanism, 1942-7, 1955-15,
1963-1, 1976-6
Satan, Puritanism on, 1953-13,
1974-23. See also witchraft
Savage, James (1784-1873),
Genealogical Dictionary (1860-
62), 1980-17
Savoy Conference (1661): Richard
Baxter and, 1972-16; Thomas
Goodwin and, 1974-8; John Owen
and, 1965-21
Saybrook, Conn., historical
geography, 1978-14
Saybrook Platform (1708), 1895-1,
1970-1, 1970-25, 1971-21
Saye and Sele, 1st Viscount (1582-
1662), 1969-6
scalp bounties, in Mass. and N.H.,
1933-2
school committees, in Mass., 1905-3
schoolmasters. See teachers (school)
schools. See education . . .

science: in colonial almanacs,
1917-2, 1971-17; education in,
1933-5; influence of Calvinism
on, 1951-10; literature of, in
American colonies, 1933-5, 1936-
6; and New England clergy, 1934-
4, 1970-40; Puritanism and, 1934-
4; and religion in 17th-century
England, 1968-19; John Winthrop,
Jr.'s contributions to, 1969-23
Scituate, Mass.: cultural
diversity in, 1980-24; mortality
in, 1972-13
Scotch-Irish element in American
Presbyterianism, 1939-3, 1964-4,
1972-6, 1972-20
Scotland. See Great Britain
Scripture. See Bible
Seekers, Roger Williams on, 1954-
2
"self," notion of, in Puritanism,
1932-4, 1976-26
self-government. See government
self-knowledge, Puritanism on,
1961-3
semiology, Puritan, 1977-7
"sentimentalism." See under
ethics
separation of powers, in American
colonies, 1953-8
Separatism: history of English,
1954-7, 1979-13; in Jacobean
Essex (England), 1973-11; in
Plymouth Colony, 1905-1;
worship in English, 1943-2.
See also Plymouth Colony; names
of individual Separatists
sermons: of John Allin, 1973-10;
in American colonies, 1936-6,
1958-7; artillery election, in
New England, 1964-13, 1965-14;
of Peter Bulkeley, 1973-10; of
Charles Chauncy (1589-1671),
1953-13, 1958-7, 1973-10; for
children, 1929-2; of John
Clarke, 1958-7; of Benjamin
Colman, 1953-13, 1963-10, 1974-
3, 1974-26; convention, in
Boston, Mass., 1971-6; of John
Cotton, 1953-13, 1958-7, 1972-
38, 1973-10, 1974-2; of Robert
Cushman, 1973-10; of John
Davenport, 1953-13, 1958-7,
1973-10; of Henry Dunster,

1961-7, 1967-30, 1975-8
wit and humor: in American
  colonies, 1938-5, 1970-15; in
  Puritan poetry, 1962-12. See
  also names of individual
  writers
witchcraft: on Long Island, 1943-
  3; in Mass., 1977-35; in New
  England, 1953-13, 1980-8. See
  also Satan; witchcraft, Salem,
  Mass.
witchcraft, Salem, Mass., (1692-
  93), 1964-7, 1974-23, 1978-11;
  Increase Mather on, 1923-6;
  portrayal of, in American
  literature, 1968-1, 1970-6
Wolcott, Roger (1679-1767),
  Poetical Meditations (1725),
  1974-6
women: in business and
  professions in American
  colonies, 1923-4; education of,
  1961-10; in New England, 1936-
  2, 1942-8, 1973-14, 1980-8,
  1980-19; poetry by colonial,
  1977-8; Puritanism and
  American, 1975-12; Puritanism
  on, 1916-2, 1936-2, 1942-8,
  1973-14, 1974-9, 1980-8;
  reading of New England, 1940-2;
  rights of, in early American
  law, 1930-3; as witches, 1980-
  8; writers in England, 1978-5;
  writers in New England, 1977-8,
  1978-5, 1978-7, 1981-14. See
  also family(ies); patriarchy;
  names of individual women
Wood, William (fl. 1629-33),
  humor of, 1938-5
Woodstock, Conn., Mass.' claim
  to, 1882-1
Woodward and Saffery survey
  (1642), 1882-1
Word of God: Richard Baxter on,
  1944-2; William Perkins on,
  1951-8; Richard Sibbes on,
  1955-7; as supreme liturgical
  criterion, 1943-2; Roger
  Williams on, 1954-2. See also
  Bible
works: Antinomian controversy nd
  covenant of, 1970-37; Richard
  Baxter on, 1955-11; John Cotton
  on, 1976-20; Thomas Goodwin on,
  1950-2; Cotton Mather on good,

1971-4; Puritanism on, 1980-7
worship, Puritanism on, 1943-
  2, 1951-6
Wright, Thomas Goddard (1885-
  1918), on Puritanism, 1971-26

Yale College, 1925-2, 1968-31;
  age of students at, 1969-2;
  Anglicans at, 1960-4 (see also
  Johnson, Samuel);
  Congregationalism at, 1942-6;
  and Conn., 1950-9; governance
  of, 1958-14; and Harvard, early
  relations of, 1972-21; library
  of, 1934-7, 1960-5; purpose of,
  1958-4; teaching of rhetoric
  at, 1936-5; teaching of science
  at, 1933-5. See also names of
  individual alumni and officials
York Co., Me., courts of, 1956-1
Young Christian's Library, The
  (1710), 1953-10

Zionism, Increase Mather on,
  1977-10